T0345031

Economics of Means-Tested Transfer Programs in the United States, Volume I

**National Bureau
of Economic Research
Conference Report**

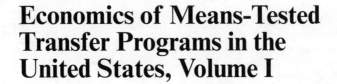

Economics of Means-Tested Transfer Programs in the United States, Volume I

Edited by **Robert A. Moffitt**

The University of Chicago Press

Chicago and London

The University of Chicago Press, Chicago 60637
The University of Chicago Press, Ltd., London
© 2016 by the National Bureau of Economic Research
All rights reserved. Published 2016.
Printed in the United States of America
25 24 23 22 21 20 19 18 17 16   1 2 3 4 5

ISBN-13: 978-0-226-37047-7   (cloth)
ISBN-13: 978-0-226-37050-7   (e-book)
DOI: 10.7208/chicago/9780226370507.001.0001

Library of Congress Cataloging-in-Publication Data

Names: Moffitt, Robert A., editor.
Title: Economics of means-tested transfer programs in the United
    States / edited by Robert Moffitt.
Other titles: National Bureau of Economic Research conference report.
Description: Chicago ; London : The University of Chicago Press,
    2016– | Series: NBER conference report | Includes bibliographical
    references and index.
Identifiers: LCCN 2016006530 | ISBN 9780226370477 (cloth : alk.
    paper) | ISBN 9780226370507 (e-book) | ISBN 9780226392493
    (cloth : alk. paper) | ISBN 9780226392523 (e-book)
Subjects: LCSH: Economic security—United States. | Income
    maintenance programs—United States. | Economic security—
    United States—Testing.
Classification: LCC HD7125 .E273 2016 | DDC 361/.05—dc23
    LC record available at http://lccn.loc.gov/2016006530

♾ This paper meets the requirements of ANSI/NISO Z39.48–1992
(Permanence of Paper).

Relation of the Directors to the
Work and Publications of the
National Bureau of Economic Research

1. The object of the NBER is to ascertain and present to the economics profession, and to the public more generally, important economic facts and their interpretation in a scientific manner without policy recommendations. The Board of Directors is charged with the responsibility of ensuring that the work of the NBER is carried on in strict conformity with this object.

2. The President shall establish an internal review process to ensure that book manuscripts proposed for publication DO NOT contain policy recommendations. This shall apply both to the proceedings of conferences and to manuscripts by a single author or by one or more co-authors but shall not apply to authors of comments at NBER conferences who are not NBER affiliates.

3. No book manuscript reporting research shall be published by the NBER until the President has sent to each member of the Board a notice that a manuscript is recommended for publication and that in the President's opinion it is suitable for publication in accordance with the above principles of the NBER. Such notification will include a table of contents and an abstract or summary of the manuscript's content, a list of contributors if applicable, and a response form for use by Directors who desire a copy of the manuscript for review. Each manuscript shall contain a summary drawing attention to the nature and treatment of the problem studied and the main conclusions reached.

4. No volume shall be published until forty-five days have elapsed from the above notification of intention to publish it. During this period a copy shall be sent to any Director requesting it, and if any Director objects to publication on the grounds that the manuscript contains policy recommendations, the objection will be presented to the author(s) or editor(s). In case of dispute, all members of the Board shall be notified, and the President shall appoint an ad hoc committee of the Board to decide the matter; thirty days additional shall be granted for this purpose.

5. The President shall present annually to the Board a report describing the internal manuscript review process, any objections made by Directors before publication or by anyone after publication, any disputes about such matters, and how they were handled.

6. Publications of the NBER issued for informational purposes concerning the work of the Bureau, or issued to inform the public of the activities at the Bureau, including but not limited to the NBER Digest and Reporter, shall be consistent with the object stated in paragraph 1. They shall contain a specific disclaimer noting that they have not passed through the review procedures required in this resolution. The Executive Committee of the Board is charged with the review of all such publications from time to time.

7. NBER working papers and manuscripts distributed on the Bureau's web site are not deemed to be publications for the purpose of this resolution, but they shall be consistent with the object stated in paragraph 1. Working papers shall contain a specific disclaimer noting that they have not passed through the review procedures required in this resolution. The NBER's web site shall contain a similar disclaimer. The President shall establish an internal review process to ensure that the working papers and the web site do not contain policy recommendations, and shall report annually to the Board on this process and any concerns raised in connection with it.

8. Unless otherwise determined by the Board or exempted by the terms of paragraphs 6 and 7, a copy of this resolution shall be printed in each NBER publication as described in paragraph 2 above.

Contents

Acknowledgments

This volume and an accompanying volume contain revised versions of papers presented at a conference at the offices of the National Bureau of Economic Research on December 4–5, 2014. The editor would like to thank NBER president James Poterba for inspiration for this project and two anonymous reviewers for the University of Chicago Press for their comments improving the chapters in the volumes. The chapters were also significantly improved by the comments and suggestions of the discussants at the conference, David Autor, David Blau, Dan Black, Richard Blundell, Amy Finkelstein, Lawrence Katz, and Jeffrey Liebman. Eugene Steuerle gave an insightful evening address at the conference as well.

Thanks also go to Carl Beck and Denis Healy for logistical and local arrangements for the conference and to Helena Fitz-Patrick for shepherding the papers through the review and publication process. Finally, the editor would like to thank the authors of the chapters for their long hours of hard work on their chapters. Any success of these volumes is to be entirely credited to them. Financial support was graciously provided by the Smith Richardson Foundation for the project. The editor also wishes to acknowledge support from the Russell Sage Foundation for work related to the project and to state that he has no other material or financial relationships relating to this research.

Introduction

Robert A. Moffitt

Issues concerning means-tested transfer programs in the United States continue to interest both researchers and policymakers. Many of the programs have evolved significantly over the last decade and a half. While some programs that had previously declined, such as the Temporary Assistance to Needy Families (TANF) program, have remained at low levels of expenditure and caseloads, many other programs have grown. Those include the Medicaid program, the Supplemental Nutrition Assistance Program (SNAP), the Earned Income Tax Credit (EITC), and subsidized housing programs. On net, more programs have grown than have declined, leading to continued increases in per capita spending on means-tested programs as a whole. Further, the Great Recession saw major increases in caseloads and spending, partly the result of automatic growth occasioned by declines in income and consequent increases in the numbers of eligible families, but partly the result of programmatic reforms enacted by Congress and signed by the president. At this writing, most, but not all, of those programmatic expansions have phased out and the overall unemployment rate has returned to prerecession levels, but whether caseloads and expenditures in the programs will decline to prerecession levels remains to be seen.

Economic research on means-tested programs has mostly focused on the determinants of participation in those programs, the causes of trends in overall caseload and expenditure growth, the effects of program participation on work incentives and other behaviors, and their potential beneficial effects on the well-being of recipients as measured by reductions in poverty

Robert A. Moffitt is the Krieger-Eisenhower Professor of Economics at Johns Hopkins University and a research associate of the National Bureau of Economic Research.

For acknowledgments, sources of research support, and disclosure of the author's material financial relationships, if any, please see http://www.nber.org/chapters/c13482.ack.

rates, increases in consumption, and positive effects on nonmonetary outcomes such as health and education, and other outcomes. The long-term trend increase in expenditures and caseloads as well as the Great Recession expansions have led to further study of the effects of the programs on these outcomes.

The chapters in the volume are revised versions of papers presented at a conference sponsored by the Smith-Richardson Foundation and convened by the National Bureau of Economic Research (NBER) in Cambridge, Massachusetts, on December 4–5, 2014. Each chapter surveys the history, policy issues, rules, caseloads, and research on one of the major programs in the US safety net. In addition, two chapters cover, respectively, employment and training programs and early childhood education programs, which are more human-capital oriented than are traditional means-tested transfer programs. The chapters represent updated versions of similar papers on each program published in a prior volume (Moffitt 2003). The goal of these chapters, like those in the earlier volume, is to provide in a single source both the institutional details of each program or set of programs of a given type, and a summary of research findings. The institutional details surrounding each program are intended to provide research economists with an introduction to the nature of each program, while the summary of research findings provides policy analysts as well as nonspecialist researchers a convenient source of learning the results of the latest studies. The technical level is kept at the level of an advanced graduate student in economics and is therefore intended to enable students conducting dissertation work as well as older researchers to follow the methods used and how they should be interpreted. The chapters also present the current policy issues under discussion for each program, another useful source of information for researchers.

This introduction has two remaining sections. The first provides an overview of current caseloads and spending in the major programs, a presentation of recent trends in those levels, and a discussion of marginal tax rates from safety net programs as a whole. The second section furnishes a short summary of each of the chapters in the volumes.

Means-Tested Transfer Programs in 2007

Table I.1 lists the major means-tested transfer programs in 2007, the last year before the Great Recession, when the caseloads and expenditures had not yet been affected by that major economic event.[1] All the programs in

---

1. Means-tested programs are defined here as programs for which core eligibility requires sufficiently low income and/or assets. Many major transfer programs like Social Security, Unemployment Insurance, and even Social Security Disability Insurance are excluded. Although often current benefits among beneficiaries in those programs are based on current earnings, income, or hours of work, core eligibility is based on having sufficient work or earnings over some historical period. Social insurance programs like these are not aimed at alleviating poverty per se, but rather at providing insurance for workers against certain types of reductions in future income.

Table I.1   Annual expenditures and caseloads in means-tested programs, FY 2007

	Type of transfer	Demographic groups covered	Expenditures (millions)	Caseloads (thousands)	Monthly expenditures per recipient (constant 2007 dollars)
Medicaid	In-kind	Families with dependent children, disabled, elderly	328,875	56,821	482
EITC	Cash	Individuals with positive earnings	48,540	24,584	165
SSI	Cash	Aged, blind, and disabled individuals	41,205	7,360	467
Housing aid	In-kind	All individuals and families	39,436	5,087	646
SNAP	In-kind	All individuals and families	30,373	26,316	96
TANF	Cash	Mostly single-mother families	11,624	4,138	234
School food programs	In-kind	Children in school	10,916	40,720	22
Head Start	In-kind	All children	6,889	908	632
WIC	In-kind	Mother, infants, and children at nutritional risk	5,409	8,285	54

Source: Ben-Shalom et al. (2012, table 1).

the table are discussed in detail in the chapters in this volume. The Medicaid program, which provides free medical care to low-income adults and children, to the elderly and disabled, and for long-term care, was by far the largest program in both expenditures and caseloads, with $328 billion in expenditures and over 56 million recipients. The second largest program by expenditure was the Earned Income Tax Credit (EITC), which provides a tax credit to families and individuals with relatively low levels of earnings, costing $48 billion in FY2007. While not always thought of as a welfare program, the EITC meets the means-tested transfer definition by its restriction to those with earned income below specified levels. The Supplemental Security Income (SSI) program, which provides cash benefits to low-income aged, blind, and disabled individuals, spent $41 billion in the same year, while almost as much, $39 billion, was spent on subsidized housing programs, which provide housing vouchers to low-income families, subsidized rent in public housing projects, and support for construction of low-income housing. The Supplemental Nutrition Assistance Program (SNAP), formerly called food stamps, which provides an allotment of funds for food expenditure for low-income families and individuals, cost $30 billion in FY 2007 and hence ranked as the fifth largest program in terms of expenditure. The Temporary Assistance to Needy Families (TANF) program, which provides cash assistance for general consumption to low-income families (mostly single mothers and children) is the most well-known program to many economists, given the amount of research that was conducted on it under its earlier name, the Aid to Families with Dependent Children (AFDC) program. However, because of contractionary reforms enacted in the 1990s, the program was only the seventh largest in the United States by 2007, with only $11 billion in expenditure—only a quarter of what was spent on the EITC, for example. The table also shows figures for school food programs (subsidized breakfasts and lunches for children from low-income families), the Head Start program (providing early education and child care for children of low-income families), and the WIC program (providing nutritional assistance to mothers, infants, and children at nutritional risk). While almost $11 billion was spent on school food programs, only $6.8 billion and $5.4 billion were spent on Head Start and WIC, respectively.

The programs differ in whether they provide a high level of benefits to a relatively small number of families, or a low level of benefits to a relatively large number of families, as shown in the last two columns of table I.1. In the former category is SSI, for example, which intends to provide cash for all consumption needs of eligible individuals. In the latter category are SNAP and school food programs, which provide only a modest benefit for food consumption only, but provide it to large numbers of adults and children. Medicaid, subsidized housing, and Head Start are quite expensive per recipient because the consumption goods they subsidize have relatively high prices, but the TANF program provides more modest benefits even though they are intended for all consumption needs. The EITC benefits are also modest despite the large scale of the program.

While the mix of different programs in the United States shown in table I.1 may seem to be a rather crazy-quilt assortment of programs with different structures and recipient groups, rather than following from some single rational design for assistance for the poor of all types, it does reflect what are commonly regarded as voter preferences in the country. For example, most programs are in-kind in nature, providing subsidies for specific consumption goods like medical care, food consumption and nutritional assistance, housing, and early childhood education. When cash is provided, it is generally not provided universally to all low-income families, but only to those with specific characteristics, like workers (the EITC) or the aged and disabled (SSI). The only quasi-general cash program in the country is the TANF program, but it has shrunk dramatically, providing only a modest level of benefits and only to a restricted set of families, again presumably reflecting disfavor for giving a general cash transfer in return for low income per se. For example, no cash program exists for poor, nonelderly and nondisabled childless nonworkers, whether single individuals or married, and only in-kind benefits are provided to other nonworkers.

Trends in Expenditure

Figures I.1 and I.2 shows trends in real per capita expenditure on means-tested programs from 1970 to 2012, both for multiple programs taken together (figure I.1) and for several of the individual major programs taken separately (figure I.2). Figure I.1 shows both a series for the top eighty-four means-tested programs through 2004 (after which the series was discontinued) and a series for the ten largest programs through the end year of 2012. Both figures show that there has been no decline in per capita spending but, instead, spending has monotonically grown, albeit at different rates in different time periods.

Five distinct periods are discernible. The first phase began in the 1960s (although not shown in the figure) and ran through the mid-1970s. In this classic period of expansion of the welfare state in the United States, the AFDC program expanded and grew, the food stamp program was extended to the nation as a whole, the SSI program was created, and housing aid was expanded. The second phase ran from the mid-1970s to the late 1980s, when expenditures flattened out, with no growth. The flattening out was a result of growth in the food stamp and housing programs offset by declines in spending on AFDC and SSI. The third phase, running from the late 1980s to the mid-1990s, saw another large increase in spending, exceeding that in the early 1970s in some cases. The growth resulted from major expansions in the EITC and in the SSI and subsidized housing programs. The fourth phase ran from the mid-1990s to 2007, with some expansion in overall spending but relatively little on the top ten programs. Spending on AFDC declined

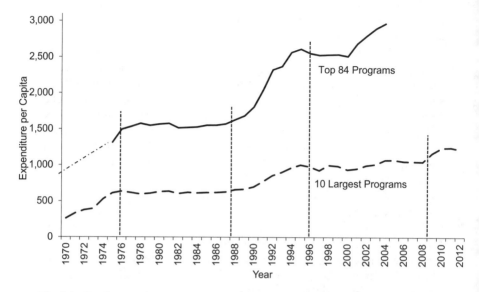

Fig. I.1   Real expenditure per capita in means-tested programs, 1970–2012 (real 2009 dollars)

Notes: The top eighty-four programs are from Spar (2006) and the ten largest programs are from authors' calculations from individual program statistics. Expenditures are sum of federal, state, and local expenditures. The top eighty-four program figures for before 1975 are extrapolated between 1968 and 1975. Top ten programs exclude Medicaid.

as it was changed to the TANF program, spending leveled off in the SSI program, housing programs, and the EITC, but a new Child Tax Credit (CTC) was introduced, pushing up spending. The Great Recession constitutes the fifth phase, where per capita spending on the ten largest programs grew by 15 percent from 2007 to 2011, arising from increases in expenditure particularly in the recently renamed SNAP program, the EITC, and SSI. The causes of the trends in expenditure for the different programs over the different periods are discussed in detail in the individual chapters in the volumes.

Both figures I.1 and I.2 exclude Medicaid expenditure growth. Per capita real spending in that program grew by 216 percent in the twenty-year period from 1970 to 1990, but continued to grow by 166 percent from 1990 to 2010. This makes the growth in aggregate spending considerably larger than implied by figure I.1. The figures also exclude expenditure on human-capital programs like employment and training programs and like child care and other early education programs. As discussed in the chapter on employment and training programs, Department of Labor funding for such programs, while very high in the 1970s from the provision of public service employment and other programs, today is quite small, even less than is spent on the TANF program, the smallest in figure I.2. There is no reliable calculation of total expenditures on all child care and early childhood education

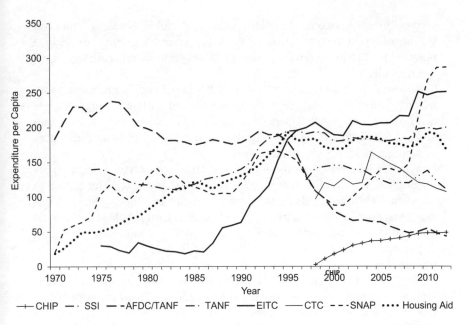

Fig. I.2   Expenditure per capita, non-Medicaid means-tested programs, 1970–2012 (real 2009 dollars)
Source: Haveman et al. (2015).

programs, either currently or historically, but the chapter on these programs in volume 2 reports total expenditure across Head Start, Early Head Start, the Child Care Development Fund, and IDEA grants that is slightly above that of TANF in 2013–2014. Clearly, expenditures on human-capital-related programs are dwarfed by those on conventional means-tested programs.

Most, but not all, of the trends in expenditure have been driven by trends in the recipient caseload rather than in expenditures per recipient. The run-ups in EITC expenditure and in spending on SNAP, for example, are primarily caseload driven. However, increases in subsidized-housing expenditure have been partially driven by the cost of housing, for subsidized housing is not an entitlement program and available slots are limited, with consequent long waiting lists (see chapter 2 by Collinson, Ellen, and Ludwig in volume 2). Moreover, while the Medicaid caseload has expanded because of expansions of eligibility, increases in medical-care prices have been at least as important in driving up the cost of the program. The decline in AFDC/TANF spending has also been primarily a result of dramatic reductions in the number of recipients, although benefits per recipient have also fallen.

These trends further illustrate the characteristics of US safety-net programs noted previously. Much of the expansion has occurred in in-kind programs, particularly Medicaid, food programs, and housing. Those programs providing cash assistance that have expanded are those targeted on specific groups (workers, the elderly, and the disabled). Cash assistance in the one program that provided assistance for general consumption needs to nonworking families, even if only mainly to single-mother families, declined dramatically.

Ben-Shalom, Moffitt, and Scholz (2012, tables 2 and 7) have shown that this evolution of expansion and contraction of different programs has resulted in a change in the distribution of expenditure by demographic group and by level of private income. This should be expected given the differences in demographic groups served shown in table I.1, for the programs that have expanded and those that have contracted have served different types of families. They find that, from 1984 to 2004, monthly transfers going to single-mother households declined by 19 percent and those going to non-employed families declined by 21 percent, while transfers going to employed families, the elderly, and the disabled grew by 61 percent, 12 percent, and 15 percent, respectively, over the same period.[2] Single-mother families with private income less than 50 percent of the poverty line saw a 37 percent decline in transfer receipt, while single-mother families as well as two-parent families with private income between 100 and 150 percent of the poverty line saw transfer increases of 93 percent.

Cumulative Marginal Tax Rates

A traditional focus of much economic research on means-tested programs concerns the magnitude of marginal tax rates (MTRs) in those programs, which measure the rate at which benefits are reduced as earnings increase and are a gauge of work disincentives. The chapters in these volumes report the individual MTRs in each program, but not what is called the "cumulative" MTR that arises when a family participates in more than one program. This section reports what is known on that issue.

For individual programs, the chapter in this volume on the Medicaid program, which does not have copays for recipients, shows that it has a zero percent MTR until the point of income eligibility is reached, after which all benefits are lost. This creates a cliff in the benefit schedule and a notch in the budget constraint where the MTR exceeds 100 percent. The SNAP program has a nominal 30 percent MTR, but is effectively 24 percent because of an earnings exclusion provision, while subsidized-housing programs have an MTR of approximately 30 percent. The SSI program has a 50 percent MTR after an income exclusion is exceeded. But the EITC provides a subsidy in its lower range, which generates an MTR that can be as high as –45 percent, but when the subsidy is eventually phased out, the MTR has a maximum of 21 percent. Most programs allow payroll and income taxes to be deducted

2. Their figures include social transfers as well as means-tested benefits, but exclude Medicaid and Medicare.

from income prior to application of the MTR, thereby reducing the impact of the two MTRs together.

Relatively few studies have been conducted that report cumulative MTRs. This is a difficult task because it depends on which programs a family participates in and it can vary markedly from state to state if the program has state-specific parameters. No comprehensive calculations have been made for all combinations of programs in which a family might participate in and for all states. However, table I.2 reports an illustration calculation of cumulative MTRs facing low-income families in 2012 who participate only in SNAP yet also face federal and state income and payroll taxes, which means that the EITC and the CTC are implicitly included as well. Since these are some of the largest programs in the safety net, they provide some sense of cumulative MTRs. The MTRs for each family vary depending on their level of earnings, whether all family members work, their level of taxable unearned income, the presence and ages of any children, marital and filing status, and other characteristics. Table I.2 reports the distribution of MTRs across all families in each earnings range, given that those MTRs vary by family. For the poorest families with earnings less than 50 percent of the poverty line, the median MTR is only 13 percent. Indeed, many families face negative MTRs because of the EITC and because they have larger numbers of children. The 90th percentile MTR for this low-income group is 35 percent, which arises mainly from families without children who are on SNAP. However, as the table shows, MTRs rise with earnings, going to medians of 24 percent for those between 50 and 100 percent of the poverty line and to 32 percent just above that line. While the 10th percentile MTRs remain modest, those taxpayers who are at the 90th percentile of taxpaying units face up to 61 percent MTRs. The higher MTRs for these relatively high-earnings families is a direct consequence of the EITC and CTC, which must be phased out. When that occurs, MTRs can be high when added to

Table I.2   **Marginal tax rates faced by US families with income below 200 percent of the poverty line participating in the SNAP program under 2012 law (percent)**

Earnings relative to the poverty line	Median	10th percentile	90th percentile
0 to 49 percent	13	–8	35
50 to 99 percent	24	13	53
100 to 149 percent	32	22	61
150 to 199 percent	31	22	51

Source: US Congressional Budget Office (2012, figure 5). The simulation estimates the MTR for each filing unit in 2012, for those families with earnings in the specified earnings-to-poverty-line range, evaluated at the point at which their family earnings are observed. The MTRs are based on federal and state income taxes, federal payroll taxes, and the SNAP benefit formula. Only nonelderly, nondisabled families with positive family earnings are included.

other positive taxes and to SNAP MTRs. But the low MTRs at low earnings and the higher MTRs at higher levels of earnings go together, and one cannot have one without the other.[3]

The major omission from these MTRs is the Medicaid program, which is the most common program received, along with SNAP, for families receiving benefits from two or more programs. Medicaid income thresholds vary by state and type of recipient family but, prior to the Affordable Care Act, thresholds were typically around 50 percent of the poverty or a little lower or higher. This implies that the MTRs shown in table I.2 are probably about right for families in the lowest earnings strata but MTRs at higher earnings levels, particularly between 50 and 100 percent of the poverty line, are considerably higher than shown. This reinforces the conclusion reached in the previous paragraph that the current means-tested transfer system imposes quite low MTRs for most of the poorest families in the United States, but considerably higher ones for the minority of families (16 percent of those below 250 percent of the poverty line) who receive benefits from multiple transfer programs.

While no time series of cumulative MTRs is available, there is little question that they have fallen significantly over time for at least two reasons. One is that most of the high cumulative MTRs calculated prior to the 1990s were a result of a 100 percent MTR in the AFDC program, and the AFDC program was the largest means-tested transfer program in the country after Medicaid at that time (see figure I.2). Further, AFDC recipients were categorically eligible for food stamps and Medicaid and were often enrolled in subsidized-housing programs, increasing the cumulative MTR for millions of recipient families. After the program was reformed in the mid-1990s, most states reduced their MTRs far below 100 percent, as the chapter on that program in this volume describes. Further, the dramatic decline in the AFDC program and its successor, TANF, means that multiple program receipt of that program with others constitutes only a small fraction of those receiving benefits today. Indeed, in 2010, 62 percent of families with income less than 250 percent of the poverty line received no benefits at all and another 22 percent received benefits from only one program (US Congressional Budget Office 2012, box 1). The remaining 16 percent received benefits from two or more, but virtually all of those families receive two benefits only, the vast majority receiving SNAP and Medicaid.[4]

The second development has been the expansion of the EITC, which, at

---

3. The CBO study had some reports of how these rates differ by presence of children and marital status, showing that families with children typically face higher MTRs than those without children, and that the dispersion of MTRs is greatest for single-mother families, who face both higher 90th-percentile MTRs as well as lower 10th-percentile MTRs.

4. Edelstein, Pergamit, and Ratcliffe (2014) report rates of multiple-benefit receipt in the middle of the first decade of the twenty-first century, and also report that the most common form of multiple receipt is of SNAP and Medicaid.

least in lower earnings ranges, provides a sizable subsidy that offsets most of the MTRs for families with children, leading to low cumulative MTRs for a large fraction of the low-income population. The introduction of a second tax credit, the Child Tax Credit in 1998, further reduces the MTR for low-income families by providing a nonrefundable credit that could only be applied against existing tax liability, thereby providing a larger credit to those with higher levels of income for those with low incomes.

Summaries of the Chapters

Each chapter in the two volumes fleshes out the details of the program and provides a summary of the research on the determinants of participation and caseload growth, as well as on the effects of program participation and programmatic reforms on behavioral outcomes.

Buchmueller, Ham, and Shore-Sheppard review the Medicaid program. They note, as did the chapter in the 2003 volume, that the program is really composed of four separate programs, covering low-income children and parents, the low-income disabled, those in nursing homes, and seniors in need of insurance coverage complementary to Medicare. They review the history of the program, which was begun in 1965 and which was, for almost thirty years, primarily provided to single-parent families receiving AFDC cash assistance and the elderly and disabled receiving SSI, but was extended to low-income children and pregnant women not receiving cash assistance starting in the 1980s. They also review in detail the many other incremental reforms of significant program features in the late 1980s and early 1990s, followed by a review of the effects of the 1996 welfare reform on the program. They then provide a status report on the current evolution of the program under the provisions of the Affordable Care Act. They also review the history and evolution of the CHIP program.

The Medicaid program has been the subject of a great deal of additional research since the 2003 volume, and more is in progress at this writing. Buchmueller, Ham, and Shore-Sheppard provide a thorough review of both the older and newer research. Their review of the more recent literature on the effects of Medicaid eligibility expansions on take-up of the program by adults and children as well as crowd-out of private insurance shows somewhat smaller estimates than did the earlier literature. The authors also review the effect of Medicaid on the purchase of private long-term care insurance, an issue of significant interest in the literature. Their discussion of the research on the effects of eligibility expansions on access to care and health of children shows that the literature provides strong support for positive effects on both, although the magnitudes are not always certain and the impacts seem larger on children in lower-income families. Impacts on adult access to care also appear positive, but effects on health itself are less conclusive. The authors also review the literature on the effects of Medicaid expansions, payment policies, reimbursement rates, and related policies on provider behavior and provision of care, finding a significant range of effects and estimated magnitudes. Their discussion of the recent literature on the effects of Medicaid on labor supply shows a wide range of estimates, ranging from zero in some studies to significant negative effects in others. Impacts of Medicaid on saving are negative for some families, but impacts on reduced household financial hardship appear positive. Finally, they review the literature on the effect of the Medicaid program and of various reforms and individual policies on family structure, finding that the effects are not very robust across studies.

Austin Nichols and Jesse Rothstein discuss the Earned Income Tax Credit (EITC) program, which provides a subsidy to families with positive earnings. The subsidy increases with earnings at low earnings levels but then is phased out as earnings rise, and eventually phases out completely for families with annual earnings of roughly $45,000 or higher (for those with two or more children). They review the familiar history of the program, which was enacted by Congress in 1975 but was made much more generous in later years. Unlike other means-tested transfer programs, the EITC is administered by the IRS and the take-up rate is very high. The authors also discuss the Child Tax Credit, which is somewhat similar in structure but covers a rather different (higher) income range. Updating the 2003 volume's discussion of the EITC, Nichols and Rothstein demonstrate the continued growth of program expenditures and recipients, discuss the expansion of the program during the Great Recession, and provide new evidence on the distribution of taxpayers over different regions of the EITC schedule and on the accuracy of EITC imputations in survey data.

In their review of the effects of the research on the effects of the EITC, the authors confirm prior findings of positive labor-supply effects for single mothers, small negative effects for married women, and essentially no labor-supply effects for men, but also discuss newer studies on those effects that provide more nuanced findings. They review new evidence on the importance of information and saliency in the take-up decision, the reasons that families seem to prefer lump sum refunds rather than collecting the credit in smaller increments over the year, the large impact of the program on reducing poverty rates, as well as notable positive effects of the EITC on adult and child health outcomes, child test scores, and educational attainment. They also describe the incidence of the EITC in the labor market, including some findings that suggest that employers capture some of the program benefits through lower equilibrium wages. Finally, they discuss proposals for reform, including more generous support for childless workers and extensions to disabled workers, and they evaluate comparisons, common in policy discussions, between the EITC and the minimum wage.

Hoynes and Schanzenbach review US food and nutrition programs, which include not only the well-known Supplemental Nutrition Assistance Program ([SNAP], formerly known as food stamps) but also the School

Breakfast Program and the National School Lunch Program (each of which supports subsidized schools meals for children from low-income families), and the Special Supplemental Nutrition Program for Women, Infants, and Children (WIC), which provides vouchers for particular nutritional foods as well as counseling, health screening, and referrals for low-income infants, young children, and pregnant and postpartum women. SNAP is the broadest and, indeed, the only means-tested transfer program in the country that provides essentially open-ended and unrestricted benefits to individuals and families of all types, basing eligibility only on need and not on family structure, disability, or other characteristic. The most important changes in the program since the 2003 volume include reforms in the states in the first decade of the twenty-first century intended to increase access to benefits, and a temporary increase in benefits during the Great Recession. As for recent reforms in the other programs in recent years, nutritional standards in both the School Breakfast Program and the National School Lunch Program have been modified, payment formulas have been altered to encourage high-poverty schools to adopt universally free meals for all students, and access to the School Breakfast Program has been expanded. The content of the food bundle provided to WIC recipients has been changed to reflect current dietary guidelines and promote consumption of fruits and vegetables. None of these reforms altered the basic structure of the programs, however.

In their literature review, the authors begin by presenting a stylized model for examining the economic impacts of the programs, in particular highlighting the range across the programs in their degree of "in-kind" versus cash structure. They then review the large volume of research on the programs and their effects on program participation, consumption, labor supply, health and nutrition, focusing on recent research that has used strong research designs. They find the research to show that the recent changes in SNAP caseloads, for example, are primarily driven by the macroeconomy, although SNAP and welfare policies have also played a role. Hoynes and Schanzenbach also review recent research on the effect of the program on food consumption and spending, finding them to be increased by the program but that the effect is essentially equivalent to the effect of cash for inframarginal households. The effects of SNAP on reducing food insecurity are, however, more mixed, and overall with less statistically significant findings. Much recent literature has focused on health effects, finding generally positive impacts on child health but more mixed results for obesity among adult participants. Recent research on the effects of the program on labor supply (based on data from the program rollout in the 1970s prior to welfare reform and the expansion in the EITC) show no significant effects overall, but significant negative effects for single-mother households. Leveraging recent expansions in the school breakfast programs, there has been a significant volume of recent research showing sharp increases in program participation, but more limited impacts on breakfast consumption and dietary quality, and decidedly mixed impacts on student test scores. Research on the National School Lunch Program on food security and body weight is quite mixed, but in the absence of experiments or programmatic changes it has been challenging to credibly identify impacts. Hoynes and Schanzenbach also review the recent literature on the WIC program. The research provides consistent evidence that WIC leads to improvements in birth outcomes, but there is much less evidence about how the program affects child nutrition and health. More recently, several studies explore the supply-side incentives generated by the program.

Ziliak reviews the Temporary Assistance for Needy Families (TANF) program, which was called the Aid to Families with Dependent Children (AFDC) program prior to 1996. He includes a new summary of the history of the program and of the major reforms in 1996 that introduced work requirements and time limits, reduced marginal tax rates on earnings, and enacted other features, and he shows the dramatic decline in the caseload that followed. He reviews the later 2005 DRA law, which changed the work requirements in the program, and he discusses the temporary additional spending allocated by Congress during the Great Recession. He shows that the "child-only" caseload has strongly increased, for an increasing proportion of cases have no adults supported by the grant, and that there has been an increase in the fraction of funds spent on in-kind activities such as child care, transportation, and work supports rather than simple cash assistance.

In his review of research on the program, he concentrates on new research conducted since the 2003 volume but also summarizes some of the research begun just after 1996 for which it is now possible to draw firmer conclusions. He finds that the literature on the causes of the caseload decline after 1996, for example, now shows somewhat greater relative effects of welfare reform policies than the macroeconomy on caseloads, but that the effect of the latter has generally declined, perhaps because of the rise of child-only families. Ziliak finds research on this issue in the Great Recession to show that the caseload became, with that recession, increasingly less responsive to the economy. His review of the effects of specific policies shows that time limits were an important contributor to caseload decline, but that the research has had difficulty fully separating the relative importance of the many components of the 1996 reforms. The large body of research on labor supply, he finds, shows that welfare reform had a positive effect on employment and hours worked of single mothers, as did a number of specific welfare-to-work experiments that were conducted. However, while the literature also shows positive effects on earnings, the declines in welfare benefits arising from leaving welfare often cancel out the earnings increases, leaving income relatively unchanged (although the literature also shows considerable heterogeneity, with some families experiencing income increases and others, decreases). Especially in more recent years, in addition, a significant number of single-mother families appear to have been made worse off and to have higher deep poverty rates. Ziliak's review of research on the effects of TANF on other outcomes shows mixed results on savings and consumption, some negative effects of the 1996 reform on health insurance coverage because of loss of Medicaid, no consistent evidence of the effect of reform on family structure and fertility, and mixed results of the effect of the reform on children, with some but not all studies showing positive effects on young children and negative effects on adolescents.

Duggan, Kearney, and Rennane review the Supplemental Security Income (SSI) program, a federal program created in 1974 that provides cash, and usually Medicaid benefits, to low-income individuals who are eligible for reasons of older age or disability. The SSI program covers three distinct populations: blind and disabled children, disabled nonelderly adults, and individuals over age sixty-five, regardless of disability status, who meet the financial criteria. Many states have supplemental SSI programs that provide additional benefits to those in federal law. The authors discuss the important literature on the determination of medical disability for adults and children and of continuing disability reviews, finding shifting definitions over time that appear to be partly responsible for rising caseloads, particularly for disabled children (the latter particularly affected by expansions in medical-eligibility criteria following the 1990 *Zebley* Supreme Court decision). They show that since the beginning of the program, the fraction of elderly adults on SSI has declined by more than half while the fraction of disabled nonelderly adults and children on SSI has risen substantially, doubling for children and younger adults. In terms of qualifying diagnoses, the authors find that in 2013, 68 percent of the child SSI caseload and 57 percent of the adult caseload had mental disorders, the rest having physical disorders.

In their review of research on SSI, the authors find that the program increases family income and reduces poverty rates and food insecurity but that the research provides mixed evidence of the effect of the child SSI program on parental labor supply and earnings. The authors also review recent research indicating that child SSI recipients who lose eligibility as an adult have subsequent very low earnings and high rates of poverty, and they review what is known for the reason for the disproportionate presence of boys in the child SSI caseload. They also review the small literature on the effect of interactions between TANF, CHIP, special education, and other programs on child SSI participation, finding that spillovers between programs likely result from financial incentives for beneficiaries and for state governments. The authors also review the sizable literature on the effects of demonstration programs over the last twenty years intended to increase work among SSI recipients, which often show little or no effect, leading to a very mixed set of results. Finally, the authors discuss many questions still to be answered in research on SSI, including the need for additional research on the long-term outcomes of child SSI recipients. In conclusion, the authors find the volume of research on the SSI program to be smaller than it should be given the importance of the program and the many important policy issues surrounding it.

Collinson, Ellen, and Ludwig discuss the many low-income housing programs in the United States, composed of public housing, privately owned subsidized housing, and tenant-based vouchers. The authors trace the history of initial but then declining support for public housing, the changing character of government subsidies for the construction of private housing for those with low and moderate incomes (especially the 1986 Low-Income Housing Tax Credit, or LIHTC), and the evolution of the 1974 housing voucher program, which is the largest housing-subsidy program for low-income households. They also provide an extensive discussion of the justification for housing programs. Their review of caseloads in the programs reveals falling numbers of households in public housing and other developments subsidized by the US Department of Housing and Urban Development, but rising numbers of those living in LIHTC developments and receiving housing vouchers. The authors also discuss the very small fraction of low-income families in the United States who actually receive subsidized-housing assistance and the existence of long waiting lists created by limits on the number of units and vouchers made available. They add a discussion of the trade-offs in providing less assistance to more households compared to the current situation as well as a discussion of targeting and priorities given the supply constraints.

The authors review existing research on housing programs, first reviewing research showing that housing subsidies do, in fact, increase housing consumption and reduce overcrowding. They also find that the research literature shows that public housing and housing vouchers have favorable effects on housing affordability, reducing the fraction of income families spend on housing, although there is little research evidence to date on the effects of the LIHTC. Their review of the evidence on the effects of housing programs on residential mobility suggests that the programs reduce it, although the number of studies is quite small. The considerably larger body of evidence on whether housing programs lead to residential locations in neighborhoods with better characteristics shows only very small effects of that kind. In their review of the effects of housing programs on other outcomes, the authors find evidence that vouchers reduce labor supply. They find little evidence that public housing and vouchers, as typically administered, do much in terms of improving neighborhood quality for families or providing measurable benefits for children. When housing vouchers improve neighborhood conditions for families, however, as in the MTO experiment, children appear to benefit substantially into adulthood.

Barnow and Smith review the wide variety of employment and training programs in the United States, ranging from programs for skill development (vocational development) to job development (public employment) to employability development (personal attitudes and attributes needed for employment) to work-experience programs (providing work experience per se). Some other programs, such as the labor exchange, are intended to match workers and jobs better or to provide counseling and assessment or information about the labor market. The authors review the long history of programs, starting in the Great Depression, but concentrate their discussion on the Workforce Investment Act (WIA) program enacted in 1998. The WIA remains the primary federal employment and training program and it was reauthorized with some changes in July, 2014, as the Workforce Innovation and Opportunity Act (WIOA). The WIA introduced many new features to the nation's training programs, greatly extending the presence of One-Stop centers where individuals can learn about and participate in a large range of program options at one time; providing new individual training accounts that were essentially vouchers for individuals to use at different training providers; mandating a fixed sequence of activities, starting with core services, then intensive ones, then training (this mandated sequence was deemphasized over time and eliminated in the 2014 reauthorization); and improving the performance management system. Studies of the implementation of WIA have shown that the One-Stop systems have been successfully established and that the individual training accounts have been very popular, but that the new performance management system had many difficult challenges and that training programs were not sufficiently engaging the local business community.

In their review of research on employment and training programs, Barnow and Smith first review the many different methodologies used to evaluate program effects and provide a discussion of data and measurement issues. Their review of research findings, concentrated on studies since the 2003 volume, indicates many estimates of positive earnings effects from the WIA program (generally interpreted as treatment effects on the treated), although often differing by gender, by whether the trainees were dislocated workers rather than other types of adults in need, and by whether the effects were long lasting rather than fading out. Their review of research on the Job Corps shows that it, alone among programs providing training to youth, has positive and substantial effects on their labor market outcomes, although the benefits fade after about five years as the control groups catch up. It also easily passes a benefit-cost criterion from the point of view of the participants. Barnow and Smith also review the evidence on the effects of the Trade Adjustment Assistance program, which provides employment and training services to those displaced by international trade, finding the program to not have statistically or substantively significant impacts on long-run labor market outcomes of the participants. The authors also review the smaller literatures on evaluation of performance measures, determinants of participation in employment and training programs, and the matching of participants to services.

Elango, García, Heckman, and Hojman review early childhood education (ECE) programs. The authors identify four different federal-funding streams for child care: the funding for Head Start and Early Head Start, the Child Care Development Fund, and the Individuals with Disabilities Education Act grants. They consider a wide variety of ECE programs, including (a) means-tested demonstration programs; (b) Head Start, the largest means-tested ECE program in the United States; (c) non-means-tested programs that have universal coverage in a local population; and (d) different types of child care. They consider four iconic demonstration programs implemented from 1962 to 1988: the Perry Preschool Project, the Carolina Abecedarian Project, the Early Training Project, and the Infant Health and Development Program. They argue that these programs have objectives and components that resemble modern high-quality ECE programs, making the conclusions drawn from them relevant. The authors also devote considerable discussion to Head Start, noting that its criterion for eligibility (poverty in terms of income) is less stringent than the criteria used for most demonstration programs (usually based on an index of disadvantage). They also review universal programs, including statewide and citywide programs in the United States, and two comprehensive evaluations of universal programs in Norway and Canada. The authors stress the difference between high-quality (center-based) and low-quality (informal, family-based) child care.

Elango and coauthors conduct an extensive review of research findings on these programs. They frame their discussion using the modern theory of skill formation and set up a framework illustrating the alternative choices that parents face for their children. They first focus on the four iconic demonstration programs, all of which were experimentally evaluated and have long-term follow-ups available. They also present their own reanalysis of the primary data sources used in those evaluations. Their review of studies of the effectiveness of Head Start considers both experimental evaluations with short-term data and quasi-experimental evaluations with long-term data. They find that, with few exceptions, ECE programs strongly boost IQ in the short run but the control group largely catches up at school entry. They argue that this catch-up in IQ does not imply that these programs are not effective, as demonstration programs have strong impacts on substantive later-life outcomes by boosting noncognitive skills. The available cost-benefit analyses of the programs are also strongly favorable. The authors stress that these positive results are obtained from populations of disadvantaged children. Then they conduct a detailed review of the most rigorous evaluations of the Head Start program (especially those addressing substitution bias, that is, the availability of good substitutes for members of control groups). They report that, contrary to some claims, Head Start has significant positive effects on many short-term and long-term child outcomes. In a review of the evaluations of universal ECE programs, the authors find that these programs have heterogeneous impacts across children in different socioeconomic statuses, with effects ranging from strongly positive for very disadvantaged children to low or even negative for non-disadvantaged children. They conclude by presenting evidence in the United States indicating that impacts are inextricably tied to program quality and to the quality of alternative home environments.

References

Ben-Shalom, Y., R. Moffitt, and J. K. Scholz. 2012. "An Assessment of the Effect of Anti-Poverty Programs in the United States." In *Oxford Handbook of the Economics of Poverty*, edited by P. Jefferson. Oxford: Oxford University Press.

Edelstein, S., M. Pergamit, and C. Ratcliffe. 2014. "Characteristics of Families Receiving Multiple Public Benefits." Research Report, Washington, DC, Urban Institute.

Haveman, R., R. Blank, R. Moffitt, T. Smeeding, and G. Wallace. 2015. "The War on Poverty: Measurement, Trends, and Policy." *Journal of Policy Analysis and Management* 34 (Summer): 593–638.

Moffitt, R., ed. 2003. *Means-Tested Transfer Programs in the United States*. Chicago: University of Chicago Press.

Spar, K. 2006. "Cash and Noncash Benefits for Persons with Limited Income: Eligibility Rules, Recipient and Expenditure Data, FY2002–FY2004." Congressional Research Service, Washington, DC.

US Congressional Budget Office. 2012. *Effective Marginal Tax Rates for Low- and Moderate-Income Workers*. Washington, DC: US Congress.

1

The Medicaid Program

Thomas Buchmueller, John C. Ham, and
Lara D. Shore-Sheppard

1.1 Introduction

In both its costs and the number of its enrollees, Medicaid is the largest means-tested transfer program in the United States. It is also a fundamental part of the health care system, providing health insurance to low-income families, indigent seniors, and disabled adults. In 2011, Medicaid covered over 68 million individuals at a cost to state and federal governments of nearly $400 billion (Centers for Medicare and Medicaid Services [CMS] 2013a). Federal Medicaid expenditures, which historically have averaged between 50 and 60 percent of total program expenditures, represent about 8 percent of the federal budget and nearly 2 percent of gross domestic product (Congressional Budget Office 2014). In 2012, the median state spent 22.4 percent of its budget on Medicaid (National Association of State Budget Officers 2013).

Because it finances different types of services for different groups of beneficiaries, it is often noted that Medicaid is essentially four public insurance programs in one (Gruber 2003). First, Medicaid is the primary source of

Thomas Buchmueller is the Waldo O. Hildebrand Professor of Risk Management and Insurance, professor and chair of business economics and professor of health management and policy at the University of Michigan, and a research associate of the National Bureau of Economic Research. John C. Ham is professor of economics and Provost's Chair at the National University of Singapore. Lara D. Shore-Sheppard is professor of economics at Williams College and a research associate of the National Bureau of Economic Research.

This chapter was prepared for the conference and volume *Economics of Means-Tested Transfer Programs in the United States*, vol. 1, organized and edited by Robert Moffitt. We are grateful to Morgan Henderson, Yuvraj Singh, and Ken Ueda for excellent research assistance and to our discussant Amy Finkelstein and other conference participants for helpful comments. For acknowledgments, sources of research support, and disclosure of the authors' material financial relationships, if any, please see http://www.nber.org/chapters/c13486.ack.

health insurance for low-income children and parents, providing coverage for a full range of outpatient and inpatient services. Second, Medicaid provides complementary insurance for low-income seniors for whom Medicare is the primary source of insurance. Third, Medicaid covers the medical expenses of low-income disabled individuals. Fourth, Medicaid is the largest source of financing for nursing home care. In addition to differences related to the characteristics and needs of different beneficiary groups, there is considerable heterogeneity across states. Although the federal government establishes important standards, states have considerable flexibility in terms of eligibility rules, the method and level of provider payment and, to a lesser extent, program benefits. Thus, it is also often argued that Medicaid is not one program, but fifty-one.

Expanded eligibility for Medicaid is a critical component of the Patient Protection and Affordable Care Act of 2010 and the Health Care and Education Reconciliation Act of 2010—together known as the Affordable Care Act (ACA). Initial projections were that roughly half of all individuals who gain insurance coverage as a result of the ACA would be enrolled in Medicaid. By establishing a new federal income standard, it was expected that the ACA would significantly reduce the variation across states in eligibility rules. However, because of the 2012 Supreme Court ruling that essentially made the ACA Medicaid expansions voluntary to states, implementation of the ACA has reduced variation in eligibility rules among expansion states while accentuating differences between states that have and have not elected to expand their programs. A number of expansion states have received waivers from the federal government allowing them to innovate on a number of dimensions. Thus, the ACA has continued not only the growth of Medicaid in terms of enrollment and expenditures, but it has contributed to the increased complexity of the program.

The ACA represents a significant inflection point for the Medicaid program, with important implications for the US health care system and for economic research on the program. The ACA eligibility expansions not only increase Medicaid enrollment and spending, but they also accelerate changes in the characteristics of individuals served by the program. As we describe below, at its inception, Medicaid eligibility was closely linked to the receipt of cash welfare benefits. Over time, this link was loosened and Medicaid eligibility limits were increased substantially for children, and to a lesser extent their parents. These expansions led to voluminous research literatures on the impact of Medicaid on a broad range of outcomes. The literature on how Medicaid affects access to care and health outcomes, especially for children, is particularly large. Multiple studies that we review in this chapter (and many more that we are not able to include) provide strong evidence that Medicaid significantly improves access to care. Several studies also suggest that this increased care leads to better health outcomes, including a reduction in infant and child mortality. The ACA eligibility expansions will largely affect nondisabled, nonelderly childless adults, a demographic group that has been underrepresented in the program. Although there has been less research on the impact of Medicaid on this population, several important studies have been published recently. The most notable are based on the randomized assignment of Medicaid eligibility in Oregon. Research based on the Oregon experiment confirms a number of results from the prior literature, such as a strong effect of Medicaid on health care utilization, while also providing evidence on other outcomes, such as financial well-being, that had previously received limited attention.

This chapter reviews the history and structure of the Medicaid program and the large body of economic research that it has spawned in the nearly half century since it was established. Section 1.2 summarizes the program's history, goals, and current rules and section 1.3 presents program statistics, mainly related to enrollment and expenditures. Then we turn to the research on the impact of Medicaid. In section 1.4 we discuss theoretical and methodological issues important for understanding these effects. Section 1.5 reviews the empirical literature, describing what has been learned thus far, investigating areas where studies seem to reach different conclusions and pointing to areas where we believe additional research would be fruitful. Section 1.6 concludes.

1.2   Program History, Goals, and Current Rules

Founded in 1965 as Title XIX of the Social Security Amendments, Medicaid is a joint state-federal program. The federal government provides the majority of the program's funding and establishes general guidelines for eligibility, services to be covered, and reimbursement rates; states provide additional funding and have some flexibility in how they administer the program in terms of eligibility levels and procedures, benefits, provider payments, and care delivery approaches. Over its fifty-year history, the program has undergone many changes and modifications, although there are characteristics of Medicaid that were present at its inception and remain important in the program today. One of these is the existence of both mandatory actions that states *must* take—groups of individuals that states must cover and services that states must provide—and optional actions that states *may* take. As a result, the program differs substantially across states with respect to eligibility, covered services, and provider reimbursement rates.

While some fundamental features of Medicaid have remained constant throughout its history, there is one key element of Medicaid that has changed in recent years. From its inception, Medicaid was available only for individuals who were actual or potential recipients of cash assistance, resulting in a means-tested program that was unavailable to large portions of the poor population. In particular, only the elderly, the disabled, or members of families with dependent children where one parent is absent, incapacitated, or unemployed (the latter only in some states) could be eligible for Medicaid. The requirement for membership in one of these groups began to be relaxed beginning with the Deficit Reduction Act of 1984, but not until the ACA was implemented was eligibility for Medicaid extended more broadly to low-income adults who were not elderly, disabled, or parents of a dependent child. The ACA thus represents both a continuation of the program as it has existed and a fundamental shift.

The history of the program can be divided into three main periods.[1] First is the period between 1965 and the early 1980s, when the program was characterized by strict limits on eligibility that were not solely income based. Since many of the features of the program established at its enactment survive in some form today, in discussing this period we also lay out the basic structure of eligibility for the program, services covered, and the structure of reimbursement. Second is the period between the early 1980s and prior to the passage of the Personal Responsibility and Work Opportunity Reconciliation Act of 1996 (PRWORA), when definitions of eligibility began to expand, although the primary route to Medicaid eligibility remained eligibility for cash assistance. In our discussion of this period we focus primarily on the incremental changes that were occurring with eligibility. Finally, there is the period beginning with the passage of PRWORA and culminating with the implementation of the ACA. During this time there were major changes in the program that resulted in the rules in place today.

We summarize the major legislative actions affecting Medicaid in table 1.1. From these legislative actions it can be seen that Medicaid is a program of fundamental tensions: between a recognition that many poor individuals lack health insurance, resulting in a desire for expanded eligibility, and concern about substantial and growing costs of the program; between a desire to compensate providers at sufficiently high levels to ensure participation and a desire to contain costs by capping provider compensation; and between giving states flexibility to design their own programs and ensuring uniform standards across the country. In addition to legislative action, Medicaid has been shaped in important ways by federal regulatory decisions and state choices. Below we discuss these important policy elements as well.

1.2.1   Implementation and Adaptation: 1965–1983

The establishment of Medicaid in 1965 grew out of earlier medical care vendor-payment programs that were linked to cash assistance receipt. These earlier programs, established by the Social Security Amendments of 1950 and expanded by the Kerr-Mills Act of 1960, had the fundamental feature continued in Medicaid of providing federal funding at state option for

---

1. Sources for this section include Congressional Research Service (1993), Gruber (2003), Schneider et al. (2002), Schneider (1997), Congressional Budget Office (2001), Urban Institute (2015), Kaiser Family Foundation (2008), US Social Security Administration (2011), Office of the Legislative Counsel (2010), Kaiser Commission on Medicaid and the Uninsured (2009), and Centers for Medicare & Medicaid Services (CMS 2013b).

Table 1.1   Major Medicaid and CHIP legislation, 1965 to 2010

Social Security Amendments of 1965	Established the Medicaid program.
Social Security Amendments of 1967	Enacted the Early and Periodic Screening, Diagnostic and Treatment (EPSDT) benefit, required for Medicaid children younger than twenty-one.
	Allowed states to extend Medicaid coverage to optional populations not receiving cash assistance, including "Ribicoff children"—individuals under twenty-one who would be eligible for AFDC if they met the definition of dependent child.
	Permitted Medicaid beneficiaries to use providers of their choice.
	Limited income eligibility standard for medically needy.
Act of 14 December 1971	Allowed states to cover services in intermediate care facilities for individuals with lower-level care needs than skilled nursing facilities.
Social Security Amendments of 1972	Enacted Supplemental Security Income (SSI) program for elderly and disabled and required states to extend Medicaid to SSI recipients or to elderly and disabled meeting state 1972 eligibility criteria ("209[b]" option).
	Repealed the Medicaid "maintenance of effort" requirement for states.
	Allowed states to cover care for beneficiaries under age twenty-two in psychiatric hospitals.
Medicare-Medicaid Anti-Fraud and Abuse Amendments of 1977	Established Medicaid Fraud Control Units.
Departments of Labor and Health, Education, and Welfare Appropriations Act for FY 1977	Enacted the Hyde Amendment, which prohibited federal Medicaid payments for medically necessary abortions except when the life of the mother would be endangered.
Mental Health Systems Act of 1980	Required most states to develop a computerized Medicaid management information system.
Omnibus Reconciliation Act of 1980 (OBRA 1980)	Enacted the Boren Amendment requiring states to pay "reasonable and adequate" rates for nursing home services instead of Medicare reimbursement rates.
Omnibus Budget Reconciliation Act of 1981 (OBRA 1981)	Enacted reduction in federal-matching percentages applicable from FY 1982–1984.
	Extended Boren Amendment payment standard to inpatient hospital services.
	Required states to make payment adjustments to hospitals serving a disproportionate share of Medicaid and low-income patients (DSH hospitals).
	Enacted section 1915(b) freedom-of-choice waiver for mandatory managed care.
	Enacted section 1915(c) home and community-based waiver.
	Eliminated special penalties for noncompliance with EPSDT requirements.
	Gave states with medically needy programs broader authority to limit coverage.

(continued)

Table 1.1 (continued)

Tax Equity and Fiscal Responsibility Act of 1982 (TEFRA)	Allowed states to impose nominal cost sharing on certain Medicaid beneficiaries and services.
Deficit Reduction Act of 1984 (DEFRA)	Required states to cover children born after September 30, 1983, up to age five in families meeting state AFDC income and resource standards.
	Required states to cover first-time pregnant women and pregnant women in two-parent unemployed families meeting state AFDC income and resource standards.
Consolidated Omnibus Budget Reconciliation Act of 1985 (COBRA)	Required states to cover pregnant women in two-parent families (whether or not unemployed) meeting state AFDC income and resource standards.
Omnibus Reconciliation Act of 1986 (OBRA 1986)	Allowed states to cover pregnant women and young children up to age five in families with incomes at or below 100 percent of federal poverty level.
	Allowed states to pay for Medicare premiums and cost sharing for low-income Medicare beneficiaries (QMBs) with incomes at or below 100 percent of federal poverty level.
	Mandated coverage of emergency services for illegal immigrants who would otherwise be eligible for Medicaid.
Medicare and Medicaid Patient and Program Protection Act of 1987	Strengthened authorities to sanction and exclude providers.
Omnibus Budget Reconciliation Act of 1987 (OBRA 1987)	Allowed states to cover pregnant women and infants in families with incomes at or below 185 percent of federal poverty level.
	Allowed states to cover children up to age eight in families below 100 percent of poverty level.
	Enacted nursing home reform provisions that phased out distinction between skilled nursing facilities and intermediate care facilities, upgraded quality of care requirements, and revised monitoring and enforcement.
	Strengthened OBRA 1981 requirements that states provide additional payment to hospitals treating a disproportionate share of low-income patients.
Medicare Catastrophic Coverage Act of 1988 (MCCA)	Required states to phase in coverage for pregnant women and infants with incomes below 100 percent of federal poverty level.
	Required states to phase in coverage of Medicare premiums and cost sharing for low-income Medicare beneficiaries (QMBs) with incomes below 100 percent of poverty level.
	Established minimum income and resource rules for nursing home residents whose spouses remain in the community to prevent "spousal impoverishment."

Family Support Act of 1988 (FSA)	Required states to extend twelve months transitional Medicaid coverage to families leaving AFDC rolls due to earnings from work.
Omnibus Budget Reconciliation Act of 1989 (OBRA 1989)	Required states to cover two-parent unemployed families meeting state AFDC income and resource standards. Required states to cover pregnant women and children under age six in families with incomes at or below 133 percent of federal poverty level. Expanded EPSDT benefit for children under twenty-one to include diagnostic and treatment services not covered under state Medicaid program for adult beneficiaries. Required states to cover services provided by federally qualified health centers.
Omnibus Budget Reconciliation Act of 1990 (OBRA 1990)	Required states to phase in coverage of children ages six through eighteen born after September 30, 1983, in families with incomes at or below 100 percent of federal poverty level. Required states to phase in coverage of Medicare premiums for low-income Medicare beneficiaries with incomes between 100 and 120 percent of federal poverty level (SLMB). Required manufacturers to give "best price" rebates to states and federal government for outpatient prescription drugs covered under Medicaid program.
Medicaid Voluntary Contribution and Provider-Specific Tax Amendments of 1991	Restricted use of provider donations and taxes as state share of Medicaid spending. Imposed ceiling on Medicaid payment adjustments to DSH hospitals (12 percent of national aggregate Medicaid spending).
Omnibus Budget Reconciliation Act of 1993 (OBRA 1993)	Established standards for state use of formularies to limit prescription drug coverage. Imposed facility-specific ceilings on the amount of payment adjustment to DSH hospitals. Tightened prohibitions against transfers of assets in order to qualify for Medicaid nursing home coverage; required recovery of nursing home payments from beneficiary estates. Established Vaccines for Children (VFC) program providing federally purchased vaccines to states.
Personal Responsibility and Work Opportunity Reconciliation Act of 1996 (PRWORA)	Replaced AFDC with Temporary Assistance for Needy Families (TANF) and severed the automatic link between cash welfare and Medicaid. Mandated coverage of families meeting AFDC eligibility standards as of July 16, 1996, while permitting coverage of higher-income families. Prohibited Medicaid coverage for legal immigrants entering the United States after August 21, 1996, and allowed states to cover these immigrants after they have been in the country for five years. Narrowed the eligibility criteria for disabled children.

(continued)

Table 1.1 (continued)

Balanced Budget Act of 1997 (BBA 1997)	Created the State Children's Health Insurance Program (SCHIP, later referred to as CHIP), allowing states to cover uninsured children in families with incomes below 200 percent of FPL who were ineligible for Medicaid.
	Allowed states to implement mandatory managed-care enrollment for most Medicaid beneficiaries without obtaining section 1915(b) waivers.
	Eliminated minimum payment standards for state-set reimbursement rates for hospitals, nursing homes, and community health centers, placed ceilings on DSH payment adjustments, and allowed states to shift the cost of Medicare deductibles and coinsurance requirements for low-income Medicare beneficiaries from their Medicaid programs to physicians and other providers.
	Allowed partial coverage of Medicare premiums for beneficiaries with incomes between 120 and 135 percent of FPL (QIs), funded via a federal block grant.
	Restored Medicaid eligibility for legal immigrants who entered the country on or before August 22, 1996, and became disabled and qualified for Supplemental Security Income (SSI) benefits thereafter.
	Restored Medicaid coverage for certain disabled children who would lose their eligibility as a result of PRWORA.
	Allowed states to provide up to twelve months of continuous eligibility for children. Allowed states to cover children presumptively until a formal determination of eligibility is made.
Ticket to Work and Work Incentives Improvement Act of 1999	Allowed states to cover working disabled individuals with incomes above 250 percent of federal poverty level and impose income-related premiums on such individuals.
Emergency Supplemental Appropriations for FY 1999	Transferred federal share of settlement funds from national tobacco litigation to states.
Breast and Cervical Cancer Treatment and Prevention Act of 2000	Allowed states to cover uninsured women with breast or cervical cancer regardless of their income and resources.
Medicare, Medicaid, and SCHIP Benefits Improvement and Protection Act of 2000 (BIPA)	Increased state-specific ceilings on DSH allotments.
	Required the Secretary of Health and Human Services to issue a final regulation restricting the amount of Medicaid payments that states may make to facilities that are operated by local governments and thus curtail the use of an accounting practice that allowed states to artificially inflate their reimbursable spending.
	Postponed the expiration of funds appropriated for SCHIP in 1998 and 1999.
	Allowed additional entities to determine presumptive eligibility.
The Jobs and Growth Tax Relief Reconciliation Act of 2003	Raised all state Medicaid matching rates by 2.95 percentage points for the period April 2003 through June 2004 as temporary federal fiscal relief for the states due to the downturn in the economy.

Medicare Prescription Drug, Improvement, and Modernization Act of 2003	Transferred drug coverage of individuals dually eligible for Medicare and Medicaid to Medicare starting in 2006. Medicaid still to provide some prescription drug coverage for the dually eligible population for prescription drugs not covered under the newly created Medicare Part D.
Deficit Reduction Act of 2005 (DRA)	Provided states with increased flexibility to make significant reforms to their Medicaid programs. Refined eligibility requirements for Medicaid beneficiaries by tightening standards for citizenship and immigration documentation and by changing the rules concerning long-term care eligibility.
Medicare, Medicaid, and SCHIP Extension Act of 2007	Reauthorized CHIP through April 2009 at then-current funding levels.
Children's Health Insurance Program Reauthorization Act of 2009 (CHIPRA)	Reauthorized CHIP through 2013 and expanded federal funding for children's coverage by $33 billion over the next four and half years. Established an upper income limit of 300 percent of the FPL for states to receive the more generous federal CHIP matching rate, with an exception for states that already had permission to cover higher-income children. Allowed states the option to expand coverage to legal immigrant children and pregnant women during their first five years in the country. Required states to cover dental services and required parity of mental health services.
Patient Protection and Affordable Care Act of 2010 (PPACA) and Health Care and Education Reconciliation Act of 2010 (HCERA)—together known as the Affordable Care Act (ACA)	Expanded Medicaid to include all individuals under age sixty-five in families with income below 138 percent of the FPL starting in 2014. (Technically, the income limit is 133 percent of the FPL, but the act also provided for a 5 percent income disregard.) The Supreme Court ruling in 2012 made this coverage expansion optional for states. Broadened availability of long-term care services and supports, starting as early as 2010 in some instances. Extended the authorization of the federal CHIP program for an additional two years, through September 30, 2015. Required states to maintain current income eligibility levels for CHIP through September 30, 2019. States prohibited from implementing eligibility standards, methodologies, or procedures more restrictive than those in place as of March 23, 2010, with the exception of waiting lists for enrolling children in CHIP.

Sources: Congressional Research Service (1993), Gruber (2003), Schneider et al. (2002), Schneider (1997), Congressional Budget Office (2001), Urban Institute (2015), Kaiser Family Foundation (2008), US Social Security Administration (2011), Office of the Legislative Counsel (2010), Kaiser Commission on Medicaid and the Uninsured (2009), and Centers for Medicare & Medicaid Services (2013).

vendor payments for the benefit of cash assistance beneficiaries. Historical accounts of the origin of Medicaid indicate that it passed Congress with very little discussion, being viewed as largely an improvement on the existing Kerr-Mills program (Moore and Smith 2005).

The combination of building on an existing program that was tightly linked to cash assistance receipt and responding to widespread concern about impoverishment through rising health care costs led to the creation of two classes of beneficiaries. The first group was the *categorically needy*: recipients of certain cash assistance programs, including Aid to the Blind, Aid to Families with Dependent Children (AFDC), and Aid to the Permanently and Totally Disabled. These programs were not only strictly means tested, but they also applied only to the blind, the elderly, the disabled, and members of families with a single parent. The second class of beneficiaries was the *medically needy*: individuals who would be categorically eligible except that their income and resources were above the eligibility cutoff, but who had sufficient medical expenses to bring their income after medical expenses below the cutoff (known as "spend down"). The goals of the program at its creation were thus to provide access to medical care to those viewed as the neediest members of society and to prevent medical expense-induced indigence among single-parent families, the disabled, and the elderly (Moore and Smith 2005; Weikel and LeaMond 1976).

As with the Kerr-Mills program that preceded it, participation in Medicaid was made optional for states, although if a state elected to participate it had to include all of the public assistance categories and all recipients within those categories, and if a state chose to have a medically needy program it had to open that program to members of all eligibility categories. Although state participation was optional, Congress included in the legislation incentives for states to participate. Federal funds for earlier medical assistance programs were scheduled to end within five years, funds were offered not only to match state expenditures but also to help pay for the administration of the Medicaid program, and states participating in the Medicaid program could use its more favorable matching rate for their other categorical assistance programs (Moore and Smith 2005). The federal match rate, or federal matching assistance percentage (FMAP), is determined annually for each state s based on a formula that compares a state's average per capita income level (Y_S) with the national average income level (Y_N): FMAP$_S$ = $1-0.45(Y_S/Y_N)^2$. According to this formula, a state where per capita income equals the national average pays 45 percent of program expenditures. No state is required to pay more than 50 percent; in most years since the start of the program between ten and fourteen higher-income states have had an FMAP of 50 percent. A state's FMAP is capped by law at 83 percent.[2]

2. Since fiscal year 1998, Washington DC's FMAP has been set permanently at 70 percent. At different times Congress has temporarily increased FMAPs in response to economic crises.

Table 1.2   States' decision on ACA and year of original implementation of Medicaid

	Not implementing ACA Medicaid expansion	Implementing ACA Medicaid expansion	Implementing a modified ACA Medicaid
1966	ID, LA, ME, NE, OK, UT, WI[a]	CA, CT, DE, HI, IL, KY, MD, MA, MN, NH[b], NM, ND, OH, RI, VT, WA, WV	MI[c], PA[d]
1967	GA, KS, MO, SD, TX, WY	NV, NY, OR	IA[e], MT[f]
1968	SC	DC	
1969	TN, VA	CO	
1970	AL, FL, MS, NC	NJ	AR[g], IN[h]
1971			
1972	AK		
1982*		AZ	

Sources: Kaiser Family Foundation State Health Facts (http://kff.org/medicaid/state-indicator/state-activity-around-expanding-medicaid-under-the-affordable-care-act/), Arizona Health Care Cost Containment System Section 1115 waiver description (http://www.azahcccs.gov/reporting/federal/waiver.aspx), and Gruber (2003); data current as of June 2015.

[a]Wisconsin amended its Medicaid state plan and existing Section 1115 waiver to cover childless adults with incomes up to 100 percent FPL in Medicaid, but did not adopt the ACA Medicaid expansion.

[b]New Hampshire implemented the Medicaid expansion as of July 1, 2014, but the state plans to seek a waiver at a later date to operate a premium assistance model.

[c]Michigan is implementing the Healthy Michigan plan using a Section 1115 waiver, under which monthly premiums and required copayments will be instituted. (See http://kff.org/medicaid/fact-sheet/medicaid-expansion-in-michigan/ for more details.)

[d]Pennsylvania is implementing a Section 1115 waiver to expand Medicaid coverage to adults under 138 percent FPL through privately managed care plans, with premiums for newly eligible adults 100–138 percent FPL. (See http://files.kff.org/attachment/medicaid-expansion-in-pennsylvania-fact-sheet for more details.)

[e]Iowa is using a Section 1115 waiver to charge monthly premiums for people with incomes between 101–38 percent FPL and another Section 1115 waiver to cover newly eligible beneficiaries with incomes at or below 100 percent FPL under Medicaid managed care. (See http://files.kff.org/attachment/medicaid-expansion-in-iowa-fact-sheet for more details.)

[f]Montana has enacted legislation adopting a modified expansion that requires premiums and copayments. The legislation requires federal waiver approval before it can go into effect.

[g]Arkansas is implementing a premium assistance model using a waiver. (See http://files.kff.org/attachment/medicaid-expansion-in-arkansas-fact-sheet for more details.)

[h]Indiana has a pending waiver for an alternative Medicaid expansion plan.

*Indicates a gap between 1982 and the preceding year.

Over half of the states began participating in the first year of the program (see the rows of table 1.2 that show which states began participating in each year), with another eleven states beginning to participate in 1967. By 1970 all but two states (Alaska and Arizona) were participating. Generosity of the FMAP was not the only factor determining when states began partici-

---

The most recent case was in 2009 as part of the American Recovery and Reinvestment Act. The FMAPs from the beginning of Medicaid through the current year may be found at http://aspe.hhs.gov/health/fmap.cfm.

pating, as some states with high match rates (including Alabama, Arkansas, and Mississippi) began participating much later than other states. For comparison, the table also shows which states have decided (as of spring 2015) to participate in the Medicaid expansion offered by the ACA; there is some correlation between deciding not to participate in the ACA at its inception and late participation in the Medicaid program. The ACA participation decision and what it entails are discussed further in the section on the most recent time period, below.

Eligibility for Families

In the initial period of Medicaid, eligibility for poor children and their families required eligibility for AFDC. To qualify for AFDC a family was required to pass stringent income and resource tests, which were far below the poverty level in most states, and generally the family must have been either headed by a single parent or have an unemployed primary earner (in states with the optional AFDC-Unemployed Parent program). An exception to the family structure requirements was created shortly after the establishment of Medicaid by the Social Security Amendments of 1967, which allowed states to extend Medicaid coverage to "Ribicoff children." Named after the senator who sponsored the legislation, these were children who did not meet the family-structure requirements for AFDC, but who nevertheless met the income and resource requirements. The income tests required that family income less disregards for work expenses and child care be below the state-determined *need standard*, an amount that differed depending on family size. Beginning in the early 1980s, additional income tests were added so that income less disregards less a small amount of earnings needed to be below the state's *payment standard* (also a function of family size) and gross income needed to be below a multiple of the state's need standard. Finally, the resource test required family resources to be below $1,000, not including the value of the home.

For illustration, calculations of the income-eligibility limits as a percentage of the poverty line for a family with three members for 1987 are shown in column (1) of table 1.3. The limits in column (1) illustrate two points: there was considerable variation in eligibility limits across states, and the income limits were well below the poverty line. Even the most generous states required family incomes to be below 85 percent of the poverty line, while the least generous states only covered families with incomes below one-third of the poverty line. (The other columns of table 1.3, which show eligibility limits for children in later years, are discussed below.)

Eligibility for Disabled Individuals

Eligibility limits for the disabled population were also fairly stringent, although somewhat less stringent than for families. From 1966 to 1972, disabled individuals needed to qualify for the Aid to the Permanently and

Table 1.3   Changes in eligibility limits for children[a]

State	Prior to expansions (1987)[b] (1)	Prior to CHIP (1997) inf. / <6 / 6–14 / 15–19 (2)	Under CHIP (2001) infants / older children (3)	Prior to ACA (2013) with CHIP (* = Medicaid limits lower) (4)	After ACA (2014)[c] with CHIP (* = Medicaid limits lower) (5)
Alabama	16	133 / 133 / 100 / 15	200 / 200	300*	317*
Alaska	82	133 / 133 / 100 / 76	200 / 200	175	208
Arizona	40	140 / 133 / 100 / 32	200 / 200	200*	205*
Arkansas	26	200 / 200 / 200 / 200	200 / 200	200	216
California	85	200 / 133 / 100 / 82	300 / 200	250*	266
Colorado	48	133 / 133 / 100 / 39	185 / 185	250*	265*
Connecticut	81	185 / 185 / 185 / 185	300 / 300	300*	323*
Delaware	43	185 / 133 / 100 / 100	200 / 200	200*	218*
District of Columbia	50	185 / 133 / 100 / 37	200 / 200	300	324
Florida	36	185 / 133 / 100 / 28	200 / 200	200*	215*
Georgia	35	185 / 133 / 100 / 39	235 / 235	235*	252*
Hawaii	56	185 / 133 / 100 / 100	200 / 200	300	313
Idaho	42	133 / 133 / 100 / 29	150 / 150	185*	190*
Illinois	47	133 / 133 / 100 / 46	200 / 185	300*	318*
Indiana	35	150 / 133 / 100 / 100	200 / 200	250*	255*
Iowa	52	185 / 133 / 100 / 39	200 / 200	300*	317*
Kansas	55	150 / 133 / 100 / 100	200 / 200	232*	250*
Kentucky	27	185 / 133 / 100 / 33	200 / 200	200*	218*
Louisiana	26	133 / 133 / 100 / 100	150 / 150	250*	255*
Maine	56	185 / 133 / 125 / 125	200 / 200	200*	213*
Maryland	47	185 / 185 / 185 / 34	200 / 200[d]	300	322
Massachusetts	67	185 / 133 / 133 / 133	200 / 200	300*	305*
Michigan	65	185 / 150 / 150 / 150	200 / 200	200*	217*
Minnesota	73	275 / 275 / 275 / 275	280 / 275	280 (inf.) / 275	288 (inf.) / 280

(continued)

Table 1.3 (continued)

State	Prior to expansions (1987)[b] (1)	Prior to CHIP (1997) inf. / <6 / 6–14 / 15–19 (2)	Under CHIP (2001) infants / older children (3)	Prior to ACA (2013) with CHIP (* = Medicaid limits lower) (4)	After ACA (2014)[c] with CHIP (* = Medicaid limits lower) (5)
Mississippi	16	185 / 133 / 100 / 34	200 / 200	200*	214*
Missouri	38	185 / 133 / 100 / 100	300 / 300	300*	305*
Montana	49	133 / 133 / 100 / 41	150 / 150	250*	266*
Nebraska	48	150 / 133 / 100 / 34	185 / 185	200	218
Nevada	39	133 / 133 / 100 / 45	200 / 200	200*	205*
New Hampshire	55	185 / 185 / 185 / 185	300 / 300	300	323
New Jersey	55	185 / 133 / 100 / 41	350 / 350	350*	355*
New Mexico	35	185 / 185 / 185 / 185	235 / 235	235	305
New York	68	185 / 133 / 100 / 87	185 / 185	400*	405*
North Carolina	36	185 / 133 / 100 / 100	200 / 200	200*	216*
North Dakota	51	133 / 133 / 100 / 100	140 / 140	160*	175*
Ohio	41	133 / 133 / 100 / 32	200 / 200	200	211
Oklahoma	43	150 / 133 / 100 / 48	185 / 185	185	210
Oregon	55	133 / 133 / 100 / 100	170 / 170	300*	305*
Pennsylvania	52	185 / 133 / 100 / 100	235 / 235	300*	319*
Rhode Island	69	250 / 250 / 250 / 250	300 / 300	250	266
South Carolina	27	185 / 133 / 100 / 18	150 / 150	200	213
South Dakota	50	133 / 133 / 100 / 100	200 / 200	200*	209*
Tennessee	21	400 / 400 / 400 / 400	400 / 400 / 100[e]	250*	255*
Texas	25	185 / 133 / 100 / 17	200 / 200	200*	206*
Utah	52	133 / 133 / 100 / 100	200 / 200	200*	205*

Vermont	79	225 / 225 / 225 / 225	300 / 300	300	318
Virginia	49	133 / 133 / 100 / 100	200 / 200	200*	205*
Washington	68	200 / 200 / 200 / 200	250 / 250	300*	305*
West Virginia	34	150 / 133 / 100 / 100	200 / 200	300*	305*
Wisconsin	75	185 / 185 / 100 / 100	185 / 185 (200 after enrlmt.)	300*	306*
Wyoming	49	133 / 133 / 100 / 55	133 / 133	200*	205*

Sources: Shore-Sheppard (2003, table 1); Heberlein et al. (2013); Kaiser Family Foundation "Medicaid and CHIP Income Eligibility Limits for Children at Application, Effective January 1, 2014," Available at http://kff.org/health-reform/state-indicator/medicaid-and-chip-income-eligibility-limits-for-children-at-application-effective-january-1-2014/ (accessed Nov 11, 2013); Kaiser Family Foundation "Medicaid and CHIP Income Eligibility Limits for Pregnant Women at Application, Effective January 1, 2014." Available at http://kff.org/medicaid/state-indicator/medicaid-and-chip-income-eligibility-limits-for-pregnant-women-at-application-effective-january-1-2014/ (accessed Nov 11, 2013).

[a]Eligibility limits are as a percent of the federal poverty threshold for that year. Note that until the ACA, eligibility limits that are apparently equal may actually differ through differences in the two states' choices of what income and resources are counted.

[b]Eligibility is through eligibility for AFDC; limits are for a family of three.

[c]Difference from prior column may solely be a result of different methods of counting income (see text).

[d]Maryland also had premium assistance eligibility to 300 percent of the poverty threshold.

[e]Tennessee had a 1115 waiver to operate TennCare. Its CHIP expansion covered children <19 born before October 1, 1983, who could not have enrolled in Medicaid before.

Totally Disabled or Aid to the Blind programs to receive Medicaid, but in the Social Security Amendments of 1972, Congress replaced the non-AFDC cash assistance programs with Supplemental Security Income for the Aged, Blind, and Disabled (SSI). Under the SSI program, the federal government funds payments and sets eligibility standards. Income eligibility for SSI is determined by comparing an individual's countable income (monthly income less disregards of $20 of any income and $65 plus one-half of the amount over $65 of earned income) to the federal benefit rate (FBR). The FBR, which was set in 1972 and has been increased by the amount of inflation since then, is roughly 74 percent of the federal poverty level (FPL). States have the option of including a state supplement, and a little less than half of the states do, which increases the income-eligibility limits in those states.

Following the introduction of SSI, Medicaid was intended to continue to be automatic for disabled individuals receiving assistance, but since the SSI eligibility standards were more lenient than what many states had in place in 1972, states could choose not to make Medicaid eligibility automatic with SSI eligibility. This option to use a state-specified standard, known as the "209(b)" option after the section of the 1972 Social Security Amendments enacting it, allowed a state to use eligibility criteria for Medicaid under disability no more restrictive than the ones it used in January 1972.[3] States choosing the 209(b) option must allow individuals to "spend down" to eligibility by deducting medical expenses incurred from countable income. States may also choose not to extend Medicaid eligibility to individuals who are eligible only for the state supplement.

In addition to income eligibility, eligibility for Medicaid under SSI or the 209(b) option also requires individuals to meet asset limits and disability standards. A full discussion of asset and disability provisions of SSI is beyond the scope of this chapter (see chapter 1 on SSI in volume 2), but there are a few elements of these provisions that are important to note. First, asset limits, unlike income limits, are not indexed for inflation, so aside from occasional increases passed by Congress they have been declining in real terms. Second, the level of disability required to receive SSI is severe: an adult must have an "inability to engage in any substantial gainful activity by reason of any medically determinable physical or mental impairment(s) which can be expected to result in death or which has lasted or can be expected to last for a continuous period of not less than 12 months," while a child will be considered disabled "if he or she has a medically determinable physical or mental impairment or combination of impairments that causes marked and severe functional limitations, and that can be expected to cause death or that has lasted or can be expected to last for a continuous period of not less than 12 months."[4]

---

3. There are eleven 209(b) states.
4. Social Security Administration, "Disability Evaluation under Social Security" (http://www.ssa.gov/disability/professionals/bluebook/general-info.htm).

Because medical expenses for the disabled are usually quite high, the medically needy provisions of Medicaid play a more important role for the disabled (and the elderly) than for the low-income families eligibility category. The medically needy are individuals who would be categorically eligible except that their countable incomes are above the relevant cutoff (for SSI or AFDC) and who have incurred sufficient medical expenses to bring their income minus expenses below the medically need income standard. (Their resources must be below the state-set medically needy resource standard; there is no "spend down" applicable to resources.) States electing to cover the medically needy not only specify the income and resource limits that apply, but may also modify their standard benefits package for the medically needy population.[5] Roughly two-thirds of states have a medically needy program.

Eligibility for the Elderly

Eligibility for the elderly population resembles eligibility for the disabled in many ways, with a key exception being the interaction with Medicare for this population. States that participate in Medicaid are required to provide supplemental coverage through Medicaid to low-income Medicare beneficiaries for services not covered by Medicare. Elderly individuals can receive SSI if they are income eligible for it (under the rules discussed above), and the same rules for Medicaid eligibility (including the 209[b] option and the requirement for states to allow spend down to eligibility) apply to elderly SSI recipients as to the nonelderly disabled. Similarly, the elderly may qualify under the medically needy provisions of their state, a common route to eligibility for individuals in nursing facilities. Further expansions of eligibility among the elderly occurred during the period of expansions in the 1980s.

Services and Reimbursement

Within federal guidelines, states choose their own eligibility standards and provider reimbursement rates, resulting in wide variation in such rates across states. The federal government requires certain medical services to be covered, including inpatient and outpatient hospital services, laboratory and X-ray services, physicians' services, and skilled nursing facilities. Beginning with the 1967 Social Security Amendments, states were mandated to cover "early and periodic screening, diagnostic, and treatment" (EPSDT) services for eligible children. States may also choose to cover services such as prescription drugs, eyeglasses, and dental care. Importantly, Medicaid is an entitlement program, so eligible individuals have the right to receive the services that states have chosen to cover, and states have the right to matching payments for the cost of those services.

However, the framers of Medicaid did not realize the significant potential costs of the program (Moore and Smith 2005; Weikel and LeaMond

5. See Schneider et al. (2002) for a detailed discussion of the various pathways onto Medicaid for different categories of disabled individuals.

1976), and already by 1967 there were moves to control expenditures. The 1967 amendments included legislation to cap eligibility among the medically needy to those with incomes at most 133 1/3 percent of the AFDC income eligibility level in a state. In addition, the 1972 amendments repealed the "maintenance of effort" requirement that had previously prevented states from reducing expenditures on Medicaid from one year to the next.

Passage of cost-control measures continued in the early 1980s. The Omnibus Budget Reconciliation Act of 1981 (OBRA 1981) implemented several changes with major long-term implications for health care providers. First, OBRA 1981 repealed the requirement that states pay Medicare hospital payment rates. Instead, states were permitted to reimburse hospitals at lower rates and to make additional payments to hospitals serving a disproportionate share of Medicaid and other poor patients. These hospitals became known as disproportionate share hospitals (DSH) and payments to them were known as "DSH payments." Second, OBRA 1981 also established new types of "Medicaid waivers" as additional potential cost-control mechanisms. A waiver is a statutorily established permission for the federal agency charged with Medicaid implementation and regulation to grant certain exceptions to the federal rules for states that apply for those exceptions. Some waiver authority had already existed, notably that granted by Section 1115 of the Social Security Act, which allows the Secretary of Health and Human Services to permit a state to use federal Medicaid matching funds to pay for a statewide demonstration covering expenditures that would otherwise not be allowable. A state seeking a Section 1115 waiver must show that its demonstration will be "budget neutral" to the federal government over the five-year period of the waiver.[6] The new waivers included section 1915(b) freedom-of-choice waivers, which allowed states to pursue mandatory managed-care enrollment of certain Medicaid populations, and section 1915(c) home- and community-based long-term care services waivers, which allowed states to cover such services for the elderly and individuals with disabilities at risk of institutional care. In addition, the Tax Equity and Fiscal Responsibility Act of 1982 expanded state options for imposing cost-sharing requirements on beneficiaries.

1.2.2   Period of Incremental Expansions: 1984–1995

Following a period of legislative focus on cost containment, beginning in the mid-1980s there was a period of legislative focus on eligibility expansion. These expansions began by relaxing some of the family structure, but not income, requirements for members of low-income families. The Deficit Reduction Act of 1984 mandated coverage of three groups—children born after September 30, 1983, first-time pregnant women, and pregnant women

6. Arizona's Medicaid program has operated under a Section 1115 waiver since its inception in 1982.

in two-parent families with an unemployed primary earner—as long as the families were income eligible for AFDC. Then beginning in 1986, a series of federal laws began to diminish the link between Medicaid eligibility and AFDC eligibility by extending Medicaid coverage to members of families with incomes above the AFDC limits. Under these expansions, Medicaid eligibility determination was different from AFDC eligibility determination in two fundamental ways: the eligibility limits were linked to the federal poverty line rather than to the AFDC limits, and there were no family structure requirements. In the Omnibus Budget Reconciliation Acts (OBRAs) of 1986 and 1987, Congress gave states the authority to raise the income thresholds for Medicaid coverage of pregnant women, infants, and very young children above the AFDC level. In addition, OBRA 1987 required states to cover all children born after September 30, 1983, who met AFDC income standards, regardless of their family composition. The Medicare Catastrophic Coverage Act (MCCA) and Family Support Act (FSA), both of 1988, required states to extend Medicaid eligibility even further. The MCCA required coverage of pregnant women and infants and permitted coverage of children up to eight years of age with family incomes below 75 percent of the poverty level. Coverage of eligible two-parent families where the principal earner was unemployed was mandated by the FSA, and the FSA also required states to extend transitional Medicaid benefits for twelve months to members of families losing cash assistance due to earnings from work. Even broader expansions took place as a result of OBRA 1989 and OBRA 1990. The OBRA of 1989 required coverage of pregnant women and children up to age six with family incomes up to 133 percent of the federal poverty level, and OBRA 1990 required states to cover children born after September 30, 1983 and under the age of eighteen with family incomes below 100 percent of the federal poverty level.

The resulting eligibility limits that states established under these mandatory and optional expansions (and in some cases with the addition of state funds) as of the beginning of 1997 are shown in column (2) of table 1.3. The increase in eligibility limits was strikingly large, with eligibility limits doubling, tripling, or increasing even more substantially over the AFDC income limits. Notably, there was substantial variation in eligibility limits by age within states, with limits being more generous for infants and least generous for older teens. The extent of within-state variation also varied, with some states having fairly similar eligibility limits across the board and others having larger differences. These differences in eligibility within and across states and over time have proven useful in examining the impacts of Medicaid on various outcomes, as discussed in section 1.3.

This period was also a time of considerable expansion in eligibility for the elderly. Recognizing that there were substantial numbers of elderly Medicare beneficiaries with incomes above the SSI cutoff level but who needed assistance with Medicare premiums and cost-sharing requirements,

OBRA 1986 permitted and the MCCA required states to phase in coverage of Medicare premiums and cost sharing for Medicare beneficiaries with incomes below 100 percent of the federal poverty level and resources at or below twice the SSI resource cutoff. States must use income- and resource-counting methodologies that are not more restrictive than those used for SSI, and may be less restrictive. These beneficiaries are known as Qualified Medicare Beneficiaries, or QMBs. The OBRA of 1990 established an additional category of Medicare-Medicaid dual eligibles, Specified Low-Income Medicare Beneficiaries, or SLMBs. States were required to provide Medicare premium assistance through Medicaid to Medicare beneficiaries with incomes between 100 and 120 percent of the FPL and with resources not exceeding twice the SSI resource level. Together, assistance to these two groups is known as the Medicare Savings Programs.

In addition to expansions in eligibility for the elderly, the MCCA included provisions to prevent "spousal impoverishment" among spouses of individuals receiving long-term care through Medicaid. These provisions have as their goal permitting the spouse still living in the community to have sufficient resources and monthly income to avoid hardship. They are triggered when one spouse enters a long-term care facility (and is likely to remain at least thirty days). The spouse remaining in the community is allowed to keep a fraction of the couple's resources and a fraction of the income received on a monthly basis. The rest is contributed to the cost of care for the institutionalized spouse. In general, due to the high cost of institutional care and the low level of income and resources required to qualify for Medicaid to pay for such care, complex rules governing transfers of assets and income were developed over this period. These rules included those attempting to discourage individuals from giving away resources to qualify for Medicaid and those intended to provide individuals in states without medically needy programs whose incomes or resources are too high to qualify for Medicaid but too low to pay for needed institutional care with ways to qualify for Medicaid. For example, such individuals may establish a Qualified Income, or Miller, trust by depositing enough income in the trust to fall below an income limit equal to 300 percent of the SSI income limit; once the individual passes away, the state receives any money remaining in the trust up to the amount Medicaid has paid on behalf of the individual (see Schneider et al. [2002] for a detailed discussion of such rules).

The period of incremental expansions was also one of substantial growth in Medicaid expenditures, as can be seen in the discussion of program statistics later in the chapter. While the increasing number of eligible individuals is one obvious source of an increase in expenditures, a key element in the increase over this time period was the increasing state use of DSH payments and related financing programs, including provider-specific taxes and intergovernmental transfers (Ku and Coughlin 1995). States developed creative financing strategies in an effort to maximize federal transfers, requiring hospitals to pay provider taxes or to make donations or intergovernmental transfers, using the revenue from these sources to make DSH payments (usually back to the providers of the taxes or transfers), and then receiving the federal match on these expenditures. Concern over rapidly rising federal expenditures on Medicaid as a result of these strategies led to the Medicaid Voluntary Contribution and Provider-Specific Tax Amendments of 1991, which essentially banned provider donations, capped provider taxes, and required such taxes to be broad based and not targeted on a quid pro quo basis, and capped DSH payments (Ku and Coughlin 1995).

Another important change that occurred during this period was a move toward the use of managed-care contracts for Medicaid enrollees, including both capitated plans such as Health Maintenance Organizations (HMOs) and noncapitated primary care case-management plans. The potential benefits for states in using Medicaid managed care include a reduction in program expenditures (through the incentive inherent in capitated plans to reduce the use of unnecessary treatments), an improvement in quality through care coordination efforts, and a reduction in the level of financial risk faced by the state (Duggan and Hayford 2013). While managed-care plans in the commercial market often reduce expenditures via contracting with providers for lower reimbursement rates, the already low reimbursement rates in fee-for-service Medicaid leave little room for savings along that dimension.

1.2.3   Major Changes: Welfare Reform to the Affordable Care Act[7]

While the mid-1980s to mid-1990s were a period of incremental changes, the changes in Medicaid since the mid-1990s have been some of the most far reaching in Medicaid's history, with three major pieces of legislation fundamentally changing the program. The first was the Personal Responsibility and Work Opportunity Reconciliation Act of 1996 (PRWORA), which eliminated the AFDC program and replaced it with the Temporary Assistance for Needy Families (TANF) program, completing the process of decoupling Medicaid for low-income families from cash assistance eligibility. Unlike AFDC, TANF eligibility does not confer automatic Medicaid eligibility. Instead, Medicaid eligibility began to be determined separately, although individuals who met the requirements for the former AFDC program were intended to continue to be entitled to Medicaid. States were required to continue using the AFDC eligibility determination processes they had in place as of July 16, 1996. Thus an individual could be eligible for Medicaid but not TANF, or vice versa.

The most important impact of the decoupling of Medicaid from TANF eligibility was the impact on coverage for low-income parents. The requirement that states continue to cover parents who would have been eligible

---

7. Additional sources for this section: Kaiser Commission on Medicaid and the Uninsured (2012, 2014a, 2014b) and Rudowitz, Artiga, and Musumeci (2014).

under the former AFDC standards (known as Section 1931 eligibility) provided a basis for further expansions to parents. For the most part, the changes due to PRWORA did not affect eligibility for children since the expansion standards for children, which were more generous than AFDC eligibility standards, remained in place. However, Medicaid enrollment among children did fall immediately following the passage of PRWORA before rising again a few years later (see section 1.3 of this chapter). Also as part of PRWORA, legal immigrants were required to wait five years before they could be eligible for federally funded Medicaid, and illegal immigrants are ineligible for Medicaid. Both groups of immigrants are eligible for emergency Medicaid, however, which covers services necessary to treat an emergency medical condition for such individuals as long as they meet all other Medicaid requirements except for their immigration status. Some states did continue to provide Medicaid coverage with state funds to legal immigrants.

Another key piece of legislation was the Balanced Budget Act (BBA) of 1997. The BBA included many smaller changes to Medicaid and introduced a new public health insurance program for low-income children. Among the smaller changes enacted in the BBA, states were allowed to provide up to twelve months of continuous eligibility for children and to cover children presumptively until a formal determination of eligibility is made. The BBA also established a new level of support for Medicare beneficiaries with higher incomes, allowing partial coverage of Medicare premiums for beneficiaries with incomes between 120 and 135 percent of FPL (known as Qualified Individuals, or QIs), funded via a federal block grant. On the expenditure and reimbursement side, the BBA eliminated minimum payment standards for state-set reimbursement rates for hospitals, nursing homes, and community health centers, placed ceilings on DSH payment adjustments, and allowed states to avoid paying Medicare deductibles and coinsurance if their Medicaid payment rates for that service are lower than Medicare's. Instead, the state pays only the Medicaid reimbursement rate, and the providers are not permitted to bill the beneficiary for the balance. This practice effectively reduces the incentive for providers to treat low-income beneficiaries (Schneider et al. 2002). The BBA also allowed states to implement mandatory managed-care enrollment for most Medicaid beneficiaries without obtaining section 1915(b) waivers.

In addition, the BBA created the State Children's Health Insurance Program (called SCHIP at the time, but since changed to CHIP; we use the later acronym throughout this chapter), which provided states with $40 billion over ten years in block-grant funding to expand publicly provided health insurance for children. The basic structure of CHIP differs from Medicaid in several ways. First, each state is given a fixed allotment (rather than an entitlement to an unlimited federal match of spending) based on the number of uninsured children in the state and the state's relative health care costs. Second, the match rate is higher than under Medicaid, ranging from 65 to

85 percent. Third, states are given more flexibility by the federal government in structuring CHIP coverage.

States had three options for their CHIP funds: they could expand their Medicaid programs to cover additional ages and income categories, design a new program, or do a combination of the two, enacting an initial Medicaid expansion (for example, to fill in gaps in coverage across the age distribution) while designing further coverage under a state program. However states could not tighten their Medicaid rules, and applicants who qualified for Medicaid under the Medicaid eligibility standards in place prior to the introduction of CHIP had to be enrolled in Medicaid. If a state expanded its Medicaid program, children eligible under the CHIP expansion became entitled to all Medicaid benefits, and the state was required to conform to all Medicaid rules. If a state created a new program (or expanded an existing state program), then the state could design new benefits packages or arrangements for services, impose limited cost sharing, and design its own eligibility rules. The state-designed programs sometimes included some cost sharing (such as small premiums or copayments), were usually (though not exclusively) operated separately from Medicaid, and often incorporated a managed-care component. In a few cases, the state plans included completely new features, such as premium assistance for employer-sponsored insurance or coverage for parents of eligible children. State CHIP plans of all types involved new outreach efforts and were required to include efforts to minimize substitution of public insurance for private insurance (known as "crowding out"). In states with non-Medicaid-expansion CHIP plans, children who had other coverage were not eligible for the CHIP expansion (such children would be eligible for Medicaid, if their family incomes were low enough). In addition, many states incorporated a waiting period of between a month and a year, depending on the state, before a child could be enrolled in the state program after having private coverage. Other anti-crowd-out measures included premiums for higher-income families and state assistance with employer-sponsored insurance premiums.

The resulting eligibility limits under CHIP as of 2001 are shown in column (3) of table 1.3. Notably, CHIP permitted states to equalize eligibility across ages within a state, and while some states continued to have higher levels of eligibility for younger children, the extent of the disparity was considerably smaller. It is also clear that states were able to increase their eligibility limits overall, in most cases to two to three times the FPL.

States were permitted to spend up to 10 percent of their block grants for items other than providing insurance, and most states used some of these funds to improve participation in public health insurance. One important change in many states was the implementation of a period of continuous coverage (usually six months or a year). This means that once children qualify for coverage, coverage continues without interruption for the entire period, even if the child's family income increases. Other important changes that many states adopted include: elimination of a requirement that family assets be below a given level, elimination of the requirement that families come to the welfare office for a face-to-face interview (allowing applications to be mailed in), making the application simpler and/or instituting a single application for both Medicaid and CHIP programs, and outreach and publicity efforts. Outreach efforts that states report implementing took many forms, including partnerships with community organizations such as schools, health clinics, and community groups to promote enrollment, placing eligibility workers who can help fill out the forms in locations other than welfare offices, instituting a toll-free hotline to help with enrollment questions, and bilingual or multilingual applications and eligibility workers.

After its first ten years, CHIP came up for renewal in 2007. Twice Congress passed bills reauthorizing CHIP, but both bills were vetoed by President Bush. One of the main areas of disagreement was over offering coverage to higher-income children, with Congress voting to offer coverage to higher-income children and the administration expressing concern about negative effects of crowd-out. In late 2007 the Medicare, Medicaid, and SCHIP Extension Act of 2007 was passed and signed, largely maintaining existing funding levels for the program on a short-term basis. Then in 2009 the Children's Health Insurance Program Reauthorization Act (CHIPRA) reauthorized the program, provided additional funding and made other significant changes. An important change related to eligibility is the removal of the five-year waiting period requirement for immigrant children and pregnant women in Medicaid and CHIP, giving states the option of receiving federal funding to provide coverage to these populations without a waiting period. The CHIPRA also changed the financing formula. Instead of being based on estimates of per capita health costs and the number of uninsured children, state allotments are now based on historical CHIP spending, with rebasing every two years and annual updates for cost inflation and population growth.

The results of the coverage expansions to children beginning in the late 1980s and continuing through CHIPRA can easily be seen in figure 1.1, an updated version of a figure from Card and Shore-Sheppard (2004). Health insurance coverage rates by family income as a percent of the poverty line among children exhibited a distinct U-shape prior to the expansions, as Medicaid was available only to the poorest children and private coverage rates did not equal or exceed Medicaid coverage rates except for children in families with incomes around 1.5 times the poverty line. Over the next twenty-five years, as the expansions took effect, insurance coverage rates smoothed out across the income distribution so that even at the lowest point coverage rates were around 85 percent, climbing above 90 percent for children with incomes above three times the poverty line.

In addition to the optional expansions in the laws discussed previously, over this period the federal government used its regulatory authority to add

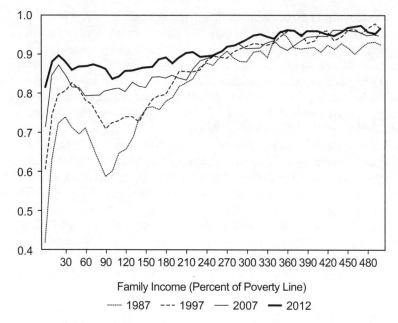

Fig. 1.1   Children's health insurance coverage rates by family income, 1987–2012
Source: Updated version of figure 1 from Card and Shore-Sheppard (2004). Data from Current Population Survey Annual Demographic File.

several provisions to the Medicaid rules or to encourage their use, permitting states to expand eligibility further.[8] The first policy shift, known as the 1902(r)(2) option after the section that was added to the Social Security Act by the MCCA, allowed states to use more liberal methods for calculating income and resources for some categories of Medicaid eligible individuals. For example, states could choose to disregard some family income or resources when determining eligibility. This raises the effective income eligibility level above the official maximum level by reducing the amount of income actually counted. Importantly, states were permitted to increase eligibility in this way for Section 1931 eligibles (low-income parents) as well as for children and pregnant women (Davidoff et al. 2004). As a result, many states' eligibility limits became considerably more generous to parents (Aizer and Grogger 2003). The second change was to encourage the use of Section 1115 waivers. In 2001 the executive branch used its regulatory authority to implement the Health Insurance Flexibility and Accountability (HIFA) waiver initiative, which encouraged states to apply for waivers that expanded

8. The federal regulatory agency with primary authority in interpreting and implementing Medicaid legislation was known as the Health Care Financing Administration (HCFA) until June 2001, when its name was changed to the Centers for Medicare and Medicaid Services (CMS).

coverage without expanding funding by using changes in benefits packages and cost-sharing provisions to help finance the expansions. In particular, some states obtained Section 1115 waivers in order to provide some coverage to childless, nondisabled adults, the only way in which such individuals could be covered under Medicaid. Because these waivers were required to be budget neutral for the federal government, they often entailed limits on benefits, higher cost sharing, or enrollment caps (Rudowitz, Artiga, and Musumeci 2014).

A somewhat less well-known change that occurred to Medicaid during this period came about because of the master settlement agreement between forty-six states and the District of Columbia and tobacco manufacturers. In the settlement, manufacturers agreed to make annual payments to the states intended to recompense them for the cost to state Medicaid programs of treating tobacco-induced illnesses (Schneider et al. 2002). In addition, the federal government allowed states to keep the federal share as well, and moreover states were permitted to use the tobacco payments to fund the state portion of Medicaid, effectively raising the federal match rate above the nominal matching rate.

The Affordable Care Act

Arguably the most far-reaching change to Medicaid is the one that was implemented most recently: the Patient Protection and Affordable Care Act of 2010 and the Health Care and Education Reconciliation Act of 2010—together known as the Affordable Care Act, or ACA. By the time of the passage of the ACA, Medicaid eligibility had expanded substantially, but was still largely limited to individuals in the original mandated groups (families, the disabled, and the elderly). As discussed above, a few states had extended eligibility under waivers to able-bodied, low-income adults who are not parents. Under the ACA, Medicaid eligibility levels for children younger than six were intended to remain largely unchanged, as were eligibility levels for pregnant women. For older children, if the state covered children with family incomes between 100 and 133 percent of the FPL under a separate CHIP plan, sometimes referred to as "stair-step" eligibility, the state was required to transition those children from separate CHIP to Medicaid. The most significant change in the ACA, however, was the potential expansion of Medicaid eligibility to adults. According to the original legislation, Medicaid was to be expanded to all adults with family incomes below 138 percent of the FPL: 133 percent of the FPL plus a 5 percent income disregard. The legislation included a higher federal match for newly eligible adults—100 percent through 2016, then phasing down to 90 percent in 2020 and following. However, the Supreme Court decision of June 2012 ruled that states would not lose existing Medicaid funds if they did not expand Medicaid for all individuals under 138 percent of the FPL, essentially making the expansion a state option. The decisions of the states about whether to participate in the Medicaid expansion are shown in the columns of table 1.2.

In addition to changes in eligibility for Medicaid, the ACA called for the creation of marketplaces ("exchanges") for the purchase of nongroup coverage, which would be federally subsidized on a sliding scale for individuals with family incomes below 400 percent of the FPL. The ACA also mandated that individuals obtain insurance coverage or pay a penalty through the tax system. Individuals who cannot obtain affordable coverage (including individuals with incomes below the FPL in states not expanding Medicaid) are exempt from the penalty.[9]

Because eligibility for premium credits through the exchanges is based on income tax rules for counting income and family size, states are required to base eligibility for Medicaid and CHIP for families and able-bodied adults on these same rules to ensure that eligibility is comparable across the different potential sources of coverage. Specifically, the tax-filing unit becomes the basis for family structure calculations, and the ACA establishes a new definition of income known as modified adjusted gross income (MAGI). The MAGI is adjusted gross income (AGI) as determined under the federal income tax, plus any foreign income or tax-exempt interest that a taxpayer receives, and untaxed Social Security benefits (see UC Berkeley Labor Center [2013] for a brief summary of the components of MAGI). Assets are not considered when determining income eligibility. Any previously existing disregards (differing by state and eligibility category) that were applied to income before it was compared to the limits were eliminated and replaced with a single disregard equal to 5 percent of the FPL. Importantly, these changes apply whether or not the state chooses to expand its Medicaid program. However, the blind, elderly, and disabled populations will continue to have financial eligibility determined using existing Medicaid rules (including both income and assets).

The use of MAGI and a fixed 5 percent disregard represents a major change in the way states calculate income eligibility for Medicaid. Prior to the ACA, under the freedom offered by the 1902(r)(2) option, states had some discretion about which types of income to count and how much income to disregard before comparing this net income level to the statutory net income eligibility standard. Thus not only does the ACA standardize the way income is counted across states, but it also changes how much of income is actually counted toward eligibility and which family members are included in the family unit whose income is being combined. Under the ACA, states were required to convert their net income standards to equivalent adjusted gross income standards using one of three possible strategies to determine

---

9. The affordability standard for individuals is that the plan should cost less than 8 percent of their household income. For other exemptions, see https://www.healthcare.gov/fees -exemptions/exemptions-from-the-fee/.

equivalence and accounting for disregards that were used previously, with the goal being to keep the number of eligible individuals approximately the same (Centers for Medicare and Medicaid Services 2012a). Because of these changes in how income and family groups are defined, however, some individuals in eligibility groups not intended to be affected by the ACA—that is, groups that were already eligible for Medicaid and were intended to remain so—may be affected.

The effects of this change to income-counting methodologies are reflected in the income-eligibility limits made public for states. In column (4) of table 1.3 we show the 2013 income eligibility limits for children, which were applied to income after state-specified disregards (that were not well publicized) were subtracted. (We show the higher of the CHIP and Medicaid eligibility limits, indicating with an asterisk states where Medicaid limits were lower than CHIP limits.) Column (5) shows the income limits in 2014 incorporating the 5 percent disregard; these income limits are applied to the family's MAGI. In most cases the apparent increase between 2013 and 2014 reflects only the change in income-counting methodology and not a true increase in eligibility.

In addition to the eligibility changes discussed above, there are some provisions of the ACA that specifically affect immigrants (Kenney and Huntress 2012). Undocumented immigrants are not eligible for Medicaid and are not eligible to purchase marketplace coverage. Such immigrants will still be eligible for emergency Medicaid and optionally for prenatal care under an option established for CHIP in 2002 allowing states to cover the unborn child (Heberlein et al. 2013). Legal immigrants in states that did not relax the five-year residency rule after being given the option in CHIPRA are still ineligible for Medicaid until they have been in the country for five years, but they may purchase coverage through the exchanges and they are eligible for the tax credit subsidies. Individuals with incomes below 100 percent of the FPL but who are ineligible for Medicaid due to the five-year rule are eligible to receive tax credits for coverage purchased through the exchanges (Stephens and Artiga 2013). They are subject to the mandate, unless they are otherwise exempt for income reasons.

Overall, Medicaid today resembles in many ways the program that was established fifty years ago, although with some key differences. It remains a state-federal partnership, with the partnership being more or less contentious in different states and for different reasons, including federal restrictions on state-desired program flexibility, federal requirements for coverage and service provisions that states may find difficult to meet in difficult economic times, and state attempts to maximize the funding obtained from the federal government. The services provided to beneficiaries have become broader and have included some important additions, although key elements remain the same. Eligibility continues to involve a categorical eligibility determination, although the eligibility pathways have become broader and more numerous.

According to the CMS there are forty-eight mandatory eligibility groups, thirty-two optional eligibility groups (including the ACA category of adults with incomes at or below 133 percent of FPL that would subsume many of the other categories), and nine medically needy categories.[10] The individual's eligibility pathway determines what income limit applies as well as which income-counting methodology will be used. The eligibility pathway also determines whether "spending down" is permitted to qualify for coverage and whether a resource test applies, and if so, which one. Immigration status and date of entry to the United States also affect eligibility. Overall, however, it is clear that the Medicaid program has moved from being a small program that covered only some of the very poorest members of society to a central part of the health care system in the United States.

1.3   Program Statistics

1.3.1   Enrollment and Expenditures

The growth of the Medicaid program is illustrated in figure 1.2, which plots Medicaid enrollment by eligibility category from 1975 to 2010. By 1975, all states but Arizona had implemented the program and total enrollment stood at 22 million people. As has been the case throughout the history of the program, children represented the largest eligibility category, accounting for 43.6 percent of total enrollment. The second-largest eligibility category consisted of nonelderly, nondisabled adults (20.6 percent of total enrollment), followed by aged beneficiaries (16.4 percent), and the disabled (11.2 percent). Enrollment remained essentially constant over the next ten years and then began to increase in the late 1980s and early 1990s as a result of eligibility expansions for pregnant women and children. In the mid-1990s the combined effect of a strong national economy and welfare-reform legislation led to declines in enrollment. Steady growth resumed early in the twenty-first century, and by 2010 more than 65 million people were enrolled in Medicaid.[11]

Over the period shown in the figure, the eligibility category with the greatest total enrollment growth was children; in 2010, children represented 48.4 percent of total Medicaid enrollment. Enrollment among nonelderly adults grew at a slightly higher rate over this period: by an average annual rate of 6.8 percent for nondisabled adults and 7.7 percent for the disabled. In 2010, these two eligibility groups represented 23.8 and 14.3 percent of total Medicaid enrollment, respectively. Enrollment grew much more slowly

10. http://www.medicaid.gov/Medicaid-CHIP-Program-Information/By-topics/Waivers /1115/Downloads/List-of-Eligibility-Groups.pdf.
11. Enrollment figures based on administrative data may differ across sources and by the type of count—for example, the number of people enrolled at a point in time or the number enrolled at any point during a given year.

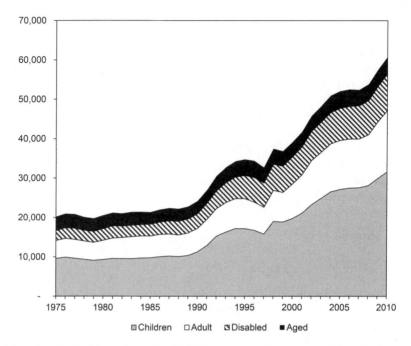

Fig. 1.2   Medicaid enrollment by eligibility category, fiscal years 1975 to 2010
Source: CMS (2012b, table 13.4).
Notes: Data for other/unknown eligibility category not shown. This category represents 6.8 percent of total enrollment in 2010. Child category includes nondisabled children and foster care children and excludes CHIP enrollment. Adult category includes nonelderly, nondisabled adults. Medicaid-eligible persons who during the year received only coverage for managed-care benefits are included, starting in fiscal year 1998.

among the aged. As a result, by 2010 this was the smallest eligibility group, accounting for 6.6 percent of total enrollment.

Open enrollment for the Affordable Care Act's new insurance options began in October 2013 for coverage that became effective in January 2014.[12] For private coverage purchased through the federal or state exchanges, the enrollment period closed at the end of March 2014 (though consumers meeting a variety of criteria could enroll after this date). Enrollment in Medicaid can take place any time during the year. By early 2015, CMS was reporting that Medicaid/CHIP enrollment had increased by between 10 and 11 million people between July–September 2013 and November 2014 (CMS 2015). As of December 2014, total Medicaid/CHIP enrollment was 69.7 million. Among the states that had implemented the ACA eligibility expansion,

12. Several states took advantage of a provision in the law allowing states to expand before 2014. These states transferred beneficiaries in existing state or local programs into Medicaid in addition to expanding coverage to previously uninsured adults (Sommers, Kenney, and Epstein 2014). According to CMS, nearly 950,000 individuals gained coverage as a result of these early expansions (CMS 2014).

enrollment had increased by nearly 9 million, an increase of roughly 27 percent. Fifteen of the expansion states experienced increases of 30 percent or more. In states that chose not to expand Medicaid eligibility, Medicaid/CHIP enrollment grew by 1.5 million or roughly 7 percent. This enrollment growth in nonexpansion states can be interpreted as a "woodwork" or "welcome mat" effect. For example, media attention to the ACA may have raised awareness of the program among people who were previously eligible, but not enrolled. In addition, enrollment may have increased among previously eligible individuals who were afraid they would be subject to a tax penalty if they did not obtain insurance.

Table 1.4 compares 2011 enrollment figures from administrative data to total population counts to calculate coverage rates for the different age groups. One important difference between table 1.4 and figure 1.2 is that the data in the table include CHIP enrollment, whereas the data in the figure do not. Out of 75.8 million people who were enrolled in Medicaid or CHIP at some point in 2011, 40.2 million were children. This figure represents just over half of all children in the United States. Measuring enrollment at a point in time yields a coverage rate of 41.3 percent for children. In 2011, the percentage of nonelderly and elderly adults with Medicaid coverage was substantially lower. The point-in-time Medicaid coverage rates calculated

Table 1.4   **Medicaid and CHIP enrollment by age, data source, and enrollment period (2011), in millions**

	Ever enrolled	Point in time	NHIS	CPS
All ages				
Total Medicaid/CHIP enrollment	75.8	60.4	50.5	50.8
Population	312.3	311	305.9	308.8
Enrollment as a percentage of population	24.3	19.3	16.5	16.5
Children under age 19[a]				
Total Medicaid/CHIP enrollment	40.3	32.4	29.5	26.3[2]
Population	78.5	78.4	78.7	74.1
Enrollment as a percentage of population	51.3	41.3	37.5	35.6
Adults 19–64				
Total Medicaid/CHIP enrollment	29.0	22.4	17.8	20.6
Population	192.1	191.4	187.4	193.2
Enrollment as a percentage of population	15.1	11.7	9.5	10.7
Adults 65 and older				
Total Medicaid/CHIP enrollment	6.5	5.6	3.1	3.9
Population	41.7	41.1	39.7	41.5
Enrollment as a percentage of population	15.5	13.7	7.9	9.4

Sources: Columns (1)–(3) are drawn from tables 16–19 from MACPAC (2014). The MACPAC report data is drawn from Medicaid Statistical Information System (MSIS) as of February 2014; CHIP Statistical Enrollment Data System data as of May 2014; the National Health Interview survey (NHIS); and US Census Bureau vintage 2012 data on the monthly postcensal resident population by single year of age, sex, race, and Hispanic origin. Column (4) is based on DeNavas-Walt, Proctor, and Smith (2012, table C-3).

[a]The CPS data are for children under eighteen years of age.

based on administrative data were 11.7 percent for nineteen- to sixty-four-year-olds and 13.7 percent for adults over age sixty-five. The last two columns report coverage estimates based on the two federal surveys that are most often used in research on health insurance: the National Health Interview Survey (NHIS) and the Current Population Survey (CPS). Although the two surveys ask about insurance coverage in different ways, they produce fairly similar estimates of coverage. Medicaid enrollment tends to be underestimated in survey data (Davern et al. 2009), as can be observed in this table. For all ages, the coverage rate in the two surveys is 16.5 percent, nearly 3 percentage points lower than the point-in-time measure based on administrative data.

Figures 1.3 and 1.4 plot expenditure data by eligibility category for the period 1975 to 2010. Figure 1.3 presents total expenditures expressed in nominal dollars, while figure 1.4 presents payments per beneficiary expressed

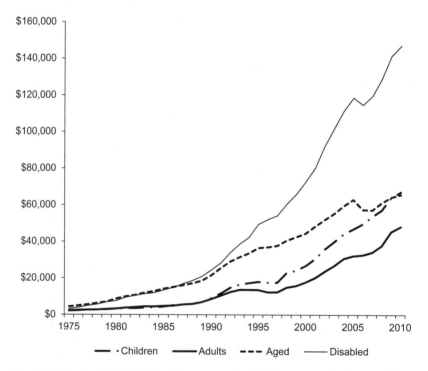

Fig. 1.3   Nominal dollar Medicaid payments by eligibility group, fiscal years 1975 to 2010

Source: CMS (2012b, table 13.10).

Notes: Beginning fiscal year 1998, expenditures capitated premiums for individuals enrolled in managed-care plans were included in this series. The SCHIP payments are excluded. As part of a 2009 revision of the national accounts classification system, components of medical care were changed, and the base year was updated to the year 2005. All personal consumption series were restated for the entire historical period to reflect the new classification structure.

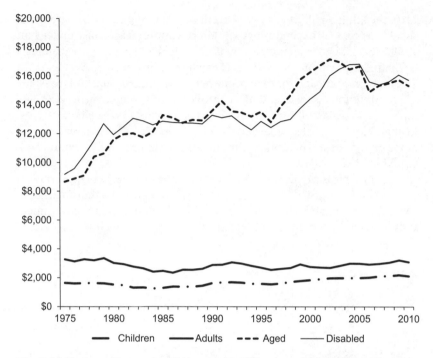

$20,000
$18,000
$16,000
$14,000
$12,000
$10,000
$8,000
$6,000
$4,000
$2,000
$0

1975   1980   1985   1990   1995   2000   2005   2010

—— Children   ——Adults   – – – Aged   —— Disabled

Fig. 1.4   Real spending per beneficiary by eligibility group, fiscal years 1975 to 2010

Source: CMS (2012b, table 13.11).

Notes: Beginning fiscal year 1998, expenditures capitated premiums for individuals enrolled in managed-care plans were included in this series. Beneficiaries covered under SCHIP and their payments are excluded. Dollar amounts are adjusted using a personal consumption expenditure index for health care services (US Department of Commerce, Bureau of Economic Analysis) expressed in fiscal year 2010 dollars. As part of a 2009 revision of the national accounts classification system, components of medical care were changed, and the base year was updated to the year 2005. All personal consumption series were restated for the entire historical period to reflect the new classification structure.

in 2010 dollars. In 1975, real ($2010) per capita spending was $9,165 for the disabled, $8,655 for the aged, $3,268 for other adults, and $1,638 for children. Because in 1975 there were more aged than disabled beneficiaries, total spending was higher for the aged. Per capita expenditures trended similarly for the two groups, but by the late 1980s total spending was greater for the disabled because of higher enrollment growth. Together the aged and disabled account for roughly 20 percent of Medicaid enrollment, but over 60 percent of program expenditures. As would be expected, per capita spending is considerably lower for nondisabled, nonelderly adults and is lowest for children. For both of these groups, the growth in total expenditures from 1975 to 2010 is driven mainly by increased enrollment. Real per capita spending for adults was actually lower in 2010 than in 1975 ($3,102 vs. $3,268). In

2010, the adult eligibility category accounted for 24 percent of enrollment and 14 percent of expenditures. Children, who represent just under half of all Medicaid beneficiaries, account for roughly 20 percent of spending.

Figure 1.5 breaks down Medicaid benefit spending by service category for the entire program and for each of the main eligibility groups. A large share of spending for disabled and aged enrollees is for long-term services and supports: 36 percent for the disabled and 66 percent for the elderly. Across all eligibility categories, Medicaid enrollees who use long-term services and supports represent 6 percent of enrollment and almost half of total spending (MACPAC 2014).

Figure 1.6 plots Medicaid and CHIP spending by the federal government and the states. As noted in section 1.2.1, the FMAP formula that determines how the financing of Medicaid is divided between the federal government and states has not changed since the start of the program. However, twice in

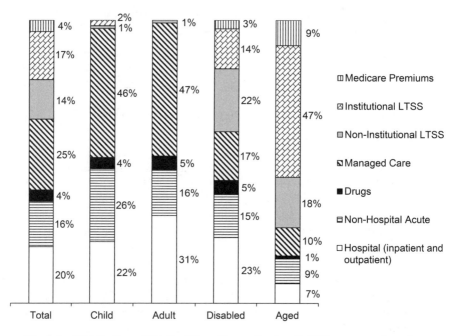

Fig. 1.5   Distribution of Medicaid benefit spending by eligibility group and service category, FY 2011

Source: Analysis of Medicaid Statistical Information System data as reported in MACPAC (2014).

Notes: The LTSS is Long-Term Services and Support, and includes federal and state funds but excludes spending for administration, Disproportionate Share Hospital payments, the territories, and Medicaid-expansion CHIP enrollees. Children and adults under age sixty-five who qualify for Medicaid on the basis of a disability are included in the disabled category. About 706,000 enrollees age sixty-five and older are identified in the data as disabled. See MACPAC (2014, figure 3) for additional notes.

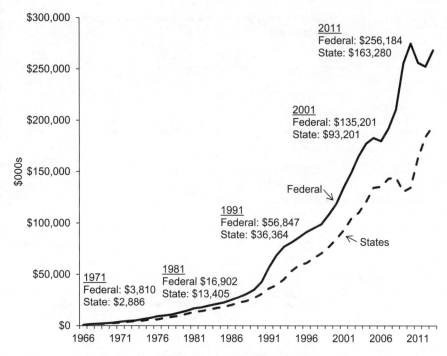

Fig. 1.6   Federal and state Medicaid expenditures, fiscal years 1966 to 2012
Source: National Health Expenditure Data, CMS (2014).

the last fifteen years Congress has temporarily increased FMAPs to provide fiscal relief to the states. In 2003, it increased the matching rates by nearly 3 percent as part of the Jobs and Growth Tax Relief Reconciliation Act. Congress increased FMAPs even more in 2009 as part of the American Recovery and Reinvestment Act (ARRA), which included $87 billion for a temporary increase in the FMAP.[13] Under ARRA, all states received at least a 6.2 percent increase in their FMAP; states that had experienced large increases in unemployment since 2006 received an additional reduction in their share of program spending. The temporary FMAP bump expired in 2011, and in 2012 the federal share of total Medicaid spending was down to 56.5 percent.

1.3.2   Provider Reimbursement

The amount that Medicaid pays providers varies across states and over time. Table 1.5 summarizes some of the variation in physician reimbursement rates. The figures come from several studies by Stephen Zuckerman

---

13. The ARRA also provided federal funds for states to provide incentives for eligible Medicaid providers to purchase and implement certified electronic health records (MACPAC 2012).

Table 1.5   Ratio of Medicaid physician fees to Medicare fees, composite fee index for selected years

	2003	2008	2012
National average			
All services	0.69	0.72	0.66
Primary care	0.62	0.66	0.59
Obstetric care	0.84	0.93	0.78
Other services	0.73	0.72	0.70
Distribution of ratio for all services by state			
Minimum	0.35	0.37	0.37
Median	0.80	0.88	0.77
Maximum	1.37	1.43	1.34
States with Medicaid/Medicare ratios:			
Less than 0.50[a]	3	3	2
0.50 to .75	18	14	19
0.75 to 1.0	26	23	27
Greater than 1.0	4	11	3

Source: Zuckerman et al. (2004); Zuckerman, Williams, and Stockley (2009); Zuckerman and Goin (2012).

Notes: Data represent the national average of Medicaid-Medicare fee indexes within given categories. Underlying source data is from the Urban Institute Medicaid Physician Fee surveys.

[a]Categories are inclusive of lower boundary.

and colleagues, who collected data on Medicaid fees for different services (Zuckerman et al. 2004; Zuckerman, Williams, and Stockley 2009; Zuckerman and Goin 2012). To provide a sense of how Medicaid compares to other payers, the reimbursement rates are expressed as a percentage of Medicare rates, which tend to be lower than private fees. The top panel reports the national average Medicaid/Medicare ratio by broad-service category. Considering all services, in 2003 Medicaid physician fees were 69 percent of Medicare fees. The national average increased to 72 percent in 2008 before falling to 66 percent in 2012. In general, Medicaid fees tend to be higher relative to Medicare for obstetric services and lower for primary care.

The bottom panel of the table gives a sense of the variation across states. In each year, the large majority of states pay physicians between 50 percent and 100 percent of what Medicare pays. Several of the states that pay more than Medicare are sparsely populated states with small Medicaid programs: Alaska and Wyoming in all three years and Idaho, Montana, Nebraska, Nevada, New Mexico, and North Dakota in 2008. At the other end of the spectrum, New Jersey and Rhode Island were the two lowest-paying states in all three years, with rates that were between 35 and 42 percent of Medicare, depending on the year. New York, which has the second largest program in terms of total enrollment, has historically also had low Medicaid rates. In 2008, New York's rates were the third lowest of all states at 43 percent of Medicare rates. In 2012, New York's Medicaid fees were 55 percent of Medicare's. California, which has roughly twice as many Medicaid enrollees as New York, has also historically had low reimbursement rates. In 2012, California paid 51 percent of Medicare rates on average.

The data summarized in table 1.5 pertain to Medicaid and Medicare patients for whom physicians are paid on a fee-for-service basis. One response states have made to the substantial budgetary pressure of Medicaid has been to encourage or require recipients to enroll in managed-care plans. As noted in section 1.2, since the early 1990s both programs have seen a significant growth in the percentage of patients who are covered by managed-care arrangements. As shown in figure 1.7, Medicaid managed-care penetration grew from 9.5 percent in 1990 to 56 percent by the end of that decade. Since then, the share of Medicaid enrollees in managed care has continued to grow, though less rapidly. By 2012, roughly three-quarters of Medicaid beneficiaries were in some form of managed care.

Recall that in the context of Medicaid, the term managed care encompasses several different types of arrangements, including comprehensive risk-based plans that received a fixed payment per member per month—that is, HMOs—as well as primary care case-management programs that pay primary care providers a monthly fee to coordinate the care of enrollees. The prevalence of these arrangements varies across eligibility categories. In FY2010, 87 percent of children were covered by managed care; 62 percent

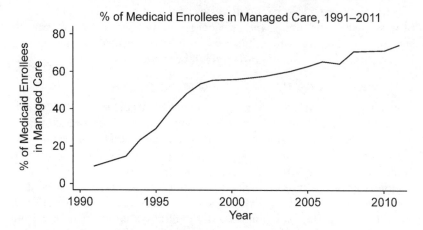

Fig. 1.7   Percent of Medicaid beneficiaries enrolled in managed-care plans, 1991–2011

Source: Medicaid Manage Care Enrollment Reports 1996, 2006, 2011.

Note: Medicaid enrollee population represents point-in-time enrollment as of June 30 for each reporting year; 1995 Medicaid enrollee population is an average over the entire year; the 1996 total Medicaid population was collected by states at the same time the managed-care enrollment data was collected instead of through HCFA-2082 reports, as was the practice in previous years.

of all Medicaid children were in a comprehensive risk-based plan.[14] Among nondisabled adults, 60.5 percent were in some form of managed care, including 46.8 percent in a risk-based plan. The disabled were slightly more likely to be in some form of managed care (63.1 percent), but much less likely to be enrolled in a comprehensive plan (28.7 percent). The aged were least likely to be in managed care overall: in 2010 40.6 percent were covered by a managed-care arrangement and 11.9 percent were in a comprehensive plan.

1.4   Review of Issues

Unsurprisingly, given the magnitude of expenditures on the Medicaid program and the sizable number of recipients, Medicaid has garnered substantial research interest covering a variety of areas.[15] An important area of research focus is the effectiveness of the program and its design, including examinations of whether Medicaid is accomplishing its intended goals of improving access to timely and appropriate medical care, improving health, and reducing the financial impact of health shocks. Research in this area has examined the impact of Medicaid eligibility and Medicaid coverage as well as the impacts of particular policy elements, such as reimbursement policy, on program effectiveness. A smaller but growing number of studies investigate the effect of Medicaid on other aspects of individual well-being, including financial well-being. There has also been an important research focus on the unintended consequences of Medicaid and its design for beneficiaries and providers, including issues of crowding out of other sources of insurance, labor supply, and provider financial impacts. In addition, the structure of the program and its relation to other means-tested programs has given rise to research on program interactions.

1.4.1   Program Take-Up and Crowd-Out

A key question in considering the impact of Medicaid is whether it is reaching individuals whom it is intended to help. As discussed above, for much of Medicaid's existence it accompanied cash assistance receipt, and thus take-up of the program was intertwined with take-up of cash assistance. However, the delinking of Medicaid from cash assistance for many eligibility groups means that take-up of Medicaid coverage can be considered separately. Moreover, Medicaid is an in-kind benefit that may duplicate insurance an eligible individual could potentially obtain privately, raising the possibility of crowding out of private health insurance. Crowding out, or the effect of public insurance availability on the propensity to have private coverage, has complex implications for individual and social welfare. For

14. Figures on managed-care enrollment by eligibility category are from MACPAC (2013, table 17).
15. The literatures on these various outcomes are large, including many more studies than we are able to cite in this review.

an individual family that is able to obtain health insurance at a significantly reduced out-of-pocket cost through Medicaid, crowding out represents a transfer of resources to that family, allowing an increase in consumption of other goods. At the societal level, such a transfer represents increased government expenditure, with the attendant deadweight losses of taxation. Moreover, transfers in the form of health insurance provision may be valued by recipients more or less than an equivalent expenditure on cash-based transfers. In addition, the interaction of Medicaid with markets for health care services and health insurance and the relationship between health insurance and employment makes the implications of crowding out even more complicated. The literature studying crowding-out and take-up has thus tended to focus on measuring the extent of these responses rather than estimating their relative costs and benefits.[16]

Simple theoretical models of take-up and crowd-out such as those discussed in Cutler and Gruber (1996) and Ham, Ozbeklik, and Shore-Sheppard (2014) suggest that an eligible family will compare the benefits and costs associated with participating in Medicaid with the benefits and costs of private insurance and will choose public coverage, private coverage, or both based on which choice maximizes utility. Take-up is defined as the enrollment response to eligibility, with estimates of take-up differing depending on whether an average take-up rate (that is, the average rate of enrollment among all eligible individuals) or a marginal take-up rate (that is, the rate of enrollment among an individual made newly eligible) is being calculated.

The basic idea of crowd-out is simple: the availability of public insurance will lead some families to substitute that coverage for private coverage. However, in practice there are multiple conceptions of crowd-out and multiple ways to measure it, leading to some confusion about which are comparable and which are not. One simple measure of crowd-out asks how making an individual eligible for Medicaid affects his or her probability of having private coverage. This measure has the advantage of being symmetric with the marginal take-up rate. In addition, it can be estimated directly along with its standard error. Another measure rescales estimates of the private response to eligibility by the take-up response to eligibility, measuring crowd-out as the reduction in private insurance coverage associated with an increase in Medicaid coverage. This measure has the characteristic that two equivalent private coverage responses to eligibility would produce different magnitudes of crowd-out, with crowd-out considered to be larger

16. While a full comparison of the costs and benefits of Medicaid to individuals and to society would be useful for evaluating Medicaid, such welfare analyses have generally not been done for Medicaid due to the difficulties inherent in valuing it, particularly the information required to conduct such an evaluation. An important exception is a recent paper by Finkelstein, Hendren, and Luttmer (2015), who conduct a welfare analysis of Medicaid provision in the context of experimental provision of insurance to low-income adults known to be uninsured. Even in this relatively straightforward context, and with a rich set of experimentally generated data, analyzing the welfare implications of Medicaid is quite challenging.

when the public coverage response to eligibility was smaller.[17] Another measure of crowd-out is the difference between the fraction of eligible children who would have private coverage if they were (counterfactually) not eligible and the fraction of those children who actually have private coverage. Still other measures use longitudinal or administrative data to look at explicit transitions out of private coverage, measuring crowd-out as the transition rate out of private coverage with eligibility.

An important concern for researchers interested in estimating take-up and crowd-out is the likely endogeneity of eligibility. This potential endogeneity arises because unobservable factors affecting eligibility are likely to be correlated with unobservable factors affecting health insurance choices, for example, attitudes toward participation in public programs, the wages and fringe benefits of jobs held by eligible and ineligible individuals, and factors affecting relative costs of obtaining private insurance or enrolling in Medicaid. Similar endogeneity concerns arise in studies of the effect of Medicaid on other outcomes. We discuss how researchers have dealt with eligibility endogeneity below when we outline the strategies researchers have used for identifying causal estimates.

1.4.2 The Effect of Public Health Insurance on Health Care Utilization and Health Status

The effect of gaining Medicaid coverage on health care utilization and health status will depend on an individual's insurance coverage and access to care prior to enrolling in the program. Relative to being uninsured, Medicaid lowers the out-of-pocket cost of all types of care. The main effect of this cost reduction will be to increase utilization, though it is possible that increased use of certain types of care may result in reduced use of others. For example, improved access to primary and preventive care may lead to health improvements that reduce hospitalizations. There is, therefore, a great interest among health services researchers in the relationship between insurance coverage and "avoidable" or "ambulatory-care-sensitive" hospital admissions. Health care utilization is less likely to increase for individuals who drop private coverage to enroll in Medicaid. In fact, because Medicaid reimbursement rates are so much lower than rates paid by private insurers, such individuals may experience reduced access to care, particularly care involving costly technologies. Consequently, the impact of Medicaid on utilization in the presence of substitution is an empirical question.

Although there is much interest in understanding how insurance coverage affects health, measuring health outcomes can be challenging. Studies focusing on ambulatory-care-sensitive hospital admissions often interpret

---

17. This ratio measure also has the problem that researchers who report it rarely provide a standard error for this measure, and it is not possible to calculate one just from the standard errors on the individual estimates.

reductions in such utilization as an improvement in health. Other studies have examined the impact of Medicaid on health directly, looking at outcomes such as blood pressure and other clinical measures of health, infant birth weight, infant or child mortality, or self-reported health status.

1.4.3   Impacts on Health Care Providers

The impact of Medicaid coverage on utilization of care and health will also depend on the willingness of different types of providers to supply services to Medicaid patients, which will depend on how Medicaid payment rates compare to what providers are paid for patients with Medicare and private insurance (Sloan, Mitchell, and Cromwell 1978). As shown in table 1.5, Medicaid fees vary across states and over time, but in general tend to be substantially lower than those for other payers. In 2011–2012, roughly 30 percent of all physicians did not accept new Medicaid patients (Decker 2013).

The effect of eligibility expansions on physicians and other providers will depend on the mix of patients they were treating prior to the expansion, the degree of crowd-out and how Medicaid payment rates compare to those of other payers. When there is little or no crowd-out, the main effects of an eligibility expansion will be on physicians who were previously treating low-income patients, including both those with Medicaid and the uninsured. Providers specializing in treating privately insured patients will be less affected. In contrast, when eligibility expansions induce a substitution of public for private insurance, many providers, including those that were not previously treating Medicaid patients, will experience the expansion as a reduction in payment rates for patients they are already seeing.

Changes in fees, whether they arise implicitly through crowd-out or directly from a change in a state's fee schedule, will have both substitution and income effects. Some research on Medicare suggests that for that program income effects are important; physicians respond to reductions in Medicare payment rates by increasing the volume of services provided (see McGuire [2000] for a good review). Such a response is less likely in the case of Medicaid given that Medicaid patients represent a smaller share of the patients seen by most physicians in private practice. When the substitution effect dominates, physicians will respond to a decrease in Medicaid fees by reducing their supply of services to Medicaid patients.

Medicaid eligibility and payment policies affect incentives for providers to invest in and use medical technology. When Medicaid accounts for a large share of patients for particular services, as is the case with obstetric care, hospitals will have less incentive to invest in costly technology, such as neonatal intensive care units, and physicians will have less incentive to provide more costly treatments.

In addition to financing roughly half of all births, Medicaid pays for a large share of nursing home care in the United States. In 2011, Medicaid was the primary payer for over 60 percent of all nursing home residents (Kaiser Commission on Medicaid and the Uninsured 2013). Therefore, Medicaid payment policy has important implications for the quality of nursing home care, though the relationship between payment rates and quality is complex. When supply-side regulations limit capacity and quality is a common good that is experienced equally by all patients in the same facility, an increase in Medicaid payments could possibly lead to a reduction in quality (Nyman 1985; Gertler 1989). The reason for this counterintuitive result is that higher payment rates will cause nursing homes to attract more Medicaid patients. Homes that were already at full capacity will therefore want fewer private-pay patients, causing them to raise price and lower quality to private-pay patients. This result relies on the existence of strict capacity constraints, which were important features of the market in the 1970s and 1980s, but have been less relevant more recently. Indeed, as we discuss below, the best evidence from recent studies is that higher Medicaid payments lead to higher-quality care.

1.4.4   Impacts on Labor Supply and Other Program Participation

From the beginning of its history Medicaid has been linked to cash assistance programs, with participation in these other programs leading to eligibility for Medicaid. When participation in a cash assistance program yields health insurance benefits as well as cash, participants would be even less likely to work than if they only received the cash payment. The Medicaid expansions of the late 1980s and onward that separated the receipt of Medicaid benefits from welfare participation meant that individuals would be less likely to choose not to work, since they could still obtain Medicaid while working. The effect of the expansions on hours is ambiguous as some parents who were working may cut their hours to qualify for Medicaid.

The potential effect of the ACA Medicaid expansion is also complex. As an effective increase in unearned income, the availability of Medicaid coverage should reduce hours of work and lower participation rates. However, the availability of subsidized private insurance for individuals and families with incomes above the FPL should reduce the incentive for workers to cut their hours in order to qualify for Medicaid. (And in states choosing not to expand Medicaid, some low-income workers will have an incentive to increase hours to qualify for private insurance subsidies.)

1.4.5   Impacts on Family Structure

There are several possible channels through which Medicaid may affect family structure. The link between AFDC eligibility and Medicaid for poor children that existed for the first twenty years of the program, and the fact that AFDC eligibility in most states was limited to single parents (effectively, single mothers) meant that marriage deprived a woman not only of an income source, but also of health insurance for herself and her children.

While marriage presumably replaced potential AFDC income with potential spousal earnings, the need to obtain health insurance for the entire family as well may have dissuaded some individuals from marrying. Thus by making eligibility for Medicaid for one's children not conditional on marital status, it is possible that the Medicaid expansions that began in the 1980s had the effect of encouraging marriage.

Medicaid might also impact family structure by affecting fertility decisions. In the framework developed by Becker (1960) and Becker and Lewis (1973), both the quantity and quality of children enter the mother's utility function. Thus covering the costs of prenatal care, delivery, and infant care lowers the price of quantity, inducing substitution in favor of quantity and causing a rise in fertility. In addition, Medicaid could also reduce miscarriages through better prenatal care. Since in this model the shadow price of children with respect to quantity is positively related to the level of quality, and vice versa, the theoretical impact of the expansions on fertility is not unambiguously positive. Expanding Medicaid to cover additional low-income children lowers the price of quality, which may lead to lower birth rates.

Another possible effect of Medicaid on fertility is the effect of Medicaid on the price of ending a pregnancy or preventing conception. Following the Hyde Amendment of 1976, federal funding of abortion under the Medicaid program was restricted to cases in which the mother's life is in danger. States have the option to cover abortions in their Medicaid program, but will not receive the federal match for them. Medicaid has covered the cost of family-planning services since 1972, and CHIP covers family-planning services for adolescents. In addition, beginning in the mid-1990s the federal government granted a number of states Section 1115 waivers to offer family-planning services under Medicaid to higher-income women or to women who otherwise would have lost Medicaid eligibility, typically postpartum. While it may seem clear that reducing the price of ending a pregnancy or preventing conception will reduce fertility, interactions between take-up, existing private provision of such services, and changes in sexual activity resulting from the change in the price make the fertility implications of such policies unclear (Kearney and Levine 2009).

1.4.6   Impacts on Financial Well-Being

There are a number of ways in which Medicaid may impact a family's financial circumstances. Because Medicaid insurance is generally offered below the fair insurance price, it can be thought of as a transfer that improves the economic circumstances of the individual through the reduction in medical insurance costs and out-of-pocket expenses that would otherwise be incurred. Medicaid also helps families avoid catastrophic losses and bankruptcies due to extreme medical expenses.

Medicaid may also affect family savings through four possible channels.

First, by reducing uncertainty about future medical expenses, Medicaid reduces the need for precautionary saving. Thus eligible households would be expected to save less (and therefore have lower assets) compared with ineligible households, all else being equal. However, to the extent that households do not expect to qualify for Medicaid indefinitely, the effect of this channel would be lessened. Second, the redistributive feature of Medicaid increases a household's available resources, and if the household's marginal propensity to save is greater than zero, this increase could lead to higher levels of asset holdings. The third channel by which the Medicaid program may affect savings levels is through the asset test that has applied to various parts of the program at various times: households might reduce their wealth holdings in order to qualify for insurance. Finally, Medicaid protects eligible families from health shocks that can drive families into debt and bankruptcy. The current research in this area has generally focused on how family medical debt, nonmedical debt, and family bankruptcy are affected by Medicaid expansions; available research indicates that it reduces a family's medical debt and probability of going into bankruptcy. In this way, Medicaid may increase a family's assets.

1.4.7   Strategies for Identifying Causal Effects

Empirical studies of all of the above questions generally aim to estimate causal effects. However, given the means-tested nature of the program, there is a fundamental challenge for research in this area as in other areas of policy evaluation: endogeneity of eligibility, enrollment, and utilization. This endogeneity arises because unobservable factors affecting eligibility for the program such as earnings ability, unobserved aspects of employment, availability of insurance from other sources, and unobserved health status, are likely to be correlated with unobservable factors that affect outcomes of interest such as health insurance choices, public program participation, and labor supply. In addition, it may be difficult to control entirely for all of the factors determining both eligibility and the outcome of interest, such as varying insurance markets, changes in the economy, and changes in the supply of providers of various types.

Due to this endogeneity, merely attempting to control for as many observable differences between groups eligible and ineligible for Medicaid as possible is unlikely to produce compelling estimates of the program's effects. Researchers working on examining the impact of Medicaid on a variety of outcomes have recognized this issue and have used a number of identification strategies to try to obtain credible empirical estimates of the program's effects. These identification strategies have taken advantage of variation arising from the fact that Medicaid parameters differ in every state. Moreover, these parameters can vary within a state either geographically (as states implement changes in one place but not in another, for example), by other subgroups in the population (by age, for example), or over time because of a policy change at the state or federal level. The variation used can be truly random, as in the experiment extending Medicaid to a subset of low-income adults in Oregon determined by lottery discussed below, or more commonly, quasi-random. Below we give a general sense of how identification is accomplished in studies of Medicaid and some important benefits and drawbacks of each approach generally; we leave a more complete discussion of the details of specific papers to the following section.

Randomized Experiment

Arguably, the strongest research design for estimating causal effects is a randomized experiment, since by design there is no correlation between individual characteristics and the policy of interest. While randomized experiments are rare in Medicaid research, an important experiment, the Oregon Health Insurance Experiment, is providing insights into key Medicaid policy questions (see, e.g., Finkelstein et al. 2012; Baicker et al. 2013). In early 2008, Oregon decided to make 10,000 additional places in its Medicaid program for low-income adults newly available. Knowing that there were insufficient funds to cover everyone who would want to enroll, the state applied for permission to use a random-assignment mechanism. Approximately 90,000 people signed up for the reservation list, and the state ran a randomized lottery on that group to determine which individuals would be permitted to apply for coverage. Individuals chosen in the lottery were allowed to apply, and all selected individuals who filled out and returned the application and who were found to be income eligible were enrolled.[18]

The researchers on the study matched an impressive wealth of data from hospital discharge records, credit records, prerandomization demographics from the sign-up list, and a follow-up survey of outcomes. Before looking at the data on outcomes for the treatment group, most analyses were prespecified and publicly archived in order to minimize concerns about data and specification mining. Since the population that received coverage through the experiment is basically the same as the population gaining eligibility through the ACA, there is a high degree of external validity with respect to that policy.

Quasi-Experiments

Other studies in the literature exploit quasi-experimental variation arising from the fact that income eligibility limits, provider reimbursement rates, and other important program features vary across states. Changes in state and federal policy create additional variation over time. Eligibility rules

18. Not all of the individuals chosen in the lottery obtained Medicaid coverage; according to Finkelstein et al. (2012) "only about 60 percent of those selected sent back applications, and about half of those who sent back applications were deemed ineligible, primarily due to failure to meet the requirement of income in the last quarter corresponding to annual income below the poverty level."

based on age create additional variation within state/year cells. Studies in the literature exploit these different "natural experiments" in various ways.

Regression Discontinuity   In recent years, regression discontinuity (RD) techniques have become a standard component of the empirical economist's toolkit for estimating program effects. Such models rely on the existence of a known cutoff or threshold in a variable (known as the "assignment" variable) with different conditions occurring for observations falling on either side of it. As long as individuals are unable to control precisely the assignment variable near the known cutoff, the RD design isolates treatment variation that is "as good as randomized" (Lee and Lemieux 2010). The examination of Medicaid, with its various eligibility cutoffs of different kinds, would seem to be a fruitful place to use an RD design, and indeed several studies have used such an approach to estimate the impact of Medicaid eligibility on insurance coverage and utilization. For example, Card and Shore-Sheppard (2004) use various discontinuities in eligibility arising from the fact that eligibility under some expansions was extended only to children of certain ages. In one formulation, they use the discontinuity in eligibility between children born before October 1, 1983, who had to meet the AFDC eligibility requirements in order to be eligible and children born after that date, who could be in two-parent families and have family income as high as the poverty level. The inability to control birthdate around that cutoff (particularly since that birthdate cutoff was not established prospectively) makes it a compelling research design.

Researchers have also applied RD methods to income cutoffs (see, e.g., de la Mata 2012; Koch 2013), although the imperfect control assumption requires more justification in the case of income. In addition, income is measured with considerably more error than birth date, and even if it is measured well, income at the time of the survey may not be the same as income at the time an individual applies for coverage. Even more importantly, as discussed above, prior to the ACA each state had complicated rules about disregards that changed the actual level of the income limits making the determination by the researcher of the correct income limit to apply to income observed in the data more difficult.

Difference-in-Differences   Several variants of a difference-in-differences (DD) research design have been used to estimate the effect of Medicaid policies. General methodological issues related to DD models have been discussed extensively elsewhere (see, e.g., Meyer 1995; Bertrand, Duflo, and Mullainathan 2004), so here we highlight the way different authors have used DD methods to leverage various sources of variation in the Medicaid program.

Given the latitude that states have in determining program parameters, an important source of variation is differences across states. For example, Gray

(2001) uses a cross-sectional DD model to estimate the effect of Medicaid physician fees on several birth outcomes. In this model, pregnant women on Medicaid are the treatment group and other pregnant women are used as a comparison group. Specifically, his regression models include a measure of Medicaid fees, an indicator variable for Medicaid coverage and the interaction of the two. Choi (2011) takes a similar approach to study the effect of adult dental benefits. The identifying assumption underlying this approach is that state-level differences in Medicaid fees or dental benefits should matter for Medicaid enrollees but not for other individuals in the state. An obvious limitation of this approach is that state Medicaid policy may be correlated with other unmeasured factors affecting the outcome, leading to biased estimates.

Other studies have used a DD strategy to compare changes over time for groups that were subject to a change in Medicaid policy to control groups who should have been unaffected, or at least less affected. The simplest application of this approach compares outcomes in two periods, "pre" and "post," for two groups, a "treatment" group that was the target of a policy change and a "control" group that should have been unaffected, or at least less affected. For example, to estimate the coverage effects of the Medicaid expansions of the late 1980s and early 1990s, Dubay and Kenney (1996) compare changes in coverage for low-income women and children, for whom income eligibility thresholds increased, with changes for low-income men, who were not the target of the eligibility expansions. In these models, identification is based on the assumption that in the absence of the Medicaid expansions, the outcomes studied would have common trends across treatments and controls.

These simple DD models do not take advantage of variation within states in eligibility rules or other program parameters. To take advantage of such variation, researchers have turned to triple difference models, with, for example, treatment and comparison groups within a state over time. For example, Garthwaite, Gross, and Notowidigdo (2014) compare insurance coverage among childless adults to other adults in Tennessee and other southern states before and after a Medicaid policy change in Tennessee that affected childless adults more than parents. Alternatively, policies may be more likely to apply to certain geographic areas within a state. For example, Aizer (2007) studies the impacts on Medicaid enrollment of community-based outreach organizations that were placed in some areas of California, but not in other areas at different times. The key identifying assumption in such models is that the trends would have been the same for treatment and control groups within a state in the absence of the policy.

Instrumental Variables   An alternative to the difference-in-differences approach that also utilizes variation arising from policy changes to identify causal effects is to use policy variables as instrumental variables. The most widely used instrumental variables approach in the Medicaid literature is the "simulated eligibility" instrument that was pioneered by Currie and Gruber (1996a, 1996b) and Cutler and Gruber (1996) and has been used in many papers since then. The idea of this approach is to summarize the exogenous variation in Medicaid eligibility by determining the fraction of a given sample that would be eligible for Medicaid under the rules applying in a particular state at a particular time. This requires detailed knowledge of the rules for Medicaid eligibility so that the eligibility for any individual in a sample can be determined based on his or her observable characteristics. In order to remove the effects of any state and time-specific economic conditions that might be correlated with both eligibility and the outcome of interest, the fraction eligible is typically determined for a random sample at the national level, and often for a fixed time period as well. This simulated fraction eligible, which is essentially an index of the expansiveness of Medicaid eligibility for each subgroup in each state and time period, can then be used as an instrument for actual (imputed) eligibility at the individual level (as in the original papers by Currie and Gruber and Cutler and Gruber) or at an aggregated (cell) level (as in Dafny and Gruber 2005).[19]

The simulated eligibility instrumental variables approach typically involves estimating a linear probability model (LPM) for the outcome of interest as a function of public insurance eligibility (*elig*), which is imputed to individuals (*i*) on the basis of observed characteristics and the eligibility rules in place for a given state and time period (*t*):

$$\text{Outcome}_{itk} = X_{it}\beta_k + \gamma_k elig_{it} + u_{itk},$$

where k denotes the particular outcome of interest, X is a vector of additional variables affecting the outcome, and u is an error term. In this framework, the effect of eligibility generally is assumed to differ across individuals and resulting coefficients on $elig_{it}$ are best interpreted as local average treatment effects (LATEs)—effects for individuals whose eligibility is affected by marginal changes in the instrument, averaged across the different marginal changes present in the data. So for example, when public coverage is the outcome of interest, the coefficient on $elig_{it}$ represents the average take-up rate among individuals made eligible, and when private coverage is the outcome of interest the coefficient is the average rate of loss of private coverage among individuals made eligible. The ratio of the latter coefficient to the former is thus the rescaled measure of crowd-out discussed earlier.

This instrument has many benefits, as its widespread adoption makes clear: it is a useful way to summarize complicated program rules in a simple but meaningful index, it is arguably exogenous along several dimensions,

---

19. Simulated eligibility has also been used in reduced-form models as an arguably exogenous index of availability of Medicaid (see, e.g., DeLeire, Lopoo, and Simon 2011).

and it has a very strong first-stage relationship with imputed eligibility. However, there are some issues that researchers who use this approach (and also the difference-in-differences methods discussed above) must consider. One is policy endogeneity: it is possible that government policy targets groups experiencing worse economic conditions or occurs in response to other factors potentially correlated with the outcome of interest, making state expansions potentially endogenous. This is a particular concern for research examining later expansions that occur purely at state initiative and arguably a smaller concern for research focusing on changes in eligibility that occurred in response to federal requirements. It is also possible that groups experiencing worse economic conditions happened to be those particularly affected by the expansions, even though the legislation was not intentionally aimed to mitigate economic conditions for these groups (Shore-Sheppard 2008). To try to account for such issues, researchers typically include state effects to account for differences across states unrelated to the expansions, time effects to control for macroeconomic shocks and economy-wide trends, and age effects to account for differences by age unrelated to the expansions. Even these fixed effects may not be enough to account for differential trends across ages or states, and if such trends are important, convincing identification may require the inclusion of two-way interactions between age, state, or time to account for them (Shore-Sheppard 2008). Even including such interactions may be insufficient if, for example, states are targeting policy at particular groups in the population in response to changes in the outcome of interest for those groups.

Finally, mismeasurement (in income, for example) or the absence of information in the data about other characteristics that would result in eligibility via other paths (such as high medical expenses that would lead to medically needy eligibility or disability) may lead to misclassification of eligibility status (Hamersma and Kim 2013). While many authors using eligibility status have noted the problem, some have suggested that using simulated eligibility as an instrument would mitigate the problem. Unfortunately, as measurement error in a binary variable cannot be classical in the sense of being uncorrelated with the true value, an IV strategy will not produce consistent estimates of the parameter of interest but may instead produce an upper bound (Black, Berger, and Scott 2000).

Another methodological issue is that as Ham, Ozbeklik, and Shore-Sheppard (2014) point out, this framework has several limitations if one is interested in heterogeneity in the response to the policy or in the effects of nonmarginal changes, and in addition the LPM approach allows an individual to have a positive probability of having public insurance even if he or she is not eligible for it. They suggest an alternative framework to deal with this issue and obtain estimates of heterogeneous effects or the effects of nonmarginal changes (discussed further below). However, their alternative approach relies on the same intuition as the simulated approach: since the rules determining Medicaid eligibility are observable, they can be used to determine who in the sample is affected by changes in policy.

1.5   Review of Research Evidence on Impacts of Medicaid

1.5.1   Eligibility, Take-Up, and Crowd-Out

Estimates for Children

A number of studies have investigated how changes in Medicaid eligibility policy affect insurance coverage, with the primary focus being changes in eligibility affecting children. One set of papers focuses on the Medicaid expansions of the late 1980s and early 1990s, while other studies consider the effect of CHIP. In addition to examining the relationship between eligibility and enrollment (take-up), these studies also estimate the effect of program eligibility on private insurance coverage (crowd-out). Table 1.6 lists studies of take-up and crowd-out, focusing primarily on studies that have been done since the Gruber (2003) review and studies done prior to the review that were instrumental in informing the research that came later.[20]

The seminal paper in the literature on Medicaid take-up and crowd-out is Cutler and Gruber's (1996) study on the effect of the eligibility expansions of the late 1980s and early 1990s. Using Current Population Survey (CPS) data for the period 1988 to 1993, they estimate linear probability models of Medicaid coverage and of private coverage as a function of eligibility using the simulated eligibility instrument discussed in the above section on instrumental variables. As noted above, the instrument is essentially an index of the generosity of Medicaid eligibility for each age group in each state and year. It is correlated with individual eligibility for Medicaid but not otherwise correlated with the demand for insurance, assuming that changes in a state's Medicaid provisions are not correlated with changes in the state's availability or price of private insurance.

In this framework, the coefficient on eligibility in the Medicaid equation can be interpreted as the average take-up rate among individuals whose eligibility is affected by marginal changes in the instrument, while the coefficient in the private equation represents the average private coverage response among these individuals. Cutler and Gruber estimate this local average take-up rate to be 24 percent and the corresponding effect of eligibility on private insurance to be 7 percent, both of which are statistically significant. As noted above, this effect on private coverage can be interpreted as a measure of crowd-out. However, Cutler and Gruber suggest scaling

20. In the table we note standard errors of estimates where they are known and correctly calculated, although we omit them from the discussion of the studies below in the interest of space.

Table 1.6 Studies of eligibility, take-up, and crowd-out[a]

Study	Data	Population	Design	Results
Cutler and Gruber (1996)	1988–1993 March CPS	Children, women of childbearing age	IV using simulated eligibility instrument. Dependent variables: private coverage, public coverage, and uninsured. Main independent variable: imputed eligibility. Variation exploited: Medicaid expansions.	For marginal eligible children: take-up 23.0 percentage points (pp.) (1.7), private decline 7.4 pp. (2.1), implies ratio of private decline to take-up 31.5 percent (s. e. not calculated),[b] uninsured decline 11.9 pp. (1.8). Women: no statistically significant changes in coverage.
Card, Hildreth, and Shore-Sheppard (2004)	SIPP and the Medi-Cal eligibility data system	Individuals in California eligible for Medicaid (children & adults)	Use administrative data to determine measurement error in SIPP reporting of Medicaid coverage.	SIPP underestimates Medicaid coverage by 10 percent. The probability of correctly reporting coverage in the SIPP for those actually covered by Medicaid is around 0.85. The probability that people who are not covered by Medicaid incorrectly report in the SIPP that they are covered is about 0.013 for the population as a whole.
Card and Shore-Sheppard (2004)	Separately use 1990–1993 panels of SIPP, 1990–1996 March CPS, and the 1992–1996 Health Interview Survey (HIS)	Children at ages around the 1989 OBRA expansion and the 1990 OBRA expansion	Use a RD design to compare children above and below the age limits set by the 1989 OBRA. Use the same strategy for the 1990 OBRA.	Find the 1990 expansion significantly increased both Medicaid and overall coverage for children just inside the eligibility limits by 7–11 pp. Find small or no effects of the 1989 OBRA. Find little or no significant level crowd-out effects.
Lo Sasso and Buchmueller (2004)	CPS 1996–2000	Children younger than age eighteen	Allow children's Medicaid eligibility from the expansions to have a different effect than those eligible due to SCHIP on private coverage, public coverage, and uninsured. Test whether the waiting period for SCHIP in many states affects the effect of SCHIP eligibility on the dependent variables.	Find take-up of eligibility due to the expansions is equal to take-up due to SCHIP (of about 9 pp.) when they do not use state * time dummies. Find take-up of SCHIP eligibility is significant (11 pp.) when they allow for state * time dummies, but only take-up due to SCHIP eligibility is significant (11 pp.) when they allow for state * time dummies. Find high levels of ratio crowd-out. Find waiting period significantly reduces Medicaid coverage and increases private coverage.
Busch and Duchovny (2005)	1995–2002 Behavioral Risk Factor Surveillance System; CPS 1996–2002 March Supplement	Household heads with children (men are included). Use two samples eligible for Medicaid—all households and low-income sample	IV using simulated eligibility instrument. Dependent variables: private coverage, public coverage, uninsured, health care utilization. Main independent variable: imputed eligibility.	Full sample—public insurance increases by 11.5 (2.2), private insurance decreases by 0.7 pp. (2.6). No insurance decreases by 10.9 pp. (2.6). Ratio crowd-out is 0.061. Low income sample—public insurance increases by 14.8 pp. (3.4). Private insurance decreases by 3.5 pp. (2.7). No insurance decreases by 11.3 pp. (3.2). Ratio crowd-out is 0.236.

(continued)

Table 1.6   (continued)

Study	Data	Population	Design	Results
Ham and Shore-Sheppard (2005b)	SIPP 1986, 1987, 1988, 1990, 1991, 1992, and 1993 panels	Children	IV using simulated eligibility instrument. Dependent variables: private coverage, public coverage. Main independent variable: imputed eligibility. Allow for dynamics.	Within baseline specification: Eligibility leads to take-up of 11.8 pp. (1.0), private insurance falls by 0.6 pp. (1.4). Thus both ratio and level crowd-out estimates are very small. Take-up of Medicaid is increased the longer a child has been eligible. Estimate both short-run and long-run effects of eligibility and find that long term is considerably bigger.
Hudson, Selden, and Banthin (2005)	Medical Expenditure Panel Survey (MEPS) 1996–2002	Children	DD approach with two treatment groups: 1. Children targeted by SCHIP and children targeted by poverty-related Medicaid Expansions. IV estimation on 4 groups of children using a modification of simulated eligibility IV approach since direct application of Cutler-Gruber approach produced unstable estimates.	Diff-in-diff for treatment group 1: Medicaid insurance increased by 8.9 pp. (2.0), private insurance decreased by 5.0 pp. (2.3), no insurance decreased by 3.9 pp. (1.9). Diff-in-diff for treatment group 2: Medicaid insurance increased by 8.3 pp. (2.8), private insurance decreased by 2.4 pp. (2.8), no insurance decreased by 6.3 pp. (2.4). IV: take-up 7.1 to 26.5 pp. (all significant), private insurance coverage declines by 14.0 to −1.25 pp. (larger values significant), ratio crowd-out 0.527 to −0.205.
Wolfe et al. (2006)	Administrative panel data from Wisconsin	Single-mother welfare leavers	Ordinary probit (standard errors corrected) estimation and random effects probit of probability of coverage for cohorts of welfare leavers before and after BadgerCare was implemented in Wisconsin. They also do a DD using fact that some cohorts were always eligible upon leaving and others became eligible later.	Ordinary probit estimates: BadgerCare increased the public health care coverage of all adult leavers by 6 pp. (0.5) to 8.0 pp. (0.6). Random effects probit effects similar. DD estimates imply public coverage increased by 17.0 pp. to 23.4 pp. (all significant).
Gruber and Simon (2008)	1996–2002 SIPP	Children birth to eighteen years old, and parents nineteen to sixty-four years old	IV using two specifications. First uses usual eligibility measure, second uses the fraction of the family eligible. Each approach has its own simulated eligibility instrument. Dependent variables: only private coverage, only public coverage, both types, uninsured. Main independent variable: eligibility or fraction of children in the family eligible.	Single-child eligibility model: eligibility raises public insurance only by 5.5 to 7.2 pp. (both significant), decreases only private by 1.1 to 1.7 pp. (both insignificant), increases private and public by 0.8 to 1.5 pp. (only significant without interactions). Ratio crowd-out 0.2 to 0.37. Family eligibility model: going from 0 percent of children eligible to 100 percent of children eligible for the family raises only public insurance by 10.9 to 15.6 pp. (both significant), decreases only private by 6.6 to 12.2 pp. (both significant), increases private and public by 2.7 pp. (both significant). Ratio crowd-out 0.61 to 0.81.

Study	Data	Method	Findings
Shore-Sheppard (2008)	CPS March supplements, 1988–1996	Uses simulated eligibility IV. Adds state * time, time * age and age * time dummies separately and together. Considers separately the effect of later expansions (than those considered by Cutler and Gruber).	Finds Cutler and Gruber's results stable except when adds age * time dummies to the specification. Take-up coefficient falls by half to 14.5 pp. (2.5). private coefficient falls to 0.5 pp. (3.1). ratio crowd-out falls to 3.4 percent. Finds later expansions have much lower take-up and ratio crowd-out.
Ham, Li, and Shore-Sheppard (2009)	SIPP 1986–1996 panels	Use a linear probability model to estimate transitions from a child being covered by public insurance to not being covered by public insurance and vice versa. Explanatory variables: demographics, TANF introduction, economic conditions, and Medicaid income limits.	Find that higher eligibility limits increase both the transitions into, and out of, public coverage. The introduction of TANF increases the transition rate out of public insurance and reduces the transition rate into public insurance. A higher unemployment rate significantly lowers the transition rate out of public insurance, but does not significantly affect the inflow. Children from more disadvantaged backgrounds have both higher inflow and outflow from public insurance.
Finkelstein et al. (2012)	Oregon's Center of Health Statistics; survey conducted by the researchers	Nonelderly Adults	Analyzes Oregon Medicaid lottery that randomly determined eligibility to volunteers for Medicaid eligibility. Looks at how lottery affected Medicaid and private insurance coverage, that is, no endogeneity or measurement error issues with eligibility. Considers several different measures of coverage; primary focus is "ever on Medicaid during the first year of the experiment." Took place at the start of the Great Recession, which may limit the applicability of the results.	People selected by lottery have a 26 pp. (0.35) increase in the probability of ever being on Medicaid. Being a member of the treatment group lowered private insurance by 0.8 pp. (0.5), hence no evidence of level or ratio crowd-out.
Gresenz et al. (2012)	2002–2009 Annual Social and Economic Supplements (ASEC) of the (CPS)	Children in families between 200 percent and 400 percent of the poverty line.	IV using simulated eligibility instrument. Dependent variables: private coverage, public coverage, uninsured. Main independent variable: imputed eligibility.	The CHIP expansions lead to a 4.1 to 4.2 pp. increase in Medicaid coverage (significant at the 1 percent level), 0.14 to 0.19 pp. decrease in private insurance coverage (all insignificant at conventional testing levels) and a 2.26 to 2.31 pp. decrease in children with no insurance (significant at the 1 percent level). Thus both level and ratio crowd-out are trivial here.

(continued)

Table 1.6 (continued)

Study	Data	Population	Design	Results
de la Mata (2012)	PSID—CDS 1997, 2002, 2007 waves	Children who were between five and eighteen years old with family income close to Medicaid income limit (on either side of the limit).	RD design. Allows for different effects at lower and higher income limits; depends on assumption of no measurement error in income. Dependent variables: public coverage and private coverage	Because of the RD approach, has numerous estimates for each treatment effect. For the lower income thresholds, Medicaid eligibility typically increases public coverage by a statistically significant 25 pp.; for the higher income thresholds, Medicaid eligibility typically increases public coverage by a marginally significant 8 pp.; for the lower income thresholds, Medicaid eligibility typically reduces private coverage by a statistically significant 27 pp.; and for the higher income thresholds, Medicaid eligibility typically reduces private coverage by a statistically insignificant 8 pp.
Hamersma and Kim (2013)	1996, 2001, and 2004 panels of the SIPP data	Parents	Estimates coverage as a quadratic function of the Medicaid thresholds. Dependent variables: private coverage, public coverage, uninsured.	Finds that the linear term in Medicaid income limits is significant and positive for no insurance and public insurance equations, while the quadratic term in income limits is significant and negative for these outcomes. For private insurance, the linear term is negative and significant, but the quadratic term is insignificant.
Bronchetti (2014)	Restricted-access National Health Interview Survey for 1998–2009	Children in immigrant families and children of natives (estimated separately)	IV using simulated eligibility instrument. Dependent variables: private coverage, public coverage, uninsured. Main independent variable: imputed eligibility.	Estimates a take-up rate of 19.2 pp. (3.8) for all children in immigrant families and 7.4 pp. (1.9) for all children of natives. The effects for private insurance (level crowd-out) are −2.8 pp. (5.0) and −3.1 pp. (1.5) for children in immigrant families and children of natives, respectively.
Dague (2014)	Administrative data from Wisconsin	Children and nonelderly adults in Wisconsin who enrolled in Medicaid from March 2008 to September 2009	Uses an RD design to study the introduction of premiums in Wisconsin's Medicaid/BadgerCare program on duration of participation in the plan. Premiums increase with income, with sharp breaks in the premium at various income levels. Uses income as reported in administrative data, so measurement error is not a problem in implementing RD approach.	Finds introducing a premium of $10 decreases the probability of a six- and twelve-month continuous spell on Medicaid by 0.129 (0.021) and 0.118 (0.0203). Finds no effect of changes in further increases in premiums (of a similar size) as the family's income increases.

Garthwaite, Gross, and Notowidigdo (2014)	CPS March Supplement 2000–2007	Childless nonelderly adults	Use DD and triple differences to examine the effect of a large number of Tennessee childless adults being excluded from Medicaid coverage in 2005. In the DD they compare Tennessee relative to other southern states; in the triple differences they compare childless adults to adults with children in Tennessee.	For the DD the take-up and level crowd-out estimates are 4.6 pp. (1.0) and 1.7 pp. (1.2), respectively; the ratio crowd-out measure is 36.2 percent (26.8). For their triple differences, the take-up and level crowd-out estimates are 7.3 pp. (1.7), and 4.3 pp. (2.4), respectively; the ratio crowd-out measure is 59.5 percent (38.4).
Ham, Ozbeklik, and Shore-Sheppard (2014)	SIPP 1986, 1987, 1988, 1990, 1991, 1992, and 1993 panels	Children younger than age sixteen. For children who have missing interviews, the first spell of continuous interviews are used.	Derive a theoretical model of take-up and crowd-out that implies one should use a switching probit model to estimate the joint probability of eligibility, public insurance, and private insurance. Such a model allows take-up and private insurance to depend on observable and unobservable family characteristics. Propose method for estimating current (nonmarginal) crowd-out as well as the effects of nonmarginal increases in Medicaid eligibility.	Find very considerable differences across demographic groups, with take-up falling as family material well-being increases. Estimate current level crowd-out (private coverage decline for currently eligible children) at 4.86 pp. (1.27). For children made newly eligible via a counterfactual 10 percent increase in Medicaid income limits (relative to their 1995 levels), estimate take-up and level crowd-out at 25.6 pp. (0.67) and 8.0 pp. (1.76).

[a]In this and the following tables, papers are listed chronologically. Papers that appeared in the same year are then listed alphabetically.

[b]We refer to this as ratio crowd-out in the rest of this table. Level crowd-out is simply the coefficient on eligibility in the private insurance coverage equation.

the private decline estimate by the estimate of the public coverage increase to measure crowd-out as the ratio of these two coefficients, obtaining an estimate of crowd-out (measured as the reduction in private insurance coverage associated with an increase in Medicaid coverage) of 31 percent. One problem with this approach is that a standard error for the crowd-out measure is generally not provided and there is not enough information in the reported results to use the delta method to calculate the standard error.[21] This is important since in many cases the numerator (the response of private insurance to Medicaid eligibility) is insignificant and imprecisely estimated. Some authors use a common bootstrap procedure to calculate the standard errors for their crowd-out estimate. However, Woutersen and Ham (2013) show that the common bootstrap procedure produces inconsistent estimates of the standard error that can be too small. They derive a procedure to obtain consistent standard errors using the bootstrap, and in the cases that they analyze they find that these consistent estimates are much larger than those produced by the common bootstrap. Thus the standard errors in the literature for the ratio crowd-out estimates are likely lower bounds on the true standard errors.

Subsequent papers have reexamined the effect of these same eligibility expansions using different data and methods. Shore-Sheppard (2008) investigates a number of critiques leveled at the Cutler and Gruber paper, using CPS data for a slightly longer period (1988–1996) and the same basic framework. Using the same data, she finds that the results are not qualitatively affected by extending the sample period or by adding state × year and age × state dummies. However, when she adds age × year dummies, either by themselves or with the other interactions, she obtains smaller estimates of take-up (between 15 and 19 percent, depending on whether other interactions are included) and crowd-out (the estimated rate of crowd-out with eligibility is between 0.5 percent and 1.2 percent, with larger standard errors). She also finds lower take-up rates when later expansions are included and small "wrong-signed" effects on private coverage.

Ham and Shore-Sheppard (2005b) replicate Cutler and Gruber's analysis using data on children from the 1986–1993 panels of the Survey of Income and Program Participation (SIPP), which has several advantages relative to the CPS, including the fact that the reference period for the insurance question is clearer and the period over which the respondent is asked to recall information is much shorter. Compared to Cutler and Gruber, they obtain smaller estimates of the marginal take-up rate (12 percent) and the effect of eligibility on private coverage (a fall of 0.6 percent), both estimated fairly precisely.

---

21. The delta method requires the covariance between the public eligibility coefficient and the private eligibility coefficient, which can be obtained by estimating the private and public coverage equations jointly.

With panel data, Ham and Shore-Sheppard (2005b) are able to estimate simple dynamic models of coverage. They find that the longer a child has been eligible for Medicaid, the more likely she is to be enrolled in Medicaid and that the immediate impact of eligibility on take-up (estimated using an endogenous lagged dependent variable as an explanatory variable) is smaller than in the static models while the long-run impact from the dynamic model is larger than in the static models. The dynamic models, like the static models, show a statistically insignificant relationship between eligibility and private coverage. Ham, Li, and Shore-Sheppard (2009) consider dynamics within the context of a two-state duration model. Specifically, they use a linear probability model and data on children using the SIPP 1986–1996 panels to estimate the factors determining entry into and exit from public insurance. Each of the two transition rates depend on demographics, economic conditions, the introduction of TANF, and Medicaid income limits. They find that higher eligibility limits for public insurance increase the transitions into, and out of, public coverage. While the latter effect seems counterintuitive, they attribute it to higher-income families, who are likely to have a greater preference for private insurance and greater opportunities for jobs with private insurance, becoming eligible and obtaining coverage when they hit hard times, but then leaving public insurance when the economy recovers.

As discussed in section 1.2, the Medicaid expansions of the late 1980s and early 1990s were the result of several legislative changes. In terms of their effect on eligibility levels, the two most important changes in Medicaid rules came from the 1989 and 1990 Omnibus Budget Reconciliation Acts, which extended Medicaid eligibility to certain children in families with incomes below 133 percent and 100 percent of the federal poverty level. A distinctive feature of these laws is that eligibility was also tied to a child's age or birthdate. The 133 percent expansion applied to all children who were under age six, while the 100 percent expansion applied to children born after September 30, 1983. These rules created stark differences in coverage options for children on either side of these age-related eligibility boundaries. Card and Shore-Sheppard (2004) use regression discontinuity models applied to data from the SIPP and the National Health Interview Survey (NHIS) to exploit this quasi-experimental variation. For the 100 percent expansion they estimate a statistically significant Medicaid take-up rate of roughly 7 to 11 percent and a statistically insignificant effect of eligibility on other coverage. For the 133 percent expansion their parameter estimates are insignificant for both outcomes.

Overall, the results from the research on Medicaid expansions prior to the implementation of CHIP indicate marginal take-up rates that are fairly modest, typically ranging between 15 and 24 percent, although lower in some cases. While there is less of a consensus on the magnitude of crowd-out, even the largest estimates of the marginal loss of private coverage with eligibility are generally below 10 percent. Measuring crowd-out as the estimates of private coverage loss rescaled by the Medicaid take-up rate may suggest that private coverage loss is more of a policy concern, although these estimates are driven as much by low levels of take-up (the denominator) as by reductions in private coverage (the numerator). Therefore, large estimates of crowd-out may not necessarily imply that a large number of people are substituting public coverage for private coverage—which is how such estimates are often interpreted—rather, they may be a symptom of low take-up of public insurance. The appropriate policy responses to a low take-up rate and a large effect of eligibility on private insurance coverage are likely to be different.

Researchers also used similar approaches to examine the effect of the CHIP eligibility expansions, which states implemented in different years between 1997 and 2000. Using CPS data, Lo Sasso and Buchmueller (2004) estimate a marginal take-up rate of 8 percent, lower than Cutler and Gruber's (1996) estimated Medicaid take-up rate, but similar to what Card and Shore-Sheppard (2004) find for the expansion of Medicaid eligibility to 100 percent of the FPL. Gruber and Simon (2008) obtain a similar estimate of the marginal take-up rate when they estimate simulated eligibility IV models using SIPP data. They provide two ratio crowd-out measures and use the common bootstrap to obtain confidence intervals for these measures. Their estimated 90 percent confidence intervals for the two measures are [0.097, 0.65] and [−0.11, 0.56], respectively, although these are likely to be lower bounds on the true confidence intervals. Hudson, Selden, and Banthin (2005), using data from the Medical Expenditure Panel Survey (MEPS), produce take-up and crowd-out estimates that are closer to those of Cutler and Gruber. Their results imply quite wide 95 percent confidence intervals for ratio crowd-out, and again these intervals are downward biased.

Lo Sasso and Buchmueller (2004) find a small and statistically insignificant effect of public insurance eligibility on private insurance. However, they also find evidence suggesting that private insurance is mismeasured. Using private nongroup insurance as the dependent variable, they find that eligibility for CHIP has a positive and significant effect on coverage. Since during this period many states either contracted with private managed-care plans to provide Medicaid benefits or designed their stand-alone CHIP plans to resemble private insurance, it is possible that some parents whose children had Medicaid or CHIP coverage said that this coverage was private when responding to the survey.[22] Gruber and Simon (2008) also find a small and

---

22. Card, Hildreth, and Shore-Sheppard (2004) examine a different issue of mismeasurement—the accuracy of reported Medicaid coverage in the SIPP. Using administrative records from California they find that the probability of correctly reporting coverage for those actually covered by Medicaid is around 85 percent, with this probability rising for low-income children. The probability that people who are not covered by Medicaid incorrectly report that they are covered is about 1.3 percent for the population as a whole, but is higher (up to 7 percent) for low-income children.

statistically insignificant effect of public insurance eligibility on private coverage. One innovation of Gruber and Simon's study is that they account for the fact that a nontrivial share of children is reported to have public and private insurance at a point in time. They find that eligibility has a positive effect on having both types of coverage.

Bronchetti (2014) estimates take-up and crowd-out effects for an even later period, 1998–2009, focusing on the different responses to changes in eligibility over this period for children in immigrant families and children of natives. Following welfare reform in 1996, which severely restricted access to public insurance eligibility among children of immigrants, in the ensuing years the implementation of CHIP, and in many states restoration of immigrant eligibility, led to an expansion of eligibility. Using the simulated IV approach and restricted-access data from the National Health Interview Survey, she runs separate take-up and crowd-out models for the two groups. She estimates the take-up response to eligibility among all children in immigrant families at a (very significant) 19.2 percentage points and among children in immigrant families with income below four times the federal poverty guidelines at an also highly significant 22.6 percentage points. For children of natives, the corresponding take-up rates are much smaller, 7.4 percentage points and 9.6 percentage points, respectively, although still quite easily distinguishable from 0. The effects of Medicaid eligibility on private insurance are estimated to be –2.8 and –5.1 percentage points (neither significant) for all children in immigrant families and those from families with income less than four times the poverty line. Among all children of natives the corresponding estimate is –3.1 percentage points (significant), while it is a statistically insignificant –2.2 percentage points for children of natives with family incomes below 400 percent of the FPL.

A recent addition to the literature on take-up and crowd-out presents an alternative to the linear probability IV models that these and many other studies use. Ham, Ozbeklik, and Shore-Sheppard (2014) develop a simple theory that suggests that one should estimate a Medicaid take-up probit equation using only data on those eligible for Medicaid, and separate probit equations for private insurance coverage for those eligible and those not eligible for Medicaid. Unlike the standard LPM approach, in this set-up the effect of Medicaid eligibility on insurance coverage will depend on a family's characteristics. Additionally, because the coefficients are constant and are not LATEs, the model can be used to make out-of-sample forecasts of the effect of raising the Medicaid income limits beyond their current levels, as well as estimating a measure of crowd-out among all of the currently eligible. This greater usefulness comes at a cost: if one wants to treat eligibility as endogenous, the computational burden of estimating the model directly becomes quite high. However, they show that there is an efficient and relatively easy to use indirect approach for estimating the model.

The authors implement the model using data on children from the 1986–

1993 SIPP panels. Their estimated effects of eligibility on coverage are precisely estimated and vary widely across the sample. The estimates show a clear pattern: eligible children from traditionally disadvantaged groups take up Medicaid at a higher rate and private insurance at a lower rate than do eligible children from typically less disadvantaged groups. Their estimates of the crowd-out effect of eligibility for the entire sample and for the different demographic groups have relatively small confidence intervals. The vast majority of crowd-out rates for the different demographic groups are statistically distinguishable from zero and negative, indicating that private and public insurance are indeed substitutes, although the degree of substitution is quite small.

This conclusion can be taken as a summary of the findings from the extensive literature on take-up and crowd-out responses to Medicaid eligibility for children: take-up responses have been small to moderate, and while some crowd-out appears to have occurred, its magnitude has been quite small and in many cases difficult to detect in the data. While there is a large range of take-up and crowd-out rates in the literature, it is important to note that different studies measure different effects. Perhaps this is not surprising given that most estimates are local average treatment effects that apply to different (but unobserved) marginal families. Even given this variability, one general result that does emerge from the literature is that marginal take-up rates are lower for families with higher incomes. The heterogeneity in response to eligibility by income and demographic group is an interesting avenue for future work. In addition, it is important for researchers interested in estimating crowd-out as the ratio of private to public eligibility coefficients to obtain consistent confidence intervals for their ratio crowd-out measures, such as by using the delta method. Given the substantial size of the confidence intervals that have been estimated and the fact that they are likely underestimates, researchers may want to reconsider the value of estimating ratio crowd-out without having very precise measures of take-up and level crowd-out to put into the ratio.

Estimates for Adults

A smaller number of studies examine the effects of changes in eligibility rules for adults. Busch and Duchovny (2005) use a standard simulated eligibility model to study expansions enacted in the wake of the 1996 welfare reform legislation, which allowed states to expand Medicaid eligibility for adults, and a policy enacted in 2000 allowing states to use unspent CHIP funds to insure low-income adults, mainly parents. They find that program eligibility raises a parent's Medicaid coverage by about 15 percentage points and reduces the probability of being uninsured by about 11 points. The estimated effect of eligibility on private coverage is small and statistically insignificant.

Hamersma and Kim (2013) also examine parental Medicaid expansions, taking a different approach to modeling the effect of eligibility on coverage. They point out that eligibility is difficult to impute accurately since the information available in the data is not all of the information used by those who make the actual eligibility determination, and they find that about 40 percent of Medicaid recipients in their sample were not assigned to be eligible by their imputation procedure. Thus they take a reduced-form approach and use as their key independent variable the state's income eligibility threshold, rather than a measure of imputed eligibility. In models where coverage is estimated as a quadratic function of the eligibility threshold they find that raising the threshold increased Medicaid coverage, but at a decreasing rate. Their results imply that an expansion in eligibility threshold by an "average" amount (about 12 percent of the federal poverty level) increases Medicaid participation by about 4 percent of baseline coverage rates. The estimated relationship between the Medicaid eligibility threshold and private coverage is not statistically significant and often has the "wrong" sign. For comparability to other studies they estimate the simulated eligibility instrument approach as well, finding estimates of marginal take-up rates that are comparable to those found for children (on the order of 15 percent) and still no evidence of crowd-out. Overall, the evidence on Medicaid expansions to parents suggests similarly sized take-up effects to those estimated for children, and no significant effect on private coverage. Since the expansions to parents tended to be focused on fairly low-income families, these results are consistent with the results from studies of the early expansions to children.

Garthwaite, Gross, and Notowidigdo (2014) study a 2005 cutback in public insurance eligibility for adults in Tennessee. The state's program, TennCare, was unique among Medicaid programs in that it offered coverage to adults, including those without children, with incomes well above the poverty line if they were uninsured or "uninsurable." In response to budget shortfalls, Tennessee tightened its eligibility rules and disenrolled approximately 170,000 adults. Garthwaite, Gross, and Notowidigdo's analysis uses data from the CPS and a difference-in-differences model that compares adults in Tennessee to adults in other southern states. They also estimate a triple-difference model that contrasts outcomes for childless adults, who were the target of the disenrollment policy, and parents, who should have been less affected. Not surprisingly, they find that public coverage fell in Tennessee relative to the comparison states. Their baseline model indicates a coverage decline of 4.6 percentage points for all adults; the triple-difference model implies a 7.3 percentage point decline for childless adults (both statistically significant). Turning to private insurance, their difference-in-differences model implies that the elimination of TennCare eligibility led to a statistically insignificant 1.7 percentage point increase in coverage, while their triple-difference specification implies a marginally significant gain of 4.3 points (p-value = .09). They estimate the ratio crowd-out measure, using a modified block-bootstrap procedure to calculate the standard errors, obtaining an estimate for the difference-in-differences model of 36.2 percent (standard error: 26.8) and for the triple difference model 59.5 percent (standard error: 38.4). Thus the resulting confidence intervals are very wide: [−16.3 percent, 88.7 percent] and [−15.7 percent, 134.8 percent], calling into question the usefulness of the ratio crowd-out measure even when correct confidence intervals are calculated.

In contrast, in the Oregon Medicaid experiment there was essentially no crowd-out. Finkelstein et al. (2012) estimate the insurance response to the Oregon lottery as the first stage in their examination of the impact of insurance on health. Their estimate is that the lottery increased Medicaid coverage by approximately 20 percent and did not reduce private coverage. Since the lottery removes the problems of endogeneity and mismeasurement from eligibility, their results have considerable credibility. At the same time, the fact that the experiment occurred during the Great Recession may limit the applicability of its results to other contexts.

Compared to children, impacts of eligibility for adults have been much less extensively researched, largely due to the fact that only recent policy changes have allowed for the identification of Medicaid effects separate from those of cash welfare or other programs. Making parents of Medicaid-eligible children eligible for Medicaid themselves appears to have clear positive impacts on coverage, with significant effects on take-up and little evidence of crowd-out. The evidence for nonparents is more equivocal, with the results from the studies that exist indicating the importance of the circumstances surrounding the conferral or removal of public coverage eligibility in determining the impact on take-up and crowd-out.

The introduction of the ACA presents opportunities to test existing estimates and models and to expand our knowledge of take-up and crowd-out behavior, since it represents a large expansion in eligibility, particularly for adults. One challenge here is that the ACA also contains a mandate to purchase insurance (or face a substantial fine), and researchers will have to adjust economic models and estimation procedures to incorporate this new provision. Under the ACA it will be important to estimate more realistic dynamic models, since the limited research in this area suggests that dynamics matter, and movement between Medicaid and other types of insurance may change as a result of the changing context for obtaining insurance.

The Impact of Other Policies Affecting Enrollment for Families

Along with changes in eligibility policy, states have implemented many other policies that have implications for take-up of the program. Some of these policies are intended to affect take-up, such as administrative reforms to make enrollment easier (presumptive eligibility, offering continuous coverage, or simplifying the application and renewal processes, for example) or outreach to encourage take-up. Other policies are intended to achieve other goals for the Medicaid program and have spillover effects on enrollment, such as the introduction of premiums, the implementation of eligibility for parents at higher income levels, or changes in physician fees. Still other policies that are not directly related to Medicaid, such as immigration enforcement, may affect Medicaid take-up.

One concern about public health insurance expansions is that eligible individuals may be unaware that they are eligible. Consequently, some states implemented information provision or outreach campaigns. An important paper on the effectiveness of outreach is by Aizer (2007) who uses data on Medicaid enrollment outreach efforts in California to address two questions: (a) how successful are various types of outreach efforts at encouraging new enrollment? and (b) what impact does this new enrollment have on ambulatory-care-sensitive hospital admissions? (The second question is discussed below in the section on utilization of care.) Outreach includes community-based application assistants (organizations trained in enrolling eligible individuals [CBOs]) and a state advertising campaign. Aizer obtained data on CBO placement and administrative data on new Medicaid enrollment by ZIP Code, race, and month for February 1996 to December 2000 among all children ages birth to fifteen. Collapsing the data to ZIP Code-year-month-race cells, she examines the impact on enrollment of the number of CBOs in a ZIP Code controlling for ZIP Code fixed effects to account for the fact that areas with more intense outreach efforts may have higher numbers of low-income children, and time fixed effects to control for general trends in enrollment over this time period, respectively. She finds significant effects of CBOs, especially for Hispanic and Asian children. The estimates suggest that an additional Spanish-language CBO increases total new monthly Medicaid enrollment for Hispanic children by 9 percent, while an additional Asian-language CBO increases enrollment by 27 percent among Asian children. The effects are larger when the CBO is also a health-care provider. She also looks at advertising, including Spanish- and English-language TV ads, using a similar approach and finds that any effect of advertising is likely small. Thus it appears that information provision is important for enrollment, but informational interventions that are targeted and accompany the ability to provide services are more effective than a general information campaign.

In addition to outreach, as eligibility limits were raised the federal government began allowing states to implement a variety of policies intended to increase enrollment among the eligible. These policies included allowing applicants to apply in different places and with simpler processes. Currie and Grogger (2002) examine whether such policies were correlated with Medicaid caseloads at the state level for the period 1990–1996 and find no statistically significant relationship. However, when they examine vital statistics data on births they find some evidence that shorter forms or being allowed to mail in forms instead of having to apply in person is associated with earlier initiation of prenatal care. Outstationing of eligibility workers is associated with inadequate prenatal care, however, suggesting that there may be omitted variables correlated with which states choose a particular policy.

A potential concern about increasing take-up for policymakers is that it may come at the cost of private coverage crowd-out, so under the CHIP program states were encouraged or required to implement policies to reduce crowd-out, such as mandatory waiting periods for previously insured children. In their analysis of the CHIP eligibility expansions, Lo Sasso and Buchmueller (2004) test for the effect of waiting periods on insurance coverage. They find that longer waiting periods decrease the probability that a child has public coverage, increase the probability of private coverage, and increase the probability of being uninsured. Thus, their results suggest that waiting periods are effective in reducing private coverage declines, though at the cost of limiting gains in the number of children with any health insurance. Wolfe and Scrivner (2005), who investigate state policy design features under CHIP using data from the 2000–2001 CPS, also find that waiting periods reduce public insurance take-up and increase the probability of being uninsured. In contrast, Gruber and Simon (2008) find no significant relationship between waiting periods and either public or private coverage. They suggest the difference may be due to differences between the data sets used in their study and that of Lo Sasso and Buchmueller (2004).

Wolfe and Scrivner (2005) find little effect for other program design variables, perhaps because there is relatively little variation in state policies over such a short time period. Bansak and Raphael (2006) compare insurance outcomes in 2001 to outcomes in 1997, just before CHIP implementation. To estimate the differential effect of state policy choices, they estimate regressions in which program design variables are interacted with an indicator variable that differentiates the pre-CHIP and post-CHIP periods. They estimate the models with state fixed effects to account for unobserved state characteristics that may be correlated with both baseline levels of insurance coverage and program features. They also find that waiting periods designed to prevent crowd-out reduce the probability a child has public insurance, and their results suggest that policies allowing for continuous enrollment increase public coverage.

Another policy that was at least partly intended to dissuade crowd-out, but was also a way to cover rising state spending on public health insurance, was the adoption of premiums for higher-income individuals. While Medicaid generally does not permit substantial amounts of cost sharing (unless a state has obtained a waiver to do so), states have more flexibility with CHIP, and during the early years of the twenty-first century several states adopted premiums. Several studies using data from selected states find a negative relationship between premiums and enrollment. Ku and Coughlin (1999/2000) find such an effect in Hawaii, Minnesota, Tennessee, and Washington. Kenney et al. (2006) examine state administrative enrollment records from 2001 to 2004–2005 from three states (Kansas, Kentucky, and

New Hampshire) and find that increases in premiums were associated with lower caseloads in all three states and with earlier disenrollment in Kentucky and New Hampshire. Similarly Marton (2007), who also studies Kentucky, finds that the introduction of premiums reduced enrollment duration, with larger effects in the first three months after the premium was introduced.

Dague (2014) uses a regression discontinuity design to study the introduction of premiums in Wisconsin's Medicaid program. Premiums in Wisconsin's program increase with income, with sharp breaks in the level of the premium at various income levels. While regression discontinuity designs with income can be problematic, as discussed above, in this case the administrative data that Dague uses permit her to observe the state's exact determination of family income, which is initially self-reported by applicants but is verified either through documentation such as paycheck stubs or direct employer verification. One issue with the administrative data that she faces is that she only observes outcomes for enrollees; however, she shows that in the case of studying the impact of premiums on enrollment spell length, selection would bias her against finding an effect. Interestingly, she finds large behavioral responses to the introduction of a relatively small premium, with a $10 premium requirement making enrollees 12–15 percentage points more likely to exit the program, but she finds very little evidence of responses to *changes* in premiums of a similar magnitude. This suggests that it is the premium *per se*, rather than its amount, which affects individual enrollment behavior.

There are two other policies that states may pursue that could have implications for enrollment in the program. First, the implementation of eligibility for parents at higher income levels than the AFDC level may encourage enrollment of children since the marginal benefit from completing the enrollment process would be higher if more individuals in the family could gain eligibility. The difficulty in examining the impact of parental eligibility expansions on children is in finding variation in parental enrollment that is uncorrelated with unobserved factors determining child enrollment. Sommers (2006) uses the March CPS matched across years, focusing on loss of coverage among children who appeared eligible in both years and modeling the probability of drop-out (loss of coverage while still eligible) as a function of parental and/or sibling coverage in year 1. He uses eligibility of the parent or sibling as an instrument for parent/sibling coverage. However, elsewhere in the literature researchers have recognized that eligibility may be endogenous, since unobserved factors that are more likely to make a parent eligible may also affect coverage. Sommers attempts to circumvent this issue by controlling for income, although the exogeneity of income is also questionable. He finds that if a parent is covered, the child is less likely to drop Medicaid, but there is no statistically significant effect of a sibling being covered.

Second, changes in physician fees may be associated with participation if, for example, raising fees leads to greater physician participation, and individuals are more likely to enroll when they believe they can obtain needed care. Indeed, Hahn (2013) estimates models of the probability of various types of coverage as a function of the ratio of Medicaid to Medicare fees and controlling for state and year fixed effects and finds that a 10 percentage point increase in the ratio is associated with a 1.24 percentage point decrease in the uninsured rate among low-income children.

Taken together, the results of research on policies intended either to encourage take-up or to deter crowd-out can best be summarized as "circumstances matter." While there is evidence of effects from a variety of the policies studied, none of the policies studied show unequivocal effects across jurisdictions, time periods, or population groups. In addition, many of the results discussed may have limited applicability to Medicaid under the Affordable Care Act, with its underlying individual mandate for coverage. However, the fact that circumstances seem to be important when examining the effects of policies to encourage take-up suggests that examining the different enrollment regimes in different states under the ACA is an important area for future research.

Finally, it is possible that policies not particularly aimed at Medicaid may have spillover effects on Medicaid participation. Using newly obtained data on immigration enforcement activity (number of deportable aliens located per noncitizen) in the 1990s across the thirty-three Immigration and Naturalization Service administrative districts, Watson (2014) estimates the impact of enforcement activity on children of noncitizens. Controlling for a number of possible confounding effects with a rich set of fixed effects and demographic variables, she finds that a 1 log point increase in enforcement efforts (about the size of the increase in enforcement between 1994 and 2000) reduces Medicaid participation by children of noncitizens relative to children of citizens by 10.1 percentage points. Her results imply that much of the observed decline in participation in Medicaid by immigrants around the time of welfare reform can, in fact, be attributed to increased enforcement of immigration law. Similarly, Sommers (2010) shows that a later (2005) change requiring proof of citizenship at the time of Medicaid application was associated with a reduction in enrollment among noncitizens, although he points out that the costs of the policy (particularly the burden on citizen applicants) are significantly larger than the savings.

Eligibility, Take-Up, and Crowd-Out in Long-Term Care

Long-term care (LTC) expenditures account for a large and growing share of total health-care spending in the United States. As noted in section 1.2, a large share of Medicaid spending for aged and disabled adults is for institutional and non-institutional LTC services. Care provided in nursing homes is a main component of LTC expenditures. Medicaid is the largest purchaser of nursing home care, accounting for roughly three-fifths of national expenditures (CMS 2014). In contrast, private health insurance accounts for only 8 percent of payments to freestanding nursing-care facilities. Why so few people purchase insurance for LTC, and the extent to which Medicaid reduces the demand for LTC insurance, are important research questions with significant policy implications.

In a series of papers, Brown and Finkelstein (2007, 2008, 2009, 2011) provide a comprehensive view of the market for LTC insurance and examine the puzzle of why so few Americans take up coverage. Brown and Finkelstein (2007) consider the potential importance of supply-side market failures as explanations by collecting the first data set on premiums for LTC. They then calculate expected costs of LTC for different groups, which allows them to ask if premiums for LTC policies are above the actuarially fair level. They find that premiums are 25–50 percent above the actuarially fair level for men, but appear close to actuarially fair for women. The existence of these excess profits for men suggests that the market has noncompetitive features. However, it is harder to explain why insurers discriminate against men in this fashion and even harder to explain why private insurance coverage rates are similar for men and women.[23] This difference in coverage between men and women only makes sense if there is an impediment on the demand side to women purchasing LTC insurance, assuming that price elasticities for the insurance are not very close to zero.

In another paper, Brown and Finkelstein (2008) investigate the demand side of the market using a calibrated life-cycle model of a consumer considering the purchase of private LTC insurance taking the supply side of the market as given. They consider the effect on consumer choice of two important aspects of how Medicaid is implemented. First, and most importantly, Medicaid is second-payer insurance and only pays what is not covered by private insurance. As a result, if consumers buy private insurance it primarily will cover expenses that Medicaid would have covered in the absence of the private insurance and thus imposes an implicit tax on private insurance expenditures; the higher the implicit tax, the less attractive private insurance is. They estimate for a man at the median of the income distribution, 60 percent of private benefits only replace expenses that Medicaid would have covered. For women, the implicit tax is even larger: almost 80 percent of private benefits go for services that Medicaid would have paid for in the absence of private coverage. (The higher implicit tax for women resolves the puzzle of why women do not buy more insurance given that they pay lower premiums relative to men than their life expectancies would merit.) Simple theory and simulations show that the demand for private insurance is decreasing in the implicit price.

Another important feature of Medicaid LTC insurance is that individu-

---

23. They note that some market imperfections may lead to quantity rationing in this market, but find no evidence of this in practice.

als/families must pass an asset test, that is, have assets under the relevant state maximum. Brown, Coe, and Finkelstein (2007) investigate the role of the asset test empirically using the restricted access version of the Health and Retirement Study (HRS) for 1996, 1998, and 2000. They examine the relationship between a family's purchase of LTC insurance and the amount of assets the family can protect under state law. They address the endogeneity of assets by regressing assets on demographic variables and state dummies and putting the predicted assets through the nonlinear formula determining protected assets to form an instrument. Thus, although they do not have an exclusion restriction they can legitimately exploit the nonlinearity of the protection formula.

Their preferred estimates suggest that a $10,000 decrease in the asset limits would decrease private LTC coverage by 1.1 percentage points. Their estimates imply that if every state moved from its current Medicaid asset eligibility requirements to the lowest (most stringent) Medicaid eligibility requirements allowed by federal law—a change that would decrease average household assets protected by Medicaid by about $25,000—demand for private LTC insurance would rise by 2.7 percentage points. While this represents a 30 percent increase in insurance coverage relative to the baseline ownership rate of 9.1 percent, it also indicates that 88 percent of households still would not hold private insurance. They also consider an even more draconian counterfactual where the lowest (most stringent) Medicaid eligibility requirements allowed by federal law are cut in half and every state moved from its current Medicaid asset eligibility requirements to the new federal limits, but this only results in a gain in private insurance coverage of 3.3 percentage points. The implication of their work is that while reducing asset limits reduces the crowding out of private insurance coverage, the gains in private coverage are quite limited.

Given that there is relatively little to be gained in terms of reducing the crowd-out of private insurance through the asset test, a natural question is how sensitive are consumers to the implicit price of private LTC insurance. In Brown and Finkelstein's (2008) simulations they find that lowering the implicit tax through a plan that allows employers to pay premiums for private LTC insurance (with this payment being nontaxable income from the employee's perspective) still leaves private insurance unattractive to the median male or female. They also note that the fact that marginal tax rates (and thus the tax subsidy) increase with wealth while the implicit tax decreases with wealth indicates the difficulty in using tax deductions to reduce the implicit tax for much of the population.

Two other studies examine policies aimed at using tax incentives to increase take-up of private LTC insurance. They both find that while the policies increased LTC coverage, the tax expenditures exceeded the savings to the Medicaid program. Courtemanche and He (2009) study the impact of a tax incentive introduced by the Health Insurance Portability and Accountability Act of 1996 (HIPAA). Under HIPAA, LTC insurance premiums can be counted as medical expenses for the purpose of itemized deductions. Using data from the HRS and a difference-in-differences research strategy, they find that the HIPAA tax incentive increased take-up of private LTC insurance by 3.3 percentage points among those who itemize medical deductions. However, since itemizers comprise only about 14 percent of the individuals in their sample, the policy increased the private LTC coverage rate by less than half a percentage point for the population as a whole. They interpret their results as implying a price elasticity for LTC insurance of –3.9. Their simulations indicate that $1 of foregone tax revenue results in only a $0.39 reduction in Medicaid expenditure. When they extrapolate their results to measure the effect of LTC premiums being fully deductible (i.e., being an above-the-line deduction), they find that private coverage would rise from 10 percent to only 13.3 percent of the eligible population.

Goda (2011) examines tax subsidies introduced in the 1990s by a number of states with the goal of shifting LTC costs away from Medicaid. In her analysis, which also uses the HRS, the dependent variable is an indicator for purchasing private long-term care insurance and her main explanatory variable is the after-tax price of $1 of private LTC insurance in terms of foregone consumption. She treats the tax price as endogenous, using a simulated instrument in the spirit of Currie and Gruber's simulated eligibility variable. The variation in this instrument comes from changes in tax subsidies for LTC insurance across states and time. Her preferred estimates imply a price elasticity with respect to the after-tax price of –3.3. However, this response to the tax subsidy is concentrated among wealthier households who generally would not have qualified for Medicaid in the absence of the incentive policy. Simulations based on her model suggest that $1 in tax expenditures produces $0.84 in Medicaid savings.

Taken as a whole, this literature suggests that Medicaid substantially reduces the demand for private long-term-care insurance and there is not much scope for improving crowd-out while making marginal changes to Medicaid LTC. However, some findings point to alternative policy approaches. Specifically, Brown and Finkelstein (2008) find in their simulations that modifying Medicaid to allow for private LTC insurance that tops up, rather than replaces, Medicaid coverage dramatically increases welfare. However, Brown and Finkelstein note that such a reform could be quite expensive in terms of additional government expenditure. Further, they argue that reforming Medicaid to reduce or eliminate the implicit tax might have limited effects if there are important demand-side factors affecting private coverage take-up such as individual myopia or relying on one's children to provide support, or if market imperfections on the supply side of the market are sufficiently serious.

1.5.2   Access, Utilization, and Health

Children, Infants, and Pregnant Women

Because women and children have historically accounted for the majority of Medicaid enrollment, much of the research examining effects on medical-care utilization and health focuses on those populations. In addition, various features of Medicaid coverage for these populations have made obtaining plausibly causal inferences more feasible. In particular, studies in this literature exploit variation arising from the eligibility expansions of the 1980s and 1990s, including an important discontinuity in eligibility rules that occurred during this period. Table 1.7 lists both seminal and some of the more recent studies from this literature.

Currie and Gruber (1996a) estimate the effect of Medicaid eligibility on several measures of health-care utilization for children, using data from the National Health Interview Survey (NHIS) from the 1984–1992 period and the simulated eligibility measure they developed as an instrumental variable calculated using data from the Current Population Survey (CPS). One outcome is the probability of not having at least one physician visit over the past twelve months. Since it is recommended that all children have an annual "well child" visit, this outcome can be seen as a general measure of access to care. Their IV estimates imply that Medicaid eligibility reduces the probability of not having a visit by nearly 10 percentage points, or roughly half of the baseline rate. They use data on the location of care to investigate whether Medicaid eligibility reduces the use of hospital emergency departments and outpatient clinics in favor of care received in physicians' offices. They find that Medicaid eligibility has a fairly large, though imprecisely estimated, effect on the probability of receiving care in a doctor's office. The estimated effect on the probability of visiting a hospital emergency department or clinic is also positive, though again not statistically significant.

Card and Shore-Sheppard (2004) examine the effect of Medicaid eligibility on the probability of having at least one doctor visit in a year using a regression discontinuity design as discussed in the above section on take-up and crowd-out, and data from the NHIS. As with their results for take-up, they find the largest (and most statistically significant) effects for the expansion of eligibility to children below poverty, with estimates suggesting that children with newly available health insurance coverage have a 60 percent higher probability of at least one annual doctor visit, although the confidence interval on this estimate is fairly wide (the standard error is 31 percent). The estimate for children eligible only under the expansion to 133 percent of the FPL, while positive, has a substantial standard error. De la Mata (2012) also uses a RD design in income, though (as discussed earlier) the use of income as the assignment variable is somewhat problematic because of unobserved differences in the income-counting methodologies across states that lead to actual income-eligibility cutoffs differing from reported cutoffs.

Table 1.7   **Studies of access, utilization, and health**

Study	Data	Population	Design	Results
Currie, Gruber, and Fischer (1995)	Vital Statistics 1979–1992; March CPS	Infants and pregnant women	State-year panel with lagged dependent variable. Dependent variables: infant mortality, Medicaid expenditures. Main independent variables: ratio of Medicaid to private fees for ob/gyns, imputed Medicaid eligibility.	Raising the fee ratio by 10 percent lowers infant mortality by 0.5 to 0.9 pp. Eligibility expansions reduced infant mortality rate but increase Medicaid expenditures, particularly for hospitals.
Currie and Gruber (1996a)	NHIS; March CPS, 1985–1993; Vital Statistics	Children	IV using simulated eligibility instrument. Dependent variables: doctor visits, state-level infant mortality. Main independent variable: imputed eligibility.	Medicaid eligibility reduces prob. of a child going without a doctor's visit in past year by one-half, raises prob. of child seeing doctor within past two weeks by two-thirds, also reduction in state-level child mortality.
Currie and Gruber (1996b)	March CPS, 1979–1992; Vital Statistics; HCFA; NSLY	Pregnant women and infants	IV using simulated eligibility instrument. Dependent variable: incidence of low birth weight, infant mortality. Main independent variable: imputed eligibility.	Medicaid eligibility changes from 1979–1992 increased the percentage of women eligible for Medicaid in case of pregnancy by 30.9 pp. A 30 pp. increase in Medicaid eligibility of pregnant women leads to an 8.5 pp. decline in infant mortality. Targeted eligibility changes are more effective than broad eligibility changes.
Joyce (1999)	Linked Medicaid administrative data and New York State birth certificates, 1989–1991	Infants and pregnant women	Stratified cross-section and IV. Dependent variables: use of prenatal services, infant birth weight. Main independent variable: Prenatal Care Assistance Program (PCAP) participation.	Participation in PCAP is associated with a 0.2 increase in the probability of enrollment in WIC, a 35 g increase in mean birth weight, and 1.3 pp. decrease in rate of low birth weight.
Gray (2001)	National Maternal and Infant Health Survey 1988	Pregnant women	Cohort difference in difference. Dependent variables: low birth weight, premature birth, infant mortality. Main independent variables: Medicaid physician fees, Medicaid coverage.	An increase in Medicaid physician fees of 10 percent relative to the mean results in 0.074 pp. reduction in risk of low birth weight, 0.035 pp. reduction in risk of very low birth weight for Medicaid-insured women.

(continued)

Table 1.7 (continued)

Study	Data	Population	Design	Results
Currie and Grogger (2002)	Vital Statistics Detailed Natality Files, 1990–1996	Universe of pregnant women	Repeated cross section Dependent variables: utilization of prenatal care, low birth weight, and infant mortality. Main independent variables: Medicaid income cutoffs, administrative reforms, welfare caseload.	Higher Medicaid income eligibility cutoffs and higher welfare caseloads increase use of prenatal care and reduce fetal deaths. No consistent effect of administrative reforms.
Card and Shore-Sheppard (2004)	SIPP, 1990–1993; HIS, 1992–1996; March CPS, 1990–1996	Children	Regression discontinuity Dependent variable: At least one doctor visit in past year. Main independent variable: income below cutoff and age in eligible range.	Children newly covered have a 60 percent higher probability of at least one annual doctor visit than in the absence of the expansion (standard error 31 percent)
Aizer, Lleras-Muney, and Stabile (2005)	Linked birth and death certificates from CA, 1989–1995	Insured pregnant women	Differences in differences Dependent variable: neonatal mortality. Main independent variables: public/private insurance status, index of hospital segregation.	Increasing access to care has small impact on neonatal mortality for entire sample; for blacks, the average decline in segregation over the sample period results in a 7 percent reduction in neonatal mortality; for twins, 12.5 percent decline; for black twins, 42 percent.
Dafny and Gruber (2005)	National Hospital Discharge Survey, 1983–1996	Children	IV using simulated eligibility instrument. Dependent variable: child hospitalizations. Main independent variable: imputed Medicaid eligibility by age group, state, and year.	A 10 pp. rise in Medicaid eligibility is associated with an 8.1 pp. increase in the unavoidable hospitalization rate, and statistically insignificant 3.2 pp. in avoidable hospitalization rate.
Aizer (2007)	Medicaid enrollment and administrative data, 1996–2000. Data set of locations of community-based application assistant locations	Children	Zip Code-race-month-year panel and IV. Dependent variables: Medicaid enrollment, avoidable hospitalizations. Main independent variable: number of community-based application assistants in the ZIP Code.	Proximity to an additional bilingual application assistant increases new monthly Medicaid enrollment among Hispanics by 7 to 9 pp., and among Asians by 27 to 36 pp. Increasing the number of children with Medicaid by 10 pp. results in 2 to 3 pp. decline in avoidable hospitalizations.

Study	Data	Sample	Method and variables	Results
Currie, Decker, and Lin (2008)	NHIS, 1986–2005	Older children	Repeated cross section. Dependent variables: utilization of care, health status. Main independent variables: household income, public insurance eligibility.	The importance of income for predicting health for older children has fallen over time. Eligibility for public health insurance increases utilization of preventative care. No effect on current health status.
Finkelstein et al. (2012)	Survey; administrative data from hospital discharge records, credit reports, and mortality records 2008–2009	Adults	Experimental. Dependent variables: self-reported health, financial strain, well-being, health-care utilization, health insurance status. Main independent variable: randomly assigned Medicaid applicant status.	Being selected by the lottery results in a 25 pp. increase in the prob. of having insurance after one year. Having insurance coverage is associated with a 2.1 pp. increase in prob. of hospital admission, a 20 pp. decline in having any out-of-pocket medical expenditure, and a .2 SD improvement in self-reported physical and mental health.
Kolstad and Kowalski (2012)	CPS, HCUP National Inpatient Sample 2004–2008, BRFSS	Hospital discharges in MA	Difference in difference. Dependent variables: insurance status, length of hospitalization, hospital costs. Main independent variables: postexpansion indicator, MA indicator.	Healthcare reform in MA decreased uninsurance by 36 percent relative to initial level, reduced length of hospitalizations. No effect on hospital cost growth.
de la Mata (2012)	PSID 1997, 2002, 2007	Children	Regression discontinuity. Dependent variables: health-care utilization, health status. Main independent variable: family income.	Medicaid eligibility increases the use of preventive health care by 11 to 14 pp., but only at low income thresholds. No significant effects on health outcomes in the short and medium run.
Miller (2012)	Acute Hospital Case Mix Databases, from the MA Division of Health Care Finance and Policy, 2002–2008	Counties in MA	Difference in difference. Dependent variables: ED use per capita. Main independent variables: 2005 uninsurance rate, expansion indicator.	MA health-care reform reduced ED usage by 5 to 8 percent, with decline concentrated for event that can be treated in a physician's office. No effect on ED use for nonpreventable emergencies.
Sommers, Baicker, and Epstein (2012)	CDC Compressed Mortality File, 1997–2007; CPS 1997–2007; BRFSS 1997–2007	Adults	Difference in difference. Dependent variables: all-cause county-level mortality, insurance coverage, incidence of delayed care due to cost, self-reported health status. Main independent variables: postexpansion indicator, expansion state indicator.	Medicaid expansions are associated with a significant 6.1 percent reduction in all-cause mortality, 3.2 pp. decrease in rate of uninsurance, 2.9 pp. decrease in rate of delay of care due to cost, and 2.2 pp. improvement in rate of self-reported health status very good or better.

(continued)

Table 1.7 (continued)

Study	Data	Population	Design	Results
Baicker et al. (2013)	Survey	Adults	Experimental Dependent variables: clinical outcomes (e.g., blood pressure), health status, health-care use, out-of-pocket medical spending. Main independent variable: randomly assigned Medicaid applicant status.	Medicaid coverage significantly increases the probability of diagnosis of diabetes, decreases the probability of positive screening for depression by 0. 915, increases use of preventative health services, nearly eliminates catastrophic out-of-pocket medical spending.
DeLeire et al. (2013)	Wisconsin's administrative Medicaid claims and enrollment databases	Childless uninsured adults	Case-crossover design Dependent variables: outpatient visits, ED visits, inpatient hospitalizations, preventable hospitalizations. Main independent variable: automatic enrollment status in "BadgerCare Plus Core Plan."	In twelve months following enrollment in public insurance program, outpatient visits increase 29 percent, ED visits increase 46 percent, inpatient hospitalizations fall by 59 percent, and preventable hospitalizations fall by 48 percent.
Bronchetti (2014)	Restricted-access National Health Interview Survey, 1998–2009	Children in immigrant families and children of natives (estimated separately)	IV using simulated eligibility instrument. Dependent variables: no doctor visit in a year, usual place for care, any hospitalization, ED visit, self-reported health status, school days missed, asthma attack. Main independent variable: imputed eligibility.	For children in immigrant families: being eligible reduces probability of no visit by 0.115 (0.047), of ED visit by 0.062 (0.030), of asthma attack by 0.020(0.011); being eligible increases probability of having a usual place of care by 0.077 (0.027) and of excellent health by 0.073. For children of natives: being eligible reduces probability of asthma attack by 0.025 (0.009) and increases probability of having a usual place of care by 0.021 (0.012).
Taubman et al. (2014)	Emergency department records from twelve Portland, OR hospitals, 2007–2009 survey	Adults	Experimental Dependent variable: Emergency department visits. Main independent variable: randomly assigned Medicaid applicant status.	Medicaid coverage significantly increases overall emergency department use by .41 visits per person, a 40 percent increase relative to average. No decline in emergency department use for any subgroups.

Study	Data source	Method	Population	Findings
Boudreaux et al. (2015)	Panel Study of Income Dynamics	Exposure to Medicaid estimated based on birth year and state of residence. Dependent variable: index of chronic health conditions	Young adults	Exposure to Medicaid in early childhood is negatively associated with chronic health conditions as a young adult.
Goodman-Bacon (2015)	Vital Statistics, Multiple Cause of Death Data Files	Difference-in-differences event study comparing states with larger and smaller changes in insurance coverage.	Children	Mortality fell significantly more for nonwhite children in high ranges of eligibility than in states with low rates of eligibility.
Wherry and Miller (2015)	National Health Interview Survey; Healthcare Cost and Utilization Project—National Inpatient Survey	IV using simulated eligibility instruments for eligibility in utero and during childhood. Dependent variables: self-reported health, obesity, hospitalization.	Young adults	Medicaid eligibility as a child is significantly associated with better self-reported health, lower rates of obesity, and lower hospitalization rates an adult.
Wherry, Miller, Kaestner, and Meyer (2015)	National Health Interview Survey; Healthcare Cost and Utilization Project—State Inpatient and Emergency Department databases	Regression discontinuity	Young adults	Medicaid eligibility associated with lower rates of hospitalization for blacks; no significant effect for whites
Wherry and Meyer (forthcoming)	Vital Statistics, Multiple Cause of Death Data Files	Regression discontinuity	Children	Medicaid eligibility associated with lower mortality for black children; no significant effect for whites

Using data on children ages five to eighteen from the Panel Study of Income Dynamics, she finds increases in the probability of at least one doctor visit of 12–14 percentage points, but only for children eligible under lower eligibility thresholds (100–185 percent of the FPL). She finds no statistically detectable effect on health, either for contemporaneous or lagged eligibility.[24]

In contrast, Bronchetti (2014) finds evidence not only of increases in health-care utilization resulting from eligibility for Medicaid and CHIP, but also some evidence of improvements in health, particularly for children in immigrant families. She estimates models of utilization and health as a function of eligibility (using a simulated eligibility instrument) on restricted-access data from the National Health Interview Survey for 1998–2009, a time period with significant expansions in eligibility for children in both immigrant and native families due to the introduction of CHIP and the relaxation of some rules preventing coverage of immigrants that had been enacted under welfare reform. Examining children in immigrant families and natives separately, she finds beneficial impacts of eligibility for both children in immigrant families and natives, but estimates for children in immigrant families show larger benefits, particularly for utilization. Specifically, for children in immigrant families she finds a 12-percentage-point reduction in the probability of no doctor visit, an 8-percentage-point increase in the probability of having a usual place for care, a 6-percentage-point reduction in the probability of an emergency department visit, and improvements in measures of self-reported health and asthma morbidity. The estimates for natives are generally smaller, and are only statistically significant for having a usual place for care and for asthma. She notes that the larger effects for children in immigrant families likely arise from the fact that such children were much less likely to have insurance coverage prior to the expansions, making this group akin to the group affected by the early Medicaid expansions of the 1980s.

Several studies examine the effect of Medicaid on inpatient utilization. As described in section 1.4, the effect on this outcome is theoretically ambiguous. On one hand, there is likely to be an access effect: by providing access to costly care that low-income patients could not otherwise afford, Medicaid should have a positive effect on inpatient utilization. At the same time, by improving timely access to primary and preventive care, Medicaid may lead to health improvements that reduce the number of "avoidable" hospitalizations for conditions like asthma, gastroenteritis, dehydration, and certain infections. An analysis by Currie and Gruber (1996a) suggests that the first of these two effects dominates: Medicaid eligibility increases the probability of having a hospital stay by about 4 percentage points, which represents

24. Other studies using different data and different research designs also find that utilization increased for children who gained eligibility for public insurance because of CHIP relative to children who did not gain eligibility (Selden and Hudson 2006; Lurie 2009; Li and Baughman 2010; Choi, Sommers, and McWilliams 2011).

nearly a doubling of the baseline rate. The NHIS data they use does not provide details on the nature of the inpatient care received, so they are not able to assess whether the Medicaid expansion reduced avoidable admissions.

Dafny and Gruber (2005) explore this issue in more detail by matching data on Medicaid eligibility measured for state/year/age group cells with data from the National Hospital Discharge Survey, adapting the simulated eligibility IV approach to these aggregate data. Their results for total hospitalizations are nearly identical to Currie and Gruber's (1996a): a 10-percentage-point increase in Medicaid eligibility increases the pediatric hospitalization rate by 8.4 percent. They then estimate separate regressions for hospitalizations classified as avoidable or unavoidable based on the prior health services literature in this area. According to their definition, roughly one-quarter of pediatric hospitalizations during the period they study were classified as avoidable. When the dependent variable is the natural log of unavoidable hospitalizations, the coefficient on the Medicaid eligibility variable is positive and significant, with a magnitude that is similar to the estimate for all hospitalizations. For avoidable hospitalizations, the coefficient on the Medicaid eligibility rate is still positive, but smaller and not significantly different from zero.

Aizer (2007) also uses IV methods to estimate the effect of Medicaid on avoidable hospitalizations, though she estimates the effect of Medicaid *enrollment* on children who were already eligible rather than the effect of eligibility. She finds that a 10 percent increase in Medicaid enrollment leads to a 2 to 3 percent decline in avoidable hospitalizations, but has no effect on hospital admissions for other conditions. These effects are large enough that the savings from reduced admissions were likely greater than the cost of the outreach program. The difference between her results and those of Dafny and Gruber may be explained by the fact that the children who gain insurance coverage because of a change in eligibility experience improved access to both outpatient and inpatient care. In contrast, since children who enrolled because of the outreach efforts already had "conditional coverage" for inpatient care in the sense that they could sign up for Medicaid if they presented at a hospital in need of acute care, the main effect of gaining coverage was improved access to primary and preventive care.

The analyses conducted by Aizer (2007) and Dafny and Gruber (2005) test for immediate effects of Medicaid coverage on proxies for child health. However, since health is a stock, it should be affected by past investments as well as current ones. Thus, to the extent that an important benefit of Medicaid is improved access to primary and preventive care, it may take time for effects on health to be realized. This is how Currie, Decker, and Lin (2008) interpret the findings of their analysis of older children using multiple years of data from the National Health Interview Survey. Using the simulated eligibility instrument approach, they find that eligibility for Medicaid significantly reduces the probability that a child does not have at least one physician visit in a year, but has no significant effect on contemporaneous health status. However, their results suggest that children who were eligible for Medicaid when they were toddlers are more likely to be in excellent health (as reported by their parents) between the ages of nine and seventeen.

Several recent working papers find evidence that having access to Medicaid as a young child leads to better health later in life. In an analysis using the Panel Study of Income Dynamics, Boudreaux, Golberstein, and McAlpine (2014) use variation across states in the timing of the introduction of the program in the 1960s to identify long-term effects among cohorts with different exposure to the program in early childhood. Miller and Wherry (2015) analyze the effect of a later coverage expansion and obtain similar results. Using a simulated eligibility instrumental variables model they find that individuals whose mothers gained eligibility as a result of the expansions for pregnant women in the late 1980s and early 1990s experienced better health outcomes as young adults. They also find a negative effect on hospitalizations for conditions that have been previously shown to be sensitive to the in utero environment, such as diabetes.

Wherry et al. (2015) exploit the same discontinuity as Card and Shore-Sheppard (2004) to investigate the effect of Medicaid eligibility as a young child on health status as a teenager and young adult. They show that poor children who were born just before September 30, 1983—the cutoff specified by OBRA 1990—enjoyed up to nearly five more years of eligibility than otherwise similar children who were born just after that date. These additional years of potential Medicaid eligibility are associated with fewer hospitalizations and emergency department visits as a young adult. Stratifying the analysis by race, they find statistically significant effects for blacks but not whites. This pattern is consistent with their finding that blacks were more likely to gain eligibility as a result of the OBRA 1990 expansions.

Several studies test for an effect of Medicaid eligibility on mortality, applying different identification strategies to data from different periods in the program's history. Focusing on the eligibility expansions of the 1980s and early 1990s, Currie and Gruber (1996a) regress the death rate by state-year-age-race cell on the imputed fraction eligible in that cell from the CPS, and using simulated eligibility for a national sample by state, year, and age as instruments, they find a reduction of 0.13 percentage points in mortality for every 10 percentage point increase in Medicaid eligibility. In their other paper focusing on the same eligibility expansions, Currie and Gruber (1996b) use vital statistics data for the period 1979–1992, to explore the impact of Medicaid eligibility changes on the fraction of births that are low birth weight and the infant mortality rate by state and year. One difference with their analysis of child mortality is that in this paper they distinguish between the earliest expansions that were aimed at women well below the poverty line and that sometimes included income increases through AFDC as well as expanded access to health insurance coverage (what they call "targeted" expansions) and later expansions aimed at women with incomes as high as the poverty line or slightly higher (what they call "broad" expansions). They find evidence both for a reduction in low birth weight incidence and a reduction in infant mortality. However, these reductions appear only to come from the earlier "targeted" expansions that might also have involved cash assistance changes; later insurance-only expansions higher up the income distribution show no statistically significant effect.

Wherry and Meyer (forthcoming) apply RD methods to the discontinuity created by the OBRA 1990 eligibility rules to examine the cumulative effect of Medicaid eligibility on child mortality several years after the OBRA 1990 expansion went into effect. In the years just after the expansion, when children born in 1983 were between the ages of eight and fourteen, there is some evidence suggesting a reduction in mortality for black children, though the estimates are imprecise and sensitive to the specification. However, between the ages of fifteen and eighteen, the mortality differences between black children born just before and just after September 30, 1983, are large and statistically significant. For this group, the results imply a 13 to 20 percent decrease in mortality from internal causes. In contrast, Wherry and Meyer find no evidence of a mortality effect for white teenagers. These racial differences resemble the pattern that Wherry et al. (2015) find using essentially the same research design to study health status. As noted in the discussion of that paper, black children were substantially more likely than white children to gain Medicaid eligibility as a result of the OBRA 1990 expansion.

A recent study by Goodman-Bacon (2015) takes yet another approach to investigate the relationship between Medicaid and child mortality. He applies a difference-in-differences event study model to state-level mortality data for the years 1959 to 1979. The key source of variation in his analysis comes from the fact that Medicaid eligibility was initially tied to the receipt of cash welfare benefits, resulting in larger coverage gains in states with higher AFDC participation rates. Prior to the introduction of Medicaid, there was no significant difference in mortality trends between "high-eligibility" and "low-eligibility" states. After the program was established, mortality fell significantly more for nonwhite infants and young children in high-eligibility states than for those in low-eligibility states. Goodman-Bacon finds no significant mortality effects for white infants or older children. Similar to the case of the OBRA 1990 expansion, a possible explanation for the way the results differ with race is that when Medicaid was implemented nonwhite children were more likely to gain coverage because they were more likely to have previously been receiving AFDC.

Like Currie and Gruber (1996a) and Wherry and Meyer (forthcoming), Goodman-Bacon finds that the overall mortality effects were driven by large declines in internal-cause mortality, especially mortality caused by infectious diseases, which during this period were typically treated with antibiotics and other drugs. One important difference between Goodman-Bacon's results and the other mortality studies has to do with the magnitudes of the estimated effects. To compare magnitudes he calculates Average Treatment Effects on the Treated (ATETs) for his analysis and those of Currie and Gruber (1996a) and Wherry and Meyer (forthcoming). The ATETs based on his difference-in-differences results imply a 24 percent mortality reduction for nonwhite children under age fourteen and a 38 percent reduction for nonwhite children between the ages of one and four. While these are large effects, they are substantially smaller than the ATETs for the other studies, which in some cases exceed 100 percent. He suggests the explanation may be that estimates based on the eligibility expansions of the 1980s may reflect additional causal mechanisms besides Medicaid.

Overall, the results from the literature thus far point to expansions in eligibility for Medicaid leading to improvements in access to care and health, although the magnitudes of the effects are sometimes difficult to pinpoint and estimates often differ for different groups or at different times. Although effects on access and utilization tend to be evident immediately, effects on health status appear to take some time to develop. Looking at the literature as a whole, it also appears that Medicaid expansions affecting more disadvantaged children tend to show more consistent positive effects. While the pattern of greater effects for lower-income children makes sense given the greater availability of alternative health insurance sources for higher-income children, the pattern is worth further exploration; in particular, it would be worthwhile to investigate whether these results are related to the way that cash assistance was a part of some expansions, but not others. This is particularly important for those researchers interested in exploring long-term effects of the health improvements discussed here.

In addition, the role of policy endogeneity in state choices is an issue that has received limited attention but is worth exploring given the frequent use of state-level variation to identify models. To the extent that state choices about how far to expand their programs reflect conditions faced by individuals in the state, estimated effects of Medicaid eligibility may also reflect state responses to these conditions. Continued examination of the impact of Medicaid and CHIP expansions on short-run and long-run health outcomes is valuable to assess more fully the impact of these programs.

Researchers have also examined the impacts of other Medicaid policy shifts, particularly payment policy, on health. Aizer, Lleras-Muney, and Stabile (2005) examine the infant mortality effects of an increase in Medicaid payments to hospitals in California through the DSH program. Pregnant women with Medicaid insurance may obtain care from different providers if providers are unwilling to treat Medicaid patients due to low reimbursement rates. Using infant-linked birth and death certificate data, Aizer, Lleras-Muney, and Stabile find that the DSH program hospital payment increase led to a substantial move by pregnant women with Medicaid insurance to hospitals with prior low use by the Medicaid population. The desegregation of hospitals by insurance type was associated with an improvement in neonatal mortality, particularly among those with the highest levels of neonatal mortality: black infants and twins. The larger effects for black infants were particularly noteworthy since black mothers were the least likely to increase their use of private hospitals, indicating the continuing existence of some barriers (informational or otherwise) to use of higher-quality care by black Medicaid recipients.

Another set of papers has examined the impact of physician fees on health outcomes. These papers use variation in fees paid to physicians either across states relative to private fees (Gray 2001), across states and time relative to private fees (Currie, Gruber, and Fischer 1995), or in the availability of enhanced prenatal care services relative to regular prenatal care services associated with the Medicaid eligibility expansion in New York (Joyce 1999). All of these papers find that higher fees are associated with improved health outcomes.

Nondisabled Adults

There has been much less research on the utilization and health effects of Medicaid for adults, even though very poor single parents have had access to Medicaid coverage since its inception, and parental Medicaid has expanded considerably in recent years. However, recent expansions to nonparents under various waivers have led to a rise in research on this population.[25] This research is of particular interest since the Medicaid expansion of the ACA will mainly affect adults, particularly childless adults, and thus these studies on programs in individual states provide valuable evidence on the likely effect of public insurance on the health-care utilization and health of this population.

The best evidence on the effect of Medicaid on health-care utilization and health for adults comes from the Oregon Health Insurance Experiment (OHIE). In three different papers (Finkelstein et al. 2012; Baicker et al. 2013; Taubman et al. 2014) the OHIE researchers estimate utilization effects using both survey and administrative data. Results from the survey data indicate sizable effects on outpatient visits and prescription drug use. Gaining Medicaid coverage through the lottery increased the probability of having an outpatient visit by 35 percent and increased the probability of filling a prescription by 15 percent. The increased visits coincided with greater receipt of recommended preventive services. Medicaid coverage led to a 20 percent increase in the likelihood of having a cholesterol test, a 15 percent increase in blood tests for diabetes, a 60 percent increase in mammograms and a 45 percent increase in the percentage of women getting a

25. Interestingly, despite the large fraction of expenditures devoted to the elderly and disabled populations, there is a dearth of research on the health and utilization effects of Medicaid for this population.

Pap test. However, although testing clearly increased, the researchers found no significant effect of Medicaid coverage on the prevalence or diagnosis of hypertension or high cholesterol levels or on the use of medication for these conditions. For diabetes, on the other hand, having Medicaid coverage significantly increased the probability of a diagnosis and the use of diabetes medication, but there was no significant effect on measures of diabetes control (Baicker et al. 2013).

There was no significant change in inpatient utilization in the survey data, though hospital discharge data indicate that Medicaid coverage increased the probability of an admission by 2.1 percentage points, a 30 percent effect relative to the mean for the control group. This effect was driven by an increase in admissions that did not originate in the emergency room. There was also a small positive effect on the intensity of inpatient treatment as measured by a composite outcome that combines the number of inpatient days, the number of procedures, and total charges.

The initial analysis of survey data indicated no significant effect of Medicaid coverage on emergency department utilization with wide confidence intervals (Finkelstein et al. 2012). However, follow-up analysis using administrative data from twelve Portland area hospitals found that Medicaid coverage increased outpatient emergency department visits by 40 percent over an eighteen-month period. There was no statistically significant increase in emergency department visits leading to an inpatient admission.[26] Additional analyses indicate that the effect of Medicaid on emergency visits was fairly consistent across different times of day and different types of care. Medicaid led to a significant increase in visits for conditions not requiring immediate care and most types of conditions where immediate care is required.

Examining general measures of health in addition to the clinical outcomes discussed above, the treatment group reported significantly better outcomes for seven different measures of self-reported physical and mental health from a survey of lottery participants, including a significant decrease in the probability of depression (Finkelstein et al. 2012). Since Medicaid enrollees' credit reports indicated significantly lower probability of having any debt in collection and particularly any medical debt in collection, and they reported significantly lower signs of financial strain in the survey, it is possible that self-reported physical and mental health may largely reflect a generally improved sense of well-being rather than physical health improve-

26. Other studies using different research designs also find a positive correlation between Medicaid coverage and emergency department utilization. For example, Shen and Zuckerman (2005) find that, controlling for observable characteristics, individuals with Medicaid coverage are twice as likely to have an emergency department visit than someone who is uninsured. Anderson, Dobkin, and Gross (2012) use a regression discontinuity approach that exploits the fact that many young adults lose private health insurance, and to a lesser extent Medicaid, when they turn nineteen. They find that there is also a significant decrease in emergency visits and inpatient admissions at that age.

ments per se (the financial results are discussed further below). Nevertheless, to the extent that health is measured by the definition of the World Health Organization ("a state of complete physical, mental, and social well-being and not merely the absence of disease or infirmity") it is clear that coverage by Medicaid improved enrollees' health.

In addition to the Oregon experiment, there are other recent state programs that provide insight on how the ACA Medicaid expansions will affect the health-care utilization of poor adults who will gain coverage. DeLeire et al. (2013) evaluate the utilization effects of a Wisconsin program, Badger-Care Plus Core, which closely resembles Medicaid. The program enrolled poor adults in Milwaukee County who tended to have high rates of chronic illness and who had previously received care at facilities reimbursed by Medicaid Disproportionate Share funds. DeLeire and colleagues find that enrollment in the new plan led to an increase in all types of outpatient utilization, including emergency department visits. In another study evaluating the utilization effect of the same program but on a rural low-income (FPL < 200 percent) population, Burns et al. (2014) found a similar effect on outpatient visits, but inconclusive results on emergency department use. One interesting contrast with the Oregon results is that when BadgerCare Plus Core was implemented in Milwaukee, inpatient utilization fell for individuals who transitioned to the new program. In particular, there was a large and significant decline in admissions for ambulatory-care-sensitive conditions. One possible explanation is that because these patients previously faced restricted access to outpatient specialty care, emergency department physicians may have admitted them in order to ensure they received diagnostic tests. With better access to specialists in outpatient settings, these admissions fell.

There have been several studies of Massachusetts' 2006 health care reform, which like the ACA increased both Medicaid and private insurance. The results from these studies paint a more optimistic picture concerning the potential for coverage expansions not only to improve access to care, but also to shift the source of care from hospitals to lower-cost settings. Miller (2012) examines the change in emergency department visits after the Massachusetts coverage expansion using preform variation in insurance-coverage rates to identify causal effects. She finds that the reforms led to a reduction in emergency department utilization of between 5 and 8 percent. Two other results are consistent with the hypothesis that patients who gained insurance coverage shifted their source of care from hospital emergency departments to physicians' offices. First, visits for nonurgent conditions account for nearly all the decline in emergency department use; Miller finds no significant effect on visits for nonpreventable emergencies like heart attacks. Second, emergency visits declined most during regular office hours when physicians' offices were likely to be open. An analysis of survey data by Long, Stockley, and Dahlen (2012) also finds that emergency department use fell after the

Massachusetts reform. And Kolstad and Kowalski (2012) find that while overall hospital admissions did not fall after the state's reforms went into effect, there was a decline in admissions coming through the emergency room and admissions for preventable conditions.

Like the Milwaukee results on inpatient admissions, Miller's finding that expanding coverage caused emergency department visits to fall can be understood by considering the services available to low-income uninsured patients before the reform. In Massachusetts, a state program, the Uncompensated Care Pool, paid for hospital care for residents with incomes less than 200 percent of the federal poverty level at no cost to the patient. Thus, when these individuals gained full insurance coverage through Medicaid, their access to office-based primary care improved, but there was little or no change in their access to an emergency department and other hospital-based facilities. The cost of emergency department use went up for some low-income individuals who gained subsidized private insurance because of the reforms, as plans sold in the Massachusetts Connector included nontrivial copays for emergency department visits.

Although the literature on health-care utilization and health status of children suggests that it may take time before the health benefits of Medicaid coverage are evident, the results of one recent study suggest that the coverage gains for low-income adults in Massachusetts may have led to a fairly immediate reduction in mortality. Sommers, Long, and Baicker (2014) estimate a county-level difference-in-differences model to examine changes in mortality in Massachusetts relative to other states. They find that the Massachusetts coverage expansion was associated with a significant decline in all-cause mortality of 8.2 deaths per 100,000 adults, approximately a 3 percent effect. Additional analyses indicate that this result is driven by a 4.5 percent decrease in deaths from causes amenable to health care. They find stronger effects for lower-income counties and counties with lower rates of insurance coverage prior to the reforms.

In a similar analysis, Sommers, Baicker, and Epstein (2012) compare all-cause county-level mortality (from mortality statistics), rates of insurance coverage and self-reported health status (from the CPS), and rates of delayed care because of costs from the Behavioral Risk Factor Surveillance System (BRFSS) for three states that substantially expanded Medicaid eligibility for adults since 2000 (New York, Maine, and Arizona) to neighboring states without expansions (Pennsylvania, New Hampshire, and New Mexico). They find that Medicaid expansions increased Medicaid coverage by 2.2 percentage points and decreased rates of uninsurance by 3.2 percentage points, and were associated with a significant reduction in all-cause mortality, particularly for older adults, nonwhites, and residents of poorer counties. In addition, the authors find reduced rates of delayed care because of costs and increased rates of self-reported health status of "excellent" or "very good."

1.5.3   Effects on Providers

Impact of Medicaid Eligibility

In most studies on how Medicaid affects medical-care utilization, the patient is the unit of analysis and the results can be interpreted mainly as demand-side effects: Medicaid reduces the pecuniary cost of receiving care, leading patients to seek more treatment. Because most of these studies identify the effect of Medicaid from either cross-sectional differences or from relatively small changes in eligibility or coverage, a partial equilibrium perspective is probably justified. However, the impact of large policy changes such as the ACA Medicaid expansions will depend on how providers respond to the resulting changes in the overall demand for care and payer mix. A small literature on how physicians and other providers respond to changes in Medicaid eligibility, coverage, and reimbursement policy sheds some light on these issues. Key studies in this literature are summarized in table 1.8.

Several studies examine the response of providers to public insurance expansions. Baker and Royalty (2000) use two years of panel data from the American Medical Association's Survey of Young Physicians to examine the impact of Medicaid eligibility expansions for pregnant women on the percentage of a physician's patients who are poor or on Medicaid. An important feature of their analysis is that they are able to distinguish between physicians in private practice and those in public health settings. They find that increased Medicaid eligibility leads public health physicians to see a greater percentage of poor patients and patients covered by Medicaid. In contrast, they find that an expansion of Medicaid eligibility has no significant impact on physicians in private practice. Survey data indicate that on the eve of the ACA Medicaid expansions, physicians in public health clinics were substantially more likely to accept new Medicaid patients than those in private practice (Decker 2013; Rhodes et al. 2014).

Two recent studies examine how pediatricians responded to the demand changes caused by the CHIP expansion (Garthwaite 2012; He and White 2013). As noted above, a share of the children who enrolled in Medicaid or stand-alone CHIP plans was covered previously by private insurance. As a result of this crowd-out, for many physicians the main effect of the CHIP expansion was a reduction in the amount they were paid for some of their existing patients. Consistent with this, both studies find that the implementation of CHIP led pediatricians to see more publicly insured patients, while at the same time reducing their weekly hours worked.

This decline in physician hours does not necessarily imply that fewer children were receiving care. Rather, physicians may have reduced their hours by spending less time with each patient. Garthwaite considers this possibility by comparing changes in visit length for pediatricians and other types of physicians between 1993 and 2002. He finds suggestive evidence that the CHIP expansion coincided with a reduction in visit length and an increase

Table 1.8   **Studies of effects on providers**

Study	Data	Population	Design	Results
Currie, Gruber, and Fischer (1995)	Vital Statistics 1979–1992; March CPS	Infants and pregnant women	State-year panel with lagged dependent variable. Dependent variables: infant mortality, Medicaid expenditures. Main independent variables: ratio of Medicaid to private fees for ob/gyns, imputed Medicaid eligibility.	Raising the fee ratio by 10 pp. lowers infant mortality by 0.5 to 0.9 pp. Eligibility expansions reduce infant mortality rate but increase Medicaid expenditures, particularly for hospitals.
Gruber, Adams, and Newhouse (1997)	Administrative Medicaid data for Tennessee and Georgia, 1985–1987	Nonelderly Medicaid recipients	Difference in difference using two states (TN and GA). Dependent variables: site of care, total Medicaid costs. Main independent variables: Residence in TN indicator, postexpansion indicator.	After TN increased its Medicaid primary care reimbursements, site of care shifted toward physicians' offices and away from free-standing clinics. Overall Medicaid program costs fell 8 percent.
Gruber, Kim, and Mayzlin (1999)	HCUP hospital discharges from nine states, 1988–1992	Medicaid discharges admitted to the hospital with a diagnosis of childbirth	Dependent variables: use of cesarean section delivery. Main independent variable: Medicaid fee differential.	Larger Medicaid fee differentials between cesarean and natural childbirth lead to higher cesarean section rates in the Medicaid population. The fee differential of Medicaid compared to private insurance can explain 1/2–3/4 of the difference in Medicaid and private cesarean section rates.
Baker and Royalty (2000)	Surveys of Young Physicians, 1987 and 1991	Private and public physicians	IV using simulated eligibility instrument. Dependent variables: percentage of patients who are poor, percentage of patients covered by Medicaid. Main independent variables: imputed Medicaid eligibility, ratio of Medicaid to private fees for total obstetrical care for vaginal delivery.	Positive effect of fees on the number of poor and Medicaid patients seen by young, private, office-based primary care physicians. Negative effect of fees on the number of poor patients seen in a public setting. Expanding eligibility increases physician services to the poor, esp. in public settings.
Duggan (2000)	Administrative data from CA Office of Statewide Health Planning and Development, 1988–1995	Acute care hospitals in CA	Panel of hospitals. Dependent variables: volume of Medicaid patients, hospital revenue. Main independent variable: DSH payments.	Private hospitals are more responsive to DSH incentives than public hospitals. Private hospitals used DSH payments to increase their holdings of financial assets, rather than improve quality of medical care for the poor.

Study	Data source	Population	Methods	Findings
Gray (2001)	National Maternal and Infant Health Survey 1988	Pregnant women	Cohort difference in difference. Dependent variables: low birth weight, premature birth, infant mortality. Main independent variables: Medicaid physician fees, Medicaid coverage.	An increase in Medicaid physician fees of 10 percent relative to the mean results in .074 reduction in the probability of a low birth weight, .035 reduction in the probability of a very low birth weight for Medicaid-insured women.
Duggan (2004)	Administrative expenditure data from CA Department of Health Services	Medicaid beneficiaries	Instrumental variable. Dependent variable: government spending and health outcomes. Main independent variables: county managed-care mandate indicator.	The switch from FFS to managed care for Medicaid recipients in CA was associated with a large increase in government spending, but no improvement in infant health outcomes.
Baicker and Staiger (2005)	Survey of Government Finances, AHA, ARF 1988–2000, Medicare claims 1989–2000	Births and heart attack patients	Repeated cross section of counties. Dependent variables: infant mortality, post-heart attack mortality. Main independent variable: effective and ineffective DSH payments per capita.	Patients in public hospitals in states where DSH funds were diverted experienced no mortality declines. Patients in hospitals in states in which DSH funds were not expropriated experienced significant declines in mortality.
Currie and Fahr (2005)	HCFA; NHIS 1989, 1992, 1993, 1994	Low-income children	Instrumental variables. Dependent variables: probability that a child has Medicaid, utilization of care. Main independent variables: Medicaid managed-care organization penetration rate. Instrument: presence of a 1915b waiver.	Black children are less likely to be covered where Medicaid managed-care organizations are more prevalent. Among those enrolled in Medicaid, higher managed-care penetration is associated with an increase in number of black children who go without doctor visits.
Kaestner, Dubay, and Kenney (2005)	National Natality files 1990–1996	Women likely to be Medicaid eligible	Repeated cross section with county and year fixed effects, state-specific linear trends. Dependent variables: prenatal-care utilization, infant birth weight, preterm birth, use of cesarean section. Main independent variable: presence of voluntary or mandatory Medicaid managed-care plans.	Among white, non-Hispanic women, Medicaid managed care was associated with a 2 pp. decrease in the number of prenatal care visits, 3 to 5 pp. increase in incidence of inadequate prenatal care. Significant increase in incidence of preterm birth (not causal). No effect on cesarean sections.

(continued)

Table 1.8   (continued

Study	Data	Population	Design	Results
Shen and Zuckerman (2005)	National Surveys of America's Families, 1997, 1999, 2002; ARF; AHA survey files; Urban Institute capitation rate surveys	Urban residents	Difference in difference with propensity score weighting. Dependent variables: continuity of care, use of preventative care, frequency of care, perception of quality. Main independent variable: Medicaid payment generosity index.	Higher Medicaid payment rates increase access and use of care for Medicaid beneficiaries. Little effect on likelihood of receiving preventative care. Significant results are sensitive to choice of control group (uninsured or privately insured).
Aizer, Currie, and Moretti (2007)	California Birth Statistical Master File, and Birth Cohort File, 1990–2000	Births	Repeated cross section with county or mother and year fixed effects. Dependent variables: insurance coverage, use of prenatal care, infant health outcomes. Main independent variable: indicator for location in Medicaid managed-care county.	The prob. a woman started prenatal care in first trimester falls 0.04 to 0.08 when required to enroll in Medicaid managed care. Medicaid managed-care plans are associated with increases in the prob. of low birth weight, prematurity, and neonatal death relative to FFS Medicaid.
Decker (2007)	NCHS National Ambulatory Medical Care Surveys, 1989, 1993, 1998, 2003; ARF	Office-based physicians, nonelderly Medicaid recipients	Repeated cross section with state and year fixed effects. Dependent variables: physician participation in Medicaid, visit duration. Main independent variable: Medicaid-to-Medicare fee ratio.	Higher Medicaid physician fees increase the number of private physicians, esp. in medical and surgical specialties, who see Medicaid patients. Higher fees reduce the difference in visit wait times between Medicaid and privately paying patients.
Decker (2009)	NHIS 1993–2004; NAMCS and NHAMCS 1993/1994, 1998/1999, 2003/2004	Population under sixty-five and not on Medicare	Difference in difference Dependent variables: volume and site of ambulatory care. Main independent variables: Medicaid-to-Medicare fee ratio, insurance status.	Reductions in Medicaid physician fees lead to a reduction in the number of physician visits for Medicaid recipients relative to the privately insured and a shift away from physicians' offices and toward hospital emergency departments for site of care.
Decker (2011)	NHIS 2000/2001, 2008/2009	Children and adolescents	Difference in difference. Dependent variable: indicator for dental visit in the past six months. Main independent variable: Medicaid dental reimbursement fee.	Increases in Medicaid dental reimbursement fees are associated with a greater use of dental care among youths covered by Medicaid: increasing from $20 to $30 leads to a 0.392 pp. increase in prob. of a Medicaid child seeing a dentist in past six months.

Study	Data	Unit of analysis	Method	Findings
Garthwaite (2012)	Community Tracking Survey, 1996/1997, 1997/1998, 2000/2001; NAMCS, 1993–2002	Physicians	Difference in difference. Dependent variables: number of hours spent on patient care, duration of patient visits. Main independent variables: simulated SCHIP eligibility, pediatric specialty indicator.	SCHIP decreased the number of hours spent on patient care, increased the percentage of pediatricians that reported seeing or accepting any Medicaid patients, increased revenues from Medicaid and led to shorter visit lengths for Medicaid patients.
Duggan and Hayford (2013)	State-level Medicaid enrollment, Medicaid managed-care enrollment, and state Medicaid expenditures, 1991–2009	States	State-year panel, with state and year fixed effects. Dependent variables: Medicaid expenditure. Main independent variable: fraction of a state's Medicaid recipients in managed-care plan.	Shifting Medicaid recipients from FFS into managed care did not on average reduce Medicaid spending. This effect varied substantially across states as a function of the state's baseline Medicaid provider reimbursement rates.
Buchmueller, Miller, and Vujicic (2014)	American Dental Association Survey of Dental Practice 1999–2011	Dental practices	Repeated cross section with state and year fixed effects. Dependent variables: publicly insured patient load, overall patient load, participation in Medicaid, wait times. Main independent variable: location in Medicaid state providing adult dental benefits.	When a state adds adults' dental benefits, dentists participate more in Medicaid, see more publicly insured patients without reducing the privately insured patient load, and make greater use of dental hygienists. Wait times increase modestly.
Buchmueller, Orzol, and Shore-Sheppard (2015)	SIPP combined with data on Medicaid dental fees, ADA Survey of Dental Practice combined with data on Medicaid dental fees	Children up to age fifteen Private dental practices Dental practices	Effect of fees identified from changes in fees conditional on state and year fixed effects.	Higher Medicaid fees increase dental visits, the probability a child has dental sealants, the probability that a dental practice treats publicly insured patients.
Freedman, Lin, and Simon (2015)	AHA Annual Survey of Hospitals, 1985–1996; ARF; March CPS	Hospitals	Hospital-county-state-year panel. Dependent variable: indicator for whether a hospital offers a NICU. Main independent variable: Simulated Medicaid eligibility of pregnant women at the state-year level	Medicaid expansions had no stat. sig. effect on NICU adoption by hospitals. In areas where more new Medicaid patients were likely to have previously been privately insured, Medicaid expansions slowed NICU adoption.

in the percentage of visits that were shorter than ten minutes. This response to the implicit reduction in fees associated with crowd-out is consistent with research by Decker (2007) on the effect of changes in Medicaid fees.

It is also possible that part of the increased demand caused by the CHIP expansions was met by nonphysician providers. A recent study examining the response of dental practices to changes in Medicaid coverage of dental benefits for adults highlights the important role that auxiliary providers play in treating Medicaid patients (Buchmueller, Miller, and Vujicic 2014). Although state Medicaid programs are required to cover dental services for children, adult dental coverage is an optional benefit that most states do not provide. The study uses repeat cross-section data from the American Dental Association's annual Survey of Dental Practice to estimate the effect of changes in Medicaid coverage policy on several supply-side outcomes: participation in the Medicaid program, the number of visits by patient insurance status and type of visit, dentists' labor supply, and the employment of dental hygienists.

The results indicate that when Medicaid covers dental care for adults, dental practices provide significantly more care to publicly insured patients. The analysis of employment practices suggests that an important way that dentists respond to increased demand from public insurance is by making greater use of dental hygienists. A ten-point increase in the percentage of a county's adults covered by Medicaid is estimated to increase the probability that a dentist employs a hygienist by 4 percent and the number of visits with hygienists by roughly 10 percent. Other results suggest that the ability of dental practices to respond to Medicaid-induced demand shocks is mediated by state scope of practice regulations. The increase in visits and the use of hygienists is greater in states where hygienists are allowed greater autonomy. A state's scope of practice environment also seems to affect the extent to which increased demand from Medicaid patients leads to crowding. In states with restrictive scope of practice regulations, an expansion of Medicaid dental coverage leads to modest but significant increases in the time that it takes to get an appointment and the average time spent by patients in the waiting room. Waiting times did not increase in states where hygienists are allowed more autonomy.

Impact of Fees

Historically, access to care has been limited by the fact that many doctors do not accept Medicaid patients. Data from the National Ambulatory Medical Care Survey indicate that in 2011–2012, two-thirds of primary care physicians and 70 percent of physicians overall accepted new Medicaid patients (Decker 2013). Because low provider participation is attributed to Medicaid's low payment rates, the ACA includes a provision that temporarily increases Medicaid payment rates for primary care to Medicare levels. A number of studies have examined the relationship between Medicaid fees and provider participation in the program. Cunningham and Nichols (2005) and Decker (2007) find that higher Medicaid fees are positively associated with the willingness of physicians to treat publicly insured patients. Baker and Royalty (2000) find such a response for private physicians in their sample. Their results suggest that higher Medicaid payments shift the site of care for low-income patients from public health settings to private physician practices. Gruber, Adams, and Newhouse (1997) find a similar result when studying the effect of increased Medicaid payments in Tennessee.

An audit study by Polsky et al. (2015) provides suggestive evidence that despite a problematic implementation, the increase in Medicaid physician payments brought by the ACA led to an improvement in access for Medicaid patients. Researchers posing as patients with different types of insurance contacted primary care practices in ten states to schedule a new-patient appointment. The calls were made during two periods: November 2012 to March 2013, just prior to the implementation of the fee increase, and mid-2014, just after the increase went into effect. Although the percentage of privately insured callers offered an appointment remained constant at 86 percent, appointment availability for Medicaid callers increased to 66.4 percent from 58.7 percent. The percentage of Medicaid callers able to schedule an appointment increased most in states where the increase to Medicare rates led to the largest increase in fees.

Because of the way that changes in payment policy can shift the site of care, increasing payment rates may or may not increase overall utilization. Some studies using cross-sectional data find a significant relationship between Medicaid payment rates and the site of care, but find no significant relationship between payment rates and overall utilization (Long, Settle, and Stuart 1986; Rosenbach 1989; Cohen and Cunningham 1995). However, other studies that analyze changes in fees suggest that access to physician services improves when Medicaid payments are increased (Gabel and Rice 1985; Shen and Zuckerman 2005; Decker 2009; White 2012).

Access problems attributed to low Medicaid fees are a significant concern in the case of dental care as dentists are even less likely than physicians to accept Medicaid (US GAO 2000). Buchmueller, Orzol, and Shore-Sheppard (2015) find that increases in Medicaid dental fees increase the percentage of dental practices that treat publicly insured patients. Their estimates imply supply elasticities of between .12 and .23, which are slightly lower than supply elasticity estimates for physicians (Baker and Royalty 2000; Decker 2007). They and Decker (2011) also find that higher Medicaid fees are positively correlated with dental visits for children. However, the magnitude of the effect is relatively small: a $10 increase in average Medicaid dental fees—a change slightly larger than the difference between the 75th and 25th percentiles for this variable—is predicted to lead to a 2 to 3 percentage point increase in the probability that a publicly insured child has at least one dental visit in a year. Because of this modest response, most of the expenditures associated with a fee increase go for inframarginal visits, making fee increases a costly way to increase utilization.

In addition to increasing access to care, higher provider reimbursement can influence the type of care that Medicaid patients receive. In most states, Medicaid pays obstetricians more for a cesarean section than for a normal delivery, though the differential is generally not as large as it is for private insurance. Gruber, Kim, and Mayzlin (1999) examine how the Medicaid fee differential affects the cesarean rate for Medicaid patients. Theoretically, the effect is ambiguous, depending on the relative magnitudes of a positive substitution effect and a negative income effect. Using 1988 to 1992 data from eleven states, they find that the substitution effect dominates: larger fee differentials lead to more cesarean deliveries.

To the extent that higher fee differentials lead physicians to overprovide cesarean sections relative to what is optimal based on clinical criteria, reducing the differential payment for performing cesarean sections will not only lower program expenditures, but will improve care quality. In other cases, however, the additional care induced by higher levels of reimbursement may be beneficial. Currie, Gruber, and Fischer (1995) use birth data aggregated to the state/year level to investigate the relationship between the ratio of Medicaid to private insurance fees and infant mortality. They find a significant negative relationship between the fee ratio and infant mortality. Gray (2001) examines the relationship between relative Medicaid fees and birth outcomes using a cross-sectional difference-in-differences approach that compares Medicaid births and non-Medicaid births. He finds that women on Medicaid are more likely to deliver infants with low birth weight, but this difference is smaller in states where Medicaid fees are higher. Higher Medicaid fees also increase the receipt of early prenatal care, which may be an important mechanism for the birth weight result.

As a result of eligibility expansions for pregnant women, today Medicaid pays for over half of all births in the United States. Freedman, Lin, and Simon (2015) examine how the changes in coverage brought about by those expansions affected hospital decisions to adopt neonatal intensive care units (NICUs). Theoretically, the way hospitals respond should depend on the extent of crowd-out. In markets with high rates of insurance coverage at baseline, increases in hospital revenue resulting from uninsured patients gaining Medicaid may be more than offset by a decline in revenue from patients who transition from private insurance to Medicaid. Such a decrease in reimbursement for deliveries will make investments in medical technologies like NICUs less profitable.

Freedman and colleagues find that while on average Medicaid expansion was not significantly related to NICU adoption, in areas where more new Medicaid enrollees were coming from private insurance Medicaid expansion led to a slowing of NICU adoption. This negative effect was most pronounced in states with the lowest Medicaid payment rates. These results are broadly consistent with earlier work by Currie and Gruber (2001) finding that increases in Medicaid eligibility increased access to costly obstetric procedures for less educated women who likely gained insurance coverage as a result of the expansion while decreasing procedure use for more highly educated women, many of whom would have had more generous private insurance in the absence of the Medicaid expansion.

Impact of Disproportionate Share Hospital Payments

Because of Medicaid's low payment rates and the fact that hospitals with large numbers of Medicaid patients also treat many uninsured patients, state Medicaid programs make disproportionate share hospital (DSH) payments to hospitals treating a high volume of low-income patients. Duggan (2000) studies how public, nonprofit and for-profit hospitals in California responded to the introduction of DSH payments in the early 1990s. His results indicate significant differences between public and private hospitals, but little difference between private nonprofit and for-profit hospitals. When DSH patients made Medicaid patients more financially attractive, there was a shift in Medicaid patients from public hospitals to private ones. At the same time, there was a reallocation of uninsured patients in the opposite direction. This pattern is consistent with private hospitals cream skimming the more profitable low-income patients.

Duggan also examines what hospitals that received DSH payments did with that windfall. For public hospitals the increased funding from Medicaid was offset essentially one-for-one by reductions in funding from state and local governments. The DSH payments led to an increase in total revenue for for-profit and nonprofit facilities, both of which used the additional funds to increase their holdings of financial assets rather than investing in new patient-care facilities. Finding no significant relationship between changes in payments arising from the DSH program and infant mortality, Duggan concludes that the increased funding did not improve health outcomes for low-income patients.

Baicker and Staiger (2005) delve more deeply into what happens when states use intergovernmental transfers to divert federal DSH payments. On average, they find that during the first decade of the DSH program states expropriated nearly half of the DSH transfers from the federal government. There was more diversion in larger states, states with more public hospitals, and states where there is a greater difference in the tendency of public and private hospitals to treat poor patients. Like Duggan (2000) they examine the effect of DSH payments on patient health outcomes, though they use differences across state expropriation behavior and hospital ownership to distinguish between "effective" DSH payments that led to net increases in hospital funding and "ineffective" payments that did not. They find that effective DSH payments led to large reductions in mortality for infants and heart attack patients, whereas DSH payments that were expropriated by state governments had no significant effect on mortality.

Impact of Managed Care

One of the most significant changes in provider reimbursement was the shift toward managed care that began in the early 1990s (figure 1.7). States moved Medicaid enrollees into managed care primarily in an attempt to better control health-care spending. Although managed care is widely credited with reducing the growth in commercial health insurance premiums, the potential for managed care to reduce Medicaid spending is not clear. There is good evidence that much of the savings achieved by commercial managed-care plans in the 1990s came from the ability of plans to negotiate lower prices with providers (Cutler, McClellan, and Newhouse 2000). Since in most states Medicaid reimbursement rates are significantly lower than private fees, price reductions are not a likely source of savings. On the other hand, Medicaid managed-care organizations may be able to reduce expenditures by managing utilization more effectively, for example, by reducing inpatient admissions or emergency department visits. However, even if such utilization efficiencies are achieved, the shift to managed-care contracting is likely to be associated with an increase in administrative costs.

Research on this issue finds little evidence that managed care has produced cost savings. Duggan (2004) examines the impact of managed-care contracting on Medicaid expenditures in California, exploiting variation arising from the way that the state implemented the policy. The state mandated twenty counties to require certain beneficiaries to enroll in managed care. These mandates were implemented on a staggered basis between 1994 and 1999. Because the timing was essentially random, Duggan uses the mandates as instruments for managed-care enrollment. He finds that, contrary to the state's objective, the managed-care mandates led to a large and statistically significant increase in spending. The point estimates suggest that the mandates increased spending by between 17 and 27 percent.

Given that California's Medicaid program long had lower-than-average provider reimbursement rates, it is perhaps not surprising that increased managed-care enrollment did not produce savings. More recent work by Duggan and Hayford (2013) provides further evidence that the effect of Medicaid managed care on program expenditures varies depending on the level of state reimbursement rates. They analyze state-level data on total Medicaid spending and Medicaid managed-care enrollment from 1991 to 2009. When they instrument for managed-care enrollment with the share of the state's population that is subject to a managed-care mandate, the estimated managed-care effect is negative but statistically insignificant. However, models in which managed-care enrollment is interacted with a measure of Medicaid fee generosity indicate that this null effect masks important heterogeneity among states. The coefficient on the interaction term is negative and significant, implying that in states where Medicaid fees are relatively high, the shift to managed care does reduce program spending. In states such as California where fees are low, managed care is associated with higher expenditures.

Several studies have examined the effect of Medicaid managed care on access to care and health outcomes. Here again, positive or negative effects are theoretically plausible. On one hand, by emphasizing coordinated primary care and making greater use of nonphysician providers, managed-care organizations may improve access to care. Improved access combined with an emphasis on prevention may lead to improved enrollee health. On the other hand, capitated payment arrangements can create an incentive to stint on care, especially for higher-risk enrollees.

Currie and Fahr (2005) use national survey data on low-income children to examine the relationship between state-level Medicaid managed-care penetration and the probability of having at least one physician visit in a year. Overall, their results indicate little relationship between Medicaid managed care and this proxy for access. Kaestner, Dubay, and Kenney (2005) use data from the National Natality Files to test for an effect of county-level Medicaid managed-care penetration on the utilization of prenatal care. Because they do not directly observe mothers' insurance status, they stratify the analysis by education and marital status, two variables that are correlated with Medicaid enrollment. For unmarried women with less than twelve years of education, they find that living in a county with a mandatory Medicaid managed-care program is negatively associated with the number of prenatal visits. However, they find generally similar results for married women with twelve to fifteen years of education, who are much less likely to have Medicaid coverage. Difference-in-differences models that treat unmarried, less educated women as the treatment group and married, more educated women as controls yield generally insignificant results.

In his study on California's county-level mandates, Duggan uses hospital discharge data to examine the effect of managed care on in-hospital infant mortality and the percentage of premature births. He finds no statistically significant effect of managed care on either outcome. Aizer, Currie, and Moretti (2007) also study birth outcomes in California over a similar period and find that managed care is associated with a lower likelihood of receiving prenatal care in the first trimester and an increased likelihood of low birth weight and neonatal mortality. They argue that the main reason for the difference between their results and Duggan's null results is that their analysis focuses more closely on women who were likely to be subject to a managed-care mandate.

Overall, the literature on the effect of Medicaid program parameters on provider behavior yields fairly consistent results. Coverage expansions and increases in reimbursement both increase the quantity of services supplied to Medicaid patients. Hospitals appear to be responsive to the incentives inherent in the DSH program, though not necessarily in ways that lead to improved outcomes for patients. And there is little evidence that the shift from fee-for-services reimbursement to managed care has led to sizable savings or improved health outcomes. Indeed, some studies suggest the opposite may be true.

With the large increases in adult coverage caused by the ACA, Medicaid will be an increasingly important source of payment for providers, including some that previously had limited experience with the program. Early evidence suggests that for hospitals in states that have implemented the ACA Medicaid expansion there has been a significant reduction in the number of uninsured patients and in the value of uncompensated care provided (DeLeire, Joynt, and McDonald 2014; Nikpay, Buchmueller, and Levy 2015). All else equal, these trends should improve the financial status of hospitals. However, in anticipation of the reduction in the number of uninsured patients, the ACA legislated reductions in the DSH program. When these reductions go into effect, for some hospitals the gain from having fewer uninsured patients will be offset, at least partially, by a reduction in DSH payments.[27]

The results of several of the studies reviewed here suggest that the impact of the ACA expansions on providers will depend on the degree of crowd-out. In cases where a large number of patients shift from private insurance to Medicaid, the main effect of the ACA could be a reduction in average payment rates. As noted above, the ACA also provided federal funding to raise Medicaid physician payment for primary care services to the level of Medicare fees, though only in fiscal years 2013 and 2014. Going forward, states will have to decide whether to use their own funds to continue this "fee bump." The decisions that states make regarding DSH and physician payment rates and the ways that providers respond to these policy choices will be an important area for future research.

Medicaid Reimbursement and Nursing Homes

As noted, Medicaid beneficiaries represent a majority of nursing home patients in the United States. There are a number of studies on how Medicaid reimbursement policy affects the nursing home market. Norton (2000) and Grabowski and Norton (2006) provide good reviews of this literature. One issue that has received considerable attention is the relationship between Medicaid payment levels and nursing home quality. As described in section 1.4.3, the relationship can be positive or negative depending on the extent to which supply-side constraints lead to a situation of excess demand. Several early studies find evidence of a negative relationship between Medicaid pay-

---

27. The DSH payment cuts were originally supposed to begin in 2014, though they have been postponed until 2017.

ment rates and input-based proxies for quality in individual states (Nyman 1985, 1988; Gertler 1989). However, more recent research finds a positive relationship between Medicaid payment rates and a number of different process and outcome-based measures of quality (Cohen and Spector 1996; Grabowski 2001, 2004; Grabowski and Angelelli 2004; Grabowski, Angelelli, and Mor 2004). In one of the more recent studies, Grabowski (2001) replicates the analysis in one of the earlier papers (Gertler 1989). Applying the methods and quality measures from the earlier study to more recent data, Grabowski finds a positive relationship between Medicaid payment and quality, which suggests that changes in market conditions are at least part of the explanation for the divergent results from the earlier and later studies. In particular, nursing home occupancy rates, an indirect indicator of excess demand, declined substantially between the mid-1970s and early 1990s.

1.5.4   Financial Impacts on Households

Given that a fundamental purpose of health insurance is to protect individuals and families from the financial burden of large medical expenditures, there is relatively little research on the effect of Medicaid on financial outcomes. However, as discussed above there are several channels through which Medicaid may affect family financial well-being, resulting in potential effects on family assets and on measures of financial strain, including bankruptcies.

Gruber and Yelowitz (1999) examine how the amount of a household's expected medical spending that is made eligible for Medicaid affects household net worth and consumption. They construct a measure of expected medical spending made eligible for Medicaid as the product of a binary eligibility variable (imputed for individual women and children in the household) and an age-gender-state-year-specific measure of both current and future medical-care spending; this product is then summed over all members of the household. To deal with the endogeneity of eligibility they create an instrument for this measure of spending in a similar fashion, replacing eligibility with simulated eligibility for a national random sample as in Currie and Gruber (1996a, 1996b). Using data from the Survey of Income and Program Participation for the 1984–1993 period, they find that Medicaid eligibility has a significant negative effect on asset holdings, estimating that a $1,000 increase in potential medical spending eligible for Medicaid leads to a fall of 0.81 percent in the odds of having positive assets and, among households with positive net wealth, a 2.51 percent decline in net wealth (median net worth is $11,171 in their sample). They also find a positive effect on consumption levels: for each $1,000 in eligible spending, they estimate that nondurable expenditures rise by 0.82 percent. The estimates are even larger for states that maintained an asset test for eligibility for women and children over this period. They conclude that parameters of the Medicaid program are a major determinant of the savings behavior of low-income households.

However, subsequent research has shed additional light on these results. Using instrumental quantile regression on Gruber and Yelowitz's data, Maynard and Qiu (2009) find that the effects of Medicaid are concentrated in the middle of the net worth distribution, disappearing entirely not only at the top end of the wealth distribution, but also for the lowest net worth households, with no discernible effect of Medicaid on the savings of the bottom 20 percent of households. Moreover, Gittleman (2011) analyzes data from the National Longitudinal Survey of Youth as well as the SIPP and finds that the results are not robust to cohort, to inclusion of some two-way interactions, and to the use of only eligible spending for the current period rather than including spending that will occur in the future assuming Medicaid rules remain the same and the family's income does not change. In addition, he finds no evidence of an effect of eligibility on wealth for later expansions. This pattern is consistent with other findings that indicate the earliest Medicaid expansions that include some AFDC eligibility and were targeted toward poorer families had the most substantial effects on a variety of outcomes.

The results on saving impacts of Medicaid for the elderly are similarly equivocal. DeNardi, French, and Jones (2010) estimate a life cycle model of saving on a sample of single, retired elderly individuals. Their focus is on explaining saving behavior among the elderly in general, so they do not model Medicaid explicitly, but they include a consumption floor that represents Medicaid and Supplemental Security Income benefits for the elderly. In simulations of their model they find that a reduction in the consumption floor results in an increase in saving among both low-income and high-income elderly. It is important to note, however, that the consumption floor in their model represents cash assistance as well as medical-spending assistance. By contrast, Gardner and Gilleski (2012) carefully include details of Medicaid eligibility in their dynamic model of long-term care arrangements, Medicaid enrollment, assets, and gifts. They find that the elderly are only responsive to a few Medicaid policies, particularly policies affecting home- and community-based services eligibility and generosity. They find small and insignificant effects of policies that affect nursing home services eligibility and generosity.

Several recent studies have focused on the impact of Medicaid on measures of financial strain. Gross and Notowidigdo (2011) exploit the variation provided by expansions between 1992 and 2004 to examine the effect of Medicaid eligibility on bankruptcies, applying a simulated eligibility instrumental variables model to state-level data. Their results imply that a 10 percent increase in Medicaid eligibility reduces personal bankruptcies by 8 percent. They then use their estimates to calibrate a theoretical model. The results of this exercise imply that out-of-pocket medical costs are pivotal in roughly a quarter of personal bankruptcies among low-income households.

In their randomized control trial in Oregon, Finkelstein et al. (2012) analyze the impact of Medicaid coverage on multiple measures of financial strain. The analyses are based on both administrative and survey data. The administrative data are from the Consumer Credit Database of the credit bureau TransUnion and include such things as delinquent credit accounts, bills sent to collection agencies, bankruptcies, liens, and judgments. The survey questions ask about medical expenditures and debt and whether respondents had to borrow money or delay paying other bills in order to pay medical bills. They find that Medicaid coverage is associated with a significant decline in the probability of having a bill sent to collection and this result is driven by a decline in medical collections. They find no significant decline in bankruptcies or liens, which are less common events that occur with a greater lag than collections. The survey results indicate large, statistically significant declines in out-of-pocket medical expenditures and the probability of having to borrow money or skip paying other bills because of medical expenses.

Mazumder and Miller (forthcoming) use similar credit report data to examine the effect of the 2006 Massachusetts health care reform on financial outcomes for those who were uninsured before the reforms. The credit report data are from the Federal Reserve Bank of New York's Consumer Credit Panel. They use a triple-difference regression model that compares consumers in Massachusetts with those in other states, and within states, compares individuals in areas with high and low rates of insurance coverage prior to the reforms. They find that the Massachusetts reform led to significant improvement in credit-risk scores while significantly reducing the fraction of debt past due, the incidence of bankruptcy in the last twenty-four months, and (at the 10 percent level) total collections.

While the impact of Medicaid on financial well-being is an important area for future research, the studies that have been done thus far point to two important conclusions. First, the existence of Medicaid and its policies can dissuade households from saving, although the effects do not seem to be particularly large and they appear to be concentrated among lower-middle-income households rather than among the poorest. Second, coverage by Medicaid reduces measured financial strain, improving household financial well-being.

1.5.5   Impact of Medicaid on Labor Supply and Program Participation

Prior to the expansions in eligibility beginning in the mid-1980s, researchers interested in identifying the effect of Medicaid on labor force and welfare participation faced the issue that it was difficult to tease out separate effects of cash payments and health insurance when one benefit always accompanied the other. To address this issue, researchers attempted to distinguish different potential values of Medicaid for different potential recipients. For example, Moffitt and Wolfe (1992) develop a proxy for the dollar value of

Medicaid for each family that takes into account actual health conditions in the family. They find that the value of Medicaid affects welfare participation, but only for families with high expected medical expenses.

By separating the receipt of Medicaid benefits from welfare participation, the eligibility expansions offered researchers the possibility of observing explicitly the impact of becoming eligible for Medicaid. Yelowitz (1995) was the first to investigate the delinking of Medicaid from welfare on AFDC participation and on labor market participation. Using data from the March CPS for 1989–1992, he examines the relationships between each of these participation decisions and the difference in the maximum income limits conferring only Medicaid eligibility for the youngest child and the maximum income limits permitting AFDC eligibility. He estimates a probit model for both AFDC participation and for labor market participation, and finds that a larger difference strongly and significantly decreases AFDC participation and increases labor market participation. He concludes that the Medicaid expansions had a strong positive effect on labor market participation of women heading families with children.

However, Ham and Shore-Sheppard (2005a) note a peculiar feature of Yelowitz's specification: the effects of the Medicaid income limits and the AFDC income limits are constrained to be equal in magnitude but opposite in sign. Ham and Shore-Sheppard show that imposing this constraint is not consistent with economic theory, since it implies that welfare benefits had no effect on labor force or welfare participation in the period prior to the decoupling of Medicaid and AFDC. They consider probit equations for AFDC and labor force participation using March CPS data from both Yelowitz's sample and a slightly longer time period (1988–1996). Using Yelowitz's specification, they generally replicate his results; however, when Medicaid and AFDC income limits are allowed to have separate coefficients, they find that only the AFDC income limits significantly affect AFDC and labor market participation. They conclude that the Medicaid expansions did not affect the labor market behavior of women heading families with children; Yelowitz's results were driven by the imposition of a constraint that is not supported by either theory or the data.

Meyer and Rosenbaum (2001) consider the effect on labor force participation of several programs simultaneously, including Medicaid. They model expected utility when working and not working and include the value of Medicaid coverage if a woman works and the value of Medicaid coverage if she does not work (using the per capita cost of Medicaid to determine the value) in their model. Using data from the CPS Outgoing Rotation Group Files and the March CPS 1984 to 1996, they find little effect of Medicaid on the employment decisions of single mothers.

The result of Ham and Shore-Sheppard (2005a) and Meyer and Rosenbaum (2001) that Medicaid coverage has no effect on labor supply is puzzling since the dollar cost of this coverage is nontrivial. However, this puzzle is potentially resolved by the finding in Finkelstein, Hendren, and Luttmer

(2015) that low-income adults value Medicaid coverage only at 20–40 percent of a dollar spent by the government. Given their results, we would not expect adding or eliminating Medicaid coverage to have large labor supply effects.

The research just discussed focusing on expansions of Medicaid to children and pregnant women found little effect of expanded Medicaid on labor supply except among families with a priori high medical costs. However, expanded availability of Medicaid may have additional effects on labor market behavior beyond participation. Hamersma and Kim (2009) investigate whether the parental Medicaid expansions increase job mobility. The idea is that if individuals obtain coverage through Medicaid, they will be more mobile since they do not need to stay on their current job just for the insurance coverage provided by the job. On the other hand, expanded eligibility could decrease mobility for those without health insurance, since there is now less pressure to move to a job that offers health insurance. Using data from the 1996 and 2001 SIPP panels they estimate a probit equation for quit behavior, which depends on the Medicaid eligibility income threshold determined by family size, state, and month, as well as controls for demographics, current labor market conditions in a state, and state and year dummies. They find that higher Medicaid thresholds lead to greater job turnover, but only among unmarried women.

While all of the research discussed in this section thus far has focused on the labor market impacts of Medicaid expansions for low-income families with children, more recent research has examined the impact of eligibility changes for low-income nondisabled adults without children that occurred in individual states, including Tennessee, Wisconsin, and Oregon. Since the ACA targeted such adults, these studies provide very useful information about the likely impacts of the ACA on the labor market, although it is important to keep in mind that the experiences of individual states may not be entirely applicable to the impacts on the country as a whole.

The study by Garthwaite, Gross, and Notowidigdo (2014) focusing on Tennessee also examines the effect the large disenrollment of childless adults on their employment. Using the same approach that they use to analyze crowd-out (a difference-in-differences model comparing adults in Tennessee to adults in other southern states and a triple-difference model contrasting outcomes for childless adults and other adults), they estimate that the forced disenrollment led to a 2.5 percentage point increase in employment using the difference-in-differences model or a 4.6 percentage point increase using the triple-difference model. (To put these results in perspective, the employment rate in the Tennessee sample was 69 percent.) Scaling by the estimated impacts on public coverage suggests that employment rose by approximately 63 percent among former TennCare enrollees. These are sizable effects, although the confidence intervals are fairly wide.

Dague, DeLeire, and Leininger (2014) study a policy change in Wisconsin, where enrollment into Wisconsin's Medicaid program for childless adults with household incomes below 200 percent of the federal poverty level was suddenly suspended in October 2009, with everyone who attempted to enroll after the cut-off date being placed on a waiting list. Dague, DeLeire, and Leininger use a regression discontinuity approach to measure the impact of this policy change. They use state administrative records on enrolled and wait-listed applicants and earnings records from Wisconsin's unemployment insurance system and compare outcomes for those who enrolled before the announcement to those who were wait listed after the announcement. Both recipients and wait-listed applicants increased their labor supply over the time period of the study, though nonrecipients increased their labor supply by more. Using wait-listed applicants as a control group implies that enrollment into public insurance led to a reduction in employment of about 5.5 percentage points (a reduction of 12 percent), with a net effect on quarterly earnings of $300.

Finally, Baicker et al. (2014) measure the labor market impacts in the Oregon lottery experiment. They estimate intent-to-treat (ITT) models that compare labor market outcomes including employment status and earnings among the treatment group to outcomes in the control group. They also estimate the impact of being covered by Medicaid (the local average treatment effect) using lottery status as the instrument for Medicaid coverage. They find no statistically significant impact of Medicaid on any of their labor market outcomes. Their point estimate for the LATE for employment is a decline of 1.6 percentage points (or about 3 percent, relative to the control group), and despite its statistical insignificance the confidence interval is tight, allowing Baicker et al. to reject a decline in employment of more than 4.4 percentage points or an increase of more than 1.2 percentage points.

Taken together, the three sets of estimates from the three different states suggest substantially different magnitudes of Medicaid effects on employment for childless adults, from close to no effect in the Oregon study, to a 12 percent reduction in employment among recipients in the Wisconsin study, to a 60 percent increase in employment among disenrollees following disenrollment in the Tennessee study. Dague et al. suggest that part of the explanation for the differences in the estimates is the economic conditions prevailing at the time of the policy changes, noting that the state unemployment rate was 5.6 percent in Tennessee in 2005, 11.1 percent in Oregon in 2009, and 8.5 percent in Wisconsin in 2010. In addition, Oregon's program was available only to individuals with incomes below the poverty level, while Tennessee's and Wisconsin's were both available to individuals with incomes up to twice the poverty level, suggesting that employment effects may be less likely when the program is targeted at lower-income individuals.

1.5.6   Effects of Medicaid on Family Structure

As discussed in section 1.4, Medicaid may well have impacts on family structure both by affecting marriage probabilities and by affecting fertility.

There has been very little research on the impact of Medicaid per se on marriage, though there is a long literature on the impact of AFDC and other cash welfare programs on marriage. The main results on the impact of Medicaid on marriage come from Yelowitz (1998), who looks at the probability a woman is married as a function of whether all of her children are age-eligible for Medicaid or whether any of her children are age-eligible using variation in eligibility by state, year, and age of child caused by the eligibility expansions for children of the late 1980s and early 1990s. He finds that women with all children eligible are 1.5 percentage points more likely to be married than women with at least one ineligible child, but he finds no effect for women with only some of their children eligible. Yelowitz notes that at least some of the effect that he finds may be due to selection into childbearing as a result of the expansions, but the results suggest that the marriage effect is likely to outweigh the selection effect.

The effect of Medicaid on childbearing is a more active research area. Studies in this area have considered three possible avenues by which Medicaid might affect fertility. First, expanded eligibility for pregnant women, infants, and children reduces the cost of having a child. Second, differences across states in whether Medicaid funds abortions may lead to differences in abortion rates. Third, the fact that Medicaid covers the cost of contraception for certain groups may reduce pregnancies.

To study the first avenue, expanded eligibility, researchers have compared birth and abortion rates for groups of women who were more or less likely to be eligible for Medicaid for exogenous reasons. Joyce and Kaestner (1996), an early paper in this area, use vital statistics data from three states and a difference-in-differences approach that compares outcomes before and after a Medicaid eligibility expansion for groups defined by race, marital status, and education level. Their results suggest that the eligibility expansion led to a decline in the abortion rate for unmarried, nonblack women with less than a high school degree, a group that was more likely to gain eligibility. However, since women with higher levels of education may still be income-eligible for the expansions, this method may result in misclassification, particularly for black women.

Joyce, Kaestner, and Kwan (1998) use state-quarter-race specific data from fifteen states and examine the association between birth and abortion rates and Medicaid expansion using indicators for the state expanding eligibility to the poverty level and for the state expanding to 185 percent of the poverty level, controlling for state, year, quarter, and state-specific linear trends. The identification is thus from changes in eligibility over time within a state. They find that increased eligibility is associated with a 5 percent increase in the birth rate for white women, but find no significant association for black women, and no effect on abortions. However, because they do not control for other changes that might be occurring within a state over the time period, their results are suggestive rather than definitive.

DeLeire, Lopoo, and Simon (2011) try to take advantage of within-state variation in eligibility by creating age-education-marital-status demographic cells and using Currie and Gruber's simulated eligibility index to obtain a measure of eligibility at the state-year-demographic-cell level. Controlling for a variety of welfare policies and the state unemployment rate in addition to the simulated eligibility index, they find fertility is positively associated with the expansions for both whites and blacks, but once they include fixed effects for demographic cells the relationship disappears entirely. Zavodny and Bitler (2010) use a similar methodology over a somewhat longer time period. They use alternatively the Medicaid eligibility threshold applying in a demographic cell or the fraction of women in a cell who would be eligible, control for additional policy changes (including the Earned Income Tax Credit), and simultaneously examine the impact of Medicaid-funding restrictions on abortion. They find some evidence of higher birth rates among whites with less than a high school education in response to expanded eligibility thresholds, but no statistically significant effect when the simulated fraction eligible is used to measure eligibility. The results from these two papers suggest that any impact of Medicaid eligibility on fertility is limited and not particularly robust.

Zavodny and Bitler do find that restrictions on Medicaid funding of abortions are associated with decreases in abortion rates and increases in birth rates. This latter result generally accords with the earlier literature on Medicaid funding of abortion (e.g., Haas-Wilson 1996; Blank, George, and London 1996; Levine, Trainor, and Zimmerman 1996; Kane and Staiger 1996), at least in finding decreases in abortion rates. The results in the literature for birth rates are somewhat more equivocal, however, with some authors finding birth-rate increases (Currie, Nixon, and Cole 1996; Zavodny and Bitler 2010) and others finding birth-rate decreases (Levine, Trainor, and Zimmerman 1996; Kane and Staiger 1996).

Researchers have also studied other possible effects of Medicaid abortion-funding restrictions. Bitler and Zavodny (2001) find no significant effect of Medicaid funding restrictions on abortion timing, while Currie, Nixon, and Cole (1996) find no evidence of an effect on birth weight. Currie, Nixon, and Cole also find suggestive evidence of policy endogeneity in Medicaid abortion-funding laws, with restrictive laws having the same effect whether or not they are enjoined by the courts and finding similar effects on high-income and low-income women. Sen (2003) finds no relationship between Medicaid funding restrictions and rates of sexually transmitted diseases among women, suggesting that Medicaid funding restrictions do not lead to increased use of safe sex behavior that prevents sexually transmitted disease, although the use of contraceptive methods such as the pill would not be detected with such an empirical strategy.

Examining contraception more directly, Kearney and Levine (2009) estimate the impact of Section 1115 waivers obtained by states to extend

Medicaid family-planning services to women who would otherwise not be eligible for them. They identify states and time periods with two types of waivers—expansions of family-planning eligibility based solely on income and extensions of family-planning eligibility to women who would otherwise lose eligibility postpartum. Using data from the Medicaid Statistical Information System and similar older data, they show that waivers, and particularly income-based waivers, were associated with larger proportions of women reported to be receiving Medicaid family-planning services. Looking at birth rates by state and year and controlling for state effects, year effects, time-changing variables for states, and state-specific linear and quadratic time trends, they find that the presence of an income-based waiver reduces births by around 2 percent for nonteens and between 4.2 and 4.7 percent for teens. They also find evidence in individual data of changes in the probability of contraceptive behavior for women in states with a waiver in effect. They find that it is a relatively cost-effective approach to reducing unwanted births.

1.6 Summary and Future Research Questions

Medicaid is a massive, multifaceted program touching almost every aspect of the health care and long-term-care delivery systems. It has achieved its objectives along many dimensions, covering a substantial percentage of the population, particularly children, increasing access to care, improving some measures of health, and providing some financial benefit to recipients. It has also, however, led to some substitution away from private insurance, particularly insurance for long-term care, and the level and nature of compensation paid to health-care providers has engendered an array of problems and concerns. Nevertheless, with the covered population expanding considerably under the ACA, Medicaid has moved from the margins to the mainstream. To conclude this chapter, we discuss some areas that we see as being important for future research.

Unsurprisingly, many of these areas concern the ACA. First, there is the question of the impact of states' decisions about whether and how to participate in the ACA expansion of Medicaid. What are the implications of these decisions in terms of fiscal pressures on states or the federal government? How much will fiscal pressures increase as Medicaid is used to finance coverage for growing subsets of the population? States' decisions also have implications for individuals, both in states that do and do not choose to participate. In nonparticipating states, one question is how is inequality in access to health care changing, and what are the implications of the continuing lack of insurance coverage for many low-income adults in terms of health and financial well-being? In participating states, the expansion of Medicaid eligibility to new groups brings new dimensions to old questions of take-up, crowd-out, labor supply, and job lock. In addition, there is the added dimension of the interaction between Medicaid and the insurance exchanges. How well integrated are the public and private dimensions of the exchanges, and how easily can individuals experiencing changes in their circumstances move from one type of coverage to another?

There are also perennial issues that are brought to the fore by the ACA, such as the relationship of the Medicaid program with providers. As we have noted, Medicaid does not compensate providers well, in general, and the question of supply of care to the insured will be an important one. In addition, there are important implications for the well-being of providers, particularly those that serve a large share of Medicaid patients, of increasing the share of Medicaid coverage in the market. Since the writers of the ACA recognized these issues and built in temporary reimbursement increases for some providers, it will be important to see how provider behavior and patient well-being are affected both by the increase and by its disappearance.

There is also the continuing and essential question of the impact of Medicaid on health. While there have been some important recent advances with the Oregon health study, health effects for adults, including for the disabled and elderly, are not well understood and thus far have been little studied. Finally, we need a better understanding of the financial impacts, again for all eligible groups, of Medicaid coverage. With expenditures of nearly $390 billion, measuring the benefits as well as the costs of this major program is crucial.

References

Aizer, Anna. 2007. "Public Health Insurance, Program Take-Up, and Child Health." *Review of Economics and Statistics* 89 (3): 400–15.
Aizer, Anna, Janet Currie, and Enrico Moretti. 2007. "Does Managed Care Hurt Health? Evidence from Medicaid Mothers." *Review of Economics and Statistics* 89 (3): 385–99.
Aizer, Anna, and Jeffrey Grogger. 2003. "Parental Medicaid Expansions and Health Insurance Coverage." NBER Working Paper no. 9907, Cambridge, MA.
Aizer, Anna, Adriana Lleras-Muney, and Mark Stabile. 2005. "Access to Care, Provider Choice, and the Infant Health Gradient." *American Economic Review* 95 (2): 248–52.
Anderson, Michael, Carlos Dobkin, and Tal Gross. 2012. "The Effect of Health Insurance Coverage on the Use of Medical Services." *American Economic Journal: Economic Policy* 4 (1): 1–27.
Baicker, Katherine, Amy Finkelstein, Jae Song, and Sarah Taubman. 2014. "The Impact of Medicaid on Labor Market Activity and Program Participation: Evidence from the Oregon Health Insurance Experiment." *American Economic Review* 104 (5): 322–28.
Baicker, Katherine, and Douglas Staiger. 2005. "Fiscal Shenanigans, Targeted Federal Health Care Funds, and Patient Mortality." *Quarterly Journal of Economics* 120 (1): 345–86.

Baicker, Katherine, Sarah L. Taubman, Heidi L. Allen, Mira Bernstein, Jonathan H. Gruber, Joseph P. Newhouse, Eric C. Schneider, Bill J. Wright, Alan M. Zaslavsky, and Amy N. Finkelstein. 2013. "The Oregon Experiment—Effects of Medicaid on Clinical Outcomes." *New England Journal of Medicine* 368 (18): 1713–22.

Baker, Laurence C., and Anne Beeson Royalty. 2000. "Medicaid Policy, Physician Behavior, and Health Care for the Low-Income Population." *Journal of Human Resources* 35 (3): 480–502.

Bansak, Cynthia, and Steven Raphael. 2006. "The Effects of State Policy Design Features on Take-Up and Crowd-Out Rates for the State Children's Health Insurance Program." *Journal of Policy Analysis and Management* 26 (1): 149–75.

Becker, Gary. 1960. "An Economic Analysis of Fertility." In *Demographic and Economic Change in Developed Countries*, Universities-National Bureau Committee for Economic Research, 209–40. New York: National Bureau of Economic Research.

Becker, Gary, and H. Gregg Lewis. 1973. "On the Interaction between the Quantity and Quality of Children." *Journal of Political Economy* 81 (2): S279–88.

Bertrand, Marianne, Esther Duflo, and Sendhil Mullainathan. 2004. "How Much Should We Trust Differences-in-Differences Estimates?" *Quarterly Journal of Economics* 119 (1): 249–75.

Bitler, Marianne P., and Madeline Zavodny. 2001. "The Effect of Abortion Restrictions on the Timing of Abortions." *Journal of Health Economics* 20 (6): 1011–32.

Black, Dan A., Mark C. Berger, and Frank A. Scott. 2000. "Bounding Parameter Estimates with Nonclassical Measurement Error." *Journal of the American Statistical Association* 95 (451): 739–48.

Blank, Rebecca M., Christine C. George, and Rebecca A. London. 1996. "State Abortion Rates the Impact of Policies, Providers, Politics, Demographics, and Economic Environment." *Journal of Health Economics* 15 (5): 513–53.

Boudreaux, Michael H., Ezra Golberstein, and Donna McAlpine. 2015. "The Long-Term Impacts of Medicaid Exposure in Early Childhood: Evidence from the Program's Origin." Unpublished Manuscript, University of Minnesota.

Bronchetti, Erin Todd. 2014. "Public Insurance Expansions and the Health of Immigrant and Native Children." *Journal of Public Economics* 120:205–19.

Brown, Jeffrey R., Norma B. Coe, and Amy Finkelstein. 2007. "Medicaid Crowd-Out of Private Long-Term Care Insurance Demand: Evidence from the Health and Retirement Survey." In *Tax Policy and the Economy*, vol. 21, edited by James M. Poterba, 1–34. Cambridge, MA: MIT Press.

Brown, Jeffrey R., and Amy Finkelstein. 2007. "Why Is the Market for Long-Term Care Insurance So Small?" *Journal of Public Economics* 91 (10): 1967–91.

———. 2008. "The Interaction of Public and Private Insurance: Medicaid and the Long-Term Care Insurance Market." *American Economic Review* 98 (3): 1083–102.

———. 2009. "The Private Market for Long-Term Care Insurance in the United States: A Review of the Evidence." *Journal of Risk and Insurance* 76 (1): 5–29.

———. 2011. "Insuring Long-Term Care in the United States." *Journal of Economic Perspectives* 25 (4): 119–42.

Buchmueller, Thomas C., Sarah Miller, and Marko Vujicic. 2014. "How Do Providers Respond to Public Health Insurance Expansions? Evidence from Adult Medicaid Dental Benefits." NBER Working Paper no. 20053, Cambridge, MA.

Buchmueller, Thomas C., Sean Orzol, and Lara D. Shore-Sheppard. 2015. "The Effect of Medicaid Payment Rates on Access to Dental Care among Children." *American Journal of Health Economics* 1 (2): 194–223.

Burns, Marguerite, Laura Dague, Thomas DeLeire, Mary Dorsch, Donna Friedsam, Lindsey Leininger, Gaston Palmucci, John Schmelzer, and Kristin Voskuil. 2014.

"The Effects of Expanding Public Insurance to Rural Low-Income Childless Adults." *Health Services Research* 49 (Suppl. 2): 2173–87.

Busch, Susan H., and Noelia Duchovny. 2005. "Family Coverage Expansions: Impact on Insurance Coverage and Health Care Utilization of Parents." *Journal of Health Economics* 24 (5): 876–90.

Card, David, Andrew K. G. Hildreth, and Lara D. Shore-Sheppard. 2004. "The Measurement of Medicaid Coverage in the SIPP." *Journal of Business & Economic Statistics* 22 (4): 410–20.

Card, David, and Lara D. Shore-Sheppard. 2004. "Using Discontinuous Eligibility Rules to Identify the Effects of the Federal Medicaid Expansions on Low-Income Children." *Review of Economics and Statistics* 86 (3): 752–66.

Centers for Medicare & Medicaid Services (CMS). Various Years. "Medicaid Managed Care Enrollment Report." http://www.medicaid.gov/Medicaid-CHIP -Program-Information/By-Topics/Data-and-Systems/Downloads/2011-Medicaid -MC-Enrollment-Report.pdf.

———. 2012a. "Letter to State Health Officials RE: Conversion of Net Income Standards to MAGI Equivalent Income Standards, December 28, 2012." http:// www.medicaid.gov/Federal-Policy-Guidance/downloads/SHO12003.pdf.

———. 2012b. "Medicare and Medicaid Statistical Supplement, 2012 Edition." http://www.cms.gov/Research-Statistics-Data-and-Systems/Statistics-Trends -and-Reports/MedicareMedicaidStatSupp/2012.html.

———. 2013a. "Medicare and Medicaid Statistical Supplement, 2013 Edition." https://www.cms.gov/Research-Statistics-Data-and-Systems/Statistics-Trends -and-Reports/MedicareMedicaidStatSupp/2013.html.

———. 2013b. "Legislative Update." http://www.cms.gov/Regulations-and -Guidance/Legislation/LegislativeUpdate/index.html?redirect=/Legislative Update/.

———. 2014. National Health Expenditures Tables. http://www.cms.gov/Research -Statistics-Data-and-Systems/Statistics-Trends-and-Reports/NationalHealth ExpendData/NationalHealthAccountsHistorical.html.

———. 2015. "Medicaid & CHIP: December 2014 Monthly Applications, Eligibility Determinations and Enrollment Report." February 23, 2015. http://medic aid.gov/medicaid-chip-program-information/program-information/downloads /december-2014-enrollment-report.pdf.

Choi, Miji, Benjamin D. Sommers, and John McWilliams. 2011. "Children's Health Insurance and Access to Care during and after the CHIP Expansion Period." *Journal of Health Care for the Poor and Underserved* 22 (2): 576–89.

Choi, Moonkyung Kate. 2011. "The Impact of Medicaid Insurance Coverage on Dental Service Use." *Journal of Health Economics* 30 (5): 1020–31.

Cohen, Joel, and Peter Cunningham. 1995. "Medicaid Physician Fee Levels and Children's Access to Care." *Health Affairs* 13:255–62.

Cohen, Joel, and William Spector. 1996. "The Effect of Medicaid Reimbursement on Quality of Care in Nursing Homes." *Journal of Health Economics* 15 (1): 23–48.

Congressional Budget Office. 2001. "Pay-As-You-Go Estimate H.R. 5661 Medicare, Medicaid, and SCHIP Benefits Improvement and Protection Act of 2000 (Incorporated in H.R. 4577, the Consolidated Appropriations Act)." September 20, 2011. http://www.cbo.gov/sites/default/files/hr5661_0.pdf.

———. 2014. "Updated Budget Projections: 2014 to 2024." April. http://www.cbo .gov/sites/default/files/45229-UpdatedBudgetProjections_2.pdf.

Congressional Research Service. 1993. *Medicaid Source Book: Background Data and Analysis* ("The Yellow Book"). Washington, DC: Government Printing Office.

Courtemanche, Charles, and Daifeng He. 2009. "Tax Incentives and the Decision to Purchase Long-Term Care Insurance." *Journal of Public Economics* 93 (1–2): 296–310.

Cunningham, Peter J., and Len Nichols. 2005. "The Effects of Medicaid Reimbursement on the Access to Care of Medicaid Enrollees: A Community Perspective." *Medical Care Research and Review* 62 (6): 676–96.

Currie, Janet, Sandra Decker, and Wanchuan Lin. 2008. "Has Public Health Insurance for Older Children Reduced Disparities in Access to Care and Health Outcomes?" *Journal of Health Economics* 27 (6): 1567–81.

Currie, Janet, and John Fahr. 2005. "Medicaid Managed Care: Effects on Children's Medicaid Coverage and Utilization." *Journal of Public Economics* 89 (1): 85–108.

Currie, Janet, and Jeffrey Grogger. 2002. "Medicaid Expansions and Welfare Contractions: Offsetting Effects on Prenatal Care and Infant Health?" *Journal of Health Economics* 21 (2): 313–35.

Currie, Janet, and Jonathan Gruber. 1996a. "Health Insurance Eligibility, Utilization of Medical Care, and Child Health." *Quarterly Journal of Economics* 111 (2): 431–66.

———. 1996b. "Saving Babies: The Efficacy and Cost of Recent Changes in the Medicaid Eligibility of Pregnant Women." *Journal of Political Economy* 104 (6): 1263–96.

———. 2001. "Public Health Insurance and Medical Treatment: The Equalizing Impact of the Medicaid Expansions." *Journal of Public Economics* 82:63–89.

Currie, Janet, Jonathan Gruber, and Michael Fischer. 1995. "Physician Payments and Infant Mortality: Evidence from Medicaid Fee Policy." *American Economic Review* 85 (2): 106–11.

Currie, Janet, Lucia Nixon, and Nancy Cole. 1996. "Restrictions on Medicaid Funding of Abortion: Effects on Birth Weight and Pregnancy Resolutions." *Journal of Human Resources* 31 (1): 159–88.

Cutler, David M., and Jonathan Gruber. 1996. "Does Public Insurance Crowd Out Private Insurance?" *Quarterly Journal of Economics* 111 (2): 391–430.

Cutler, David, Mark McClellan, and Joseph Newhouse. 2000. "How Does Managed Care Do It?" *Rand Journal of Economics* 31 (3): 526–48.

Dafny, Leemore, and Jonathan Gruber. 2005. "Public Insurance and Child Hospitalizations: Access and Efficiency Effects." *Journal of Public Economics* 89 (1): 109–29.

Dague, Laura. 2014. "The Effect of Medicaid Premiums on Enrollment: A Regression Discontinuity Approach." *Journal of Health Economics* 37:1–12.

Dague, Laura, Thomas DeLeire, and Lindsey Leininger. 2014. "The Effect of Public Insurance Coverage for Childless Adults on Labor Supply." NBER Working Paper no. 20111, Cambridge, MA.

Davern, Michael, Jacob Klerman, David Baugh, Kathleen Thiede Call, and George Greenberg. 2009. "An Examination of the Medicaid Undercount in the Current Population Survey: Preliminary Results from Record Linking." *Health Services Research* 44 (3): 965–87.

Davidoff, Amy, Anna S. Sommers, Jennifer Lesko, and Alshadye Yemane. 2004. "Medicaid and State-Funded Coverage for Adults: Estimates of Eligibility and Enrollment." Kaiser Commission on Medicaid and the Uninsured Policy Brief, Urban Institute. https://kaiserfamilyfoundation.files.wordpress.com/2013/01/medicaid-and-state-funded-coverage-for-adults-estimates-of-eligibilty-and-enrollment-report.pdf.

Decker, Sandra L. 2007. "Medicaid Physician Fees and the Quality of Medical Care of Medicaid Patients in the USA." *Review of Economics of the Household* 5 (1): 95–112.

———. 2009. "Changes in Medicaid Physician Fees and Patterns of Ambulatory Care." *Inquiry* 46 (3): 291–304.

———. 2011. "Medicaid Payment Levels to Dentists and Access to Dental Care among Children and Adolescents." *Journal of the American Medical Association* 306 (2): 187–93.

———. 2013. "Two-Thirds of Primary Care Physicians Accepted New Medicaid Patients in 2011–12: A Baseline to Measure Future Acceptance Rates." *Health Affairs* 32 (7): 1183–87.

De La Mata, Dolores. 2012. "The Effect of Medicaid Eligibility on Coverage, Utilization, and Children's Health." *Health Economics* 21 (9): 1061–79.

DeLeire, Thomas, Laura Dague, Lindsey Leininger, Kristen Voskuil, and Donna Friedsam. 2013. "Wisconsin Experience Indicates That Expanding Public Insurance to Low-Income Childless Adults Has Health Care Impacts." *Health Affairs* 32 (3):1037–45.

DeLeire, Thomas, Karen Joynt, and Ruth McDonald. 2014. "Impact of Insurance Expansion on Hospital Uncompensated Care Costs in 2014." ASPE Issue Brief, September 24. http://aspe.hhs.gov/sites/default/files/pdf/77061/ib_Uncompensated Care.pdf.

DeLeire, Thomas, Leonard M. Lopoo, and Kosali I. Simon. 2011. "Medicaid Expansions and Fertility in the United States." *Demography* 48 (2): 725–47.

DeNardi, Mariacristina, Eric French, and John B. Jones. 2010. "Why Do the Elderly Save? The Role of Medical Expenses." *Journal of Political Economy* 118 (1): 39–75.

DeNavas-Walt, Carmen, Bernadette D. Proctor, and Jessica C. Smith. 2012. "Income, Poverty, and Health Insurance Coverage in the United States: 2011." US Census Bureau, Current Population Reports, P60–243, Washington, DC, US Government Printing Office.

Dubay, Lisa C., and Genevieve M. Kenney. 1996. "The Effects of Medicaid Expansions on Insurance Coverage of Children." *Future of Children* 6 (1): 152–61.

Duggan, Mark G. 2000. "Hospital Ownership and Public Medical Spending." *Quarterly Journal of Economics* 115 (4): 1343–73.

———. 2004. "Does Contracting out Increase the Efficiency of Government Programs? Evidence from Medicaid HMOs." *Journal of Public Economics* 88 (12): 2549–72.

Duggan, Mark, and Tamara Hayford. 2013. "Has the Shift to Managed Care Reduced Medicaid Expenditures? Evidence from State and Local-Level Mandates." *Journal of Policy Analysis and Management* 32 (3): 505–35.

Finkelstein, Amy, Sarah Taubman, Bill Wright, Mira Bernstein, Jonathan Gruber, Joseph P. Newhouse, Heidi Allen, Katherine Baicker, and the Oregon Health Study Group. 2012. "The Oregon Health Insurance Experiment: Evidence from the First Year." *Quarterly Journal of Economics* 127 (3): 1057–106.

Finkelstein, Amy, Nathaniel Hendren, and Erzo Luttmer. 2015. "The Value of Medicaid: Interpreting Results from the Oregon Health Insurance Experiment." NBER Working Paper no. 21308, Cambridge, MA.

Freedman, Seth, Haizhen Lin, and Kosali Simon. 2015. "Public Health Insurance Expansions and Hospital Technology Adoption." *Journal of Public Economics* 121:117–31.

Gabel, Jon, and Thomas Rice. 1985. "Reducing Public Expenditures for Physician Services: The Price of Paying Less." *Journal of Health Politics, Policy and Law* 9 (4): 595–609.

Gardner, Lara, and Donna B. Gilleskie. 2012. "The Effects of State Medicaid Policies on the Dynamic Savings Patterns and Medicaid Enrollment of the Elderly." *Journal of Human Resources* 47 (4): 1082–127.

Garthwaite, Craig L. 2012. "The Doctor Might See You Now: The Supply Side Effects of Public Health Insurance Expansions." *American Economic Journal: Economic Policy* 4 (3): 190–215.

Garthwaite, Craig, Tal Gross, and Matthew J. Notowidigdo. 2014. "Public Health Insurance, Labor Supply, and Employment Lock." *Quarterly Journal of Economics* 129 (2): 653–96.

Gertler, Paul J. 1989. "Subsidies, Quality, and the Regulation of Nursing Homes." *Journal of Public Economics* 38 (1): 33–52.

Gittleman, Maury. 2011. "Medicaid and Wealth: A Re-Examination." *B.E. Journal of Economic Analysis and Policy* 11 (1): 1–25.

Goda, Gopi Shah. 2011. "The Impact of State Tax Subsidies for Private Long-Term Care Insurance on Coverage and Medicaid Expenditures." *Journal of Public Economics* 95 (7–8): 744–57.

Goodman-Bacon, Andrew. 2015. "Public Insurance and Mortality: Evidence from Medicaid Implementation." Working Paper, University of Michigan.

Grabowski, David C. 2001. "Medicaid Reimbursement and the Quality of Nursing Home Care." *Journal of Health Economics* 20 (4): 549–69.

———. 2004. "A Longitudinal Study of Medicaid Payment, Private-Pay Price and Nursing Home Quality." *International Journal of Health Care Finance and Economics* 4 (1): 5–26.

Grabowski, David C., and Joseph J. Angelelli. 2004. "The Relationship of Medicaid Payment Rates, Bed Constraint Policies, and Risk-Adjusted Pressure Ulcers." *Health Services Research* 39 (4p1): 793–812.

Grabowski, David C., Joseph J. Angelelli, and Vincent Mor. 2004. "Medicaid Payment and Risk-Adjusted Nursing Home Quality." *Health Affairs* 23 (5): 243–52.

Grabowski, David, and Edward Norton. 2006. "Nursing Home Quality of Care." In *The Elgar Companion to Health Economics*, edited by Andrew Jones, 296–305. Cheltenham, UK: Elgar Publishing, Inc.

Gray, Bradley. 2001. "Do Medicaid Physician Fees for Prenatal Services Affect Birth Outcomes?" *Journal of Health Economics* 20 (4): 571–90.

Gresenz, Carole Roan, Sarah E. Edgington, Miriam Laugesen, and José J. Escarce. 2012. "Take-Up of Public Insurance and Crowd-Out of Private Insurance under Recent CHIP Expansions to Higher Income Children." *Health Services Research* 47 (5): 1999–2011.

Gross, Tal, and Matthew J. Notowidigdo. 2011. "Health Insurance and the Consumer Bankruptcy Decision: Evidence from Expansions of Medicaid." *Journal of Public Economics* 95 (7–8): 767–78.

Gruber, Jonathan. 2003. "Medicaid." In *Means-Tested Transfer Programs in the United States*, edited by Robert Moffitt. Chicago: University of Chicago Press.

Gruber, Jonathan, Kathleen Adams, and Joseph P. Newhouse. 1997. "Physician Fee Policy and Medicaid Program Costs." *Journal of Human Resources* 32 (4): 611–34.

Gruber, Jon, John Kim, and Dina Mayzlin. 1999. "Physician Fees and Procedure Intensity: The Case of Cesarean Delivery." *Journal of Health Economics* 18 (4): 473–90.

Gruber, Jonathan, and Kosali Simon. 2008. "Crowd-Out 10 Years Later: Have Recent Public Insurance Expansions Crowded Out Private Health Insurance?" *Journal of Health Economics* 27 (2): 201–17.

Gruber, Jonathan, and Aaron Yelowitz. 1999. "Public Health Insurance and Private Savings." *Journal of Political Economy* 107 (6): 1249–74.

Haas-Wilson, Deborah. 1996. "The Impact of State Abortion Restrictions on Minors' Demand for Abortions." *Journal of Human Resources* 31 (1): 140–58.

Hahn, Youjin. 2013. "The Effect of Medicaid Physician Fees on Take-Up of Public

Health Insurance among Children in Poverty." *Journal of Health Economics* 32 (2): 452–62.

Ham, John C., Xianghong Li, and Lara Shore-Sheppard. 2009. "Public Policy and the Dynamics of Children's Health Insurance, 1986–1999." *American Economic Review (Papers and Proceedings)* 99:522–26.

Ham, John C., I. Serkan Ozbeklik, and Lara Shore-Sheppard. 2014. "Estimating Heterogeneous Takeup and Crowd-Out Responses to Existing Medicaid Income Limits and Their Nonmarginal Expansions." *Journal of Human Resources* 49 (4): 872–905.

Ham, John C., and Lara Shore-Sheppard. 2005a. "Did Expanding Medicaid Affect Welfare Participation?" *Industrial and Labor Relations Review* 58(3): 452–70.

———. 2005b. "The Effect of Medicaid Expansions for Low-Income Children on Medicaid Participation and Private Insurance Coverage: Evidence from the SIPP." *Journal of Public Economics* 89 (1): 57–83.

Hamersma, Sarah, and Matthew Kim. 2009. "The Effect of Parental Medicaid Expansions on Job Mobility." *Journal of Health Economics* 28 (4): 761–70.

———. 2013. "Participation and Crowd Out: Assessing the Effects of Parental Medicaid Expansions." *Journal of Health Economics* 32 (1): 160–71.

He, Fang, and Chapin White. 2013. "The Effect of the Children's Health Insurance Program on Pediatricians' Work Hours." *Medicare & Medicaid Research Review* 3 (1): E1–32.

Heberlein, Martha, Tricia Brooks, Joan Alker, Samantha Artiga, and Jessica Stephens. 2013. "Getting into Gear for 2014: Findings from a 50-State Survey of Eligibility, Enrollment, Renewal, and Cost-Sharing Policies in Medicaid and CHIP, 2012–2013." Washington, DC, Kaiser Commission on Medicaid and the Uninsured, January. https://kaiserfamilyfoundation.files.wordpress.com/2013/05/8401.pdf.

Hudson, Julie L., Thomas M. Selden, and Jessica S. Banthin. 2005. "The Impact of SCHIP on Insurance Coverage of Children." *INQUIRY: The Journal of Health Care Organization, Provision, and Financing* 42 (3): 232–54.

Joyce, Theodore. 1999. "Impact of Augmented Prenatal Care on Birth Outcomes of Medicaid Recipients in New York City." *Journal of Health Economics* 18 (1): 31–67.

Joyce, Theodore, and Robert Kaestner. 1996. "The Effect of Expansions in Medicaid Income Eligibility on Abortion." *Demography* 33 (2): 181–92.

Joyce, Theodore, Robert Kaestner, and Florence Kwan. 1998. "Is Medicaid Pronatalist? The Effect of Eligibility Expansions on Abortions and Births." *Family Planning Perspectives* 30 (3): 108–27.

Kaestner, Robert, Lisa Dubay, and Genevieve Kenney. 2005. "Managed Care and Infant Health: An Evaluation of Medicaid in the US." *Social Science & Medicine* 60 (8): 1815–33.

Kaiser Commission on Medicaid and the Uninsured. 2009. "State Children's Health Insurance Program (CHIP): Reauthorization History." February. https://kaiserfamilyfoundation.files.wordpress.com/2013/01/7743–02.pdf.

———. 2012. "An Overview of Recent Section 1115 Medicaid Demonstration Waiver Activity." Policy Brief, May. https://kaiserfamilyfoundation.files.wordpress.com/2013/01/8318.pdf.

———. 2013. "Overview of Nursing Facility Capacity, Financing and Ownership in the United States in 2011." Fact Sheet, June. http://kff.org/medicaid/fact-sheet/overview-of-nursing-facility-capacity-financing-and-ownership-in-the-united-states-in-2011/.

———. 2014a. "A Closer Look at the Impact of State Decisions Not to Expand

Medicaid on Coverage for Uninsured Adults." April. https://kaiserfamily
foundation.files.wordpress.com/2014/04/8585-a-closer-look-at-the-impact
-of-state-decisions-not-to-expand-medicaid.pdf.

———. 2014b. "Medicaid Moving Forward." June. https://kaiserfamilyfoundation
.files.wordpress.com/2014/06/7235-07-medicaid-moving-forward2.pdf.

Kaiser Family Foundation. 2008. "Medicaid: A Timeline of Key Developments." https://kaiserfamilyfoundation.files.wordpress.com/2008/04/5-02-13
-medicaid-timeline.pdf.

Kane, Thomas J., and Douglas Staiger. 1996. "Teen Motherhood and Abortion
Access." *Quarterly Journal of Economics* 111 (2): 467–506.

Kearney, Melissa S., and Phillip B. Levine. 2009. "Subsidized Contraception, Fertility, and Sexual Behavior." *Review of Economics and Statistics* 91 (1): 137–51.

Kenney, Genevieve, R. Andrew Allison, Julia F. Costich, James Marton, and Joshua
McFeeters. 2006. "Effects of Premium Increases on Enrollment in SCHIP: Findings from Three States." *Inquiry* 43 (4): 378–92.

Kenney, Genevieve, and Mike Huntress. 2012. "Affordable Care Act: Coverage
Implications and Issues for Immigrant Families." ASPE Issue Brief, April, US
Department of Health and Human Services, Office of the Assistant Secretary for
Planning and Evaluation. https://aspe.hhs.gov/basic-report/affordable-care-act
-coverage-implications-and-issues-immigrant-families.

Koch, Thomas G. 2013. "Using RD Design to Understand Heterogeneity in Health
Insurance Crowd-Out." *Journal of Health Economics* 32 (3): 599–611.

Kolstad, Jonathan, and Amanda Kowalski. 2012. "The Impact of Health Care
Reform on Hospital and Preventive Care: Evidence from Massachusetts." *Journal
of Public Economics* 96 (11): 909–29.

Ku, Leighton, and Teresa A. Coughlin. 1995. "Medicaid Disproportionate Share
and Other Special Financing Programs." *Health Care Financing Review* 16 (3):
27–54.

———. 1999/2000. "Sliding Scale Premium Health Insurance Programs: Four
States' Experiences." *Inquiry* 36 (4): 471–80.

Lee, David S., and Thomas Lemieux. 2010. "Regression Discontinuity Designs in
Economics." *Journal of Economic Literature* 48:281–355.

Levine, Phillip B., Amy B. Trainor, and David J. Zimmerman. 1996. "The Effect of
Medicaid Abortion Funding Restrictions on Abortions, Pregnancies and Births."
Journal of Health Economics 15 (5): 555–78.

Li, Minghua, and Reagan Baughman. 2010. "Coverage, Utilization, and Health Outcomes of the State Children's Health Insurance Program." *Inquiry* 47 (4): 296–314.

Long, Stephen, Russell Settle, and Bruce Stuart. 1986. "Reimbursement and Access to
Physicians' Services under Medicaid." *Journal of Health Economics* 5 (3): 235–51.

Long, Sharon K., Karen Stockley, and Heather Dahlen. 2012. "Massachusetts Health
Reforms: Uninsurance Remains Low, Self-Reported Health Status Improves as
State Prepares to Tackle Costs." *Health Affairs* 31 (2): 444–51.

Lo Sasso, Anthony T., and Thomas C. Buchmueller. 2004. "The Effect of the State
Children's Health Insurance Program on Health Insurance Coverage." *Journal of
Health Economics* 23 (5): 1059–82.

Lurie, Ithai. 2009. "Differential Effect of the State Children's Health Insurance Program Expansions by Children's Age." *Health Services Research* 44 (5): 1504–20.

Marton, James. 2007. "The Impact of the Introduction of Premiums into a SCHIP
Program." *Journal of Policy Analysis and Management* 26 (2): 237–55.

Maynard, Alex, and Jiaping Qiu. 2009. "Public Insurance and Private Savings: Who
is Affected and by How Much?" *Journal of Applied Econometrics* 24:282–308.

Mazumder, Bhashkar, and Sarah Miller. Forthcoming. "The Effects of the Massachusetts Health Reform on Household Financial Distress." *American Economic Journal: Economic Policy.*

McGuire, Thomas. 2000. "Physician Agency." In *Handbook of Health Economics,* edited by Culyer and Newhouse. Amsterdam: North Holland.

Medicaid and CHIP Payment and Access Commission (MACPAC). 2012. Report to the Congress on Medicaid and CHIP. March. https://www.macpac.gov/wp-content/uploads/2015/01/2012–03–15_MACPAC_Report1.pdf.

———. 2013. Report to the Congress on Medicaid and CHIP. June. https://www.macpac.gov/wp-content/uploads/2015/01/2013–06–15_MACPAC_Report.pdf.

———. 2014. Report to the Congress on Medicaid and CHIP. June. https://www.macpac.gov/wp-content/uploads/2015/01/2014–06–13_MACPAC_Report.pdf.

Meyer, Bruce D. 1995. "Natural and Quasi-Experiments in Economics." *Journal of Business & Economic Statistics* 13 (2): 151–61.

Meyer, Bruce D., and Dan T. Rosenbaum. 2001. "Welfare, the Earned Income Tax Credit, and the Labor Supply of Single Mothers." *Quarterly Journal of Economics* 116 (3): 1063–114.

Miller, Sarah. 2012. "The Effect of Insurance on Emergency Room Visits: An Analysis of the 2006 Massachusetts Health Reform." *Journal of Public Economics* 96 (11): 893–908.

Miller, Sarah, and Laura Wherry. 2015. "The Long-Term Effects of Early Life Medicaid Coverage." Unpublished Manuscript, University of Michigan.

Moffitt, Robert, and Barbara Wolfe. 1992. "The Effect of the Medicaid Program on Welfare Participation and Labor Supply." *Review of Economics and Statistics* 74 (4): 615–26.

Moore, Judith D., and David G. Smith. 2005. "Legislating Medicaid: Considering Medicaid and Its Origins." *Health Care Financing Review* 27 (2): 45–52.

National Association of State Budget Officers. 2013. "State Expenditure Report: Examining Fiscal 2011–2013 State Spending." https://www.nasbo.org/sites/default/files/State Expenditure Report %28Fiscal 2011–2013 Data%29.pdf.

Nikpay, Sayeh, Thomas Buchmueller, and Helen Levy. 2015. "Early Medicaid Expansion in Connecticut Stemmed the Growth in Hospital Uncompensated Care." *Health Affairs* 34 (7): 1170–79.

Norton, Edward. 2000. "Long-Term Care." In *Handbook of Health Economics,* edited by Anthony Culyer and Joseph Newhouse, 955–94. Amsterdam: Elsevier.

Nyman, John. 1985. "Prospective and 'Cost-Plus' Medicaid Reimbursement, Excess Medicaid Demand, and the Quality of Nursing Home Care." *Journal of Health Economics* 4 (3): 237–59.

———. 1988. "Excess Demand, the Percentage of Medicaid Patients, and the Quality of Nursing Home Care." *Journal of Human Resources* 23 (1): 76–92.

Office of the Legislative Counsel, US House of Representatives. 2010. Compilation of Patient Protection and Affordable Care Act, Washington, DC. http://housedocs.house.gov/energycommerce/ppacacon.pdf.

Polsky, Daniel, Michael Richards, Simon Basseyn, Douglas Wissoker, Genevieve Kenney, Stephen Zuckerman, and Karin Rhodes. 2015. "Appointment Availability after Increases in Medicaid Payments for Primary Care." *New England Journal of Medicine* 372 (6): 537–45.

Rhodes, Karin, Genevieve Kenney, A. B. Friedman, Brendan Saloner, C. C. Lawrence, D. Chearo, Douglas Wissoker, and Daniel Polsky. 2014. "Primary Care Access for New Patients on the Eve of Health Care Reform." *Journal of the American Medical Association Internal Medicine* 174 (6): 861–69.

Rosenbach, Margo. 1989. "The Impact of Medicaid on Physician Use by Low-Income Children." *American Journal of Public Health* 79 (9): 1220–26.

Rudowitz, Robin, Samantha Artiga, and MaryBeth Musumeci. 2014. "The ACA and Recent Section 1115 Medicaid Demonstration Waivers." Kaiser Commission on Medicaid and the Uninsured Issue Brief. http://kff.org/medicaid/issue-brief/the-aca-and-medicaid-expansion-waivers/.

Schneider, Andy. 1997. "Overview of Medicaid Provisions in the Balanced Budget Act of 1997, P.L. 105–33." Center on Budget and Policy Priorities Report, September 8. http://www.cbpp.org/archives/908mcaid.htm.

Schneider, Andy, Risa Elias, Rachel Garfield, David Rousseau, and Victoria Wachino. 2002. "The Medicaid Resource Book." The Kaiser Commission on Medicaid and the Uninsured. http://kff.org/medicaid/report/the-medicaid-resource-book/.

Selden, Thomas, and Julie Hudson. 2006. "Access to Care and Utilization among Children: Estimating the Effects of Public and Private Coverage." *Medical Care* 44 (5): 19–26.

Sen, Bisakha. 2003. "A Preliminary Investigation of the Effects of Restrictions on Medicaid Funding for Abortions on Female STD Rates." *Health Economics* 12 (6): 453–64.

Shen, Yu-Chu, and Stephen Zuckerman. 2005. "The Effect of Medicaid Payment Generosity on Access and Use among Beneficiaries." *Health Services Research* 40 (3): 723–44.

Shore-Sheppard, Lara D. 2003. "Expanding Public Health Insurance for Children: Medicaid and the State Children's Health Insurance Program." In *Changing Welfare*, edited by Rachel A. Gordon and Herbert J. Walberg, 95–118. New York: Kluwer Academic Publishers.

———. 2008. "Stemming the Tide? The Effect of Expanding Medicaid Eligibility on Health Insurance Coverage." *B.E. Journal of Economic Analysis & Policy* 8 (2): 1–35.

Sloan, Frank, Janet Mitchell, and Jerry Cromwell. 1978. "Physician Participation in State Medicaid Programs." *Journal of Human Resources* 13:211–45.

Sommers, Benjamin D. 2006. "Insuring Children or Insuring Families: Do Parental and Sibling Coverage Lead to Improved Retention of Children in Medicaid and CHIP?" *Journal of Health Economics* 25 (6): 1154–69.

———. 2010. "Targeting in Medicaid: The Costs and Enrollment Effects of Medicaid's Citizenship Documentation Requirement." *Journal of Public Economics* 94 (1–2): 174–82.

Sommers, Benjamin D., Katherine Baicker, and Arnold M. Epstein. 2012. "Mortality and Access to Care among Adults after State Medicaid Expansions." *New England Journal of Medicine* 367 (11): 1025–34.

Sommers, Benjamin D., Genevieve M. Kenney, and Arnold M. Epstein. 2014. "New Evidence on the Affordable Care Act: Coverage Impacts of Early Medicaid Expansions." *Health Affairs* 33 (1): 78–87.

Sommers, Benjamin D., Sharon K. Long, and Katherine Baicker. 2014. "Changes in Mortality after Massachusetts Health Care Reform: A Quasi-Experimental Study." *Annals of Internal Medicine* 160 (9): 585–93.

Stephens, Jessica, and Samantha Artiga. 2013. "Key Facts on Health Coverage for Low-Income Immigrants Today and under the Affordable Care Act." Washington, DC, Kaiser Commission on Medicaid and the Uninsured, March. https://kaiserfamilyfoundation.files.wordpress.com/2013/03/8279–02.pdf.

Taubman, Sarah L., Heidi L. Allen, Bill J. Wright, Katherine Baicker, and Amy N. Finkelstein. 2014. "Medicaid Increases Emergency-Department Use: Evidence from Oregon's Health Insurance Experiment." *Science* 343 (6168): 263–68.

UC Berkeley Labor Center. 2013. "Modified Adjusted Gross Income under the Affordable Care Act." Fact Sheet. http://laborcenter.berkeley.edu/pdf/2013/MAGI_summary13.pdf.

US General Accounting Office (US GAO). 2000. "Factors Contributing to Low Use

of Dental Services by Low-Income Populations." GAO/HEHS-00–149. http://
www.gao.gov/new.items/he00149.pdf.

US Social Security Administration Office of Retirement and Disability Policy. 2011.
"Annual Statistical Supplement to the Social Security Bulletin, 2011." http://www
.ssa.gov/policy/docs/statcomps/supplement/2011/supplement11.pdf.

Urban Institute. 2015. "Safety Net Almanac: Medicaid Legislative History." http://
safetynet.urban.org/safety-net-almanac/Medicaid-CHIP/Medicaid-Legislative
-History.cfm.

Watson, Tara. 2014. "Inside the Refrigerator: Immigration Enforcement and Chilling Effects in Medicaid Participation." *American Economic Journal: Economic
Policy* 6 (3): 313–38.

Weikel, M. Keith, and Nancy A. LeaMond. 1976. "A Decade of Medicaid." *Public
Health Reports* 91 (4): 303–38.

Wherry, Laura, and Bruce Meyer. Forthcoming. "Saving Teens: Using a Policy Discontinuity to Estimate the Effects of Medicaid Eligibility." *Journal of Human
Resources.*

Wherry, Laura, Sarah Miller, Robert Kaestner, and Bruce Meyer. 2015. "Childhood
Medicaid Coverage and Later Life Health Care Utilization." NBER Working
Paper no. 20929, Cambridge, MA.

White, Chapin. 2012. "A Comparison of Two Approaches to Increasing Access to
Care: Expanding Coverage versus Increasing Physician Fees." *Health Services
Research* 47 (3–1): 963–38.

Wolfe, Barbara, Thomas Kaplan, Robert Haveman, and Yoonyoung Cho. 2006.
"SCHIP Expansion and Parental Coverage: An Evaluation of Wisconsin's Badger
Care." *Journal of Health Economics* 25 (6): 1170–92.

Wolfe, Barbara, and Scott Scrivner. 2005. "The Devil May Be in the Details: How
the Characteristics of SCHIP Programs Affect Take-Up." *Journal of Policy Analysis and Management* 24 (3): 499–522.

Woutersen, Tiemen, and John C. Ham. 2013. "Calculating Confidence Intervals for
Continuous and Discontinuous Functions of Estimated Parameters." Cemmap
Working Paper no. 23/13, Department of Economics, University College London.

Yelowitz, Aaron S. 1995. "The Medicaid Notch, Labor Supply, and Welfare Participation: Evidence from Eligibility Expansions." *Quarterly Journal of Economics*
110 (4): 909–39.

———. 1998. "Will Extending Medicaid to Two-Parent Families Encourage Marriage?" *Journal of Human Resources* 33 (4): 833–65.

Zavodny, Madeline, and Marianne P. Bitler. 2010. "The Effect of Medicaid Eligibility
Expansions on Fertility." *Social Science & Medicine* 71 (5): 918–24.

Zuckerman, Stephen, Joshua McFeeters, Peter Cunningham, and Len Nichols. 2004.
"Changes in Medicaid Physician Fees, 1998–2003: Implications for Physician
Participation." *Health Affairs* w374–84.

Zuckerman, Stephen, Aimee Williams, and Karen Stockley. 2009. "Trends in Medicaid Physician Fees, 2003–2008." *Health Affairs* 28 (3): w510–19.

Zuckerman, Stephen, and Dana Goin. 2012. "How Much Will Medicaid Physician
Fees for Primary Care Rise in 2013? Evidence from a 2012 Survey of Medicaid
Physician Fees." Kaiser Family Foundation Issue Brief. December. http://kff.org
/medicaid/issue-brief/how-much-will-medicaid-physician-fees-for/.

The Earned Income Tax Credit

Austin Nichols and Jesse Rothstein

2.1 Introduction

The Earned Income Tax Credit ([EITC]; sometimes referred to as the "Earned Income Credit," or [EIC]) is in many ways the most important means-tested transfer program in the United States. Introduced in 1975, it has grown to be one of the largest and least controversial elements of the US welfare state, with 26.7 million recipients sharing $63 billion in total federal EITC expenditures in 2013. Moreover, the federal EITC is supplemented by the Child Tax Credit, which has a similar structure and is comparable in size (though more tilted toward higher-income families), and by state and local EITCs in at least twenty-five states and several municipalities.

Judged as an antipoverty program, the EITC is extremely successful. Hoynes and Patel (2015) find that EITC receipt is concentrated among families whose incomes (after other taxes and transfers) would otherwise be between 75 percent and 150 percent of the poverty line. An analysis of the new Census Bureau supplemental poverty measure (Short 2014), designed to include the effects of transfer programs on families' disposable income,

Austin Nichols is principal scientist at Abt Associates. Jesse Rothstein is professor of public policy and economics and director of the Institute for Research on Labor and Employment at the University of California, Berkeley, and a research associate of the National Bureau of Economic Research.

We thank Apurna Chakraborty and Darian Woods for excellent research assistance. The chapter has benefited from comments and suggestions from Richard Blundell, Chye-Ching Huang, Robert Greenstein, Hilary Hoynes, Chuck Marr, Robert Moffitt, Emmanuel Saez, Arloc Sherman, and John Wancheck, though none are responsible for the content. We are especially grateful to Margaret Jones of the US Census Bureau for providing the tabulations of nonpublic matched CPS-IRS data discussed in section 2.3. For acknowledgments, sources of research support, and disclosure of the authors' material financial relationships, if any, please see http://www.nber.org/chapters/c13484.ack.

indicates that income from refundable tax credits (primarily but not exclusively the EITC) reduces the number of people in poverty by over 15 percent. The impact on children is even more dramatic: income from refundable tax credits reduces child poverty by over one-quarter. No other program—save perhaps Social Security retirement benefits—approaches this impact. Moreover, as we discuss below, the income that the EITC provides has important impacts on parent and child health, and on children's academic achievement.

For all its size and importance, the EITC is atypical when seen as a transfer program. It began life not as a carefully considered effort to alleviate poverty but as a legislative blocking maneuver, used by Senator Russell Long (D-LA) to defuse proposals in the late 1960s and early 1970s for a negative income tax (see Hotz and Scholz 2003). It has long received bipartisan support, with expansions authorized by both Democratic and Republican congresses and under each of the last five presidents. In recent years, prominent members of both parties have called for EITC expansions. Then House of Representatives Budget Committee Chair (now Speaker of the House) Paul Ryan's July 2014 discussion budget calls the EITC "[o]ne of the federal government's most effective anti-poverty programs," and proposes more than doubling the generosity of the EITC for childless workers. President Obama's 2016 budget proposal included similar expansions. It is reasonable to suspect that Ryan and Obama do not agree on much else where means-tested transfers are concerned.

The EITC is also distinguished by its administration and incentives. It is administered by the Internal Revenue Service, not ordinarily thought of as an agency focused on fighting poverty or on distributing government spending. There are no government caseworkers, and take-up rates are substantially higher than in many other antipoverty programs. On the other hand, recipients often rely on for-profit tax preparers, sometimes paying high fees to have their tax returns prepared or for short-term loans against their eventual EITC refunds. And where a common critique of means-tested transfers is that they create incentives to masquerade as a person of limited means by reducing labor supply, the EITC's primary incentive is to *increase* labor supply. Indeed, one concern about the EITC is that it too may induce labor supply in the targeted population, reducing wages and allowing employers of low-skill workers to capture a portion of credit expenditures.

Early research on the EITC (ably reviewed by Hotz and Scholz [2003]) focused on understanding the program's labor-supply effects in a static setting. Even by the time of Hotz and Scholz's review, however, the research literature was broadening to consider effects on marriage and fertility, skill formation, and consumption. Since then, the literature has become even more diffuse, encompassing a wide array of issues including the role of tax preparers; compliance and gaming of the tax code; information and so-called "behavioral" impacts on participation; the role of the EITC as an automatic stabilizer; and effects of the program on pretax wages, on recipients' health, and on children's long-run outcomes.

In section 2.2, we review the history and rules of the EITC, along with its younger and less-well-known sibling, the Child Tax Credit (CTC). We also discuss the goals of the program, both as articulated by the politicians who have supported it and as can be inferred from the program's design. Section 2.3 presents statistics on the growth, take-up, and distribution of the EITC.

Section 2.4 reviews a number of issues surrounding the program. We return to the rationale for the program's design. In the 1960s, a number of reformers advocated a negative income tax (NIT), which would provide a universal basic income to those without other sources of income that would be taxed away as other income rose. In contrast to other antipoverty programs with extremely high implicit tax rates at low earnings levels, the NIT was designed to have a modest marginal tax rate over a wide phaseout range. This was appealing both to the designers of the war on poverty and to conservatives who worried about disincentives created by traditional means-tested antipoverty programs, and had supporters as diverse as Lyndon Johnson's Office of Economic Opportunity (though not Johnson himself), Richard Nixon, and Milton Friedman.

The EITC in some ways resembles an NIT, and is often thought of as a version of the latter, but it differs in important ways. We discuss reasons for that difference, and rationalizations of an EITC structure as an optimal response to deviations from the simple model that gave rise to the NIT. We also review the incentives that the EITC might be expected to create, as well as concerns about interactions with other programs and with cyclical variation.

Section 2.5 reviews the empirical literature regarding the EITC. We begin by examining evidence on participation in the program and compliance with credit rules, largely from administrative audit studies. This section also discusses the "Advance EIC" program that (until 2011) allowed recipients to receive their credits as increments to their paychecks throughout the year rather than as a lump-sum tax refund. Take up of this program—which could be seen as a free loan against a future credit—was extremely low. This is quite puzzling given the prevalence of "refund anticipation loans" that speed access to tax refunds but charge very high interest rates.[1]

Next, we turn to studies of the effects of the credit on recipients' well-being. Researchers have documented beneficial effects on poverty, on consumption, on health, and on children's academic outcomes. The magnitude of these effects is large: millions of families are brought above the poverty line, and estimates of the effects on children indicate that this may have extremely important effects on the intergenerational transmission of pov-

---

1. As we discuss below, pressure from federal bank regulators has sharply curtailed the supply of refund anticipation loans, which are widely seen as usurious.

erty as well. Taking all of the evidence together, the EITC appears to benefit recipients—and especially their children—substantially, though there is some evidence of unintended consequences (e.g., on marriage and fertility) as well.

Third, we consider the impact of the credit on the labor market. There is an overwhelming consensus in the literature that the EITC raises single mothers' labor force participation. There is also evidence of a *negative*, but smaller, effect on the employment of married women, who may take advantage of the credit to stay home with their children. There is little evidence of any effects on men, and estimated effects on the number of weeks or hours that women work, conditional on participating at all, are much smaller than those on participation. Indeed, most evidence on the intensive margin derives from effects on *reported* earnings among self-employed workers who face negative marginal tax rates and thus incentives to inflate their earnings, which are difficult to verify, though we discuss some recent work that finds evidence of effects on the non-self-employed as well.

Section 2.5 also considers the EITC's effect on pretax wages. Standard tax incidence models emphasize that the economic impacts of taxes may differ from the statutory incidence, and a straightforward application of the canonical model implies that a portion of the EITC's incidence may be on the purchasers of the subsidized product—labor—rather than on the sellers. This fact was not prominent in early discussions of the EITC, but has been the subject of several studies in the last decade. Although none of the evidence is airtight, it appears that employers of low-wage labor are able to capture a meaningful share of the credit through reduced wages. This comes to some extent at the expense of low-skill workers who are not eligible for the credit (due, for example, to not having children; although there is a credit schedule for childless workers, it is much less generous than that for families with children).

Finally, we discuss the EITC's role within a larger economy and constellation of transfer programs. We discuss work on interactions with other programs and with economic conditions. Of particular interest, given the Great Recession of 2007–2009 and the subsequent period of extreme weakness in the labor market, is the potential role of the EITC as a countercyclical stabilizer. Going into the Great Recession, it was not clear what to expect from this. On the one hand, the EITC is available only to those who work, so it might not be expected to do much to help those who are involuntarily jobless. On the other hand, because the credit is computed based on calendar-year earnings, partial year unemployment would be expected to generate larger credits for many recipients (whose credits are declining in their earnings) and to make many others eligible who would not have qualified had they worked the whole year. It is thus an empirical question whether the EITC will expand or contract in recessions. A few very recent studies have shed light on this. The results are not encouraging—perhaps not surprisingly, as countercyclical stabilization has never been one of the primary goals of the program.

A second important interaction is with the minimum wage. The minimum wage and the EITC represent two quite different ways to help, in President Clinton's words, "make work pay," and the political debate often places them in opposition to one another. But it is not clear that the two should be seen as alternatives, as tax incidence considerations may create important complementarities between the two: in the absence of a binding minimum wage, EITC-induced labor supply increases drive down the market wage, enabling employers to capture a portion of the credit. A higher minimum wage can thus make the EITC more effective. In a neoclassical model, much depends on how a limited number of jobs are rationed among job seekers. Under certain assumptions, the optimal policy combines a generous EITC with a high minimum wage.

The EITC has evolved substantially since its introduction: since 1991, the credit has been more generous for families with two or more children than for those with just one; since 2009 it has been more generous still for families with three or more children and more generous for married couples than for single parents (though these provisions are set to expire in 2017); a small credit was added in 1994 for families without children; and there has been repeated experimentation with the administration and enforcement of the credit. Section 2.6 discusses proposals for further reform, including those aimed at reducing marriage penalties or at expanding the reach of the EITC to noncustodial parents or to childless tax filers (who currently are eligible for a maximum credit of less than 10 percent that available to families with two or more children).

2.2   History, Rules, and Goals

2.2.1   History and Goals

There have been a number of excellent studies of the history of the EITC, including Liebman (1998), Ventry (2000), Moffitt (2003, 2010), and Hotz and Scholz (2003). Our brief discussion here cannot do it justice, and readers are referred to those studies—on which we draw heavily—for more information.

The EITC grew out of the 1960s War on Poverty. As the welfare state grew, some—both supporters and critics—became concerned that a patchwork of means-tested antipoverty programs would both leave important holes and create perverse incentives that discouraged work and encouraged permanent dependency. The latter issue is familiar from debates over the Aid for Families with Dependent Children (AFDC) program, since replaced by Temporary Aid for Needy Families (TANF): because AFDC was aimed at nonworkers and benefits were generally reduced dollar-for-dollar for any earnings, recipients contemplating work would quickly realize that the effective wage—the amount by which their incomes would rise for each hour worked—was zero.

One solution was to target the program carefully at populations—for example, low-skill, single mothers—who could not be expected to work in any case (Akerlof 1978). But even in the target population many might be capable of finding jobs, and there would surely be those who needed help despite not being in one of the defined target groups. Moreover, as programs multiplied to serve many different needy populations, often with overlapping eligibility criteria, the disincentive problem sometimes got worse: those who participated in multiple programs could face extremely complex effective tax schedules, with many "cliffs" where marginal rates were well in excess of 100 percent. Average effective tax rates, while generally lower, were nevertheless quite high. A recipient subject to such a schedule, with most of her potential earnings subject to clawback as her benefits phased out, might reasonably decide to remain out of work even if she had other options.

One resolution to this problem might have been to try to improve program "tagging," while accepting that no tagging system would be perfect and that any means-tested program would have some distortionary effect. But this would have been inconsistent with a longstanding moral aversion in America to welfare dependency and commitment to work as the route out of poverty. President Johnson's 1964 Economic Report argued that while it would be possible to alleviate poverty solely through cash aid to the less fortunate, "this 'solution' would leave untouched most of the roots of poverty. . . . It will be far better, even if more difficult, to equip and permit the poor of the Nation to produce and earn" their way out of poverty (Council of Economic Advisers 1964).

This made it attractive to find an antipoverty program that would limit work disincentives. Leading economists of the period supported a negative income tax (NIT) on this basis (see, e.g., Friedman 1962; Lampman 1965; Tobin 1966). An NIT would have provided a baseline transfer to each eligible recipient, even if they did not work, that would be reduced at less than a one-for-one rate with recipients' earnings. Because the effective tax rate under an NIT is less than 100 percent, recipients would see higher total incomes if they worked than if they did not, and would thus face modest incentives to work, albeit weaker than in the absence of any program. Friedman (1962) was a prominent proponent of an NIT, advocating that it should be made universal and should replace the grab bag of other antipoverty programs.[2] President Nixon proposed an NIT, the Family Assistance Plan (FAP), in 1969.

But NITs have two important drawbacks. First, they are extremely expen-

2. Another prominent proposal at the time was a "guaranteed annual income," or GAI. To modern eyes, the distinction between a universal NIT and a GAI is not entirely clear. Although GAIs nominally did not phase out, someone would have to pay positive taxes to fund them, and the associated marginal tax rates do not appear economically different than a phase-out of the NIT. Nevertheless, NIT proponents—in particular Friedman (2013)—were hostile to GAIs (Ventry 2000, fn. 17).

sive, with many benefits going to nonemployed individuals who might not face great need (e.g., to early retirees or those in school). Second, like welfare they permit some individuals to withdraw voluntarily from work in order to live on the dole. Thus, while the disincentive to enter the labor market is smaller than with traditional welfare, for many observers even an NIT would not do enough to promote work. Indeed, it is not necessarily the case that an NIT leads to more labor supply than does a traditional welfare program with a 100 percent phase-out rate: while the NIT effective tax rate is lower, this necessarily means that the phase-out range reaches higher into the income distribution, and the net effect is theoretically ambiguous. Moreover, where traditional welfare had rules designed to require work from those who were able, the NIT can be seen as legitimizing the choice not to work. Nixon's FAP proposal attempted to address this by requiring that adults in recipient families register at employment offices for work, training, or vocational rehabilitation, and also provided expanded day care and transportation services to make it easier to combine work with child-rearing. However, this did not satisfy critics.

Senator Russell Long (D-LA) was a leader of the anti-FAP faction. In 1970 he proposed a "workfare" program as an alternative to FAP. Long's proposal would have provided a small guaranteed income to those judged unemployable (e.g., the blind, disabled, aged, and mothers of very young children). Those judged employable would have been eligible for work and training opportunities, wage subsidies, and even income maintenance payments when work was unavailable.

Long continued to attach versions of his proposal to various legislative vehicles. The 1972 iteration of his proposal closely resembled the modern EITC. Nonworkers would have received nothing, but workers would have seen their earnings matched at a 10 percent rate, up to a maximum match of $400 ($2,229 in 2013 dollars) for a worker earning $4,000 per year. This match was explicitly designed to offset Social Security payroll taxes, then rising quickly and seen as quite regressive. (The subsidy rate, however, would have been substantially higher than the payroll tax rate, then under 6 percent.) For those with earnings above $4,000, the subsidy would have been taxed away at $0.25 per additional dollar earned, reaching zero for earnings above $5,600. This was a much lower phase-out rate—and thus a longer phase-out range—than the 50 percent rate in most NIT proposals.

Long's work bonus was finally enacted in 1975, with his originally proposed subsidy rate of 10 percent and $400 maximum credit but with a lower, 10 percent phase-out rate that stretched the eligibility range up to an annual income of $8,000. Only families with children were eligible, and the program was initially authorized for only one year. Importantly, it was enacted as part of the Tax Reduction Act of 1975, largely concerned with tax cuts as a means of providing economic stimulus, not as part of a broad-based reform of the welfare state. Thus, where NIT proponents had advocated it as a replacement for other transfer programs, the EITC was enacted as a supplement to the existing constellation of programs.

Long's temporary program was reauthorized, and was made permanent in 1978. That year, the maximum credit was increased to $500, the phase-out rate was increased slightly, and the credit schedule was modified to add a "plateau" range. Eligible families with earnings between $5,000 and $6,000 received the maximum credit of $500. The credit was reduced by 12.5 cents for every dollar of earnings above $6,000, finally disappearing when earnings reached $10,000. Another important change was the introduction of an "advance payment" option, whereby workers who signed up could receive their credit as small payments in each paycheck rather than as a lump-sum tax refund in the spring. As we discuss below, however, this option was never much used, despite substantial marketing efforts in the 1990s, and was discontinued in 2011.

The program was largely stable between 1978 and 1986, but because it was not indexed to inflation the real value of the maximum credit fell by 18.2 percent. The Tax Reform Act of 1986 returned the credit to the same real value as in 1975 and provided for inflation indexing going forward. The phase-in rate was also increased, to 14 percent, while the phase-out rate was cut to its original level of 10 percent. The plateau was also dramatically widened in 1988, extending to $9,840. Because the phase-out rate was unchanged, this meant that credits were available all the way up to $18,576 in annual earnings ($36,579 in 2013 dollars).

The next big change came in 1990, when the credit was used to offset undesirable distributional consequences of other components of the 1990 tax bill. The maximum credit was expanded by $646, phased in over three years; phase-in and phase-out rates were both increased; and a separate, more generous schedule was introduced for families with two or more children. The latter has been a permanent feature ever since.

Perhaps the most notable change in the EITC's history came as part of the 1993 budget. In his first State of the Union address, President Clinton announced a principle that full-time work at the minimum wage should pay enough to keep the family income, inclusive of the EITC and food stamps but net of payroll taxes, above the poverty line. To help achieve this, the EITC was increased sharply, particularly for families with two or more children for whom the credit was roughly doubled. By 1996, the phase-in rate was 40 percent (34 percent for families with only one child), the maximum credit was over $3,500 ($2,150 for smaller families; these are $5,197 and $3,192, respectively, in 2013 dollars), and families with incomes as high as $28,500 ($42,315 in 2013 dollars) could receive credits.

The 1993 budget also included a conceptually important change in the program, introducing a credit schedule for families without children. The maximum credit was only $481 (in 2013 dollars), about 15 percent of the one-child maximum, and the credit phased out at a very low income (just over $14,000 in current dollars). Another conceptually important change was introduced in 2002, when separate (though not wildly different) schedules were introduced for married couples than for single parents. As we discuss below, further modifications along these lines are at the center of current discussions about EITC reform.

The final set of changes to date came with the American Recovery and Reinvestment Act (ARRA) of 2009. Maximum credits were increased slightly; a new, more generous schedule was introduced for families with three or more children; and the married couple schedule was extended substantially in an effort to reduce marriage penalties for two-earner couples. All of these were made as temporary changes, originally set to expire in 2010, but since extended to 2017.

Figure 2.1 provides one illustration of the growth of the program. It shows the EITC schedule for a single parent with two qualifying children in 1979, 1993, 1996, and 2014, with both incomes and credits converted to real 2013 dollars. The real maximum value of the credit was 52 percent higher in 1993 than in 1979, though in 1993 the maximum credit was attained with a lower real income and the phase-out range extended to a higher level. By 1996, the real value of the credit had more than doubled, and the maximum income at which the credit could be received had risen further still. One implication

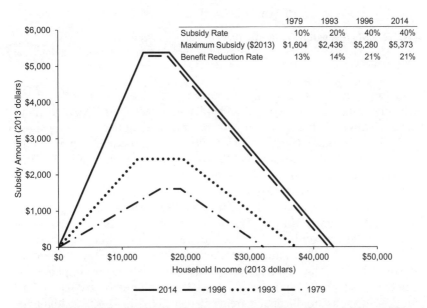

	1979	1993	1996	2014
Subsidy Rate	10%	20%	40%	40%
Maximum Subsidy ($2013)	$1,604	$2,436	$5,280	$5,373
Benefit Reduction Rate	13%	14%	21%	21%

Fig. 2.1   The EITC schedule for single parents with two qualifying children (1979, 1993, 1996, and 2014)

Sources: US Government Publishing Office (2004); Internal Revenue Service and US Department of the Treasury (2014).

Notes: Calculations assume no unearned income.

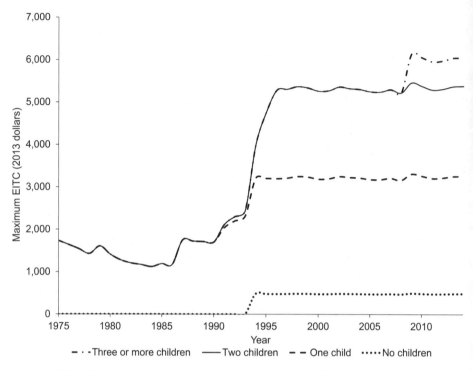

Fig. 2.2   Maximum real credit over time, by number of children
Sources: US Government Publishing Office (2004); Internal Revenue Service Publication no. 596 (various years).

is that marginal tax rates for most recipients—the slope of the sides of the schedule trapezoids—roughly doubled between 1993 and 1996, becoming more negative for those with very low incomes and more positive for those with higher incomes. Changes since 1996—at least for single parent families with two children, as depicted here—have been minimal, and the 2014 schedule is quite similar to that in 1996.

Figure 2.2 provides another look at the program's history. It again shows that the 1993 expansion (phased in through 1996) was by far the most dramatic in the program's history. We can also see here substantial expansions in 1986, 1990, and (only for families with three or more children) 2009.

Not visible in either figure are changes in the married-couple schedules starting in 2002. The income levels at which the credit begins to phase out and then at which it disappears were $1,000 higher for married couples than for head-of-household (single parent) filers in 2002–2004, $2,000 higher in 2005–2007, $3,000 higher in 2008, and $5,000 higher in 2009, rising with inflation since then.

The Taxpayer Relief Act of 1997 introduced a new program, the Child Tax Credit (CTC). It is structurally similar to the EITC, though it targets higher-income families: as of 2013, it is available to families with incomes as high as $130,000, with maximum credits available at incomes as high as $110,000. The maximum credit has been $1,000 (in nominal dollars) since 2003. Although this credit is only a fraction of the EITC, the CTC's broader reach means that total expenditures are comparable ($55 billion for the CTC vs. $64 billion for the EITC in 2012).

The CTC, unlike the EITC, is not fully refundable. For many recipients, this is not relevant—they earn enough to face meaningful income tax liabilities, and the CTC merely offsets those. But for lower-income families affected by the EITC, income tax liabilities are low and the refundability of the credit is key to its value. The refundable portion of the CTC is known as the Additional Child Tax Credit, and is limited to 15 percent of earned income less a fixed threshold. This threshold was initially set at a relatively high level, preventing most low-income families from receiving meaningful refunds via the CTC. But in 2009, ARRA reduced the threshold to $3,000. This allowed more taxpayers to claim the additional child tax credit and increased the amount of refundable credits, making the schedule similar to the EITC's. Like the ARRA EITC provisions, the reduced CTC threshold was originally set to expire at the end of 2010, but has since been extended through 2017.

Figure 2.3 shows the combined schedules of the EITC and CTC by fam-

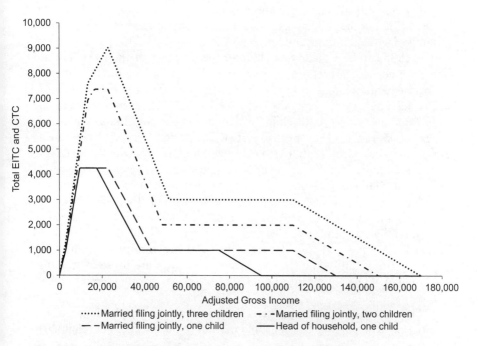

Fig. 2.3   Combined EITC and Child Tax Credit schedules, 2013

Sources: US Government Publishing Office (2011); Internal Revenue Service (2013).

Notes: Figure includes only the refundable portion of the Child Tax Credit. Calculations assume that adjusted gross income equals earned income.

ily type, counting only the refundable portion of the CTC for low-income families. (The credit calculations assume that families have zero unearned income or exclusions from adjusted gross income.) It shows that the CTC's schedule has the same trapezoidal structure as the EITC, but that it extends much farther into the income distribution.

2.2.2 Rules

Eligibility

Eligibility for the EITC is based on the family structure and the family's earnings and income.

The primary family structure criterion is the presence of "qualifying" children in the household. A qualifying child must be younger than nineteen (twenty-four if a full-time student, or any age if totally disabled); the child, grandchild, or foster child of the tax filer or his or her sibling; and a resident of the household for at least half of the tax year.[3] When the EITC was introduced, it was available only to families with qualifying children. A more generous credit for families with two or more qualifying children was added in 1991, and a yet more generous credit for those with three or more children was added in 2009 (though the latter is currently set to expire in 2017). Since 1994, families without qualifying children can be eligible for the credit, but the childless credit remains much less generous than that for families with qualifying children (figure 2.2).

A child can be a qualifying child for the purposes of the EITC but not for the dependent exemption, and vice versa, as the two impose different requirements relating to residency and support. Most importantly, noncustodial parents are generally ineligible for the EITC, even if they provide substantial support to the child, but can in some circumstances claim children as dependents. (Recent changes to the dependency criteria have reduced noncustodial parents' ability to claim children as dependents, narrowing but not eliminating the discrepancy.) Some states have experimented with noncustodial parent credits; we discuss these in section 2.6.

The second eligibility requirement is earned income. To qualify for a non-zero credit, this must be positive, and must be below a threshold that varies with family size (and, recently, with filing status). In 2014, this threshold was $48,378 per year for a family of two children with two parents filing jointly. Importantly, the relevant income measures are those for the tax-filing unit. Thus, for married couples both spouses' earnings count toward the threshold.

There are also secondary criteria that are less central to the design of the program. The parents' tax filing and marital status affects EITC eligibility:

---

3. As with many aspects of tax rules, there are exceptions and qualifications that apply to unusual cases. We do not attempt to be comprehensive.

non-filers and married couples who file separately cannot claim the EITC, and since 2002 married couples who file jointly are subject to a somewhat more generous credit than are head-of-household (unmarried) filers.

Finally, families with unearned income (e.g., interest or dividends) can be ineligible for the EITC, even if earnings are below the threshold. Families with total income from interest, rent, dividends, capital gains, and other "passive" sources above $3,300 are ineligible for the credit, as are those with adjusted gross income ([AGI]—roughly equal to total taxable income) above the earned income threshold.

Claiming

Obtaining the credit requires filing a tax return. Many families must do so anyway, so for these the claiming requirement is not burdensome. Some EITC recipients with low incomes, however, might not otherwise be required to file returns.

For families with positive tax liabilities from the regular income tax or the self-employment tax, the EITC is used to offset these liabilities. When the EITC exceeds other liabilities, however, it is refundable. Over 85 percent of EITC claimants receive all or part of their credit as a refund, and a similar proportion of credit dollars are refunded (IRS 2014g).

The portion of the EITC in excess of tax liabilities is distributed as a lump sum following the filing of the family's tax return just as if withholding was set too high. Not surprisingly, EITC recipients tend to file their returns earlier than do other families, and the majority of EITC refunds are distributed in February. The IRS typically issues refunds within a few weeks.

A substantial majority of EITC claimants use third-party tax preparers to file their tax returns (Chetty, Friedman, and Saez 2013; Greenstein and Wancheck 2011). Some receive assistance from nonprofit tax preparation services such as the Volunteer Income Tax Assistance (VITA) program, though many use for-profit services, of which H&R Block is perhaps the best known. The EITC has supported rapid growth in for-profit tax preparation services in low-income neighborhoods. These services typically charge modest fees for preparing returns, but in the past have made much of their revenue from expensive "refund anticipation loans" (RALs), originated by the tax preparer or by an affiliated bank, that provide the tax refund (including the refundable EITC) immediately upon filing the return. These speed access to the refund by only a few weeks, and often carry usurious effective annual interest rates.

The IRS estimates that 15 million EITC recipients used paid tax preparers in 2013, and one study estimates total tax preparation fees at $2.75 billion (IRS SPEC 2014; Wu 2014). Fees and interest for RALs and other forms of loans against returns amounted to perhaps $500 million more (IRS SPEC 2014; Wu 2014). Combining these, fees accounted for about 5 percent of total EITC expenditures. This is a substantial reduction from years past, due largely to a sharp reduction in RALs since 2007 (IRS SPEC 2014; Wu 2014); this in turn is due in large part to bank exit from the RAL market following a crackdown by bank regulators. To put EITC fees in context, 5 percent is much smaller than the administrative share of costs for traditional transfer programs, implying that a larger share of EITC expenditures reach recipients, though the EITC is unusual in that much of the administrative cost is borne by recipients rather than by the government.

Since 2012, no traditional bank has offered RALs. Although RALs are still available from some nonbank lenders (such as tax preparation firms), their prevalence has fallen by a factor of ten or more (IRS SPEC 2014; Wu 2014). They have been replaced by an alternative product, the refund anticipation check (RAC), which facilitates access to refunds for recipients without checking accounts at a cost about half of that of an RAL.

From 1979 to 2010, the IRS offered an alternative mechanism for delivering the credit, known as the "Advance EIC." Recipients who expected to receive an EITC could sign up by submitting an IRS form to their employer. Once this form was filed, the EITC would appear as credits (negative deductions) on the worker's weekly, biweekly, or monthly paycheck. The Advance EIC thus treated the EITC like any other form of taxes, adjusting the withholding rate to match the expected end-of-year tax liability, though the required withholding rate was generally negative, yielding supplements to each paycheck. As with other withholding, it amounted to an interest-free loan against the eventual return. The Advance EIC was never used by more than a few percent of EITC recipients (GAO 2007), and was eliminated beginning in tax year 2011. We discuss potential explanations for the unpopularity of the Advance EIC in section 2.5.2.

Credit Schedules

Table 2.1 shows the EITC schedule over time, for selected years. As illustrated in figure 2.1, the schedule consists of three segments: a "phase-in" range, over which the credit increases in proportion to the amount earned (so the marginal tax rate, equal to minus one times the slope of the schedule, is negative); a "plateau," where the maximum credit is paid (so the marginal tax rate is zero); and a "phase-out" range, where the credit is reduced in proportion to the difference between earnings and the end of the plateau range (so the marginal tax rate is positive). The phase-out range ends at the point where the credit is reduced to zero; families with earnings above that amount are not eligible for the credit.

The schedule is slightly more complex for families with unearned income. When earnings place the family in the plateau or phase-out ranges and adjusted gross income (including unearned income) exceeds earned income, the credit is based on the latter.

The Child Tax Credit (CTC) has a similar form, though eligibility for the CTC depends on only adjusted gross income (AGI), not on earnings, and the credit is not refundable unless earnings exceed a threshold (set at

Table 2.1 **Earned Income Tax Credit parameters, 1975–2015 (selected years), in 2013 dollars**

Calendar year	Credit rate (percent)	Minimum income for maximum credit	Maximum credit	Phase-out rate (percent)	Phase-out range[a] Beginning income	Ending income
2015[b]						
No children	7.65	6,580	503	7.65	8,240	14,820
One child	34.00	9,880	3,359	15.98	18,110	39,131
Two children	40.00	13,870	5,548	21.06	18,110	44,454
Three children	45.00	13,870	6,242	21.06	18,110	47,747
2014[b]						
No children	7.65	6,480	496	7.65	8,110	14,590
One child	34.00	9,720	3,305	15.98	17,830	38,511
Two children	40.00	13,650	5,460	21.06	17,830	43,756
Three children	45.00	13,650	6,143	21.06	17,830	46,997
2009						
No children	8.31	6,483	496	7.65	8,111	14,594
One child	36.92	9,718	3,304	15.98	17,830	38,508
Two children	43.43	13,649	5,460	21.06	17,830	43,755
Three children	48.86	13,649	6,143	21.06	17,830	46,995
2003[a]						
No children	9.69	6,318	484	7.65	7,900	14,218
One child	43.05	9,483	3,225	15.98	17,383	37,559
Two children	50.64	13,306	5,323	21.06	17,383	42,656
1996						
No children	7.65	6,266	480	7.65	7,839	14,105
One child	34.00	9,398	3,195	15.98	17,238	37,235
Two children	40.00	13,199	5,280	21.06	17,238	42,308
1995						
No children	7.65	6,267	480	7.65	7,842	14,109
One child	34.00	9,416	3,201	15.98	17,258	37,291
Two children	36.00	13,207	4,754	20.22	17,258	40,772
1994						
No children	7.65	6,288	481	7.65	7,860	14,147
One child	26.30	12,182	3,204	15.98	17,291	37,341
Two children	30.00	13,243	3,974	17.68	17,291	39,763
1993						
One child	18.50	12,494	2,312	13.21	19,668	37,160
Two children	19.50	12,494	2,436	13.93	19,668	37,160
1992						
One child	17.60	12,486	2,198	12.57	19,659	37,144
Two children	18.40	12,486	2,298	13.14	19,659	37,144
1991						
One child	16.70	12,212	2,039	11.93	19,242	36,346
Two children	17.30	12,212	2,112	12.36	19,242	36,346
1990	14.00	12,138	1,699	10	19,125	36,118
1989	14.00	6,500	910	10	10,240	19,340
1988	14.00	6,240	874	10	9,840	18,576
1987	14.00	12,468	1,745	10	14,191	31,646
1985–86	11.00	10,726	1,180	12.22	13,944	23,598
1979–84	10.00	12,995	1,299	12.5	15,594	25,990
1975–78	10.00	15,841	1,584	10	15,841	31,683

[a]Beginning in 2002, the values of the beginning and ending points of the phase-out range were increased for married taxpayers filing jointly. The values for these taxpayers were $1,000 higher than the listed values from 2002 to 2004, $2,000 higher from 2005 to 2007, $3,000 higher in 2008, $5,000 higher in 2009, $5,010 higher in 2010, $5,080 higher in 2011, $5,210 higher in 2012, $5,340 higher in 2013, $5,430 higher in 2014, and $5,520 higher in 2015.
[b]Nominal dollars for 2014 and 2015.

$3,000 since 2009). The CTC reaches much farther into the income distribution, however: where families with earnings above $51,567 are ineligible for the EITC, three-children, two-parent families can receive the CTC with incomes as high as $165,000 (figure 2.3).

State EICs

A number of states have incorporated Earned Income Credits into their own income tax systems. Typically, these are refundable (or sometimes nonrefundable) credits equal to a specified percentage of the tax filer's federal EITC. As of 2014, twenty-four states and the District of Columbia had credits, ranging from 4 percent (for a family with one child in Wisconsin) to 40 percent (in the District of Columbia) of the federal credit (IRS 2014d). These states are listed in table 2.2. New York City and Montgomery County, Maryland, have also adopted substate credits.

Because state and local credits are (nearly always) specified as shares of the federal credit, recipients face even more negative marginal tax rates over the phase-in portion of the schedule and even larger positive rates over the phase-out than are produced by the federal schedule alone.

A few states have experimented with credits that go beyond a partial match of the federal credit. In particular, New York State and Washington, DC have also introduced EITCs for noncustodial parents, who are not generally eligible for the federal credit.

Interactions

The EITC's administration through the tax code, as a function of earned income, means that EITC eligibility is not directly affected by participation in most other programs. One exception is unemployment insurance benefits: these are not counted as earned income but do count toward adjusted gross income (AGI), and so can reduce a family's credit or even make a family ineligible for the credit.

Most federal means-tested benefit programs do not count EITC refunds as income, even when (before 2011) the refund is received as negative paycheck deductions. Programs in this category include Supplemental Security Income (SSI), Medicaid, the Supplemental Nutritional Assistance Program ([SNAP], formerly known as food stamps), Veteran's benefits, Head Start, and new benefits under the Affordable Care Act. However, individual states decide whether the EITC counts as income in their TANF programs (only Connecticut does, and only for advance EITC), LIHEAP, child-care subsidies, and all state-funded, means-tested benefit programs.

Even when the EITC payment does not count as income, it can still count against asset limits if it is saved rather than spent immediately, though there is typically a grace period (of around nine to twelve months) after receipt. Following the 2008 Farm Bill, tax refunds that are deposited in qualified retirement plans and education savings accounts do not count as assets in determining SNAP eligibility. Effectively, then, EITC recipients are encour-

Table 2.2   **State Earned Income Tax Credits, tax year 2014**

State	Percentage of federal credit
Refundable tax credits	
Colorado	10
Connecticut	30
District of Columbia	40
Illinois	10
Indiana	9
Iowa	14
Kansas	18
Louisiana	3.5
Maryland	25*
Massachusetts	15
Michigan	6
Minnesota	Average 33
Nebraska	10
New Jersey	20
New Mexico	10
New York	30
Oklahoma	5
Oregon	6
Vermont	32
Wisconsin	4 (one child); 11 (two children); 34 (three children)
Nonrefundable tax credits	
Delaware	20
Maine	5
Ohio	5
Virginia	20
Partially refundable tax credits	
Rhode Island	25
City and county tax credits (refundable)	
New York City	5
Montgomery Cty (MD)	19

* Maryland offers a nonrefundable credit of up to 50 percent of federal EITC or a refundable credit of up to 25 percent of federal EITC.

Sources: Internal Revenue Service (2014b); Tax Credits for Working Families (2011); Stokan (2013).

aged either to deposit their refunds in tax-protected accounts—perhaps unlikely for low-income families—or to spend them quickly, rather than to set them aside as short- or medium-term savings against unanticipated shocks.

When EITC recipients participate in other programs as well—a particularly common situation since the recent recession (Nichols and Zedlewski 2011)—the total effective marginal tax rate (MTR) can be much different than the relatively simple schedule illustrated in figure 2.1. This can dramatically alter marginal incentives. Indeed, many authors (e.g., Moffitt 2003)

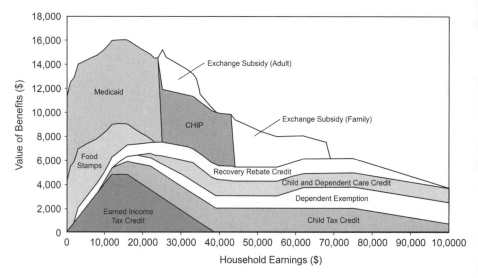

Fig. 2.4   Universally available tax and transfer benefits: single parent with two children in Colorado, 2008 (from Maag et al. 2012)

Source: Reproduced from Maag et al. (2012), figure 1. Reprinted with permission from the National Tax Journal. Tax and transfer rules are for 2008 with hypothetical exchange plans in 2014 added in. Health value estimates are based on Medicaid spending and insurance premiums as reported by the Kaiser Family Foundation.

have emphasized the possibility that the negative MTR associated with the EITC's phase-in region may serve to offset positive MTRs created by other programs.

Maag et al. (2012) calculate total effective marginal tax rates (due to taxes and benefit reductions) across a wide variety of programs. Figure 2.4 reproduces their figure 1, showing how the combined value of all universally available taxes and transfers varies with earnings for single parents with two children in Colorado. It is clear here that the EITC is only a small part of the overall picture. At the same time, the EITC phase-in, plateau, and phase-out regions are clearly visible even in the cumulative tax and transfer schedule (represented by the top line in the figure), mostly because the EITC phase-in region ends before the phase-out regions of the other programs really begin to affect net income.

Additional complexity comes from other taxes and nonuniversal programs, not included in figure 2.4. Most obviously, essentially all earners will pay payroll taxes on the first dollar earned. The combined tax rate for federal payroll taxes is 7.65 percent if only the worker's share is counted or 15.3 percent if the employer share is counted as well. The latter offsets just over one-third of the negative phase-in MTR for a two-child family. State payroll taxes (e.g., unemployment insurance taxes, levied on the employer) would add a bit more to this.

Maag et al. (2012) extend their analyses to include state income taxes and TANF, each of which varies by state, along with state rules for the universal programs (including, for example, variation in fair market rents, used for SNAP benefit calculations). When they do this, they find wide variation across states and families. For example, in Connecticut, moving from zero gross earnings to poverty-level gross earnings incurs an overall effective tax of 2.0 percent for a single parent of two who has Medicaid, but negative 10 percent for a single parent of two without Medicaid (but with ACA credits). The mean effective MTR, across states, is positive but small at low incomes, but many states have substantially negative effective MTRs while others have large positive rates. See also Hanson and Andrews (2009), who describe how effective tax rates on earnings due to benefit reductions depend on complex interactions across SNAP, SSI, and TANF, and on state policy choices regarding each of these programs. One implication is that for some families the EITC phase-in rate does serve to offset positive effective marginal tax rates (including benefit reduction rates) arising for other programs. But this holds only in some states, and only for families that participate in all possible programs. This is unusual. In more typical cases the net marginal tax rate is substantially negative in the EITC phase-in range.

Enforcement and Noncompliance

In theory, the EITC is much easier to enforce than are other transfer programs, simply because the IRS receives so much third-party reporting of relevant information (e.g., earnings). Indeed, the Department of the Treasury (Treasury Inspector General for Tax Administration 2011) estimates that EITC administrative costs are only about 1 percent of benefits provided, much less than for other programs (which can have administrative costs as high as 20 percent).

Noncompliance issues with the EITC center around three factors that are *not* covered by third-party information returns: claiming of the credit based on nonqualifying children, self-employment income, and filing status.

A qualifying child for the EITC must be younger than nineteen (or twenty-four, if a full-time student) or permanently and totally disabled, and must live with the taxpayer for more than half the year. The residency criterion differs from that used elsewhere in the tax code; for example, dependent exemptions are based on which parent provided financial support and not on where the child resides (though 2004 changes to dependency rules moved the two sets of criteria closer to harmony). As we discuss in section 2.5.2, a large share of EITC noncompliance occurs when a noncustodial parent claims the credit based on a child who does not qualify due to the residency test.

Another substantial portion of noncompliance appears to derive from the *over*statement of income among the self-employed, who gain more in additional EITC by increasing reported income to the end of the phase-in region than they lose through other tax obligations. A third category occurs when taxpayers claim the wrong filing status: a head-of-household return that claims the EITC becomes noncompliant if the IRS judges that it should have been filed as married-filing-separately.

As a result of noncompliance, a substantial amount of refundable credits are issued in error each year, which has led Congress to demand ever-increasing scrutiny of EITC recipients. It should be noted, though, that the rates of noncompliance and amounts of dollars paid in error are small relative to other segments of taxpayers. A reduction in tax liability due to misreporting receipts or expenses among a high-income, self-employed person who is well above the phase-out range of the EITC will usually dwarf the increase in a refundable credit amount issued to a low-income taxpayer who overreports net earnings from self-employment (IRS 2006). However, the former's reduction in tax liability is less salient to some Congressional observers than is the latter's increase in payment, though the impact on the federal budget is identical.

2.2.3   Comparison to Other Countries

The US EITC has parallels in programs in place in many other developed countries. One that is often discussed is the United Kingdom's Working Families Tax Credit (Blundell and Hoynes 2004). Like the EITC, it is available only to those who work. It does not have a phase-in negative marginal tax rate, however; rather, it is available only to those who meet minimum weekly hours requirements.

Enumerating the universe of EITC-like programs (often referred to as "in-work tax credits") is difficult, as similar tax structures can appear quite different depending on how the portions are labeled. (Consider, for example, the "program" consisting of the combination of payroll taxes, the EITC, and the TANF and food stamps benefit phase-out ranges.) Table 2.3 presents one effort to enumerate EITC-like programs in the Organisation for Economic Co-operation and Development (OECD). We restrict attention to programs that are generally available (so not limited to, for example, the long-term unemployed) and either refundable or small enough to be fully offset by other taxes. There is a great deal of heterogeneity here. The US program stands out as more generous than many and as having one of the largest phase-in rates.

2.3   Program Statistics

The numbers of EITC recipients and aggregate EITC outlays have both grown sharply since the program's introduction. Figure 2.5 shows these two series. There are notable spikes in 1988, 1991, 1994–1996, 2000, and 2009, each due to changes in the EITC schedule. A comparable series for CTC outlays is shown as well. Here, we see a sharp increase following 2003 tax law changes but relative stability since 2004.

Table 2.3   In-work tax credits in the OECD

Country	Target group	Maximum value (in 2010 PPP USD)	Max. phase-in rate (%)	Max. phase-out rate (%)	Maximum income for eligibility (percent of average wage)	Family structure criterion
Belgium	Individual	2,471	*	28	61	N
Canada	Families	1,377	25	15	57	N
Finland	Individual	3,923	51	5	240	N
Finland	Individual	714	5	1	223	N
France	Family	1,298	8	19	90	Y
Germany	Individual	573	10	10	23	N
Hungary	Individual	1,444	17	12	187	N
Ireland	Family	14,863***	**	60	97	Y
Italy	Individual	2,359	None	7	197	Y
Korea	Family	1,426	15	24	46	Y
Netherlands	Individual	1,752	12	1	Infinite	N
New Zealand	Family	2,080	**	20	186	Y
New Zealand	Individual	347	**	13	100	N
Slovak Republic	Individual	1,257	**	16	Infinite	Y
Spain	Individual	556	None	10	****	N
Sweden	Individual	2,241	32	None	Infinite	N
United Kingdom	Family	6,667	**	39	53	Y
United States	Family	5,038	40	21	88	Y

Sources: OECD (2011, 2014, 2015); Owens (2005); World Bank (2014).

Notes: Table includes only programs that are generally applicable, without restrictions to specific subpopulations (e.g., the long-term unemployed). Where schedules vary with family structure, values shown are for families with two children.

*Not applicable or phase-in rate is not well defined (e.g., due to interactions with other taxes).

**No phase-in rate but available only if meet minimum hours or earnings criterion.

***Calculated on the basis of one earner working nineteen hours per week at the minimum wage.

****Not reported by OECD.

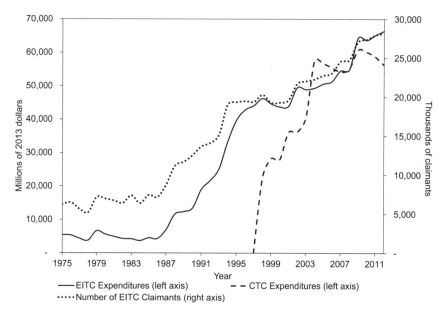

Fig. 2.5   Number of EITC recipients and total EITC and CTC outlays, by year
Sources: Internal Revenue Service (2014a, e); Tax Policy Center (2014, 2015).
Notes: Child Tax Credit expenditures include the Additional Child Tax Credit.

Figures 2.6 and 2.7 show the distribution of EITC and CTC recipient returns and expenditures by income level.[4] (Note that the two figures use somewhat different income bins, and that the CTC figure does not show counts of households due to the difficulty of counting unduplicated participation in the refundable and nonrefundable portions.) Clearly, the EITC pays its benefits to substantially lower-income tax units on average. Most EITC recipients have family incomes under $20,000, though the dollar-value-weighted distribution is somewhat higher as the very lowest income families are eligible for only small credits. By contrast, most CTC payments go to families with incomes above this point. Fully 8.8 percent of payments go to families with incomes above $100,000.

Most evidence on the demographic characteristics of EITC recipients comes from the Annual Social and Economic Supplement (ASEC) to the Current Population Survey (CPS). Table 2.4 shows the distribution of tax units across EITC schedule ranges in the 2012 CPS ASEC, by the characteristics of the tax filer and the filing unit. Not surprisingly, families without children are overwhelmingly unlikely to receive any EITC, and when they do the average amounts are small. Larger families are both more likely to

4. The IRS statistics treat the CTC and the Additional CTC (the refundable portion) as separate programs, so it is not possible to compute counts of unduplicated tax returns. Our estimates of expenditures combine the value of CTCs used to offset other taxes with the value of Additional CTC refunds.

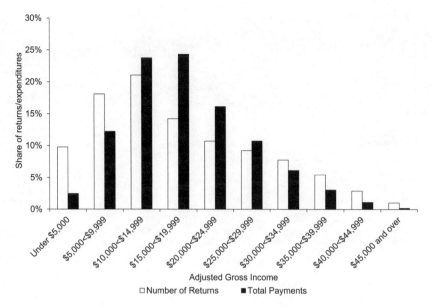

Fig. 2.6   Income distribution of EITC recipients, unweighted and weighted by payment received, 2012
Source: Internal Revenue Service (2014f).

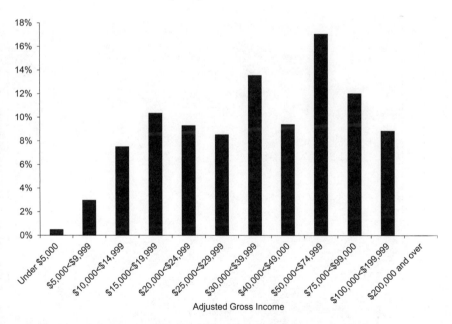

Fig. 2.7   Income distribution of CTC recipients, weighted by payment received, 2012
Source: Internal Revenue Service (2014h).

Note: Figure reflects the CTC-weighted income distribution, corresponding to the "total payments" series in figure 2.6.

Table 2.4 EITC eligibility by demographic characteristics

	Percent in each credit range					Mean EITC in each range ($1,000s)		
	Zero income, zero EITC	Phase-in	Plateau	Phase-out	Positive income, zero EITC	Phase-in	Plateau	Phase-out
All families	5.9	4.3	2.7	9.2	77.9	1.6	3.5	1.9
By number of children in family								
Zero	7.6	2.9	0.9	4.1	84.5	0.2	0.5	0.2
One	3.9	7.9	11.4	23.2	53.6	1.5	3.2	1.6
Two	2.8	7.6	4.8	19.9	65.0	3.0	5.2	2.7
Three or more	2.1	5.6	3.9	15.0	73.5	3.3	5.8	3.4
By family structure								
Single, no children	7.2	3.8	0.7	5.2	83.1	0.2	0.5	0.2
Single, with children	4.6	11.9	7.6	22.1	53.9	2.5	4.1	2.5
Married, no children	8.3	1.3	1.3	2.2	86.9	0.2	0.5	0.2
Married, with children	1.5	3.1	5.0	16.5	73.9	3.0	4.7	2.6
By imputed tax return type								
Joint, both < 65	1.9	2.3	3.8	10.0	82.0	2.3	3.9	2.4
Joint, one	9.0	2.5	3.6	4.3	80.6	0.7	1.3	1.0
Joint, both 65+	26.4	0.2	0.1	0.5	72.9	2.3	3.2	1.0
Head of household	3.1	19.9	11.8	38.2	27.1	2.6	4.2	2.5
Single	6.7	3.4	0.6	4.8	84.5	0.2	0.5	0.2
By race/ethnicity of primary taxpayer								
White only	6.9	3.0	1.7	6.6	81.8	1.3	3.1	1.7
Black only	5.3	7.8	3.9	13.3	69.6	1.7	3.6	1.9
Hispanic	3.1	6.9	6.3	17.8	65.8	2.0	3.9	2.1
Other	4.0	4.3	2.5	9.0	80.3	1.6	3.1	1.8
By education of primary taxpayer								
Less than HS	11.0	10.6	7.3	18.7	52.4	1.8	4.0	2.1
HS graduate	8.2	5.3	3.7	11.5	71.4	1.5	3.5	1.9
Some college	5.1	4.4	2.4	9.7	78.5	1.6	3.4	1.9
BA or better	3.4	1.5	0.9	4.1	90.0	1.2	2.8	1.5
By age of primary taxpayer								
Age 15–29	1.2	5.6	3.8	8.0	81.5	1.7	3.4	1.9
Age 30–44	1.5	6.0	3.9	15.8	72.9	1.9	4.3	2.2
Age 45–59	2.3	3.7	2.1	8.7	83.2	1.1	2.8	1.5
Age 60–74	14.4	1.6	1.1	3.0	79.8	0.6	1.4	0.6
Age 75 plus	42.1	0.2	0.3	0.6	56.9	1.7	1.8	0.9

Source: Authors' analysis of the 2012 CPS ASEC.

Table 2.5   **Number of EITC claims and dollars spent, IRS data versus Current Population Survey (2011)**

Number of qualifying children	IRS		CPS		CPS/IRS (%)	
	Returns (millions)	Dollars (millions)	Returns (millions)	Dollars (millions)	Returns	Dollars
0	6.886	1,821	6.528	1,672	94.8	91.8
1	10.094	22,201	5.357	10,253	53.1	46.2
2	7.498	26,010	5.166	15,557	68.9	59.8
3+	3.433	12,874	4.050	14,778	118.0	114.8
All	27.912	62,906	21.101	42,260	75.6	67.2

Source: http://www.irs.gov/uac/SOI-Tax-Stats-Individual-Income-Tax-Returns and authors' calculations using CPS ASEC (March 2012) data.

receive the credit and receive larger credits when they do. Tax filers who are nonwhite, who have less education, and who are of child-rearing age are all overrepresented among EITC recipients.

An important caveat to these data—and to all CPS-based analyses of EITC recipients—is that the CPS does not survey respondents about their EITC receipt but rather imputes it based on the family structure and self-reported annual income. This may lead to errors: in some cases, the CPS will impute the credit to families that are ineligible or that do not claim the credit, and in other cases the CPS will fail to assign the credit to a family that in fact receives it. The dimensions of these potential errors are not well understood, despite the large amount of EITC research that depends on CPS imputations of credit participation.

Table 2.5 presents aggregate comparisons. We show estimates of the number of tax returns and the total credit received by families with different numbers of children, first using IRS records and then using the CPS. The CPS yields only about three-quarters as many EITC recipient families as are seen in the tax return data, and only about two-thirds as much spending. Relative undercounts in the CPS are concentrated among one and two child families; families with three or more children are overcounted in the CPS, while those with zero children are roughly comparable between the two sources. It is not clear, however, whether discrepancies reflect misclassification of families or misreporting of income in the CPS, or overclaiming of the credit on tax returns.

To shed further light on the limits of the CPS imputation, we turn to tabulations of CPS data, linked at the tax-unit level to actual tax returns (Jones 2015).[5] Columns (2) and (3) of table 2.6 estimate the characteristics of

5. We are extremely grateful to Margaret Jones of the Census Bureau for providing these tabulations. They are based on 75,963 tax return records and 115,281 W-2 records matched to 143,099 CPS records, covering about 95 percent of taxpayers (weighted). The CPS records with imputed earnings (22 percent) or no linkage possible (7 percent) are excluded.

Table 2.6   **Concordance between EITC simulations based on tax return income and CPS income**

	Distribution of families (column %)			Probability elig. in CPS, if elig. in IRS	Probability elig. in IRS, if elig. in CPS
	All	EITC elig. (CPS)	EITC elig. (IRS)		
All households	100	100	100		
By number of children in family					
Zero	65.8	32.2	26.0	42.7	32.9
One	8.9	23.6	34.6	57.9	82.8
Two	12.2	24.4	26.4	62.9	87.4
Three or more	13.1	19.8	13.0	57.4	85.4
By imputed tax return type					
Joint, both < 65	33.9	33.9	28.6	42.0	75.5
Joint, one or both 65+	8.4	2.0	1.5	40.5	53.4
Head of household	8.6	37.5	45.4	67.8	86.3
Single	49.1	26.6	24.5	48.4	57.1
By race/ethnicity of primary taxpayer					
White only	66.5	46.4	45.5	53.6	61.4
Black only	11.6	18.0	19.3	60.6	69.4
Hispanic	14.9	28.8	28.2	54.1	60.1
Other	7.0	6.8	7.0	54.9	57.4
By education of primary taxpayer					
Less than HS	8.8	20.0	18.6	51.9	59.1
HS graduate	27.7	35.2	35.5	53.1	61.0
Some college	31.2	31.8	32.2	60.8	65.9
BA or better	32.3	13.1	13.7	52.0	60.4
By age of primary taxpayer					
Age 15–29	23.0	24.7	27.6	51.9	64.7
Age 30–44	28.0	44.6	43.1	61.1	65.4
Age 45–59	27.7	25.0	23.8	51.4	58.0
Age 60+	21.4	5.8	5.5	41.7	45.8
By annual weeks worked					
0–25	24.9	27.8	25.7	38.3	43.5
26–49	11.6	18.1	16.7	67.4	69.8
50–52	63.6	54.2	57.5	59.1	69.8
By usual hours per week (if worked)					
0–19	5.2	19.5	34.6	48.0	51.4
20–34	14.8	22.2	16.8	68.3	69.8
35+	80.0	58.3	48.5	55.8	68.9
By hourly wage of primary taxpayer (if worked)					
< $10/hour	22.0	50.2	58.0	53.5	56.1
$10–15/hr.	21.5	28.6	21.4	61.8	75.2
$15–20/hr.	16.3	13.8	11.7	61.2	73.5
$20+/hr.	40.2	7.4	8.9	42.5	66.9

Source: Authors' analysis of 2012 CPS ASEC and Jones (2015).

Notes: Columns (1)–(2) from CPS. Column (3) is based on matched CPS-IRS data, and uses Form 1040 income measures in place of the CPS measures. Column (4) shows the share of tax units that appear EITC eligible when IRS data are used who are also eligible when CPS data are used, while column (5) shows the converse. The IRS simulations are based on 75,963 tax return records and 115,281 W-2 records matched to 143,099 CPS records, covering about 95 percent of taxpayers (weighted). The CPS records with imputed earnings (22 percent) or no linkage possible (7 percent) are excluded.

EITC-eligible taxpayers, first using the CPS income measures to impute eligibility and then repeating the imputation using tax values. Characteristics of all tax units are shown in column (1) for comparison. In these columns, entries represent column percentages within each type of characteristic.

Columns (4) and (5) of table 2.6 present another type of comparison. In column (4), we show the likelihood that a tax unit who is eligible for the EITC using the tax values will also appear to be eligible when CPS values are used, while column (5) presents the converse. The low probabilities in columns (4) and (5) may raise questions about the validity of CPS imputations, but the same probabilities seem relatively high when we take into account the high prevalence of discrepancies in reported and matched administrative data on earnings in most surveys (Nichols, Smith, and Wheaton 2011; Cristia and Schwabish 2009). The consistency of EITC imputations based on reported or matched earnings are also high relative to comparisons of reported and matched data on transfer income (e.g., Meyer, Mok, and Sullivan 2015; Meyer and Mittag 2014). Nevertheless, the low concordance of survey and administrative measures of EITC eligibility are important to bear in mind when assessing the validity of studies based on a survey measure of EITC eligibility or receipt. Fortunately, although individual-level concordance between the two data sources is quite imperfect, columns (2)–(3) suggest that analyses of the average characteristics of EITC recipients are not likely to be affected dramatically by this.

2.4   Review of Issues Surrounding the Program

In this section, we review a number of issues related to the program. We focus on issues that might arise in theory, assuming optimizing agents with full information and the ability to choose labor supply continuously with a fixed wage, and use these to discuss potential rationales for the program's structure. The assumptions are obviously unrealistic. Section 2.5 discusses the empirical evidence regarding many of the predicted impacts; while many have support in the data, for others—particularly those regarding changes in the hours of work of those who are participating in any case—the evidence is weaker.

2.4.1   Labor Supply Incentives

As noted above, the EITC's treatment of nonworkers is an important source of its popularity among politicians and policymakers, for two related reasons: credits go to poor workers and not to poor (unmarried) nonworkers who can be demonized as "takers," and the credit does not penalize work the way that more traditional programs often do. But labor supply disincentives can only be shifted around, not totally avoided, in means-tested transfers, and the incentives created by the EITC are complex. The EITC's structure can be expected to encourage labor force participation among single parents, but to discourage it for many would-be secondary earners in married couples. Among workers, some face incentives to work more, while many more face incentives to work less. We consider each of these incentives in turn.[6]

We begin with the case of a single parent faced with a decision whether to work at all. If she does not work, she will not receive an EITC (though she may receive TANF, food stamps, or other transfers). If she does, and if her earnings are less than $38,511 per year (for a one-child family), she will receive a positive EITC. This will offset other taxes if any are owed, and will be refunded if they are not. Clearly, the EITC tilts this decision in favor of working. For an individual whose potential earnings are below the end of the phase-in range, the effective negative tax rate equals the full EITC phase-in rate (net of rates imposed by other taxes or transfers), so the impact on the return to work is large.

For married couples, the incentives can go the other direction. Consider a sequential labor supply decision, where one spouse chooses his/her labor supply before the other. If the primary earner will earn enough to take the family out of the phase-in range on his own, then the second mover can only reduce the family's credit by working, and the EITC thus reduces net returns to work. Importantly, the effective positive tax rate here is smaller in magnitude than the negative rate faced by single parents: it can never be bigger than the EITC phase-out rate (again, adjusted to account for other taxes and transfers), and will often be much smaller.

At the intensive margin—the choice of the number of hours to work per week or the number of weeks to work per year—incentives depend on where in the schedule the family falls. Workers in families on the phase-in range face incentives to work more, while those in the phase-out range (and even some who would earn slightly above the eligibility threshold in the absence of the credit) are encouraged to work less in order to obtain a larger EITC payment. One might also expect negative, albeit smaller, effects in the plateau region, where there is no substitution effect but income effects will generally lead to less work.

As this makes clear, there is really only one unambiguous pro-work incentive in the EITC: single parents are encouraged to work at least a bit each year rather than to remain out of the labor force. This is perhaps not surprising, as it is exactly this intended response that motivated the design of the program. But other groups face much more complex incentives.

This discussion focuses on static labor supply decisions. There are interesting dynamic effects as well, deriving from the EITC's dependence on calendar year earnings. Sole earners face incentives to spread their work out across as many calendar years as possible, while secondary earners can face an opposite incentive to alternate years in and out of the labor force rather

6. Our discussion is informal. See Hotz and Scholz (2003) for a more formal treatment.

than working part time but consistently. This requires a perhaps unrealistic level of knowledge of the tax code and ability to time one's employment. Slightly more realistically, if individuals are not able to perfectly forecast their earnings within a calendar year, they can face incentives either to raise labor supply during the autumn (if they are still in the phase-in range) or to reduce it (if they have reached the phase-out range).

In the longer run, the EITC—like any means-tested transfer or progressive tax schedule—reduces the return to human capital. The reason is simple: an initial human capital investment decision depends on anticipated future income if one does or does not make the investment. The EITC is likely to have more value if the investment is not made, as earnings in that case will be lower and thus future EITC payments will be larger. The existence of the program thus reduces the net return to education, and could in theory reduce investment. Similar considerations suggest a dynamic channel, beyond the static incentive created by the marginal tax rate, by which the EITC could reduce labor supply among younger workers: if an important part of the return to work is via the accumulation of experience that will lead to higher wages later in life, and if the EITC reduces the net return to higher future pre-tax wages, then it may reduce the incentive to work in early career "training" jobs. This effect depends importantly on the specific model of human capital investment, however—predictions can be reversed if the relevant investment is made in classrooms rather than on the job. It is worth emphasizing that these are theoretical predictions; empirical evidence is quite limited (though see Heckman, Lochner, and Cossa 2003).

The self-employed face additional incentives. These mostly relate to reporting—where traditional workers' earnings are reported to the IRS by the employer, self-employed workers must report their own earnings, and often must make arbitrary accounting decisions about how to allocate business income between earnings and profits. Those in the phase-out range of the EITC schedule, and even some with earnings above the end of that range, can face an incentive to hide or reclassify some earnings in order to maximize their credit. Moreover, those in the phase-in range face incentives to *raise* their reported earnings. This is because the EITC phase-in rate is higher, in absolute value, than the additional payroll taxes that would need to be paid on the additional reported earnings. Similar incentives apply to those choosing between formal and informal (i.e., under the table) work—the EITC raises the return to being paid formally, though it can also incentivize shifting a portion of compensation under the table for those in the phase-out range (Gunter 2013).

There is no third-party reporting of self-employment income (nor, obviously, of informal sector earnings), making it harder to enforce accurate reporting here. Moreover, what enforcement mechanisms there are are aimed at detecting underreporting of income, not overreporting, so it is very difficult to detect workers who overreport their self-employment income.

2.4.2   Why Structure a Program This Way?

As the above discussion of the EITC's history makes clear, the program's various goals have long been in tension. Of course, one goal of all means-tested transfer programs is to transfer income to the poor. But why the particular structure of the EITC? Specifically, why use negative marginal tax rates on the first dollar of earnings to distort labor supply decisions? Why base the schedule on total income of the tax filing unit? And why such a comparatively stingy schedule for families without children? These design choices have a number of potential rationalizations.

As we discussed in section 2.2.2, the EITC creates negative average and marginal tax rates on work in its phase-in range that are too large in magnitude, for most recipients, to be fully offset by the positive rates imposed by payroll taxes and the phaseout of other means-tested transfers. A natural explanation for this is that at least some supporters of the program have an explicit goal of encouraging more work than would be obtained even without distortions. Evidently, (some) policymakers place a lower social welfare weight on the leisure of single mothers than do the women themselves. This explanation could rationalize the evident aversion to subsidizing voluntary nonemployment across a variety of programs. The question then arises: Why might policymakers' social welfare functions have this feature? One potential source is paternalism—a view that poor women are not able to maximize their own utilities. Another potential explanation, implicit in many discussions but rarely voiced explicitly, is that policy is attempting to force women to internalize a positive externality associated with their labor (Acs and Toder 2007).

One such externality is on government budgets. There may be a social interest in more work than would be chosen in the absence of any tax and transfer distortions, if this leads to more government revenue that can be used elsewhere. This consideration leads to "optimal tax" analyses that attempt to balance the benefits of tax revenue with the costs of distorting individual choice. Saez (2002) argues that when labor-supply decisions are made primarily along the intensive margin (about how many hours to work per year) the optimal transfer policy resembles a negative income tax, with a base transfer that is taxed away as earnings rise above zero, but that when the extensive margin (about whether to work at all) labor supply elasticity is large, then an EITC-like structure can be optimal.[7]

A key assumption in Saez's (2002) model is that labor supply is the binding constraint. Ongoing work by Kroft et al. (2016) shows that when the labor market is slack the optimal transfer schedule is more like the NIT and less like the EITC. A related point is that Saez (2002) assumes that pretax wages are invariant to the tax schedule. Rothstein (2010) notes that the EITC's

7. See also Blundell (2006) and Blundell et al. (2009).

effect on wages partially offsets its redistributive intent, while the NIT's ability to redistribute is magnified by its wage effects. We discuss this issue in section 2.4.3.

A second potential externality is on children. Low family incomes may have negative effects on children, who bear no responsibility for their parents' economic circumstances, and this can create an argument for public intervention. But the most direct intervention to address this would be cash welfare, not the EITC.[8] A more compelling argument for the EITC's negative phase-in tax rate needs to tie the externality to the work decision itself. It is plausible that parents do not fully internalize the long-term negative consequences for their children of modeling low work attachment. If so, incentivizing work among low-income parents may protect some children from coming to believe that nonparticipation in the labor market is a viable life course. This notion of parents modeling good work behavior for children played a central role in Bill Clinton's narrative around "ending welfare as we know it" and in expanding the EITC. Recent state-level innovations in noncustodial benefits (discussed in section 2.6) are also consistent with this view.

Another potential source of a child-related externality concerns the quality of child care provided by stay-at-home mothers, relative to that which would be obtained if the mother worked. There is emerging evidence that center-based child care can be superior—in the sense of producing better child outcomes—to the at-home care provided in many low-income families (Heckman, Pinto, and Savelyev 2013; Kline and Walters 2016; Feller et al. 2016). If so, subsidizing work via the EITC can perhaps be justified as a means of improving the quality of children's environments. (Though note that in practice, the alternative to at-home care is often not a well-run center but an informal arrangement with a neighbor or grandmother.) An attractive feature of this argument is that it can rationalize the fact that the EITC's generosity rises with the number of children and perhaps even the work disincentives that the EITC creates for married mothers: if married women, in contrast to single mothers, provide better at-home care than can be obtained on the market, encouraging them to remain out of the labor force can be optimal. But the EITC is an awfully indirect way of addressing child-care externalities, even granting the strong assumptions implicit in the above discussion. It would be more straightforward to subsidize (or provide directly) high-quality, center-based care for the children of mothers deemed likely to provide poor care at home (see chapter 4 in volume 2).

8. Many higher-income mothers appear to believe that a stay-at-home parent is better for young children than is paid child care. If the same is true for low-income families, this can be seen as a negative externality associated with maternal employment, and constitutes an affirmative argument for unconditional over conditional transfers. But there is at least some evidence that paid child care is beneficial for low-income children (see, e.g., Deming 2009; Puma et al. 2012).

A largely distinct set of questions about the EITC relates to its unusual placement within the tax code, rather than in traditional social welfare agencies. This, too, has a number of potential explanations. First, it symbolically links the credit to participation in the formal economy, likely producing smaller stigma for recipients than do welfare programs. Second, it provides a simple means of administering the credit without the large overhead of caseworkers and other staff needed for traditional means-tested transfers. Third, there is a political advantage to implementing a transfer through the tax code: refundable tax credits are not always perceived as spending, and do not count toward congressional spending caps.

Administration of the EITC through the tax system does impose limitations, however: because income taxation is at the family level in the United States, so is EITC eligibility. This creates some perverse incentives. In particular, as we discuss above and in section 2.5.4, many potential secondary earners face positive (and sometimes large) marginal tax rates from the first dollar they earn, simply because their spouses' earnings are enough to put the family in the EITC phase-out range. This could be avoided with individual credit schedules. But this is not practical, given the family basis of the rest of the US income tax code. A more practical, though imperfect, alternative is to use a different schedule for married couples than for single parents, as was implemented in 2002. This can be expensive, however, as it means giving the credit to many families that elect to keep one spouse at home and are less needy than their per-adult market earnings imply.

2.4.3   Incidence

Labor supply impacts are only the beginning of the EITC's potential effect in the labor market. Standard public economic theory implies that policies that affect labor supply decisions will have follow-on effects on other labor market outcomes, including market wages. In particular, a negative effective tax rate that encourages increased labor force participation will lead to a decline in pretax wages. This implies that a portion of the money spent on the EITC will be captured by employers of EITC recipients and of other workers competing in the same labor markets as the recipients. We develop this idea in the simplest possible case; readers are referred to Rothstein (2010) and Fullerton and Metcalf (2002) for more elaborate models.

In general, nonlinear income taxes make it difficult to define a single hourly or annual net-of-tax wage. We focus on a simple model with a single linear tax, levied on the worker, that introduces a fixed wedge between the pretax wage w and the posttax wage ω: $\omega = w(1 - \tau)$. Given the evidence discussed below that the primary labor supply effect of the EITC is for single mothers on the extensive margin, it is useful to think of individual labor supply decisions as binary—participate or not—and thus to think of τ as the average tax rate on potential earnings, which is negative under the EITC.

The EITC, like other personal income taxes, is levied on the worker rather than on the employer. Thus, labor supply should depend on ω. A simple representation of total labor supply is:

(1) $$L^S = \alpha \omega^\sigma,$$

where $\sigma \geq 0$ represents the elasticity of labor supply. Labor demand depends on the pretax wage that is actually paid by the employer, with elasticity $\rho < 0$:

(2) $$L^D = \beta w^\rho.$$

So long as the labor supply elasticity is positive and demand is less than fully elastic, a portion of the subsidy $-w\tau$ will accrue to employers through reduced pretax wages. Given the simple supply and demand equations above, the equilibrium pretax wage and quantity are

(3) $$w = \alpha^{-1/(\sigma-\rho)}\beta^{1/(\sigma-\rho)}(1-\tau)^{-\sigma/(\sigma-\rho)}$$

and

(4) $$L = \alpha^{-\rho/(\sigma-\rho)}\beta^{\sigma/(\sigma-\rho)}(1-\tau)^{-\sigma\rho/(\sigma-\rho)}.$$

This implies a posttax wage of

(5) $$\omega = \alpha^{-1/(\sigma-\rho)}\beta^{1/(\sigma-\rho)}(1-\tau)^{-\rho/(\sigma-\rho)}.$$

In other words, employers capture a portion $f \equiv \sigma/(\sigma - \rho) > 0$ of the EITC subsidy. Workers receive a subsidy—ω is increasing in $|\tau|$—but less than would be obtained were wages fixed. Specifically, recipients receive only $(1 - f)$ of every dollar spent, and labor supply increases in proportion only to $(1 - f)\tau$ rather than to the full subsidy τ.

This simple model assumes that all workers are eligible for the subsidy. Rothstein (2010) extends the model to consider a labor market (e.g., low-skill women's labor) in which some workers are eligible and some are not. Importantly, insofar as ineligible workers are perfect substitutes for eligible workers, both see their wages decline by the same amount. In this case, the decline in the pretax wage is proportional to the product of the share of labor in the market supplied by subsidized workers and the above fraction f. This means that subsidized workers keep a larger share of the subsidy that is intended for them the smaller is their share of the workforce. Nevertheless, the share of the subsidy payment that is captured by employers is unaffected by the workforce composition.

Of course, the total amount received has to equal the amount spent. The difference is made up by unsubsidized workers. These workers' pretax wages decline, with no subsidy to compensate. The decline in the per-worker or per-hour wage, w, is proportional to the product of the subsidized share of the labor force with f. However, the total transfer from unsubsidized workers to employers is larger the *smaller* is the share of subsidized workers in the labor market.

Translated into real-world terms, this means that the EITC—and any other policy that increases labor supply—functions in part as a subsidy to employers of the workers in question. As the target recipients of the EITC tend to be relatively low income, the employer share of the incidence flows to employers of low-skill labor. This effect leads Lee and Saez (2012) to argue that the minimum wage is a complement to the EITC, as a binding minimum wage can prevent employers from capturing the credit.

There has been some confusion in the literature about the mechanism by which this incidence effect arises. It does *not* depend on the employer knowing that the worker is receiving the EITC. In a neoclassical model of the labor market, an individual worker's wage is unaffected by the specific factors influencing that worker's labor supply. Rather, the wage is set by the overall balance of supply and demand in the market, and thus by the *average* worker's labor supply.

One implication is that incidence considerations cannot explain the low take-up of the Advance EITC (discussed further below), at least in a neoclassical model. It is possible that violations of that model's assumptions would allow employers to discriminate against workers who claim the Advance credit (and thus reveal that they are EITC recipients). But the neoclassical model's insight that any such discrimination is limited by the worker's ability to take another job with an employer who pays the going wage seems likely to be relatively robust.

2.4.4   Non-Labor-Market Incentives

Beyond the EITC's labor supply effects, it has the potential to distort decisions on other margins. As mentioned above, it can reduce the effective returns to education. (It may improve children's educational outcomes, however, through direct effects of family resources.) It also incentivizes fertility for many low-income workers. Finally, it has complex effects on the incentives to marry. The EITC creates a marriage penalty for many dual-earner couples, who might receive the credit if filing as two unmarried taxpayers but collectively have too high earnings to receive it as a married couple. (The extension of the schedule for married taxpayers in 2002 partially offsets this, but by no means completely.) In other cases, the EITC can encourage marriage—for example, between a nonworking custodial mother and a working father who would be nonresident in the absence of the credit.

In general, empirical evidence of perverse effects on potential recipients' marriage, fertility, and educational attainment decisions is thin (though there is stronger evidence of positive effects on children's outcomes.) We discuss this evidence in section 2.5.3.

2.4.5   Consumption and Income Smoothing

EITC recipients nearly always receive their credits as lump-sum payments in the spring. This has implications for savings and consumption.

In a standard neoclassical model of household finances, families should borrow and save to smooth their consumption through the year, and the lump-sum nature of the EITC should have no implications for consumption decisions. But this model is not a good characterization of typical low-income households, not least because these households are often unable to borrow at reasonable interest rates (as evidenced by the high take-up of extremely high-interest, refund anticipation loans). If credit constraints are binding, a lump-sum payment has a smaller effect on the household's utility than would a series of smaller payments throughout the year.

Until 2010, the Advance EIC allowed recipients to receive the credit as part of their regular paychecks. But take-up of this option was extremely low, under 1 percent of all returns receiving the EITC. The low take-up rate was somewhat surprising, given the prevalence of refund anticipation loans. The decision to take these loans can only be rationalized if recipients have extremely high discount rates or, more plausibly, if they are severely credit constrained; either would seem to make a zero interest loan from the IRS attractive. We return to this topic in section 2.5.2.

2.4.6   Interactions with Other Programs and the Macroeconomy

We discussed interactions between eligibility for the EITC and for other means-tested transfers in section 2.2.2. The EITC also interacts with other policies aimed at making work pay, most importantly the minimum wage. Political discussions often treat the EITC and minimum wage as alternative ways of accomplishing this goal—each increases the take-home pay of low-skill workers, though the transfer is financed by the government in one case and by the employer in the other.

But it is not clear that the EITC and minimum wage should be seen as substitutes rather than complements. As discussed in section 2.4.3, employers may be able to capture a portion of the EITC through reduced equilibrium market wages. Minimum wages can constrain this effect, placing more of the incidence on the intended recipient.

On the other hand, insofar as minimum wages lead to labor market rationing, they can make it harder for those hoping to receive the EITC to actually find jobs.[9] The preponderance of evidence indicates that minimum wage increases have minimal impacts on the quantity of labor demanded (e.g., Allegretto, Dube, and Reich 2008), indicating perhaps that a competitive model does not apply (Manning 2003) or that adjustments take place along a different dimension than wages and quantity transacted, for example, a quality of work dimension.

As the Great Moderation of the 1990s and early twenty-first century was replaced by the Great Recession in 2007, interest in the cyclical properties

---

9. Lee and Saez's (2012) result that the optimal policy combines the EITC and minimum wage depends on their assumption that rationing is efficient: that limited jobs go to those job seekers who receive the largest surplus from employment at the minimum wage.

of transfer programs has grown. It is not clear ex ante whether the EITC is pro-cyclical or countercyclical. On the one hand, labor market slack makes it harder for people hoping to obtain the EITC to find jobs, and thus can be expected to reduce EITC eligibility and payments. On the other hand, however, weak labor market conditions generally lead to higher rates of part-year and part-time work. This could make many higher-wage individuals eligible for the credit, where they would not be with full-time, full-year earnings. The cyclical properties of the credit are thus an empirical question.

2.5   Research on the EITC

In this section, we review empirical evidence about the use and effects of the EITC. Nearly all of the potential impacts discussed in section 2.4 have been the subject of at least some serious research, though in some cases the evidence is not as conclusive as one would like and in others there is reasonably conclusive evidence that the predicted impact is small. We begin with evidence on participation rates and noncompliance. We then turn to what we view as the central question: How does the EITC impact participants' well-being? After reviewing various dimensions of well-being, we examine the effect of the EITC on the labor market, including the most-studied topic concerning the EITC: its impact on recipients' labor supply. Finally, we consider evidence on interactions. In our view, the most interesting question here concerns the EITC's potential role in offsetting cyclical fluctuations in employment and earnings, so we focus on this.

2.5.1   Methodology

The studies discussed in this section use a variety of methodological approaches to identify the effects of the EITC. One strategy is common enough, and raises enough issues that cut across categories of outcomes, to be worth a special note. This is the difference-in-differences research design. We discuss it briefly here, taking as our example the estimation of the effect of the EITC on participants' health.

A major challenge for any program evaluation is to distinguish the impacts of the program under study from those of other factors that may be coincident with program participation but causally independent. For example, a comparison of EITC recipients with individuals who are ineligible for the EITC due to too-high earnings may confound the EITC with that of other factors that lead to earnings differences between the groups.

Many researchers attempt to avoid this problem—known as "omitted variable bias"—via a method known as "difference-in-differences," or DD. This method attempts to remove the confounding influence of omitted factors affecting income by subtracting an estimate of the omitted variable bias obtained from a comparison between two groups that are *not* differentially treated by the EITC but are otherwise similarly situated to the EITC "treatment" and "control" groups.

For example, one common empirical strategy is based on the comparison between single mothers with two or more children and those with just a single child in the post-1996 period, when the former group was eligible for a much more generous EITC than was the latter. As single parents with multiple children may differ in many ways from those with only children, the simple comparison does not provide a credible estimate of the effect of the more generous credit schedule. A DD estimator acknowledges this, and uses differences among the two groups prior to 1993—when they faced similar schedules—to separate the influence of the program from that of the unmeasured factors that might influence the two groups' relative outcomes.

Specifically, let $Y_{2+,1996}$ represent the average outcome for women with two or more children in 1996; $Y_{1,1996}$ represent the average outcome for women with single children in the same year; and $Y_{2+,1993}$ and $Y_{1,1993}$ represent the corresponding average outcomes in 1993. There are two simple differences estimators available. The first contrasts multiple-child families with single-child families in 1996:

$$(6) \qquad D_{\text{famsize}} = Y_{2+,1996} - Y_{1,1996}.$$

The second contrasts multiple-child families in 1996 and 1993:

$$(7) \qquad D_{\text{timing}} = Y_{2+,1996} - Y_{2+,1993}.$$

Neither of these provides credible evidence on the effects of the EITC. The first may be confounded by differences among families of different sizes, while the second may be confounded by changing economic conditions between 1993 and 1996. But the two strategies can be combined to form a difference-in-differences estimator:

$$(8) \qquad DD = (Y_{2+,1996} - Y_{1,1996}) - (Y_{2+,1993} - Y_{1,1993})$$
$$= (Y_{2+,1996} - Y_{2+,1993}) - (Y_{1,1996} - Y_{1,1993}).$$

This will identify the impact of the EITC expansion on the relative outcomes of multiple-child families if any underlying trends in outcomes are similar for families of different sizes (or, equivalently, if any underlying differences between family-size groups are stable over time).

Much of the available evidence about the impacts of the EITC comes from research designs of this type, exploiting either the relative expansion of the EITC for large families in 1996 or the introduction of state EITCs in some but not all states. If the requisite common-trends assumption holds, studies using this type of design can identify the effect of EITC expansion on the outcome of interest (e.g., health).[10]

But there are two challenges. One is that the common-trends assumption may be incorrect. The strong labor market of the late 1990s may have

---

10. There are other formal requirements. In particular, one must assume that policy changes in one state or group do not affect other jurisdictions or workers. This is a version of the Stable Unit Treatment Value Assumption (Rubin 1986).

differentially affected less-skilled women, and single mothers with multiple children may have lower skill levels, on average, than do single mothers without children. Or the child-care provisions of welfare reform may have had different implications for women with only children than for those with multiple children, for whom child-care costs presumably loom larger. Another violation would occur if state EITCs were introduced in response to changing conditions or expectations.

A second challenge lies in interpreting the source of any EITC effect, once it is isolated. It is tempting to assume that an EITC effect on, for example, maternal health reflects the impact of additional income and the goods and services (e.g., health care) that it can purchase. But this may be incorrect. The EITC expansion has effects on other outcomes as well, most notably labor supply. Thus, the basic DD estimate for maternal health combines the pure effect of income on health, holding all else constant, with the effect of additional work. The EITC effect should be interpreted to include effects operating through (for example) changes in time use, access to employer-provided health insurance, and the mental health consequences of employment. This issue arises as well in many of the studies of other outcomes discussed below, whether based on the DD research design or on another strategy.

Unfortunately, there is no good solution. One can control for labor force participation in analyzing health impacts, but the resulting estimates are difficult to interpret. This is known as the "intermediate outcome problem." Absent an independent source of variation in each potential mediating channel, parsing the mechanisms that produce the reduced-form causal effects identified via a simple DD analysis is in general not possible.

2.5.2   Participation and Compliance

Participation and Take-Up

Relative to many other transfer programs, take-up of the EITC among eligible families is quite high, in large part due to its administration through the tax code. Scholz (1994) estimates the take-up rate for the EITC in 1990 at 80 to 86 percent. By contrast, the 2004 take-up rate for Temporary Assistance for Needy Families (TANF) was 42 percent, the rate for the food stamp program (now SNAP) was 55 percent, and take-up of the Supplemental Security Income program was 46 percent (HHS 2007).

The EITC take-up rates have changed over time, due in part to increasing knowledge of the program and changing program rules. Scholz's (1994) estimate of take-up in 1990 likely overstates the current rate, as it was prior to the expansion of the EITC to childless individuals, for whom take-up rates are lower, and during a period when the IRS semiautomatically issued the credit to filers who appeared eligible but did not claim the credit. Plueger (2009) estimates a 75 percent take-up rate for the EITC in 2005.

Jones (2014a) uses IRS data linked to the Current Population Survey to examine how take-up rates vary with family structure, credit segment, and economic conditions. She estimates that the overall take-up rate rose from 77 percent to 79 percent between 2005 and 2009, and that take-up rates were similar for single and joint filers. The 2009 figure matches the IRS's own estimate for 2010, from matched IRS-American Community Survey data (IRS 2014c).

Jones finds dramatic differences in take-up for taxpayers at different positions on the EITC schedule: the take-up rate was above 80 percent for those on the plateau and phase-out segments of the schedule, but under 70 percent for those on the phase-in. The discrepancy is largest for those with the smallest credits: in the phase-out range, those eligible for small credits were as likely to claim them as were those eligible for larger credits, but in the phase-in range take-out rates were quite low for those eligible for small credits—under 40 percent for those eligible for credits under $100. This is likely attributable to low tax-return-filing rates among those with very low earnings, for who filing is often not required. Blumenthal, Erard, and Ho (2005), examining audited tax data, find a similar pattern. Among filers with a legal responsibility to file, the fraction that claimed the EITC rose from 89 to 94 percent between 1988 and 1999, while in households with no filing requirement the claiming rate rose from under 40 percent to 50 percent over the same period.

There are also substantial differences in take-up rates by demographic characteristics of the taxpayer. Jones (2014a) finds that working women had higher take-up rates (81 percent in 2005 and 82 percent in 2009) but that working men's take-up rate increased by more (from 72 percent to 76 percent). Take-up rates were much higher for those with children (82–86 percent, depending on the year and number of children) than for those without, though again the latter group's take-up rate increased by much more (from 56 percent to 65 percent). Using the 1999 National Survey of America's Families, Ross Phillips (2001) finds that low-income Hispanic parents are much less likely to know about the EITC than other low-income parents, and that among low-income parents who know about the EITC, Hispanics are less likely to have ever received the credit.

These differences in take-up rates across groups raise concerns about implications for horizontal equity. However, large changes in the composition of the eligible population over time can influence the overall take-up rate and take-up rates by subgroup, and the impact of these compositional shifts is not well understood. Reliable data that include both eligibility and receipt are very hard to come by, but some emerging research is beginning to disaggregate shifts over time in eligibility and receipt. Jones (2014a) finds that joint filers, taxpayers with more children, and men experienced increasing rates of eligibility between 2005 and 2009, but eligibility rates fell for those with less education. Jones (2014b) uses the 2006 CPS matched to tax data from 2005 through 2011 to examine changes in eligibility and finds that less-educated, unmarried women experienced a greater hazard of eligibility loss due to movement to zero annual earnings compared to other labor market groups.

There may also be interactions of EITC take-up with participation in other programs. Caputo (2006) finds that food stamp receipt tripled the odds of filing for the EITC, but finds no significant correlations with SSI or TANF receipt. In contrast, Jones (2014a) finds that SNAP and unemployment insurance benefits were strongly positively associated with receipt of the EITC conditional on eligibility, but SSI was strongly negatively associated (TANF was negatively associated with take-up of the EITC but not statistically significantly so).

Noncompliance

Overclaiming of the EITC has been a persistent concern with the program. A major issue, as discussed above, is the definition of qualifying children. It can be challenging for potential recipients to know whether their children qualify. Enforcement is also challenging for the IRS, as many components of the qualifying child definition are not readily observed.

McCubbin (2000) uses an IRS sample of 2,046 returns filed in 1994 that were subjected to additional scrutiny to estimate a 26 percent rate of overclaiming (though standard enforcement measures would be expected to reduce that rate to 20.7 percent). The rates of overclaiming may be overstated in the administrative data, however, as filers who request reconsideration of credit denials succeed in overturning nearly half of IRS rulings (National Taxpayer Advocate 2004). A more recent IRS study of audited 2006–2008 returns (Internal Revenue Service 2014h) found a preenforcement overclaiming rate between 28.5 percent and 39.1 percent of all EITC dollars claimed, depending on assumptions made about taxpayers who did not participate in the audit. This was not significantly different from what was found in an earlier 1999 study.

McCubbin (2000) finds that most of the overclaiming is due to filers claiming real but nonqualifying children. Despite subsequent changes intended to simplify the qualifying child rules, this remains the most common source of error in the more recent study. Residency test failures are the most common, suggesting that many noncustodial parents claim a child who should have been claimable only by the custodial parent. In the recent data, between 13 and 27 percent of all children claimed for the EITC were claimed in error (Internal Revenue Service 2014h).

Liebman (2000) examines the nature of compliance errors by matching the 1991 March Current Population Survey (CPS) to respondents' 1990 tax returns. This was prior to the introduction of the EITC schedule for families without children, and also predates IRS efforts to reduce overclaiming of dependent children. He finds that 11 to 13 percent of apparently EITC-eligible families who claimed children as dependents on their tax returns did not report having children in the home on the CPS survey. A portion of this reflects timing—a child could have been present in the house for six months, as required to qualify for the EITC, without being there at the time of the March CPS survey. But there appear to be discrepancies that cannot be explained this way.

The IRS Publication 596 lists a multitude of examples in which many economists would have trouble identifying who was eligible to claim the credit, and many situations in which multiple filers could claim different credits with choices over who claims qualifying children. The optimal choice is often hard to determine. Greenstein and Wancheck (2011, 3) conclude that "EITC overpayments most commonly result from misunderstanding of how to apply the EITC's intricate rules regarding who may claim a child, especially in changing family situations involving separated, divorced, or three-generation families." The IRS has recently modified the dependent child definitions, but as noted above qualifying child errors remain common.

McCubbin (2000) reports that incorrect filing status accounted for 31 percent of EITC overclaiming in 1994. Most of these errors occurred on returns for which the IRS changed the filing status of the sampled taxpayer from single or head of household to married filing separately (who are not eligible for the EITC) or to married filing jointly (who are eligible but often receive a smaller or zero credit). McCubbin finds no support for the argument of Schiffren (1995) that the refundability of the credit contributes to noncompliance, and National Taxpayer Advocate (2009) supports the notion that other factors matter far more. In more recent data, returns with filing status errors account for only about one-sixth of overclaims (Internal Revenue Service 2014h). A more common error in the 2006–2008 returns is income misreporting, which occurred on two-thirds of returns with identifiable errors, but accounted for only one-quarter to one-third of overclaimed dollars. The bulk of this misreporting relates to self-employment income, which cannot be checked against information reports as can traditional wage income.

Information

Surveys of low-income tax filers at free tax preparation sites by Bhargava and Manoli (2015) indicate that many eligible filers are unaware of the credit and its incentives (see also Maag 2005; Romich and Weisner 2002; Ross Phillips 2001; Smeeding, Ross Phillips, and O'Connor 2000). Forty-three percent of eligible filers are not aware of the program and 33 percent of eligible filers aware of the credit believe they are ineligible. (Note, however, that a taxpayer need not be aware of the credit to receive it, particularly when a third party assists with tax preparation.) A majority (61 percent) of eligible, aware filers underestimate the size of the credit, by an average of 83 percent. They also substantially overestimate the likelihood of an audit: the actual audit rate is 1.8 percent, but the median respondent believed the rate to be 15 percent.

An important implication of this is that behavioral responses to the credit may be substantially muted relative to what would be obtained if all taxpayers were aware of the incentives they actually face. Tach and Halpern-Meekin (2014) interview 115 EITC recipients and find that they tend not to understand the marginal incentives embodied in the credit, and not to differentiate the credit from their overall tax refund (see also Chetty and Saez 2013). They are unlikely to change their employment or marital status in response to tax incentives, but rather try to maximize their refunds by listing zero exemptions and deductions on their W-4s, filing returns as head of household rather than as married, and dividing children among the tax returns of multiple caregivers.

Bhargava and Manoli (2015) examine whether informational barriers help explain incomplete take-up of the EITC, using an experiment in which the IRS mailed letters providing information to filers who failed to claim the credit but seemed likely to be eligible. Fourteen percent of nonclaimants claimed the credit after receiving a mailing with a "textually dense, two-sided document that emphasizes eligibility requirements repeated later in the worksheet," meant to mimic traditional IRS communications. A simplified design increased take-up by an additional 9 percentage points, while a mailing that clearly displayed the benefits of claiming increased take-up to 28 percentage points (5 percentage points more than the simplified form alone).

The Advance EITC

Until 2011, EITC recipients could choose to receive a portion of their credit with each paycheck rather than as a lump sum at tax filing time, via the Advance EIC program. Note that a taxpayer with positive non-EITC tax liability can do this to some extent by reducing withholding. But since most EITC recipients have negative net income tax liability, this still leaves most of the value of the credit to be paid as a refund the following spring. The Advance EIC allowed for *negative* withholding from the weekly, biweekly, or monthly paycheck. But take-up of this option was very low, only 1–2 percent of EITC claimants, leading to its cancellation.

Several explanations for the failure of the Advance EIC program have been offered (Holt 2008). One is that recipients were unaware of the Advance EIC option. Jones (2010) conducted a field experiment aimed in part at this explanation: employees at a single large firm were randomly assigned to receive Advance EIC information and enrollment forms in the workplace. This treatment raised participation rates only to 1.6 percent (from a base of around 0.6 percent). This echoes the results of an earlier IRS study in which EITC recipients were mailed information about the Advance option (IRS 1999), and demonstrates rather conclusively that lack of information about the Advance option cannot account for its unpopularity.

A second explanation is that recipients may have preferred that their employers not know that they were receiving the EITC. There is no reason for an employer to ever find out that a worker is receiving the regular credit, as workers claim the credit directly from the IRS, but signing up for the Advance EIC required submitting a withholding election form to the employer. The experimental treatment protocol used by Jones (2010) attempted to address this by requiring all employees to turn in forms, whether or not they wanted to enroll; this would have disguised the employee's choice from the manager, if not from the human resources office.

The remaining candidate explanation is that recipients *prefer* to receive the EITC as a lump sum, treating it as a (zero interest) savings mechanism that allows them to accumulate larger balances than they would be able to amass if faced with the temptation to spend the credit as it came in. Some behavioral models posit that individuals have difficulty committing to saving plans, and that forced savings can be valued for this reason. Much of the survey evidence discussed above can be interpreted to support this view.

The Jones (2010) experiment included a second treatment arm aimed at understanding the role of forced savings motives. Employees were encouraged to sign up to have their Advance EITC payments deposited directly into a 401(k) plan. This led to a roughly 4 percentage point increase in retirement plan participation, but did not appreciably increase take-up of the Advance EIC. This seems to rule out motivations related to a desire to commit to long-term savings. However, 401(k) balances are highly illiquid; Jones' (2010) experiment would not identify a motivation to commit to medium-term savings (e.g., toward the purchase of durable goods).

The United Kingdom's Working Tax Credit (formerly the Working Families' Tax Credit, or WFTC) is a useful analogy. These payments are disbursed on a monthly or biweekly basis. Brewer, Saez, and Shephard (2010) note the absence of a market for financial vehicles that would allow recipients to commit to saving their credits, in contrast to the (formerly) robust market in refund anticipation loans in the United States. This is further suggestive evidence against forced savings explanations for the unpopularity of the Advance EIC.

Brewer, Saez, and Shephard (2010) point instead to uncertainty as an important factor. A worker who expects to have several jobs over the course of the year, or whose hours vary unpredictably, may not be able to accurately forecast her eventual credit eligibility. Signing up for the Advance EIC could expose her to end-of-year liabilities if she turns out to have overestimated. This could be costly for a family with limited or no access to credit markets and/or ability to commit to precautionary saving. (Note that Jones' [2010] 401(k) treatment would not address this concern, as it would be difficult to access 401(k) balances to pay end-of-year tax liabilities.) In 2005, the United Kingdom changed its credit system to base eligibility primarily on the prior year's income, accepting some reduction in targeting efficiency for the sake of reducing overpayments that would need to be squared up later.

Once again, however, concerns about eventual liabilities cannot fully explain the lack of take-up of the Advance EIC. Reforms introduced in 1993 limited the amount of the EITC that could be received in advance, making large overpayments unlikely, but had little effect on take-up.

Jones (2012) points out that the low take-up of the Advance EIC is only a part of a larger overwithholding puzzle. He documents that average tax refunds to EITC recipients *exceed* the average size of the credit, as many recipients elect positive withholding from their paychecks that is then refunded, along with the EITC, at the end of the year. This is potentially consistent with forced withholding or uncertainty explanations, but not at all with explanations related to information about or the mechanics of the Advance EIC. He interprets the patterns to indicate that inertia is a large component of the explanation—that taxpayers, particularly low-income taxpayers, take many years to adjust their withholding to account for changes in their tax liability.

2.5.3   Impacts on Well-Being

Poverty and Consumption

The expansion of the EITC in the mid-1990s was associated with a large decline in child poverty rates, almost completely reversed in the Great Recession. The decline had a number of causes, welfare reform and the strong economy of that period among them. Nichols (2006, 2013) attributes nearly all of the changes in child poverty rates since the 1990s to changing work patterns of parents, where changing family structure was the dominant driver in the 1970s and 1980s. Several studies have found that the EITC was an important contributor due to its work incentives (Haskins 2008; CBO 2007). Neumark and Wascher (2001) find that the introduction of state EITCs is associated with increases in the likelihood that families with sub-poverty-level earnings in one year have earnings levels above the poverty threshold in the next year.

These studies capture only EITC effects that operate through changes in labor supply and pretax earnings, as these are the basis for the official poverty measure. The first-order consequence of the EITC—that the credit itself alleviates families' hardship—is not counted in official poverty calculations. The Census Bureau has developed a new Supplemental Poverty Measure (SPM) that includes taxes and cash and noncash benefits in family resources. The Census Bureau estimates that the SPM poverty rate was 15.5 percent in 2013, but would have been 18.4 percent without the EITC and CTC (Short 2014; see also CEA 2014). The effect on child poverty is even stronger: the SPM poverty rate for those under eighteen years of age was 16.4 percent, but would have been 22.8 percent without the refundable tax credits. Based on these numbers, the EITC can be credited with lifting 9.1 million people, including 4.7 million children, out of poverty.[11] The effects on total poverty are far larger than those of any other single program except Social Security, and the effects on child poverty are the largest without exception.

Hoynes and Patel (2015) conduct a similar analysis, focusing on single mothers but expanding the scope to consider effects on other income thresholds. They find that EITC receipt is concentrated among families whose incomes (after other taxes and transfers) would be between 75 percent and 150 percent of the poverty line, and that the credit has large effects on the overall income distribution (for single-mother families) in this range but small or zero effects below 75 percent or above 250 percent of poverty.

There has been extensive research on the ways that EITC recipients spend their refunds. Barrow and McGranahan (2000) and Goodman-Bacon and McGranahan (2008) use data from the Consumer Expenditure Survey to examine monthly consumption patterns of EITC-eligible households. They find that these households spend more on durable goods in February, relative to other months and to other households. The biggest category of extra expenditures is vehicles. The authors interpret this as consistent with the program's pro-work goals, though there is no direct evidence that the extra vehicle expenditures are to facilitate commuting to work. They also find effects on furniture, appliances, and household goods. These patterns are consistent with estimates of the effects of other tax refunds on short-run consumption (Souleles 1999; Parker et al. 2013), so do not seem to be specific to the EITC population. They are also consistent with self-reports of prospective EITC recipients (Smeeding, Ross Phillips, and O'Connor 2000), who also say that they plan to devote some of their refunds to savings—the purchase of durable goods is a form of saving—or to paying off bills (Mendenhall et al. 2012). Gao, Kaushal, and Waldfogel (2009) find that each dollar in EITC generosity reduces single mothers' average debt by a statistically significant but small four cents.

Given their low incomes, EITC recipients are unlikely to be using their refunds to build substantial nest eggs. Athreya, Reilly, and Simpson (2010) find that EITC recipients have about one-fifth the wealth of non-EITC recipients (who generally have higher incomes). The lowest quarter of EITC recipients have negative average wealth, whereas the bottom quarter of nonrecipient households have positive average wealth. Debt-to-income ratios of households receiving the EITC are much higher than those of nonrecipients.

Health

Another way to assess the EITC's value for families is to examine objective measures of well-being. Health status is the most obvious, though clearly not all of the beneficial effects of the EITC will be captured through the

11. We are grateful to Hilary Hoynes for these calculations.

relatively crude health measures that are available. Evans and Garthwaite (2014; see also Boyd-Swan et al. 2013) examine EITC effects on women's health, using difference-in-differences models for women with multiple children relative to those with just a single child before and after the 1993 EITC expansion. They find that the expansion improved the mental health and self-reported health status of women with multiple children relative to those with fewer. They also find improvements in biological markers of health status, particularly those indicative of inflammation.

Other studies have examined the effect of the EITC on infant or child health (Baker 2008; Hoynes, Miller, and Simon 2015; Baughman 2012; Strully, Rehkopf, and Xuan 2010). Hoynes, Miller, and Simon (2015) find that EITC expansions reduce the incidence of low birth weight, a widely used indicator of poor infant health. Their results indicate that each $1,000 in EITC income reduces low birth weight by 7–11 percent. The effects do not appear to operate through increased insurance coverage, but increased access to prenatal care may play a role, as may reductions in maternal smoking and drinking. Baughman and Duchovny (2016) also test for but do not find an effect on insurance coverage of children ages birth to five years. But they do find that state EITCs are associated with shifts from public to private coverage and with increases in self-reported health status for older children.

As noted above, it is difficult to determine whether health effects reflect the additional income the EITC provides or the impact of increased labor force participation. Evans and Garthwaite (2014) find that estimated health effects are basically unchanged by the inclusion of controls for employment status. This appears to suggest that the EITC effect on health is not working through the employment channel, but this conclusion is necessarily tentative absent a research design that can isolate women who would have been working with or without the expanded EITC.

Marriage and Fertility

The EITC creates incentives for low-income, one-earner couples to legally marry, while for low-income, two-earner families the incentive is to cohabit without marriage. The incentives can be very large as a percentage of total income for many low-income families. The EITC expansions could thus be partly responsible for increased cohabitation rates in low-income, two-earner families. There may be both income and substitution effects at work here: increased financial resources due to the EITC may free some women from the pressure to enter into unpromising marriages, even aside from any effect operating through the change in the size of the marriage penalty or bonus.

Dickert-Conlin and Houser (1998) show that the EITC, while subsidizing marriage for poor families and penalizing marriage for near–poor families, did not overcome the large marriage penalties for poor families that arise from phasing out benefits in the transfer system. Holtzblatt and Rebelein (2000) calculate that the EITC subsidized marriage on average for families earning less than $15,000, but created or added to marriage penalties, again on average, for higher-income families. The majority of EITC-induced marriage penalties are seen in couples whose combined incomes were above the EITC's eligibility threshold but would not have been had the couple not been married. As the EITC was expanded, incentives to marry increased for some due to larger marriage bonuses and decreased for others due to larger marriage penalties.

Unfortunately, the evidence to date can support only tentative conclusions about the presence and size of behavioral distortions in this area. One issue is the difficulty of disentangling direct effects from those operating through labor-supply decisions, as income, fertility, and work are all jointly determined. On top of this, there were numerous changes during the 1990s in the tax and transfer system, with offsetting effects on marriage and fertility incentives. Given state dependence in the relevant outcomes—someone who has a child one year cannot un-have it the next year when the tax incentive has changed—it is much harder to tease apart the separate effects of the various factors than for annual choices like labor supply. Moreover, while it is relatively straightforward to measure a household's actual EITC eligibility, it is quite difficult to compute the counterfactual credit that would be obtained with a different family structure. Nearly all estimates of responses to marriage and fertility incentives rely on not-very-accurate estimates of the magnitude of the incentive faced by a particular family. Thus, the empirical evidence is largely inconclusive, though it generally points to small effects.

Past work on incentives embedded in the tax and transfer system finds modest impacts on marriage (e.g., Alm and Whittington 1999; Moffitt 1994; Hoynes 1997). Ellwood (2000) finds no evidence in the 1975 to 1999 CPS that the marriage rates of women with low predicted wages, who presumably faced marriage bonuses due to EITC expansions, increased relative to women with higher predicted wages, who presumably faced marriage penalties on average.

Estimates in Rosenbaum (2000) suggest that the EITC can have large negative effects on marriage, but the estimates are sensitive to the way tax costs are specified in the model and many are statistically insignificant. Eissa and Hoynes (2004) use repeated cross sections in the CPS to estimate that a $1,000 increase in the cost of marriage decreases the marriage rate by 1.3 percentage points but simulate that EITC expansions increased marriage rates by 1 to 5 percent for families with income below $25,000 and reduced marriage rates by 1 percent for families with incomes between $25,000 and $75,000. Herbst (2011) finds that increases in the EITC are associated with very small reductions in the rate of new marriages, and finds no relationship between EITC amounts and new divorces. Dickert-Conlin and Houser (2002) use linear fixed-effect models in SIPP data from October 1989 to

December 1995 to estimate that a $100 increase in a woman's EITC (not the benefits to marriage arising from the EITC) lowers her probability of being married by less than half a percentage point, though the sign is reversed when instrumenting for EITC using policy variation applied to baseline characteristics.

One fundamental problem with much of this work is that marriage should be affected by the difference in utility (often proxied by net income, though work disutility also plays a role) between the married state and the single state, not the EITC received in one state. We do not observe the difference for single women because we do not know the characteristics of her counterfactual spouse, or the behavioral responses that would accompany marriage. Thus, many analyses of marriage penalties and bonuses (e.g., Holtzblatt and Rebelein 2000) are based on samples of women who are actually married but could see higher (lower) after-tax incomes if divorced due to the elimination of the penalty (bonus). Their statuses may not be representative of those who are not married.

Michelmore (2014) addresses this issue by predicting the earnings of unobserved potential spouses for unmarried, non-college-educated women ages eighteen to fifty, using data on single men from the 2001, 2004, and 2008 Survey of Income and Program Participation (SIPP) and probabilities of assortative mating from the CPS. She exploits the changes to credits in the first decade of the twenty-first century that reduced marriage penalties, and finds that $1,000 in expected loss of EITC benefits is associated with a 1.8 percentage point decrease in the likelihood of marrying and 1.1 percentage point increase in the probability of cohabiting over multiple years. However, the confidence intervals do not account for the imputation of unobserved spouse characteristics, so the true intervals for these estimates might well overlap zero.

It is difficult to avoid the conclusion that effects of the EITC on marriage are poorly understood. Most confidence intervals include zero, but impacts could easily be one or two percentage points per thousand-dollar change in the net marriage penalty/bonus. A possible explanation for the generally small estimated effects could be lack of knowledge about the presence and magnitude of marriage incentives (Tach and Halpern-Meekin 2014).

Evidence regarding effects on fertility is similarly inconclusive. Because the EITC is more generous for families with more children, nearly all recipients face incentives to have more children, and low-income individuals and couples without children face incentives to begin families. Baughman and Dickert-Conlin (2009) find very small impacts of the EITC expansions of the 1990s on birth rates, but higher first birth rates among married women and lower first births among unmarried women. Effects by marital status are potentially confounded by effects on marriage, and Baughman and Dickert-Conlin interpret their estimates as suggestive evidence that the larger EITC encouraged marriage among single women.

Children's Educational Outcomes

In addition to impacts on child health discussed above, a recent literature examines the impact of the EITC on children's educational achievement and attainment. There are strong associations of income in general with educational outcomes (e.g., Rothstein and Wozny 2013), implying that EITC-sized resource changes could have very large impacts on children in families receiving the credit. The social welfare implications of improved child outcomes are dramatic (Chetty et al. 2011; Heckman et al. 2010), and have the potential to swamp other more proximate impacts.

Dahl and Lochner (2012) use an instrumental variables strategy that leverages EITC expansions to identify the effect of additional family income in data from the Children of the National Longitudinal Survey of Youth. They find that a $1,000 increase in family income due to EITC expansions raises combined math and reading test scores by about 6 percent of a standard deviation. The EITC's test score impacts appear to be larger for boys, for younger children (under twelve), for black or Hispanic children, and for children whose parents are unmarried.

As above, the interpretation of these estimates is hazardous, as the EITC may have impacts on children that operate through channels other than family disposable resources. A particular concern for child outcomes is effects operating through changes in maternal labor supply. There is evidence that increased work among more educated mothers may hurt student achievement, while increased work among less educated mothers may improve student achievement. This would be expected if the average quality (in terms of productivity for educational outcomes) of the nonfamily care used when the mother works is lower than that of the in-home care that a more educated mother would otherwise provide, but higher than that of the care that would be provided by less educated mothers. Since the EITC primarily affects less educated families, the labor-supply effects may exert an independent positive effect, on average, on children's outcomes.

This may help to explain the magnitude of Dahl and Lochner's estimates. To put them in perspective, they are larger than the cross-sectional association between permanent family income and student test scores (Rothstein and Wozny 2013), which one might expect to be upward biased due to omitted factors. They are also somewhat larger, though not dramatically so, than earlier estimates identified from the same population. One analysis of welfare experiments in the 1990s found that a $1,000 increase in annual income increased young children's achievement by about 5 percent of a standard deviation, on average (Duncan, Morris, and Rodrigues 2011). Like the EITC, the treatments studied in these experiments affected both income and maternal labor supply, and this estimate does not distinguish between these channels.

Another informative comparison is to the effects of educational interventions. For example, a well-known class-size-reduction experiment cost about $12,000 per pupil (in 2007 dollars) and increased student test scores by only 0.17 standard deviations (Dynarski, Hyman, and Schanzenbach 2013). Dahl and Lochner's estimates imply that simply giving the money to families—with no restriction that it be spent on children's education—increases test scores by over four times as much.

Dahl and Lochner attribute their large effects to the fact that IV estimates avoid downward bias from measurement error in family income (though so do the Rothstein and Wozny [2013] and Duncan, Morris, and Rodrigues [2011] estimates); to the declining marginal effect of income, implying that EITC payments to low-income families will have larger than average effects; to an inferred propensity to use lump-sum credits for educationally productive investments; and to the persistence of income shocks due to changes in the EITC schedule, which likely signal increased expected income for many years in the future.

That said, there are reasons to be concerned about the causal interpretation of Dahl and Lochner's estimates. Their instruments are rather weak, a situation that can lead to inconsistent and misleading results (Bound, Jaeger, and Baker 1995; Stock and Yogo 2010). Moreover, because indirect EITC effects on family structure and labor supply may move in different directions for different families, the Dahl and Lochner estimates cannot be interpreted as local average treatment effects for any well-defined subpopulation.

Still, it seems likely that EITC expansions did improve children's test score outcomes to a degree that is likely to translate into substantially better life outcomes. It is especially reassuring that other authors have recently found impacts that are generally in line with (or even larger than) Dahl and Lochner's estimates. For example, Chetty, Friedman, and Rockoff (2011) use the nonlinearity of the EITC schedule to identify the effect of EITC receipt on New York City schoolchildren's test scores, controlling for a smooth polynomial in AGI. (This can be seen as an informal version of a "regression kink" design, discussed below.) They find that $1,000 in EITC income raises test scores by 0.06–0.09 standard deviations. One would expect that Chetty, et al.'s design would capture the effect of transitory variation in the EITC, where Dahl and Lochner's captures the effect of a permanent increase, so the Chetty et al. results imply substantially larger effects.

There is also evidence of effects on educational attainment—the amount of education obtained—as distinct from achievement on standardized tests during the process. Michelmore (2013) uses state EITC variation and data from the Survey of Income and Program Participation (SIPP) to find that a $1,000 increase in the maximum EITC is associated with eighteen to twenty-three-year-olds in likely EITC-eligible households being 1 percentage point more likely to have ever enrolled in college and 0.3 percentage points more likely to complete a bachelor's degree. The association is driven by individuals younger than twelve at the time of state EITC implementation, and there is no apparent effect of the EITC expansions on older children.

Similarly, Maxfield (2013) uses the National Longitudinal Survey and finds an increase in the maximum EITC of $1,000 increases math achievement by about 7 percent of a standard deviation, increases the probability of high school completion at age nineteen by about 2 percentage points, and increases the probability of completing one or more years of college by age nineteen by about 1.4 percentage points. The apparent effects of EITC expansions are larger for boys and minority children, and the effects on educational outcomes are larger for children who were younger during the expansion.

Manoli and Turner (2014) use a regression kink design (RKD) to study the effect of EITC refunds in the senior year of high school on subsequent college enrollment. The RKD estimator exploits the fact that an extra dollar of earnings is associated with thirty-four to forty cents in additional EITC for a family in the credit schedule's phase-in range, but with no change in EITC for a family in the plateau range. Thus, if the EITC affects enrollment then the relationship between income and enrollment should be stronger below the kink point that separates the two ranges than above it. Manoli and Turner find this to be the case; the magnitude of the effect implies that an extra $100 of EITC rebate in the senior year of high school increases college enrollment by 0.2 to 0.3 percentage points. (Because the RKD identifies the EITC's effect from very small variations, we report the effect per $100. But if one is willing to extrapolate from this design, the overall effect of the program on college enrollment is quite large.)

Taking all of the estimates together, there is robust evidence of quite large effects of the EITC on children's academic achievement and attainment, with potentially important consequences for later-life outcomes. Indeed, the effects are large enough to demand an explanation for the relatively small estimates of effects of family income on student outcomes that come from non-EITC settings. We do not see this issue as fully resolved.

There is one notable area of conflict among the EITC studies. Several of the studies (including Dahl and Lochner 2012; Michelmore 2013; Maxfield 2013) find that effects are concentrated among younger children, and that EITC payments received when children are older have small or zero effects. It is not clear how to reconcile this with the large estimates of Manoli and Turner (2014), which come from variation in the credit received by the families of college seniors, or with Chetty et al.'s (2011) finding that the EITC has larger effects on middle school than on elementary school students. The resolution has important implications for theories of child development.

2.5.4   Labor Market Impacts

An enormous literature in the 1990s examined the labor-supply effects of the EITC, particularly on single mothers (e.g., Eissa and Liebman 1996; Meyer 2002; Meyer and Rosenbaum 2001). Much of this work exploited the large expansion of the program (enacted in 1993), especially for families with two or more children, though some studies instead exploited variation in state-level credits.

There is remarkable consensus around a few key results. In particular, essentially all authors agree that the EITC expansion led to sizable increases in single mothers' employment rates, concentrated among less skilled women and among those with more than one qualifying child. Effects on hours of work, and on male labor supply at either margin, were generally small. We review the key results from this early literature below, but refer readers to Hotz and Scholz (2003; see also Eissa and Hoynes 2006, 2011; Hoynes 2009; Meyer 2008, 2010) for a more comprehensive review. We attempt to be more complete in our review of the somewhat smaller post-2003 literature.

Labor Supply—Extensive Margin

A substantial share of the evidence regarding the EITC's labor-supply effects derives from the 1993 EITC expansion and the historic increase in single mothers' employment during the mid-1990s. This is illustrated in figure 2.8, panel (A): for the decade and a half before 1993, the annual employment rate for unmarried women with children hovered around 70 percent, similar to that for married mothers. By 2001, the single-mother employment rate rose to above 80 percent, similar to that for women without children. It remained elevated through the onset of the Great Recession, but has collapsed since. (This collapse appears to reflect increased rates of school enrollment and/or reduced rates of working while in school among single mothers; it is largely absent in an alternative series that excludes students.)

Many studies identify the EITC's effect based on contrasts between women with a single child and those with two or more children, exploiting the 1993 expansion's relative generosity for multi-child families. Figure 2.8, panel (B) shows employment rates for single women, separately for families with zero, one, two, and three or more children. We see here that the mid-1990s increases are concentrated in larger families, consistent with them being attributable to the EITC. The most recent data also shows a suggestive increase in the employment of women with three or more children, consistent with an effect of the 2009 expansion of the credit for these women, though given the turbulence of recent macroeconomic conditions it is probably too early to draw firm conclusions.

Given the clear patterns in the 1990s, it is not surprising that studies based on the 1993 expansion indicate that the EITC raises single mothers' employment rates. Meyer and Rosenbaum (2001) find that this expansion raised single mothers' annual employment rates by 3.1 percentage points, over one-third of the total increase relative to single childless women between 1992 and 1996. This implies an extensive-margin labor supply elasticity around 0.7. Other studies come to similar conclusions. Dahl, DeLeire, and Schwabish (2009) find that more generous EITC benefits are associated with

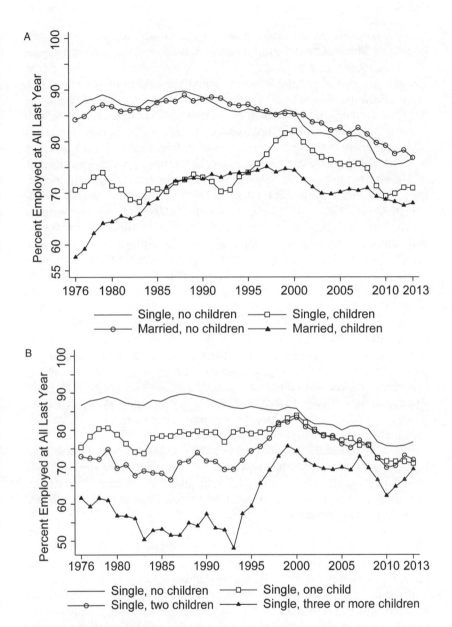

Fig. 2.8 Female employment rates over time

Source: Authors' analysis of the Current Population Survey Annual Social and Economic Supplement (CPS ASEC, also known as the March CPS).

Note: Panel (A): by marital status and presence of children; panel (B): unmarried women, by number of children.

higher year-over-year earnings growth for those who are employed, suggesting that the additional employment is not coming via "dead-end" jobs with little room for advancement.

There are two important concerns about the studies of the mid-1990s expansion. First, as discussed above, studies that identify the effects of the EITC from comparisons between women with a single child and those with two or more children implicitly assume that other policy changes would not have had differential effects on families of different sizes, though this may not be true. There were a great many other things happening during the mid-1990s that might have contributed to the rise in employment, including in particular welfare reform and the strong economy of the late 1990s, and these may have had heterogeneous effects. In particular, the returns to work net of child-care costs are likely to be quite different for women with multiple children than for those with a single child, and for those with young children not yet eligible for public school than for those with older children. This implies differential selection into nonparticipation under any fixed regime, and likely differences in the effects of welfare reform that could easily mirror the expected effects of the EITC by family size. Looney and Manoli (2016) argue that the increase in the 1990s in the relative labor force participation rates of multiple-child single mothers—the main evidence for EITC effects—reflects increases in participation of mothers with children under age five rather than anything about the number of children itself.

A related concern is that the labor supply outcomes seen in the mid-1990s studies might be specific to that time period. In particular, one might expect to see larger effects of work incentives in tight labor markets, as in the mid- to late-1990s, than when there is more slack.

While the literature has not conclusively ruled out either of these concerns, what evidence there is is encouraging. Estimated labor supply effects appear to be quite robust across different time periods (including studies identified from pre-1993 expansions), and studies that exploit state EITC expansions also find similar effects.[12]

The consensus interpretation is not without dissenters, however. Mead (2014) argues that the change in incentives induced by the 1993 EITC expansion was *not* responsible for moving single mothers into the labor force. He relies on survey evidence indicating that potential beneficiaries did not understand or even know of the EITC and that welfare administrators did not credit the EITC with declines in welfare rolls. Mead is generally dismissive of the "several statistical studies that credit the EITC with much, even most, of the rise in work levels among welfare mothers" (22) and claims that "whether the EITC drove welfare recipients to work in the '90s is ultimately

---

12. One exception is Cancian and Levinson (2006), who find no labor supply response to the 1995 introduction of a generous EITC supplement in Wisconsin for women with three children.

a question about human motivation, and on this matter economic analysis alone cannot be trusted to provide a complete answer" (27).

We find Mead's arguments unconvincing. Even if nonworking potential recipients of the expanded EITC knew nothing about it, the EITC could still have had an effect by reducing exit from the labor force among those who had worked and received the credit in an initial year. Low-income workers have high rates of exit and entry, so a modest impact on labor force exit can accumulate into a large change in the stock of labor force participants. The studies on participation are generally silent on the specific mechanism for the observed changes, but it seems plausible given general ignorance about tax policy that impacts on net income are realized after the fact and influence subsequent behavior, keeping many single mothers in the labor force who otherwise would have exited.

Early studies focused on single mothers because the program was most obviously targeted at them and because the predicted effects for that group are relatively straightforward. Eissa and Hoynes (2004), however, point out that the predicted and realized effects for married couples are quite different. In particular, the EITC generally imposes positive average tax rates on a secondary earner's earnings, so is expected to reduce work in this group. Eissa and Hoynes find that EITC expansions between 1984 and 1996 reduced married women's labor force participation rate by about 1 percentage point, with larger effects for subgroups facing the strongest disincentives. This effect is, of course, much smaller than the positive effect on single mothers, small enough not to be visible in figure 2.8, panel (A). The larger number of married mothers, however, means that even a small effect can have important aggregate implications.

Labor Supply—Intensive Margin

Most research on the EITC's labor-supply effects in the last decade has focused on the intensive margin—the choices of the number of weeks to work per year and the number of hours to work per week among those who would work in any case.

Many of the early studies that documented large extensive margin effects for single mothers examined effects on average annual hours worked among workers as well. These generally found very small or zero effects. But standard difference-in-differences research designs are not ideally suited to this question. Estimated effects on mean hours of work among those with some participation combine behavioral effects on those who would have worked in any case with composition effects driven by differences between this group and those who are brought into participation by the EITC expansion. These composition effects may confound true intensive-margin responses.

This has motivated more structural analyses of labor supply (Blundell and MaCurdy 1999). These are based on parametric specifications of the individual's utility function and on assumptions that observed choices are utility maximizing. If the utility function is correctly specified, observed choices can be used to identify its parameters, and these in turn can be used to compute behavioral effects on intensive-margin labor supply net of composition changes. This is easier said than done, however. In particular, it is difficult to incorporate into structural models a realistic distinction between labor force participation and hours of work decisions that allows for meaningfully different responses on the two margins. A typical approach is to discretize the labor supply choice, making zero supply (nonparticipation) one among a small number of choices (Keane and Moffitt [1998]; Blundell et al. [2000]; though Heim [2010] is an exception). More recent models also incorporate potential dynamic effects and incentives (Blundell et al. 2016), which are difficult to study using reduced-form methods.

An advantage of these models is that they yield estimates of structural parameters that can be used to simulate the impacts of policies that have not yet been tried, where the results of reduced-form studies are harder to generalize outside of the specific setting. Blundell et al. (2000), for example, use estimates from a structural labor-supply model to predict the impact of the United Kingdom's Working Families' Tax Credit (WFTC), a rough analogue of the EITC that is available only to individuals meeting minimum hours of work requirements, before data on its actual effects were available.

Set against this major advantage is that structural estimates are often heavily dependent on parametric assumptions, often made for reasons of computational tractability rather than because they are believed to be particularly plausible. This makes it difficult to assess the credibility of the specific parameter estimates, either within the sample or for out-of-sample predictions. Perhaps for this reason, fully structural estimates have not been prominent in the recent literature on the EITC's labor-supply effects, though they have played a larger role in assessments of the UK's WFTC and related programs (Blundell et al. 2009; Blundell and Hoynes 2004).

The US literature has focused on more reduced-form methods, with substantial recent attention to the development of strategies that can identify intensive-margin behavioral responses without a great deal of parametric structure. An example is Saez (2010). Saez notes that standard labor-supply models predict that intensive-margin responses will vary across the different segments of the EITC schedule: those in the phase-in range will increase their labor supply, those in the phase-out range will reduce it, and those in the plateau will likely show smaller responses. This implies that the EITC should lead to "hollowing out" of the earnings distribution around the third kink, at the end of the phase-out range of the schedule, and to "bunching" around the first and second kinks.

This is illustrated for several hypothetical individuals in figure 2.9. The curved lines illustrate indifference curves between leisure and consumption that would generate traditional labor supply responses. The person whose preferences are depicted in panel (A) would have chosen labor supply

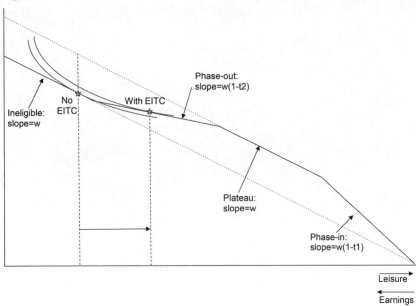

A Consumption

Phase-out:
slope=w(1-t2)

No
EITC   With EITC

Ineligible:
slope=w

Plateau:
slope=w

Phase-in:
slope=w(1-t1)

Leisure

Earnings

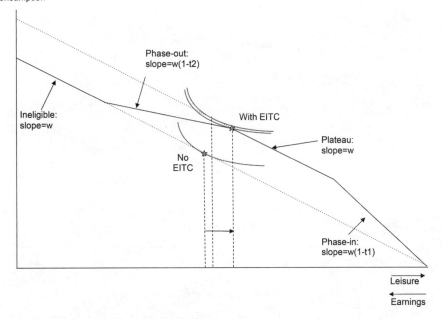

B Consumption

Phase-out:
slope=w(1-t2)

With EITC

Ineligible:
slope=w

Plateau:
slope=w

No
EITC

Phase-in:
slope=w(1-t1)

Leisure

Earnings

Fig. 2.9   Labor supply responses to the EITC

Note: Panel (A): "hollowing out" at the third kink point due to labor supply reductions; panel
(B): "bunching" at the second kink point due to labor supply reductions.

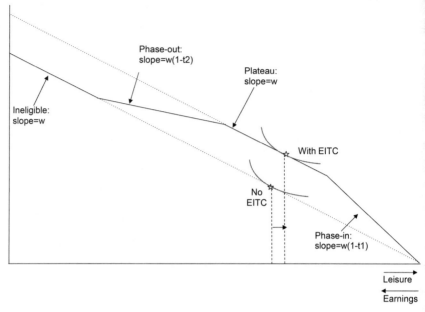

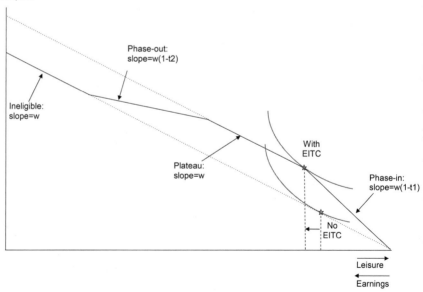

Fig. 2.9   (cont.)
Note: Panel (C): no clear effect on the distribution in the plateau range; and panel (D): "bunching" at the first kink point due to labor supply increases.

above the maximum level for credit eligibility had the credit not existed, but responds to the program by reducing her labor supply into the phase-out range in order to receive a credit. This response leads to "hollowing out" of the earnings distribution around the point where the credit disappears, due to nonconvexity of the budget set here.

By contrast, panel (B) shows the indifference curves for an individual who would have chosen labor supply sufficient to place her in the phase-out range before the expansion, but who after the expansion locates herself at the "kink" point between the plateau and the phase-out regions. This sort of response will lead to a point mass in the earnings distribution at this kink, as a range of individuals shift from just above the kink to locate exactly at it.

Panel (C) shows a third individual who would have been in the plateau range before the expansion. For this person, the expansion represents a pure income effect, with no distortion to the relative price of leisure. Income effects may produce increases or reductions in labor supply, but these are not likely to be large. Finally, the individual depicted in panel (D) would have located in the phase-in range without the credit, and substitution effects lead her to increase her labor supply in response to the credit, creating a second point mass at the first schedule kink.

This figure illustrates the unambiguous prediction that if the intensive margin elasticity is nonzero, a measurable fraction of the population will relocate from the phase-in and phase-out ranges to the first and second kink points when the EITC is expanded, while others will reduce labor supply to move from the region beyond the end of the EITC eligibility range onto the phase-out segment. Assuming that underlying preferences are smoothly distributed, then, one can measure the size of the intensive-margin labor supply elasticity by the excess mass of the earnings distribution located at or near the convex kink points, relative to an estimate of the mass near these points in the counterfactual. (In principle, it would also be possible to construct an estimate from the "missing" mass around the nonconvex kink at the end of the phase-out segment.)

Carrying out this exercise, Saez (2010) finds little sign of bunching at the EITC kink or at other, similar thresholds in the tax schedule. This is consistent with the other evidence that intensive-margin labor supply elasticities are small, though it could also indicate that people are simply unaware of their marginal tax rates or unable to choose their total annual earnings with much precision (as would occur if people had less-than-full ability to predict their December hours or earnings earlier in the year).

There is one group for which Saez does find substantial evidence of bunching: the self-employed. Individuals with positive self-employment income are very disproportionately likely to have earnings at or very near the first kink point of the EITC schedule, at the end of the phase-in range. Interestingly, there is no sign of bunching even in this group at the second kink point (at the beginning of the phase-out range), nor of a hollowing out of the density at the third (at the end of the phase-out range), though the standard model would predict all three.

As Saez points out, the total marginal tax rate, combining the EITC and other taxes (e.g., payroll taxes), is generally negative in the phase-in range (see the discussion in section 2.2.2). This means that an individual or family with earnings below the first kink point would come out ahead by reporting to the IRS *higher* earnings than it actually had. Alternatively, a family that would underreport its income in the absence of the EITC would face an incentive not to do so—up to the first kink point—in its presence. The self-employed likely have a fair amount of latitude over how much income to report, as there is no external check on their reported earnings. Thus, Saez suggests that the bunching he observes likely reflects decisions to report casual earnings (e.g., from babysitting) that would not have been reported to the IRS in the absence of the EITC. This is consistent with evidence from LaLumia (2009) that reported self-employment income has grown over time among EITC recipients, and that this income tends to increase the EITC payment rather than reduce it.

One potential explanation for the general failure to find meaningful intensive-margin effects is that EITC recipients are only vaguely aware of the program rules, and may not realize the incentives they face. Chetty and Saez (2013) report on an information experiment conducted on clients of the H&R Block tax preparation firm. Tax preparers were asked to spend a few minutes with randomly selected clients explaining the EITC rules and the marginal incentives that the client faced. Chetty and Saez measure the effect of this treatment on the subsequent year's earnings and EITC payment. They find only small effects on average. When they focus on the subsample of preparers who seem to have been particularly effective at explaining the marginal incentives, they find somewhat larger effects: treatment by these preparers increased EITC payments the next year by about 3 percent, on average. These effects are concentrated among the self employed, though Chetty and Saez find effects on wages as well.

This at least suggests that intensive-margin responses may be depressed by lack of information about the marginal tax rate, though in our eyes the treatment-group responses remain quite small regardless. For taxpayers with two children in the phase-in range, where the marginal tax rate is 40 percent, a 3 percent increase in EITC payments due to moving from zero knowledge to full knowledge of the incentives corresponds to an intensive-margin labor supply elasticity of about $0.03/0.40 = 0.075$. This calculation is inexact in many ways—not all participants are in the phase-in range, some may have known about their tax rates even without the treatment, or may not have fully understood them with it, and so forth. But even a full accounting for all of these factors would be unlikely to yield an implied intensive-margin elasticity even in the ballpark of the extensive-margin elasticities discussed above.

Chetty, Friedman, and Saez (2013) build on the Saez (2010) and Chetty and Saez (2013) papers to construct another measure of intensive-margin responses based on labor supply of new parents. Because families with children are eligible for a much more generous credit than those without, individuals who have just had a child—or who expect to have one later in the calendar year—face incentives to change their labor supply from what was optimal before parenthood. Thus, Chetty et al. measure the frequency with which the change in labor supply from the year before to the year of a first child's birth has the effect of increasing the family's EITC. An important advantage of this measure is its sensitivity to realistic labor-supply responses. It may be difficult for respondents to bunch precisely if they do not have exact control over their hours of work or have a hard time predicting their end-of-year earnings when they make labor-supply decisions earlier in the year, but they may nevertheless be responding to the EITC's intensive-margin elasticities by moving themselves further up the schedule than they would otherwise wind up being.

Using this measure, Chetty, Friedman, and Saez (2013) estimate an average intensive-margin earnings elasticity around 0.14 in the phase-out region and 0.31 in the phase-in region. They also find that the response is correlated across geographic areas with a Saez-style (2010) measure of the amount of bunching at the first kink point among the self-employed. They interpret the latter variation as deriving from differences in awareness of the EITC schedule and the incentives it creates, and thus the covariation between the two measures as an indication that intensive-margin responses are depressed by a lack of information. In ZIP Codes in the top decile of bunching among the self-employed, they estimate intensive-margin elasticities of 0.29 in the phase-out region and 0.84 in the phase-in.

The discrepancy with prior estimates that generally fail to find meaningful intensive-margin responses likely has several potential explanations. One is the limitations of difference-in-differences estimates of intensive-margin responses, discussed above, which may have masked true responses in earlier work. A second is that past work focuses primarily on the phase-out range—as discussed above, policymakers and researchers are more concerned with tax-induced reductions in work effort than with increases. Chetty et al.'s estimate of the intensive-margin response in this range is quite small. Many past studies could not have identified effects of this magnitude.

On the other hand, there are also reasons to be concerned about the generalizability of Chetty et al.'s results, which are identified from the specific population of new parents in the calendar year in which a first child is born. These individuals may have unusual latitude to respond to tax incentives on the intensive margin, simply by delaying or accelerating their return to work following parental leave. Other workers may find it more challenging to adjust their hours worked. Chetty et al. present event-study evidence that effects persist (but do not grow) for several years after the child's birth. But many of the families in question will have additional children in that interval, so will be facing more generous schedules with stronger incentives than in the initial year. Thus, constant effects imply a declining labor-supply elasticity.

These considerations lead us to conclude that the true intensive-margin elasticity is probably positive, but small, on average. Even Chetty, Friedman, and Saez's (2013) estimate of an average intensive elasticity of 0.14 in the phase-out range, in a population that might be expected to be unusually responsive, is several multiples smaller than consensus estimates of the extensive-margin elasticity around 0.7 to 1.0. There may be a somewhat higher elasticity in the phase-in range, though it is also possible that this reflects reporting along the lines of the reporting choices that lead to bunching among the self-employed. Chetty, Friedman, and Saez (2013) assume that wage and salary workers do not have latitude over reporting, but this is not clear: they may be able to work under the table, or simply to fail to report (some of) their tip income. In any event, even if all of the phase-in response is real, it remains much smaller than the extensive elasticity.

Chetty et al. find much larger responses in ZIP Codes where the self-employed exhibit a high degree of bunching. Their interpretation is that intensive-margin labor-supply elasticities with respect to known incentives are reasonably large, but that it is only in these ZIP Codes that knowledge of the credit is widespread. Under this view, average elasticities are small only because people in more typical ZIP Codes are generally unaware of their marginal tax rates, but there are other possible interpretations. Chetty et al.'s bunching measure could equally well be interpreted not as a measure of knowledge of the tax schedule, but as a proxy for access to advisers with financial interests in maximizing recipients' refunds and/or a willingness to bend the rules to do so. This is supported by the geographic distribution: bunching is high in the southern United States, consistent with other evidence that social capital and rule-following are relatively low in this region. If this interpretation is correct, responses in high-knowledge areas may not actually reflect taxpayers' underlying preferences or even their true labor supply, and expanding this form of knowledge may not be welfare improving.

Incidence

Hotz and Scholz (2003) concluded that there was only one major EITC-related topic that had not received serious scholarly attention: the economic incidence of the credit. The topic has received some attention since, but remains understudied.

The empirical evidence reviewed above suggests that single mothers have increased their labor supply substantially in response to EITC expansions, with any negative intensive-margin effects dominated by the extensive-margin effects, and that any effects on married women were small by comparison. Standard tax incidence models (section 2.4.3) have two key predictions in this setting. First, the increase in labor supply should have reduced pretax wages. Second, the decline in wages should be observed both for EITC recipients and for others who are close substitutes for them in production (that is, who compete in the same labor markets).

This second prediction presents a challenge for studies of wage effects. Recall the standard research design for studying labor-supply responses to the EITC, contrasting single mothers with one versus two or more children in periods where the EITC schedule became relatively more generous for the latter. This design cannot be used to identify the effect of the credit on wages: insofar as single-child and multiple-child mothers participate in the same labor markets, one would expect any wage effects of the EITC to be the same for the two.

Identifying wage effects thus requires an empirical strategy that compares two separate labor markets, with different EITC-induced labor-supply shocks, which are distinct enough that participants in the two are not close substitutes in production, but nevertheless similar enough that one can credibly distinguish EITC effects on the difference between the two from other determinants of wages. This is a tough order.

Leigh (2010) exploits the introduction of state-level EITCs in a difference-in-differences framework. His identifying assumption, not unreasonable, is that it is difficult for employers to substitute workers in different states, at least in the short term. He finds that a 10 percent increase in the EITC—through, for example, the introduction of a state EITC equal to 10 percent of the federal credit—leads to a 5 percent reduction in pretax wages for high school dropouts and a 2 percent reduction for high school graduates, with no effect on the wages of college graduates. These wage effects are similar for eligible and ineligible members of these groups, as predicted by the incidence model above.

In interpreting these surprising effects, Leigh focuses on the ratio of the effect of the EITC on labor supply to the effect on wages. Comparing equations (4) and (3), this ratio equals the elasticity of labor demand; Leigh estimates that it is around –0.3.

But examining only the ratio of the two coefficients obscures an important part of the story. Assuming that the labor demand curve is not upward sloping, equation (5) indicates that a reduction in the effective tax rate unambiguously raises net-of-tax wages, and equation (4) indicates that pretax wages can fall by no more than the average subsidy rate across all workers in the labor market. Leigh's estimates are not consistent with these restrictions. The federal EITC phase-in rate is around 40 percent, so a 10 percent increase in the EITC corresponds to an earnings subsidy of 4 percent or less. Leigh finds that this reduces the pretax wage of high school dropouts by 5 percent. Moreover, only one-quarter of these workers are EITC eligible. Thus, Leigh's estimates imply that employers capture approximately 500 percent of total EITC spending, and that state EITCs reduce the after-tax incomes not just of ineligible workers but of eligible workers as well. This cannot occur through pure incidence channels.

To be clear, we do not criticize Leigh's approach or methods. Both are reasonable, particularly relative to other feasible solutions. But they yield somewhat unreasonable results. One possible interpretation is to note that the 5 percent wage effect has a standard error of a bit over 1 percent, so we cannot reject that net-of-tax wages for eligible workers were constant. But even this requires a wage effect quadruple what would be seen with wholly inelastic labor demand.

Rothstein (2008) uses a different strategy to estimate wage effects of the EITC. He focuses on the 1993 national expansion of the program, but notes that any labor market effects of this expansion should be concentrated in the low-skill labor markets where EITC recipients participate. He thus examines differences in single women's wage trends by skill level (proxied by position in the wage distribution) for evidence of EITC effects. He finds that low-skill women's relative pretax wages *rose* in the mid-1990s, where the incidence model predicts a decline, but that the rate of relative increase was slower than in the prior period. Under an assumption that technical change was increasing the relative demand for low-skill women's labor at a constant rate over the late 1980s and early 1990s, the impact of the EITC can be identified from the change in the relative rate of earnings growth. He estimates that the pattern of wage and labor supply changes over the mid-1990s are consistent with a total labor supply elasticity around 0.7, driven by the extensive margin, and a labor demand elasticity around –0.3.

Eissa and Nichols (2005) examine trends in 10th percentile wages for single mothers. They find no indication that these were affected by EITC expansions, but suggest that the EITC's effects may be masked by the floor placed on wages by the minimum wage. Finally, Azmat (2008) examines wage effects of the United Kingdom Working Families' Tax Credit (WFTC). As discussed above, the WFTC is administered via workers' paychecks, so employers know which workers are and are not receiving the credit. Azmat finds that participating workers' pretax wages fell relative to those of non-participants in the same workplaces. Insofar as the two groups of workers are substitutes in production, the standard model implies that wage effects should be identical (and that the contrast cannot identify the incidence effect), so Azmat's evidence points to employer discrimination that is ruled out in neoclassical models but may be possible if employers are monopsonistic.

While each of these studies makes a valiant effort to identify wage effects of the EITC, we think—each of us having authored or coauthored one of them—that they are collectively far from decisive. There is room for much more work on the topic. Unfortunately, given the identification challenges discussed above, we are not optimistic that the problem will be resolved in the near term.

In the absence of a clean identification strategy for the EITC's effects on wages, a more promising approach might be to rely on external estimates of the labor-demand elasticity to calibrate a calculation of the distributional effects of the EITC. This is done by Rothstein (2010). With an extensive-margin labor-supply elasticity of 0.75, an intensive-margin elasticity of zero, a labor demand elasticity of -0.3, and the observed distribution of eligible and ineligible workers across labor markets (defined by skill levels), he finds that employers capture about $0.36 of each dollar spent on the program through reduced wages. Workers' after-tax incomes rise by only $0.73—$1 in EITC payments, plus $0.09 from increased labor supply, less $0.36 in reduced wages per hour worked. Importantly, there are large distributional effects within the group of workers. The eligible workers themselves receive a net transfer (EITC payment less wage effect) of $0.83. After-tax incomes rise by $1.07, with the additional $0.24 coming from increased labor supply (with only second-order effects on recipients' utility). But ineligible workers lose $0.18 through reduced wages and $0.16 through the induced reductions in labor supply.

Table 2.7 illustrates the effects on four demographic groups: single mothers, single women without children, married mothers, married women without children, and employers. Rothstein (2010) assumes that labor markets are segmented by gender, age, education, and marital status. He focuses exclusively on female labor markets. As there are few single fathers and married men are more likely to be primary than secondary earners, there are unlikely to be meaningful EITC effects on the male labor market. In the single women labor market, the EITC induces a substantial increase in the amount of labor supplied, driving down wages and negatively impacting childless workers. Employers capture nearly 100 percent of total spending, so all of the transfer received by EITC-eligible workers is paid for with

Table 2.7   Simulations of EITC incidence

Group	Intended EITC transfer	Change in earnings due to			Change in after-tax income	Change in welfare
		Labor supply	Wages	Total		
Single women						
With children	+0.55	+0.35	−0.31	+0.04	+0.59	+0.24
Without children	0	−0.20	−0.23	−0.43	−0.43	−0.23
Employers						+0.54
Married women						
With children	+0.45	−0.10	+0.14	+0.04	+0.49	+0.59
Without children	0	+0.04	+0.05	+0.09	+0.09	+0.05
Employers						−0.19

Notes: Calculations are based on the estimates of Rothstein (2010, table 5, panel [a]) and correspond to $1 in EITC spending distributed across single and married women with children in proportion to their share of actual EITC spending.

transfers away from ineligible workers. In the married women market, however, the EITC's initial effect is to reduce total labor supply. Wages thus rise modestly, with positive impacts on childless workers and transfers away from employers.

These simulations are far from decisive. Among other limitations, the assumption that single and married women participate in distinct labor markets is not well supported.[13] But the general conclusion that labor-supply subsidies in competitive labor markets are in part captured by employers is almost certainly robust. This has important policy implications. In particular, Saez's (2002) conclusion that an EITC structure is approximately optimal depends on the incidence of the credit falling exclusively on the worker. Incidence considerations strengthen the argument for negative income tax-like structures, with positive transfers at zero earnings and less negative tax rates at low earnings. (This could be implemented as an EITC plus a separate welfare program for nonworkers that phases out over the EITC phase-in range.) They also militate for combining the EITC with other policies aimed at limiting employer capture, such as the minimum wage (Lee and Saez 2012).

2.5.5   Interactions

Interactions with Cash Welfare

The EITC is in many ways a substitute for cash welfare, both in the minds of its political backers and in the trends in caseloads and expenditures over time. Moreover, the major expansion of the EITC in the mid-1990s roughly coincided with welfare reform, and with a large increase in the labor force participation of single mothers. Interactions between the programs are thus of interest, though mostly historically: TANF is a shadow of the former AFDC program, and is no longer a major component of the antipoverty portfolio.

Grogger (2004) studies transitions onto and off of welfare in the 1990s. He identifies the effect of EITC benefits on these transitions both from variation in state EITCs and from changes in the relative generosity of the federal EITC across different family sizes. He finds that higher EITC benefits are associated with lower probabilities of entering welfare. However, there is no association with the likelihood of exiting welfare, suggesting that work subsidies were not a major "pull" factor in the decline in welfare caseloads. This is consistent with our interpretation of Mead's (2014) survey results, discussed in section 2.5.4.

---

13. Rothstein (2010) also presents estimates in which there is just one labor market for each education-age group of women. This does not change the amount of the credit that employers are able to capture, though it does change the distribution of benefits across demographic groups: wage losses are smaller, so eligible workers see larger increases in their after-tax incomes, but are spread across larger groups of ineligible workers.

Hotz, Mullin, and Scholz (2010) find that EITC expansions may have had important effects on former welfare recipients' labor force participation. Studying a sample drawn from California's database of welfare recipients, they find that the differential expansion of the EITC for families with two or more children raised employment rates of multiple-child families by 3.4 percentage points relative to families with one child. They conclude that this is consistent with an employment elasticity around 1.3, at the upper end of the range of previous studies. They do not examine transitions from welfare to work directly, so their estimates are also consistent with the EITC's effect operating through reduced exit from work rather than through increased entry.

Labor Market Interactions

The EITC also likely interacts importantly with labor market institutions, including unemployment insurance, disability insurance, and the minimum wage. There has been relatively little work on these interactions. Neumark and Wascher (2011) use variation in state EITCs and state minimum wages in a difference-in-differences framework to examine the interaction between these two policies. In models for low-skill single mothers' employment and earnings, they find positive interaction effects of the generosity of the state EITC with the level of the minimum wage. They find some evidence of a negative interaction effect on employment of low-skilled, childless men and women. In qualitative terms, the pattern of results appears consistent with what one would expect the impact of the EITC to be in a labor market subject to a binding minimum wage: labor supply increases, wages are largely unaffected, and jobs are rationed. It is not clear from Neumark and Wascher's (2011) reported results how to interpret the magnitudes, however.

LaLumia (2013) examines interactions of the EITC with unemployment at the individual level. She finds that unemployment spells that coincide with the receipt of EITC refunds last longer, consistent with the presence of important liquidity effects on job search behavior (Chetty 2008; Card, Chetty, and Weber 2007).

Bitler, Hoynes, and Kuka (2016) also study interactions between the EITC and unemployment, but at a macroeconomic level. Specifically, they ask whether EITC recipiency and payments rise in business-cycle downturns. As noted earlier, this relationship is theoretically ambiguous: labor market slack may reduce the number of would-be EITC claimants who are able to find work, but may also lead to more eligibility among involuntary part-year workers whose wages are too high to qualify for the EITC with full-year work or among married couples who could qualify for the credit with one earner but not with two. Bitler et al. find that higher unemployment rates are associated with more recipiency and payments for married couples, implying that the second effect dominates for this group, but that the net effect is negative but statistically insignificant for single individuals. This implies that the EITC plays a weaker countercyclical stabilization role than do explicitly countercyclical programs like unemployment insurance or traditional means-tested transfers like TANF and SNAP.

2.6   Proposed Modifications

The EITC is generally seen as a successful program, but it is by no means perfect. We are aware of a number of serious proposals to modify the program in various ways.

2.6.1   Changes within the Same Basic Structure

There have been a number of proposals to expand the EITC, either as a whole or for particular groups. Recently, these discussions have centered on the temporary EITC expansions (a larger credit for three-child families and an extended schedule for married couples) introduced in 2009, which are currently due to expire in 2017. President Obama's 2016 budget proposal would make these permanent.

Discussions of expanding the EITC often occur against the backdrop of a proposed increase in the minimum wage. Opponents of minimum wage increases frequently argue that the EITC is a superior alternative. But this reflects an unsupported assumption that the two programs are substitutes. The incidence considerations above imply that they are best thought of as complements, and that increases in the EITC strengthen the case for raising the minimum wage (Lee and Saez 2012; Konczal 2013).

One area of recurrent concern is incentives for noncustodial parents. A focus in this area has been to create incentives for the payment of child support, by allowing these parents to receive the credit but conditioning it on the payment of child support (Primus 2006). Noncustodial parent credits have recently been implemented in New York and Washington, DC. A regression discontinuity evaluation of New York's noncustodial parent credit finds increased work and payment of child support in full for noncustodial parents just eligible for the credit (Nichols, Sorensen, Lippold 2012). An ongoing experiment in New York City is designed to test a credit-like conditional transfer for childless workers in certain subgroups, including noncustodial parents.

A more consequential change would be to expand the EITC for childless workers more generally. This has attracted support of late from both President Obama and prominent Republicans (notably Representative Paul Ryan, now chair of the House Ways and Means Committee). President Obama's most recent proposal, part of his 2016 budget, would double the childless worker credit and extend the phase-out range, as well as extend the age ranges at which taxpayers are eligible.

Berlin (2007) proposes a more radical modification in the structure of the EITC. He would make EITC eligibility depend on individual earnings, without regard to marriage or children. This would eliminate the second worker penalty, alter marriage and fertility incentives, and generate tens of billions of dollars in additional credit payments, mostly to married couples. The expansions of the plateau for taxpayers married filing jointly during the first decade of the twenty-first century have made the proposal cheaper to implement, but budgetary concerns make implementation of the proposal unlikely. A related, more incremental recent proposal from Kearney and Turner (2013) would allow secondary earners to deduct a portion of their earnings. This would also reduce the second worker penalty and effectively extend the EITC schedule to higher earnings levels for two-earner families.

Several authors have proposed rationalizing the definitions of children across tax and transfer rules (e.g., Maag 2011), which would reduce compliance costs. As noted above, recent changes in dependent rules move in this direction. But other recent policies have moved in the opposite direction. For example, the Affordable Care Act extended health insurance under parental policies to age twenty-five, a threshold that has not been used for other programs.

2.6.2   Administration of the EITC

An important source of policymakers' dissatisfaction with the EITC revolves around its arrival as a lump-sum payment, months after the period that it nominally covers. This is surely an important brake on the credit's ability to cushion families against income shocks, and it creates an opportunity for financial services firms to capture a portion of the credit via expensive financial instruments. It seems clear that the EITC would be more effective as a means of supporting low-wage families if it could somehow be delivered more evenly through the year. But the desire to do this runs up against the failure of the Advance EITC program.

Nevertheless, the ambition to change the method of payment remains, and several proposals or demonstrations have arisen in recent years. For example, the Periodic Earned Income Tax Credit Payment Pilot Project, begun in 2014 by the Center for Economic Progress, Chicago Mayor Rahm Emanuel, the Chicago Housing Authority, and the University of Illinois at Urbana-Champaign, aims to explore whether a quarterly advance credit (structured as a loan but treated as an advance on the credit) can help balance families' needs for a savings vehicle with the need for extra resources during the year. The Center for American Progress (Vallas, Boteach, and West 2014) recently proposed allowing workers to access a small portion of their EITC early so they do not have to rely on predatory lending products, an idea adopted in 2015 by Senator Sherrod Brown from Ohio.

However, it is clear that there would be real drawbacks from any such effort. The payment of means-tested health insurance subsidies under the Patient Protection and Affordable Care Act (PPACA, or Obamacare) is a useful analogy. Eligibility for subsidies depends on annual family income, just like the EITC. But because the subsidies are meant to make health insurance affordable, they are paid out gradually through the year. This means that families that overestimate their eligibility for subsidies may be faced with large bills at tax time. At this writing, it is not clear how this will be handled.

It is easier to see a route toward reducing the role of for-profit tax preparers in the administration of the EITC. Recent bank regulation efforts have largely eliminated refund anticipation loans, though there are still other financial products designed to capture a portion of the tax refund. The IRS encourages claimants to simply write "EITC" on their tax returns rather than attempting to calculate it, presumably in part to simplify returns so that recipients do not need to engage preparers. Moreover, there exist in many areas not-for-profit tax preparation services for those who still need assistance.

2.6.3   EITC Expansion for Workers with Disabilities

There have been several recent proposals for a new EITC aimed exclusively at workers with a documented work-limiting disability. For example, the Disability Policy Panel of the National Academy of Social Insurance in 1996 recommended the creation of a refundable Disabled Worker Tax Credit (Oi 1996, 122). The impetus for the proposals is the pending exhaustion of the Social Security Disability Insurance (SSDI) trust fund and the perceived disconnect between the expressed desire to work among beneficiaries of SSDI and the ineffectiveness of current strategies to encourage work. While one in six SSDI beneficiaries say they would like to earn their way off the rolls within five years, the take-up rate for the Ticket to Work incentive is under 2 percent (Stapleton et al. 2008).

Huang and Schmeiser (2012) and Rutledge (2014) examine the likely impact of EITC expansions on people with work-limiting disabilities and find an increase in labor force participation among workers with resident children compared to those without. While the 1 percent increase estimated by Rutledge does not differ significantly from zero, it is consistent with a large impact on a subset of these individuals and no impact on most. He also finds an impact on the intensive margin, as workers with disabilities and resident children work more.

Gokhale (2014) proposes a more significant intervention, combining a refundable credit with dramatic changes in SSDI program rules that would eliminate the cliff in eligibility and instead impose a smooth effective tax on additional earnings starting with the first dollar. While this proposal would almost certainly encourage more work, the more effective it is, the more costly it becomes, and its main effect is to transfer program costs out of SSDI and into refundable tax credits, with different budget-scoring rules. A policy that would deliver equivalent benefits monthly instead of annually could be administered through an altered Supplemental Security Income (SSI) program, which has no trust fund limitation but is scored as a spending program rather than a negative tax. Policy innovations through SSI could be implemented through state waivers as well, to encourage state experimentation in developing the most effective innovation.

2.7 Conclusion

The EITC has become the centerpiece of the US safety net, dwarfing other means-tested programs in terms of the number of beneficiaries, total expenditures, or poverty-reduction impacts.

Research in the last two decades has documented large positive impacts on net incomes for low-income families who work and dramatic improvements in well-being among children in those families. The EITC expansions of the 1990s seem to have increased work among single parents, though they may have induced some secondary workers to cut back. Recent research has documented extremely important benefits for children's educational achievement and attainment. The generally positive impacts found for the EITC have led to broad political support and a raft of proposals to expand its reach.

The exact form of the credit evolves frequently. Recent changes reducing marriage penalties may have increased marriage rates among some low-income families, and experimental state-level credits aimed at noncustodial parents seem to have increased work and payment of child support.

The advantage of an earned income tax credit over a negative income tax or equivalent transfer policy (e.g., cash welfare with a less than 100 percent claw-back rate) depends on the effectiveness of the EITC at moving people into work, and on the desirability of that outcome. During an exceptionally weak job market, expanding the size of the EITC is less attractive as people induced to enter the labor market are more likely to move into unemployment rather than employment, or to displace other potential workers. Moreover, even in stronger markets some of the benefit of larger credits accrues to employers through reduced pretax wages, at least if the credits are not accompanied by increased minimum wages. Nevertheless, the political attractiveness of tax credits relative to spending programs appears undiminished. Thus, we should expect more policy variation in the future.

In the last decade, research on the EITC has broadened beyond the initial focus on single mothers' labor supply to consider a wide variety of other outcomes. We discuss here a few topics that, while not necessarily understudied, remain less than completely resolved. These would be our priorities for future research.

On the labor-supply front, a better understanding of intensive margin responses would be quite valuable. How generalizable are Chetty, Friedman, and Saez's (2013) results to a population beyond first-time parents? Another important question in this area concerns the form of intensive margin responses: Do these come through changes in hours worked per week or through changes in weeks worked per year? The latter is in some sense an extensive margin effect; given other evidence of strong extensive margin effects, it would be unsurprising if much of the apparent intensive margin responsiveness reflected effects on weeks worked (including those that occur via changes in job durations).

Another set of important topics for further research concerns the effects of the EITC on human capital accumulation. What are the mechanisms that underlie the large effects on children's academic achievement and attainment discussed in section 2.5.3? Are there dynamic effects on recipients' own long-run productivity, perhaps operating through more stable labor force attachment or through crowd-out of formal education by increased employment? Does the availability of the EITC affect potential future recipients' educational investment decisions in the pre-labor-market stage of life?

A third set of topics concerns the nature of gaming, manipulation, and tax evasion that leads to bunching among the self-employed at the EITC kink point. What, exactly, is going on here? Are people working more to qualify for the maximum credit, reporting their actual income more completely, or fabricating income for the purpose of receiving the credit?

Among topics that have not been much studied to date, we think that one of the most important concerns the interaction of the EITC with the new health insurance marketplaces created under the Affordable Care Act, and in particular with the new means-tested subsidies for insurance purchase. This bears study as the new health insurance regime takes shape.

Finally, as the EITC has become an ever-larger share of the US antipoverty portfolio, more research is needed into the people who are *not* reached. How many people fail to qualify for the EITC due to extended spells of unemployment, to work-limiting disabilities, or to other barriers to employment? How do they make ends meet?

References

Acs, Gregory, and Eric Toder. 2007. "Should We Subsidize Work? Welfare Reform, the Earned Income Tax Credit and Optimal Transfers." *International Tax and Public Finance* 14 (3): 327–43.

Akerlof, George A. 1978. "The Economics of 'Tagging' as Applied to the Optimal Income Tax, Welfare Programs, and Manpower Planning." *American Economic Review* 68 (1): 8–19.

Allegretto, Sylvia, Arindrajit Dube, and Michael Reich. 2008. "New Estimates of Minimum Wage Effects after Correcting for Spatial Heterogeneity and Selectivity." Working Paper, Institute for Research on Labor and Employment, University of California, Berkeley, March.

Alm, James, and Leslie A. Whittington. 1999. "For Love or Money? The Impact of Income Taxes on Marriage." *Economica* 66:297–316.

Athreya, Kartik B., Devin Reilly, and Nicole B. Simpson. 2010. "Earned Income Tax Credit Recipients: Income, Marginal Tax Rates, Wealth, and Credit Constraints." *Economic Quarterly* 96 (3): 229–58.

Azmat, Ghazala. 2008. "The Incidence of an Earned Income Tax Credit: Evaluating the Impact on Wages in the UK." Working Paper, Barcelona, University Pompeu Fabra, March.

Baker, Kevin. 2008. "Do Cash Transfer Programs Improve Infant Health: Evidence from the 1993 Expansion of the Earned Income Tax Credit." Working Paper, University of Notre Dame.

Barrow, Lisa, and Leslie McGranahan. 2000. "The Effects of the Earned Income Tax Credit on the Seasonality of Household Expenditures." *National Tax Journal* 53 (4, part 2): 1211–43.

Baughman, Reagan A. 2012. "The Effects of State EITC Expansion on Children's Health." Carsey Institute at the Scholars' Repository Paper no. 168, Durham, NH, Carsey Institute, May.

Baughman, Reagan A., and Stacy Dickert-Conlin. 2009. "The Earned Income Tax Credit and Fertility." *Journal of Population Economics* 22 (3): 537–63.

Baughman, Reagan A., and Noelia Duchovny. 2016. "State Earned Income Tax Credits and the Production of Child Health: Insurance Coverage, Utilization, and Health Status." *National Tax Journal* 69:103–32.

Berlin, Gordon L. 2007. "Rewarding the Work of Individuals: A Counterintuitive Approach to Reducing Poverty and Strengthening Families." *Future of Children* 17 (2): 17–42.

Bhargava, Saurabh, and Dayanand Manoli. 2015. "Psychological Frictions and the Incomplete Take-Up of Social Benefits: Evidence from an IRS Field Experiment." *American Economic Review* 105 (11): 1–42.

Bitler, Marianne P., Hilary Hoynes, and Elira Kuka. 2016. "Do In-Work Tax Credits Serve as a Safety Net?" *Journal of Human Resources* doi:10.3368/jhr.52.2.0614-6433R1.

Blumenthal, Marsha, Brian Erard, and Chih-Chin Ho. 2005. "Participation and Compliance with the Earned Income Tax Credit." *National Tax Journal* 58 (2): 189–213.

Blundell, Richard. 2006. "Earned Income Tax Credit Policies: Impact and Optimality." *Labour Economics* 13:423–43.

Blundell, Richard, Mike Brewer, Peter Haan, and Andrew Shephard. 2009. "Optimal Income Taxation of Lone Mothers: An Empirical Comparison of the UK and Germany." *Economic Journal* 199 (February): 101–21.

Blundell, Richard, Monica Costa Dias, Costas Meghir, and Jonathan M. Shaw. 2016. "Female Labour Supply, Human Capital and Welfare Reform." Cowles Foundation Discussion Paper no. 1892RR. New Haven, CT.

Blundell, Richard, Alan Duncan, Julian McCrae, and Costas Meghir. 2000. "The Labour Market Impact of the Working Families' Tax Credit." *Fiscal Studies* 21 (1): 75–104.

Blundell, Richard, and Hilary W. Hoynes. 2004. "Has 'In-Work' Benefit Reform Helped the Labor Market?" In *Seeking a Premier Economy: The Economic Effects of British Economic Reforms, 1980–2000*, edited by David Card, Richard Blundell, and Richard B. Freeman, 411–59. Chicago: University of Chicago Press.

Blundell, Richard, and Thomas MaCurdy. 1999. "Labor Supply: A Review of Alternative Approaches." *Handbook of Labor Economics,* vol. 3 (part A), edited by Orley C. Ashenfelter and David Card, 1559–695. Amsterdam: North-Holland.

Bound, John, David A. Jaeger, and Regina M. Baker. 1995. "Problems with Instrumental Variables Estimation When the Correlation between the Instruments and the Endogenous Explanatory Variable is Weak." *Journal of the American Statistical Association* 90 (430): 443–50.

Boyd-Swan, Casey, Chris M. Herbst, John Ifcher, and Homa Zarghamee. 2013. "The Earned Income Tax Credit, Health, and Happiness." IZA Discussion Paper no. 7261, Bonn, Germany, Forschungsinstitut zur Zukunft der Arbeit, March.

Brewer, Mike, Emmanuel Saez, and Andrew Shephard. 2010. "Means-Testing and Tax Rates on Earnings." In *Dimensions of Tax Design*, (The Mirrlees Review), edited by Stuart Adam, Tim Besley, Richard Blundell, Steve Bond, Robert Chote, Malcolm Gammie, Paul Johnson, Gareth Myles, and James Poterba, 90–173. Oxford: Oxford University Press.

Cancian, Maria, and Arik Levinson. 2006. "Labor Supply Effects of the Earned Income Tax Credit: Evidence from Wisconsin's Supplemental Benefit for Families with Three Children." *National Tax Journal* LIX (4): 781–800.

Caputo, Richard K. 2006. "The Earned Income Tax Credit: A Study of Eligible Participants vs. Non-Participants." *Journal of Sociology and Social Welfare* 33 (1): 9–29.

Card, David, Raj Chetty, and Andrea Weber. 2007. "The Spike at Benefit Exhaustion: Leaving the Unemployment System or Starting a New Job?" *American Economic Review* 97 (2): 113–18.

Chetty, Raj. 2008. "Moral Hazard versus Liquidity and Optimal Unemployment Insurance." *Journal of Political Economy* 116 (2): 173–234.

Chetty, Raj, John Friedman, Nathaniel Hilger, Emmanuel Saez, Diane Whitmore Schanzenbach, and Danny Yagan. 2011. "How Does Your Kindergarten Classroom Affect Your Earnings? Evidence from Project STAR." *Quarterly Journal of Economics* 126 (4): 1593–660.

Chetty, Raj, John N. Friedman, and Jonah Rockoff. 2011. "New Evidence on the Long-Term Impacts of Tax Credits." November. Washington, DC: US Internal Revenue Service. https://www.irs.gov/pub/irs-soi/11rpchettyfriedmanrockoff.pdf.

Chetty, Raj, John N. Friedman, and Emmanuel Saez. 2013. "Using Differences in Knowledge across Neighborhoods to Uncover the Impacts of the EITC on Earnings." *American Economic Review* 103 (7): 2683–721.

Chetty, Raj, and Emmanuel Saez. 2013. "Teaching the Tax Code: Earnings Responses to an Experiment with EITC Recipients." *American Economic Journal: Applied Economics* 5 (1): 1–31.

Congressional Budget Office (CBO). 2007. "Changes in the Economic Resources of Low-Income Households with Children." CBO Paper no. 2602, Washington, DC, Congress of the United States Congressional Budget Office, May.

Council of Economic Advisers (CEA). 1964. *The Annual Report of the Council of Economic Advisers*. January. Washington, DC: Council of Economic Advisers.

———. 2014. "The War on Poverty 50 Years Later: A Progress Report." In *The Annual Report of the Council of Economic Advisers*. March. Washington, DC: Council of Economic Advisers.

Cristia, Julian P., and Jonathan A. Schwabish. 2009. "Measurement Error in the SIPP: Evidence from Administrative Matched Records." *Journal of Economic and Social Measurement* 34 (1): 1–17.

Dahl, Gordon B., and Lance Lochner. 2012. "The Impact of Family Income on Child Achievement: Evidence from the Earned Income Tax Credit." *American Economic Review* 102 (5): 1927–56.

Dahl, Molly, Thomas DeLeire, and Jonathan Schwabish. 2009. "Stepping Stone or Dead End? The Effect of the EITC on Earnings Growth." IZA Discussion Paper no. 4146, Bonn, Germany, Forschungsinstitut zur Zukunft der Arbeit, April.

Deming, David. 2009. "Early Childhood Intervention and Life-Cycle Skill Development: Evidence from Head Start." *American Economic Journal: Applied Economics* 1 (3): 111–34.

Dickert-Conlin, Stacy, and Scott Houser. 1998. "Taxes and Transfers: A New Look at the Marriage Penalty." *National Tax Journal* 51 (2): 175–217.

———. 2002. "EITC and Marriage." *National Tax Journal* 55 (1): 25–40.

Duncan, Greg J., Pamela A. Morris, and Chris Rodrigues. 2011. "Does Money Really Matter? Estimating Impacts of Family Income on Young Children's Achievement with Data from Random-Assignment Experiments." *Developmental Psychology* 47 (5): 1263–79.

Dynarski, Susan, Joshua Hyman, and Diane Whitmore Schanzenbach. 2013. "Experimental Evidence on the Effect of Childhood Investments on Postsecondary Attainment and Degree Completion." *Journal of Policy Analysis and Management* 32 (4): 692–717.

Eissa, Nada, and Hilary W. Hoynes. 2004. "Taxes and the Labor Market Participation of Married Couples: The Earned Income Tax Credit." *Journal of Public Economics* 88 (9): 1931–58.

————. 2006. "Behavioral Responses to Taxes: Lessons from the EITC and Labor Supply." In *Tax Policy and the Economy*, vol. 20, edited by J. M. Poterba, 74–110. Cambridge, MA: MIT Press.

————. 2011. "Redistribution and Tax Expenditures: The Earned Income Tax Credit." *National Tax Journal* 64 (2, part 2): 689–730.

Eissa, Nada, and Jeffrey B. Liebman. 1996. "Labor Supply Response to the Earned Income Tax Credit." *Quarterly Journal of Economics* 11 (2): 605–37.

Eissa, Nada, and Austin Nichols. 2005. "Tax-Transfer Policy and Labor-Market Outcomes." *American Economic Review* 95 (2): 88–93.

Ellwood, David T. 2000. "The Impact of the Earned Income Tax Credit and Social Policy Reforms on Work, Marriage, and Living Arrangements." *National Tax Journal* 53 (4, part 2): 1063–105.

Evans, William N., and Craig L. Garthwaite. 2014. "Giving Mom a Break: The Impact of Higher EITC Payments on Maternal Health." *American Economic Journal: Economic Policy* 6 (2): 258–90.

Feller, Avi, Todd Grindal, Luke Miratrix, and Lindsay Page. 2016. "Compared to What? Variation in the Impacts of Early Childhood Education by Alternative Care-Type Settings." Forthcoming, *Annals of Applied Statistics*.

Friedman, Milton. 1962. *Capitalism and Freedom*. Chicago: University of Chicago Press.

————. 2013. "The Case for a Negative Income Tax: A View from the Right." In *Basic Income: An Anthology of Contemporary Research*, edited by Karl Widerquist, Jose A. Noguera, Yannick Vanderborght, and Jurgen De Wispelaere, 11–16. Oxford: Wiley-Blackwell.

Fullerton, Don, and Gilbert E. Metcalf. 2002. "Tax Incidence." In *Handbook of Public Economics*, vol. 4, edited by A. J. Auerbach and M. Feldstein, 1787–872. Amsterdam: North-Holland.

Gao, Qin, Neeraj Kaushal, and Jane Waldfogel. 2009. "How Have Expansions in the Earned Income Tax Credit Affected Family Expenditures?" In *Welfare Reform and Its Long-Term Consequences for America's Poor*, edited by James P. Ziliak, 104–39. Cambridge: Cambridge University Press.

Gokhale, Jagadeesh. 2014. "SSDI Reform: Promoting Gainful Employment While Preserving Economic Security." *Cato Institute Policy Analysis* 762 (October): 1–35.

Goodman-Bacon, Andrew, and Leslie McGranahan. 2008. "How Do EITC Recipients Spend Their Refunds?" *Economic Perspectives* 32 (2): 17–32.

Greenstein, Robert, and John Wancheck. 2011. "Earned Income Tax Credit Overpayment and Error Issues." Center on Budget and Policy Priorities, Washington, DC, April. http://www.cbpp.org/research/earned-income-tax-credit-overpayment -and-error-issues.

Grogger, Jeffrey. 2004. "Welfare Transitions in the 1990s: The Economy, Welfare, Policy, and the EITC." *Journal of Policy Analysis and Management* 23 (4): 671–95.

Gunter, Samara. 2013. "State Earned Income Tax Credits and Participation in Regular and Informal Work." *National Tax Journal* 66 (1): 33–62.

Hanson, Kenneth, and Margaret Andrews. 2009. "State Variations in the Food Stamp Benefit Reduction Rate for Earnings: Cross-Program Effects from TANF and SSI Cash Assistance." *USDA Economic Research Service* EIB-46.

Haskins, Ron. 2008. "Making Work Pay—Again." In *Big Ideas for Children: Investing in Our Nation's Future*, 183–90. Washington, DC: First Focus.

Heckman, James J., Lance Lochner, and Ricardo Cossa. 2003. "Learning-By-Doing vs. On-The-Job Training: Using Variation Induced by the EITC to Distinguish between Models of Skill Formation." In *Designing Inclusion: Tools to Raise Low-End Pay and Employment in Private Enterprise*, edited by Edmund S. Phelps, 74–130. Cambridge: Cambridge University Press.

Heckman, James J., Seong Hyeok Moon, Rodrigo Pinto, Peter Savelyev, and Adam Yavitz. 2010. "A New Cost-Benefit and Rate of Return Analysis for the Perry Preschool Program." In *Childhood Programs and Practices in the First Decade of Life*, edited by Arthur J. Reynolds, Arthur J. Rolnick, Michelle M. Englund, and Judy A. Temple, 366–80. New York: Cambridge University Press.

Heckman, James, Rodrigo Pinto, and Peter Savelyev. 2013. "Understanding the Mechanisms through Which an Influential Early Childhood Program Boosted Adult Outcomes." *American Economic Review* 103 (6): 2052–86.

Heim, Bradley T. 2010. "The Impact of the Earned Income Tax Credit on the Labor Supply of Married Couples: A Structural Estimation." Working Paper, Indiana University.

Herbst, Chris M. 2011. "The Impact of the Earned Income Tax Credit on Marriage and Divorce: Evidence from Flow Data." *Population Research Policy Review* 30:101–28.

Holt, Stephen D. 2008. "Periodic Payment of the Earned Income Tax Credit." Brookings Institution Background Paper, Washington, DC, Brookings Institution. June.

Holtzblatt, Janet, and Robert Rebelein. 2000. "Measuring the Effect of the EITC on Marriage Penalties and Bonuses." *National Tax Journal* 53 (4, part 2): 1107–33.

Hotz, V. Joseph, Charles H. Mullin, and John Karl Scholz. 2010. "Examining the Effect of the Earned Income Tax Credit on the Labor Market Participation of Families on Welfare." Working Paper, University of Wisconsin-Madison, June.

Hotz, V. Joseph, and John Karl Scholz. 2003. "The Earned Income Tax Credit." In *Means-Tested Transfer Programs in the United States*, edited by Robert A. Moffitt, 141–97. Chicago: University of Chicago Press.

Hoynes, Hilary W. 1997. "Does Welfare Play Any Role in Female Headship Decisions?" *Journal of Public Economics* 65:89–117.

———. 2009. "The Earned Income Tax Credit, Welfare Reform, and the Employment of Low-Skill Single Mothers." In *Strategies for Improving Economic Mobility of Workers: Bridging Research and Practice*, edited by Maude Toussaint-Comeau and Bruce D. Meyer. Kalamazoo, MI: Upjohn Press.

Hoynes, Hilary W., Douglas L. Miller, and David Simon. 2015. "Income, the Earned Income Tax Credit, and Infant Health." *American Economic Journal: Economic Policy* 7 (1): 172–211.

Hoynes, Hilary W., and Ankur Patel. 2015. "The Earned Income Tax Credit and the Distribution of Income." NBER Working Paper no. 2134, Cambridge, MA.

Huang, Jun, and Maximilian D. Schmeiser. 2012. "Does the Earned Income Tax Credit Crowd Out the Employment of People with Disabilities? Evidence of the Single Mothers from the 1990s." Unpublished Manuscript, Columbia Business School, December.

Internal Revenue Service (IRS). 2006. "Individual Income Tax Underreporting Gap Estimates, Tax Year 2001." Posted February 14. http://www.irs.gov/pub/irs-utl /tax_gap_update_070212.pdf.

———. 2009. *2009 Annual Report to Congress, vol. 2: Research and Related Studies.* December. Washington, DC: Internal Revenue Service.

———. 2013. 1040 Instructions 2013, page 59. Posted December 24. http://www.irs .gov/pub/irs-prior/i1040gi-2013.pdf.

———. 2014a. "All Returns: Tax Liability, Tax Credits, and Tax Payments." Table 3.3, Publication no. 1304. http://www.irs.gov/file_source/pub/irs-soi/12in33ar.xls.

———. 2014b. "Compliance Estimates for the Earned Income Tax Credit Claimed on 2006–2008 Returns." Research, Analysis & Statistics Report, Publication 5162. August.

———. 2014c. "EITC Participation Rate by States." Posted January 16. http://www .eitc.irs.gov/EITC-Central/Participation-Rate.

———. 2014d. "States and Local Governments with Earned Income Tax Credit." Posted August 11. http://www.irs.gov/Individuals/States-and-Local-Governments -with-Earned-Income-Tax-Credit.

———. 2014e. "Table 1: Individual Income Tax Returns: Selected Income and Tax Items for Tax Years 1999–2012." Posted May 9. http://www.irs.gov/uac/SOI-Tax -Stats-Historical-Table-1.

———. 2014f. "Table 2.5: Returns with Earned Income Credit, by Size of Adjusted Gross Income." Tax Year 2012 in SOI Tax Stats—Individual Statistical Tables by Size of Adjusted Gross Income. Posted July. http://www.irs.gov/file_source/pub /irs-soi/12in25ic.xls.

———. 2014g. "Table 2.5 Returns with Earned Income Credit, Tax Year 2012." In SOI Tax Stats—Individual Income tax. Statistics of Income Division, Publication no. 1304. Posted May 14. http://www.irs.gov/uac/SOI-Tax-Stats-Individual -Income-Tax-Returns.

———. 2014h. "Table 3.3: All Returns: Tax Liability, Tax Credits, and Tax Payments, by Size of Adjusted Gross Income, Tax Year 2012." In Tax Year 2012 in SOI Tax Stats—Individual Statistical Tables by Size of Adjusted Gross Income. Posted July. http://www.irs.gov/file_source/pub/irs-soi/12in33ar.xls.

Internal Revenue Service (IRS) SPEC. 2014. Return Information Database for Tax Year 2012 (returns filed in 2013). January.

Internal Revenue Service (IRS), and US Department of the Treasury. 1999. "Advance Earned Income Tax Credit: 1994 and 1997 Notice Study: A Report to Congress." August. Washington DC: IRS.

———. 2004. "Earned Income Credit (EIC) for Use in 2004 Returns." Publication no. 596. http://www.irs.gov/pub/irs-prior/p596—2004.pdf.

———. 2005. "Earned Income Credit (EIC) for Use in 2005 Returns." Publication no. 596. http://www.irs.gov/pub/irs-prior/p596—2005.pdf.

———. 2006. "Earned Income Credit (EIC) for Use in 2006 Returns." Publication no. 596. http://www.irs.gov/pub/irs-prior/p596—2006.pdf.

———. 2007. "Earned Income Credit (EIC) for Use in 2007 Returns." Publication no. 596. http://www.irs.gov/pub/irs-prior/p596—2007.pdf.

———. 2008. "Earned Income Credit (EIC) for Use in 2008 Returns." Publication no. 596. http://www.irs.gov/pub/irs-prior/p596—2008.pdf.

———. 2009. "Earned Income Credit (EIC) for Use in 2009 Returns." Publication no. 596. http://www.irs.gov/uac/EITC-Eligibility-Rules-for-2009-Tax-Year -Outlined.

———. 2010. "Earned Income Credit (EIC) for Use in 2010 Returns." Publication no. 596. http://www.irs.gov/pub/irs-prior/p596—2010.pdf.

————. 2011. "2011 Tax Year EITC Income Limits, Maximum Credit Amounts and Tax Law Changes." http://www.irs.gov/Individuals/2011-Tax-Year-EITC-Income -Limits,-Maximum-Credit—Amounts-and-Tax-Law-Updates.

————. 2012. "2012 EITC Income Limits, Maximum Amounts and Tax Law Changes." http://www.irs.gov/Individuals/2012-EITC-Income-Limits,-Maximum -Credit—Amounts-and-Tax-Law-Updates.

————. 2013. "2013 EITC Income Limits, Maximum Amounts and Tax Law Changes." http://www.irs.gov/Individuals/2013-EITC-Income-Limits,-Maximum -Credit—Amounts-and-Tax-Law-Changes.

————. 2014. "Earned Income Credit (EIC) for Use in 2014 Returns." Publication no. 596. Posted December 14. http://www.irs.gov/pub/irs-pdf/p596.pdf.

Jones, Damon. 2010. "Information, Preferences and Public Benefit Participation: Experimental Evidence from the Advance EITC and 401(k) Savings." *American Economic Journal* 2 (2): 147–63.

————. 2012. "Inertia and Overwithholding: Explaining the Prevalence of Income Tax Refunds." *American Economic Journal: Economic Policy* 4 (1): 158–85.

Jones, Margaret R. 2014a. "Changes in EITC Eligibility and Participation, 2005–2009." CARRA Working Paper no. 2014–04, Washington, DC, US Census Bureau, July.

————. 2014b. "The EITC over the Business Cycle: Who Benefits?" Working Paper. Washington, DC, US Census Bureau, November.

————. 2015. Personal communication via e-mail. February 23.

Keane, Michael, and Robert Moffitt. 1998. "A Structural Model of Multiple Welfare Program Participation and Labor Supply." *International Economic Review* 39 (3): 553–89.

Kearney, Melissa S., and Lesley J. Turner. 2013. "Giving Secondary Earners a Tax Break: A Proposal to Help Low- and Middle-Income Families." The Hamilton Project Discussion Paper no. 2013–07, December. http://www.hamiltonproject .org/papers/giving_secondary_earners_a_tax_break.

Kline, Patrick, and Christopher Walters. 2016. "Evaluating Public Programs with Close Substitutes: The Case of Head Start." Forthcoming, *Quarterly Journal of Economics.*

Konczal, Mike. 2013. Interview with Dube; EITC and minimum wage as complements. *Next New Deal.* Posted February 15, 2013. http://www.nextnewdeal.net /rortybomb/interview-dube-eitc-and-minimum-wage-complements.

Kroft, Kory, Kavan Kucko, Etienne Lehmann, and Johannes Schmieder. 2016. "Optimal Income Taxation with Unemployment and Wage Responses: A Sufficient Statistics Approach." Unpublished Manuscript, Boston University.

LaLumia, Sara. 2009. "The Earned Income Tax Credit and Reported Self-Employment Income." *National Tax Journal* 62 (2): 191–217.

Lampman, Robert J. 1965. "Approaches to the Reduction of Poverty." *American Economic Review* 55 (1, part 2): 521–29.

Lee, David, and Emmanuel Saez. 2012. "Optimal Minimum Wage Policy in Competitive Labor Markets." *Journal of Public Economics* 96 (9): 739–49.

Leigh, Andrew. 2010. "Who Benefits from the Earned Income Tax Credit? Incidence among Recipients, Coworkers and Firms." *B. E. Journal of Economic Analysis & Policy* 10 (1). DOI: 10.2202/1935-1682.1994.

Liebman, Jeffrey B. 1998. "The Impact of the Earned Income Tax Credit on Incentives and Income Distribution." In *Tax Policy and the Economy,* vol. 12, edited by James Poterba, 83–119. Cambridge, MA: MIT Press.

————. 2000. "Who Are the Ineligible EITC Recipients?" *National Tax Journal* 53 (4, part 2): 1165–86.

Looney, Adam, and Day Manoli. 2016. "Are There Returns to Experience at Low-

Skill Jobs? Evidence from Single Mothers in the United States over the 1990s." Upjohn Institute Working Paper 16–255. Kalamazoo, MI: W. E. Upjohn Institute for Employment Research. http://dx.doi.org/10.17848/wp16-255.

Maag, Elaine. 2005. "Disparities in Knowledge of the EITC." *Tax Notes* (March): 1323.

———. 2011. "Tax Simplification: Clarifying Work, Child, and Education Incentives." *Tax Notes* 130 (28): 1587–96.

Maag, Elaine, C. Eugene Steurle, Ritadhi Chakravarti, and Caleb Quakenbush. 2012. "How Marginal Tax Rates Affect Families at Various Levels of Poverty." *National Tax Journal* 65 (4): 759–82.

Manning, Alan. 2003. *Monopsony in Motion: Imperfect Competition in Labor Markets.* Princeton, NJ: Princeton University Press.

Manoli, Day, and Nick Turner. 2014. "Cash-on-Hand and College Enrollment: Evidence from Population Tax Data and Policy Nonlinearities." NBER Working Paper no. 19836, Cambridge, MA.

Maxfield, Michelle. 2013. "The Effects of the Earned Income Tax Credit on Child Achievement and Long-Term Educational Achievement." Job Market Paper, Michigan State University, November.

McCubbin, Janet. 2000. "EITC Noncompliance: The Misreporting of Children and the Size of the EITC." *National Tax Journal* 53 (4): 1135–64.

Mead, Lawrence M. 2014. "Overselling the Earned Income Tax Credit." *National Affairs* 21:20–33.

Mendenhall, Ruby, Kathryn Edin, Susan Crowley, Jennifer Sykes, Laura Tach, Katrin Kriz, and Jeffrey R. Kling. 2012. "The Role of Earned Income Tax Credit in the Budgets of Low-Income Families." *Social Service Review* 86 (3): 367–400.

Meyer, Bruce D. 2002. "Labor Supply at the Extensive and Intensive Margins: The EITC, Welfare and Hours Worked." *American Economic Review* 92 (2): 373–79.

———. 2008. "The US Earned Income Tax Credit, Its Effects, and Possible Reforms." Working Paper no. 2008:14, Institute for Labour Market Policy Evaluation, Uppsala, Sweden, Swedish Ministry of Employment, May.

———. 2010. "The Effects of the Earned Income Tax Credit and Recent Reforms." *Tax Policy and the Economy*, vol. 24, edited by Jeffrey R. Brown, 153–80. Chicago: University of Chicago Press.

Meyer, Bruce D., and Nikolas Mittag. 2014. "Misclassification in Binary Choice Models." NBER Working Paper no. 20509, Cambridge, MA.

Meyer, Bruce D., Wallace K. C. Mok, and James X. Sullivan. 2015. "The Under-Reporting of Transfers in Household Surveys: Its Nature and Consequences." Unpublished Manuscript. June. http://harris.uchicago.edu/sites/default/files/AggregatesPaper.pdf.

Meyer, Bruce D., and Dan T. Rosenbaum. 2001. "Welfare, the Earned Income Tax Credit, and the Labor Supply of Single Mothers." *Quarterly Journal of Economics* 116 (3): 1063–114.

Michelmore, Katherine. 2013. "The Effect of Income on Educational Attainment: Evidence from State Earned Income Tax Credit Expansions." Working Paper, Institute for Research on Poverty. http://www.irp.wisc.edu/newsevents/seminars/Presentations/2013-2014/Michelmore_Draft_September_2013.pdf.

———. 2014. "EITC and Union Formation: The Impact of Expected Spouse Earnings." Working Paper, Cornell University.

Moffitt, Robert. 1994. "Welfare Effects on Female Headship with Area Effects." *Journal of Human Resources* 29 (2): 621–36.

———. 2003. "The Negative Income Tax and the Evolution of US Welfare Policy." *Journal of Economic Perspectives* 17 (3): 119–40.

———. 2010. "Economics and the Earned Income Tax Credit." In *Better Living through Economics*, edited by John J. Siegfried, 88–109. Cambridge, MA: Harvard University Press.

National Taxpayer Advocate. 2004. "Earned Income Tax Credit (EITC) Audit Reconsideration Study." *National Taxpayer Advocate 2004 Annual Report to Congress*, vol. 2. Washington, DC, Internal Revenue Service, December.

———. 2009. "2009 Annual Report to Congress." US Treasury Department Publication no. 2104, (Rev. 12-2009), Catalog no. 23655L, Washington, DC.

Neumark, David, and William Wascher. 2001. "Using the EITC to Help Poor Families: New Evidence and a Comparison with the Minimum Wage." *National Tax Journal* 54 (2): 281–318.

———. 2011. "Does a Higher Minimum Wage Enhance the Effectiveness of the Earned Income Tax Credit?" *Industrial and Labor Relations Review* 64 (4): 712–46.

Nichols, Austin. 2006. "Understanding Recent Changes in Child Poverty." Urban Institute Series A, no. A-71, Washington, DC, The Urban Institute, August.

———. 2013. "Explaining Changes in Child Poverty over the Past Four Decades." Low-Income Working Families Discussion Paper no. 2, Washington, DC, The Urban Institute, September.

Nichols, Austin, Karen Smith, and Laura Wheaton. 2011. "Analysis of Income Data Quality on the CPS ASEC." Technical report under contract with the US Census Bureau. Presented at the Association of Public Policy Analysis and Management conference on November 4, 2011, Washington, DC, The Urban Institution.

Nichols, Austin, Elaine Sorensen, and Kye Lippold. 2012. "The New York Noncustodial Parent EITC: Its Impact on Child Support Payments and Employment." Urban Institute Paper, Washington, DC, The Urban Institute, June.

Nichols, Austin, and Sheila Zedlewski. 2011. "Is the Safety Net Catching Unemployed Families? Perspectives on Low-Income Working Families." Urban Institute Brief no. 21, Washington, DC, The Urban Institute.

Organisation for Economic Co-operation and Development (OECD). 2011. *Taxation and Employment 2011*. OECD Tax Policy Studies no. 21. Paris: OECD Publishing.

———. 2014. *OECD Tax Database Explanatory Annex, Part I: Taxation of Wage Income.* http://www.oecd.org/ctp/tax-policy/Personal-Income-Tax-rates _Explanatory-Annex-2014.pdf.

———. 2015. *Employment-Conditional Benefits.* http://www.oecd.org/social/soc /Employment-conditional%20benefits.xlsx.

Oi, Walter, Y. 1996. "Employment Benefits for People with Diverse Disabilities." In *Disability, Work and Cash Benefits*, edited by Jerry L. Mashaw, Virginia Reno, Richard V. Burkhauser, and Monroe Berkowitz, 103–29. Kalamazoo, MI: W. E. Upjohn Institute for Employment Research.

Owens, Jeffrey. 2005. "Fundamental Tax Reform: The Experience of OECD Countries." Background Paper no. 47, Washington, DC, Tax Foundation.

Parker, Jonathan A., Nicholas S. Souleles, David S. Johnson, and Robert McClelland. 2013. "Consumer Spending and the Economic Stimulus Payments of 2008." *American Economic Review* 103 (6): 2530–53.

Plueger, Dean. 2009. "Earned Income Tax Credit Participation Rate for Tax Year 2005." IRS Research Bulletin, 151–95, Washington, DC, Internal Revenue Service. https://www.irs.gov/pub/irs-soi/09resconeitcpart.pdf.

Primus, Wendell. 2006. "Improving Public Policies to Increase the Income and Employment of Low-Income Nonresident Fathers." In *Black Males Left Behind*, edited by Ronald B. Mincy, 211–48. Washington, DC: Urban Institute Press.

Puma, Mike, Stephen Bell, Ronna Cook, Camilla Heid, Pam Broene, Frank Jenkins, Andrew Mashburn, and Jason Downer. 2012. "Third Grade Follow-Up to the

Head Start Impact Study Final Report." OPRE Report no. 2012–45, Washington, DC, Office of Planning, Research and Evaluation, Administration for Children and Families, US Department of Health and Human Services, October.

Romich, Jennifer L., and Thomas S. Weisner. 2002. "How Families View and Use the Earned Income Tax Credit: Advance Payment versus Lump-Sum Delivery." In *Making Work Pay: The Earned Income Tax Credit and Its Impact on American Families*, edited by Bruce D. Meyer and Douglas Holtz-Eakin, 366–92. New York: Russell Sage Foundation.

Rosenbaum, Dan T. 2000. "Taxes, the Earned Income Tax Credit, and Marital Status." Prepared for the 1999–2000 ASPE Census Bureau Small Grants Sponsored Research Conference, May 18–19, 2000, Washington, DC.

Ross Phillips, Katherine. 2001. "Who Knows about the Earned Income Tax Credit?" In *New Federalism: National Survey of America's Families* Series B, no. B-27, January. Washington, DC: Urban Institute.

Rothstein, Jesse. 2008. "The Unintended Consequences of Encouraging Work: Tax Incidence and the EITC." Working Paper, Princeton University.

———. 2010. "Is the EITC as Good as an NIT? Conditional Cash Transfers and Tax Incidence." *American Economic Journal: Economic Policy* 2 (1): 177–208.

Rothstein, Jesse, and Nathan Wozny. 2013. "Permanent Income and the Black-White Test Score Gap." *Journal of Human Resources* 48 (3): 509–44.

Rubin, Donald B. 1986. "Statistics and Causal Inference: Comment: Which Ifs Have Causal Answers." *Journal of the American Statistical Association* 81 (396): 961–62.

Rutledge, Matthew S. 2014. "Would a Refundable Tax Credit Increase the Labor Supply of Impaired Adults?" Working Paper, Center for Retirement Research at Boston College.

Saez, Emmanuel. 2002. "Optimal Income Transfer Programs: Intensive versus Extensive Labor Supply Responses." *Quarterly Journal of Economics* 107 (3): 1039–73.

———. 2010. "Do Taxpayers Bunch at Kink Points?" *American Economic Journal: Economic Policy* 2 (3): 180–212.

Schiffren, Lisa. 1995. "America's Best-Kept Welfare Secret." *American Spectator* April: 24–29.

Scholz, John Karl. 1994. "The Earned Income Tax Credit: Participation, Compliance, and Antipoverty Effectiveness." *National Tax Journal* 47 (1): 64–87.

Short, Kathleen. 2014. "The Supplemental Poverty Measure 2013." Current Population Reports, Washington, DC, US Census Bureau, October.

Smeeding, Timothy M., Katherin Ross Phillips, and Michael O'Connor. 2000. "The EITC: Expectation, Knowledge, Use, and Economic and Social Mobility." *National Tax Journal* 53 (4, part 2): 1187–209.

Souleles, Nicholas S. 1999. "The Response of Household Consumption to Income Tax Refunds." *American Economic Review* 89 (4): 947–58.

Stapleton, David, Gina Livermore, Craig Thornton, Bonnie O'Day, Robert Weathers, Krista Harrison, So O'Neil, Emily Sama Martin, David Wittenburg, and Debra Wright. 2008. "Ticket to Work at the Crossroads: A Solid Foundation with an Uncertain Future." Mathematica Policy Research Paper no. 8977, Washington, DC, Mathematica Policy Research, Inc.

Stock, James H., and Motohiro Yogo. 2010. "Testing for Weak Instruments in Linear IV Regressions." In *Identification and Inference for Econometric Models*, edited by Donald W. K. Andrews and James H. Stock, 80–108. Cambridge: Cambridge University Press.

Strully, Kate W., David H. Rehkopf, and Ziming Xuan. 2010. "Aspects of Prenatal Poverty on Infant Health: State Earned Income Tax Credits and Birth Weight." *American Sociological Review* 75 (4): 534–62.

Tach, Laura, and Sarah Halpern-Meekin. 2014. "Tax Code Knowledge and Behavioral Responses among EITC Recipients: Policy Insights from Qualitative Data." *Journal of Policy Analysis and Management* 33 (2): 413–39.

Tax Policy Center. 2013. "Earned Income Tax Credit Parameters, 1975–2015." Posted November 3. http://www.taxpolicycenter.org/taxfacts/displayafact.cfm?Docid=36.

———. 2014. "Real Federal Spending on EITC, CTC and Welfare: FY1975–2011." http://www.taxpolicycenter.org/taxfacts/displayafact.cfm?Docid=266.

———. 2015. "Earned Income Tax Credit: Number of Recipients and Amount of Credit, 1975–2012." Posted January 20. http://www.taxpolicycenter.org/taxfacts/displayafact.cfm?Docid=37.

Tobin, James. 1966. "The Case for an Income Guarantee." *Public Interest* 15:31–41.

Treasury Inspector General for Tax Administration. 2011. "Reduction Targets and Strategies Have Not Been Established to Reduce the Billions of Dollars in Improper Earned Income Tax Credit Payments Each Year." Report no. 2011-40-023, Washington, DC, Treasury Inspector General for Tax Administration, February.

US Census Bureau. 2013. "Current Population Survey." March. https://www.census.gov/cps/data/.

US Department of Health and Human Services (HHS). 2007. "Indicators of Welfare Dependence: Annual Report to Congress." Washington DC: HHS.

US Government Accountability Office (GAO). 2007. "Advance Earned Income Tax Credit: Low Use and Small Dollars Paid Impede IRS's Efforts to Reduce High Noncompliance." Report no. GAO-07-1110, Washington, DC, US GAO, August.

US Government Publishing Office (GPO). 2004. "Table 13–12: Earned Income Credit Parameters, 1965–2003." In *Background Material and Data on Programs within the Jurisdiction of the Committee and on Ways and Means* (Green Book). Section 13—Tax Provisions Related to Retirement, Health, Poverty, Employment, Disability and other Social Issues. Posted March 1. http://www.gpo.gov/fdsys/pkg/GPO-CPRT-108WPRT108-6/pdf/GPO-CPRT-108WPRT108-6-2-13.pdf.

———. 2011. *26 U.S.C. 24—Child Tax Credit.* https://www.gpo.gov/fdsys/granule/USCODE-2011-title26/USCODE-2011-title26-subtitleA-chap1-subchapA-partIV-subpartA-sec24.

Vallas, Rebecca, Melissa Boteach, and Rachel West. 2014. "Harnessing the EITC and Other Tax Credits to Promote Financial Stability and Economic Mobility." Washington, DC, Center for American Progress, October. https://cdn.americanprogress.org/wp-content/uploads/2014/10/EITC-report2.pdf.

Ventry, Dennis. 2000. "The Collision of Tax and Welfare Politics: The Political History of the Earned Income Tax Credit, 1969–1999." *National Tax Journal* 53 (4, part 2): 983–1026.

World Bank. 2014. *PPP Conversion Factor, GDP (LCU per International $).* World Development Indicators. http://data.worldbank.org/indicator/PA.NUS.PPP?order=wbapi_data_value_2010+wbapi_data_value+wbapi_data_value-first&sort=asc.

Wu, Chi Chi. 2014. "It's a Wild World: Consumers at Risk from Tax-Time Financial Products and Unregulated Preparers." NCLC Paper, Boston, MA, National Consumer Law Center, February.

3

US Food and Nutrition Programs

Hilary Hoynes and Diane Whitmore Schanzenbach

Concerns about adequate nutrition figure prominently in discussions of the health and well-being of America's disadvantaged populations. In 2014, 15.4 percent of persons and 20.9 percent of children lived in households reported as food insecure—meaning conditions such as worrying about whether food would run out, food not lasting, not being able to afford balanced meals, skipping meals, or not eating enough (Coleman-Jensen et al. 2015). At the same time, Americans' diet quality has been persistently low and unchanging over time (Wang et al. 2014) and more than a third of adults and 17 percent of children are obese (Ogden et al. 2014).

To address these problems, a range of US food and nutrition programs are provided by the US Department of Agriculture. Spending on the largest eight programs totaled $99 billion in 2014; by comparison, the Earned Income Tax Credit cost $64 billion (in 2012). In this survey, we focus on the four largest of these programs, including the Supplemental Nutrition Assistance Program ([SNAP], previously known as food stamps), the Special Supplemental Nutrition Program for Women, Infants, and Children (WIC), the National School Lunch Program (NSLP), and the School Breakfast Program (SBP).

Hilary Hoynes is professor of economics and public policy and holds the Haas Distinguished Chair in Economic Disparities at the University of California, Berkeley, and is a research associate of the National Bureau of Economic Research. Diane Whitmore Schanzenbach is associate professor of education and social policy at Northwestern University and a research associate of the National Bureau of Economic Research.

We thank Dorian Carloni, Elora Ditton, and Andrea Kwan for excellent research assistance. We appreciate comments provided by Marianne Bitler, Jeffrey Liebman, Robert Moffitt, Zoe Neuberger, Dottie Rosenbaum, and James Ziliak. For acknowledgments, sources of research support, and disclosure of the authors' material financial relationships, if any, please see http://www.nber.org/chapters/c13488.ack.

There are many features that are common to the four food and nutrition programs. The programs are all means tested, that is, they are limited to individuals living in households with limited income (and sometimes limited assets). The programs share the goal of assuring adequate nutrition. Notably, while much of the US social safety net is provided at the state or local level, food and nutrition programs are federal, thus providing a basic floor for protecting individuals and families that is similar across all states.

However, there are also important ways in which the programs differ. First, the programs vary in their targeted populations, from near-universal eligibility for SNAP to the narrowly defined age groups eligible for WIC. Second, the income cutoffs for eligibility vary across the programs with higher income limits (185 percent of the federal poverty line) for WIC compared to SNAP (130 percent of the federal poverty line). Third, the programs also vary by the degree to which the benefits are provided "in kind," from largely unrestricted vouchers in SNAP, to more targeted vouchers in WIC, to direct provision of meals that are required to conform to nutrition guidelines in the school feeding programs. Fourth, the programs vary by whether they phase out gradually (SNAP) or abruptly as income increases (the others). Together, these factors affect how the programs impact the family's budget, and as we describe in section 3.3 below, how they are to be modeled in the canonical means-tested program budget constraint framework. Notably, the programs also layer on top of each other so that a family may be receiving benefits from multiple programs at once, and also may lose access to one or more of them abruptly (e.g., during school vacations, or when a child ages out of WIC).

We begin our survey with a description of these four central food and nutrition programs, their history, the rules under which they operate, as well as providing program statistics. SNAP is by far the largest program at a cost of $74.2 billion in 2014. Nearly one in seven Americans participated in SNAP in 2014, and the program lifted 4.7 million people, including 2.1 million children, out of poverty in 2014 (Short 2014). SNAP is the most universal of the programs, in that there is no additional targeting to specific groups beyond income and asset eligibility criteria. Additionally, SNAP is the most unrestricted as the program provides vouchers that can be used to purchase most foods at grocery stores or other authorized retailers. Average monthly benefits in 2014 amounted to $257 per household, or $125 per person. This translates to benefits worth about $4.11 per person per day.

The WIC program is more narrowly targeted in terms of both population served and types of goods that can be purchased with benefits. In 2014, $6.2 billion was spent on WIC. As the name implies, benefits are targeted to infants, young children, and pregnant and postpartum women. The WIC benefits can be used to purchase infant formula and other specific food items such as milk, cereal, and juice as specified in the WIC bundle. Additionally, WIC provides nutrition education and referrals to health care and other social services. Over half of US infants receive WIC benefits.

The school breakfast and lunch programs (SBP and NSLP) provide free or low-cost meals to low-income children. Students from higher-income families may also participate in the program through the purchase of meals, and these meals receive subsidies (though much smaller ones) as well. Forty percent of school children receive free or reduced price lunches and 56.6 percent of school children overall participate in the NSLP. The combined cost of these programs in 2014 totaled $15 billion.

We go on, in section 3.3, to discuss the theoretical issues around these programs. Each of the food and nutrition programs can be analyzed through standard economic frameworks to explore predicted effects on food consumption and labor supply. The applicable frameworks and predictions differ somewhat due to the design of the programs—such as how "in kind" the benefits are and whether they are phased out gradually or are all or nothing. We pay particular attention to the difference in incentives for programs with "value vouchers" (as in SNAP) versus those with "quantity vouchers" (as in WIC). An important distinction of programs with quantity vouchers is the lack of sensitivity to price, leading to incentives for firm mark up and increases in program costs. More generally, as with other means-tested transfer programs, these programs face the usual trade-off in balancing the protective aspects of the programs to improve dietary intake and reduce food insecurity against their distorting incentives such as reduced labor supply.

In section 3.4 we provide a comprehensive summary of the research on these programs, with particular emphasis on the work published since Currie (2003). We begin by discussing the challenges for identification and an overview of the different empirical approaches taken in the literature. A central challenge for evaluation of the effects of food and nutrition programs is that commonly used quasi-experimental approaches, relying on variation across states and reforms over time, are not easily applied. This stems from the federal structure of these programs and the relatively limited changes over time. Further, a comparison of participants to nonparticipants is problematic due to selection into the program and its relationship to poverty and disadvantage. Additionally, with respect to the food stamp program, the universal nature of the program means there are no ineligible groups to serve as controls, which is another common approach in the quasi-experimental literature. Nonetheless, researchers have found sources of variation—such as exploiting geographic variation in access, sharp differences in eligibility, and program rule changes—to credibly identify program impacts in some cases. We provide a summary of the literature on our four central food and nutrition programs, focusing on studies with credible, design-based approaches. Throughout our review, we pay particular attention to studies that examine the impact and relevance of these programs for the nonelderly population.

Overall, our review of SNAP studies shows that macroeconomic conditions are a key determinant for tracking caseloads and expenditures over time, with less role for changes in program policies. Additionally, studies have investigated the impacts of SNAP on a wide range of economic and health outcomes, including their impacts on food insecurity, dietary quality, consumption patterns, obesity, and labor market participation. In general, the studies with the most credible designs have found results on take-up and consumption that are consistent with economic theory predictions. SNAP increases family resources and studies show that the program leads to increases in food and nonfood spending. Furthermore, the increases in food spending from the relatively unrestricted SNAP benefits appear to be similar to if the program was provided as cash. Studies consistently show that SNAP reduces food insecurity and increases health at birth, and greater exposure to SNAP in early life leads to improvements in medium-term and long-term health. The evidence for effects of SNAP on contemporaneous health for children and adults is more mixed, however.

The literature on WIC is primarily aimed at estimating the effects of the program on health at birth. The most credible design-based studies show consistent evidence that WIC leads to improvements in outcomes such as average birth weight, the incidence of low birth weight, and maternal weight gain. There is much less evidence about how the program affects outcomes for children, who are eligible for benefits through age five. Recent work on firm incentives explores interesting and important issues arising due to the quantity voucher nature of the program.

Most research on the NSLP has focused on how the program impacts dietary intake, and also obesity rates. The results have been somewhat mixed, with generally more positive impacts for lower-income students. The research on the SBP has increased dramatically over the past twenty years, in part taking advantage of the expansion of the program during this time first to schools that previously did not offer the program, and then by expanding access within schools to a wider range of students. The former generally shows positive program impacts, while the latter finds strong improvements in participation but more mixed effects on dietary quality and student outcomes.

We conclude by discussing new developments and current policy discussions. We identify areas that are unexplored and discuss areas that are ripe for future research.

3.1   History of the Programs and Rules

Table 3.1 provides a brief overview of the four food and nutrition programs that we study in this chapter: SNAP (formerly the food stamp program), Special Supplemental Nutrition Program for Women, Infants, and Children (WIC), National School Lunch Program (NSLP), and School Breakfast Program (SBP). While all of the programs share the goal of assuring

Table 3.1   Overview of US food and nutrition programs and rules

Program and date of introduction	Federal cost (2014)	Population served	Benefits	Eligibility requirements
Supplemental Nutrition Assistance Program (SNAP) formerly FSP	74.2 billion	Low-income households	Monthly benefit issued electronically via Electronic Benefit Transfer (EBT) card account and calculated based on Thrifty Food Plan	Household gross monthly income < 130 percent of poverty line
1961: pilot 1975: permanent program		46.5 million individuals/ month (2014)	Maximum monthly allotment through 2015: $194 for a one-person household, $511 for a three-person household, and $925 for a six-person household; 2014 average monthly benefit per person = $125.35, per household = $256.98	Meet countable resource limit of $2,250 or $3,250 for elderly or disabled; TANF, SSI, and GA recipients eligible; legal, qualified aliens may be SNAP eligible; some households may be required to meet employment, service, and training requirements; individuals without a Social Security number, most postsecondary students, and strikers are not eligible
2009: ARRA provisions (expired 10/2013)			13.6 percent increase in maximum food stamp benefit	Temporarily allowed states to suspend eligibility time limits on ABAWDs
Special Supplemental Nutrition Program for Women, Infants, and Children (WIC)	6.2 billion	Low-income pregnant or postpartum women, infants (< 1), and children (< 5)	Food instrument or cash-value voucher (some states on EBT) to purchase specified nutritious foods rich in protein, iron, calcium, vitamins A, C, and D; nutrition education; screening and referrals to health care and other social services	Pregnant, postpartum, or breastfeeding women, infants, or children < 5; must be individually determined to be at "nutritional risk" by a health professional; meet state residency requirement; gross income ≤ 185 percent of FPL
1972: pilot 1974: permanent program		8.26 million individuals (2014)	Food package assignment varies by situational need	WIC eligibility priority system
National School Lunch Program (NSLP)	11.4 billion	Low-income children	Nutritionally balanced daily lunches conforming to the latest *Dietary Guidelines for Americans* standards; 1/2 daily nutrition requirements	Free lunch if income ≤ 130 percent of poverty line; reduced-price lunch if income ≤ 185 percent of poverty line
1946		19.2 million children receiving free lunch; 2.5 million receiving reduced-price lunch (2014)	Avg. reimbursement rate = $3.06/free meal, $2.66/ reduced-price meal, in schools where 60 percent or more of meals are subsidized and meeting Healthy, Hunger-Free Kids Act requirements (SY14/15)	SNAP recipients automatically qualify for free meals

(continued)

Table 3.1   (continued)

Program and date of introduction	Federal cost (2014)	Population served	Benefits	Eligibility requirements
School Breakfast Program (SBP) 1966: pilot 1975: permanent program	3.7 billion	10.6 million children receiving free breakfast; 1.0 million children receiving reduced-price breakfast (2014)	Nutritionally balanced daily breakfast meeting latest *Dietary Guidelines for Americans* standards Avg. reimbursement rate = $1.93/free meal, $1.63/reduced-price meal, at school in severe need (SY14/15)	Free breakfast if income ≤ 130 percent of poverty line; reduced-price breakfast if income ≤ 185 percent of poverty line SNAP recipients automatically qualify for free meals
Child and Adult Care Food Program (CACFP)	3.1 billion	3.9 million average daily attendance	Reimbursements for meals and snacks that conform to meal patterns (approved centers receive $1.62/free breakfast; $2.98/free lunch; $2.98/free supper; $0.82/free snack)	Centers are operated by public, private nonprofit, and certain for-profit organizations
1968: day care		Children in day care	(see above)	Centers must provide nonresidential care services and be licensed/approved by state
1976: family care		Children (twelve years of age or younger)	(see above)	Facilities must be licensed/approved and provide nonresidential child-care services in a group or family home setting
1987: adult care		Adults in care (functionally impaired or over age sixty, or older)	(see above)	Centers must provide services to adults who are functionally impaired or over age sixty, provide community-based programs, provide nonresidential services, and be licensed/approved to provide adult day-care services
2010: at-risk care (all states)		At-risk children (age eighteen and younger)	(see above)	Centers must primarily provide care for children after school or on weekends, holidays, or school vacations during school year; provide organized scheduled activities; include education or enrichment activities; be located in area near public school w/ 50 percent or more of income ≤ 185 percent of poverty line

Program	Amount	Population served	Benefits / Reimbursement	Eligibility requirements
Summer Food Service Program (SFSP)	465.6 million	2.7 million children/day	Free meals that meet nutrition guidelines to all participating children at approved sites; enrichment activities	Child's participation at: open site = 50% or more of families w/ incomes at or below 185% of FPL; enrolled site = 50% or more of children enrolled in activity program are eligible for F/RP school meals; camp site = free meals only to children who qualify for F/RP meals
1968: pilot; 1975: permanent		Low-income children eighteen years old and younger at approved SFSP sites	Reimbursement rates for rural or self-prep sites = $2.08/breakfast, $6.35/lunch or supper, $0.87/snack; for all other sites = $2.04/ breakfast, $3.59/lunch or supper, $0.85/ snack	
Special Milk Program (SMP)	10.5 million	50.0 million half-pints milk served to low-income children	Reimbursement for half-pints milk	Children that meet income guidelines for free meals who attend a school or institution that does not participate in other federal child nutrition meal service programs
1971: permanent program			Reimbursement rate: $0.23/half pint	
Fresh Fruit and Vegetable Program (FFVP)	153.3 million	Children at elementary schools w/a high percentage of F/RP meal eligibles	Free fresh fruit and vegetables for students outside of normal school meal time frames	Elementary school must have high percentage of students certified for F/RP meals and participate in NSLP
2002: pilot; 2008: permanent program			Schools receive between $50–$75 per student for the school year	Priority to high-need schools

Source: The SNAP eligibility requirements are from http://www.fns.usda.gov/snap/eligibility; NSLP and SBP reimbursement rates from http://www.fns.usda.gov/cn/NAPs14–15.pdf; program statistics from http://www.fns.usda.gov/data-and-statistics; WIC eligibility requirements from http://www.fns.usda.gov/wic/wic-eligibility-requirements; WIC benefits from http://www.fns.usda.gov/wic/wic-eligibility-requirements; SNAP benefits from http://www.fns.usda.gov/node/9320: School meal eligibility guidelines from http://www.fns.usda.gov/school-meals/income-eligibility-guidelines; SFSP info from http://www.fns.usda.gov/sfsp/frequently-asked-questions-faqs#4; SFSP rates from http://www.fns.usda.gov/sfsp-reimbursement-rates; CACFP info from http://www.fns.usda.gov/cacfp/child-and-adult-care-food-program; CACFP rates from http://www.fns.usda.gov/cacfp/reimbursement-rates; SMP data from http://www.fns.usda.gov/sites/default/files/pd/11smhpfy.pdf; SMP expenditures from http://www.fns.usda.gov/sites/default/files/pd/smsummar.pdf; SMP reimbursement rates from http://www.fns.usda.gov/sites/default/files/cn/NAPs14–15.pdf; SMP info from http://www.fns.usda.gov/sites/default/files/SMP_Quick_Facts_0.pdf; and FFVP program info from http://www.fns.usda.gov/sites/default/files/handbook.pdf.

adequate nutritional intake among at-risk populations and each is means tested, the programs differ in terms of the population served, and the nature of the program provided. SNAP is the largest program, reaching an average of 46.5 million persons at a total annual cost of $74.2 billion in 2014. It is the most unrestricted, providing a debit card to facilitate purchases of most food items in the grocery store and extending benefits to the broadest population. On the other hand, WIC is highly prescribed benefit, largely consisting of quantity vouchers to purchase very specific bundles. Additionally, the program is highly targeted, extending benefits only to pregnant and postpartum women, infants, and children under age five. In 2014, WIC served just under 2 million women and 6.3 million children at a cost of $6.3 billion. The school lunch and breakfast programs provide free and reduced-price meals to eligible school-age children. In 2014, the lunch program served 21.7 million low-income children at a cost of $9.6 billion and the breakfast program served 11.6 million low-income children at a total cost of $3.6 billion.[1]

3.1.1   Program History and Rules: SNAP

Overview of Program

SNAP has features consistent with traditional means-tested transfer programs. Eligible households must satisfy income and asset tests. Maximum benefits are assigned based on household size, and actual benefits received are reduced as income increases based on the benefit-reduction rate (or tax rate) calculated through the benefits formula. The similarities with other US means-tested programs end there.

Unlike virtually all means-tested programs in the United States, SNAP eligibility is not limited to certain targeted groups such as families with children, aged, and the disabled.[2] Second, SNAP is a federal program with all funding (except 50 percent of administrative costs) provided by the federal government, eligibility and benefit rules determined federally, and comparably few rules set by the states (particularly prior to welfare reform).[3] Third, the income eligibility threshold and benefits are adjusted for changes in prices each year.[4] Fourth, the benefit-reduction rate is 30 percent of net income (lower than AFDC/TANF) and the program serves both the working and nonworking poor. Its universal eligibility (i.e., eligibility depends

1. These costs only include spending on free and reduced-price meals. In 2014 total spending, including paid meals, was $11.4 and $3.7 billion for lunch and breakfast, respectively.
2. The program is not quite universal: notably undocumented immigrants are not eligible for SNAP. Additionally, as discussed below, there are restrictions on receipt for able-bodied adults age eighteen to forty-nine without dependents.
3. In other public assistance programs such as TANF and Medicaid, states determine fundamental parameters such as the income eligibility cutoffs and (for TANF) benefit levels.
4. Benefits are tied to the cost of a "market basket of foods which if prepared and consumed at home, would provide a complete, nutritious diet at minimal cost," the so-called Thrifty Food Plan, and then indexed for increases in prices.

only on need) combined with the fact that benefits and caseloads rise freely with need (i.e., it expands during recessions, since the program is an entitlement and expenditures are not capped) have elevated SNAP to its status as the fundamental safety net program in the United States.

Benefits take the form of "value vouchers" in that they provide a dollar amount that can be used to purchase most foods from grocery stores that are foods designed to be taken home and prepared. In other words, most grocery store foods can be purchased with the exceptions of goods such as hot foods intended for immediate consumption, vitamins, paper products, pet foods, alcohol, and tobacco. Starting in the late 1980s and completed by 2004, states transitioned to delivery of benefits by Electronic Benefit Transfer (EBT) cards, eliminating the use of paper vouchers. In 2008, the program name was changed from the food stamp program to the Supplemental Nutrition Assistance Program (SNAP). Some states have different names for the program, such as California's "CalFresh."

Eligibility and Benefits

Like other safety net programs, SNAP is designed to ensure a basic level of consumption in low-income families. Consequently, a traditional income-support program will feature a "guarantee"—that is, a benefit level if the family has no income. As earnings or income increases, benefits are reduced resulting in an implicit tax rate on earnings (called the benefit-reduction rate or BRR).

Unlike most means-tested benefit programs in the United States, SNAP is broadly available to almost all households with low incomes. The eligibility rules and benefit levels vary little within the United States, and are largely set at the federal level. Eligible households must meet three criteria: gross monthly income does not exceed 130 percent of the poverty line, net income (income after deductions) does not exceed the poverty line, and "countable" assets do not exceed $2,250 (or $3,250 for elderly, disabled).[5] Additionally, most nonworking, nondisabled childless adults ages eighteen to forty-nine (referred to as able-bodied adults without dependents or ABAWD) are limited to three months of benefits within a three-year period. The eligibility unit is the "household unit" and consists of people who purchase and prepare food together. After initial eligibility, households must be recertified every six to twenty-four months.

A stylized version of the benefit formula is presented in figure 3.1 for a family of a fixed size. A key parameter of the formula is the cost of food under the USDA's Thrifty Food Plan, which we also term the "needs standard." The maximum SNAP benefit amount (represented as the horizontal

---

5. As described below, the gross income test rules have recently been relaxed through expansions in categorical eligibility. For SNAP, countable assets exclude homes and retirement plans, and the extent to which vehicles are counted varies across states. The SNAP recipients who receive SSI or TANF are excluded from the SNAP asset test.

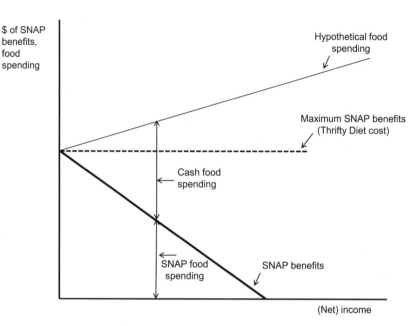

Fig. 3.1   Stylized representation of SNAP benefit formula
Source: Hoynes, McGranahan, and Schanzenbach (2015).

line in the figure) is typically set equal to the needs standard.[6] The SNAP benefit is designed to fill the gap between the needs standard and the cash resources available to a family to purchase food. A family with no income receives the maximum benefit amount, and is expected to contribute nothing out of pocket to food purchases. Total food spending, depicted by the upward-sloping line labeled "hypothetical food spending" increases with income since food is a normal good.[7] Total food spending thus equals the maximum benefit level for a family with no other income source. As a family's income increases, they are expected to be able to spend more of their own cash on food purchases, and SNAP benefits are reduced accordingly. The slope of the SNAP benefits line in figure 3.1 is the BRR, which is currently set at 0.3. The benefit formula is thus as follows:

(1)   Benefits = Max_Benefit − 0.3 * (Net_Income).

The SNAP benefit level as a function of net family income is represented by the downward-sloping line in the figure. Finally, the family's out-of-

6. Congress can set maximum benefits equal to some multiple of the needs standard. For example, the American Recovery and Reinvestment Act of 2009 temporarily raised maximum benefits to be 113.6 percent of the needs standard.

7. As drawn here, we assume the marginal propensity to consume food out of income is lower than the marginal tax rate, and we assume that SNAP is valued the same as cash for food purchases.

pocket spending on food is the vertical distance between the SNAP benefits line and the food spending line.

Net income is calculated as cash pretax income less the following deductions: a standard deduction, a 20 percent deduction from earned income, an excess shelter cost deduction, a deduction for child-care costs associated with working/training, and a medical cost deduction that is available only to the elderly and disabled. Because of these deductions, in practice the benefit-reduction rate (the effective tax rate) out of gross income is lower than 0.3 (we present data on this below). Notably, the income measures used for SNAP eligibility use a *cash, pretax* measure and therefore do not include in-kind benefits (e.g., housing assistance) or tax credits including the EITC or the Child Tax Credit. Net income does include cash transfers such as Social Security, disability income, unemployment insurance, and TANF.

Central policy issues include whether the needs standard is set at an appropriate level, and whether the benefit-reduction rate is appropriate (Institute of Medicine [IOM] 2013). It is worth pointing out that this 0.3 (statutory) benefit-reduction rate is substantially lower than that experienced by other safety net programs such as disability and TANF.

History, Reforms, and Policy Changes

Currie (2003) provides a detailed history of the food stamp program. We briefly touch on some of the important elements of the history and discuss more recent policy changes.

The modern food stamp program began with President Kennedy's 1961 initiation of pilot food stamp programs in eight impoverished counties.[8] The pilot programs were later expanded to forty-three counties in 1962 and 1963. The success with these pilot programs led to the Food Stamp Act of 1964, which gave local areas the authority to start up the food stamp program in their county. As it remains today, the program was federally funded and benefits were redeemable at approved retail food stores. In the period following the passage of the Food Stamp Act, there was a steady stream of counties initiating food stamp programs and federal spending on the FSP more than doubled between 1967 and 1969. Support for requiring counties to participate in FSP grew due to a national spotlight on hunger (Berry 1984). This interest culminated in the passage of 1973 Amendments to the Food Stamp Act, which mandated that all counties offer FSP by 1975.[9]

Figure 3.2 plots the population-weighted percent of counties with a FSP

8. A more detailed history timeline can be found here: http://www.fns.usda.gov/sites/default/files/timeline.pdf.

9. Prior to the food stamp program, some counties provided food aid through the Commodity Distribution Program (CDP). The main goal of the CDP was to support farm prices and farm income by removing surplus commodities from the market. The CDP was far from a universal program. It never reached all counties. The food basket contained a limited range of products, the distribution was infrequent, and distribution centers were difficult to reach.

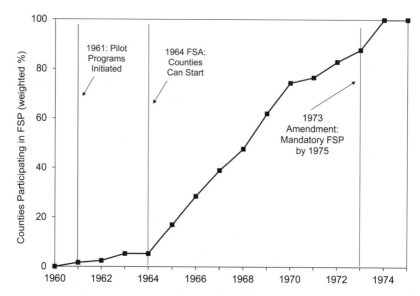

Fig. 3.2   Cumulative percent of counties with Food Stamp Program, 1960–1975
Source: Hoynes and Schanzenbach (2009). Weighted by 1970 county population.

from 1960 to 1975.[10] During the pilot phase (1961–1964), FSP coverage increased slowly. Beginning in 1964, program growth accelerated; coverage expanded at a steady pace until all counties were covered in 1974. There was substantial heterogeneity in timing of adoption of the FSP, both within and across states. The map in figure 3.3 shades counties according to date of FSP adoption (with darker shading denoting a later start-up date).

Compared to the dramatic reforms (AFDC) and expansions (EITC) of income support programs that have characterized the last two decades, the programmatic aspects of food stamps have remained fairly stable over time. A major change took place in the 1977 Food Stamp Act reauthorization with the elimination of the purchase requirement. Prior to this law change, families were required to make cash payment upfront (the "purchase requirement") to receive their food stamp benefits. The presence of (or elimination of) this feature did not change the net value of the benefits a family received, yet food stamp caseloads increased substantially after the removal of the purchase requirement.[11]

The 1996 welfare-reform legislation left the core structure of the food stamp program relatively unaffected, but did limit benefits for legal immi-

10. Counties are weighted by their 1970 population. Note this is not the food stamp case-load, but represents the percent of the US population that lived in a county with a FSP.

11. That is, if the family was deemed able to afford to spend $60 on food, but the cost of the thrifty food plan was $80, the family could purchase $80 in food stamps for the cash price of $60. Under today's program, a similar family would simply receive $20 in food stamps and would not have to outlay any cash.

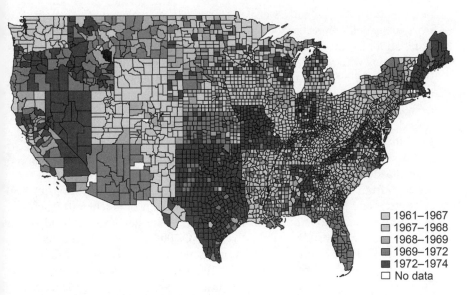

Fig. 3.3   Food stamp start date, by county
Source: Hoynes and Schanzenbach (2009).

grants (who were deemed ineligible until they accumulated ten years of work history)[12] and able-bodied adults without dependents eighteen to forty-nine (who were typically limited to three months of benefits in a three-year period) and eliminated benefits for convicted drug felons.[13] The legislation included a temporary waiver of the time limits in places with high unemployment rates or "insufficient jobs." A 1998 agriculture bill restored food stamp eligibility to some legal immigrant children, disabled persons, the blind, and the elderly (those who had arrived in the United States prior to welfare reform). Later, the 2002 Farm Bill restored food stamp eligibility to all legal immigrant children and disabled persons, regardless of their time of residence in United States, and to legal immigrant adults in the country for five

12. The CBO estimated that welfare reform's changes to food stamps that did not address immigrants would reduce spending on food stamps by $23 billion from 1997 to 2002. Most of the savings came from imposing the work requirement, reducing maximum benefits across the board, and changing allowable deductions when calculating net income. See http://www.cbo .gov/sites/default/files/1996doc32.pdf.

13. As discussed in Bitler and Hoynes (2013), prior to welfare reform, there was a "bright line" that distinguished between legal immigrants and unauthorized residents in determining eligibility for safety net programs. Legal immigrants were eligible for most safety net programs on the same terms as citizens while unauthorized immigrants were not. There were exceptions: unauthorized immigrants maintained eligibility for free and reduced-price school lunch and breakfast, WIC, emergency Medicaid, and state-funded emergency programs. In addition, refugees and asylum seekers also sometimes faced different rules than others. Finally, in response to the postwelfare reform reductions in immigrant eligibility for food stamps, some states chose to maintain coverage for legal immigrants with state-funded replacement coverage (known as "fill-in" programs).

or more years. Additionally, welfare reform reduced the maximum benefit, froze many deductions used in calculating net income, and mandated that states adopt Electronic Benefit Transfer.

Beginning with regulatory changes in 1999 and continuing with the 2002 Farm Bill, the USDA has allowed states to implement policies aimed at improving access to benefits, particularly for working families. This came from the observation that the process of signing up for food stamps takes considerable time and, in particular for working families, getting to the benefits office can be a significant barrier to access to the program. This has led to redesigning income-reporting requirements (increasing the time between recertifications, reducing income reporting between recertifications), moving away from in-person meetings for determining eligibility (instead using call centers and online applications), as well as relaxing of asset limits (such as vehicle ownership). Additionally, during this time states also expanded "broad-based categorical eligibility" (US GAO 2007) whereby states extend SNAP eligibility to households whose gross income is above 130 percent of the poverty line (above gross income test), but with disposable income below the poverty line (meet the net income test). They also can relax the asset limits. However, the benefit formula remained fixed (as the maximum benefit less 30 percent of net income); this implies that any expanded eligibility would be for those with large deductions to gross income (such as families with high child care and shelter costs).

In 2008, the food stamp program was renamed the Supplemental Nutrition Assistance Program (SNAP). Legislative reforms at that time also included excluding certain tax-preferred education savings and retirement accounts from the calculation of the asset test, and indexing of the asset limits to inflation.

The American Recovery and Reinvestment Act of 2009 (federal stimulus or ARRA) increased the maximum SNAP benefit by 13.6 percent. Due to ordinary SNAP nominal benefit changes and additional legislation, the benefit increase was sunset in October 2013. In addition, because unemployment rates rose to high levels during the Great Recession, in most states the three-month time limit on able-bodied childless adults was temporarily suspended as allowed at state option during periods of high unemployment under the rules adopted with welfare reform.

3.1.2   Program History and Rules: WIC

Overview of Program

The goal of the Special Supplemental Nutrition Program for Women, Infants, and Children (WIC) is to improve the nutritional well-being of low-income pregnant and postpartum women, infants, and children under the age of five who are at nutritional risk by providing nutritious foods to supplement diets, nutrition education, and referrals to health care and social services. More specifically the program aims to improve birth outcomes, support the growth and development of infants and children, and promote long-term health in all WIC participants. The WIC program also provides nutritional services and education.

Eligibility and Benefits

Eligibility for WIC requires satisfying categorical eligibility and income-eligibility requirements. Five types of individuals are categorically eligible for WIC: pregnant women, postpartum women for six months after birth, breastfeeding women with an infant under twelve months, infants, and children under age five. Benefits are assigned separately for each group, so, for example, an income-eligible family consisting of a pregnant woman, infant, and child under age five would receive three WIC benefits. Income eligibility dictates that participants must live in households with family incomes below 185 percent of the poverty line or become eligible through participation in another welfare program (with income eligibility below 185 percent of poverty line) such as TANF or SNAP. Under the federal rules, immigrants are eligible for WIC under the same circumstances as natives.[14] Additionally, participants must be deemed to be at nutritional risk; risk factors include low maternal weight gain, inadequate growth in children, anemia, dietary deficiencies, heavy weight, and other nutrition-related medical conditions.[15] However, virtually all financially eligible persons appear to satisfy this requirement (Ver Ploeg and Betson 2003). After initial eligibility, recertification is generally required every six months. Like SNAP, WIC benefits take the form of vouchers and many states currently use (or are in planning stages to use) debit cards for distributing benefits. The vast majority of WIC participants access the food packages by redeeming vouchers or using EBT at participating retail outlets.[16]

The WIC benefits differ from food stamp benefits in two key ways. First, the WIC benefit does not vary with countable income, and thus there is no benefit-reduction rate that reduces the benefit as countable income rises. Instead, as with programs such as Medicaid, recipients who are income and categorically eligible receive the full WIC benefit (an "all or nothing" benefit package). Second, the WIC bundle is restricted to specific items; the WIC approved foods are chosen because they contain substantial amounts of protein, calcium, iron, or vitamins A or C. The approved foods include juice, fortified cereal, eggs, cheese, milk, dried legumes or peanut butter, and canned fish. Table 3.2 summarizes the current elements of the food package

14. States have the discretion to deny benefits to immigrants, though as of this writing none have implemented explicit restrictions (http://www.fns.usda.gov/sites/default/files/wic/WICRegulations-7CFR246.pdf).

15. Risk factors can also include homelessness and migrancy, drug abuse, and alcoholism.

16. Alternatively, a few state agencies purchase the items in bulk and make them available through distribution centers or through home delivery.

Table 3.2	WIC food packages (maximum monthly allowances)	
Food package	Recipient	Food
I	Infants, fully formula fed (birth to five months)	WIC formula: 823 fl. oz. reconstituted liquid concentrate (birth to three months) WIC formula: 896 fl. oz. reconstituted liquid concentrate (four to five months)
	Infants, partially breastfed (birth to five months)	WIC formula: 104 fl. oz. reconstituted powder (birth to one month) WIC formula: 388 fl. oz. reconstituted liquid concentrate (one to three months) WIC formula: 460 fl. oz. reconstituted liquid concentrate (four to five months)
II	Infants, fully formula fed (six to eleven months)	WIC formula: 630 fl. oz. reconstituted liquid concentrate Infant cereal: 24 oz. Baby food fruits and vegetables: 128 oz.
	Infants, partially breastfed (six to eleven months)	WIC formula: 315 fl. oz. reconstituted liquid concentrate Infant cereal: 24 oz. Baby food fruits and vegetables: 128 oz.
	Infants, fully breastfed (six to eleven months)	Infant cereal: 24 oz. Baby food fruits and vegetables: 256 oz. Baby food meat: 77.5 oz.
III	Infants, fully formula fed (birth to eleven months)	WIC formula: 823 fl. oz. reconstituted liquid concentrate (birth to three months) WIC formula: 896 fl. oz. reconstituted liquid concentrate (four to five months) WIC formula: 630 fl. oz. reconstituted liquid concentrate (six to eleven months) Infant cereal: 24 oz. (six to eleven months) Baby food fruits and vegetables: 128 oz. (six to eleven months)
	Infants, partially breastfed (birth to eleven months)	WIC formula: 104 fl. oz. reconstituted powder (birth to one month) WIC formula: 388 fl. oz. reconstituted liquid concentrate (one to three months) WIC formula: 460 fl. oz. reconstituted liquid concentrate (four to five months) WIC formula: 315 fl. oz. reconstituted liquid concentrate (six to eleven months) Infant cereal: 24 oz. (six to eleven months) Baby food fruits and vegetables: 128 oz. (six to eleven months)
IV	Children: one to four years old	Juice, single strength: 128 fl. oz. Milk: 16 qt.* Breakfast cereal: 36 oz. Eggs: 1 dozen Fruits and vegetables: $8.00 in cash value voucher Whole wheat bread: 2 lb.** Legumes, 1 lb. dry or 64 oz. canned OR peanut butter, 18 oz.

Table 3.2   (continued)

Food package	Recipient	Food
V	Pregnant and partially breastfeeding women (up to one year postpartum)	Juice, single strength: 144 fl. oz. Milk: 22 qt.* Breakfast cereal: 36 oz. Eggs: 1 dozen Fruits and vegetables: $10.00 in cash value voucher Whole wheat bread: 1 lb.** Legumes, 1 lb. dry or 64 oz. canned AND peanut butter, 18 oz.
VI	Postpartum women (not breastfeeding, up to six months postpartum)	Juice, single strength: 96 fl. oz. Milk: 16 qt.* Breakfast cereal: 36 oz. Eggs: 1 dozen Fruits and vegetables: $10.00 in cash value voucher Legumes, 1 lb. dry or 64 oz. canned OR peanut butter, 18 oz.
VII	Fully breastfeeding women (up to one year postpartum)	Juice, single strength: 144 fl. oz. Milk: 24 qt.* Breakfast cereal: 36 oz. Cheese: 1 lb. Eggs: 2 dozen Fruits and vegetables: $10.00 in cash value voucher Whole wheat bread: 1 lb.** Fish, canned: 30 oz.*** Legumes, 1 lb. dry or 64 oz. canned AND peanut butter, 18 oz.

Source: USDA Federal Register/vol. 79, no. 42/March 2014/; Rules and Regulations accessed http://www.fns.usda.gov/sites/default/files/03–04–14_WIC-Food-Packages-Final-Rule.pdf.
* Allowable options for milk alternatives are cheese, soy beverage, tofu, and yogurt (partially). No whole milk for > 2 years.
** Allowable options for whole wheat bread are whole grain bread, brown rice, bulgur, oatmeal, whole-grain barley, soft corn, or whole wheat tortillas.
*** Allowable options for canned fish are light tuna, salmon, sardines, mackerel, and Jack mackerel.

and the specified maximum monthly allowance of WIC foods (separately for each eligibility group). For example, children ages one to four receive vouchers for juice (128 fluid ounces), milk (16 quarts), breakfast cereal (36 ounces), eggs (one dozen), whole wheat bread (2 pounds), and legumes/peanut butter. Infants are eligible for formula (if not exclusively breast fed), infant cereal, and baby food. Postpartum women have access to breastfeeding services. In addition, in 2009 WIC added a "cash value voucher" (CVV), here shown as $8 ($10) for fruits and vegetables for children (women).

This discussion makes clear that WIC then is primarily a quantity voucher and thus households do not face price incentives for these goods (the exception is the CVV for fruits and vegetables). In part to address this, an increasing number of states require participants to limit purchases to the cheapest available items or store brands in the authorized grocery outlet. More generally, WIC purchases may be limited by product type, product size, and brand. An important special case of this is for infant formula, which is a large part of WIC food costs. In 2010, spending on formula for WIC totaled almost $1 billion out of a total program food cost of $4.6 billion (USDA FNS 2013). Under current regulations, state WIC agencies typically award a contract to a single manufacturer of infant formula in exchange for a rebate for each can of infant formula purchased by WIC participants. These rebates are very high, ranging from 77 to 98 percent of the wholesale price. The formula market is highly concentrated—with only three firms—and more than half of all formula sold in the United States goes to WIC participants (Oliveira, Frazão, and Smallwood 2013).

In addition to the food benefits, WIC provides participants with health screenings, nutrition education, and referrals to other social services.

Importantly, WIC is not an entitlement program; SNAP on the other hand has been a fully funded entitlement program since it went national in 1975. Congress makes appropriations for WIC, which in principle could lead to shortfalls in the number of people that can be served. In recent times (since 1997), these allocations have been sufficient to meet demand for the program and thus in practice it has operated as an entitlement program.

Also, WIC has an unusual administrative structure that operates at the federal, state, and local levels. The program is federally funded and operated through the USDA. The USDA provides grants to support food benefits, nutrition services, and administration to ninety WIC agencies (covering the fifty states, Washington, DC, US territories, and Indian Tribal Organizations). The state agencies then contract with local WIC-sponsoring agencies located primarily in state and county health departments. These local sponsoring agencies then provide benefits directly or through local services sites at community health centers, hospitals, schools, mobile vans, and other locations.

History, Reforms, and Policy Changes

Currie (2003) provides a detailed history of WIC. We briefly touch on some of the important elements of the history and discuss more recent policy changes.[17]

The WIC program was first established as a pilot program in 1972 as an amendment to the Child Nutrition Act of 1966. The program was developed in direct response to policy recommendations highlighting health deficits among low-income individuals that might be reduced by improving their access to food. It was further recognized that, by providing food at "critical times of development" to pregnant and lactating women and young children, it might be possible to prevent a variety of health problems (Oliveira

---

17. Much of this section is drawn from Oliveira et al. (2002).

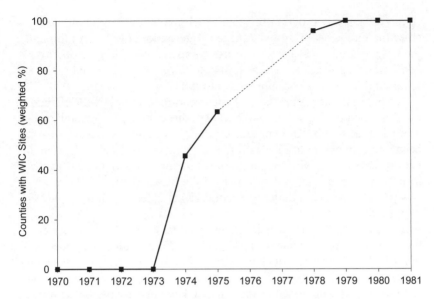

Fig. 3.4   Cumulative percent of counties with WIC programs, 1970–1981
Source: Hoynes, Page, and Stevens (2011). Weighted by 1970 county population. Missing data for 1976 and 1977.

et al. 2002). The program became permanent in 1975. The WIC program was intended to provide targeted benefits to its eligible population, and was not intended to replace food stamp benefits for them. The authorizing legislation specifically did not preclude a person from WIC participation if they were already receiving food stamps.

The WIC sites were established in different counties between 1972 and 1979, with legislation requiring that the program be implemented first in "areas most in need of special supplemental food" (Oliveira et al. 2002). The first WIC program office was established in January 1974 in Kentucky, and had expanded to include counties in forty-five states by the end of that year.[18] Figure 3.4 shows the population-weighted percent of counties with WIC programs in place. The graph shows steady expansion in the program between the years 1974–1978.

The Child Nutrition and WIC Reauthorization Act of 1989 established automatic eligibility for WIC for families participating in food stamps, Medicaid, or Aid to Families with Dependent Children. At this time, the WIC income-eligibility limits exceeded the limits in these other programs. The policy change led to an expansion of WIC and in some ways turned

18. Participation in the commodity distribution program, however, disqualified individuals from WIC participation (Oliveira et al. 2002). The CDP was being phased out during the 1970s as the FSP expanded to a national program.

it into a "gateway program through which many low-income households enter the public health system" (Macro International 1995). Additionally, the act required WIC agencies to use competitive bidding or other cost-containment policies to reduce costs of infant formula. Finally, the act required the USDA to promote breastfeeding.

For the first thirty-plus years of the program, there was little change in the WIC food package. The food packages throughout this period included a very limited number of items: juice, infant cereal, milk, cheese, eggs, dried beans, and peanut butter. The only major change to the food package in this period was in 1992 with the addition of an enhanced WIC food package including canned tuna and carrots for fully breastfeeding mothers, which was part of a growing desire to encourage breastfeeding among the WIC population.

In the late 1990s and early in the twenty-first century there was a growing view that this very narrow food package did not adequately meet current dietary guidelines (which are updated every five years). Additionally, concerns grew about significant changes in the food supply at grocery outlets (such as the increased availability of low-cost, energy-dense foods), the growing prevalence of obesity, and whether WIC foods were culturally appropriate for all participants. The USDA's Food and Nutrition Service set a goal to determine cost-neutral changes to WIC food packages based on information about the nutrition needs of WIC participants. This led to a report by the Institute of Medicine (IOM 2005), with new food packages introduced in 2009 and adopted in 2014. The IOM report identified that WIC packages should increase their coverage of nutrients such as iron, vitamin E, potassium, and fiber, and also provide more access to fruits and vegetables. Particular attention was aimed at encouraging breastfeeding through expanding the food package for breastfeeding mothers. The modified rules added flexible vouchers for fruit and vegetables (e.g., $8.00 per month for a child, $10.00 for pregnant and breastfeeding women), decreased juice and milk allotments, and added milk alternatives (cheese, yogurt, tofu) and whole grains. Table 3.2, as presented above, describes this recently adopted WIC food bundle. The Institute of Medicine is now reviewing the WIC food package to update it to reflect the latest nutrition science and dietary guidelines for Americans.

3.1.3   Program History and Rules: National School Lunch Program

Overview of Program

The school lunch program provides federal cash and commodity support for meals served to children at public and private schools, and other qualifying institutions. There is a three-tiered system based on a child's household income that determines the level of federal payments made to schools. Unless the school has adopted a universal free-meals plan, this system also typically determines the student's price category (free, reduced price, or paid).

Schools receive both cash and in-kind payments for meals served. In 2014/15, schools received federal cash subsidies equal to $2.98 per free lunch, $2.58 per reduced-price lunch, and $0.28 per paid lunch.[19] If the share of free or reduced-price lunches served at the school exceeds 60 percent (in a base year two years prior to the current year), then per-meal cash subsidies are increased by two cents per meal.[20] As described below, schools are eligible for additional payments of six cents per meal if they document that their lunches meet nutritional guidelines. In addition, schools receive commodity foods worth $0.2475 for each lunch served, regardless of the price category. Schools may also receive bonus commodities from the USDA's purchase of surplus commodities if they are available.

Benefits and Eligibility

Under traditional eligibility, children from households with incomes less than 130 percent of the federal poverty line receive lunches free of charge, while those from households with incomes between 130 percent and 185 percent of the federal poverty line are eligible for reduced-price meals, which have a maximum allowable price charged to students of $0.40. Children from households with incomes above 185 percent of the federal poverty line may purchase so-called "paid meals." Individual school districts have discretion to set their own prices for paid lunches, which are priced on average less than $2.50 per meal. Some children are additionally eligible for free meals based on categorical eligibility criteria, or if their school has adopted a universal free-meal program. Regardless of household income, children are deemed to be categorically eligible for free meals if their family receives benefits through SNAP or the Food Distribution Program on Indian Reservations (FDPIR), TANF, if the child is a foster, homeless, runaway, or migrant, or if the child is in Head Start. Students are offered the same components of school lunch regardless of their price category, and are allowed some choice to refuse components they are offered.

In recent years, there has been expansion in the use of direct certification of students for free meals using other data sources instead of requiring families to fill out application forms at schools. Direct certification can take the form of data matching or, in the case of homeless, migrant, runaway, or foster children, using a list provided to the school meals program by an appropriate official. States are required to conduct direct certification using SNAP data, but are not required to conduct direct certification using other

---

19. Payment levels are higher in Alaska and Hawaii.
20. Some states provide additional supplementary funding.

sources (e.g., TANF or FDPIR rolls).[21] The 2010 Healthy, Hunger-Free Kids Act provides incentives to states that show "outstanding performance" or "substantial improvement" in directly certifying students for free meals through these methods. In addition, as described below, students who are not income eligible or categorically eligible for free meals may receive them for free if their school has adopted a universal free-lunch program.

History, Reforms, and Policy Changes

Predecessors to the National School Lunch Program (NSLP) date back to the Great Depression, when the government began to distribute surplus farm commodities to schools with large populations of malnourished students. In 1946 Congress passed the National School Lunch Act (Gunderson 1971, see also table 3.3). The act's statement of purpose indicates that a non-profit school lunch program should be established "as a measure of national security" with the dual purposes "to safeguard the health and well-being of the Nation's children and to encourage the domestic consumption of nutritious agricultural commodities and other food." Under the act, commodities were distributed and cash payments were made to states according to a formula that was a function of per capita income and population. The NSLP was significantly amended in 1962 to adjust the funding formula to become a function of both the program participation rate and the "assistance need rate" that was a function of the state's average per capita income (Hinrichs 2010).

In recent years there have been legislative changes both regarding payment formulas and nutrition standards. In terms of payment formulas, there have been several recent efforts to reduce administrative costs for the payment process. Under the typical approach to eligibility, families are required to apply for the lunch subsidy, and then schools must track daily meal participation by price category. The alternative reimbursement provisions save schools the administrative costs of both processing applications and also daily tracking of meals served by price category. One such provision available to schools is the Community Eligibility Provision (CEP), which was phased in starting in 2011 and became available nationally in the 2014/15 school year. This policy allows schools to provide free meals to all of its students if they can document that at least 40 percent of their students are categorically eligible for free meals. If a school opts for the CEP, the federal government reimburses X percent of school meals at the free rate, where X equals 1.6 times the share of students who are categorically eligible at the school. Remaining meals served are reimbursed at the paid-lunch rate, and schools must cover any shortfall between costs and reimbursements with

21. Under USDA demonstration projects, a few states are allowed to use Medicaid data for direct certification, but only if the household's income is at or below 133 percent of the federal poverty line (Levin and Neuberger 2014).

Table 3.3   **NSLP and SBP history**

1946	National School Lunch Act
	Congress passes to make school lunch program permanent
	A. Serve lunches meeting the minimum nutritional requirements prescribed by Secretary of Agriculture
	B. Serve meals without cost or at reduced cost to children of need
	C. Operate program on a nonprofit basis
	D. Utilize commodities declared by the secretary to be in abundance
	E. Utilize commodities donated by the secretary
	F. Maintain proper records of all receipts and expenditures to be reported to state agency
1952	1st Amendment to change appropriations in AK, HI, P.R., V.I., and Guam
1962	Amended fund to be apportioned on basis of participation rate and assistance need rate
1966	Child Nutrition Act
	A. Program expanded and strengthened
	B. Special Milk Program added
	C. School Breakfast Program two-year pilot begins
1971	Congress specifies SBP to target schools in which there are children of working mothers and from low-income families
1973	SBP restructured reimbursement from grant to a specific per-meal reimbursement
1975	SBP becomes permanent with emphasis on schools in severe need
1998	Child Nutrition Reauthorization Act increases federal subsidies for child nutrition programs
2004	Child Nutrition and WIC Reauthorization Act of 2004
	A. Required all school districts receiving federal funds for meal programs to create wellness policies
2010	Healthy, Hunger-Free Kids Act
	A. Improves nutrition with a focus on childhood obesity reduction
	B. Increases access
	C. Increases program monitoring
	D. Increases funding

Source: NSLP history from http://www.fns.usda.gov/sites/default/files/NSLP-Program%20History.pdf; SBP history from http://www.fns.usda.gov/sbp/program-history.

nonfederal funds. Under the CEP, a school must provide both breakfast and lunch free to all students.

Two alternatives (referred to as "Provision 2" and "Provision 3") allow schools to serve free meals to all students enrolled at the school, while only requiring the collection of applications for free or reduced-price eligibility every four years. Provision 2 allows a school to determine the fraction of meals it serves at each price tier during one base year, then applies the same ratio of reimbursement rates to all meals served for the following three years. Under the Provision 3 option, a school counts meals served by type during the base year, and then may receive the same level of cash payments and commodities in the subsequent three years regardless of the number of meals served. Under these provisions, a school may decide to provide lunch, breakfast, or both meals for free to all students. Likely in part due to these administrative alternatives, the share of schools offering universal free lunches has increased.

The 2010 Healthy, Hunger-Free Kids Act made major changes to nutrition standards for school lunches, as shown in table 3.4. Under prior nutrient standards, schools were required to serve at least a minimum number of calories per meal, and the standard varied by student age from 633 calories in grades K–3 to 785 calories in grades 4–12. Schools were also required to insure that no more than 10 percent of calories came from saturated fats. There were also requirements for minimum levels of daily fruits and vegetables, meats, grains, and milk. Updated program rules have imposed new calorie guidelines, imposing both minimum and maximum calorie rules.

Table 3.4   Current NSLP and SBP rules (post Healthy, Hunger-Free Kids Act implementation)

I.		New dietary guidelines established by USDA
	A.	Fluid milk restrictions: unflavored milk can be 1 percent or fat free; flavored milk must be fat free
	B.	No added trans fat or zero trans fat
	C.	Avg. saturated fat content per meal (averaged across week) must be less than 10 percent of total calories
	D.	Fruits and vegetables minimum requirement increase
	E.	Avg. calories per meal (averaged across week) must fall within defined ranges for each age/grade group
	F.	Serve a variety of vegetables from each of these groups every week: dark green, red/orange, legumes, starchy and "all other"
	G.	Half of grain items offered must be "whole grain rich"
	H.	Number of servings of grain items and meat/meat alternates offered must be within the weekly ranges for each age/grade group
	I.	Minimum daily portion sizes and minimum weekly serving requirements for each food group
	J.	Reduce sodium content
II.		Simplifications to direct certification process and increased access
	A.	Foster children automatically eligible
	B.	Community eligibility: areas of high poverty qualify for universal free meals
III.		Payments and reimbursement changes
	A.	Increased lunch reimbursement rate by six cents for meals that meet nutrition standards
	B.	Requires school districts to gradually increase price of paid lunches to offset new costs
IV.		Increased authority to USDA
	A.	Regulation of competitive foods
	B.	Nutritional standards applicable to all food sold in schools
V.		Requires schools to make free potable water where meals are served
VI.		Increased program monitoring
VII.		Privacy protection for individual completing application

Source: USDA Comparison of Previous and Current Regulatory Requirements under Final Rule, http://www.fns.usda.gov/sites/default/files/comparison.pdf; Summary of the Healthy, Hunger-Free Kids Act of 2010 from http://www.fns.usda.gov/sites/default/files/PL111–296_Summary.pdf.

Table 3.5   **Previous and current school meal caloric standards**

Previous (pre-HHFKA)	Current (post-HHFKA)
Lunch	
Grades K–3	Grades K–5
Min: 633	Min: 550
Max: none	Max: 650
Grades 4–12	Grades 6–8
Min: 785	Min: 600
Max: none	Max: 700
Grades 7–12 (optional)	Grades 9–12
Min: 825	Min: 750
Max: none	Max: 850
Breakfast	
Grades K–12	Grades K–5
Min: 554	Min: 350
Max: none	Max: 500
	Grades 6–8
	Min: 400
	Max: 550
	Grades 9–12
	Min: 450
	Max: 600

Source: Comparison of previous and current regulatory requirements under final rule from Nutrition Standards in the National School Lunch and School Breakfast Programs (published January 26, 2012).

For many grades, the new maximum allowable calories were set below the previous calorie floor (see table 3.5). The new rules also include stronger requirements for daily and weekly food group servings, including weekly requirements for a variety of vegetables (such as dark green, red/orange, and starchy), restrictions on the fat content of milk, and a phased-in requirement to use only whole grain rich grains. Schools that meet these enhanced nutrition requirements receive an additional six-cent payment per meal. In addition, the act gave the USDA authority to set nutritional standards for all foods sold in school during the school day, including in vending machines, school stores, and a la carte lunch items. The research literature evaluating the impacts of the policy changes on participation in the program at the individual or school level is sparse to date.

3.1.4   Program History and Rules: School Breakfast Program

Overview of Program

The school breakfast operates in a similar manner to the lunch program, though participation is lower. The SBP provides federal cash support (but, unlike the NSLP, no additional commodity support) for meals served to children at public and private schools and other qualifying institutions. The same approach is employed as in the NSLP, in which a three-tiered system based on a child's household income determines the level of federal payments made to schools, and typically also determines the student's price category.

In 2014/15, schools received federal cash subsidies equal to $1.62 per free breakfast, $1.32 per reduced-price breakfast, and $0.28 per paid breakfast.[22] If the share of free or reduced-price breakfasts served at the school exceeds 40 percent (in a base year two years prior to the current year), then the school is eligibility for "severe need" payments, which increase the per-meal cash subsidies by thirty-one cents per meal for free and reduced-price meals. About three-quarters of breakfasts served in the SBP receive this "severe need" payment.

Benefits and Eligibility

The eligibility rules are the same for breakfast and lunch, and a single eligibility determination is made for each child that covers both meals. The current maximum allowable price for reduced-price breakfast is $0.30. Children from households with incomes above 185 percent of the federal poverty line may purchase so-called "paid meals." The categorical eligibility criteria (whereby participation in selected means-tested transfers automatically confer eligibility for SBP) are the same as they are for the school lunch program.

History, Reforms, and Policy Changes

The SBP was established in 1966 as a two-year pilot program. It originally provided categorical grants to provide payments to schools that served breakfast to "nutritionally needy" students. In 1973, the program was amended to replace the categorical grant with the per-meal payment system used today. It was permanently authorized in 1975.

New program rules adopted after the 2010 Healthy, Hunger-Free Kids Act made substantial changes to breakfast standards. Under prior nutrient standards, schools were required to serve at least 554 calories at breakfast. Under the new standards, breakfast calories were required to fall within a specified range, from 350–500 for grades K–5 to 450–600 for high school students. Similar to the changes made to the lunch nutrient standards, new rules required more fruits and vegetables, a switch to whole grains, and imposed restrictions on the fat content of milk. The act also authorized grants that can be used to establish or expand school breakfast programs.

Other Food and Nutrition Programs

There are four other child nutrition programs (see table 3.1), and together they comprise about 4 percent of spending on food and nutrition programs overall or about one-quarter of the total federal spending on child nutrition

22. Reimbursements are higher in Alaska and Hawaii.

programs). These programs provide meals for children and other vulnerable groups outside of school and during the summer, or provide additional food items to children.

The Child and Adult Care Food Program (CACFP) provides meals and snacks to children in day care facilities, as well as to functionally impaired adults receiving care in nonresidential adult day care centers and to the elderly (e.g., through Meals on Wheels). Participation in 2014 totaled 3.9 million children and adults, and total federal spending was $3.1 billion. The Summer Food Service Program (SFSP) supports meals and snacks served to children at schools, camps, and other organizations during the summer when school is not in session. In 2014, the program served 160 million meals to 2.7 million children (measured in July, the peak participation month) at a cost of $465.6 million. The Fresh Fruit and Vegetable Program (FFVP) provides resources for elementary schools to serve fresh fruits and vegetables as snacks outside of regular lunch and breakfast times. Schools apply to participate in the program, which is targeted to schools with high enrollments of free- and reduced-price-meal-eligible students. Participating schools receive an annual allotment of $50 to $75 per student. In 2014/15, the FFVP had $153 million in spending. The Special Milk Program (SMP) provides subsidized milk, primarily to schools, childcare institutions, and camps that do not participate in other federally subsidized child nutrition programs. The cost in 2014 was $10.5 million.

3.2   Program Statistics and Recipient Characteristics

3.2.1   Program Statistics: SNAP

In 2014, SNAP expenditures totaled $74.2 billion and served 46.5 million persons (or 22.7 million households). This translates to participation by more than one out of seven Americans. The average monthly benefit in 2014 amounted to $257 per household, $125 per person, or $4.11 per person per day. Overall, SNAP is the largest cash or near-cash means-tested safety net program in the United States.

Table 3.6 presents data on SNAP participation and expenditures over time. Total expenditures (in real 2014 dollars) increased from $28.0 billion in 1990 to $74.2 billion in 2014. Average monthly participation follows a similar path, moving from 20 million persons in 1990 to 46.5 million in 2014. The bottom of the table presents SNAP participants as a percent of the total US population—it has ranged from 8.1 percent in 1990 down to 6.2 percent in 2000, to 14.8 percent in 2014.

The take-up rate of SNAP, calculated as the fraction of the eligible population that is participating in the program, is fairly high at 79 percent in 2011 (Cunnyngham 2014). The take-up rates vary significantly across groups, with elderly individuals having considerably lower take-up rates than other groups. The take-up rates also vary substantially across states in the United

Table 3.6   Expenditures and caseload in food and nutrition programs

	1990	1995	2000	2005	2010	2012	2013	2014
Expenditures (billions $2014)								
SNAP	28.0	38.2	23.4	37.7	74.1	80.9	81.2	74.2
WIC	3.8	5.3	5.4	6.0	7.0	6.9	6.5	6.2
NSLP	5.8	6.9	7.6	8.6	10.6	10.7	11.2	11.4
SBP	1.1	1.6	1.9	2.3	3.1	3.4	3.6	3.7
Average monthly participation (millions persons)								
SNAP	20.0	26.6	17.2	25.6	40.3	46.6	47.6	46.5
Annual participation (millions persons)								
WIC (total)	4.5	6.9	7.2	8.0	9.2	8.9	8.7	8.3
Women	1.0	1.6	1.7	2.0	2.1	2.1	2.0	2.0
Infants	1.4	1.8	1.9	2.0	2.2	2.1	2.0	2.0
Children	2.1	3.5	3.6	4.0	4.9	4.7	4.6	4.3
NSLP (total free, reduced, and full paid meals)	24.1	25.7	27.3	29.6	31.8	31.7	30.7	30.5
Free meals	9.8	12.4	13.0	14.6	17.6	18.7	18.9	19.2
Reduced-price meals	1.7	1.9	2.5	2.9	3.0	2.7	2.6	2.5
SBP (total free, reduced, and full paid meals)	4.1	6.3	7.6	9.4	11.7	12.9	13.2	13.6
Free meals	3.3	5.1	5.7	6.8	8.7	9.8	10.2	10.6
Reduced-price meals	0.22	0.37	0.61	0.86	1.0	1.0	1.0	1.0
Caseload (as % relevant population)								
SNAP	8.1	10.1	6.2	8.7	13.2	15.0	15.2	14.8
WIC								
Women (as % of all women ages 18–44)	1.9	2.9	3.1	3.6	3.9	3.7	3.6	3.5
Children 1–4	13.5	21.7	23.0	24.6	28.3	29.6	28.5	26.9
Infants < 1	35.3	46.5	48.5	50.5	52.9	53.4	53.8	51.9
NSLP (as % of children ages 5–17)								
Free and reduced-price meals	25.0	28.0	29.1	32.6	38.4	39.5	39.7	40.0
Free meals	21.4	24.4	24.5	22.7	32.8	34.5	35.0	35.4
All meals	52.5	50.2	51.5	55.3	59.2	58.3	56.6	56.2
SBP (as % of children ages 5–17)								
Free and reduced-price meals	7.6	10.7	12.0	14.3	18.1	19.9	20.6	21.3
Free meals	7.2	10.0	10.8	12.7	16.2	18.0	18.8	19.5
All meals	8.8	12.4	14.3	17.4	21.7	23.7	24.4	25.2

Sources: http://www.fns.usda.gov/sites/default/files/pd/SNAPsummary.xls; CPI is from EROP http://www .gpoaccess.gov/eop/tables10.html; population is from EROP http://www.gpoaccess.gov/eop/2010/B34.xls and Census Department http://www.fns.usda.gov/sites/default/files/pd/17SNAPfyBEN$.xls; http://www.fns.usda .gov/sites/default/files/pd/SNAPsummary.xls. Additional spreadsheets provided by Candy Mountjoy (Candy .Mountjoy@fns.usda.gov), Maeve Myers (maeve.myers@fns.usda.gov), and Gene Austin (Gene.Austin@fns .usda.gov); http://www.fns.usda.gov/sites/default/files/pd/10sbcash.xls, http://www.fns.usda.gov/sites/default /files/pd/16SNAPpartHH.xls; http://www.fns.usda.gov/sites/default/files/pd/34SNAPmonthly.xls, http://www .fns.usda.gov/sites/default/files/pd/15SNAPpartPP.xls; and http://www.fns.usda.gov/sites/default/files/pd/06sl cash.xls.

States with higher rates in New England, the upper Midwest and the Pacific Northwest, and lower rates in the Mountain Plains, the Far West, and Texas (Cunnyngham 2014). Take-up rates have varied substantially over time: from 75 percent in 1994, down to 59 percent after federal welfare reform (in 2000), to 54 percent in 2002, then increasing to 67 percent in 2006 and

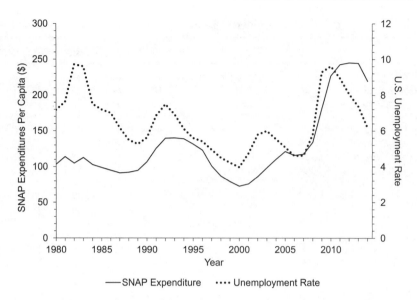

— SNAP Expenditure   ···· Unemployment Rate

Fig. 3.5   Real per capita expenditures for SNAP, 1980–2014 (real 2014 dollars), with US unemployment rate

Source: USDA SNAP data: http://www.fns.usda.gov/pd/supplemental-nutrition-assistance-program-snap. Unemployment rates from http://data.bls.gov/pdq/SurveyOutputServlet. For definitions of recessionary periods, see Bitler and Hoynes (2016).

Note: Per capita SNAP expenditures are calculated using the US population as the denominator (not per SNAP recipient) and inflation adjusted using the US Bureau of Labor Statistics' CPI inflation calculator.

79 percent in 2011 (Cunnyngham 2002, 2010; Cunnyngham, Sukasih, and Castner 2014).

Figure 3.5 plots annual SNAP expenditures from 1980 to 2014, in real 2014 dollars. We normalize by the total US population in each year, thereby generating real per capita (not per recipient) expenditures. The figure also includes the annual US unemployment rate. During this period, per capita real spending on SNAP was relatively flat in the 1980s, increased in the early 1990s, and then fell dramatically through the late 1990s. Since that time, spending has increased steadily. Overall, the program shows a countercyclical pattern, increasing in the recessions in the early 1990s, early 2000s, and especially notable, in the Great Recession.

Table 3.7 presents summary characteristics for SNAP recipient units and how they vary over time. The top panel of the table relates to all SNAP recipients and the bottom panel limits to SNAP recipient units without any elderly (age sixty or more) individuals. These tabulations are based on administrative data from the USDA Quality Control (QC) files. In 2012, about 45 percent of SNAP recipient units included children, down from about 60 percent in 1996. Female-headed households with children as a

Table 3.7   Characteristics of SNAP recipients

	1996	2000	2005	2010	2012
All food stamp households					
Share with children	60	54	54	49	45
Share female heads with children	39	35	32	26	24
Share with elderly members	16	21	17	16	17
Share of individuals < 18	47	47	47	44	43
Share of individuals > = 65	9	10	7	5	6
Share no elderly, no kids, no disabled	15	11	16	24	25
Share with gross monthly income below poverty	91	89	88	85	82
Share with no cash income	10	8	14	20	20
Share with any earnings	23	27	29	30	31
Share with no net income	25	20	30	38	38
Multiple program participation; share with income from:					
AFDC/TANF	37	26	15	8	7
General assistance	6	5	6	4	3
SSI	24	32	26	21	20
Social Security	19	25	23	21	23
Unemployment insurance	2	2	2	7	5
Veterans benefits	1	1	1	1	1
Food stamp households without elderly members					
Share with children	70	67	64	57	54
Share female heads with children	46	43	38	30	29
Share with elderly members	0	0	0	0	0
Share with gross monthly income below poverty	92	89	89	87	85
Share with no cash income	12	10	16	22	23
Share with any earnings	26	33	35	34	37
Multiple program participation; share with income from:					
AFDC/TANF	43	32	17	9	8
General assistance	7	5	6	4	3
SSI	17	24	20	16	16
Social Security	9	14	14	13	14
Unemployment insurance	2	2	2	8	6
Veterans benefits	1	1	1	1	0
Effective tax rate on:					
Earned income	18	15	16	15	15
Unearned income	19	17	17	17	16

Source: Authors' tabulations of SNAP Quality Control Data. Available at http://hostm142.mathemati-campr.com/fns/.

share of the total caseload are also falling over time, from 39 percent in 1996 to 24 percent in 2012. About 17 percent contain an elderly individual, and that share has not changed much over time. The share with no children, elderly, or disabled persons (a proxy for the able-bodied adults without dependents) has increased from 15 percent in 1996 to 25 percent in 2012. An increasing share of the caseload combines benefit receipt with employment. About 31 percent of households currently have earned income, a rate that is up 8 percentage points since 1996. On the other hand, some 20 percent have no cash income, up from 10 percent in 1996 (for an in-depth analysis of this issue, see Peterson et al. [2014]). Thirty-eight percent of households have no net income (income after allowable deductions), up from 25 percent in 1996.

At the bottom of the bottom panel of table 3.7, we present the effective tax rates faced by (nonelderly) SNAP recipients. These are calculated using the QC data and follow the methods used in Ziliak (2008). The effective tax rate is the average of the marginal tax rates faced by SNAP households—marginal because it is calculated on their observed income amounts, and average because it is averaged over households. Table 3.7 shows that the effective tax rate on earned income is 15 percent in 2012, down slightly from 18 percent in 1996. The tax rate on unearned income is somewhat higher at 16 percent in 2012. In light of the discussion above, it is important to point out that this is the tax rate within SNAP only (as opposed to the cumulative tax rate experienced across multiple programs). To the extent that SNAP recipients have children and very low earnings, then the negative marginal tax rates in the EITC will reduce the cumulative tax rates below the SNAP effective tax rate. On the other hand, those with higher earnings (e.g., perhaps in the phaseout of the EITC) would experience cumulative tax rates in excess of the SNAP effective tax rate. See Moffitt (2015) for further discussion of multiple participation rates.

Given the patchwork of US means-tested programs, it is of interest to examine the propensity to participate in multiple programs, especially in light of concerns about cumulative work disincentives (Congressional Budget Office 2012; Mulligan 2012).[23] It is also interesting to examine this over time given welfare reform and the many changes in the safety net. The food stamp quality control data (table 3.7) track all resources that count as income for determining SNAP benefits, practically this translates to *cash* income programs. In 2012, only 7 percent of SNAP recipients have income from TANF, down from 37 percent in 1996 on the eve of welfare reform. The share with income from SSI and Social Security has stayed relatively steady; in 2012, 20 and 23 percent of SNAP units received SSI and Social Security, respectively. If you limit to recipient units without elderly individuals, the share with Social Security (which we interpret as likely including SSDI) has increased, from 9 percent in 1996 to 14 percent in 2012. Few food stamp recipients have income from UI (5 percent), general assistance (3 percent), or veteran's payments (1 percent). Although receipt of UI among SNAP recipients units is low, the data show a notable increase in the Great Recession (from 2 percent in 2005 to 7 percent in 2010). While the QC data are valuable, they are limited because they only track sources of income relevant for determining SNAP benefits. Moffitt (2015) uses the Survey of Income and

---

23. As discussed in Moffitt (2015), Parrott and Greenstein (2014), and elsewhere, in many analyses citing high cumulative marginal tax rates, the calculations assume that families are participating in all programs. This, as we discuss below, it not consistent with the data.

Table 3.8   Food stamps maximum benefits by household size (2014)

Household size	Net income (100% of poverty line) ($)	Gross income (130% of poverty line) ($)	Maximum benefit ($)
1	973	1,265	194
2	1,311	1,705	357
3	1,650	2,144	511
4	1,988	2,584	649
5	2,326	3,024	771
6	2,665	3,464	925
7	3,003	3,904	1,022
8	3,341	4,344	1,169
Each additional person	(+) 339	(+) 440	(+) 146

Source: Income eligibility standards from http://www.fns.usda.gov/sites/default/files/FY15_Income_Standards.pdf; maximum allotments from http://www.fns.usda.gov/sites/default/files/FY15_Allot_Deduct.pdf.
Notes: Includes contiguous states, District of Columbia, Guam, and the Virgin Islands. Does not include Hawaii or Alaska.

Program Participation and studies multiple program participation across a wider range of programs. He finds that (in 2008) 30 percent of nondisabled, nonelderly SNAP families receive WIC, more than half receive the EITC, and 21 percent receive subsidized housing.

Table 3.8 presents maximum monthly SNAP benefits by household size for 2014. A household of four has a maximum monthly benefit of $649, while a household of size two has a maximum benefit of $357. Annualizing these amounts, maximum benefits correspond to between 27 and 33 percent of the federal poverty line.

As discussed above in section 3.1.1, the SNAP benefit formula has changed little over time, other than adjusting for annual changes in the price of food. Interest in the adequacy of the SNAP benefit has increased over time and led to a recent Institute of Medicine report (IOM 2013). Hoynes, McGranahan, and Schanzenbach (2015) explore SNAP benefit adequacy by examining the food spending patterns across families of differing income and composition. They argue that the maximum benefit level is inappropriate on at least two fronts: the Thrifty Food Plan (TFP) is based on outdated assumptions, and the family size adjustment does not reflect differences in spending patterns. First, consider the TFP, which is set at $632 per month for a typical family of four in 2013. Recall that maximum benefits are set based on the TFP, and the program aims to ensure that households have adequate resources to purchase this "target" spending level. Based on an analysis of the Consumer Expenditure Survey, they show that over the past twenty years, the majority of families with incomes below 200 percent of the poverty line spent more than the TFP amount. They argue this is in part due to the fact that the TFP is based on assumptions regarding how much cooking is done from scratch that are increasingly unrealistic and out of line with time-use data. Second, they show that differences in actual spending patterns across family size are much steeper than are accounted for by the benefit multipliers. Since the average SNAP household size is 2.3, this suggests that many families are receiving benefits based on a formula that understates their needs.

3.2.2   Program Statistics: WIC

In 2014, WIC expenditures totaled $6.2 billion and served 8.3 million persons. The costs break down into $4.3 billion for food and $1.9 billion for nutrition services and administration.[24] Average monthly federal food cost per person in 2014 amounted to $43.65, or $1.44 per person per day. The WIC caseload breaks down to be 10 percent pregnant women, 13 percent postpartum or breastfeeding women, 24 percent infants, and 53 percent children (USDA 2014). The average cost per recipient varies little across groups, from $49.36 per infant, to $49.16 per breastfeeding woman, to $36.94 per child (USDA 2014). A given family may have multiple members with WIC benefits (for example, a pregnant mother, her infant, and her child age three would have three WIC packages) and the total value of the WIC package to a family accumulates across individuals.

Table 3.6 presents data on WIC participation and expenditures over time. The WIC program has increased over this period from 4.5 million recipients in 1990 to 8.3 million in 2014. The total cost increased from 3.8 billion (2014$) in 1990 to 6.2 billion in 2014. The growth seems to be fairly similar across the subgroups of women, infants, and children. The bottom of table 3.6 presents program participation rates, where we express the number of participants as a percent of the relevant demographic group. So, for example, the WIC infant (child) caseload is a percent of all persons less than one year (between one and four).[25] We express the women caseload as a share of women ages eighteen to forty-four. Both infant and child caseloads have increased over this period. Fully 26.9 percent of children ages one to four received WIC in 2014, up from 13.5 percent in 1990. Participation is higher for infants, likely due to the high cost of infant formula, more than half of infants in the United States in 2014 received WIC benefits. In 2014, 3.5 percent of women ages eighteen to forty-four received WIC, though this figure is an underestimate of potential participation since we do not condition on pregnant, postpartum, or breastfeeding women in the denominator.

Figure 3.6 plots the real spending on WIC annually from 1980 to 2014. Again, we normalize by the total US population to create a per capita (not per participant) measure. The WIC expenditures exhibit a fairly steady rise in the 1990s consistent with the expansions in the 1989 WIC reauthorization

24. We omit additional WIC spending on items other than food and nutrition services, including program evaluation, special projects, and infrastructure.

25. These are participation rates, not take-up rates, because they do not condition on income eligibility.

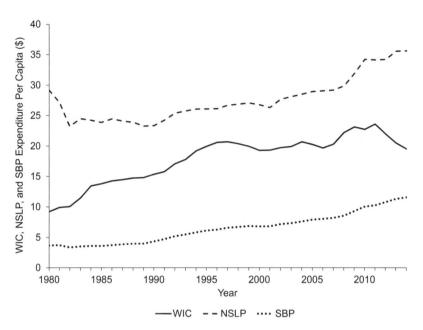

Fig. 3.6   Real per capita expenditures for WIC, NSLP, and SBP, 1980–2014 (real 2014 dollars)

Source: USDA WIC, NSLP, and SBP program data, http://www.fns.usda.gov/pd/wic-program and http://www.fns.usda.gov/pd/child-nutrition-tables.

Note: Per capita expenditures are calculated using the US population as the denominator (not per program recipient) and inflation adjusted using the US Bureau of Labor Statistics' CPI inflation calculator.

act. Costs slowed in the late 1990s, perhaps due to welfare reform (and the overall "chilling" effect that followed) as well as the strong labor market. After a relatively flat period, a countercyclical pattern with the Great Recession and recovery is evident at the end of the period.

Table 3.9 presents summary characteristics for WIC recipient units in 2012 (the most recent year available) and, for comparison, 1994. Despite the income-threshold of 185 percent of the poverty line (higher than SNAP, for example), fully 37 percent of WIC recipients have income below 50 percent of the poverty line ("extreme poverty"). Seventy-three percent have incomes below 100 percent of the poverty line, and 92 have income below 150 percent. The distribution of recipients by income has not changed much between 1994 and 2012. One notable change in the caseloads is the rise of breastfeeding women as a share of all women on the program, which has increased from 17 percent in 1994 to 29 percent in 2012. We also explore the extent of multiple-program participation among WIC recipients. In 2012, only 9 percent of WIC recipients have income from TANF, down from 29 percent in 1992 (prior to welfare reform). The share with income from SNAP has been

Table 3.9   Characteristics of WIC recipients

	1994	2012
Income below 50% FPL	42	37
Income below 100% FPL	74	73
Income below 150% FPL	91	92
Percent of women participants who are:		
Pregnant	52	43
Breastfeeding	17	29
Postpartum	31	28
	100	100
Multiple program participation; percent with income from:		
TANF	29	9
SNAP	40	37
Medicaid	58	72
SNAP and Medicaid	35	33
No TANF/SNAP or Medicaid	36	24

Source: "WIC Participant and Program Characteristics 2012: Final Report" FNS, USDA, December 2013 and "WIC Participant and Program Characteristics 1994" FNS, USDA. Observations with missing data are excluded from the tabulations.

relatively steady; in 2012, 37 percent of WIC units received SNAP compared to 40 percent in 1992. Participation in Medicaid among WIC recipients was very high at 72 percent in 2012, up from 58 percent in 1992, reflecting the substantial expansions in Medicaid for pregnant women and children.

3.2.3   Program Statistics: NSLP

The National School Lunch Program (NSLP) serves lunch to almost 30 million students—56 percent of the total student population (see table 3.6). Almost all public schools offer the NSLP, which in 2014 cost $11.4 billion with average participation of 19.2 million children in free, 2.5 children in reduced-price, and 8.8 million in paid lunch. Overall, including the free, reduced-price, and paid categories, over 5 billion lunches were served. As shown in the bottom of table 3.6, 40 percent of all school-age children received free or reduced-price lunch in 2014, up from 25 percent in 1990. The share of students receiving school lunch for free (among those eating school lunch) has grown over time from 41 percent in 1990 to 63.6 percent in 2014. Overall, participation (free, reduced price, or paid as share of all school-age children) has edged down somewhat in the last few years from its historic peak of 59 percent in 2010.

After adjusting for inflation, spending on NSLP has almost doubled since 1990. This reflects an increase in the number of school-age children, an increase in spending per lunch, and a trend toward increased participation rates. The increased spending per lunch has been driven by a combination of increased costs and policy changes. Per-meal spending on child nutrition programs increases annually because payment levels are indexed according to the Food Away from Home series of the CPI-U. Commodity payments are inflated according to the Price Index of Foods used in schools and institutions. (Payments are legislated not to decrease, so if food prices decline in a year, there is no adjustment to these costs). In recent years, the price index for food away from home has grown more quickly than overall inflation (measured by the price index for personal consumption expenditures). In addition, the 2010 Healthy, Hunger-Free Kids Act increased cash payments by six cents per meal for schools that meet the new, more stringent nutrition requirements.

3.2.4   Program Statistics: SBP

There have been recent—and highly successful—attempts to expand access to the SBP. As shown in table 3.6, between 1990 and 2014 the total number of students receiving the SBP more than tripled (compared to a 27 percent increase in the number of NSLP participants). At the same time, the share of school-age children receiving free or reduced-price breakfast also increased sharply, from 7.6 percent in 1990 to 21.3 percent of children in 2014. Some of this has been driven by increases in participation rates of schools in the program in 2014. Schanzenbach and Zaki (2014) calculate from the NHANES that in 2009/10 almost three-quarters of children attended a school that offered the SBP, up from approximately half of students in the 1988–1994 wave. An additional portion has been driven by policies to expand take-up by students, including providing breakfast for free to all students before school or introducing Breakfast in the Classroom programs. In 2014, 85 percent of participants received the SBP either for free or at reduced price.

3.2.5   Summary Measures across Programs

Figure 3.7 summarizes the programs, presenting the total program costs and total program recipients in 2014. Considering our four central food and nutrition programs (SNAP, WIC, NSLP, and SBP) as well as the other smaller programs in table 3.1, total spending amounted to about 100 billion dollars in 2014 and about 95 million total participants benefited from these programs. (Given multiple program participation, the total unique recipients would be less than 95 million.) Considering the programs together, figure 3.7 shows that SNAP is clearly the largest program—in terms of both people reached and program cost. In 2014, expenditures on SNAP were over six times as large as the NSLP and almost twelve times as large as WIC. The number of SNAP recipients was about two times those receiving free or reduced-price NSLP and over five times WIC. However, these comparisons ignore the fact that SNAP is universal, while NSLP and WIC are targeted on specific demographic groups. Using this lens, the figures in the bottom of table 3.6 show that SNAP has the *smallest* reach among the programs.

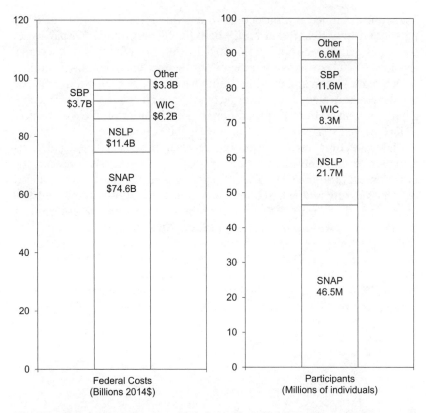

Fig. 3.7   Federal expenditures and number of recipients by program (2014)

Note: "Other" includes the Child and Adult Care Food Program (CACFP), the Summer Food Service Program (SFSP), the Special Milk Program (SMP), and the Fresh Fruit and Vegetable Program (FFVP). Participation for NSLP and SBP only includes free and reduced-price lunch participants. Participation data is missing from SMP and FFVP and is not included in this graph.

Half of all infants and almost 30 percent of children ages one to four receive WIC, over 20 percent of school-age children receive free or reduced-price breakfast, and 40 percent receive free or reduced-price lunch. By contrast, SNAP is received by 15 percent of the population.

Figure 3.8 shows how program participation for the food and nutrition programs varies by income level. In particular, the figure plots household participation in SNAP, NSLP, and WIC (alongside EITC as a comparison) as a function of household private income to poverty level (truncating at eight times income to poverty).[26] The figure is based on tabulations of the 2014 Current Population Survey corresponding to data for calendar year

26. The figure is adopted using the approach in Bitler and Hoynes (2016). See that paper for details on the sample and measurement.

2013, and is limited to households with children headed by a nonelderly person. Overall, SNAP and NSLP have the highest household participation rates, with lower household participation rates for WIC. Of course, this lower WIC participation rate reflects the fact that eligibility is limited to pregnant women and children through age four. Participation in SNAP is most concentrated at the lower income levels, reflecting its lower income eligibility limits. The WIC program has a much flatter profile with respect to income, reflecting the higher income eligibility limits.

Figure 3.9 compares antipoverty effects of the programs. The calculations are based on the Supplemental Poverty Measure (SPM), first released by the census in 2011 (Short 2011). The SPM provides an alternative to the official poverty measure and is based on a comprehensive after-tax and transfer-income resource measure that includes the value of noncash government transfers. Here we use the 2014 SPM (Short 2014) and plot the number of children removed from poverty for all government tax and transfer programs tracked in the SPM. This is a static calculation, essentially zeroing out the income source and recalculating family income and poverty status assuming all else (e.g., earnings, other income sources) remain constant. SNAP removes 2.1 million children from poverty, second only to the combined

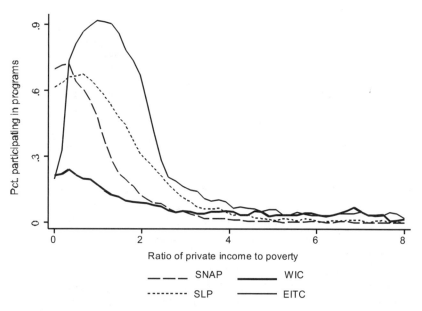

Fig. 3.8   Household participation in food and nutrition programs by household income to poverty, households with children headed by nonelderly individual (2013)
Source: Adapted from Bitler and Hoynes (2016). Authors' tabulations of 2014 Current Population Survey capturing data for 2013 calendar year. Kernel density plot of household program participation, by ratio of household private income to poverty. Sample includes nonelderly household heads in households with children.

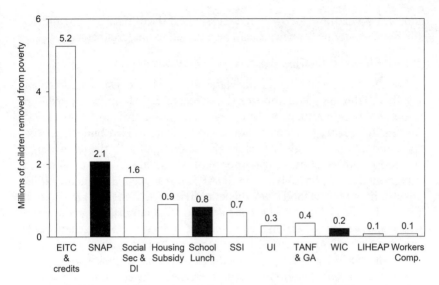

Fig. 3.9   Millions of children removed from poverty by program, 2014
Source: Authors' tabulation of Short (2014).

effects of the EITC and Child Tax Credit that together remove 5.2 million children from poverty. By comparison, the NSLP removes 0.8 million children from poverty and WIC removes 0.2 million children from poverty.[27] Although not shown here, calculations for the entire population show that SNAP removes a total of 4.7 million people from poverty, making SNAP the third largest US antipoverty program after Social Security and the Earned Income Tax Credit.

3.3   Review of the Issues Surrounding the Programs

Each of the food and nutrition programs can be analyzed through standard economic frameworks. The applicable frameworks differ somewhat, though, because the programs differ in terms of the degree to which the benefits are provided in kind. Closest to cash, SNAP takes the form of a value voucher and can be used to purchase most foods, while the more targeted WIC takes the form of a quantity voucher limited to specific foods, and the school meals programs offer meals directly. As with other means-tested transfer programs, these programs face the usual trade-off in balancing the protective aspects of the programs to improve dietary intake and reduce hunger and food insecurity against their distorting incentives such as reduced labor supply. We start by discussing SNAP because it is the largest program and has been

27. With underreporting of SNAP and other food and nutrition programs, these are underestimates of the total antipoverty effects (Tiehen, Jolliffe, and Smeeding 2013).

most researched, and follow with discussions of the other programs and how the basic economic framework can be adapted to analyze them.

3.3.1   Effects of In-Kind Benefits on Food Consumption

We begin by presenting the neoclassical model of consumer choice and use this to discuss predictions for the effects of SNAP on family spending patterns.[28] Figure 3.10, panel (A) presents the standard Southworth (1945) model, in which a consumer chooses to allocate a fixed budget between food and all other goods. The slope of the budget line is the relative price of food to other goods. In the absence of SNAP, the budget constraint is represented by the line AB. When SNAP is introduced, it shifts the budget constraint out by the food stamp benefit (divided by food price) B_F/P_F to the new budget line labeled ACD. The first, and most important, prediction of the neoclassical model is that the presence of, or increase in the generosity of, the SNAP transfer leads to a shift out in the budget constraint. The transfer does not alter the relative prices of different goods, so can be analyzed as a pure income effect, and predicts an increase in the consumption level of all normal goods. Thus, the central prediction is that food stamps, like an increase in disposable income or a cash transfer, will increase both food spending and nonfood spending.

However, SNAP benefits are provided as a voucher that only can be used toward food purchases. Canonical economic theory predicts that in-kind transfers like SNAP are treated as if they are cash as long as their value is no larger than the amount that a consumer would spend on the good if she had the same total income in cash. Returning to figure 3.10, panel (A), there is a portion of the budget set that is not attainable with SNAP that would be attainable with the cash-equivalent value income transfer. (We are assuming that the resale of these vouchers is not possible.) In other words, because the benefits B_F are provided in the form of a food voucher, this amount is not available to purchase other goods, and thus we would expect a consumer to purchase at least B_F amount of food. Thus paying benefits in the form of a food voucher leads to a budget constraint with a kink point.

Figure 3.10, panel (B) illustrates how consumption responds to the receipt of SNAP benefits. In the absence of SNAP, a typical consumer purchases some mix of food and nonfood goods, choosing the bundle that maximizes her utility and exhausts her budget constraint. This is represented as point A_0^*, with the consumer purchasing food in the amount F_0. After SNAP is introduced, the budget constraint shifts outward and the consumer chooses the consumption bundle represented by point A_1^*. Note that consumption of both goods increases and food consumption goes up by less than the full

28. See also Currie and Gahvari (2008) for an excellent overview of the economics of in-kind transfer programs.

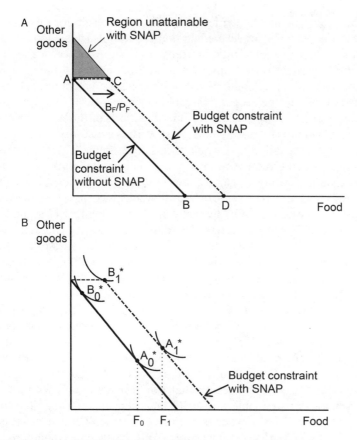

Fig. 3.10   Effects of SNAP on consumption

Note: Panel (A): budget set shift; panel (B): consumer's utility maximization response to SNAP.

SNAP benefit amount. Such a consumer is termed "inframarginal" and the canonical model predicts that SNAP will increase food spending the same amount as if the SNAP benefits were paid in cash. As discussed further below, the predicted impacts of proposed policy changes, such as calls to restrict purchases of certain goods with SNAP benefits, hinges on what proportion of recipients are inframarginal.

There are two important exceptions to the SNAP-as-cash model, though. The first is for consumers that prefer relatively little food consumption. In the absence of SNAP, such a consumer may choose the consumption bundle labeled B_0^* in panel (B). When SNAP is introduced, this consumer spends only his benefit amount on food, preferring to use all available cash resources to purchase other goods as represented at point B_1^*. If benefits were paid in cash instead of as a food voucher, the consumer would opt to purchase less food and could obtain a higher level of utility. As a result, for this type of consumer, the canonical model predicts that SNAP will increase food spending by more than an equivalent cash transfer would. Another exception to the standard model comes from behavioral economics and predicts that SNAP may not be equivalent to cash if households use a mental accounting framework that puts the benefits in a separate "category."[29]

We can extend this approach to consider the effects of the WIC program. There are two important distinctions. First, WIC is a quantity voucher, not a value voucher. So while SNAP would award, for example, $100 to purchase food, WIC instead gives a voucher for sixteen quarts of milk (and other items). Second, there are specified goods that are provided by the voucher (this can also include a restriction on the allowable package sizes in the WIC package). We present the WIC budget constraint in figure 3.11 and adapt the SNAP graph by putting "targeted subsidized goods" (e.g., items in table 3.2) on the x axis and all other goods (which also includes much of the food budget as well as nonfood goods) on the y axis. The no program budget constraint again is AB, and the budget set shifts out by the WIC quantity voucher Q_W. Note the contrast to SNAP, where the value voucher shifts out the budget constraint by B_F/P_F. Thus, for SNAP, the recipient faces price incentives: choosing lower-priced goods increases the value of the SNAP benefit. In contrast, with WIC, recipients are price insensitive; their budget constraint (and potential increase in utility due to the program) is affected only by the quantity Q_W, regardless of the price of those goods P_W.

As with SNAP, there is a region that would be attainable with a cash transfer that is not attainable with WIC, and there are inframarginal consumers and constrained consumers. However, because WIC is such a specified bundle, we expect that a larger share of WIC participants (compared to SNAP recipients) will be constrained and at point C.

Additionally, as discussed in Meckel (2014), vendors face incentives to charge WIC recipients a mark up on the WIC packages (because of recipients' price inelasticity). This would amount to fraud and could be sanctioned if caught. Vendors may also choose to compete on products (quantity and diversity) to gain market share given that price competition is not available (McLaughlin 2014).

School lunch and breakfast programs are even more specified. We model

---

29. There are other reasons that may explain why SNAP leads to different effects on food consumption compared to ordinary case income. It is possible that the family member with control over food stamp benefits may be different from the person that controls earnings and other cash income. If the person with control over food stamps has greater preferences for food, then we may find that food stamps lead to larger increases in food consumption compared to cash income. Alternatively, families may perceive that food stamp benefits are a more permanent source of income compared to earnings. Finally, Shapiro (2005) finds evidence of a "food stamp cycle," whereby daily caloric and nutritional intake declines within weeks since their food stamp payment suggests a significant preference for immediate consumption.

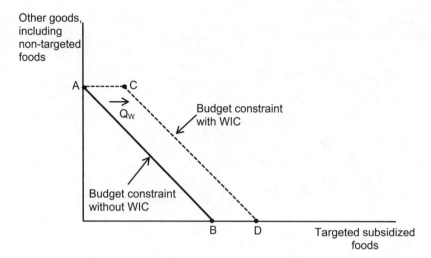

Fig. 3.11   Effects of WIC on consumption

these as "take it or leave it" benefits—if you are eligible for a free lunch then you have the choice to consume the lunch or use private resources for lunch.[30] This is illustrated in figure 3.12 with the targeted subsidized good (e.g., school lunch) on the x axis and all other goods on the y axis. We represent the school lunch option as a single point, and as the quality of the lunch increases the point shifts out. Some consumers will chose the private option, and others will chose the public option. As the quality of the public option increases, more will switch into the lunch program.

Unlike SNAP, the WIC and school feeding programs are explicitly targeted at certain groups (pregnant women, infants, children age one to four, school-age children). In the context of families, it is possible—perhaps likely—that the program will have spillover benefits to other family members who are not explicit recipients. This could happen with WIC because the goods purchased with the vouchers could be shared with the family. Additionally, since the programs shift out the family's total budget constraint, this "income effect" could lead to an increase in consumption of other foods or other goods that benefit the family more broadly. Additionally, WIC's nutrition education component may lead to changes in the composition of food consumption for the entire family.

30. In their chapter on housing programs in volume 2, Ellen and Ludwig discuss the possibility that a take-it-or-leave-it benefit will reduce consumption of the targeted good. While theoretically possible in the case of food consumption, we think this is not likely. Food consumption is more straightforward to top up (e.g., snacks, supplemental lunch foods brought from home or purchased) than housing is.

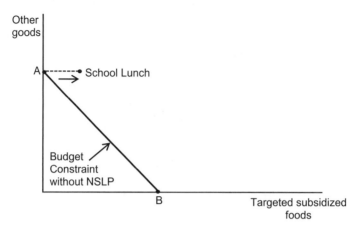

Fig. 3.12   Effects of NSLP on consumption

3.3.2   Effects of FNP on Food Insecurity, Diet, and Health

As discussed above, SNAP and the other food and nutrition programs increase household resources. If health is a normal good, then increases in resources due to food and nutrition programs should increase health. With this framing, an increase in resources could lead to changes in health through many channels. One obvious channel is through improvements in nutrition. The income effect, in principle, could also encourage behaviors that could harm health, such as smoking or drinking.[31] Health improvements may work through other channels as well, for instance improving nutrition education, increasing services (for WIC), and reducing stress (e.g., financial stress).

There also may be linkages between access to food and nutrition programs in utero and in childhood and later-life health and human capital outcomes. Causal mechanisms by which early childhood events affect later life are best understood for nutrition. For example, undernourished children may suffer from anemia and listlessness. This may reduce their ability to invest in learning during childhood and may harm their long-run earnings and other outcomes. Poor early-life nutrition may also directly harm long-run outcomes through altering the body's developmental trajectory. There is an emerging scientific consensus that describes critical periods of development during early life that "program" the body's long-term survival outcomes (Barker 1997; Gluckman and Hanson 2004). During development the fetus (and postnatally the child) may take cues from the current environment to predict the type of environment it is expected to face in the long run, and in some cases adapts its formation to better thrive in the expected environ-

---

31. Even though recipients cannot purchase cigarettes directly with FSP benefits, the increase in resources to the household may increase cigarette consumption.

ment (Gluckman and Hanson 2004). A problem arises, however, when the realized environment differs substantially from the predicted environment. For example, if nutrients are scarce during the prenatal (or early postnatal) period, the developing body therefore predicts that the future will also be nutritionally deprived. The body may then invoke (difficult-to-reverse) biological mechanisms to adapt to the predicted future environment. For example, the metabolic system may adapt in a manner that will allow the individual to survive in an environment with chronic food shortages. This pattern is termed the "thrifty phenotype" and is sometimes referred to as the Barker hypothesis. The problem arises if, in fact, there is not a long-run food shortage and nutrition is plentiful. In that case, the early-life metabolic adaptations are a bad match to the actual environment and will increase the likelihood that the individual develops a metabolic disorder, which can include high blood pressure (hypertension), type 2 diabetes, obesity, and cardiovascular disease. To summarize, a lack of nutrition in early life leads to higher incidence of metabolic syndrome, thus greater access to food and nutrition programs in early life and childhood may reduce metabolic syndrome in adulthood.

3.3.3 Effects on Labor Supply

We begin by considering the effect of SNAP on labor supply. As discussed above, SNAP benefits have the structure of a traditional income support program, with a guaranteed income benefit that is reduced with family income at the legislated benefit-reduction rate. Recipients are allotted a benefit amount B equal to the difference between the federally defined maximum benefit level for a given family size (i.e., G, the guarantee amount) and the amount that the family is deemed to be able to afford to pay for food on its own according to the benefits formula (30 percent of cash income, less deductions). We illustrate the labor-leisure trade-off with and without food stamps in figure 3.13. Like other means-tested programs, SNAP alters the household's labor-leisure trade-off increasing after tax and transfer income at earnings up to the break-even point. The SNAP benefits are largest at zero hours of work, and benefits are reduced as income and earnings are increased, leading to an implicit tax rate on earned income. The benefit-reduction rate in the food stamp program is 30 percent.

In figure 3.13, the x axis measures the amount of leisure consumed, and the y axis measures total income including the SNAP benefit.[32] The "no benefit" budget constraint is a straight line with a slope equal to the individual's wage w. The individual has a certain amount of unearned income (U), and the budget constraint is represented by the line CAL. The simple static labor-

---

32. By shifting out the budget constraint by the full SNAP benefit we assume households treat the benefit as cash. We also assume, for simplicity, that there are no other welfare programs in place.

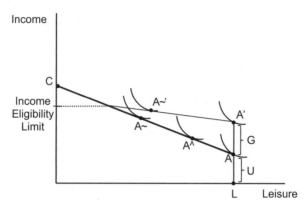

Fig. 3.13   Income-leisure trade-offs and SNAP
Source: Hoynes and Schanzenbach (2012).

supply model states that an individual maximizes her utility subject to this budget constraint, and assuming a positive labor-supply choice, chooses some combination of consumption of goods and leisure at points illustrated for consumers with different preferences by $A^\sim$ and $A^\wedge$. If her offer wage is below her reservation wage (the slope of the indifference curve at zero hours of work), then it will be optimal to remain out of the labor force, as illustrated by point A (at maximum leisure choice L, or hours = 0).

Adding SNAP alters the budget constraint to line $CA'L$ by adding nonlabor income G (the maximum benefit level or the "guarantee"), and rotating the slope of the budget constraint to $w(1 - t)$ where t is the benefit reduction rate (that is, the tax rate on benefits) as income increases ($t = 0.3$). For the individual supplying zero hours of work and consuming only leisure, consumption opportunities increase by the SNAP "guarantee" amount G. At the income eligibility threshold (labeled on the y axis) you earn enough such that benefits have been fully taxed away.

As is well known, this combination of a guaranteed income and benefit-reduction rate leads unambiguously to predictions of reductions in the intensive and extensive margins of labor supply. In this case, both the income effect of the benefit as well as the income and substitution effect from the benefit-reduction rate leads, unambiguously, to a predicted decline in employment (extensive margin), hours worked (intensive margin), and (if wages are fixed) earnings. In addition, family *cash* income (which as measured does not include food stamp benefits) would also be predicted to fall. Of course, family total after transfer income including food stamps is likely to increase.

Referring back to figure 3.13, our representative individual who was, prior to the introduction of the food stamp program, in the labor force and consuming at point $A^\sim$ is predicted to increase their leisure (reduce their hours worked), choosing a consumption bundle $A^{\sim\prime}$. Alternatively, it is possible

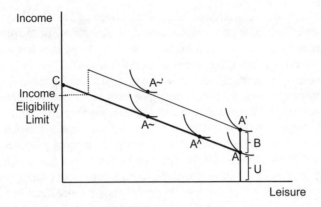

Fig. 3.14   Income-leisure trade-offs and WIC/NSLP

that the combination of the negative income and substitution effects can push them out of labor market to point A'.

Figure 3.14 adapts the labor-leisure diagram to model WIC and the school feeding programs. For these programs a household receives a fixed benefit B for all income levels up to the eligibility limit (e.g., 185% of poverty line for WIC). Thus the budget set shifts out by a constant amount and creates a "notch" or cliff where the household reaches the eligibility limit. The qualitative predictions for labor supply are the same as for SNAP—reductions in the intensive and extensive margins of labor supply. In this case, many households face a pure income effect while higher-income households face the incentive to reduce their labor supply to obtain eligibility.[33]

Additionally, as discussed in Currie and Gahvari (2008), in-kind programs such as SNAP or WIC might *increase* labor supply, depending on the degree of complementarity between the subsidized good (here food and nutrition) and labor supply. This has had limited testing in the empirical literature.

3.4   Review of Results of Research on the Programs

3.4.1   Challenges for Identification and Overview of Empirical Approaches

A central challenge for evaluation of the effects of food and nutrition programs is that commonly used quasi-experimental approaches are not easily applied. First, food and nutrition programs are federal and exhibit little variation across states such as been used in the analysis of AFDC and TANF. Second, the programs have not seen repeated reform or expansions

---

33. For the NSLP, there would be one notch at 130 percent of poverty where the household goes from free lunch to reduced-price lunch, then a cliff at 185 percent of poverty, where they lose eligibility for reduced-price lunch.

such as has been used in analysis of the Earned Income Tax Credit. Finally, with respect to the food stamp program, the universal nature of the program means there are no ineligible groups to serve as controls, which is another common approach in the quasi-experimental literature.

Early studies use comparisons between participants and nonparticipants to estimate the effect of food and nutrition programs. Many researchers (Bitler 2015; Currie 2003; Bitler and Currie 2005; Ludwig and Miller 2005) have drawn attention to the fact that selection into participation in these programs is nonrandom. If program recipients are healthier, more motivated, or generally positively selected, then comparisons between the participants and nonparticipants could produce positive program estimates even if the true effect is zero. Conversely, if program participants are more disadvantaged, or generally negatively selected than nonrecipients, such comparisons may understate the program's impact.

Bitler (2015) provides a recent analysis to examine the selectivity of SNAP recipients. She examines detailed health data from NHANES and NHIS and shows that SNAP recipients have worse diets and nutritional intake, higher levels of obesity and underweight, and worse child health and adult health when compared to all nonrecipients or income-eligible nonrecipients. Thus, it seems clear that SNAP recipients are negatively selected. Bitler and Currie (2005) provide evidence that WIC recipients are negatively selected among a sample of Medicaid recipients, in terms of their education, marital status, smoking behavior, obesity, labor market, and program participation.

There are several approaches to solving this fundamental identification problem. First, some studies make use of the limited policy variation across areas. For SNAP, this includes variation due to welfare reform (especially for examining immigrants versus natives) and state SNAP policies (length of recertification periods, fingerprinting, vehicle asset exemptions, and broad-based categorical eligibility). In some cases, these state policy rules may not change much from year to year, which limits their suitability as instruments. This approach is used in instrumental variable settings, essentially providing instrument-driven variation in program participation. Policy variation is also used in reduced-form approaches.

Second, other studies take a historical approach and use program introduction, relying on variation across areas during the rollout years of the program. As discussed above, both the food stamp program and WIC were introduced at different points across counties in the United States. This allows for an event study or difference-in-difference approach to evaluate the programs, essentially using untreated counties as controls for treated counties. The validity of this approach relies on the exogeneity of the timing of the rollout across areas.[34]

---

34. This approach has also been used to analyze many other aspects of the Great Society and Civil Rights era (Ludwig and Miller 2007; Finkelstein and McKnight 2008; Bailey 2012; Cascio et al. 2010; Almond, Chay, and Greenstone 2006; Goodman-Bacon 2014).

A third approach is to use longitudinal data and control for family, person, or sibling fixed effects. This approach nets out time-invariant effects. For example, in an analysis of siblings, family fixed effects generate estimates by comparing outcomes among siblings who participated in the program compared to outcomes among those who did not. There are drawbacks to this approach. Between-birth changes in economic or health conditions of other family members may be correlated with between-sibling differences in program participation. Additionally, within-family comparisons are likely to exacerbate measurement-error problems that bias estimates toward zero (Griliches 1979). There also may be spillover effects from the participating sibling to the nonparticipating sibling, which will lead to underestimates of the program's true effect. In such cases, selection biases will not be eliminated. Another longitudinal differencing approach uses an individual fixed effects estimator, which compares outcomes for those who switch (into or out of) program participation. Of course, there could be some third factor that affects both transitions into (or out of) program participation and outcomes.

Fourth, some studies use regression discontinuity approaches, comparing those in a small band above the eligibility threshold to those in a small band below the eligibility threshold. The validity of the approach requires a sharp change in participation at the discontinuity that is not correlated with other changing variables. This approach can be applied to income eligibility for WIC and school feeding programs where a recipient is either eligible or not eligible for the entire bundle of benefits. This approach would not generally be appropriate for SNAP because, empirically, participation smoothly falls as income rises (the benefit falls as income rises). It also can be applied to age discontinuities in eligibility for the other food and nutrition programs. In practice, regression discontinuity studies based on differences across income-based eligibility criteria may not be valid given that income can be manipulated, which invalidates the RD approach (one no longer has randomness across the threshold).

Fifth, randomized experiments could in principle capture the effect of food and nutrition programs (or more likely, changes in program policies). In practice, in the past decades there is not much such evidence, with notable exceptions in the Healthy Incentives Pilot (Bartlett et al. 2014) and School Breakfast Program Pilot Project (Bernstein et al. 2004), both further described below. Finally, another approach uses matching methods to control for selection, essentially relying on "selection on observables."

In order to focus our review of the literature on the studies with the most credible evidence, we limit our discussion to papers that use the "design-based" approaches discussed above. The most common study that would not pass this criterion would be simple comparisons, either with or without regression controls, of FNP recipients and nonrecipients.

3.4.2   Research on Food Stamp Program

SNAP Participation

As we showed in table 3.6 and figure 3.5, participation in and expenditures on SNAP have varied significantly over time. One consistent strand in the literature seeks to understand the determinants of these changes in the program (table 3.10 provides a catalog of the papers we review). The literature has explored the role of the macroeconomy, changes in SNAP policies, changes in related program policies (especially welfare reform), and changes in demographics. The papers in this area typically leverage variation across states and over time in labor market conditions (e.g., unemployment rates, employment-to-population ratios) and program polices. As outlined above, SNAP is primarily a federal program and has less variation across states than other parts of the US means-tested safety net (such as Medicaid or TANF). The available state-varying policies for SNAP include length between required recertification, immigrant eligibility following welfare reform, presence or absence of restrictions for ABAWD, and the broad-based categorical eligibility expansions of the early twenty-first century.

Overall, the macroeconomy consistently ranks as the largest contributor to changes in SNAP caseloads. However, SNAP and welfare policies have also played a role. Welfare reform and reductions in SNAP certification periods led to reductions in SNAP caseloads in the 1990s (Currie and Grogger 2001; Kabbani and Wilde 2003; Ziliak, Gundersen, and Figlio 2003; Figlio, Gunderson, and Ziliak 2000). Additionally, changes in immigrant access to the safety net during the welfare reform period also led to reductions in SNAP participation (Borjas 2004; Haider et al. 2004; Kaestner and Kaushal 2005; Bitler and Hoynes 2013).

Ganong and Liebman (2013) examine the large increase in SNAP caseloads in the Great Recession and find that local economic conditions explain about two-thirds of the increase in SNAP with a much smaller role for SNAP policy changes (e.g., expansions for broad-based categorical eligibility).[35] Ziliak (2015) finds a larger role for policy, perhaps accounting for 30 percent of the caseload change. Bitler and Hoynes (2016) find that the countercyclical effect of SNAP as measured by the effect of the unemployment rate on the SNAP caseload was larger in the Great Recession compared to the early 1980s recession (although the difference was not statistically significant).

SNAP and Consumption

The first-order prediction is that SNAP, by shifting out the budget set, should lead to an increase in food (and nonfood) spending. This is confirmed

---

35. When examining the earlier period, especially the Bush expansions in the early twenty-first century, Ganong and Liebman (2013) find more of a role for policy changes in explaining the growth of food stamp caseloads.

Table 3.10   **Studies of the Supplemental Nutrition Assistance Program**

Study	Data	Design	Results
		Studies of determinants of SNAP participation	
Bitler and Hoynes (2016)	Administrative data: SNAP caseloads by state and month 1980–2013, normalized by state × year population	State panel fixed effects model Main independent variable: UR and interactions for subperiods	For full period a 1 percentage point increase in the UR leads to a 3.4 percent increase in caseloads per capita; larger effects (though not statistically different) in the Great Recession
Currie and Grogger (2001)	CPS 1981–1999 and administrative data on state-year SNAP caseloads	State panel fixed effects model Main independent variables: UR, SNAP policy variable (recertification length), welfare reform	Caseload decreases due to welfare reform, reduction in UR, and reductions in recertification period
Figlio, Gundersen, and Ziliak (2000)	Administrative data: food stamp caseloads, state × year 1980–1998	State panel fixed effects model Main independent variables: UR (and lags), growth of EPOP (and lags), SNAP policies, welfare policies	Reduction in SNAP in 1990s due primarily to economy and less to welfare reform
Ganong and Liebman (2013)	SIPP 2007–2011 Administrative county SNAP data: 1990–2011	State (or county) fixed effects model, including models with lags Independent variables include: UR (and lags), SNAP policy, welfare policy	Most of the increase in SNAP between 2007–2011 is due to the macroeconomy; SNAP relaxing of income and asset limits in early twenty-first century (broad-based categorical eligibility) accounts for 8 percent of the increase in enrollment; relaxing of ABAWD accounts for 10 percent
Kabbani and Wilde (2003)	Administrative data: Food Stamp Quality Control Data, 1990–2000, state × year	State panel fixed effects model Main independent variables: UR (and lags), SNAP policy variable (share of persons facing recertification periods ≤ 3 months)	Increase in 10 pp. of share ≤ 3 months leads to a 2.7 percent reduction in caseload/pop; reduced error rates by 0.8 pp.
Ziliak (2013)	CPS 1980–2011 $N = 5,552,486$ individuals residing in 2,053,018 households pooled across all years (173,515 persons in a typical yr. across sample period)	State fixed effects model, including models with lags Independent variables include: UR (and lags), SNAP policy, welfare policy	Increase in participation from 2007–2011—50 percent due to higher UR, 30 percent due to policy changes, remainder due to demographics and other
Ziliak, Gundersen, and Figlio (2003)	Administrative data: annual state caseloads 1980–1999	State panel fixed effects model; estimated static and dynamic (including lags) Main independent variables include: state-year UR, welfare policies	A 1 percentage point increase in the unemployment rate leads to a 2.3 percent increase after one year and 8 percent decrease in the long run; a 10-percentage-point increase in the share of a state's population waived from rules limiting food stamp receipt among ABAWDs results in a 0.5 percent increase in contemporaneous caseloads

(continued)

Table 3.10 (continued)

Study	Data	Design	Results
		Studies of impact on consumption	
Beatty and Tuttle (2014)	CEX 2007–2010; limit sample to households with total expenditures ≥ 150 percent of average expenditures of SNAP recipients $N = 29,000$ household quarters	Difference-in-difference design comparing SNAP recipients to nonrecipients before and after SNAP benefit increases (the ARRA 2009 increase in SNAP benefits being the largest increase); matching method used to improve control group; model the effect of an increase in benefits using an Engel curve approach	The ARRA policy change (increase in SNAP benefit of 13.6 percent) led to a 6.0 percent increase in food at home; no significant effects on food away from home
Blundell and Pistaferri (2003)	PSID 1978–1992; male-headed married couples age twenty-five to sixty-five in stable households $N = 2,469$ unique households	Panel data model with household fixed effects and parametric modeling for (permanent income shock, measurement error in income, measurement error in consumption and taste); framework allowed for self-insurance, in which consumers smooth idiosyncratic shocks through saving; also considered the complete markets assumption in which all idiosyncratic shocks are insured	The effect of permanent income shocks on consumption declines by about one-third with SNAP
Bruich (2014)	Grocery store-level scanner data from 2012–2014; 431 grocery stores from Los Angeles, CA, Atlanta, GA, and Columbus, OH	Difference-in-difference model (using variation in SNAP share at the stores) to examine the expiration of the SNAP benefits in ARRA	Due to 2013 SNAP benefit cuts, on average, SNAP households in CA, GA, and OH lost $20 dollars in benefits (per month), resulting in a $5.91 decline in SNAP households monthly spending; each $1 of cuts reduced grocery store expenditure by $0.37, implying a marginal propensity to consume food out of food stamps of 0.30
Gundersen and Ziliak (2003)	PSID 1980–1999, household heads, at risk of SNAP samples: (a) income < 130 percent FPL, (b) income over < 130 percent FPL, (c) average income in bottom quartile of sample average income $N = 8,485$ unique households	Panel data model with household fixed effects; model 1 is first difference in log income, with an analysis of variance of the residual; model 2 is an IV of change in log consumption on the change in log income (instruments are changes in the head's labor supply)	Among families at risk of SNAP receipt, food stamps reduced income volatility by about 12 percent and food-consumption volatility by about 14 percent

Study	Data	Method	Findings
Hoynes and Schanzenbach (2009)	PSID 1968–1978; three samples: (a) all nonelderly headed households, (b) nonelderly headed household with < twelve years of education, (c) female-headed households. $N = 39,623$ family-year observations	Difference-in-difference and event-study model using rollout of SNAP across counties between 1961 and 1975; triple difference using across-group variation (e.g., high vs. low potential SNAP participation) as third differencing	Total food consumption increases with introduction of FSP; MPC out of FSP is 0.163 and MPC out of cash income is 0.087
Kim (2014)	CEX 2007–2011	Difference-in-differences model; month and year fixed effects; low-income households as a treatment group	The increase in SNAP benefits due to ARRA leads to increases in food spending and increases in spending on nonfood (housing, transportation, entertainment), the increase in food expenditure is slightly less than the full SNAP benefit increase ($18–$24/person monthly benefit increase and $13/person expenditure increase)

Studies of impact on food insecurity

Study	Data	Method	Findings
Borjas (2004)	CPS-FSS 1995–1999	Estimate effect of public assistance receipt on FI using welfare reform in two-sample IV, comparing noncitizens versus natives. Instrument = triple difference between state × year × citizenship status	Reduction in proportion of welfare recipients by 10 percentage points increased FI by about 5 percentage points
DePolt, Moffitt, and Ribar (2009)	Longitudinal data from the Three-City Study (Boston, Chicago, and San Antonio); low-income families (below 200 percent of the poverty line). $N = 2,973$ person-year observations	Use household fixed effect model, identifying effects of SNAP participation of off switchers (on or off program); multiple-indicator, multiple-cause models	Participation in SNAP is associated with fewer food hardships
Gibson-Davis and Foster (2006)	ECLS-K, fall 1998 and spring 1999; households with incomes < 130 percent of FPL. $N = 4,276$	Propensity score matching with two models	Food stamps do not decrease the probability of being food insecure, although they lessen the severity of the problem according to some models
Gregory, Rabbitt, and Ribar (2013)	CPS-FSS 2009–2011, households ≤ 130 percent FPL	Three designs to estimate effect of SNAP on FI: (a) propensity-score matching, (b) one year apart longitudinal estimators, (c) IV (instruments: household head being a noncitizen, SNAP certification interval in state)	Propensity score and longitudinal models show positive effect of SNAP on FI; inconsistent results for IV

(continued)

Table 3.10 (continued)

Study	Data	Design	Results
Mykerezi and Mills (2010)	1999 PSID; samples: (a) ≤ 150 percent FPL (N = 1,608), (b) ≤ 200 percent FPL (N = 2,237), (c) ≤ 250 percent FPL (N = 2,837)	IV model, estimate of SNAP on FI; also relate loss of SNAP (involuntary, "due to government office decision") to change in FI. Instrument: state SNAP underpayment rate and overpayment rate	FSP participation lowers FI by 19 percent (cross-section IV using state policy variables could capture other aspects of state)
Ratcliffe, McKernan, and Zhang (2011)	1996, 2001, 2004 SIPP panels; low-income households (< 150 percent of poverty threshold)	IV using state SNAP policies as instrument: use of biometric technology, outreach spending, full immigrant eligibility, and partial immigrant eligibility	SNAP reduces the likelihood of being food insecure by 30 percent and very food insecure by 20 percent
Schmidt, Shore-Sheppard, and Watson (2015)	CPS 2001–2009, families w/at least one child under eighteen, < 300 percent of the poverty line, no immigrants, particular focus on single-parent families. N = 28,189 (first stage, December). N = 68,702 (second stage, March)	IV approach, effect of program benefits on FI; instrument actual benefits with simulated benefits eligibility and potential benefit calculator	$1,000 in potential benefits (benefits for which a family is eligible) reduces low food security by 2 percentage points on a base rate of 33 percent; a treatment on the treated $1,000 in benefits reduces low food security by 4 percentage points
Shaefer and Gutierrez (2013)	SIPP 1996, 2001, 2004, households with children and < 150 percent FPL	IV with instrument: state-year share < three-month short recertification; implementation of biometric technology	SNAP reduces household food insecurity by 12.8 percentage points
Wilde and Nord (2005)	CPS-FSS 2001–2002, longitudinally linked. N = 17,331 matched households	Household fixed effects using transitions onto and off of SNAP	Transitions into SNAP associated with transitions into FI
Yen et al. (2008)	1996–1997 National Food Stamp Program Survey. N = 2,179 households	IV approach to estimate effect of SNAP participation on FI. Instruments: state policy variables (recertification length, EBT availability), pop. share of immigrants and four dummy variables on stigma to capture the effect of welfare stigma: whether the individual had avoided telling (people about receiving food stamps), shopped at stores (they are) unknown, (been treated with) disrespect shopping (with food stamps), or (been treated with) disrespect telling (people about being on food stamps)	Participation in SNAP reduces FI by 0.4 percentage points (7 percent)

Study	Data	Description	Findings
Studies of impacts on child health outcomes			
Almond, Hoynes, and Schanzenbach (2011)	National Vital Statistics data on births 1968–1977	Difference-in-difference and event study analysis of food stamp program rollout; examine effects of exposure to SNAP on birth outcomes, low birth weight	SNAP exposure leads to significant reduction in low birth weight births; no significant effects for infant mortality
Currie and Moretti (2008)	Vital statistics data on California births 1960–1974	Difference-in-difference analysis of food stamp program rollout in California; examine effects of exposure to SNAP on birth weight	SNAP exposure leads to reduction in birth weight
East (2015a)	National Vital Statistics data on births 2000–2007; NHIS 1998–2013, children ages six to sixteen	Difference-in-difference using immigrants' eligibility across states and over time; triple difference with children of natives; examine effect of exposure to SNAP in utero on health at birth, and exposure from time in utero to age five on health outcomes at ages six to sixteen	SNAP increases average birth weight and reduces low birth weight; early-life access improves parent-reported health at ages six to sixteen and insignificant estimates on school days missed, doctor visits, and hospitalizations but signs indicate improvements
Gibson (2004)	NLSY-79 child sample N = 3,831 (girls) N = 4,012 (boys), person-years	Examine effects of SNAP participation over past five years on overweight, by gender and age; family and child fixed effects	Mostly insignificant effects, but signs indicate reduction in overweight for boys and increase in overweight for girls
Kreider et al. (2012)	NHANES 2001–2006, children 2–17 in households w/income < 130% FPL N= 4,418	Partial identification bounding methods to address selection and measurement error (underreporting) of SNAP; range of models with weaker and stronger assumptions	Under weakest nonparametric assumptions, cannot rule out positive or negative effects of SNAP on obesity; tightest bounds indicate beneficial effects of SNAP
Schmeiser (2012)	NLSY-79, children ages five to eighteen N = 8,409 (boys) N = 8,144 (girls)	Examine effects of SNAP participation over past five years on distribution of BMI via IV Instruments: state-level SNAP policies including recertification period length, fingerprinting, and vehicle asset exclusions	SNAP participation significantly reduces BMI for most child gender-age groups
Vartanian and Houser (2012)	PSID 1968–2005	Sibling fixed effects model to relate childhood participation in SNAP to adult BMI	Positive effect of childhood SNAP participation on adult BMI
Studies of impact on adult health outcomes			
Fan (2010)	NLSY79 1985–1988 N = 6,111	Use propensity score weighting to construct control group along with within-person variation in SNAP participation; estimate both short-term (one-year participation) and long-term (three-year participation) treatment effects	No significant effects of SNAP on obesity rate, overweight rate, or BMI

(continued)

Table 3.10 (continued)

Study	Data	Design	Results
Gibson (2003)	NLSY79, ages twenty to forty $N = 13,390$	Examine effects of SNAP participation (past year, past nine years) on obesity; individual fixed effects	Current and longer-term SNAP participation increased obesity for women
Hoynes, Schanzenbach, and Almond (2016)	PSID 1968–2009	Difference-in-difference and event study analysis of food stamp program rollout; examine effects of childhood exposure to SNAP on adult health and economic outcomes	SNAP exposure, especially in early childhood (age ≤ 4) leads to significant reduction in metabolic syndrome in adulthood; SNAP exposure throughout childhood leads to improvements in economic outcomes for women but not men
Kaushal (2007)	NHIS 1992–2000	Estimate effect of SNAP on obesity using welfare reform in two-sample IV, comparing immigrants to natives. Instrument: triple difference between state × year × citizenship status	Insignificant effect of SNAP on obesity
Meyerhoefer and Pylypchuk (2008)	Medical Expenditure Panel Survey 2002–2003, adults age eighteen to sixty-four eligible for FSP $N = 6,644$	Individual fixed effects and IV instruments: state-level SNAP policies including expenditures on outreach, fingerprinting, recertification length	SNAP leads to increase in overweight and obesity for women; no significant effects for men (instrument does not vary over time, so could capture cross-sectional geographic effects)
		Studies of impact on labor supply	
East (2015b)	Current Population Survey 1995–2007, Working-age adults with high school education or less	Difference-in-difference analysis of immigrants' eligibility across states and over time; triple difference with natives	For married and single women employment declines; for married men employment not affected but hours of work declines
Hoynes and Schanzenbach (2012)	PSID 1968–1978, family head < 65 $N = 48,168$ family-years. Three samples: (a) all nonelderly headed households, (b) nonelderly headed household with < 12 years of education, and (c) female-headed households	Difference-in-difference and event study model using rollout of SNAP across counties between 1961 and 1975; triple difference using across-group variation (e.g., high vs. low potential SNAP participation) as third differencing	Hours of work and employment decline with SNAP introduction, with the largest effects for female-headed households

in the empirical literature. The model also predicts that for inframarginal households, SNAP should lead to a similar increase in food spending compared to equal-sized cash transfer. There was significant attention to this question in the 1980s and 1990s, typically using observational approaches (comparing recipients to nonrecipients) and suffering from the biases due to selection discussed above. Overall, many of these early papers found that SNAP recipients consume more food out of SNAP than they would with an equivalent cash transfer (Currie 2003).

More recent papers, however, based on research designs that are able to isolate causality have found evidence more consistent with the canonical model. As reviewed in Currie, RCTs on "cash-out" experiments in the 1990s found little difference in food spending between the group receiving benefits in cash versus in food vouchers. The reanalysis by Schanzenbach (2007) finds that the mean treatment effect is a combination of no difference in food spending among inframarginal recipients, and a substantial shift in consumption toward food for the relatively small group of stamp recipients who are constrained. Overall, these experiments provide evidence on the difference between cash and vouchers, but do not provide estimates for the broader question of how providing SNAP benefits (by increasing family disposable income) affects food spending or consumption more broadly.

Hoynes and Schanzenbach (2009) use the initial rollout of the food stamp program to quasi-experimentally examine the effects on food spending. As discussed above, the program's introduction took place across the approximately 3,000 US counties between 1961 and 1975. Consistent with the theoretical predictions discussed in section 3.3.1, they find that the introduction of FSP leads to a decrease in out-of-pocket food spending and an increase in overall food expenditures. They estimate a marginal propensity to consume food out of food stamps of 0.16 for all nonelderly and 0.30 for female-headed households. The estimated marginal propensity to consume food out of food stamp income is close to the marginal propensity to consume out of cash income. In addition, consistent with economy theory those predicted to be constrained (at the kink in the food/nonfood budget set) experience larger increases in food spending with the introduction of food stamps.

Several recent studies have used the changes in SNAP benefits from the economic stimulus (ARRA) whereby benefits were temporarily increased between April 2009 and October 2013. Beatty and Tuttle (2014) use a difference-in-difference approach, and using nonrecipients as controls (with matching methods) they find using the Consumer Expenditure Survey that the 13.6 percent increase in benefits leads to a 6 percent increase in food at home. Kim (2014) uses the same approach and data and finds that, consistent with the theoretical predictions, the increase in SNAP benefits leads to increases in food spending and increases in spending on nonfood (housing, transportation, entertainment). Bruich (2014) uses grocery-store-level scanner data and a difference-indifference model (using variation in SNAP share at the stores) to examine the expiration of the ARRA increase in SNAP benefits. On average, SNAP households lost $17 dollars in benefits (per month) and Bruich's estimates imply a marginal propensity to consume food out of food stamps of 0.30.

A second set of studies examines the effects of food stamps on consumption, with the focus on estimating the insurance effects of the program. Blundell and Pistaferri (2003) use longitudinal data from the PSID to examine how SNAP mitigates the effect of shocks to permanent income on consumption and income volatility. Gundersen and Ziliak (2003) use an IV approach to examine how log income changes affect log consumption. Both studies show that SNAP provides important consumption protection. Gundersen and Ziliak find that SNAP receipt reduced income volatility by 12 percent and food consumption volatility by 14 percent. Blundell and Pistaferri find that the effect of permanent income shocks decline by about one-third with SNAP.

SNAP and Food Insecurity

Food hardship measures were developed by the USDA in response to the National Nutrition Monitoring and Related Research Act of 1990 with an interest in "access at all times to enough food for an active, healthy life" (Coleman-Jensen et al. 2012). The first measures were released in 1995 and currently a household's "food security" (or insecurity) status is determined through a battery of questions asked during the December CPS as part of the Food Security Supplement (CPS-FSS). There are ten questions asked of all households, and an additional eight questions asked of households with children. There are four kinds of questions: those that capture anxiety or perception that the food budget or supply is inadequate in quantity. There are also questions that capture whether food is perceived to be inadequate in quality. A group of questions are more quantitative in nature, asking about instances where food intake was reduced or weight loss occurred associated with reduced food intake. One set of these questions pertains to adults and the other to children in the household. Answering more of these questions affirmatively indicates a more severe degree of food insecurity. For example, a household is considered to have "very low food security among children" if five or more of the eight child-centered food security questions are answered affirmatively (Nord 2009).

There are several existing reviews of the literature of SNAP and food insecurity [FI] (e.g., Currie 2003; Gregory, Rabbitt, and Ribar 2015). Here we focus on the research since Currie's review that meets our research design criteria.

One set of studies use instrumental variable approaches, typically using state SNAP policies as instruments (Yen et al. 2008; Mykerezi and Mills 2010; Shaefer and Gutierrez 2013; Ratcliffe, McKernan, and Zhang 2011). A commonly employed instrument is the state's SNAP certification length, and while it is not a very strong instrument it may be valid on excludability grounds. A second instrument leverages variation in state policies toward immigrant SNAP coverage or overall immigrant participation in the program. This is more powerful but less likely to be excludable. The results vary across studies, typically finding that SNAP participation leads to decreases in FI (that is, they improve outcomes) but many are not statistically significant.

Two studies use IV approaches but broaden the analysis to examine effects of public assistance (rather than only SNAP). Borjas (2004) uses welfare reform and the relatively large reduction in program participation among immigrants in a triple-difference IV, essentially using state by year by citizenship status as the instrument. Schmidt, Shore-Sheppard, and Watson (2015) use a simulated program benefit (using detailed benefit calculators) as an instrument for actual benefits to identify the effects of benefit income on FI. Both studies find that program participation (or benefits) leads to reductions in FI.

A second approach uses a household fixed effects and longitudinal data, essentially identifying the effects of SNAP on FI using switchers into and out of SNAP (Depolt, Moffitt, and Ribar 2009; Wilde and Nord 2005). This approach may not be credible, given that transitions into SNAP may be correlated with other factors that negatively affect FI. Compared to the IV approach, these studies are more likely to find a positive association between SNAP and FI. A final approach uses propensity score matching (e.g., Gibson-Davis and Foster 2006), often finding a positive association between SNAP and FI.

Overall, the literature on SNAP and FI finds a wide range of results, some finding positive association, some negative, and some insignificant. This range is well illustrated in the recent review and replication work in Gregory, Rabbitt, and Ribar (2015) showing a range of estimates for propensity score matching, longitudinal and IV approaches in one sample. The range of estimates illustrates well the challenge for causal identification in evaluating the effects of food and nutrition programs.

SNAP and Child and Adult Health

The literature on child and adult health takes a similar path to the literature on food insecurity. Studies use family and child fixed effects, instrumental variables, and propensity score matching. In this setting there are also studies that leverage the historical rollout of SNAP. As above, we review the studies since Currie (2003) that meet our research design criteria. The recent review by Meyerhoefer and Yang (2011) is also a useful reference.

Studies of the effect of SNAP on child BMI find varying effects, depending to some degree on the estimation approach. Gibson (2004) uses child and family fixed effects and finds SNAP leads to a reduction in overweight for boys but an increase for girls. Vartanian and Houser (2012) use a similar approach but relate childhood exposure to adult BMI, finding a beneficial effect of SNAP. Schmeiser (2012) uses an IV approach, with state SNAP policies (recertification period, fingerprinting, vehicle asset exemptions) as instruments, and finds that SNAP reduces BMI for most gender-age groups. Kreider et al. (2012) address selection into and measurement error of SNAP using a bounding approach and find quite substantial bounds that generally cannot rule out positive or negative effects of SNAP on BMI.

Similar approaches are used to examine effects on adult health. Gibson (2003) uses an individual fixed effects approach and finds SNAP participation increased obesity among women, though as noted above the fixed effects approach may not be credible if transitions into SNAP are correlated with other factors that directly affect health. Fan (2010) extends this approach and adds propensity score matching and finds no significant effect of SNAP on obesity, overweight, or BMI. Meyerhoefer and Pylypchuk (2008) combine individual fixed effects and IV and find SNAP leads to increases in obesity for women but no significant effects for men. Their instruments—state SNAP policies—do not vary over time so these effects could be capturing state cross-sectional correlations. Kaushal (2007) extends Borjas's (2004) study and uses welfare reform as an instrument for SNAP; she finds insignificant effects of SNAP on obesity of immigrants.

There is a small set of studies that examine the effect of SNAP on birth outcomes; thereby examining the effects of SNAP on pregnant women. Currie and Moretti (2008) use the county roll out of FSP in California and find that FSP introduction was associated with a *reduction* in birth weight, driven particularly by first births among teens and by changes for Los Angeles County. Almond, Hoynes, and Schanzenbach (2011) extend that work and examine the effects of the program rollout across all counties in the United States, finding that infant outcomes improve with FSP introduction. Changes in mean birth weight were small, but impacts were larger at the bottom of the birth weight distribution, reducing the incidence of low birth weight among the treated by 7 percent for whites and 3 percent for blacks. They also find that the FSP introduction leads to a reduction in neonatal infant mortality, although these results rarely reach statistical significance. East (2015a) utilizes changes in immigrants' eligibility across states and over time as the result beginning with 1996 welfare reform and extending through subsequent legislation in the early twenty-first century. She finds that parental access to SNAP in utero improves health at birth. Additionally, she finds that increases in SNAP access between conception and age five improves parent-reported health at ages six to sixteen (with suggestive evidence of reductions in school days missed, doctor visits, and hospitalizations at ages six to sixteen).

Hoynes, Schanzenbach, and Almond (2016) extend their SNAP rollout design and estimation approach to estimate the relationship between childhood access to the food stamp program and adult health and human capital outcomes. They find that access to the FSP in utero and in early childhood leads to a large and statistically significant reduction in the incidence of "metabolic syndrome" (obesity, high blood pressure, heart disease, diabetes) as well as an increase in reporting to be in good health. The results show little additional protection beyond the age of four, consistent with the importance of early life in the development of the metabolic system. They also find for women, but not men, that access to food stamps in early childhood leads to an increase in economic self-sufficiency.

Overall, we have more confidence in the approaches using instruments based on state policies and the quasi-experimental estimates from program rollouts, and these studies tend to find positive or null impacts of SNAP on health. The estimates relying on within-family or within-individual variation in SNAP participation are more likely to find harmful estimates, and are subject to the concern that changes in unobservables are simultaneously driving SNAP participation and negative health outcomes.

SNAP and Labor Supply

Hoynes and Schanzenbach (2012) use county variation in the rollout of food stamps to identify the impact of food stamps on labor supply. Using the PSID, they use a difference-in-difference approach (using counties without food stamps as controls) and find no significant impacts on the overall sample, but among single-parent households with a female head—a group much more likely to participate in the program—they find a significant intent-to-treat estimate of a reduction of 183 annual hours (treatment-on-the-treated reduction of 505 annual hours). They find no significant impacts of the FSP on earnings or family income, though the estimates are imprecise.

Using variation across states and over time in immigrants' eligibility for SNAP, East (2015b) studies the effect on the labor supply of foreign-born single women and married couples, who both participate in the program at high rates. She finds individuals reduce labor supply when eligible: the largest effects are among married and single women who reduce employment, whereas the effects for married men are smaller and are concentrated along the intensive margin (hours of work). Other than East (2015b), to our knowledge, there is no other study that meets our research design criteria that estimates the impact of SNAP on labor supply in the era after welfare reform and the expansion of EITC.

3.4.3   Research on WIC

Given the targeted nature of WIC, the literature naturally focuses on the impact of WIC on birth outcomes, breastfeeding, and nutritional intake. (See table 3.11 for the catalog of the WIC studies we review.) There is also attention on the health of pregnant women and children less than age five. In the earlier volume, Currie (2003) reviews the literature and it generally concludes that women who participate in WIC give birth to healthier

Table 3.11   **Studies of the Special Supplemental Nutrition Program for Women, Infants, and Children (WIC)**

Study	Data	Design	Results
Studies of determinants of WIC participation and selection			
Bitler and Currie (2005)	Pregnancy Risk Assessment Monitoring System (PRAMS), 1992–1999, Medicaid paid births $N = 60{,}731$	Comparison of WIC versus non-WIC within sample of Medicaid-funded births; examine impacts on WIC participation and effect of WIC on birth outcomes	WIC participants are negatively selected w/adverse measures for education, age, marital status, presence of father, smoking, obesity, employment, and housing characteristics; WIC participation is associated w/improved birth outcomes: 6–7 percent more likely to have begun prenatal care in the first trimester; 2 percent less likely to bear infants who are below the 25th percentile of weight given gestational age or to bear infants of low birth weight
Bitler, Currie, and Scholz (2003)	CPS survey 1998–2001, administrative WIC counts 1992–2000	State fixed effects panel analysis using variation in labor market characteristics and WIC policies by state and year	State unemployment rates and poverty rates are not important determinants of state WIC caseloads; the presence of WIC policies such as requiring proof of income (before required nationally) and stricter program rules lower participation
Corsetto (2012)	Administrative WIC counts, 1990–2010	State fixed effects panel analysis using variation in unemployment rate by state and year	No relationship between state unemployment rates and WIC participation for full period (1990–2010); modest countercyclical effect for 2000–2010
Rossin-Slater (2013)	Administrative birth records, Texas, 2005–2009, linked to administrative records on openings and closings of WIC clinics $N = 612{,}694$	IV-maternal fixed effect model Instrument: ZIP Code presence of WIC clinics	The presence of a WIC clinic in a mother's ZIP Code of residence during pregnancy increases her likelihood of WIC food receipt by about 6 percent; access to WIC increases pregnancy weight gain, birth weight (by 22–32 g), and breastfeeding (4 percentage points for mothers with high school degree or less)

Studies of effects on pregnancy and birth outcomes

Bitler and Currie (2005)	Pregnancy Risk Assessment Monitoring System (PRAMS), 1992–1999, Medicaid paid births $N = 60,731$	Comparison of WIC versus non-WIC within sample of Medicaid-funded births; examine impacts on WIC participation and effect of WIC on birth outcomes	WIC participants are negatively selected with adverse measures for education, age, marital status, presence of father, smoking, obesity, employment, and housing characteristics; WIC participation is associated with improved birth outcomes: 6–7 percent more likely to have begun prenatal care in the first trimester, and 2 percent less likely to bear infants who are below the 25th percentile of weight given gestational age or to bear infants of low birth weight
Currie and Ranjani (2014)	Administrative birth records, New York City, 1994–2004 $N = 1.2M$	Maternal fixed effects model	WIC leads to improved birth outcomes: increased birth weight and reduced preterm birth, small for gestational age, and low weight gain; effects found for subsample of full-term births (to address gestational age bias)
Figlio, Hammersma, and Roth (2009)	Administrative birth data, Florida, 1997–2001, women age eighteen to forty-four, matched to school records of their older siblings (to identify "marginally eligible" and "marginally ineligible" families) and WIC records (to identify date of WIC participation) $N = 2,530$ marginally ineligible and 1,744 marginally eligible (multiple-birth families where there is at least a six-year gap in age between two siblings)	Difference-in-differences and event study approach, using variation in eligibility (marginally ineligible versus marginally eligible, using longitudinal data on free and reduced-price lunch status of older sibling) and a policy change (increasing income-reporting requirement); also estimated as IV where the instrument is the interaction of postpolicy change and marginal eligibility	WIC reduces low birth weight but has no effect on average birth weight, gestational age, or premature birth

(_continued_)

Table 3.11 (continued)

Study	Data	Design	Results
Hoynes, Page, and Stevens (2012)	National Vital Statistics data on births 1971–1975, 1978–1982	Difference-in-differences and event study analysis of county-level WIC program rollout; examine effects of exposure to WIC on birth outcomes, low birth weight	WIC exposure leads to significant increase in average birth weight and a decrease in low birth weight births; effect on average birth weight range from 2–7 grams among infants born to mothers with low education levels (treatment on the treated effects of 18–29 grams)
Joyce, Gibson, and Colman (2005)	New York City administrative birth data, 1988–2001, Medicaid paid births $N > 800,00$ births	Comparison of WIC versus non-WIC within sample of Medicaid-funded births; examine impacts on WIC participation and effect of WIC on birth outcomes	WIC participation leads to improvements in birth weight, low birth weight, and gestational age; no impacts on weight for gestational age; largest effect for African Americans
Rossin-Slater (2013)	Administrative birth records, Texas, 2005–2009, linked to administrative records on openings and closings of WIC clinics $N = 612,694$	IV-maternal fixed effects model Instrument: ZIP Code presence of WIC clinics	The presence of a WIC clinic in a mother's ZIP Code of residence during pregnancy increases her likelihood of WIC food receipt by about 6 percent; access to WIC increases pregnancy weight gain, birth weight (by 22–32 g), and breastfeeding (4 percentage points for mothers with high school degree or less)
		Studies of the effects of WIC vendors	
McLaughlin (2014)	In-store product survey for California A50 vendors; individual vendor FI redemptions for California; locations of WIC vendors in California; wholesale costs of WIC goods	Two-part modeling approach: (a) establish incentives for brand competition, and (b) test intensity of brand competition using IV	Vendors compete on products (brand profile, range, and diversity of products) as well as choosing locations consistent with Hotelling-like incentives
Meckel (2014)	Nielsen Consumer Panel 2005–2009; administrative data on WIC groceries in Texas; Texas birth certificates	Difference-in-difference design using variation in the timing of EBT rollout across counties to assess causal effects	With EBT implementation, prices charged to non-WIC recipients increase; vendor participation and individual participation in WIC declines

infants than nonparticipants. Here, we update the literature since the Currie review, again limiting to studies that meet our research design criteria.

WIC Participation

We begin our review with studies on the determinants of WIC participation. As with the early SNAP literature, the early WIC literature often relied on comparisons of the birth outcomes of women participating in WIC versus not participating. To explore the validity of this approach, several studies explore the characteristics of WIC participants. Bitler and Currie (2005) found that WIC participants (among women with Medicaid-funded births) are negatively selected revealed through measures of education, age, marital status, presence of father, smoking, obesity, employment, and housing characteristics.[36] Currie and Rajani (2014) extend this analysis and examine the characteristics of WIC participation among mothers who switched WIC participation status between births. They found that women receive WIC when they are younger, unemployed, or unmarried. Identifying these changes are important for evaluating the validity of the maternal fixed effects design. Rossin-Slater (2013), examining variation due to the openings and closings of WIC clinics, finds evidence that participation increases with proximity to a clinic. Two studies examine the cyclicality of WIC participation, finding little relationship between state unemployment and poverty and state WIC caseloads (Bitler, Currie, and Scholz 2003; Corsetto 2012).

WIC and Health Outcomes

The next panel reviews the literature on pregnancy and birth outcomes. Recent studies have used several different approaches to address the fundamental selection problem. One approach taken is to compare outcomes among more narrowly defined treatment and control groups (e.g., Bitler and Currie 2005; Joyce, Gibson, and Colman 2005; Joyce, Racine, and Yunzal-Butler 2008; Figlio, Hamersma, and Roth 2009). Bitler and Currie (2005) create a control group based on Medicaid-funded births and find that WIC leads to higher average birth weight and a reduction in being small for gestational age. Figlio, Hamersma, and Roth (2009) identify groups marginally eligible versus marginally ineligible for WIC (obtained by matching birth records to older sibling free and reduced-price lunch records). They find WIC reduces the incidence of low birth weight but has no effect on average birth weight, gestational age, or premature birth.

Another approach employs maternal fixed effects models, controlling for unobserved family background characteristics by comparing outcomes among siblings who participated in WIC to outcomes among those who did not. Currie and Rajani (2014) use a maternal fixed effects model applied to

---

36. Women eligible for Medicaid are categorically eligible for WIC. Limiting to Medicaid-funded births identifies a sample where all women are eligible for WIC.

administrative data from NYC from 1994–2004 and find that WIC leads to reductions in low birth weight and being small for gestational age, but an increase in medical care use.

Joyce, Racine, and Yunzal-Butler (2008) discuss the possibility of a *gestational age bias* in this literature. They point out that women whose pregnancies last longer have more opportunity to enroll in WIC. If this is true (which they demonstrate using administrative data), then it leads to a mechanical relationship between WIC participation and longer gestation, biasing the results toward a positive effect of WIC. Currie and Rajani (2014) address this concern by estimating results on the subsample of full term births; they find smaller effects but still conclude that WIC improves birth outcomes.

An alternative approach is to use the introduction of WIC in the 1970s. Hoynes, Page, and Stevens (2011) use differences in the timing of rollout by county to examine impacts of WIC on infant health. Using a difference-in-differences analysis, where the control counties have not yet adopted WIC, they find that rollout of the WIC program led to an increase birth weight and a decline in low birth weight. Rossin-Slater (2013) extends this analysis by combining geographic access with a maternal fixed effects approach. In particular, she uses administrative data from Texas combined with detailed information about the opening and closing of WIC clinics from 2005 to 2009; her approach is identified across mothers who had varying access to WIC clinics across births. She finds WIC improves pregnancy weight gain, birth weight, and breastfeeding initiation.

There are few studies that leverage variation in WIC policy changes. This is in large part due to the minimal variation across states and over time in the program rules. Bitler and Currie (2005) find lower take-up for states in which proof of income is required (prior to the federal mandate) and higher take-up for states with higher WIC package prices. However, they find these to be relatively weak instruments. With the more recent changes to WIC, it might be reasonable to reexamine the potential for using state policy variation to identify the effects of WIC.

The studies above are all focused on pregnant women and outcomes at birth. Yet pregnant women account for less than a quarter of WIC participants (table 3.9), half are children ages one to four, and another quarter are infants. There are many outcomes of interest here, notably rates of breastfeeding, nutritional intake, food security, child weight gain, and general health. However, there is a dearth of studies that use credible designs to evaluate WIC on children. Reflecting on the designs used in the analysis of birth outcomes (e.g., maternal fixed effects, geographic and time variation in presence of WIC clinics), it appears possible to apply similar approaches to examine child health. However, this would likely require rich administrative data, combining child health records, linked across siblings, and family WIC participation. The birth records data, with fine geographic identifiers, and WIC participation data, with the ability to link births across mothers, provide this information. But it is much less common to have these linkages for child health data. Any analysis of the effects of WIC on child health would have to grapple with the interesting question as to the possibility of spillovers to other noncovered family members. This could occur either though the sharing of WIC bundles or an income effect of WIC benefits. It could also possibly work through the nutritional education component of the program.

WIC and Market Factors

The supply side of the WIC market is less developed in the literature. There is a small literature on the infant formula market that starts with the stunning fact that over half of all US infant formula is purchased through the WIC program (Oliveira, Frazão, and Smallwood 2013). Further, because WIC is a quantity voucher benefit, recipients are not sensitive to price. This creates clear incentives for producers to price above marginal cost, especially in this highly concentrated market. Amid concerns about the rising costs of formula, the WIC program moved to a system whereby manufacturers bid on the contract to be the formula provider for the state. In exchange for the right, manufacturers pay a rebate on the formula; in practice the rebates are large, averaging 85–90 percent of wholesale price. Recent studies find that market shares increase substantially for firms that land the state contract (Huang and Perloff 2014; Oliveira, Frazão, and Smallwood 2013), and Davis (2012) finds that the winning firm sees its share of the sales to non-WIC customers increase by 50–60 percent.

Meckel (2014) examines the incentives for vendor fraud with WIC. Because WIC recipients are price insensitive, vendors face incentives to price discriminate by charging higher prices to WIC recipients. She uses the rollout of EBT in WIC across Texas counties and finds that with EBT (which makes it harder to engage in fraud), prices charged to non-WIC recipients increase. Additionally, EBT sparks a decline in both vendor participation and individual participation in WIC. McLaughlin (2014) explores vendor competition given that they cannot compete on price (due to price insensitivity of WIC participants). Using a sample of WIC vendors in California, he finds that vendors compete on products (brand profile, range, and diversity of products) as well as choosing locations consistent with Hotelling-like incentives.

Another aspect to the supply side has to do with the nature of foods available in stores where WIC recipients shop. Andreyeva (2012) provides an interesting case study analysis of how product stock changed in WIC-authorized grocery and convenience stores after the recent alteration of the WIC packages. There was a substantial increase in stocking of healthy foods; for example, 8 percent of WIC-authorized convenience and grocery stores had any whole wheat/whole grain bread at baseline, while 81 percent did so after the revisions took effect (over the same time, non-WIC stores increased whole wheat/whole grain bread from 25 percent to 35 percent).

3.4.4   Research on NSLP

Most research on the National School Lunch Program has focused on how the program impacts dietary intake and obesity rates. Because the NSLP is virtually universally available, and most policy changes are implemented at the federal level, there are relatively few examples of credible quasi-experiments in the literature. Most of the research employs difference-in-difference between siblings, or across periods when the NSLP is or is not available. It is worth noting that none of the studies reviewed in this section have used data collected after the 2012–2013 implementation of the Healthy, Hunger-Free Kids Act that dramatically overhauled nutrition standards for school meals. Table 3.12 catalogs the studies we review.

NSLP and Dietary Quality

Gleason and Suitor (2003) compare observations of dietary intake for an individual across multiple days that vary by whether the student does or does not receive a school lunch, and find mixed evidence on nutrition intake. They find that NSLP increases the consumption of fat, protein, and six types of vitamins and minerals, but that it has no overall impact on total calories eaten at lunch or over a twenty-four-hour period. Nord and Romig (2006) compare intake during the summer versus the school year for families with school-age versus preschool-age children, and find that NSLP availability significantly reduces the rate of food insecurity.

NLSP and Child Health and Education Outcomes

Several papers have investigated the relationship between NSLP participation and childhood obesity. The results are estimated at different ages and at different points on the income distribution, and find mixed results. Schanzenbach (2009) finds that children ineligible for a free or reduced-price lunch who go on to consume school lunch enter kindergarten with similar body weights when compared to children who do not consume school lunch, but that NSLP participants become comparatively heavier as their exposure to school lunch increases. In addition, she uses the income cutoff for receipt of reduced-price lunch and finds that both NSLP participation and body weight discretely increase at the cutoff. Millimet, Tchernis, and Husain (2010) find similar results using the same data.

On the other hand, Gundersen, Kreider, and Pepper (2012) use a Manski-style partial identification approach and find that receipt of free or reduced-price lunch improves child health and substantially reduces obesity rates. Mirtcheva and Powell (2013) use children who change their participation in NSLP between waves in the PSID, and find that NSLP has no effect on body weight in either direction.

Dunifon and Kowaleski-Jones (2003) compare siblings who differ in their NSLP participation decisions. In the ordinary least squares (OLS), NSLP

Table 3.12   **Studies of the National School Lunch Program**

Study	Data	Design	Results
Studies of impact on dietary quality and food insecurity			
Gleason and Suitor (2003)	CSFII 1994–1996, individual dietary recall data, children age six to eighteen	Individual fixed effects, comparing dietary intake on day ate school lunch with day did not eat school lunch	No impact on calories at lunch or over twenty-four hours; increased consumption of fat and protein; decreased consumption of added sugars; increased intake of six vitamins and minerals
Nord and Romig (2006)	CPS-FSS 1995–2001, survey alternates monthly in year	Difference-in-differences estimate of food insecurity during summer versus school year for families with preschool versus school-age children	Food insecurity relatively higher in the summer for households with school-age children; difference smaller in states that provide more summer food service lunches
Studies of impact on child health outcomes			
Gundersen, Kreider, and Pepper (2012)	NHANES 2001–2004, individual data	Nonparametric partial identification	Receipt of free and reduced-price lunches reduces the incidence of poor health by at least 3.5 percentage points, and reduces obesity by at least 4 percentage points
Mirtcheva and Powell (2013)	PSID Child Development Supplement 1997 and 2003, individual panel data, children ages six to eighteen	Individual-level fixed effects, change in participation across waves	No significant effect of NSLP participation on body weight for the full sample or by gender
Schanzenbach (2009)	Early Childhood Longitudinal Data, K–5, individual panel data	Change over time; regression discontinuity at eligibility for reduced-price lunch	NSLP increases obesity rates by 1 pp./year in change regression; increases obesity in RD
Studies of impact on student achievement			
Dunifon and Kowaleski-Jones (2003)	PSID Child Development Supplement 1997, individual data, children age six to twelve	Sibling fixed effects, comparing health, behavior, and achievement outcomes across siblings who differ in NSLP participation	Negative OLS relationship between NSLP participation and child outcomes appears to be driven by unmeasured family-specific factors; no between-sibling differences in outcomes predicted by NSLP participation
Hinrichs (2010)	Outcomes from 1976–1980 NHIS and 1980 census, state-level factors predicting treatment including funding, participation, per capita income, and population ages five to seventeen	IV exploiting change in funding formula over time, across states	Increasing NSLP exposure by 10 percentage points increased completed education by .365 years for women, and nearly one year for men

participation predicts more behavioral problems, increased health limitations, and lower math test scores. When sibling comparisons are employed, the coefficients decline in magnitude and are no longer statistically significant, suggesting the OLS correlations in part reflect unobserved family characteristics.

In the spirit of the program rollout literature described in the SNAP section above, Hinrichs (2010) leverages changes in NSLP funding formulas during the early years of the program to estimate the long-run impacts of the expansion of the program. He finds that increasing NSLP exposure in a state by 10 percentage points increases completed education by nearly one year for males, and one-third of a year for females. On the other hand, NSLP did not appear to have long-term health impacts.

3.4.5   Research on SBP

As shown in table 3.6, participation in the SBP has increased dramatically over the past twenty years. In particular, many more schools have adopted the program during this time period, or have adopted policies aimed at increasing availability and take-up of the program. The literature has been active in recent years, and table 3.13 lists the studies we review.

Bhattacharya, Currie, and Haider (2006) use variation in school participation in the SBP prior to the recent increase in participation to identify the impacts of the program on children and their families. Using a difference-in-differences setup, they compare students observed during the school year versus when they are on school vacation, by whether or not their school offered the SBP. They find that SBP does not impact the number of calories consumed nor the likelihood that a student eats breakfast, but it does improve dietary quality as measured by the Healthy Eating Index and in blood serum. The income transfer implied by the SBP does not appear to spill over and improve dietary quality for other household members, however. Modeling school selection into the SBP and bounding the potential for individual-level unobservables to confound the effect, Millimet, Tchernis, and Husain (2010) find that the SBP reduces childhood obesity.

Some states have statutes requiring participation in the SBP for schools that meet at least some threshold (which varies across states, typically between 10 and 40 percent) of eligibility for free or reduced-price meals. Frisvold (2012) uses these thresholds to construct difference-in-differences and RD estimates of the impact of SBP for schools near the thresholds. He finds that SBP improves achievement in math and reading, and that participation improves the nutritional content of breakfast.

Evidence on the SBP has increased recently as researchers have used policy changes aimed at expanding the program to identify its impacts. In particular, to address (perceived) stigma associated with participation in the school breakfast program and in response to incentives from the USDA, some districts have begun (or stopped) offering universal free school breakfast instead of the standard program that provides free breakfast only to

Table 3.13   Studies of the School Breakfast Program

Study	Data	Design	Results
		Studies of determinants of participation	
Leos-Urbel et al. (2013)	Individual data: test scores, attendance, meal participation NYC public elementary and middle schools, 2002–08	Triple-difference approach, using difference in timing of introduction of universal free breakfast and difference across student eligibility for free meals prior to policy change	Universal free breakfast increased breakfast participation both for students who experienced a decrease in the price of breakfast and for free-lunch-eligible students who experienced no price change; small positive effect on attendance for black and Asian students; no impacts on student test scores
Ribar and Haldeman (2013)	Individual data: test scores and attendance in Title I Elementary schools in Guilford County, North Carolina	Difference-in-difference study of termination of UFB program in some schools	Termination of UFB reduced SBP participation substantially; largest reductions for students not eligible for free or reduced-price meals; no change in test scores
Schanzenbach and Zaki (2014)	Individual data: participation and outcomes, students grades 2–6 in 153 elementary schools in six districts	Random assignment within matched-pair schools to universal free breakfast or traditional program; compare within matched-pair schools that opt for cafeteria breakfast or breakfast in classroom	Universal free breakfast increases participation in SBP, larger participation effects for BIC; no change in likelihood of eating breakfast; few impacts on measures of dietary quality, health, or achievement outcomes
		Studies of impacts on dietary quality and food insecurity	
Bhattacharya, Currie, and Haider (2006)	NHANES-III 1988–1994, five- to sixteen-year-olds, individual data	Difference-in-differences comparing students in school to those on school vacation, across schools that do and do not offer SBP	No impact of SBP on the calories consumed or on probability student eats breakfast; improves nutritional quality as measured on HEI and in blood serum; no measured positive spillover effects for other household members
Crepinsek et al. (2006)	Individual data: dietary recall study, students grades 2–6 in 153 elementary schools in six districts	Random assignment within matched-pair schools to universal free breakfast or traditional program	Treatment school students more likely to consume a nutritionally substantive breakfast; no change in twenty-four-hour dietary intakes or in the rate of breakfast skipping
Millimet, Tchernis, and Husain (2010)	Early Childhood Longitudinal Data, K–5 1998–99 $N = 13{,}531$	Growth from kindergarten entry; selection model for school participation in SBP; Altonji et al. approach to assess selection on unobservables	School breakfast decreases obesity; school lunch increases obesity
		Studies of impact on student achievement	
Dotter (2012)	Individual data: achievement, attendance, behavior in San Diego elementary schools, 2002–2011	Difference-in-differences on UFB and BIC introduction across schools that were versus were not treated	UFB increased achievement in math (0.15 SD) and reading (0.10 SD); larger gains where fewer students were previously participating; no incremental effect of BIC versus UFB
Frisvold (2012)	Test score data from 2003 National Assessment of Educational Progress; school SBP availability, consumption, attendance, and behavior from ECLS-K	States require schools to participate in SBP if the school exceeds a threshold percent eligible for free/reduced-price meals; thresholds differ across states; difference-in-difference and RD around thresholds	SBP improves test scores in math (0.09 SD) and reading (0.05–0.12 SD), and improves the nutritional content of breakfast
Imberman and Kugler (2014)	Individual data: test scores and attendance (2003–2010) and BMI (2009–2010) in a large urban school district in the southwest United States	Difference-in-difference using quasi-random timing of introduction of new Breakfast in the Classroom program; all schools eventually treated	Exposure to BIC for one or more weeks increases achievement in math by 0.09 SD and reading by 0.06 SD; no impact on grades or attendance

students who are income eligible for a subsidy. There is substantial evidence that universal free breakfast (UFB) has increased participation rates. Leos-Urbel et al. (2013) find that expansion of the UFB program in New York City schools increased participation rates for those previously ineligible for breakfast subsidies, and also for free-breakfast students. This suggests that the UFB program may also reduce stigma associated with participation. They find small positive impacts of the program on attendance rates, but no impact on test scores. Ribar and Haldeman (2013) use the termination of UFB in some schools but not others in a North Carolina district, and find a decline in participation that was largest for students who were not income eligible for free breakfasts.

The USDA sponsored a large randomized-controlled trial of UFB, and collected information on impacts on participation, dietary intake, health, behavior, and achievement. Crepinsek et al. (2006) analyze the experimental data and find that students who attend a school randomly assigned to receive UFB are more likely to consume a nutritionally substantive breakfast; the program has no impact on twenty-four-hour dietary intakes or on the rate of breakfast skipping.

While UFB increases take-up rates, the limitation remains that in order to participate in the breakfast program a student generally has to arrive at school prior to the start of classes. To remove this barrier, another recent policy innovation has been to serve breakfast in the classroom (BIC) during the first few minutes of the school day. The BIC eliminates the need for students to arrive to school early to participate in the school breakfast program, and dramatically increases participation in the SBP. This program has recently gained momentum, with major expansions in cities such as Washington, DC, Houston, New York City, Chicago, San Diego, and Memphis, and a flurry of research studies on the impacts of the program.

Imberman and Kugler (2014) investigate the very short-term impacts of the introduction of a BIC program in a large urban school district in the southwestern United States. The program was introduced on a rolling basis across schools, and the earliest adopting schools had the program in place for up to nine weeks before the state's annual standardized test was administered. They find increases in reading and math test scores on the order of 0.06 and 0.09 standard deviations, respectively, but no impact on grades or attendance. Additionally, there was no difference in impact on test scores between those schools that had adopted the program for only one week versus those that had the program for a longer time. The pattern in the results led the authors to speculate that the test score impacts were driven by short-term cognitive gains on the day of the test due to eating breakfast and not underlying learning gains.

Schanzenbach and Zaki (2014) reanalyze the USDA's experimental data described above to separately investigate the impact of the BIC program. They find few positive impacts on measures of dietary quality, and no positive impacts on behavior, health, or achievement measured after one to three years of treatment. They find some evidence of health and behavior improvements among specific subpopulations. Dotter (2012), on the other hand, finds stronger impacts of the staggered introduction of a BIC program in elementary schools in San Diego. Using a difference-in-differences approach based on the introduction of the program, he finds that BIC increases test scores in math and reading by 0.15 and 0.10 standard deviations, respectively. He finds no test score impacts on schools that previously had universal free breakfast, and no impacts on attendance rates.

3.5 Conclusions and Future Directions

A pressing concern for policymakers is whether food and nutrition programs are doing an adequate job of enhancing and protecting the nutrition status of Americans. Despite the patchwork of nutrition programs available, many recipients either suffer food insecurity, consume diets that fall short of dietary guidelines, or both. There are many holes in the research literature, and better answers to these unresolved questions could give policymakers guidance on ways to potentially improve the programs. We conclude this chapter with our thoughts on open research questions. We organize these comments into three categories: programs and policy (basic program impacts), the role of market incentives, and potential insights from behavioral economics to enhance the effectiveness of the programs.

3.5.1 Programs and Policy

As described in the sections above, while there have been recent strides in our understanding of the causal impacts of food and nutrition programs, there are many holes to be filled in terms of our knowledge about what food and nutrition programs do. For example, although over three-quarters of WIC participants are infants and children, little is known about the health impacts of WIC on these populations. In addition, little is known about the effects of the $388 million in nutrition education or $100 million in employment and training programs in SNAP (figures from CBO [2012]). Recent policy changes also need evaluation; for example, the impacts of stricter nutrition standards for school meals adopted under the Healthy, Hunger-Free Kids Act on participation and outcomes are yet to be understood. The act also imposed restrictions on "competitive foods" sold in schools that could have important impacts on participation, child health, and educational outcomes. Similarly, the impacts of the recent change in the WIC food basket on take-up and participant outcomes need study. In addition, the impacts of the relaxation of the gross income test in SNAP—which expanded eligibility to households with earnings above 130 percent of the poverty line that have high deductions for shelter costs, child care, and medical costs—are in need of study.

In addition, the interactions between these and other safety net programs are not well understood. Bitler and Hoynes (2016) show that in the postwelfare reform world, SNAP played a large and important role in protecting families from falling into poverty in the Great Recession. Further, they find that TANF is providing much less protection in response to economic downturns than it did prior to welfare reform (when the program was called AFDC). As a result, SNAP's role in insuring consumption in the face of economic downturns appears to be evolving and growing. Have the responses to the work disincentives of SNAP changed in the era after welfare reform, in which TANF's role in the safety net has been displaced by the EITC? How have the time limits on ABAWD participants in SNAP changed work incentives? Does SNAP play a more important role in alleviating food insecurity and other measures of material hardship because it is paid out monthly instead of the EITC's annual lump-sum payment? In a broader sense, is it optimal to have the current patchwork of programs, or would it be better to combine or streamline the programs somehow?

There is a recent and growing literature on the medium- and long-run effects of providing food and nutrition programs in utero and in early childhood. We have much more to learn about the potential benefits of these programs on health and well-being in the long run, and when in the life cycle is the most important time to provide these benefits.

A few recent papers focus on understanding the recent SNAP caseload dynamics, as motivated by the increase in SNAP in the Great Recession. Studies by Bitler and Hoynes (2016) and Ganong and Liebman (2013) show that a significant share of the increase in SNAP in the Great Recession can be explained by the severity of the labor market contraction. As of this writing, as the labor market is recovering, SNAP caseloads are declining. It will be of interest to understand whether these dynamics continue. Relatively little is understood about the duration and frequency of participation spells. What are the income dynamics that correlate with households' entry to and exit from the program? Given the trade-offs between incentives, protection, and the administrative costs of enrolling a household in SNAP, are the program rules set optimally?

In addition, the Institute of Medicine (IOM 2013) set out a variety of research questions on the adequacy of SNAP benefits that have not been answered. Since a high proportion of SNAP recipients experience food insecurity at some point during the year, are there changes that could enhance the program's effectiveness in this regard? For example, are the funding formula's parameters set appropriately? Important areas of study include whether the earnings disregard is adequate, the impact of the cap on the shelter-cost deduction to net income, and whether the assumptions of the amount of home production of meals implicit in the Thrifty Food Plan are reasonable in an era with higher shares of the caseload employed.

3.5.2   The Role of Market Incentives (for Participants and Firms)

More work is also needed in understanding the price elasticity of demand for various goods (e.g., healthy foods). There is some recent evidence on this question from the Healthy Incentives Pilot conducted in Massachusetts (Bartlett et al. 2014). This small-scale, randomized-controlled trial gave the treatment group a $0.30 rebate for each dollar of SNAP benefits spent on fruits and vegetables (subject to a maximum subsidy). The evaluation shows that the price subsidy led to a 25 percent increase in consumption of fruits and vegetables. It would be useful to know how consumption would respond to different levels of price subsidies, and whether the results are different if they are offered at all participating retailers or limited to farmers markets only. It would also be useful to know how and for whom consumption patterns would change under targeted price subsidies compared to other policy changes with equivalent cost, such as an increase in the maximum benefit levels or an increase in the earnings disregard. Along a similar line, Just and Price (2013) find that children are more likely to eat fruits or vegetables at lunch in school if they are given a cash incentive, and impacts are more than twice as large if they are offered a quarter as a nickel.

More work is needed to understand how to design programs that are efficient and incentive-compatible for vendors. For example, SNAP and WIC benefits make use of normal channels of trade, and can be redeemed at a large number of retail stores. What are ways to promote lowest-price redemption of WIC vouchers given that WIC is a quantity voucher? How would the efficiency and effectiveness of the program be changed if the benefits were altered such that recipients could respond to the price of the goods (e.g., by turning the program into a dollar-value voucher that could be used for targeted goods)? For school meals, how have revenues responded to the new nutrition standards, and if meals are losing revenue, from what sources are schools making up the shortfall? What combination of incentives and regulations improve the provision of healthy school meals, and does that vary by whether the meals service is run by the district or contracted to a private vendor?

3.5.3   Insights from Behavioral Economics

Another direction for research is testing whether existing economic models accurately capture participant behavior, or if models that incorporate behavioral economics insights are more appropriate. The USDA is interested in pursuing these avenues, and recently funded a Center for Behavioral Economics and Healthy Food Choice Research.

For example, some policy advocates have suggested altering the types of goods that can be purchased with SNAP benefits, such as excluding sugar-sweetened beverages or allowing purchase of hot foods. Under the canonical model, inframarginal consumers would not be predicted to alter their consumption of these goods regardless of whether SNAP benefits can be used to purchase the items. Does actual behavior adhere to the canonical model prediction, or would recipients alter their consumption of the targeted goods in response to these potential "nudges"? In 2010, New York City requested a waiver from the USDA to ban the purchase of a wide range of sugar-sweetened beverages with SNAP benefits. While the waiver was rejected, a well-designed demonstration project would provide useful evidence on the matter. Even if such policies do not alter behavior, there may be scope for other well-targeted nudges to encourage healthier food consumption.

There is more to learn about the importance of the "food stamp cycle" first documented by Shapiro (2005). In particular, the data show that as the number of days pass since a family receives their (monthly) food stamp payment, food consumption, calories, nutritional intake, and food expenses decline. The decline is especially notable in the last week of the food stamp cycle. Hastings and Washington (2010) find results consistent with this using grocery-store-scanner data. These findings have caused some policy interest in paying out benefits more frequently, for example, twice per month. Using a population shopping at commissaries on military bases, though, Zaki (2014) documents a similar decline in daily food purchasing patterns late in the pay period when paychecks are distributed twice per month. This suggests that more frequent payments of benefits may not be more effective at encouraging consumption smoothing. A better understanding of the interactions between the frequency of payments, self-control, and consumption smoothing would give us important insights into the economic decision making among low-income populations that could be incorporated in our food and nutrition programs and policies.

3.5.4   Final Conclusions

It is encouraging that in recent years there has been an increase in the study of food and nutrition programs using designs that attempt to isolate causal impacts of the programs. Nonetheless, many important questions remain that are unlikely to be answered by quasi-experimental analyses. To provide compelling answers on the impacts of these important programs, the USDA should be open to expanding access to administrative data and implementing well-designed social experiments.

References

Almond, D., K. Y. Chay, and M. Greenstone. 2006. "Civil Rights, the War on Poverty, and Black-White Convergence in Infant Mortality in the Rural South and

Mississippi." Working Paper no. 07*04 MIT Department of Economics, Cambridge, MA, December.

Almond, D., H. W. Hoynes, and D. W. Schanzenbach. 2011. "Inside the War on Poverty: The Impact of Food Stamps on Birth Outcomes." *Review of Economics and Statistics* 93 (2): 387–403.

Andreyeva, T. 2012. "Effects of the Revised Food Packages for Women, Infants, and Children (WIC) in Connecticut." *Choices* 27 (3). http://www.choicesmagazine
.org/choices-magazine/theme-articles/an-evaluation-of-food-deserts-in-america
/effects-of-the-revised-food-packages-for-women-infants-and-children-wic
-in-connecticut.

Bailey, M. J. 2012. "Reexamining the Impact of Family Planning Programs on US Fertility: Evidence from the War on Poverty and the Early Years of Title X." *American Economic Journal Applied Economics* 4 (2): 62.

Barker, D. J. 1997. "Maternal Nutrition, Fetal Nutrition, and Disease in Later Life." *Nutrition* 13 (9): 807–13.

Bartlett, S., J. Klerman, P. Wilde, L. Olsho, C. Logan, M. Blocklin, M. Beauregard, and A. Enver. 2014. *Evaluation of the Healthy Incentives Pilot (HIP): Final Report.* Food and Nutrition Service, US Department of Agriculture, September. Cambridge, MA: Abt Associates.

Beatty, T. K., and C. Tuttle. 2014. "Expenditure Response to Increases in In-Kind Transfers: Evidence from the Supplemental Nutrition Assistance Program." *American Journal of Agricultural Economics.* doi: 10.1093/ajae/aau097, http://ajae.oxfordjournals.org/content/early/2014/11/21/ajae.aau097.

Bernstein, L. S., J. E. McLaughlin, M. K. Crepinsek, and L. M. Daft. 2004. *Evaluation of the School Breakfast Program Pilot Project: Final Report.* Nutrition Assistance Program Report Series no. CN-04-SBP, Office of Analysis, Nutrition, and Evaluation, Food and Nutrition Service, US Department of Agriculture, Alexandria, VA, December.

Berry, J. M. 1984. *Feeding Hungry People: Rulemaking in the Food Stamp Program.* New Brunswick, NJ: Rutgers University Press.

Bhattacharya, J., J. Currie, and S. J. Haider. 2006. "Breakfast of Champions? The School Breakfast Program and the Nutrition of Children and Families." *Journal of Human Resources* 41 (3): 445–66.

Bitler, M. 2015. "Health and Nutrition Effects of SNAP: Selection into the Program and a Review of the Literature." In *SNAP Matters: How Food Stamps Affect Health and Well-Being,* edited by J. Bartfeld, C. Gundersen, T. Smeeding, and J. Ziliak. Redwood City, CA: Stanford University Press.

Bitler, M., and J. Currie. 2005. "Does WIC Work? The Effects of WIC on Pregnancy and Birth Outcomes." *Journal of Policy Analysis and Management* 24 (1): 73–91.

Bitler, M. P., J. Currie, and J. K. Scholz. 2003. "WIC Eligibility and Participation." *Journal of Human Resources* 38:1139–79.

Bitler, M., and H. W. Hoynes. 2013. "Immigrants, Welfare and the US Safety Net." In *Immigration, Poverty, and Socioeconomic Inequality,* edited by David Card and Steven Raphael. New York: Russell Sage Foundation.

———. 2016. "The More Things Change, The More They Stay the Same? The Safety Net and Poverty in the Great Recession." *Journal of Labor Economics* 34 (S1): S403–44.

Blundell, R., and L. Pistaferri. 2003. "Income Volatility and Household Consumption: The Impact of Food Assistance Programs." *Journal of Human Resources* 38:1032–50.

Borjas, G. J. 2004. "Food Insecurity and Public Assistance." *Journal of Public Economics* 88 (7): 1421–43.

Bruich, G. 2014. "The Effect of SNAP Benefits on Expenditures: New Evidence from

Scanner Data and the November 2013 Benefit Cuts." Unpublished Manuscript, Harvard University, September.

Cascio, E., N. Gordon, E. Lewis, and S. Reber. 2010. "Paying for Progress: Conditional Grants and the Desegregation of Southern Schools." *Quarterly Journal of Economics* 125 (1): 445–82.

Coleman-Jensen, A., M. Nord, M. Andrews, and S. Carlson. 2012. "Household Food Security in the United States in 2011." Economic Research Report no.141, Washington, DC, Economic Research Service, US Department of Agriculture.

Coleman-Jensen, A., M. Rabbitt, C. Gregory, and A. Singh. 2015. "Statistical Supplement to Household Food Security in the United States in 2014." Administrative Publication no. 069, Washington, DC, Economic Research Service, US Department of Agriculture.

Congressional Budget Office. 2012. "Effective Marginal Tax Rates for Low- and Moderate-income Workers." Washington, DC, November.

Corsetto, L. 2012. "Food and Nutrition Program Cyclicality." Unpublished Manuscript, University of California-Davis.

Crepinsek, M. K., A. Singh, L. S. Bernstein, and J. E. McLaughlin. 2006. "Dietary Effects of Universal-Free School Breakfast: Findings from the Evaluation of the School Breakfast Program Pilot Project." *Journal of the American Dietetic Association* 106 (11): 1796–803.

Cunnyngham, K. 2002. "Trends in Food Stamp Program Participation Rates: 1994 to 2000." Contract no. 53–3198–9-008, Washington, DC, Mathematica Policy Research.

———. 2010. "State Trends in Supplemental Nutrition Assistance Program Eligibility and Participation among Elderly Individuals." Washington, DC, Mathematica Policy Research.

———. 2014. "State Supplemental Nutrition Program Participation Rates in 2011." Contract no. AG-3198-K-13–0006, Washington, DC, Food and Nutrition Service, US Department of Agriculture, February.

Cunnyngham, K, A. Sukasih, and L. Castner. 2014. "Empirical Bayes Shrinkage Estimates of State Supplemental Nutrition Assistance Program Participation Rates in 2009–2011 for All Eligible People and the Working Poor." Washington, DC, Mathematica Policy Research, March.

Currie, J. 2003. "US Food and Nutrition Programs. In *Means-Tested Transfer Programs in the United States*, edited by R. A. Moffitt, 199–289. Chicago: University of Chicago Press.

Currie, J., and F. Gahvari. 2008. "Transfers in Cash and In-Kind: Theory Meets the Data." *Journal of Economic Literature* 46 (2): 333–83.

Currie, J., and J. Grogger. 2001. "Explaining Recent Declines in Food Stamp Program Participation [with comments]." *Brookings-Wharton Papers on Urban Affairs: 2001* 203–44.

Currie, J., and E. Moretti. 2008. "Did the Introduction of Food Stamps Affect Birth Outcomes in California?" In *Making Americans Healthier: Social and Economic Policy as Health Policy*, edited by R. Schoeni, J. House, G. Kaplan, and H. Pollack. New York: Russell Sage Press.

Currie, J., and I. Rajani. 2014. "Within-Mother Estimates of the Effects of WIC on Birth Outcomes in New York City." NBER Working Paper no. 20400, Cambridge, MA.

Davis, D. 2012. "Bidding for WIC Infant Formula Contracts: Do Non-WIC Customers Subsidize WIC Customers?" *American Journal of Agricultural Economics* 94 (1): 80–96.

DePolt, R. A., R. A. Moffitt, and D. C. Ribar. 2009. "Food Stamps, Temporary

Assistance for Needy Families and Food Hardships in Three American Cities." *Pacific Economic Review* 14 (4): 445–73.

Dotter, D. 2012. "Breakfast at the Desk: The Impact of Universal Breakfast Programs on Academic Performance." Unpublished Manuscript, University of California, San Diego.

Dunifon, R., and L. Kowaleski-Jones. 2003. "The Influences of Participation in the National School Lunch Program and Food Insecurity on Child Well-Being." *Social Service Review* 77 (1): 72–92.

East, Chloe. 2015a. "The Effect of Food Stamps on Children's Health: Evidence from Immigrants' Changing Eligibility." Unpublished Manuscript, University of California, Davis.

———. 2015b. "The Labor Supply Response to Food Stamp Access." Unpublished Manuscript, University of California, Davis.

Fan, M. 2010. "Do Food Stamps Contribute to Obesity in Low-Income Women? Evidence from the National Longitudinal Survey of Youth 1979." *American Journal of Agricultural Economics* 92 (4): 1165–80.

Figlio, D. N., C. Gundersen, and J. P. Ziliak. 2000. "The Effects of the Macroeconomy and Welfare Reform on Food Stamp Caseloads." *American Journal of Agricultural Economics* 82 (3): 635–41.

Figlio, D., S. Hamersma, and J. Roth. 2009. "Does Prenatal WIC Participation Improve Birth Outcomes? New Evidence from Florida." *Journal of Public Economics* 93 (1): 235–45.

Finkelstein, A., and R. McKnight. 2008. "What Did Medicare Do? The Initial Impact of Medicare on Mortality and Out of Pocket Medical Spending." *Journal of Public Economics* 92 (7): 1644–68.

Frisvold, D. E. 2012. "Nutrition and Cognitive Achievement: An Evaluation of the School Breakfast Program." Discussion Paper no. 1402–12, Institute for Research on Poverty, Madison, WI, August.

Ganong, P., and J. B. Liebman. 2013. "The Decline, Rebound, and Further Rise in SNAP Enrollment: Disentangling Business Cycle Fluctuations and Policy Changes." NBER Working Paper no. 19363, Cambridge, MA.

Gibson, D. 2003. "Food Stamp Program Participation is Positively Related to Obesity in Low-Income Women." *Journal of Nutrition* 133 (7): 2225–31.

———. 2004. "Long-Term Food Stamp Program Participation is Differentially Related to Overweight in Young Girls and Boys." *Journal of Nutrition* 134 (2): 372–79.

Gibson-Davis, C. M., and E. M. Foster. 2006. "A Cautionary Tale: Using Propensity Scores to Estimate the Effect of Food Stamps on Food Insecurity." *Social Service Review* 80 (1): 93–126.

Gleason, P. M., and C. W. Suitor. 2003. "Eating at School: How the National School Lunch Program Affects Children's Diets." *American Journal of Agricultural Economics* 85 (4): 1047–61.

Gluckman, P. D., and M. A. Hanson. 2004. *The Fetal Matrix: Evolution, Development and Disease*. Cambridge: Cambridge University Press.

Goodman-Bacon, A. J. 2014. "Public Insurance and Mortality: Evidence from Medicaid Implementation." Working Paper, University of Michigan.

Gregory, C., M. Rabbitt, and D. C. Ribar. 2015. "The Supplemental Nutrition Assistance Program and Food Insecurity." In *SNAP Matters: How Food Stamps Affect Health and Well Being*, edited by J. Bartfeld, C. Gundersen, T. Smeeding, and J. Ziliak. Redwood City, CA: Stanford University Press.

Griliches, Z. 1979. "Sibling Models and Data in Economics: Beginnings of a Survey." *Journal of Political Economy* 87 (5, part 2): S37–64.

Gunderson, G. W. 1971. *History of the National School Lunch Program.* FNS 63, Food and Nutrition Service, USDA. Washington, DC: US Government Printing Office 1971 0-429-783. http://www.fns.usda.gov/nslp/history.

Gundersen, C., B. Kreider, and J. Pepper. 2012. "The Impact of the National School Lunch Program on Child Health: A Nonparametric Bounds Analysis." *Journal of Econometrics* 166 (1): 79–91.

Gundersen, C., and J. P. Ziliak. 2003. "The Role of Food Stamps in Consumption Stabilization." *Journal of Human Resources* 38:1051–79.

Haider, S. J., R. F. Schoeni, Y. Bao, and C. Danielson. 2004. "Immigrants, Welfare Reform, and the Economy." *Journal of Policy Analysis and Management* 23 (4): 745–64.

Hastings, J., and E. Washington. 2010. "The First of the Month Effect: Consumer Behavior and Store Responses." *American Economic Journal: Economic Policy* 2 (2): 142–62.

Hinrichs, P. 2010. "The Effects of the National School Lunch Program on Education and Health." *Journal of Policy Analysis and Management* 29 (3): 479–505.

Hoynes, H. W., L. McGranahan, and D. W. Schanzenbach. 2015. "SNAP and Food Consumption." In *SNAP Matters: How Food Stamps Affect Health and Well Being,* edited by J. Bartfeld, C. Gundersen, T. Smeeding, and J. Ziliak. Redwood City, CA: Stanford University Press.

Hoynes, H., M. Page, and A. H. Stevens. 2011. "Can Targeted Transfers Improve Birth Outcomes? Evidence from the Introduction of the WIC Program." *Journal of Public Economics* 95 (7): 813–27.

Hoynes, H. W., and D. W. Schanzenbach. 2009. "Consumption Responses to In-Kind Transfers: Evidence from the Introduction of the Food Stamp Program." *American Economic Journal: Applied Economics* 1 (4): 109–39.

———. 2012. "Work Incentives and the Food Stamp Program." *Journal of Public Economics* 96 (1): 151–62.

Hoynes, H. W., D. W. Schanzenbach, and D. Almond. 2016. "Long Run Impacts of Childhood Access to the Safety Net." *American Economic Review* 106 (4): 903–34.

Huang, R., and J. M. Perloff. 2014. "WIC Contract Spillover Effects." *Review of Industrial Organization* 44 (1): 49–71.

Imberman, S. A., and A. D. Kugler. 2014. "The Effect of Providing Breakfast in Class on Student Performance." *Journal of Policy Analysis and Management* 33 (3): 669–99.

Institute of Medicine (IOM). 2005. *WIC Food Packages: Time for a Change.* Washington, DC: National Academies Press.

———. 2013. *Supplemental Nutrition Assistance Program: Examining the Evidence to Define Benefit Adequacy.* Washington, DC: National Academies Press.

Joyce, T., D. Gibson, and S. Colman. 2005. "The Changing Association between Prenatal Participation in WIC and Birth Outcomes in New York City." *Journal of Policy Analysis and Management* 24 (4): 661–85.

Joyce, T., A. Racine, and C. Yunzal-Butler. 2008. "Reassessing the WIC Effect: Evidence from the Pregnancy Nutrition Surveillance System." *Journal of Policy Analysis and Management* 27 (2): 277–303.

Just, D. R., and J. Price. 2013. "Using Incentives to Encourage Healthy Eating in Children." *Journal of Human Resources* 48 (4): 855–72.

Kabbani, N. S., and P. E. Wilde. 2003. "Short Recertification Periods in the US Food Stamp Program." *Journal of Human Resources* 38:1112–38.

Kaestner, R., and N. Kaushal. 2005. "Immigrant and Native Responses to Welfare Reform." *Journal of Population Economics* 18 (1): 69–92.

Kaushal, N. 2007. "Do Food Stamps Cause Obesity? Evidence from Immigrant Experience." *Journal of Health Economics* 26 (5): 968–91.

Kim, J. 2014. "Changes in Low-income Household's Spending Pattern in Response to the 2009 SNAP Benefit Increase." Unpublished Manuscript, University of Michigan.

Kreider, B., J. V. Pepper, C. Gundersen, and D. Jolliffe. 2012. "Identifying the Effects of SNAP (Food Stamps) on Child Health Outcomes When Participation is Endogenous and Misreported." *Journal of the American Statistical Association* 107 (499): 958–75.

Leos-Urbel, J., A. E. Schwartz, M. Weinstein, and S. Corcoran. 2013. "Not Just for Poor Kids: The Impact of Universal Free School Breakfast on Meal Participation and Student Outcomes." *Economics of Education Review* 36:88–107.

Levin, M., and Z. Neuberger. 2014. *Improving Direct Certification Will Help More Low-Income Children Receive School Meals.* Washington, DC: Center on Budget and Policy Priorities.

Ludwig, J., and D. L. Miller. 2007. "Does Head Start Improve Children's Life Chances? Evidence from a Regression Discontinuity Approach." *Quarterly Journal of Economics* 122 (1): 159–208.

Ludwig, J., and M. Miller. 2005. "Interpreting the WIC Debate." *Journal of Policy Analysis and Management* 24 (3): 691–701.

Macro International. 1995. *The WIC Dynamics Study, Volume 1, Final Report.* US Department of Agriculture, Food and Consumer Service, Washington, DC, February.

McLaughlin, P. 2014. "Incentives for Non-Price Competition in the California WIC Program." Working Paper, University of California-Davis, May.

Meckel, K. 2014. "Is the Cure Worse than the Disease? Unintended Consequences of Fraud Reduction in Transfer Programs." Working Paper, Columbia University, November.

Meyerhoefer, C. D., and Y. Pylypchuk. 2008. "Does Participation in the Food Stamp Program Increase the Prevalence of Obesity and Health Care Spending?" *American Journal of Agricultural Economics* 90 (2): 287–305.

Meyerhoefer, C. D., and M. Yang. 2011. "The Relationship between Food Assistance and Health: A Review of the Literature and Empirical Strategies for Identifying Program Effects." *Applied Economic Perspectives and Policy* doi: 10.1093/aepp /ppr023. http://aepp.oxfordjournals.org/content/early/2011/08/10/aepp.ppr023.

Millimet, D. L., R. Tchernis, and M. Husain. M. 2010. "School Nutrition Programs and the Incidence of Childhood Obesity." *Journal of Human Resources* 45 (3): 640–54.

Mirtcheva, D. M., and L. M. Powell. 2013. "National School Lunch Program Participation and Child Body Weight." *Eastern Economic Journal* 39 (3): 328–45.

Moffitt, R. 2015. "Multiple Program Participation and SNAP." *SNAP Matters: How Food Stamps Affect Health and Well Being,* edited by J. Bartfeld, C. Gundersen, T. Smeeding, and J. Ziliak. Redwood City, CA: Stanford University Press.

Mulligan, C. B. 2012. *The Redistribution Recession: How Labor Market Distortions Contracted the Economy.* New York: Oxford University Press.

Mykerezi, E., and B. Mills. 2010. "The Impact of Food Stamp Program Participation on Household Food Insecurity." *American Journal of Agricultural Economics* 92 (5): 1379–91.

Nord, M. 2009. *Food Insecurity in Households with Children: Prevalence, Severity, and Household Characteristics.* Economic Information Bulletin no. 56, Washington, DC, US Department of Agriculture, September.

Nord, M., and K. Romig. 2006. "Hunger in the Summer: Seasonal Food Insecurity and the National School Lunch and Summer Food Service Programs." *Journal of Children & Poverty* 12 (2): 141–58.

Ogden, C. L., M. Carroll, B. Kit, and K. Flegal. 2014. "Prevalence of Childhood and

Adult Obesity in the United States, 2011–2012." *Journal of the American Medical Association* 311 (8): 806–14.

Oliveira, V., E. Frazão, and D. Smallwood. 2013. *Trends in Infant Formula Rebate Contracts: Implications for the WIC Program, EIB-119.* Washington, DC: US Department of Agriculture, Economic Research Service.

Oliveira, V., E. Racine, J. Olmsted, and L. M. Ghelfi. 2002. *The WIC Program: Background, Trends, and Issues.* Food Assistance and Nutrition Research Report no. 27, Washington, DC, Food and Rural Economics Division, Economic Research Service, US Department of Agriculture, September.

Parrott, S., and R. Greenstein. 2014. "Policymakers Often Overstate Marginal Tax Rates for Lower-Income Workers and Gloss over Tough Trade-Offs in Reducing Them." Washington, DC, Center on Budget and Policy Priorities, December.

Peterson, A., B. McGill, B. Thorn, A. Suchman, and D. Ribar. 2014. "Examining the Growth of the Zero-Income SNAP Caseload: Characteristics, Circumstances, and Dynamics of Zero-Income SNAP Participants. Volume I: Cross-Sectional and Longitudinal Findings, 1993–2008." Contract no. AG-3198-C-11–0008, Insight Policy Research, Food and Nutrition Service, US Department of Agriculture, Alexandria, VA.

Ratcliffe, C., S. M. McKernan, and S. Zhang. 2011. "How Much Does the Supplemental Nutrition Assistance Program Reduce Food Insecurity?" *American Journal of Agricultural Economics* 93 (4): 1082–98.

Ribar, D. C., and L. A. Haldeman. 2013. "Changes in Meal Participation, Attendance, and Test Scores Associated with the Availability of Universal Free School Breakfasts." *Social Service Review* 87 (2): 354–85.

Rossin-Slater, M. 2013. "WIC in Your Neighborhood: New Evidence on the Impacts of Geographic Access to Clinics." *Journal of Public Economics* 102:51–69.

Schanzenbach, D. W. 2007. "What Are Food Stamps Worth?" Working Paper, University of Chicago.

———. 2009. "Do School Lunches Contribute to Childhood Obesity?" *Journal of Human Resources* 44 (3): 684–709.

Schanzenbach, D. W., and M. Zaki. 2014. "Expanding the School Breakfast Program: Impacts on Children's Consumption, Nutrition and Health." NBER Working Paper no. 20308, Cambridge, MA.

Schmeiser, M. D. 2012. "The Impact of Long-Term Participation in the Supplemental Nutrition Assistance Program on Child Obesity." *Health Economics* 21 (4): 386–404.

Schmidt, L., L. Shore-Sheppard, and T. Watson. 2015. "The Effect of Safety Net Programs on Food Insecurity." *Journal of Human Resources.*

Shaefer, H. L., and I. A. Gutierrez. 2013. "The Supplemental Nutrition Assistance Program and Material Hardships among Low-Income Households with Children." *Social Service Review* 87(4): 753–79.

Shapiro, J. M. 2005. "Is There a Daily Discount Rate? Evidence from the Food Stamp Nutrition Cycle." *Journal of Public Economics* 89 (2): 303–25.

Short, K. 2011. "The Research Supplemental Poverty Measure: 2010." *Current Population Reports*, (P60–241), Washington, DC, US Department of Commerce, Economics and Statistics Administration, US Census Bureau, November.

Short, K. 2014. "The Research Supplemental Poverty Measure: 2014." *Current Population Reports*, (P60–254), Washington, DC, US Department of Commerce, Economics and Statistics Administration, US Census Bureau.

Southworth, H. M. 1945. "The Economics of Public Measures to Subsidize Food Consumption." *Journal of Farm Economics* 27 (1): 38–66.

Tiehen, L., D. Jolliffe, and T. Smeeding. 2013. "The Effect of SNAP on Poverty."

Discussion Paper Series no. DP2013–06, University of Kentucky Center for Poverty Research, October.

US Government Accountability Office (GAO). 2007. "Food Stamp Program: FNS Could Improve Guidance and Monitoring to Help Ensure Appropriate Use of Non-Cash Categorical Eligibility." Report no. GAO-07–465, Washington, DC, March.

US Department of Agriculture (USDA). 2013. "Special Supplemental Nutrition Program for Women, Infants, and Children Food Package Cost Report, Fiscal Year 2010." Washington, DC, Food and Nutrition Service, US Department of Agriculture, August.

US Department of Agriculture (USDA), Food and Nutrition Service. 2014. WIC Program Data, Monthly Data-State Level of Participation by Category and Program Costs [data set]. http://www.fns.usda.gov/pd/wic-program.

Vartanian, T. P., and L. Houser. 2012. "The Effects of Childhood SNAP Use and Neighborhood Conditions on Adult Body Mass Index." *Demography* 49 (3): 1127–54.

Ver Ploeg, M., and D. Betson. 2003. *Estimating Eligibility and Participation for the WIC Program.* Washington, DC: National Academies Press.

Wang, D. D., C. W. Leung, Y. Li, E. L. Ding, S. E. Chiuve, F. B. Hu, and W. C. Willett. 2014. "Trends in Dietary Quality among Adults in the United States, 1999 through 2010." *JAMA Internal Medicine* 174 (10): 1587–95.

Wilde, P., and M. Nord. 2005. "The Effect of Food Stamps on Food Security: A Panel Data Approach." *Applied Economic Perspectives and Policy* 27 (3): 425–32.

Yen, S. T., M. Andrews, Z. Chen, and D. B. Eastwood. 2008. "Food Stamp Program Participation and Food Insecurity: An Instrumental Variables Approach." *American Journal of Agricultural Economics* 90 (1): 117–32.

Zaki, M. 2014. "Access to Short-Term Credit and Consumption Smoothing within the Paycycle." Working Paper, Department of Economics, Northwestern University.

Ziliak, J. 2008. "Effective Tax Rates and Guarantees in the Food Stamp Program." A report to the Food and Nutrition Research Program, Economic Research Service, US Department of Agriculture, April.

Ziliak, J. P. 2015. "Why Are So Many Americans on Food Stamps? The Role of the Economy, Policy, and Demographics." In *SNAP Matters: How Food Stamps Affect Health and Well Being,* edited by J. Bartfeld, C. Gundersen, T. Smeeding, and J. Ziliak. Redwood City, CA: Stanford University Press.

Ziliak, J. P., C. Gundersen, and D. N. Figlio. 2003. "Food Stamp Caseloads over the Business Cycle." *Southern Economic Journal* 69 (4): 903–19.

4 Temporary Assistance for Needy Families

James P. Ziliak

4.1 Introduction

The provision of public assistance to families with children in America faced a watershed moment with the passage of the Personal Responsibility and Work Opportunity Reconciliation Act of 1996 (PRWORA); PRWORA replaced the Aid to Families with Dependent Children (AFDC) program, which was an entitlement funded via a federal-state matching grant, with Temporary Assistance for Needy Families (TANF), which is no longer an entitlement and is financed with a fixed federal block-grant to the states. The impetus for reform had been building for at least the two decades prior to passage, but took on greater currency with the dramatic growth in AFDC caseloads in the early 1990s, with then-Governor Clinton's vow to "end welfare as we know it" during the 1992 presidential campaign, and with states' expansive experimentation with waivers from federal AFDC rules during President Clinton's first term in office (Haskins 2007). The state waivers included some elements from prior reform efforts—such as work requirements for benefit eligibility and sanctions for failing to work or participate in a training program—but with teeth. In addition, some states adopted radical new features such as time limits on benefit receipt. Not to be out-

James P. Ziliak holds the Carol Martin Gatton Endowed Chair in Microeconomics in the Department of Economics and is founding director of the Center for Poverty Research at the University of Kentucky.

I thank Robert Paul Hartley, Alexa Prettyman, and Lewis Warren for research assistance. I also thank Marianne Bitler, Peter Germanis, Colleen Heflin, Robert Moffitt, Shana Moore, Donna Pavetti, Liz Schott, Steve Ziliak, seminar participants at the NBER, and two anonymous reviewers for helpful comments. For acknowledgments, sources of research support, and disclosure of the author's material financial relationships, if any, please see http://www.nber .org/chapters/c13483.ack.

done, the Congress jumped on the reform bandwagon and codified some of the waivers into PRWORA, but also added their own twist, including the move to block-grant financing. These policy changes led to a flurry of social science research on the effects of the reform on welfare participation, employment, consumption, saving, health, family structure, and maternal and child well-being. The aim of this chapter is to review the research on the TANF program, with a particular emphasis on those studies conducted since the surveys by Blank (2002, 2009), Moffitt (2003), and Grogger and Karoly (2005).

I first begin with a brief history of the TANF program, including sources and uses of funds, eligibility, and benefits. Welfare at the founding of America was very much the purview of local and state jurisdictions, not too unlike the program today. State, and in some cases local, governments under TANF have great leeway in determining who is eligible for assistance and for how long, and the size and composition of the assistance package. This has resulted in substantial heterogeneity across states in terms of income and asset limits for eligibility, work requirements, time limits, sanctions, benefit levels, among others. One key distinction is that the early programs of the 1800s were wholly funded at the local level (and later the local and state level), whereas today TANF is funded by both federal and state tax dollars. Congress appropriates an annual block grant to states of $16.5 billion, and each year states are required to spend at least 75 percent of their FY1994 outlays on cash assistance. Positioned in between the present program, and the nineteenth century city and county programs, was AFDC. The AFDC program began as a program for children of widows and destitute mothers as part of President Roosevelt's New Deal, and was gradually expanded to include the parent (usually the mother) and then the second parent (with additional restrictions) in the assistance unit with passage of the 1988 Family Support Act. The TANF program returned to the states the authority to determine eligibility, and while all states allow eligible children and custodial parent to join, a few categorically deny aid to the second parent. Funding for AFDC was initially a grant-in-aid from the federal government, which was then converted to a federal-state matching grant with the introduction of Medicaid in 1965. The block grant of TANF is akin to the grant-in-aid funding mechanism as it is a targeted appropriation with restrictions attached, though unlike TANF, the former grant-in-aid was technically an entitlement.

I next turn to a discussion of trends in the level and composition of participation and spending under TANF. Participation peaked in 1994 with over 14 million recipients on AFDC, but then plummeted nearly 40 percent over the next three years during the final two years of the waiver era and first year of TANF. Perhaps surprisingly, participation has fallen an additional 50 percent, even through much of the Great Recession, so that by 2013 just over 4.1 million persons were on assistance, a level comparable to 1964. Moreover, in 1960, nearly eight in ten recipients of AFDC were children, and this fell to just over six in ten by 1980. However, by 2013, 7.5 out of 10 recipients of TANF were children, once again suggesting the program is "regressing to the (historical) mean." Here, however, I issue a cautionary note. A fundamental shift between the AFDC and TANF programs, and one that poses a challenge for measurement and evaluation, is that in a typical year for AFDC seventy cents of every dollar spent was in the form of cash assistance. Under TANF, it is just the reverse. Today, 70 percent of appropriations are in the form of in-kind transfers such as childcare subsidies, transportation assistance, tax credits, mental health and substance use counseling, among others. Because TANF law only requires states to report how many individuals receive cash assistance, not in-kind support, the decline in participation is overstated because cash and in-kind assistance caseloads were combined under AFDC. As a result, comparing inflation-adjusted total spending on AFDC to TANF shows that while spending is lower today than before welfare reform, it is lower by a more modest 18 percent.

The authorizing legislation for TANF stated four main goals: (a) to provide assistance to needy families so that children may be cared for in their own homes or in the homes of relatives; (b) to end the dependency of needy parents on government benefits by promoting job preparation, work, and marriage; (c) to prevent and reduce the incidence of out-of-wedlock pregnancies and establish annual numerical goals for preventing and reducing the incidence of these pregnancies; and (d) to encourage the formation and maintenance of two-parent families. I use these goals as the organizing framework for the next section of the chapter on the theoretical behavioral issues under TANF. While many of the issues overlap that of the AFDC program, the details of the behavioral models under TANF necessarily differ because of programmatic reforms, especially those policies that affect decisions over time such as work requirements, time limits, and expanded asset tests. As such I adopt a life-cycle model of decision making under uncertainty to describe how participation, labor supply, consumption, saving, health, fertility, and marriage are likely to respond in the face of the new complex set of TANF rules. Here I highlight distinctions between predictions from the static and life-cycle models. For example, the static model of labor supply generally predicts that work requirements will lead to an increase in aggregate work hours. The life-cycle model, however, is less clear depending on whether one introduces endogenous human capital formation, and if so, whether work is treated as complementary to human capital as in a "learning-by-doing" model of Weiss (1972) or as a substitute for human capital as in a Ben Porath (1967) "on-the-job training" model. For readers with less formal training in economics, the more technical material on behavioral issues can be skipped without loss of generality.

The theoretical discussion is then followed by a comprehensive review of the empirical literature on TANF. This includes first-generation welfare-reform research on the economy versus policy debates surrounding the decline in welfare participation and rise in employment, as well as more second-generation studies on consumption, saving, health insurance and health outcomes, family structure, and child well-being. Research on TANF draws from a wide cross-section of the social sciences, and while economists contributed heavily to the evaluation of the program, there was significant new effort from other disciplines such as demography, sociology, developmental psychology, political science, and social work. Where practicable, I try to bring this wider research literature into the review. I devote significant attention to issues of model identification. Much of the research is nonexperimental and of the single-equation variety that utilizes cross-state over time variation in welfare policies to estimate the effect of reform on the outcome of interest. However, with the introduction of time limits and work requirements, there has been a renewed interest in specifying and estimating structural life-cycle models, and I discuss those contributions as well.

In the final section, I attempt to summarize lessons learned about the effects of welfare reform on family well-being among low-income Americans, where I argue that with few exceptions beyond work and welfare participation, the evidence to date is either too mixed or too thin to draw definitive conclusions. This leads to a discussion of and call for future research needs as we approach the twentieth anniversary of welfare reform.

4.2   Program History and Rules

The roots of the present day TANF program lie in colonial America where public relief was the legal responsibility of the local government (town or county) and financed at the local level, typically via a property tax (Ziliak and Hannon 2006). Eligibility was also determined by local, or in a few cases, state governments. Assistance was provided both in the form of "outdoor relief," that is, cash payments and in-kind transfers to those living independently, as well as in the form of "indoor relief," which generally meant institutionalization into almshouses. The provision of outdoor relief came under great pressure from groups like the Charity Organization Society after the deep recessions of the 1870s and 1880s swelled the rolls, and in response dozens of cities either eliminated or reduced outdoor relief and replaced it with voluntary assistance from private charities and religious organizations (Katz 1986; Ziliak 2004). By the start of the twentieth century most state and local governments turned away from poorhouses as a viable form of assistance, owing to the record of deplorable conditions and questionable success in aiding the poor. Likewise, private charity as a primary means of relief fell out of favor after the 1893–1894 recession, and in its place came the ascendance of state-funded and administered outdoor-relief programs. One such program was known as Mothers' Pensions, which provided assistance to impoverished widowed mothers with young children, and indeed, by 1920 forty states offered the program (Skocpol 1992).

The financial burden of these pensions on states surged with the onset of the Great Depression, and this led to the federalization of the pension program with passage of the Social Security Act of 1935 (P.L. 74–271), that among other things, created the Aid to Dependent Children program (ADC). The stated purpose of the ADC program was to "release from the wage-earning role the person whose natural function is to give her children the physical and affectionate guardianship necessary not alone to keep them from falling into social misfortune, but more affirmatively to rear them into citizens capable of contributing to society" (Green Book 2008, 7-2). Keeping in line with the mothers' pension program, the ADC program's focal target population was widowed mothers with young (preteen) dependent children. However, with passage of the 1950 amendment to the Social Security Act, coverage was extended to impoverished mothers caring for a child, not just those widowed (Fishback and Thomasson 2006). Reflecting that expanded reach, ADC was renamed Aid to Families with Dependent Children (AFDC) as part of the 1962 Public Welfare Amendments. These amendments also extended, at state option, assistance to those families with a second adult (usually a father) who was present and unemployed or underemployed (and not necessarily permanently disabled), creating two streams of assistance, the AFDC-Basic and AFDC-Unemployed Parent (AFDC-UP) programs.

Although nominal work requirements were introduced into the AFDC program in 1967, as well as "rehabilitative services" a decade earlier, the work requirements were rarely enforced and thus for most recipients the program provided assistance for mothers (and/or families with an unemployed parent) for care in the home. This emphasis changed, however, with passage of the Family Support Act of 1988 (FSA), which required most welfare mothers without a child under age three to engage in education, work, or training under the Job Opportunities and Basic Skills Training Program (JOBS). The Family Support Act also required all states to participate in the AFDC-UP program (only about half the states did so until that point), and it also created childcare programs and associated subsidies for those mothers engaging in training or transitioning from welfare to work (Green Book 2008, 7-4). Since the 1960s, states had been granted authority to request waivers from federal program rules under Section 1115 of the Social Security Act to experiment (usually via demonstration projects) with their welfare programs, but few exercised the option prior to the Reagan administration in the mid-1980s. On the heels of the FSA, however, caseloads began to explode (for reasons unrelated to FSA, see Ziliak et al. [2000]; Blank [2001]), and thus by 1992 twelve states were authorized to receive waivers. By the end of President Clinton's first term in 1996, the number of states with approved waivers leapt to forty-three. These state initiatives set the stage for Congress to act, and on August 22, 1996, Clinton signed PRWORA into law, which eliminated AFDC and created its replacement, TANF. The authorizing legislation for TANF expired in 2002, and after a series of continuing resolutions, the program was renewed for another five years with the Deficit Reduction Act of 2005. Since 2010, TANF has operated on annual continuing resolutions. Table 4.1 contains a timeline of legislation affecting the TANF program, while table 4.2 provides a summary of key differences between AFDC and TANF, including some amendments to the initial law as part of the Deficit Reduction Act of 2005. See Ziliak and Hannon (2006) for a historical timeline of major welfare legislation from the 1601 Elizabethan Poor Laws through TANF, Moffitt (2003) for ADC through TANF, and Hahn and Frisk (2010) for changes to TANF as part of DRA 2005.

4.2.1   Financing

Leading up to the creation of the ADC program, funding for mothers' pensions and the precursors of indoor and outdoor relief were strictly a function of local and state governments. The Great Depression and passage of the Social Security Act of 1935 changed that, but only slowly. Specifically, in the early 1930s the federal government provided large grants to states to cope with the swelling rolls of needy families and displaced workers, which was then codified into the creation of Social Security, Unemployment Insurance, and ADC (Fishback and Thomasson 2006). Participation in ADC was voluntary among the states, and assistance came in the form of grants-in-aid. To qualify for federal assistance, states had to submit plans to the Social Security Board for approval, which required, among other things, that the program be made available in all political jurisdictions of the state and that the state participate financially in the program (Bucklin 1939). The grants were capped at one-third of the program cost, up to $6 per month for the first dependent child and $4 per month for each additional child. In the first year of 1936, twenty-seven states received federal funds covering just 12 percent of total costs, and this reached forty-one states and 27 percent of total cost by 1939 (Bucklin 1939, table 4). Although Congress appropriated roughly $25 million for the ADC program in its first year, it was essentially an open-ended obligation designed to meet need (Ruggles et al. 1998).

Title XIX of the Social Security Act in 1965, which created the Medicaid and Medicare programs, changed financing of AFDC from a grant-in-aid to an explicit matching formula based on the Federal Medical Assistance Percentage (FMAP) used in determining a state's financial liability for its Medicaid program. Transitioning from the grant-in-aid to the open-ended FMAP was contingent on the state adopting Medicaid, the latter of which was adopted by all states but Arizona by 1972 (Gruber 2003). Specifically, the federal share of a state's AFDC benefit payments was determined by the matching formula

Table 4.1   **Major legislation regarding the TANF program, 1996–September 2012**

Date	Title of legislation	Main provisions
August 22, 1996	Personal Responsibility and Work Opportunity Reconciliation Act	Established the block grant of Temporary Assistance for Needy Families. Appropriated funds for the block grant through FY2002.
August 5, 1997	Balanced Budget Act of 1997	Raised the cap limiting the counting of vocational educational training and teen parents engaged in education from 20 percent of those considered engaged in work to 30 percent of those considered engaged in work, and temporarily removed from that cap teen parents through FY1999; set the maximum allowable TANF transfer to Title XX social services at 10 percent of the block grant (rather than one-third of total transfers); and made technical corrections to P.L. 104–93. P.L. 105–33 also established the $3 billion over two years (FY1998 and FY1999) Welfare-to-Work (WTW) grant program within TANF, but administered by the Department of Labor at the federal level, with local administration by state workforce investment boards and competitive grantees.
November 19, 1997	Adoption and Safe Families Act	Reduced the contingency fund appropriation by $40 million.
June 9, 1998	Transportation Act for the 21st Century	Permitted the use of federal TANF funds to be used as matching funds for reverse commuter grants.
November 29, 1999	Consolidated Appropriations Act for 2000	Broadened eligibility for recipients to be served by the WTW grant program and added limited authority for vocational educational or job training to be WTW activities.
	Consolidated Appropriations Act for 2001	Gave grantees two more years to spend WTW grant funds (a total of five years from the date of the grant award).
March 9, 2002	Job Creation and Worker Assistance Act	Extended supplemental grants and contingency funds, both of which had expired on September 30, 2001, through FY2002. (Supplemental grants were extended at FY2001 levels.)
February 8, 2006	Deficit Reduction Act of 2005	Extended most TANF grants through FY2010 (supplemental grants expire at the end of FY2008); eliminated TANF bonus funds; established competitive grants within TANF for healthy marriage and responsible fatherhood initiatives; revised the caseload reduction credit; and required HHS to issue regulations to develop definitions for the statutory activities that count toward the TANF work participation standards as well as verify work and participation in activities.
February 17, 2009	American Recovery and Reinvestment Act	Established a $5 billion Emergency Contingency Fund (ECF) to reimburse states for increased costs associated with the 2007–2009 recession for FY2009 and FY2010. The fund reimbursed states, territories, and tribes for 80 percent of the increased costs of basic assistance, nonrecurrent short-term benefits, and subsidized employment. The law also permitted states to "freeze" caseload reduction credits at prerecession levels, allowed states to use TANF reserve funds for any benefit or service (before it was restricted to assistance), and extended supplemental grants through the end of FY2010.

(continued)

Table 4.1 (continued)

Date	Title of legislation	Main provisions
December 8, 2010	Claims Resolution Act of 2010	Extended basic TANF funding through the end of FY2011, September 30, 2011, but reduced funding for the contingency fund and provided supplemental grants only through June 30, 2011. Also required some additional reporting on work activities and TANF expenditures.
September 30, 2011	Short-Term TANF Extension Act	Extended basic TANF funding for three months, through December 31, 2011. No funding was provided for supplemental grants.
December 23, 2011	Temporary Payroll Tax Cut Continuation Act of 2011	Extended basic TANF funding for two months through February 29, 2012.
February 22, 2012	Middle Class Tax Relief and Job Creation Act of 2012	Extended basic TANF funding for the remainder of FY2012 (to September 30, 2012). It also prevented electronic benefit transaction access to TANF cash at liquor stores, casinos, and strip clubs; states would be required to prohibit access to TANF cash at automated teller machines (ATMs) at such establishments. It also required states to report TANF data in a manner that facilitates the exchange of that data with other programs' data systems.

Notes: Additional, but unnamed legislation includes:

P.L. 107–229 extended TANF basic grants, supplemental grants, bonus funds, contingency funds, and other related programs through December 20, 2002. Signed into law December 20, 2002. Other "temporary extensions" of TANF grants were made in: P.L. 107–294, through March 30, 2003 (November 22, 2002); P.L. 108–7, through June 30, 2003 (February 20, 2003); P.L. 108–40, through September 30, 2003 (June 30, 2003); P.L. 108–89, through March 31, 2004 (October 1, 2003); P.L. 108–210, through June 30, 2004 (March 31, 2004); P.L. 108–262, through September 30, 2004 (June 30, 2004); P.L. 108–308, through March 31, 2005 (September 30, 2004); P.L. 109–4, through June 30, 2005 (March 25, 2005); and P.L. 109–19, through September 30, 2005 (July 1, 2005).

P.L. 108–99 rescinded all remaining unspent WTW formula grant funds, effectively ending the WTW grant program. Signed into law January 23, 2004.

P.L. 109–68 provided extra funding to help states provide benefits to families affected by Hurricane Katrina, allowing states to draw upon contingency funds to assist those displaced by the hurricane; allowing directly affected states to receive funds from the loan fund, with repayment of the loan forgiven; and suspending penalties for failure to meet certain requirements for states directly affected by the hurricane. Also, temporarily extended TANF grants through December 30, 2005. Signed into law September 21, 2005.

P.L. 109–61 extended TANF grants through March 30, 2006. Signed into law December 30, 2005.

P.L. 110–275 included an extension of TANF supplemental grants through the end of FY2009. Signed into law July 15, 2008.

P.L. 111–242, the first continuing appropriations resolution for FY2011, extended TANF funding through December 3, 2010. Signed into law September 30, 2010. P.L. 111–290, the second continuing resolution, continued TANF funding authority through December 18, 2010. Signed into law December 4, 2010.

P.L. 112–75, the Continuing Appropriations Resolution, 2013 extended TANF funding through March, 2013, at FY2012 levels. Signed into law September 28, 2012.

Table 4.2   **Comparison of AFDC, TANF 2000, and TANF 2013**

Date	AFDC	TANF 2000	TANF 2013
Financing	Matching grant	Block grant	
Eligibility	Children deprived of support of one parent or children in low-income, two-parent families (AFDC-UP)	Children in low-income families as designated by state; AFDC-UP abolished. Minor mothers must live with parents; minor mothers must also attend school	
Immigrants	Illegal aliens ineligible	Aliens ineligible for five years after entry and longer at state option	
Form of aid	Almost exclusively cash payment	States free to use funds for services and noncash benefits	
Benefit levels	At state option	Same	
Entitlement status	Federal government required to pay matched share of all recipients	No individual entitlement	
Income limits	Family income cannot exceed gross income limits	No provision	
Asset limits	Federal limits	No provision	
Treatment of earnings disregards	After four months of work, only a lump sum $90 deduction plus child care expenses; and nothing after twelve months	No provision	
Time limits	None	Federal funds cannot be used for payments to adults for more than sixty months lifetime (20 percent of caseload exempt)	

(continued)

Table 4.2 (continued)

Date	AFDC	TANF 2000	TANF 2013
Work requirements	Parents without a child under three required to participate in JOBS	Exemptions from work requirements are narrowed and types of qualified activities are narrowed and prespecified (generally excludes education and classroom training) and must be twenty hours/week rising to thirty hours/week for single mothers	Thirty hours/week for single mothers or twenty hours/week with children under age six; fifty-five hours/week for two-parent families with federally funded childcare or thirty-five hours/week with no childcare. Supplemental educational activities can make up ten hours/week for single mothers without children under age six or five hours/week for two-parent families; vocational education training (twelve-month lifetime limit) and community service (structured programs meeting certain criteria) are considered core activities
Work requirement participation requirements	JOBS participation requirements	Participation for work requirements rise to 50 percent by FY 2002	Participation rates adjusted downward based on caseload declines since 2005 instead of 1995; applicable caseloads include SSP-MOE
Childcare	Guaranteed for all JOBS participants	No guarantee, but states are given increased childcare funds	
Sanctions	General provisions	Specific provisions mandating sanctions for failure to comply with work requirements, child support enforcement, schooling attendance, and other activities	
Child support	States required to allow first $50 of child support received by mother to not reduce benefit	No provision	

Source: Burke (1996).

$$(1) \qquad FMAP = 1 - 0.45 * \left(\frac{\text{State per capita income}}{\text{National per capita income}} \right)^2,$$

or that the federal share is inversely proportional to the square of the state's per capita income relative to the national per capita level.[1] If state per capita income is the same as the aggregate level then the federal share is 55 percent, but if state income exceeds the national level then the FMAP is set at a floor of 50 percent. In the last full year of AFDC in 1996 the matching rate was 50 percent for eleven states plus the District of Columbia, and averaged about 60 percent across all states, with Mississippi receiving the largest federal subsidy of 78 percent (Green Book 1998). Because of the relative permanence of a state's location in the national income distribution, the FMAPs remained fairly stable across the three decades in use for the AFDC program. During this period, upward of ten states devolved some share of their costs to the local level, reaching as high as 50 percent in both New York and North Carolina.

One of the most fundamental changes with welfare reform was that the federal open-ended obligation to states under AFDC, that implicitly rose and fell with the health of the state's macroeconomy, was severed with the creation of the TANF program. Funding for TANF is now provided to states primarily as a fixed block grant (basic block), a grant-in-aid much more in spirit with funding under ADC, along with a supplemental grant and a recession-related contingency grant (Green Book 2008; Falk 2012; Schott, Pavetti, and Finch 2012). The basic block grant to states is based on the maximum of federal expenditures on cash assistance, emergency aid, and job training under AFDC over the four fiscal years 1992 to 1995, and totaled $16.5 billion across all states and the District of Columbia. The grant is fixed in nominal dollars, and thus the real value of the grant has declined by over a quarter since 1997. Congress appropriated supplemental grants to those states that were deemed disadvantaged by the reliance on the FMAP in the early 1990s, in particular those states with high population-growth rates and those that provided very low cash benefits relative to their poverty rates under AFDC. In total seventeen states qualified for supplemental grants, which were funded at $319 million per year from 2001 to 2011, but subsequently have been dropped (Falk 2012). A $2 billion contingency fund was established with PRWORA to those states that met an "economic need test," defined as an excess unemployment rate or food stamp caseload growth, and spending on TANF out of its own funds in excess of what the state spent in FY1994.[2] Monthly payments out of the contingency fund are capped at

---

1. For more detail on the FMAP see Kaiser Commission on Medicaid and the Uninsured (2012).

2. The specific economic need test is for (a) the three-month seasonally adjusted unemployment rate to be at least 6.5 percent and at least 10 percent higher than the corresponding three-month period in either of the prior two years; or (b) for the food stamp caseload (renamed

1.67 percent of a state's basic block grant. The contingency fund ran out in FY2010 during the Great Recession, highlighting the lack of buoyancy of the basic block-grant structure to respond to economic need compared to the matching-grant funding under AFDC. States did, however, gain access to an "emergency" TANF fund of $5 billion for FY2009–2010, and a new allocation of $612 million was added to the contingency fund in each of FY2012–FY2014 (Falk 2012; OFA 2014).

The TANF legislation mandated that states continue to provide financial support for low-income families as a condition for receipt of the basic block, known as the maintenance-of-effort (MOE) requirement. Specifically, states are required to spend annually at least 75 percent of the outlays on cash assistance, emergency aid, and job training incurred as part of their contribution to AFDC funding in FY1994.[3] In the aggregate this totals to $10.4 billion (Falk 2012). States can count any state, local, or "third party" nongovernmental spending (e.g., spending by food banks or domestic violence shelters) directed toward needy families as long as it is tied to at least one of the four goals of TANF (Schott, Pavetti, and Finch 2012; Germanis 2015). Indeed, states can reduce direct spending on TANF while simultaneously increasing the use of third-party funds to count as MOE, such as Georgia where third-party funds now make up 40 percent of MOE while nominal cuts in direct spending were implemented (Schott, Pavetti, and Finch 2012). If it is a new activity beyond prior commitments under AFDC, then the state needs to demonstrate that it is in excess of FY1995 spending on that activity. One such example of new spending used by many states to meet MOE is refundable State Earned Income Tax Credits (EITC)—by 2011 twenty-one states were using TANF/MOE to fund a state EITC (Schott, Pavetti, and Finch 2012). Failure to meet the state MOE results in a dollar-for-dollar reduction in the basic block grant in the ensuing fiscal year. This was a nonissue for most states, especially post-DRA 2005 when TANF law was changed to allow states to utilize excess MOE spending toward meeting their work participation rate requirements, as was done by thirty-two states in FY2007 (Hahn and Frisk 2010).

4.2.2   Uses of Funds

Broadly speaking, TANF funds (including MOE) may be spent for the purpose of providing support in the form of "assistance," that is, cash and near-cash benefits, and "nonassistance" such as childcare, transportation,

---

Supplemental Nutrition Assistance Program [SNAP] after FY2008) over the prior three-month period to be at least 10 percent higher than the adjusted caseload over the same three-month period in FY1994 or FY1995. The adjustment is determined by excluding those cases deemed ineligible for food stamps as part of PRWORA, for example, legal immigrants in the country for less than five years.

3. The state MOE rises to 80 percent of FY1994 AFDC spending if the state fails to meet its work participation requirement.

work supports, employer subsidies, refundable state EITCs, education and training programs, counseling, nonrecurrent benefits such as diversion payments, and Individual Development Accounts (OFA 2013). As discussed in the next section, states are only obligated to report on the number of persons served in assistance cases, but do not have reporting requirements on the number of persons receiving nonassistance. This poses a real challenge for evaluation of program reach given that two-thirds of current spending in TANF is on nonassistance.

States have considerable leeway on how to design and distribute program benefits, including using different eligibility criteria for different programs within TANF. States may transfer up to a combined 30 percent of the TANF basic grant to the Child Care and Development Block Grant (CCDBG) and the Social Services Block Grant (SSBG). Transfers to the SSBG may be available to families up to twice the poverty line, and spending out of the basic grant on "healthy marriages" and preventing out-of-wedlock pregnancies are potentially open to families regardless of income level as long as it is nonassistance spending (Schott, Pavetti, and Finch 2012). Indeed, PRWORA bestowed enough flexibility to states that ten chose to devolve some of these programmatic decisions to the county-level government.

The state MOE funds may be "commingled" with the federal block grant, "segregated" from the block grant but spent on the state TANF program, or "separated" from federal funds and operated outside of the TANF program (known as separate state programs [SSP]) (OFA 2013). The distinction lies in the degree to which the MOE funds are subject to federal rules. Commingled funds are subject to the full spectrum of federal TANF rules, while segregated and separated are subject to progressively fewer federal rules.[4] For example, neither segregated nor separate funds are subject to the federal five-year time limit, but segregated funds do face federal restrictions for individuals convicted of certain drug felonies, whereas separate funds are exempt (Lower-Basch 2011, table 2).

4.2.3   Eligibility and Benefits

Eligibility for AFDC was restricted to needy children under age eighteen who were deprived of parental support owing to parental absence, incapacitation, or unemployment.[5] Funds were also available for the child's caretaker (usually the mother), and for another adult deemed essential to the child's

---

4. Some states operate solely state-funded programs (SSF), which are funded outside of TANF and MOE and thus not subject to any of the federal rules. They are designed to assist those families facing difficulty meeting work requirements such as two-parent families or those with significant barriers to employment (but not so severe as to gain an exemption under TANF). A Government Accountability Office survey of states indicated that as of 2010 twenty-nine states operated SSFs, most of which began after enactment of DRA 2005 (Hahn and Frisk 2010).

5. Children were no longer eligible upon their eighteenth birthday, unless they were a full-time student, then benefits were paid until their nineteenth birthday.

welfare (usually the unemployed father). It was not possible for an AFDC recipient to also receive support from Supplemental Security Income (SSI), though families could blend benefits, with some on AFDC and some on SSI. Undocumented immigrants were ineligible, as were children that received foster care payments.

Economic eligibility under AFDC was determined by the family's income and liquid and vehicle assets, the upper limits of which were set by the federal government. Income of all family members was generally deemed to the child, and the monthly gross income was not permitted to exceed 185 percent of the state's monthly "need standard."[6] Net, or countable income, was not allowed to exceed 100 percent of the need standard. States did not have leeway in determining what counted as income without a waiver, but what was left unspecified in federal law was the definition of "need standard." Roughly half the states defined need in terms of minimum subsistence compatible with decency and health, another 40 percent defined need in terms of a budgetary shortfall relative to the state's assistance standard, and the remainder either specified need by statutory mandate or simply as having no support (Chief 1979). There was substantial cross-state variation in need standards, some of which likely reflected differences in cost of living and some political choice, though the real value of the need standard for the median state declined by 38 percent over the last three decades of the program (Green Book 1998). Currently, TANF no longer requires that states establish a need standard, though most states continue to do so. However, only fourteen states in 2012 applied some variant of the "185 percent of need" for the gross income limit. Most states under TANF adopted a more stringent test, and in some cases dropped the gross income test altogether (Kassabian et al. 2013). For example, in 2012 West Virginia applied a 100 percent of need for a gross income test, while Alabama applied a 100 percent of the payment standard (see definition below) for the monthly net income limit, which was only $215 for a family of three.

States were initially given some latitude in setting real property and vehicle asset limits used in determining benefit eligibility under AFDC. Indeed, prior to the Omnibus Budget Reconciliation Act of 1981, there was substantial state-specific heterogeneity in asset limits, but by 1984 only five states had vehicle limits below the allowable federal maximum of $1,500, and nine states had nonhousing, nonburial personal property limits below the federal maximum of $1,000. By 1994, all states but two had their asset limits set equal to the federal maximum (California and Iowa had received welfare waivers prior to 1994). Under TANF, states once again have the flexibility to set the liquid and vehicle asset limits for eligibility. As shown in table 4.3,

6. Some income sources were exempt. For example, after passage of the FSA in 1988 EITC refunds were no longer counted as income, and were exempt from treatment as a liquid asset for two months after receipt (Green Book 1998). In addition, the gross income limit was dropped to 150 percent of need for a few years after OBRA 1981, before returning to 185 percent.

Table 4.3   State policy choices in the TANF program as of 2012

State	Family cap[b]	Liquid asset limit[c]	Vehicle asset test[c]	Diversion payment amount[d]
Alabama	No	None	All	None
Alaska	No	2,000/3,000[1]	All	3 months
Arizona	Yes	2,000	All	3 months
Arkansas	Yes	3,000	One	3 months
California	Yes	2,000/3,000[1]	4,650[f]/driver	Varies
Colorado	No	None	All	Varies
Connecticut	Yes	3,000	9,500[e]	3 months
Delaware	Yes	10,000	All	$1,500
District of Columbia	No	2,000/3,000[1]	All	3 months
Florida	Yes	2,000	8,500[e]	Varies
Georgia	Yes	1,000	1,500/4,650[e]	None
Hawaii	No	5,000	All	None
Idaho	No	5,000	One	3 months
Illinois	No	2,000/3,000/+50	One	None*
Indiana	Yes	1,000/1,500	5000[e]	None
Iowa	No	2,000/5,000	One	None
Kansas	No	2,000	All	$1,000
Kentucky	No	2,000	All	$1,300
Louisiana	No	None	All	None
Maine	No	2,000	One	3 months
Maryland	No	None	All	3 months
Massachusetts	Yes	2,500	10,000[f]/5,000[e]	None
Michigan	No	3,000	All	3 months
Minnesota	Yes	2,000/5,000	15,000[f]	Varies
Mississippi	Yes	2,000	All	None
Missouri	No	1,000/5,000	One	None
Montana	No	3,000	One	None
Nebraska	No	4,000/6,000	One	None
Nevada	No	2,000	One	Varies
New Hampshire	No	1,000/2,000	One/driver	None
New Jersey	Yes	2,000	All[f]	$1,550
New Mexico	No	3,500	All	$2,500
New York	No	2,000/3,000[1]	4,650[f]/9,300[f]	Varies
North Carolina	Yes	3,000	All	3 months
North Dakota	Yes	3,000/6,000/+25	One	$1,720
Ohio	No	None	All	None
Oklahoma	No	1,000	5,000[e]	None
Oregon	No	2,500	10,000[e]	None
Pennsylvania	No	1,000	One	3 months
Rhode Island	No	1,000	One/adult	None
South Carolina	Yes	2,500	One/driver	None
South Dakota	No	2,000	One	2 months
Tennessee	Yes	2,000	4,600[e]	$1,200
Texas	No	1,000	4,650 of all[f]	$1,000
Utah	No	2,000	All	3 months
Vermont	No	2,000	One/adult	4 months

(*continued*)

Table 4.3   (continued)

State	Family cap[b]	Liquid asset limit[c]	Vehicle asset test[c]	Diversion payment amount[d]
Virginia	Yes	None	All	4 months
Washington	No	1,000	5,000[e]	$1,250
West Virginia	No	2,000	One	3 months
Wisconsin	No	2,500	10,000[e]	$1,600
Wyoming	No	2,500	One	None

Source: Welfare Rules Databook (2014).

[a]WRD (2014). Table L5 Maximum Monthly Benefit for a Family of Three with No Income, 1996–2012 (July).

[b]WRD (2014). Table IV.B.1 Family Cap Policies, July 2012.

[c]WRD (2014). Table I.C.1 Asset Limits for Applicants, July 2012; Table IV.A.3 Asset Limits for Recipients, July 2012. Note: Vehicle asset may be equity value or fair-market value depending on state.

[d]WRD (2014). Table I.A.1 Formal Diversion Payments, July 2012.

[e]Equity value of the vehicle.

[f]Fair-market value of the vehicle.

Note: Many states have separate policies regarding different types of vehicles, such as income-producing vehicles, recreational vehicles, and vehicles that are used as homes. See the Welfare Rules Database for more information on these policies.

[1]Units including an elderly person may exempt $3,000; all other units exempt $2,000.

*Note: Illinois diversion payments.

WRD (2014) indicates Illinois has a diversion payment program but lacks information on the maximum amount, how often one can receive it, or period of ineligibility after payment; it only indicates "Yes" for program, "Cash" for form of payment, and "No" for payment counts toward time limit. Footnote 17: "An applicant who has found a job that will make him or her ineligible for cash assistance, or who wants to accept a job and withdraw his or her application for assistance, is eligible for a one-time payment to begin or maintain employment." Http:// www.cfs.purdue.edu/cff/documents/family_data/abt_associates_repor.pdf indicates no diversion program, and http://www.acf.hhs.gov/programs/ofa/resource/tanf-financial-data-fy-2012 shows Illinois has no expenditures for nonrecurring benefits in 2012, but it did in 2005, 2010, and 2011.

most states raised the ceiling on liquid assets, and five states eliminated that test altogether.[7] Moreover, with few exceptions, states now exempt at least one vehicle from the test if it is used to meet basic needs or to transport a disabled dependent, and nineteen states exempt all vehicles when determining initial eligibility. For most of the states, the published goal of increasing asset and vehicle limits associated with TANF was to promote welfare-to-work transitions and saving among low-income households, consistent with TANF goal (b) listed in the introduction.

What set TANF apart from its predecessor was the introduction of a

---

7. The information in tables 3–5 come from the Welfare Rules Databook in Kassabian et al. (2013), which is a rich resource containing a vast amount of detail on the specific policies adopted by states over time.

host of new eligibility rules and limits. Most of the new program features evolved out of state-level experiments conducted in the early 1990s via waivers from federal regulations granted by the US Department of Health and Human Services. For example, as shown in table 4.3, thirty-two states offer formal diversion programs that steer eligible applicants away from the official caseload and instead toward a lump-sum payment, typically valued at three months of the maximum benefit for a given family size. This policy is targeted primarily to those potential cases in need of very short-term assistance, and where the adult caretaker is comparatively "job ready." In most states, diversion is voluntary, but also limited to two or three times in a lifetime, and if accepted, usually entails a period of ineligibility for the regular TANF program of three to twelve months, though in seven states the client is immediately eligible. In addition, seventeen states impose a family cap on the size of the benefit, which means that the size of the benefit is restricted in some form from increasing when a child is born into or enters a preexisting assistance unit. In most cases states do not increase the benefit at all, though there are a few exceptions. Two states (New Hampshire and North Dakota) no longer allow two-parent cases, two others impose new restrictions if the second parent is not disabled, and nine still require the additional tests under the old AFDC-UP program, that is, the hours and work history tests, and a waiting period (Kassabian et al. 2013, 20).

The policies that garnered the most attention, and controversy, were work requirements, sanctions, and time limits. Work requirements came to the fore in AFDC after passage of the Family Support Act, which mandated that adult caretakers with dependents over age three enroll in JOBS training programs. As summarized in table 4.2, the TANF law stipulated that the adult must participate in work activities, and at least half of the caseload must be engaged in thirty hours of work-related activity by FY2002 (twenty hours if there is a single parent or caretaker relative of a child under age six). These activities include, among others, unsubsidized employment, subsidized private- or public-sector employment, on-the-job training, job search and job readiness assistance (for a maximum of six weeks), community service programs, vocational educational training (twelve months maximum), and education directly related to employment for recipients without a high school diploma or equivalent. With the Deficit Reduction Act of 2005, 50 percent of all adults in a state receiving assistance in TANF, and 90 percent of two-parent households, must participate in more tightly specified and counted work activities (Parrott et al. 2007). Those percentages are lowered if TANF caseloads fall below their 2005 levels and/or the state spends on MOE in excess of their mandated 75 percent (Hahn and Frisk 2010). States have the flexibility to decide what work activities count, at how many hours per week, and whether certain persons may be exempt from work requirements. The latter most often involve those working full time in unsubsidized jobs, the elderly, the ill or incapacitated or caring for such a person, and expectant mothers in their third trimester. However, states generally may not exclude these persons when calculating their work participation rates.

Nineteen states now require some form of mandatory job search at the point of benefit application, and in fourteen of those states the sanction for noncompliance is to deny the application. Moreover, if a client is not participating in their assigned work activities, then that case generally faces sanctions, ranging from the adult being removed from the case for a fixed period of time, the family benefit being reduced by a fixed percentage, or the whole family being removed. The initial sanction in twenty states calls for full removal of the benefit and/or case closure, typically for one to three months. After repeat noncompliance, all but three states either close the case or remove the entire family from the benefit. In Idaho, Michigan, Mississippi, Pennsylvania, and Washington the latter sanction is permanent.

The TANF program imposed a maximum lifetime limit of sixty months of federal benefits for families with an adult recipient, though states have the option of imposing more stringent limits, or even extending assistance beyond the five years provided the support is out of state MOE funds. Federal law exempts child-only cases from the time limit. Table 4.4 summarizes state time-limit policies as of 2012. Thirty-four states adhere to the basic sixty-month federal policy (with some deviations, such as benefit receipt in twenty-four out of every sixty months), six limit assistance to forty-eight months, two limit to thirty-six months, and four limit to twenty-four months or less. After the federal sixty-month limit is reached, Massachusetts, New York, Vermont, and the District of Columbia offer unlimited benefits out of nonfederal funds subject to various restrictions. Moreover, five states only time limit the adult on the case and continue to provide assistance to the child-only case. States may also exempt 20 percent of their caseload from the sixty-month federal limit. The bottom panel of table 4.4 highlights that nine states have more complicated time limits, such as Nevada, which staggers twenty-four months of receipt followed by twelve months of ineligibility.

Beyond the standard income, asset, work, and time limits, many states also opted to impose additional behavioral requirements on the children or adults, or both. For example, adults may be subject to drug testing, while children may be required to maintain a minimum grade point average or attendance (thirty-six states), to receive immunizations (twenty-four states), and to receive regular health check-ups (seven states) (Kassabian et al. 2013, table III.A.1). Failure to adhere to any of these varied rules and regulations could result in sanctioning of the TANF case for noncompliance. The form of the sanction depends of the activity where the noncompliance occurs, but can entail temporary removal of the adult from the benefit allotment for several months or more, to as severe as permanent removal of the full family from the rolls.

Like most transfer programs, the basic cash benefit amount in AFDC,

Table 4.4   State lifetime TANF limits, July 2012

States	Lifetime limits
34: AK, AL, CO, HI, IA, IL, KY, LA, MD,* ME, MN, MO, MS, MT, NC, ND, NE, NH, NJ, NM, NV, OH,[a] OK, OR,* PA, SC, SD, TN, TX,* VA, WA, WI, WV, WY	60 months
6: CA,* FL, GA, KS, MI, RI	48 months
2: DE, UT	36 months
4: AR, AZ, ID, IN*	24 months
1: CT	21 months
4: DC,[b] MA, NY, VT	Unlimited; state sponsored after 60 months

	Intermittent limits
3: LA, MA, RI	24 of 60 months
1: SC	12 of 120 months
1: NV	24 months; followed by 12 months of ineligibility
1: VA	24 months; followed by 24 months of ineligibility
1: NC	24 months; followed by 36 months of ineligibility
1: OH	36 months; followed by 24 months of ineligibility
1: TX*	12/24/36 months; followed by 60 months of ineligibility

Source: Welfare Rules Databook (2014).
(For original table, see p. 166–67 of Welfare Rules Databook. State TANF policies as of July 2012.pdf.)
[a]After receiving thirty-six months of assistance, the case is closed; however, it is possible to receive twenty-four additional months of benefits if the unit has not received benefits for at least twenty-four months and can demonstrate good cause for reapplying.
[b]After sixty months, the unit remains eligible if the net income falls below the reduced-payment level. Benefits are reduced to 80 percent of the payment level for the unit size.
* Only adult benefits are terminated; otherwise, benefits are terminated for the entire unit.

and its successor TANF, is determined by the maximum benefit amount (G), the rate (t) at which the benefit is reduced as earned and unearned income (Y) increases, and the level and sources of income that can be excluded (D) from benefit determination:

$$(2) \qquad \text{Benefit} = G - t * (Y - D).$$

In the AFDC program, the maximum benefit was set at the state level, and as presented in table 4.5 there was considerable state variation in generosity, reflecting both income and cost-of-living differences and also voter preferences for redistribution (Ribar and Wilhelm 1999). This variation has continued in the TANF program. Just over half the states increased the nominal maximum guarantee since enactment of PRWORA, but even still there has been an across-the-board decline in the inflation-adjusted value of the maximum payment. As seen in the last column of table 4.5 the real

Table 4.5   AFDC/TANF maximum benefit for a three-person family by state, 1970–2012

	Jul-70[a]	Jul-75	Jul-80	Jul-85	Jan-90[b]	Jan-95[b]	Jul-01[b]	Jul-12[b]	Percent change[c]
Alabama	$65	$108	$118	$118	$118	$164	$164	$215	−30
Alaska	328	350	457	719	846	923	923	923	−41
Arizona	138	163	202	233	293	347	347	278	−58
Arkansas	89	125	161	192	204	204	204	204	−52
California	186	293	473	587	694	607	645	638	−28
Colorado	193	217	290	346	356	356	356	462	−50
Connecticut	283	346	475	569	649	680	543	576	−57
Delaware	160	221	266	287	333	338	338	338	−56
District of Columbia	195	243	286	327	409	420	379	428	−54
Florida	114	144	195	240	294	303	303	303	−44
Georgia	107	123	164	223	273	280	280	280	−45
Hawaii	226	428	468	468	602	712	570	610	−43
Idaho	211	300	323	304	317	317	293	309	−69
Illinois	232	261	288	341	367	367	377	432	−61
Indiana	120	200	255	256	288	288	288	288	−49
Iowa	201	294	360	360	410	426	426	426	−55
Kansas	222	321	345	391	409	429	429	429	−59
Kentucky	147	185	188	197	228	228	262	262	−62
Louisiana	88	128	152	190	190	190	240	240	−43
Maine	135	176	280	370	453	418	461	485	−24
Maryland	162	200	270	329	396	366	439	574	−25
Massachusetts	268	259	379	432	539	579	618	618	−51
Michigan (Wayne County)	219	333	425	417	516	459	459	492	−53
Minnesota	256	330	417	528	532	532	532	532	−56
Mississippi	56	48	96	96	120	120	170	170	−36
Missouri	104	120	248	274	289	292	292	292	−41
Montana	202	201	259	354	359	401	494	504	−47
Nebraska	171	210	310	350	364	364	364	364	−55

Nevada	121	195	262	285	330	348	348	383	−33
New Hampshire	262	308	346	389	506	550	600	675	−46
New Jersey	302	310	360	404	424	424	424	424	−70
New Mexico	149	169	220	258	264	357	389	380	−46
New York	279	332	394	474	577	577	577	770	−42
North Carolina	145	183	192	246	272	272	272	272	−60
North Dakota	213	283	334	371	386	409	477	427	−58
Ohio	161	204	263	290	334	341	373	450	−41
Oklahoma	152	217	282	282	325	324	292	292	−60
Oregon	184	337	282	386	432	460	503	506	−42
Pennsylvania	265	296	332	364	421	421	403	403	−68
Rhode Island	229	278	340	409	543	554	554	554	−49
South Carolina	85	96	129	187	206	200	203	216	−46
South Dakota	264	289	321	329	377	417	430	555	−56
Tennessee	112	115	122	153	184	185	185	185	−65
Texas	148	116	116	167	184	184	201	263	−63
Utah	175	252	360	376	387	414	474	498	−40
Vermont	267	322	492	583	662	638	629	640	−50
Virginia	225	268	310	354	354	354	320	320	−70
Washington	258	315	458	476	501	546	546	478	−61
West Virginia	114	206	206	249	249	249	453	340	−37
Wisconsin	184	342	444	533	517	517	628	608	−30
Wyoming	213	235	315	360	360	360	340	602	−40
Median State	232	279	321	401	539	645	389	427	−51

Source: For 1970–1995: Green Book (1998, tables 7–14); for 2001 and 2012: Welfare Rules Databook (2014) Table L5 Maximum Monthly Benefit for a Family of Three with No Income, 1996–2012 (July).

[a]Data on three-person families were not published or reported before 1975. Thus, the 1970 data were derived by reducing the reported four-person need standard by the proportional difference between three- and four-person AFDC need standards as shown in the July 1975 DHEW reports.

[b]CRS survey data.

[c]Real percentage change, calculated assuming a 2012 PCE value of 106.01 relative to the 1970 value of 22.325.

benefit declined from 24 to upward of 70 percent between 1970 and 2012, and for the median state it fell by 51 percent. Although the need standard under AFDC was supposed to reflect some minimum monthly threshold of income necessary to meet basic needs, most states did not tie the maximum benefit to the need standard, but instead utilized a so-called payment standard, and as of 1996, thirty states had payment standards below the need standard (Green Book 1998). And in a dozen of these states, the maximum benefit was below the payment standard. The implication is that even though the household may have passed the gross and income tests, along with the two asset tests, they may not have qualified for any positive benefit if there was a significant discrepancy between the need standard and the maximum guarantee, G. Under TANF, the need standard is no longer required by law, and only twenty states in 2012 relied on the payment standard to set the maximum, and utilized the basic formula in equation (2) for benefit determination.[8]

The statutory benefit reduction rate, t, on earned income after deductions under AFDC was cut from 100 percent to 67 percent in 1967, only to be raised back to 100 percent as part of OBRA 1981. The statutory tax rate on unearned income was also 100 percent. These tax rates were applied to net (countable) income. Earnings of most household members were counted as gross income, and likewise for nonlabor income, though several sources were exempt such as SSI and food stamps. The monthly deductions allowed included a $90 work expense disregard, followed by a disregard of $30 and one-third of remaining earnings. After four months of consecutive earnings, recipients were no longer eligible for the one-third disregard, so the disregard was simply $120. After eight additional months of consecutive earnings, recipients were no longer eligible for the $30 disregard, so the disregard was $90, after which earnings were taxed at 100 percent.

Under welfare reform most states nominally embraced the "making work pay" philosophy by expanding earnings disregards so that recipients could retain more of the monthly benefit if they worked. Table 4.6 summarizes the state disregard policy as of 2012. There it is evident that states have adopted a diverse set of policies, ranging from no disregards allowed in Arkansas and Wisconsin, to 100 percent of earnings disregarded (at least in the early months) in the case of eight states. Most, however, continue to allow recipients to deduct a flat dollar amount, and then a certain percentage of earnings thereafter. Across all jurisdictions listed in table 4.6, the average earnings disregard rate is 39 percent, and this rises to 50 percent among those with nonzero rates. This increased generosity in treatment of

8. Kassabian et al. (2013, table II.A.2) As noted on p. 94 in this document, "owing to the complexity of state programs, identifying the payment standard and maximum benefit is no longer clear. States may include multiple standards in the benefit calculation, depending on the type or amount of income."

Table 4.6   **Monthly benefit earnings disregards in TANF, July 2012**

State	Flat disregard ($)	Percent of remainder	Months applicable
Alabama	0	100	1–12
	0	20	>12[a]
Alaska	150	33	1–12
	150	25	13–24
	150	20	25–36
	150	15	37–48
	150	10	49–60
	150	0	>60
Arizona—All, except JOBSTART	90	30	All
Arizona—JOBSTART	0	100	All[b]
Arkansas	No disregards; flat grant amount		All
California	112	50	All
Colorado	0	66.7	1–12
	120	33.3	13–16
	120	0	17–24
	90	0	>24
Connecticut	0	100 up to FPL	All
Delaware	120	33.3	1–4
	120	0	5–12
	90	0	>12
District of Columbia	160	66.7	All
Florida	200	50	All
Georgia	120	33.3	1–4
	120	0	5–12
	90	0	>12
Hawaii	20%, $200	55	1–24
	20%, $200	36	>24
Idaho	0	40	All
Illinois	0	75	All
Indiana	0	75	All
Iowa	20%	58	All
Kansas	90	60	All
Kentucky	0	100	1–2[c]
	120	33.3	3–6
	120	0	7–14
	90	0	>14
Louisiana	1,020	0	1–6[d]
	120	0	>6
Maine	108	50	All
Maryland	0	40	All
Massachusetts—Nonexempt	120	50	All
Massachusetts—Exempt	120	33.3	All
Michigan	200	20	All[e]
Minnesota	0	38	All
Mississippi	0	100	1–6
	90	0	>6

(continued)

Table 4.6   (continued)

State	Flat disregard ($)	Percent of remainder	Months applicable
Missouri	90	66.7	1–12
	90	0	>12
Montana	200	25	All
Nebraska	0	20	All
Nevada	0	100	1–3
	0	85	4–6
	0	75	7–9
	0	65	10–12
	max($90, 20%)	0	>12
New Hampshire	0	50	All
New Jersey	0	100	1
	0	75	2–7
	0	50[f]	>7
New Mexico	125	50	All[g]
New York	90	50	All
North Carolina	0	100	1–3[h]
	0	27.5	>3
North Dakota	max($180, 27%)	50	1–6
	max($180, 27%)	35	7–9
	max($180, 27%)	25	10–13
	max($180, 27%)	0	>13
Ohio	250	50	All
Oklahoma	240	50	All[i]
Oregon	0	50	All
Pennsylvania	0	50	All
Rhode Island	170	50	All
South Carolina	0	50	1–4[j]
	100	0	>4
South Dakota	90	20	All
Tennessee	250	0	All[k]
Texas	120	90 (up to $1,400)	4 out of 12 months[l]
	120	0	>4 out of 12[l]
Utah	100	50	All
Vermont	200	25	All[m]
Virginia	147	20	All[n]
Washington	0	50	All
West Virginia	0	40	All
Wisconsin	No disregards; flat grant amount.		All
Wyoming	200	0	All[o]

Source: Welfare Rules Databook (2014). Table L4. Earned Income Disregards for Benefit Computation, 1996–2012 (July) or table II.A.1. Earned Income Disregards for Benefit Computation, July 2012, or table II.A.2 Benefit Determination Policies, July 2012.

Notes: The table describes benefit computation disregards for recipients. If the disregards differ for applicants, it is footnoted.

[a]The earned income disregard cannot be applied to the earnings of an individual receiving assistance beyond the sixtieth month under an exemption or extension.

Table 4.6   (continued)

[b]In addition to the 100 percent disregard of all subsidized JOBSTART wages, recipients can disregard the standard $90 and 30 percent of the remainder for any non-JOBSTART earned income.

[c]Recipients are eligible for the one-time 100 percent disregard if they become newly employed or report increased wages acquired after approval.

[d]The six months in which the extra $900 is disregarded need not be consecutive, but the recipient may use this extra disregard in no more than six months over the course of his or her lifetime.

[e]At application to determine initial eligibility, 20 percent disregard is used. Once determined eligible and for ongoing benefits, a 50 percent disregard is used for benefit computation.

[f]These disregards apply to individuals working twenty or more hours a week. Individuals employed fewer than twenty hours a week may disregard 100 percent in the first month of employment and 50 percent thereafter. However, if an individual's hours increase to twenty hours during the first six months, he or she may disregard 75 percent for the remainder of the six-month period. The 100 percent disregard is only applicable once every twelve months, even if employment is lost and then regained.

[g]Two-parent units may disregard $225 and 50 percent of the remainder.

[h]The 100 percent disregard is available only once in a lifetime and may be received only if the recipient is newly employed at a job that is expected to be permanent for more than twenty hours a week.

[i]These disregards apply to individuals working full time, defined as twenty hours a week for recipients caring for a child under age six and thirty hours a week for all other recipients. Individuals working less than full time may disregard $120 and 50 percent of the remainder.

[j]The 50 percent disregard is available only once in a lifetime and may only be applied to consecutive months.

[k]If a parent marries while receiving assistance, the unit may choose to exclude the new spouse from the unit for three months. At the end of the three-month period, however, the new spouse becomes a mandatory member of the assistance unit, and his or her income is counted in benefit computation calculations.

[l]Once the recipient has received four months (they need not be consecutive) of the 90 percent disregard, he or she is not eligible to receive the disregard again until the TANF case has been denied and remains denied for one full month, and twelve calendar months have passed since the denial. The twelve-month ineligibility period begins with the first full month of denial after the client used the fourth month of the 90 percent disregard. The earnings of a TANF recipient's new spouse are disregarded for six months if the total gross income of the budget group does not exceed 200 percent of the federal poverty level.

[m]These disregards apply to recipients with income from unsubsidized employment or a combination of subsidized and unsubsidized employment. For recipients with earnings from subsidized employment only, the disregard is $90.

[n]The disregard varies by family size; for one to three family members, the disregard is $147. For four members, the disregard is $155; for five members, the disregard is $181; and for six or more family members, the disregard is $208.

[o]Married couples with a child in common may disregard $400.

earnings was tempered by the decision to retain statutory benefit-reduction rates of 100 percent. In fact, for seven states the benefit was set at a fraction of the difference between the need (or payment) standard and net income; for example, South Carolina only awards 28.1 percent of the difference.

Research by Lurie (1974), Hutchens (1978), Fraker, Moffitt, and Wolf (1985), McKinnish, Sanders, and Smith (1999), and Ziliak (2007) indicated that the "effective" (or average marginal) tax rate that AFDC recipients faced was generally only 40–50 percent of the statutory rate. This gap between statutory and effective rates could be the result of cross-state variation in disregards stemming from state policy choices, by caseworker discretion and/or error, or by shifting composition of income among recipients. Under

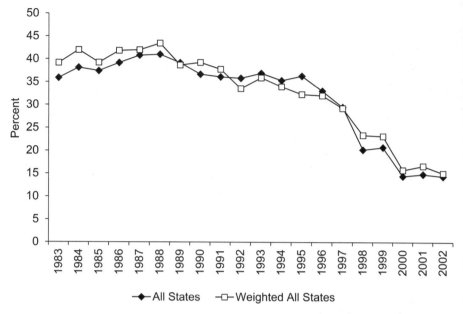

Fig. 4.1   Effective AFDC/TANF earned income tax rates, 1983–2002
Source: Ziliak (2007).

AFDC states did not have the option of setting disregard standards absent a waiver from federal rules, and thus the latter two reasons likely account for most of the statutory-effective gap. As depicted in figure 4.1, after passage of PRWORA the effective rate fell by half in the first five years, whether one considers the rate in terms of the average state (unweighted) or the average recipient (weighted by number of AFDC/TANF recipients). Ziliak (2007) shows that the reduction in these rates were most pronounced among the states that adopted the most aggressive welfare reform policies, suggesting that the observed decline in effective rates reflected state policy.

4.3   Program Statistics

Figure 4.2 presents the time series of expenditure on the AFDC/TANF program from its inception in 1936 until 2012.[9] Real spending, based on the 2012 Personal Consumption Expenditure Deflator, surged from $6.8 billion in 1960 to $23.8 billion in 1970. Moffitt (1987) showed that while part of this growth is attributable to the growth of female-headed families, rising maximum benefit guarantees, and declines in the benefit reduction rate in

9. The figure reports actual spending, and does not include the transfers out of the federal TANF grant to CCDF and SSBG allowed after 1996.

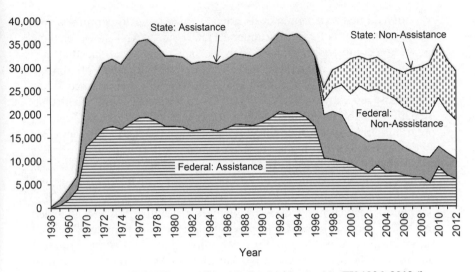

Fig. 4.2   The AFDC/TANF expenditures by level and category, FY 1936–2012 (in millions of 2012 dollars)

1967, the lion's share is unexplained by economic forces. The leading non-economic explanations include possible shifts in cultural attitudes toward welfare, and a series of court orders that liberalized access to welfare for cohabiting couples, along with passage of the Civil Rights Act of 1964 that forbade discrimination in the allocation of federal funds, including access to welfare among African Americans (Gordon and Batlan 2011). Real spending increased another $12 billion to $36 billion in 1977, but then subsequently fell by about $5 billion over the next five years, first from a growing economy in the late 1970s, and then tightening of eligibility and benefit rules with OBRA 1981. Real spending flatlined for the rest of the 1980s, until the run up in spending from 1990–1993, which we will see below was in response to a strong surge in caseloads. With the strong economy, implementation of welfare waivers, and then welfare reform, expenditures fell by one-third in the three-year period after 1994. After that, total spending rebounded by 2000 and then more or less remained flat, though there was a temporary increase in FY2010 when emergency TANF spending of $5 billion was made available as part of the American Recovery and Reinvestment Act of 2009 (ARRA). Real total spending in 2012 of $28.9 billion lies in between the amount spent between 1971 and 1972, which is in stark contrast to all other programs in the social safety net that saw significant growth in real spending over the past four decades (Bitler and Hoynes 2010; Moffitt and Scholz 2010; Ziliak 2015).

The other aspect of figure 4.2 that stands in stark contrast with the past is the shifting composition of spending from cash assistance to in-kind non-assistance after welfare reform. Although not delineated in the figure as it was not recorded on a regular basis, nonassistance typically comprised one-fourth to one-third of spending under AFDC. Under TANF, however, there has been a complete reversal. As early as 2000, one-half of spending was directed to assistance and the other half to nonassistance, and by the end of the decade two-thirds of spending was in the form of nonassistance. While states must generally use TANF dollars to support needy families with children, they are able to set different criteria for assistance versus nonassistance programs, and as such often direct nonassistance funds to a broader cross section of families (i.e., higher income), suggesting the program may be less target efficient. Indeed, federal and state cash assistance continued its secular decline, even through the Great Recession (except for FY2010) and total spending was propped up only by nonassistance spending via state MOE.

Figure 4.3 depicts how federal TANF and state MOE funds were allocated in FY2012. Only 36 percent was spent on basic assistance and work-related activities, in contrast to the 59 percent reported for FY1999 in figure 5.4 of Moffitt (2003). Moreover, 8 percent of funds were transferred out to TANF to the CCDBG and SSBG, about 12 percent of funds were allocated to childcare (most in the form of nonassistance subsidies), another

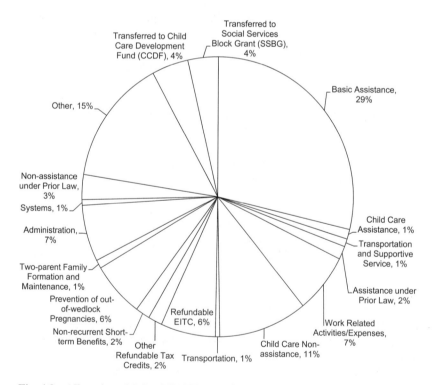

Fig. 4.3   Allocation of federal TANF and state maintenance of effort funds, FY2012

8 percent were allocated to refundable EITC and child tax credits, 7 percent to address goals (c) and (d) of TANF to reduce out-of-wedlock pregnancy and encourage two-parent families, and a sizable 15 percent of funds were allocated to "other." This catch-all category includes child welfare payments and services, early childhood education, counseling for domestic violence, mental health, and addiction, and TANF program expenses, among others (OFA 2013).

Figures 4.4A and 4.4B shed some light into the trends underlying spending by depicting the evolution of TANF caseloads and recipients from 1960 to 2013.[10] Also reported are the fraction of total cases and fraction of total recipients that are designated as children. This is important because child-only cases are not subject to federal time limits and work requirements. The trends in spending in figure 4.2 track closely the trends in caseloads and recipients in figures 4.4A and 4.4B from 1960 until 1997, but whereas total spending rebounded and then remained relatively stable in real terms in the ensuing decade, caseloads continued to decline. The disconnect stems from the fact that post-TANF states are only required to report the number of cases and recipients receiving assistance, and not the number of persons served in nonassistance. This inhibits greatly our ability to evaluate welfare reform. Most researchers and members of the policy and advocacy communities hone in on the caseload trends, but this ignores the fact that scores of individuals also receive help in the form of nonassistance and do not show up in the caseload counts. Also of note in figure 4.4A is the fourfold increase in the fraction of cases that are child only from 10 percent in 1990 to over 40 percent in 2013. This has led to a "return to normal" in terms of the composition of recipients to about 75 percent children found in the 1960s.

The aggregate caseload trends mask some important heterogeneity in state experiences. For example, in the mid-to-late 1980s aggregate AFDC caseloads held fairly steady, but as documented in Ziliak (2002), this overlooks the fact that nearly half the states experienced declines in caseloads, and the other half experienced increases, such that in the aggregate they cancelled out. Figure 4.5 presents maps depicting caseload change in the welfare reform era, first from 1993 to 2000, and then from 2000 to 2013. In the boom years of the late 1990s, most states had declines of 50 percent or more in caseloads, with Hawaii the lone state to see an increase in caseloads. Over the last decade, however, there is greater divergence across states. Oregon and Maine, for example, had an increase in caseloads of 120 percent or more, while Illinois and Texas had declines of over 70 percent. To be certain, what is most notable in the bottom panel of figure 4.5 is the vast majority of states had declines in cash assistance during a very weak economic period, in sharp contrast to the huge increase in food stamp usage.

---

10. The figure includes participants in separate state programs starting in FY2000. The SSPs contribute only 5.8 percent to the total caseload in an average year.

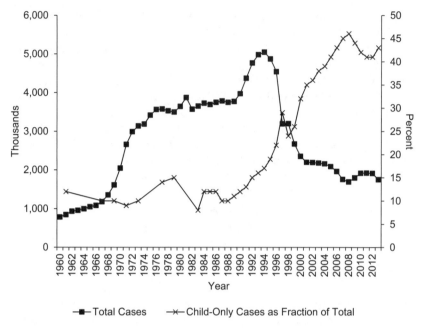

Fig. 4.4A Trends in total and child-only AFDC/TANF caseloads, 1960–2013

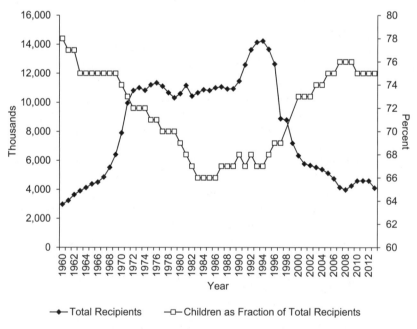

Fig. 4.4B Trends in total and child AFDC/TANF recipients, 1960–2013

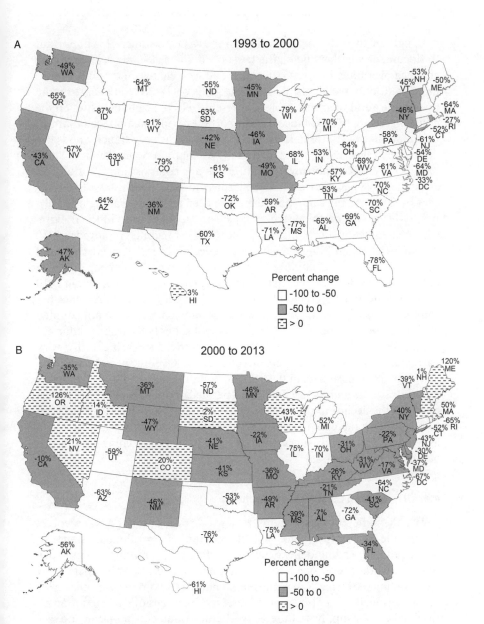

Fig. 4.5 Change in AFDC/TANF caseloads by state

Sources: University of Kentucky Center for Poverty Research http://www.ukcpr.org/AvailableData.aspx>; caseload figures are population adjusted. (For original data, see "TANF_map_data_UKCPR_ACF-OFA.xlsx".)

In light of the substantial declines in the cash assistance, it is important to document whether the characteristics of the caseload recipients have changed over time. Figure 4.4 depicted one such change in the shift toward more child-only recipients. Because the goals of TANF were geared more toward the adult recipient, table 4.7 presents selected characteristics on the adults in receipt of assistance. It is important to once again recall that this information is only available for those receiving cash assistance, and is not necessarily reflective of the entire adult caseload on nonassistance. There has been a marked downward shift in the age composition of adults on assistance—48 percent were under age thirty in 1996, but this rose to 59 percent by 2010. At the same time there has been a skill upgrading of adults twenty-five years and older with a 6 percentage point drop in the fraction who are high school dropouts. While the fraction of adults employed in 2010 is double the rate in 1996, there has been a decline over the past decade, and since the fraction of unemployed fell as well, there is now a higher percentage not in the labor force. Note that the employment rate of 22 percent in 2010 seems low given the presence of nominal 50 percent work requirements, but some activities that count toward work-requirement goals are not counted as "employment," and in FY2010 thirty-eight states had earned a sufficient number of so-called caseload-reduction credits to reduce their effective work participation rates below 25 percent (OFA 2013). Over the past decade there has been an increase both in the fraction of adults that are married or never married, and a decline in the fraction separated or divorced. Perhaps consistent with the decline in the average age of an adult recipient, there has been a concomitant increase in the fraction of children under age one receiving assistance. Both trends suggest that cash assistance is reaching a more vulnerable population today.

4.4   Research on the TANF Program

The thematic emphasis of my review of research on TANF revolves around the four statutory goals of the program of providing assistance to needy families, ending dependence on welfare by promoting job preparation and work, preventing and reducing out-of-wedlock pregnancies, and encouraging the formation of and maintenance of two-parent families. This necessarily leads to a discussion of research on program participation and caseloads, labor supply, welfare-to-work transitions, consumption and saving, health, fertility, child well-being, and marriage. Initially Congress was clearly most interested in ending dependence and promoting work with the emphasis on caseload reductions, work requirements, and time limits, but by the time TANF was reauthorized in DRA 2005, there was heightened interest among some on the secondary goals of out-of-wedlock pregnancies and healthy marriage.

While many of the issues overlap that of the AFDC program, the details

Table 4.7   Selected characteristics of TANF families, 1996–2010

	1996	2000	2005	2010
Age of adult recipients, percent[a]				
Under 20	5.8	7.1	7.3	7.9
20–29	42.3	42.5	47.1	51.3
30–39	35.3	32.1	28.1	25.4
40–49	16.6*	14.7	14.2	12.1
Over 49		3.6	3.2	3.3
Percent adults > = 25 with less than HS education[b]	18.3	15.9	14.8	12.9
Other assistance[c]				
Living in public housing	8.8	17.7	18.4	13.1
Receiving SNAP or donated food	89.3	79.9	81.5	82.4
Employment status, percent of adults[c]				
Employed	11.1	26.4	23.2	22.3
Unemployed	—	49.2	50.4	46.8
Not in the labor force	—	24.3	26.4	30.9
Marital status, percent of adults[c]				
Single	—	65.3	68.8	70.0
Married	—	12.4	10.7	14.4
Separated	—	13.1	11.8	9.6
Widowed	—	0.7	0.6	0.5
Divorced	—	8.5	8.1	5.5
Family size[c]	2.8	2.6	2.4	2.4
Percent child-only families[c]	—	32.7	42.6	44.0
Percent whose youngest child is:[d]				
Ages 1–2	24.7	20.3	20.3	23.0
Under age 1	10.6	13.6	14.5	14.8

Source: USDHHS (2014) and Characteristics and Financial Circumstances of TANF Recipients (online).

[a]USDHHS (2014, table IND 3a). "Number and Percentage of the Total Population Receiving AFDC/ TANF by Age: 1970–2011."

[b]USDHHS (2014, table WORK 4). "Percentage of Adults Ages 25 and over by Level of Educational Attainment: Selected Years."

[c]USDHHS (2014, table TANF 7). "Characteristics of AFDC/TANF Families: Selected Years 1969—2011."

[d]Administration for Children and Families, Office of Family Assistance, Characteristics and Financial Circumstances of TANF Recipients (data inflated by fraction of nonmissing). (http://archive.acf.hhs.gov /programs/ofa/character/.) (Date accessed: June 24, 2014).

*Data in this year is only available for age groups 40–45 and >45, so this figure represents > = 40.

Suggested citations:

US Department of Health and Human Services (2014). Administration for Children and Families, Office of Family Assistance, Characteristics and Financial Circumstances of TANF Recipients (http://archive .acf.hhs.gov/programs/ofa/character/) (Date accessed: June 24, 2014).

For original tables from the 13th Annual Report to Congress, see "13th TANF Report to Congress. Welfare indicators and risk factors (2014).pdf".

For original tables from AFC-OFA online, see url links below:

Table 11. AFDC Families by age of the youngest child in the assistance unit (http://archive.acf.hhs.gov /programs/ofa/character/FY96/AX11.PDF).

Table I-32. Temporary Assistance for Needy Families—Active Cases—Percent Distribution of TANF Youngest Child Recipient by Age Group, October 1999—September 2000 (http://archive.acf.hhs.gov /programs/ofa/character/FY2000/132.htm).

Table 34. Temporary Assistance for Needy Families—Active Cases—Percent Distribution of TANF Youngest Child Recipient by Age Group, October 2004—September 2005 (http://archive.acf.hhs.gov /programs/ofa/character/FY2005/tab18.htm).

Table 34. Temporary Assistance for Needy Families—Active Cases—Percent Distribution of TANF Youngest Child Recipient by Age FY2010 (http://www.acf.hhs.gov/sites/default/files/ofa/appendix_ys _final.pdf).

of the behavioral models under TANF necessarily differ because of programmatic reforms, especially those policies that affect decisions over time such as work requirements, time limits, and expanded asset tests. Moffitt (1992, 2003) provides a comprehensive review of the AFDC models, and thus I first review the underlying behavioral issues within the general TANF paradigm, followed by a survey of results. Organizing the behavioral issues within the context of the TANF goals necessarily leads to some subjective decisions. For example, I discuss child support and childcare under goal (d) on two-parent families, along with child well-being, though these could equally fall under goals (a) and (b) as policies designed to foster work and reduce dependence.

4.4.1   Review of Behavioral Issues

Because the goals of TANF aspire to affect a wide array of family outcomes, and the various requirements and incentives that underlie those goals affect budget constraints over time, I begin with a life-cycle model under uncertainty. Although much of the research on the TANF program has been in reduced form, there have been some important developments in structural models (Swann 2005; Keane and Wolpin 2002a, 2002b, 2010; Chan 2013) that followed on the heels of prior static models of AFDC (Moffitt 1983; Hoynes 1996; Keane and Moffitt 1998), and this section relies on this paradigm as an organizing framework. This is useful because it offers the chance to highlight where and how the program is likely to affect decision making over time. Because TANF is restricted to households with dependent children, and historically most adult caretakers have been single women, it is standard to specify the model from the perspective of the mother as the householder, and I follow the literature in this modeling approach.

Specifically, consider a model whereby in each period the woman chooses consumption of medical (S_t) and nonmedical (C_t) goods and services, whether to work and how much (N_t), whether to join TANF (P_t), whether to have a child (F_t), and whether to marry (M_t) in order to maximize the present discounted value of uncertain utility defined over nonmedical spending, leisure (L_t), and the stock of health (H_t). The dynamic optimization problem facing the woman is

$$(3) \qquad V\left(A_t, K_t, H_t\right) = U\left(C_t, L_t, P_t, F_t, M_t, H_t\right) + \beta E_t\left[V_{t+1}\right],$$

where K_t is the stock of human capital; $\beta = 1/(1 + \rho)$ is the discount factor based on rate of time preference (ρ); and E_t is the time t expectations operator reflecting uncertainty over future income, fertility, marriage, and health. Similar to the health model of Grossman (1972), there is no direct utility from medical spending, only indirectly via its effect on the stock of health.

Income comes from four potential sources: interest income on the prior period assets ($r_t A_t$), where r_t is a time t interest rate on composite assets; labor earnings ($w_t N_t$), where w_t is the before-tax hourly wage rate; nonwelfare, nonlabor income, $Y_t(M_t)$, that is a function of marital status and thus may include the earnings of the spouse or other household members; and welfare benefits $\text{TANF}_t(f_t(a_t),F_t,w_tN_t,N_t,Y(M_t),r_tA_t,A_t)$, which are a function of the current size and age structure of the family ($f_t(a_t)$), fertility, labor and non-labor income (including interest income), work, and the stock of assets. Age-adjusted family size and fertility are important as they potentially affect the size of the maximum benefit guarantee and also lead to study of time limits and family caps. Earnings and nonlabor income enter because of the limits for eligibility, and likewise for the stock of assets. This presents opportunities for research on how benefit reduction rates, earnings disregards, and income and asset tests affect the decisions to work, consume, save, and participate. Moreover, work enters separately from earnings to capture the influence of work requirements and training programs.

Income can be spent on nonmedical consumption at price p_t^C, on medical services at the price p_t^S, on tax payments that are assessed to earned and unearned income (but not welfare) and that are affected by the age and size of the family via credits and deductions $R_t \equiv R(w_tN_t,Y(M_t),r_tA_t;f_t(a_t))$, or the income can be saved and carried forward to the next period. Consumption is adjusted by an adult equivalence scale, $e(f_t(a_t))$, to reflect that there are potential economies to scale within the household. The resulting asset accumulation constraint is:

$$(4)\quad A_{t+1} = (1+r_t)\left(A_t + w_tN_t + Y(M_t) + P_t * \text{TANF}_t - \frac{p_t^C C_t}{e(f_t(a_t))} - \frac{p_t^S S_t}{e(f_t(a_t))} - R_t \right).$$

In the ensuing subsections I elaborate on the model and how it can be modified to address specific policies of interest. For parsimony, I do not spell out all possible state variables and instead focus on those most relevant to focal research questions.

Goal 1. To Provide Assistance to Needy Families: Income and Asset Tests

The first goal of TANF is to support needy families, and as such I initially examine how the basic eligibility structure of the benefit—notably income and asset tests—affects the decision to participate in the program. Specifically, based on the model above, the decision to participate in TANF in period t occurs if and only if

$$(5)\quad P_t^* = V\left(A_t,K_t,H_t \mid P_t = 1\right) - V\left(A_t,K_t,H_t \mid P_t = 0\right) > 0,$$

which says that the family participates in TANF if the value from participation exceeds that obtained from nonparticipation. Implicit in the calculation are the costs of participation that come in the form of time and money (e.g., queuing for benefits and thus missing work) and psychic costs such as stigma (Moffitt 1983). The family must be needy as determined by the gross and net income tests, and the liquid and vehicle asset tests, which implies that the decision to participate is made jointly with work, consumption, fertility, and marriage decisions.

To begin, assume that fertility, marriage, and health are exogenous and thus taken as given. This is consistent with most static models of labor supply and welfare participation, and permits us to focus on the benefit structure. In the presence of income and asset limits that vary by state of residence k in time t the benefit formula for family i can be written as

$$(6) \qquad \text{TANF}_{ikt} = G_{ikt} - t_{kt}\left(w_{it}N_{it} + r_t A_{it} + Y_{it} - D_{ikt}\right)$$

$$w_{it}N_{it} + r_t A_{it} + Y_{it} < Y_{kt}^{\text{gross}}$$

$$w_{it}N_{it} + r_t A_{it} + Y_{it} - D_{ikt} < Y_{kt}^{\text{net}}$$

$$A_{it} < A_{kt}^{lim}$$

$$\text{Car}_{it} < \text{Car}_{kt}^{lim}$$

where the maximum guarantee (G_{ikt}) varies by family size within a given state and year, and labor income, interest income, and other nonlabor income are all subject to benefit taxation (t_{kt}) after deductions that vary by family, state, and year (D_{ikt}). In order to qualify, gross income must be below the state-specific gross limit, net income must be below the net limit, the stock of liquid wealth must be below the state-specific limit, and the market value of the car (Car_{it}) must be below a separate state-specific limit. Notably, states have discretion in whether to count the EITC as nonlabor income (or a resource) in determining the size of the benefit. Most do not count it as income, though most do count it as a resource after several months.

In the absence of TANF (and taxation) and other interest and nonlabor income, the within-period budget line facing the mother is depicted in figure 4.6 as the line segment $\overline{ae}$. The slope of this segment is the real gross hourly wage rate, $-(w_{it}/p_t^C)$. With TANF, along with a 100 percent benefit-reduction rate and no deductions, the budget constraint facing the mother is the line $\overline{Gbe}$. If the mother does not work and thus has zero net income, she qualifies for the maximum benefit, G. If she combines welfare and work along segment $\overline{Gb}$ then her TANF benefit is reduced dollar for dollar. Once she reaches point b, her benefit is zero, and earnings above this point make her ineligible and she returns to her original budget line. As noted previously, all states except Arkansas and Wisconsin have set $t_{kt} = 1$; however, with the exception of the latter two states, all allow earnings deductions of some form. Arkansas and Wisconsin each offer a flat grant amount that goes to zero once the family reaches the income limit in the state, which creates a "notch" in the budget line $\overline{dd'}$. In those two states, TANF has a pure nonlabor income effect of reducing the incentive to work when moving from segment $\overline{ad'}$ to segment $\overline{Gd}$, and can produce jump discontinuities for those located on $\overline{d'b}$ akin to that found in Medicaid. The more typical scenario is similar to that facing a mother in California where the first $112 per month are disregarded—

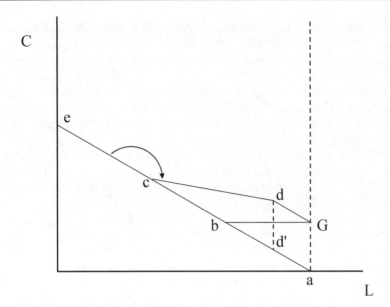

Fig. 4.6   Static budget constraint under TANF

segment $\overline{Gd}$—and thereafter 50 percent of earnings is disregarded along segment $\overline{dc}$ until she reaches the state's income limit. Even though the statutory benefit-reduction rate is 100 percent, the effective rate in California is half that amount so that for each dollar earned the benefit only declines by 0.5. Variations on this schedule are found in most states, which helps account for the trend decline in effective rates shown in figure 4.1. However, whether this wedge between statutory and effective tax rates stimulates labor supply is not known a priori because of potentially offsetting substitution and income effects among the eligibles. Moreover, the lower effective tax rate makes previously ineligible persons along segment $\overline{bc}$ newly eligible, and in this case the substitution and income effects work in tandem to reduce the incentive to work on the margin. The nonconvexity of the budget constraint Gdc also opens up the possibility that workers just above the income limit at point c may reduce effort and join the program. Of course, once one layers additional transfer programs on top of TANF, some of which may interact with TANF such as food stamps, the budget constraint becomes considerably more complex (Moffitt 2015).

Cash assistance in TANF offers families insurance against income shocks, which means that there is a consumption floor, $\underline{C}$, below which spending will not fall. In a model with uncertainty, this floor on consumption can then result in a reduced need to self-insure for precautionary reasons. Moreover, the explicit limits placed on liquid and vehicle assets may also discourage families from saving (Hubbard, Skinner, and Zeldes 1995; Powers 1998;

Ziliak 2003; Hurst and Ziliak 2006). Both of these effects can lead to "over-consumption" and suboptimal asset accumulation over the life cycle.

To see the possible implications of the consumption floor on intertemporal consumption choice, consider a simple two-period model in figure 4.7. Ignoring equivalence scales and setting the price of consumption to 1, the mother will choose to consume more in periods with low interest rates, and thus the trade-off between current and future consumption is reflected by the budget segment $\overline{adb}$ with slope $-(1 + r)$. Suppose that in period 1 the mother has no assets at the start of the period and her only source of income out of which to consume is labor earnings, $w_1 N_1$. She is notified at the start of the first period that with certainty she will be laid off at the end of the period. In the absence of welfare, her optimal consumption choice is found at point c*, which means that $C_1 < w_1 N_1$ and she will carry savings forward to period 2 so that $C_2 = (1 + r)(w_1 N_1 - C_1)$. Now suppose that TANF is available that offers a consumption floor $\underline{C}$ for those with low earnings. In period 1 her earnings are too high to be eligible, but with no earnings in period 2 she is income eligible. This implies that instead of a potential decline in income flow in period 2 of $(r^*(w_1 N_1 - C_1)/w_1 N_1) - 1)$ percent, it only falls by $(r^*[(w_1 N_1 - C_1) + \text{TANF}_2]/w_1 N_1) - 1)$ percent. However, suppose that TANF also imposes asset limits that make the mother categorically ineligible in period 2 if the stock of wealth $(A_2 = (w_1 N_1 - C_1))$ is too high. This asset limit creates incentives to consume more in period 1 than otherwise would be the case in the absence of the limit, and thus the mother may instead opt for point c** in figure 4.7. In the more general case of uncertainty over earnings,

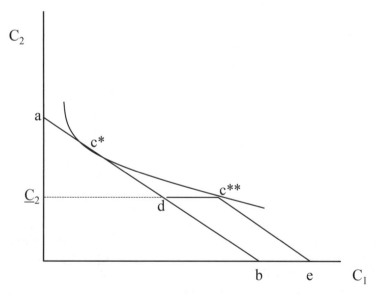

Fig. 4.7   Effect of consumption floor and asset tests on intertemporal consumption

say because of employment volatility over the business cycle, the life-cycle model predicts that the mother will self-insure in order to protect against an income shock. However, the presence of $\underline{C}_2$ reduces the need to save for precautionary reasons, and the presence of the asset test only serves to reinforce that disincentive to save.[11]

State policy choices before and after welfare reform may have further affected the intertemporal consumption and saving decision. For the better part of three decades most states have allowed the real value of the maximum benefit to erode (see table 4.5), which means that in figure 4.7 $\underline{C}_2$ has shifted down toward the origin, reducing consumption insurance and making c** suboptimal compared to c*. At the same time states liberalized asset tests (see table 4.3), including six states that eliminated it altogether, which means the mother is no longer indifferent between c* and c** because c** results in too low of saving. On top of this there is a potentially important interaction between the asset tests and income tests. Under uncertainty and a 100 percent benefit-reduction rate, if the mother knows that any dollar carried over from one period to the next results in a dollar for dollar reduction in benefits then there is little value in saving in the event that she needs to join the program. After PRWORA the statutory tax rate on interest income remains 100 percent, and most states do not provide exemptions to this saving unless it is in a certain class (e.g., Individual Development Accounts are untaxed in most states). However, Ziliak (2007) shows that the effective tax rate on unearned income plummeted after welfare reform, suggesting that there might be more exemptions than official policy would dictate. Moreover, as depicted in figure 4.6 and detailed in table 4.6, most states increased earnings disregards, making higher-income (and wealth) individuals potentially eligible for benefits. Taken together—lower real guarantees, higher asset limits, and higher earning disregards—all suggest that saving and the asset position of the typical mother on welfare should be higher in TANF than under AFDC.

Goal 2. To End Dependence on Welfare: Human Capital,
Work Requirements, and Time Limits

The second goal of TANF is to end dependence on welfare by promoting job preparation and work, and to achieve this goal states shifted TANF resources away from cash assistance and toward in-kind job training and other basic skills training, and at the direction of Congress, established work requirements and time limits. What activities count as work related varies greatly across states and time, but most states allow at least ten hours of

11. The fact that interest income gets taxed by the TANF program also creates a time non-separability in the household budget constraint, complicating identification and estimation of consumption and labor supply choice. This has not been addressed in the welfare literature, though see Blomquist (1985) for theoretical treatment and Ziliak and Kniesner (1999) for estimates in the general case of income taxation.

weekly education and training to count toward the established work-related activity requirement (Kassabian et al. 2013, table III.B.2). Moreover, a typical guideline is that nonexempt adult caretakers are required to work at least thirty hours per week as soon as possible after entering the system, and no later than after twenty-four months of benefit receipt.

In the static model of labor supply, minimum work requirements are generally expected to increase aggregate hours among the adult welfare population. Take, for example, a nonexempt single mother with two children living in California in 2012. The budget constraint facing the family is depicted in figure 4.8, under the assumption that there is no other nonlabor income. California offers a $638 maximum monthly guarantee, a fixed monthly earnings disregard of $112, and a variable earnings disregard of 50 percent that makes the effective benefit-reduction rate (brr) 50 percent. This means that the "break-even" income level—the point at which income eligibility stops—is $1,388 per month (= $638/0.5 + 112). California requires a minimum of thirty-two hours of work activity per week, or 128 hours per month. This means that anything to the right of N_{min} is infeasible if she wishes to be on the program. The state minimum wage in 2012 was $8 per hour, so that if the mother has a minimum-wage job and works the mandated thirty-two hours per week her monthly earnings are $1,024. She is income eligible for TANF and qualifies for a benefit of $182 per month. However, if she earns above $10.84 per hour and meets the work requirement by spending all her hours in paid employment then she is income ineligible. If she works forty hours per week then the maximum wage she can receive is $8.67 per hour

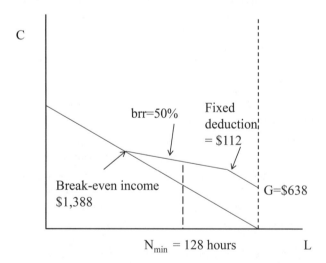

Fig. 4.8   **Work requirements under TANF for single mother with two kids in California as of 2012**

in 2012. The implication then is that if the mother is not exempt from work requirements then only very low-wage workers are eligible for TANF, and if they sign up for the program then aggregate hours of work will increase under the work requirement. However, if they do not sign up, but enter the labor force, then we again would expect aggregate labor supply to rise. The exception to this prediction could occur if a sizable fraction do not join TANF and do not work—so-called disconnected mothers—then it is less clear whether the state will realize higher labor supply under work requirements (Turner, Danziger, and Seefeldt 2006).

Because the goal of reducing dependence brings time to the forefront, the life-cycle model can provide additional insight into how work requirements might affect labor supply choice over time. The key modeling decision is whether to characterize subsidized and/or unsubsidized work, as well as job training and education programs, as "learning-by-doing" skill formation as in Weiss (1972) or as "on-the-job training" as in Ben Porath (1967). As elucidated in Heckman, Lochner, and Cossa (2003) the distinction between the two models is important to our understanding of the effects of policies like work requirements (their application was to the EITC). In the Weiss model, training and work are complements because skill is acquired by virtue of doing your job. Following Shaw (1989), suppose we specify the observed wage (w_t) as the product of a human capital stock (K_t) and the unobserved rental rate on human capital (q_t), $w_t = q_t K_t$. In each period the mother inherits a stock of human capital that depreciates at rate δ_K. New investment occurs on the job through learning by doing that depends on hours worked and the level of human capital, $x(N_t K_t)$. Human capital evolves according to the law of motion

(7) $$K_{t+1} = (1 - \delta_K) K_t + x(N_t, K_t),$$

and using the wage equation to replace the capital stock in equation (7) yields

(8) $$\frac{w_{t+1}}{q_{t+1}} = (1 - \delta_K) \frac{w_t}{q_t} + x\left(N_t, \frac{w_t}{q_t}\right).$$

Equation (8) shows that wages tomorrow are a function of wages today along with new human capital investment. The introduction of work requirements pulls nonworkers into the labor force (assuming they remain on TANF), and work today feeds directly into higher wages tomorrow. That is, work requirements create a nonseparability in the lifetime budget constraint in the learning-by-doing model. Returning to figure 4.8, note that if the mother would choose to work N_{min} in the absence of TANF, then the introduction of TANF will reduce labor supply and skill formation both from the income effect induced by the provision of the transfer and the substitution effect given that the marginal wage rate in TANF is $0.5*w$. Thus, work requirements only lead to higher future wages for those induced to work more in the current period in the learning-by-doing model.

In the standard Ben Porath model, work and skill formation are substitutes in the current period because each hour in training implies a forgone hourly wage. That is, in equation (7) we replace N_t with $(1 - n_t/N_t)$, where n_t/N_t is the fraction of time spent in training. Increasing the amount of time in training reduces the fraction of time in work. If the mother would choose N_{min} in the absence of the work requirement, then introducing TANF with the requirement will make training relatively more attractive. This is because the opportunity cost of training is lower under TANF due to the 50 percent benefit-reduction rate lowering the net wage compared to the no-TANF constraint. Moreover, if this human capital development generates higher future wages placing the mother above the break-even income level, then training is that much more attractive. Whether and to what extent work requirements are complements or substitutes hinges on the state of residence and the extent to which training substitutes for work. For example, in Utah if the children are at least six years old then the mother is required to work thirty hours per week, ten of which may be in the form of education. This means that two-thirds of the work requirement is complementary with work, and one-third rivalrous. If the children are under age six then the work requirement is twenty hours per week and all hours must be spent in work and thus training is complementary via learning by doing.

Like work requirements, the study of time limits is most conducive in the life-cycle framework. As noted in table 4.4, the federal lifetime limit for benefits is five years, though in eighteen states the limit is either less than five years and/or clients face intermittent limits prior to reaching the maximum. As a consequence the timing of work and benefit receipt is closely linked to the age composition of the children in the family, and ultimately, fertility decisions (Grogger and Michalopoulos 2003; Swann 2005; Chan 2013). The value function in equation (3) now must be modified to include a fourth state variable, the stock of years on welfare, D_t, that evolves as

$$(9) \qquad\qquad D_t = D_{t-1} + P(a_t),$$

where D_{t-1} denotes the total number of years on TANF leading up to time period t, and $P(a_t)$ is a modified indicator variable of whether the family is on welfare in time t as a function of the age composition of the children in the family (a_t). Equation (6), which describes the TANF benefit formula, now requires the additional constraint that $D_t \le D_{kt}^{lim}$, which says that total time on welfare cannot exceed the state- and year-specific time limit.

Most of the research on time limits have not incorporated asset tests, and thus TANF only distorts saving via its effect as a consumption floor. Indeed, it is generally assumed that the mother survives hand to mouth so that there is no self-insurance and thus TANF is the sole means of support in the event of a negative employment shock. This means that the timing of benefit receipt hinges crucially on the age of the youngest child. Since eligibility ends when the age of the youngest child reaches age eighteen, this means that the five-year time limit is not binding if the youngest child is age thirteen or older (but this is raised to age sixteen and older in the five states with a two-year or less time limit). However, if the child is younger than age thirteen, then there are incentives for the mother to "bank" her benefits. That is, we expect countercyclical participation in TANF to be greater in families with young children compared to families with only adolescents. Holding business-cycle conditions constant, we also expect labor supply to be higher when the child is younger.

This benefit-banking effect is confounded, however, in the presence of work requirements, learning by doing, saving, and asset tests. First, with work requirements there are technically no periods with nonemployment coupled with TANF benefits since work, or at least work-related activities, are a prerequisite of benefit receipt. The exception is that in most states mothers are exempt from work requirements when the child is young (usually age one and under), and this creates countervailing incentives to deplete benefits when the child is young. Second, as the benefit-banking model predicts greater work effort when young, this also means that there will be future wage growth via learning by doing à la equation (8), and this wage growth could render the family income ineligible when it comes time to apply. Third, if the mother saves then we expect self-insurance to be greater when the child is young under benefit banking because this is the period of highest labor supply, though this self-insurance will be attenuated by the consumption floor of TANF. Moreover, with asset tests, this self-insurance may render the family ineligible when the time comes to join the program. All told, we expect benefit-banking effects to be strongest in states with relatively lenient work requirements, income limits, and asset limits. Because child-only cases are not subject to time limits, benefit banking should not apply to these assistance units.[12]

Goal 3. To Prevent and Reduce Out-of-Wedlock
Pregnancies: Family Caps and Maternal Health

The rise of out-of-wedlock childbearing came to national attention with the publication of the Moynihan Report in 1965 (US Department of Labor 1965). The report focused on the challenges facing the black family, where it was noted with alarm that nearly one in four black children were born out of wedlock in 1963. This trend continued over the next two decades, rising to 60 percent by the early 1980s, and today stands at 71 percent (Child Trends 2014). At the time of the Moynihan Report, only 4 percent of births to white

---

12. The other approach to avert the time limit is via the diversion program, if available in the state. Two-thirds of states have formal diversion programs, and only three of those count the payment against the lifetime limit.

mothers were out of wedlock. This percentage increased dramatically by the early 1980s, and by 2013 was over seven times the rate five decades earlier with about 30 percent of births outside of marriage. The comparable rates in 2013 are 53 percent among Hispanics and 17 percent among Asians and Pacific Islanders.

This significant change in child bearing led some commentators to lay blame squarely on the doorstep of AFDC (Murray 1984). The critique of the program focused on the fact that since eligibility was restricted to those families with children, and benefits were provided with relatively few strings attached, it created a viable option for child birth outside of marriage. Indeed, the structure of the benefit formula is such that $\partial \text{TANF}_t / \partial Y(M_t) < 0$; that is, income from a spouse (or noncustodial parent via child support) increased net income and thereby reduced the size of the benefit, all else equal. At the same time, because need standards and thus potential benefits increased with the size of the family unit, $\partial \text{TANF}_t / \partial f(a_t) > 0$, there were implicit incentives to have more children.

As shown in figure 4.3, 6 percent of total TANF and MOE spending in 2012 was targeted to programs aimed at reducing out-of-wedlock child-birth. Some of these efforts are "sticks" and some are "carrots." The most obvious stick is the introduction of family caps. Nearly 40 percent of states at some point under TANF have introduced family caps that limit or restrict the size of the benefit increase when an additional child is born so that effectively $\partial \text{TANF}_t / \partial f(a_t) = 0$. In the context of the asset accumulation constraint of equation (4), lifetime wealth will fall with an additional child on TANF because the benefit remains fixed, but equivalized consumption, $(p_t^C C_t) / e(f(a_t))$, increases. This negative wealth effect in turn should increase labor supply, partially offsetting the loss in assets, but typically well below a full offset. Many states also imposed new behavioral rules that increase the effective cost of children, and therefore reduce the demand. These rules include requiring that the children meet attendance quotas at school and/or a minimum grade point average, that the children receive all required immunizations, and that the children meet health-screening requirements.

Most of the spending on efforts to reduce out-of-wedlock births are carrots, coming in the form of home-visiting programs, education programs, media campaigns, family planning, abstinence education, and youth services (Green Book 2008). Within these categories, many can be characterized as investments in mothers' health. This is underscored further when considering the 15 percent "other" spending category in figure 4.3, which includes, among others, mental health services, drug and alcohol addiction treatment, and domestic violence counseling and prevention. Returning to the life-cycle model in equations (3) and (4), which includes the stock of health, assume that in each period the mother inherits a stock of health capital that depreciates at rate δ_H. Health can be replenished by devoting leisure time

(L_t) to exercise, purchasing medical services (S_t), and receiving in-kind services from TANF. Health capital then evolves according to

(10) $$H_{t+1} = (1 - \delta_H) H_t + y(S_t, L_t, \text{TANF}_t),$$

where $y(L_t, S_t, \text{TANF}_t)$ is the health investment production function that is akin to the standard Grossman (1972) model but modified to include the services received in TANF.[13] Equation (10) makes explicit that participation in TANF can offer an additional channel to improve lifetime well-being beyond providing a consumption floor via health promotion. These health services may interact positively with human capital, thereby increasing lifetime earning potential.

Goal 4. To Encourage the Formation and Maintenance of Two-Parent Families: Child Support and Child Well-Being

In the original ADC program, benefits were confined to the child, and then the 1950 amendment to the Social Security Act allowed the mother to be part of the assistance unit as well (technically the caretaking parent). This was then extended, at state option, to the second natural parent with the advent of the AFDC-UP program in 1961. In the late 1960s there were several Supreme Court decisions that implicitly extended eligibility to cohabiting couples. One decision eliminated so-called man-in-the-house rules that disqualified otherwise eligible mothers from receiving AFDC because of coresidence with a man who was not the natural father of the child, while another decision ruled unconstitutional the inclusion of income from the cohabiting male in benefit determination without proof that his income was used to support the mother and children (Moffitt, Reville, and Winkler 1998). The Family Support Act of 1988 extended the 1961 amendment by no longer making the AFDC-UP optional and mandated all states implement it by 1990. Each of these changes was designed to promote family unity, and this goal was codified as one of the four pillars of TANF.

The promotion of marriage (or at least cohabitation) and family stability is built on the belief, backed up by evidence, that children (and adults) do better on average in two-parent families than in single-parent families—higher incomes and wealth, and lower poverty and mortality (Waite 1995)—and ultimately from the policymakers perspective, lower transmission of welfare across generations.[14] This is most readily captured in the framework of the Becker-Tomes (1979) model of intergenerational mobility whereby

13. The concept of leisure in this framework differs from leisure in the standard labor supply model, where leisure represents nonmarket time. The Grossman (1972) model separates total time into time for work, time for health, time for producing the household good, and time for sickness.
14. Whether marriage causes these positive outcomes or whether there is self-selection of better-qualified parents into marriage is still an active line of inquiry.

during childhood the parent(s) allocates income between their own consumption and investment in the human capital of the child. The more income that is invested in the child the more economically mobile the child will be in adulthood. In a simple regression context we get

$$(11) \qquad ln\text{TANF}^{\text{Child}}_{\text{Adulthood}} = \beta ln\text{TANF}^{\text{Parent}}_{\text{Childhood}} + X\theta + u,$$

where $ln\text{TANF}^{\text{Child}}_{\text{Adulthood}}$ is the natural log of TANF income that the child receives in adulthood, $ln\text{TANF}^{\text{Parent}}_{\text{Childhood}}$ is the natural log of TANF income that the parent receives while the child is growing up, X is a vector of family and child control variables, and u is an error term. The coefficient β is the intergenerational correlation of TANF incomes—as $\beta \rightarrow 0$ the intergenerational link of welfare is broken. Children growing up in two-parent families, all else equal, receive proportionately more investment in terms of time and money in their human capital, and thereby have greater odds of economic mobility in later life.

In terms of the life-cycle model of equations (3) and (4), in any given period the mother will choose to marry if and only if the value function while married exceeds that not married. Whether or not she also combines marriage with TANF will be made with the knowledge that the income and asset limits are the same whether she is married or not, and given that the prospective spouse is expected to bring both income and assets into the family, this will make eligibility for TANF less likely. Moreover, her spouse's income, $Y(M_t)$, will count against the size of the benefit if they qualify. Under TANF, depending on state of residence, she may not qualify for benefits if she is married (New Hampshire and North Dakota), or eligibility may be confined to only those fathers with less than full-time attachment to work (Maine, Mississippi, South Dakota, and Tennessee). These features create disincentives to marry, or at least to not marry "well."

In most states the resources used to meet this goal were directed toward responsible fatherhood initiatives, which often are in the form of employment and training services for noncustodial fathers (Green Book 2008). The idea here is that if that the father has steady employment and earnings, there will be a greater chance of regular child support payments to assist the family, and that there will also be positive role model effects passed from father to child (e.g., a lower β in equation [11]). Under AFDC only $50 per month in child support was disregarded from the benefit (known as the child-support pass through) and the remainder was retained by the state and thus effectively taxed at 100 percent. This high tax rate created strong disincentives both to paternity establishment and to formal child support, conditional on paternity being established. This disincentive is exacerbated by the fact that recipients are required to surrender their child support income to the state, and then states determine how much to pass through. States adopt this policy in part because they are required to return a percentage (based on the state's FMAP) of this income to the federal government (Kassabian et al. 2013). After **PRWORA**, seven states retained the basic $50 pass through, seven others raised the pass through to anywhere between $75 and $200 per month, and seven additional states no longer explicitly count child support (100 percent pass through). The remainder adopted some other policy, including not passing through any child support. In short, only a small number of states made a concerted effort to align their TANF program with enhanced child support payments. This cross-state variation offers an opportunity to test whether child well-being is higher among the TANF population in those states with more generous pass through policies.

Arguably the most significant investment in child well-being under TANF is the expansion of childcare subsidies. As documented in figure 4.3, 12 percent of TANF funds were directly spent on childcare in 2012 (1 percent on cash subsidies; 11 percent in kind), and an additional 4 percent of TANF funds were transferred to the Child Care Development Fund. The latter are less restrictive in terms of income eligibility and thus are more likely to assist children in two-parent families than TANF childcare funds (though in both cases the subsidies are only for children under age thirteen). Whether received directly as cash or in kind, childcare assistance can be viewed as a wage subsidy, such that the net wage of the mother on TANF is $w_t\left(1 - brr_t + t_t^c\right)$, where t_t^c is the effective hourly subsidy rate from childcare. The childcare subsidy attenuates the disincentive to work from the benefit reduction rate, which should increase labor force entry and may also increase hours of work provided that the substitution effect dominates the income effect. The evidence from the childcare literature seems to confirm both of these predictions (e.g., Berger and Black 1992; Blau and Currie 2006; Tekin 2007). Moreover, this literature shows that children generally do better in model, center-based care than informal (home-based) care on a host of cognitive and noncognitive measures (Morris et al. 2009; Blau and Currie 2006; Bernal and Keane 2011). However, it was estimated that in FY2009 only one in six children eligible for CCDF or TANF childcare received assistance (OFA 2013). This helps explain why in calendar years 2012–2013, out-of-pocket childcare costs ate up nearly 20 percent of the median annual earnings of single-mother families with children under age five, and upward of one-third in states like Massachusetts (Ziliak 2014).

4.4.2   Review of Results

Across the spectrum of programs in the social safety net, AFDC was historically the most heavily researched. This stemmed in part because it was the primary means of cash assistance for low-income families with young children from the 1960s through the 1980s, coupled with the fact that it was one of the few programs that provided cross-state variation in key design parameters such as the maximum benefit guarantee and effective benefit-reduction rates that were crucial for nonexperimental evaluation. In the aftermath of welfare reform, research on the program exploded as

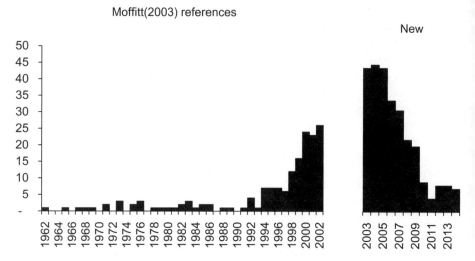

Fig. 4.9   **AFDC/TANF book and journal citations by year**

depicted in figure 4.9. This research activity persisted for a full decade after reform and has only tapered off in recent years. The figure only captures part of the story, however, because it only covers peer-reviewed books and journal articles and omits the scores of unpublished working papers as well as technical reports written by evaluation firms, think tanks, and government agencies (and undoubtedly published works overlooked by the author). The growth in research was spurred on by the vast breadth of reforms, funding for demonstration projects, the advent of new data sets such as the Three-City Study and Fragile Families, annual conferences such as Association of Public Policy and Management, National Association of Welfare Research and Statistics, and the Welfare Research and Evaluation Conference, and the democratization of research effort. The research during the AFDC era was heavily dominated by economists, and while economists continued in this tradition after welfare reform, there was a large influx of new research by demographers, development psychologists, political scientists, sociologists, and social workers pulled in by opportunity to study outcomes beyond participation decisions and labor supply such as child development, health, immigration, and the political economy of program implementation.

In this section the primary focus is on TANF research not covered in Moffitt (2003), though there will be some overlap of material as well as from the surveys of Grogger and Karoly (2005) and Blank (2009). It is not possible to review all the papers identified in figure 4.9; instead, emphasis is on a subset of papers representative of the broad range of research topics spanning participation and caseloads, labor supply and welfare-to-work, income and poverty, consumption and saving, health, fertility and marriage, and child development.

Participation and Caseloads

The adoption of AFDC waivers that introduced time limits, work requirements, sanctions, expanded earnings disregards, and asset limits in the early 1990s spawned a flurry of research focused primarily on the decline in welfare participation between 1993 to 1996, as this was the key policy outcome of interest at the time (Council of Economic Advisers 1997; Figlio and Ziliak 1999; Moffitt 1999; Bartik and Eberts 1999; Ziliak et al. 2000; Blank 2001). Research on participation prior to this had mostly emphasized the roles of demographic factors, along with cross-state variation in maximum guarantees and effective tax rates, in predicting welfare use, and relied on cross-sectional data (Barr and Hall 1981; Moffitt 1983; Robins 1986; Hoynes 1996). When a time dimension was incorporated, it was most often in the context of estimating the determinants of welfare spells (Blank 1989; Fitzgerald 1991; Hoynes and MaCurdy 1994).

Economy versus Policy Debate. This new research took a more macro approach, utilizing administrative data on the number of AFDC cases (or recipients) per capita in each state over time to estimate the relative roles of the business cycle versus welfare waivers in accounting for the large decline in participation. These nonexperimental studies took advantage of the differential timing and types of welfare waivers implemented by states, along with state and regional differences in business cycles as measured by unemployment rates and/or employment growth. There was agreement that the strong macroeconomy in the mid-1990s was the most important factor behind the decline in caseloads, but there were considerable discrepancies across studies in whether and to what extent welfare waivers affected the decline.

For example, the CEA (1997) and Blank (2001) attributed between a quarter and a third of the decline to welfare waivers, while Ziliak et al. (2000) attributed none. Ziliak et al. found that states with time limits and behavioral responsibility waivers experienced declines in caseloads, while other states with work requirements and expanded disregards and asset limits had increases, and in the aggregate they canceled out. The studies differed in several respects. The CEA and Blank studies each used annual state panel data, while Ziliak et al. used monthly state panels. Moreover, the former studies only admitted dynamics in the model via lags of the business cycle (the CEA also had policy lead variables), while the latter study included lags in both the business-cycle measures and the dependent variable (log of per capita caseloads). In their reconciliation study, Figlio and Ziliak (1999) attributed the majority of the difference to the inclusion of lagged caseloads, which were found to be highly significant both economically and statistically. Specifically, lagged caseloads had the effect of heightening the influence of the business cycle and attenuating the influence of policy. In most of the caseload studies around 25 percent of the variation was left unexplained by the business cycle and state welfare policy choices. The remainder was attributed to other policies such as the expansion of the EITC that made work more attractive relative to welfare (Meyer and Rosenbaum 2001) and enhanced child-support enforcement (Huang, Garfinkel, and Waldfogel 2004).

In the wake of these early studies several others followed up with a deeper examination of caseload dynamics. Grogger, Haider, and Klerman (2003) used household-level data from the SIPP to ask the question of whether the decline in the 1990s came via reduced entry and/or increased exit. That is, at any given time the caseload is a function of the stock of caseloads from the prior period along with the flows on and off between periods. They found that exits increased during the 1990s, but nearly half the decline was driven by a reduction in entry. Hoynes (2000), Klerman and Haider (2004) and Haider and Klerman (2005) used rich micro caseload data from the state of California to examine caseload flows. Because the data come from a single state they were not able to address the economy versus policy issue directly, and instead focused on the local economy alone. Hoynes found that local labor demand conditions at the county level—lower unemployment, higher employment per population, higher average wages—were a key driver of exits off AFDC spells.

Klerman and Haider utilized the data to estimate Markov-chain models to pin down the proper dynamic structure of the caseload. Their theoretical model predicted that static models need to include many lags of regressors along with interactions among them to be consistent with the Markov model, suggesting that the models of the CEA and Blank studies were insufficient in their controls for dynamics. As for dynamic models, Klerman and Haider found that a single lag of the dependent variable is also not sufficient, and these models must include long lags of explanatory variables for the model to be consistent with duration dependence in welfare spells. For example, Ziliak et al. included three lags of the dependent variable, six lags of the economy, and four lags of welfare waivers in their model, using the Schwarz criterion to select the lag structure. Applying their results to California, Klerman and Haider found that local unemployment rates explained about 50 percent of the decline in caseloads, about double the estimate they obtain from a standard static model like the CEA. Haider and Klerman go further in finding that the caseload decline in California was due more to declining entry rates than exits. Frogner, Moffitt, and Ribar (2009) use longitudinal data from the Three-City Study, which followed 2,400 low-income women with children from 1999–2005 in Boston, Chicago, and San Antonio, and found that exit rates from TANF were high, and that entry and reentry rates were very low, consistent with Haider and Klerman.

Most of the participation research examining the economy versus policy

debate focused on the years leading up to passage of PRWORA. Grogger and Karoly (2005), in their survey of the literature, concluded that of
those studies examining the first few years after PRWORA, TANF policies
accounted for about 20 percent of the decline in caseloads, and that the
macroeconomy remained the main driver. There were a couple of exceptions
using more recent data. Fang and Keane (2004) used repeated cross sections of the CPS from 1980–2002 to estimate a host of welfare-reform policies interacted with several household demographic characteristics on the
decision to participate in AFDC/TANF. They found that policies mattered
much more than the economy for the 1993–2002 period, especially work
requirements. However, they only included static controls for the economy
(state unemployment rate, average wage at the 20th percentile) and thus fall
into the critiques of Ziliak et al. (2000) and Klerman and Haider (2004).
Danielson and Klerman (2008) used monthly state caseload data from 1990–
2005, focusing on time limits, diversion, sanctions, and financial-incentive
policies. While they do include a lag structure for both the macroeconomy
and welfare policies, they do not include lags of the dependent variable.
However, they do a more careful job of accounting for differential reporting of separate state programs in construction of the dependent variable
caseloads. They found that from 2000–2005 welfare policies accounted for
more of the caseload change than the economy; however, over 80 percent
of the variation is left unexplained by these two factors. This was not the
case in the first-generation caseload research on the waiver period. Perhaps
part of the weakening of the models stems from the fact that take-up rates
of cash benefits have plummeted from 79 percent in the last year of AFDC
to 36 percent in 2007 (Loprest 2012), which itself is a likely policy outcome
that is not adequately captured. Moreover, with the surge in child-only cases,
many on the rolls are not subject to the same macroeconomic and policy
forces as under AFDC, when it was the norm for both the adult and child
to be on assistance.

There are only two caseload studies that I am aware of that include the
years of the Great Recession. Bitler and Hoynes (2010) use both monthly
administrative data on state caseloads from 1980–2009, as well as annual
survey data from the Current Population Survey, to examine the effect of
the economy and welfare reform on AFDC/TANF (along with other outcomes). Their estimates from static models suggest that TANF (assistance)
caseloads are no more responsive to business-cycle conditions after welfare
reform, though in some specifications the caseload is less responsive to the
economy. In a follow-up analysis, Bitler and Hoynes (forthcoming) extend
the data through 2012 where they confirm the lack of responsiveness of
TANF to the Great Recession, especially expenditures, and as a consequence
extreme poverty is more cyclical than in past recessions. They do not offer
a decomposition analysis of economy versus policy, which is perhaps the
correct choice given the identification challenges of evaluating TANF as a

bundle (see below). However, it remains an open question as to whether the models with the additional variation induced by the Great Recession can account for changes in TANF more akin to the waiver studies, or whether the more pessimistic assessment of Danielson and Klerman (2008) carries the day.

The Bitler and Hoynes (2010, forthcoming) papers also shed light on a related, but distinct, literature that examines fiscal-federalism incentives facing states in the provision of social assistance (Gramlich and Laren 1984; Moffitt 1990; Chernick 1998; Chernick and McGuire 1999; Powers 2000; Ribar and Wilhelm 1999; Brueckner 2000; McGuire and Merriman 2006). Specifically, under the basic block grant of TANF, states are responsible for the full marginal cost of additional spending once the grant is exhausted, whereas under the matching-grant system of AFDC they only covered a fraction of additional spending as determined by the FMAP. Thus, under TANF the "price" of welfare is higher, and all else equal, we expect state spending on cash assistance to fall relative to AFDC. At the same time, states that rely heavily on a progressive income tax to support spending tend to have more volatile revenue streams, and in the event of a downturn, revenues fall creating an income effect that also depresses spending on welfare just as the need for assistance accelerates. The price effect suggests that there should be a (secular) decline in state spending on cash assistance after welfare reform, while the income effect suggests that states should be less willing to increase spending during recessions under the block grant. Chernick (1998) predicted such effects, though the early evidence in McGuire and Merriman (2006) was not conclusive. Part of this might be due to the fact that states accumulated surpluses in the first half dozen years after welfare reform and could carry these forward to future fiscal years, and part due to state MOE requirements. McGuire and Merriman also argued that TANF has become an increasingly smaller share of state spending and thus is less elastic as a consequence. However, with an additional decade of data the evidence in Bitler and Hoynes is quite persuasive that both price and income effects have lead to a reduced responsiveness of TANF to economic need compared to AFDC. That said, the financing models focus on state spending, and since Bitler and Hoynes did not direct their attention to this literature, they did not separate out state-only spending from spending commingled with federal dollars, and thus future work should separate these funding streams to more accurately examine the model predictions from block grants.

Specific Policy Studies.   One of the challenges facing evaluation of TANF as a complete package is that the policy was implemented across all states within roughly eighteen months. This is distinct from the waiver period when policies were implemented over a four-year period, with some states not adopting waivers at all, and thus offering more variation to separate the effect of the economy versus policy on participation (Bitler, Gelbach, and

Hoynes 2003). While most of the first-generation papers estimated disaggregated policy effects—sanctions, time limits, work requirements, incentives—and some included interactions between the economy and policy (e.g., Bartik and Eberts 1999; Ziliak et al. 2000) or the economy and demographics (Moffitt 1999), this was crucial for identification in the TANF era. That is, it became necessary to either utilize qualitative differences in the stringency of program rules or to exploit variation over the business cycle or demographic groups to identify policy effects post PRWORA. This in turn makes it more challenging to aggregate up to a total "welfare reform effect," leading some to instead focus on the contributions of individual policies on the decline via counterfactual simulations (Fang and Keane 2004; Danielson and Klerman 2008).

The most prominent of these policy-centric papers are on time limits. For example, Grogger (2003, 2004) implemented a reduced-form version of the dynamic model proposed by Grogger and Michalopoulos (2003) using data from the CPS from 1979 to 2000. He exploited the prediction of the federal five-year lifetime limit that single mothers with only older children (age thirteen and older) should exhaust their benefits more rapidly than mothers with younger children since the latter have an incentive to "bank" their benefits in case of a (more) rainy day in the future. He implements this by interacting the time-limit variable with a variable that equals 0 if the youngest child is age thirteen or older and equals the deviation of the age of the youngest child from thirteen if the child is under age thirteen. Grogger finds no overall effect of time limits on welfare use, but significant effects on the age-dependent interaction term such that a mother whose youngest child is ten years old reduced participation by 2 percentage points. His estimates suggest that time limits accounted for about one-eighth of the decline in welfare participation between 1993 and 1999. Mazzolari (2007) extended the Grogger model to account for the fact that his specification is valid only at the point of implementation, but as time passes one also must control for the stock of remaining benefits (see equation [9] above). She also attempted to disentangle behavioral from mechanical effects of the limits (Ashenfelter 1983), the latter of which can arise from state variation in exemptions from the limits. Using data from the 1990 through 2001 panels of the Survey of Income and Program Participation (SIPP), she estimated that from 1996 to 2003 time limits reduced welfare use by 25 percent, 5 percentage points of which (i.e., 20 percent of the total) was from behavioral effects. This is perhaps not surprising in that Loprest (2012) reports that only 2 percent of cases were closed in FY2009 for reaching the time limit.

The forward-looking aspects of time limits have also led to a few attempts at estimating structural models of life-cycle behavior (Keane and Wolpin 2002b, 2010; Swann 2005; Fang and Silverman 2009; Chan 2013). These papers are distinct from the others in the literature because the welfare decision is made jointly with labor supply decisions, and perhaps marriage and fertility choices. As such they will be mentioned in later sections under those respective topics. All the papers use exclusively prewelfare reform data (Panel Study of Income Dynamics from 1968–1992 for Swann; National Longitudinal Survey of Youth from1979–1991 for Keane and Wolpin and Fang and Silverman) except for Chan, who uses data both pre- and post-welfare reform (SIPP panels for 1992, 1993, and 1996). However, by formally modeling the structural preferences and budget constraints facing the women they are able to conduct detailed counterfactual simulations of how behavior likely changed under TANF. For example, Swann (2005) estimated that a five-year time limit leads to a 9 percent reduction in the caseload, but a 60 percent reduction in the number of person-years on welfare, one-third of which is a behavioral response from forward-looking behavior. Chan (2013) estimated a smaller 37 percent reduction in person-years within ten years of implementation; however, he also attributed at least a third of this effect to a behavioral response. Thus, incorporating forward-looking behavior has the effect of increasing the importance of time limits on the welfare decisions of mothers.

Beyond time limits, sanctioning policy took renewed prominence in the research literature. For example, Wu et al. (2006) used administrative longitudinal caseload data spanning 1997–2003 from the state of Wisconsin to examine the extent and consequences of sanctioning policy. They found that nearly two-thirds of women on welfare faced a noncompliance for work requirement sanction over a four-year period, but because most of the sanctions were short term and partial, the most common transition for this group was back to welfare within a month or two after a sanction. They also found that Hispanics and African Americans were more likely to be sanctioned than whites. This racial gap in sanctioning was also found in Schram et al. (2009), who used a hypothetical "audit study" of case managers in Florida. Their audit study is unique in this literature, and involved a Web-based survey of Florida Welfare Transition case managers whereby the managers were presented with various rule-violation scenarios and randomly assigned client characteristics. The authors found that African American mothers, more so than Latinas, were likely to face sanctions compared to white mothers. This result was corroborated in actual administrative data outcomes in Fording, Soss, and Schram (2007), especially for longer spells on welfare where black clients faced sanction rates of 22 to 35 percent higher in month nine of a spell compared to white clients.

The PRWORA limited access to assistance for legal immigrants arriving after passage of the law until after five years of residence, and left it to state discretion on whether current legal immigrants would be eligible (illegal immigrants have always been denied benefits). This provision stemmed from a concern that the large increase in low-skilled immigration in the 1980s and early 1990s might be in response to generous welfare benefits (Haskins 2009). Such concerns with welfare migration have a long history with welfare, starting at least with the Law of Settlement and Removal of 1662 whereby local officials in England could force individuals and families to return to their home parishes if they became dependent prior to proof that they contributed to the well-being of the community (Hansan 2011). The evidence on whether there is such endogenous immigration or internal migration in response to welfare generosity in the United States is mixed (Borjas 1999; Gelbach 2004; Kaushal 2005; McKinnish 2007; Kennan and Walker 2010).

Several studies examined trends in welfare participation among immigrants before and after passage of PRWORA, including testing whether there was a "chilling effect" on participation among immigrants, that is, a voluntary withdrawal from the program even though eligible owing to misinformation or perhaps fear (Fix and Passel 1999; Lofstrom and Bean 2002; Haider et al. 2004; Kaestner and Kaushal 2005; Capps, Fix, and Henderson 2009). While most of the studies examining the early years after reform found evidence that immigrants reduced participation more than native born after welfare reform, this may be due more to differential response of immigrants to the strong labor market of the late 1990s (Lofstrom and Bean 2002; Haider et al. 2004). However, in a recent paper, Bitler and Hoynes (2013) compared immigrant and native-born participation rates in TANF in 2008–2009 to AFDC rates for comparable groups in 1994–1995, and while the difference-in-difference estimates suggest lower participation rates of 2–3 percent among immigrants than natives, the differences are not significant.

Because there are so many possible policy variables that capture different aspects of welfare reform, attempts to include them all, or even a sizable subset, has been met with little success owing to collinearity problems. As a consequence, some have attempted to summarize the policies in a more parsimonious manner, such as the aggressiveness of the reforms ranging from "lenient" to "severe" (Ellwood 1999; Meyer and Rosenbaum 2001; Soss et al. 2001; Grogger and Karoly 2005; McKernan, Bernstein, and Fender 2005; De Jong et al. 2006). Ellwood (1999) proposed a measure of aggressiveness that captured the changing odds that people of a given earnings level in a given state would receive public assistance. To construct the measure he used data from the Current Population Survey over the period 1984–1992 to estimate a probit model of AFDC participation among single parents in each state as a function of age, education, race, state unemployment, earnings, and a linear trend. Then he predicted the likelihood of receiving aid using the same demographic and state-level variable but with data from the 1997 and 1998 CPS under the proviso that AFDC program rules were the same as in the base period of 1984–1992. The difference between the actual and predicted decline in AFDC participation between 1991–1992 and 1997–1998 is used as the metric of aggressiveness.

Meyer and Rosenbaum's (2001) approach consists of whether (a) the real AFDC benefit fell at least 25 percent between 1986 and 1997; (b) whether the state imposed a time limit waiver; (c) whether the state imposed full family sanctions for failure to comply with JOBS requirements; and (d) whether any persons were terminated for failure to meet a requirement under AFDC waivers. States that satisfied at least three of the four criteria were defined as most aggressive. Grogger and Karoly (2005) considered several alternative metrics of aggressiveness, including where (a) a state is deemed aggressive if it had one or more waivers implemented between 1992 and 1996 (see their table 4.1), (b) a state is deemed aggressive if it had three or more waivers implemented between 1992 and 1996, or (c) a state is deemed aggressive if all four studies on state sanctions policies summarized in their table 4.2 agree that the state's (full family benefit) sanction policy is stringent during the 1992 to 1996 period. De Jong et al. (2006) coded seventy-eight policies from the Welfare Rules Database from lenient to stringent, and then applied factor analysis that identified fifteen leading policies. In a bid for greater parsimony they conducted a second-order factor analysis that resulted in three broad categories of policies: eligibility requirements, behavioral responsibilities, and eligibility limits and exemptions.

There have only been limited attempts to use these indices to predict welfare caseloads. The Council of Economic Advisors (CEA 1999) updated their earlier study to include two years post-TANF and found that states with more stringent job-sanctioning policies had larger declines in caseloads than those employing more lenient policies. Schmidt and Sevak (2004) used data from the CPS for calendar years 1987–1996 and found that states that implemented more aggressive reforms saw a 21 percent increase in participation in Supplemental Security Income (SSI), suggesting that states partially shifted the burden from their budgets to the federal budget. Cadena, Danzinger, and Seefeldt (2006) used data from the CPS for the years 1994 to 2003 to construct three-year moving averages of TANF participation among single mothers with at least one dependent child and with no more than high school for each state. They then estimated the effects of the De Jong et al. indices on participation, finding that they have no predictive power once one controls for state fixed effects. They present some suggestive evidence that the lack of power in the De Jong et al. measure might be due to its omission of the AFDC/TANF maximum benefit guarantee, which has historically been a key proxy of state generosity.

Labor Supply and Welfare-to-Work

Concomitant with the surge of research on participation in TANF was research on employment. This follows hand in hand with the second goal of TANF to end dependence and promote work. While several studies were national in focus, much of this research was fueled by area studies on welfare leavers or eligibles from demonstration projects, focused surveys, and administrative data. The demonstration projects, several of which were conducted during the welfare waiver era, included the California Greater

Avenues for Independence (GAIN), Florida's Family Transition Program (FTP), Connecticut's Jobs First, Minnesota's Family Investment Plan (MFIP), Milwaukee's New Hope program, and Wisconsin's Child Support Demonstration Evaluation (CSDE).[15] The most prominent focused surveys were fielded after welfare reform, including the Three-City Study, the Fragile Families and Child Well Being Survey, and the Women's Employment Study (WES). And in a relatively new turn of events, several states such as California, Florida, Georgia, Illinois, Maryland, Michigan, Missouri, New York, North and South Carolina, Tennessee, Washington, and Wisconsin opened up their administrative records to academics and evaluation firms to evaluate how former welfare recipients were faring in the labor market. In this section I first discuss observational studies, both reduced form and structural, followed by leavers studies and demonstrations. These research strands follow rich histories on AFDC starting in the 1960s as national household surveys such as the CPS, the NLS, and PSID were coming on line at the same time as the negative income tax experiments were fielded in Gary, Indiana, New Jersey, and Seattle and Denver (SIME/DIME).

Employment.   In the wake of welfare reform, most of the new observational studies on employment with a national focus were reduced form, and they relied heavily on the pre-TANF period for identification. Instead of emphasizing the effects of maximum benefit guarantees and benefit-reduction rates as was typical with the earlier AFDC research, these studies examined the overall effect of welfare waivers (or TANF) on the extensive and intensive margins of employment. Moffitt (1999) used CPS data from 1977–1995 and found that only less skilled mothers (i.e., those with a high school diploma or less) responded to welfare waivers. Mothers who dropped out of high school increased work by sixty-eight hours annually, while those with a diploma increased annual hours by forty-one hours. Schoeni and Blank (2000) extended the CPS data four more years through 1999, and found that waivers increased employment rates for high school dropout mothers by 2 percentage points on a baseline rate of 53 percent, the number of weeks worked increased by one week, and weekly hours increased by one (the mean hours per week were sixteen). They found no labor supply response among the less skilled in the three years after TANF was passed.

Grogger (2003) used the same CPS data and a slightly modified model as he also included the time limit and time limit interacted with the age of the

15. Canada's Self-Sufficiency Project (SSP) was conducted at the same time. The SSP was a randomized control trial conducted in New Brunswick and British Columbia that provided earnings supplements (akin to the US EITC) for up to three years to long-term welfare recipients if they found full-time work and left welfare within one year of random assignment. Thirty-six percent of the treatment group found full-time work, and had an employment rate that was 61 percent higher than the control group at the three-year follow up. See Michalopoulos et al. (2002) for details.

youngest child, along with the overall reform variable and controls for the EITC. He found that employment rates overall increased by 2.6 percentage points by non-time-limit welfare reforms, and the time limit boosted the employment rate of mothers with children by 0.34 percentage points for each year the child was under age thirteen. And while time limits did not boost annual weeks worked, the non-time-limit reforms did by about 2.6 weeks. Kaushal and Kaestner (2001) use just four years of CPS data spanning 1995–1999 and employ a difference-in-differences estimator. They found that employment rates of less skilled unmarried mothers increased about 7 percentage points in response to time limits, or about 14 percent over the baseline. This larger effect from time limits compared to Grogger may result both from a different specification of time limits (Kaushal and Kaestner only use a dummy variable, not a direct function of age of child as in Grogger) and their use of a comparison group of married women, which may impart bias if there are endogenous marriage responses to welfare reform. Fang and Keane (2004) attribute more of the growth in employment between 1993 and 2002 to the EITC and macroeconomy than welfare reform, but still a sizable 27 percent to the combined effects of work requirements (17 percent) and time limits (10 percent).

Meyer and Rosenbaum (2001) employ a quasi-structural approach to estimating employment rates, again using CPS data but for years 1984–1996. Their approach is considered "quasi-structural" because they model the employment decision as a function of the difference between expected income from work and from nonwork, where income is specified as a detailed function of the parameters governing the tax and transfer system and thus affecting the woman's budget constraint. They also use a difference-in-differences estimator, but in this case use single, childless women as the main comparison group, again under the assumption that fertility decisions are unrelated to welfare. While they found that expansions of the EITC accounted for over 60 percent of the growth in employment over their sample period, they also found that welfare waivers accounted for about 15 percent, and even more if the counterfactual period is restricted to 1992–1996. This larger effect is consistent with Kaushal and Kaestner, and perhaps reflects the use of a comparison group. Indeed the effect of any termination waiver on the employment decision is about 25 percent lower when they exclude a comparison group (compare their table IV, column [5] to table V, column [6]).

As discussed in the last section, the introduction of time limits spurred on the estimation of structural models of labor supply to capture the joint decisions of welfare and work when mothers are forward looking. Although these studies, with the exception of Chan (2013), restricted estimation to the prewelfare waiver era, and thus do not incorporate key elements of reform in the budget constraint, they simulated how employment was expected to change under stylized scenarios resembling welfare reform. For example,

Swann (2005) conducted counterfactual simulations of cutting the effective benefit reduction via earnings disregards, introducing a five-year lifetime limit on benefits and a two-year work-requirement time limit, and the latter two combined. He found that a 10 percent reduction in the benefit-reduction rate had little effect on employment choices, consistent with the AFDC literature, but the introduction of a five-year time limit lead to a 67 percent reduction in the probability of being on welfare with no work, and a 46 percent reduction of combining welfare and work. Interestingly, though, the group with the largest increase was single mothers neither working nor on welfare. This estimate is consistent with the rise of so-called disconnected women (Blank and Kovak 2009). However, when he combined the benefit time limit with the work requirement time limit his model predicted that the most common "state" for the mother is to be single, working, and not on welfare. Keane and Wolpin (2010), in their simulations, found that a five-year benefit time limit likewise had a smaller effect on the probability of working than a twenty-five-hour per week work requirement after six months, but they also found that most of these women remained eligible for welfare because the higher earnings did not offset the lower welfare, a result found in earlier work by Moffitt (1983) and Hoynes (1996).

Chan (2013) extended the prior two structural papers by explicitly modeling the rules affecting AFDC and TANF, including work requirements and time limits, along with food stamp rules, federal and state taxes (inclusive of the EITC), and the payroll tax. Like Meyer and Rosenbaum (2001) before him, he used repeated cross sections over time (from the SIPP, not CPS), and thus allowed the welfare and tax parameters to change across states over time, assisting in the identification of model parameters beyond cross-state variation alone. His model is quite complicated, allowing for multiple program participation, with and without work, state dependence in those program/work decisions, a distribution of job offer arrival probabilities, and a version of learning by doing such that lagged work status (not the stock of experience as in Keane and Wolpin [2010]) affected the wage and job-offer arrival. Interestingly, his model predicted that the employment response to job offers was ten times larger than the elasticity of employment with respect to the wage, and likewise, program participation responses were much larger for job offers than actual wages. This suggests demand-side conditions matter greatly for the welfare and work decisions of mothers, a result that Hoynes (2000) found in her analysis of welfare spells in California. When he used the structural estimates to decompose changes in welfare and employment from 1992–1999, he found that the macroeconomy was the most important reason for the increase in employment, accounting for nearly half, and that the time limit accounted for about 6 percent of the increase, followed by the EITC, and then work requirements. His estimates yielded a larger "total" effect of welfare policy on employment compared to the modal estimate surveyed in Grogger and Karoly (2005), with the exception of Fang and Keane (2004).

The latter study's large estimate of work requirements likely stemmed from their parsimonious specification of the macroeconomy.

Welfare-to-Work.   The "Riverside Miracle" framed much of the debate surrounding welfare reform, and how to transition mothers from welfare to work. In 1988 the evaluation firm MDRC was contracted to conduct a randomized control trial of the effectiveness of the California GAIN program in six counties (Riccio and Friedlander 1992; Riccio, Friedlander, and Freedman 1994). The GAIN program was the official JOBS program for the state, and depending on how the participant scored on a basic reading and math test, they were assigned either to programs emphasizing additional human-capital development (HCD) if the score was below a threshold or to programs emphasizing "work first" such as job-search assistance. Counties were given great leeway to design programs that suited their needs, and as such, Riverside tended to emphasize work first, while Alameda, Los Angeles, and San Diego counties emphasized HCD. Three years after random assignment, treatment group members in Riverside experienced 63 percent more quarters of employment and a comparable gain in earnings compared to control-group members. This treatment effect was three times larger than that found in the counties focused on HCD. The miracle of Riverside served as a platform for many states (and countries) as they designed their new welfare programs. Indeed the tension of work-first versus HCD is found in Goal (ii) of TANF where the aim is to end dependence by at once promoting "job preparation" *and* "work."

Hotz, Imbens, and Klerman (2006) noted that the treatment effects across the GAIN sites could differ because of differences in populations served, how treatment was assigned, and in local economic conditions. They proposed a new method of how to evaluate differential effects of alternative treatments such as HCD and work first. Using these methods they then re-examined the results of GAIN by focusing on impacts nine years after random assignment, which should be a sufficiently long period for HCD to have an effect. They found that much of the "Riverside Miracle" was not due to the work-first strategies of the GAIN program in the county, rather it was an anomalous result of a very strong local economy three to five years post assignment. Moreover, by six years after assignment the longer-run gains in employment were more pronounced for those treated with an HCD approach than work-first, suggesting that HCD programs may impart long-term benefits for mothers leaving welfare.

Dyke et al. (2006) applied some of these ideas to administrative data in Missouri and North Carolina to examine the effects of assessment, job-search and readiness training, and intensive training on employment outcomes for up to sixteen months after entry into TANF. Those individuals receiving intensive training gained skills more akin to HCD than the more work-first oriented assessment and job-search training. They employed matching estimators, as well as difference-in-differences with matching as recommended by Smith and Todd (2005) to sweep out individual fixed effects, and found that work-first strategies fade out over time while HCD programs increase in effectiveness on labor market outcomes.

Mueser, Stevens, and Troske (2009) followed up on this work, but instead relied on administrative data from the states of Missouri and Maryland. They examined the demographic composition, employment, and welfare recidivism of three cohorts of welfare leavers—leavers in FY1993, FY1997, and FY2002. Using the three separate cohorts permitted the authors to compare welfare recipients before welfare reform, during its implementation, and six years later. The data from Missouri and Maryland are not nationally representative, but the trends were strikingly similar to national trends in welfare, employment, and economic growth. Mueser et al. found little change in the demographic composition of the caseload across cohorts, but employment rose and persisted even into the 2001 recession, not only among leavers but also current recipients and new entrants, the latter of which was consistent with work requirements and perhaps states adopting a more work-first strategy. That the demographic composition at a point in time was little changed is not incongruent with the results from the Three-City Study by Frogner, Moffitt, and Ribar (2009). They found that from 1999–2005 the group of mothers who stayed on TANF became much more select—they worked less, had lower rates of marriage, and reported worse health and higher rates of disability than other mothers. Moffitt and Stevens (2001) found similar results in an earlier analysis of CPS data. This suggests that stayers face particular disadvantages well beyond the typical recipient.

Indeed, Danziger et al. (2000) brought the issue of barriers to employment for welfare leavers to the fore after reform in their analysis of data from WES, which is a longitudinal survey of 753 women on welfare in an urban county in Michigan that was collected in five waves from 1997–2003. They reported that women unable to transition quickly in a work-first environment generally faced multiple barriers including physical and mental health problems, victimization from domestic violence, and lack of access to (any) reliable transportation. Of the fourteen barriers that they assessed, 37 percent of mothers had two to three barriers, and 24 percent had four to six barriers. Their regression estimates suggested that a mother in the latter category had a 20 percentage point lower odds of working at least twenty hours per week than a mother in the former category of two to three barriers.

Bloom, Loprest, and Zedlewski (2011) reported on a series of random assignment demonstration evaluations of programs adopted in various states over the past decade designed to address some of these barriers to employment. The programs reflected a mix of approaches to address the barriers, with some emphasizing a learning-by-doing philosophy where work experience is the key to overcome barriers, and others emphasizing assessment, training, and counseling in a more HCD approach. They concluded that the evidence across the ten programs reviewed was mixed, some positive short-run impacts on employment, but not so positive or unknown impacts in the longer term. In fact the work-first models tended to exhibit poor employment results over time, and while the HCD models emphasizing treatment suggested that service use increased, the corresponding employment effects are not known. One potentially promising model was implemented in rural Nebraska ("Building Nebraska Families") that involved home visits every week or two by a highly trained professional with a master's degree. The overall employment effect was zero, but it was positive for the hardest to serve facing multiple barriers, suggesting the need for future evaluation of more intensive and targeted strategies on the most disadvantaged.

Earnings and Income

Does work "pay" for former welfare recipients? This was an oft-raised question in the aftermath of welfare reform. The record of earnings gains of welfare leavers under the former AFDC program was not encouraging. However, the 1996 reform was being implemented in one of the strongest periods of economic growth in the post–World War II era, and there were complementary reforms that occurred simultaneously; notably, the expansion of the EITC in 1993–1996 and the introduction of the State Children's Health Insurance Program (SCHIP) in 1997 that provided insurance to children in families whose income is low but too high to qualify for Medicaid. It was hoped that the strong economy and other policy reforms, combined with the pull of liberalized earnings disregards and asset limits, as well as the push of work requirements and time limits, would lead to earnings and income gains of single mothers, both those on the program and at risk of joining.

The initial results of the welfare-reform bundle on earnings and income were not especially promising. In a descriptive study, Primus et al. (1999) examined changes in the earnings and disposable income (inclusive of EITC, food stamps and housing assistance, less federal and state tax payments) of female-headed households from 1993 to 1995 and again from 1995 to 1997 from the March CPS. They found that among families in the bottom 20 percent of the single-mother family disposable-income distribution, earnings increased by one-third and disposable income by 14 percent during welfare waiver/pre-TANF era, but then disposable income fell an average of $580, or 7 percent, after passage of PRWORA. Of the decline, 20 percent was lower earnings and 80 percent was lower means-tested transfers. Among those mothers in the second quintile of the income distribution, their earnings continued to rise from 1995–1997, but total disposable income was unchanged due to the clawback of transfers.

The Primus et al. study did not control for any confounding factors, but both Moffitt (1999) and Schoeni and Blank (2000) did control for other factors such as the state business cycle, demographics, and welfare reform.

Moffitt (1999) found that in the pre-PRWORA period (1977–1995) the state-specific welfare waivers led to an average increase in annual earnings of $274, or about 2–3 percent above the mean, but all of this gain was among mothers with a high school diploma or more. He found no effect on family income. Schoeni and Blank (2000), who used CPS data through 1998, found a significant welfare-reform-induced increase in own and family earnings for women with less than high school in the waiver period; however, there was no additional increase after the passage of PRWORA. They did find evidence that welfare reform both in the waiver period and the TANF period reduced the incidence of poverty for the subpopulation of less-skilled women. It is not clear whether the difference between the Moffitt and Schoeni and Blank studies comes from the extra three years in the latter study, or the fact that they exclude those with zero earnings and incomes and use logarithms instead of levels. While Grogger (2003) finds no specific effect of time limits, or age-adjusted limits, on earnings and income, he did find a modest overall reform effect on both, especially if he drops 0s and uses logs of the dependent variable.

Several early studies highlighted the importance of heterogeneity of welfare reform effects, whether by place in the income distribution or education attainment. These ideas were formalized in a few recent papers, most prominently in Bitler, Gelbach, and Hoynes (2006a). They used data from MDRC's random assignment evaluation of Connecticut's Jobs First program, which was implemented between January 1996 and February 1997 and in the field until the end of 2000. Jobs First features a twenty-one-month benefit time limit—the shortest in the nation (see table 4)—along with one of the most generous earnings disregards policies (see table 6). In the static model of labor supply Jobs First generates heterogeneous predictions across the distribution, ranging from no effect at the bottom, to positive effects in the middle, to possibly negative effects at the top of the distribution resulting from behavioral-induced reductions in labor supply. They test these predictions using an inverse probability weighted quantile treatment effects estimator, where the weights are based on propensity score model of the probability of assignment to Jobs First.[16] Bitler, Gelbach, and Hoynes (2006a) find results on earnings consistent with theory, and when they apply the estimator to total income, they find significantly negative effects at the 20th–40th quantiles, and positive effects between the median and 75th quantile.[17] Bollinger, Gonzalez, and Ziliak (2009) generalized the

16. Even though assignment to Jobs First was random, Bitler, Gelbach, and Hoynes (2006a) used weights because of some evidence of pretreatment differences in earnings and welfare income across treatment and control groups.

17. Lamarche and Hartley (2014) test the robustness of Bitler et al. by admitting person-specific latent heterogeneity and reestimating with a panel-quantile estimator. They confirm the results, except at the top of the distribution of earnings where they do not find evidence of fade out, perhaps suggesting that latent preferences for work (or stigma of welfare) induces these women to not pull back effort in the presence of Job First.

Bitler et al. estimates in their study of single-mother families in the March CPS from 1979–2004. They estimated the effects of welfare reform, the business cycle, and interactions of the two, as well as with education attainment of the mother, for various quantiles of both the earnings and disposable income distributions. They found that TANF raised disposable incomes an average of 8 percent among higher-skilled mothers, and raised earnings among low-skilled mothers in the lower half of the distribution by as much as 20 percent, but also resulted in a significant equal-sized loss of after-tax total income among the low skilled. The earnings gains among the low skilled a decade after the implementation of TANF have been more than offset by losses in transfer income.

Leaver Studies.   Adding to the mixed signals of the effects of reform on earnings and income are the findings from leaver studies. Cancian et al. (2002) used two cohorts of leavers in the state of Wisconsin, one from AFDC in 1995 and a second from TANF in 1997, and examined the mother's own earnings and incomes as well as family-level outcomes. Although they found that earnings were substantially higher in the quarter one year after exit compared to the quarter prior to leaving, these earnings gains were wiped out by losses in other income so that total income (both own and family) was lower and poverty rates higher.

This is contrasted with the results in Danziger et al. (2002), who used data from WES and thus followed a single cohort of leavers in a Michigan county from 1997–1999. They found a substantial 63 percent increase in net income for "wage reliant" mothers who were working and not on welfare compared to "welfare reliant" mothers who stayed on welfare and were not working, though even among the former nearly half remained in poverty. Moffitt and Winder (2005) used the first two waves of the Three-City Study (1999 and 2001) to look at the same issues, but found a much smaller gain (14 percent) among working leavers. They argued that this was due to lower receipts of "other family income" among their sample participants compared to those in WES. This was also true among disconnected leavers (not in work or on welfare), but again this group is better off in the WES. Moreover, mothers who combined welfare and work were no worse off than those strictly wage reliant, again contrary to Danziger et al. In response, Danziger and Wang (2005) wrote a rejoinder and found that their earlier results from WES were largely robust, though smaller in magnitude, if the contributions of other members were excluded. While likely not the last word on the issue, Frogner, Moffitt, and Ribar (2009, 169) added the 2005 wave of the Three-City analyses of Moffitt and Winder and concluded that:

> On the critical issue of whether "work pays," which we define as having occurred when the increase in a leaver's own earnings after leaving welfare

exceed the loss of benefits, we find that it does so for employed leavers. However, it does not do so overall; when leavers as a whole are considered, employed and nonemployed combined, increases in average own-earnings are completely offset by declines in TANF and Food Stamp benefits. Incomes for leavers rise, on average, but this is because of increases in other household members' earnings and increases in disability payments. But, on average, going off welfare does not result in sufficient work to compensate for the loss of benefits.

Where there is evidence that work pays for low-skilled women, it comes from demonstrations that involved intensive training of both clients and case managers, assistance finding full-time work, and generous wage supplements such as in MFIP, New Hope, and SSP (Knox, Miller, and Gennetian 2000; Michalopoulos et al. 2002; Duncan, Huston, and Weisner 2008; Duncan et al. 2009).

Antipoverty Effects.   Taken together, the results from leaver studies, demonstrations, and from national samples suggest that many women were worse off financially after welfare reform, especially at the bottom of the distribution. But this result becomes clear only if data post-2000 are brought to bear. Recall that Schoeni and Blank (2000) found that both waivers and TANF resulted in lower family poverty in CPS data through 1998. The latter result was corroborated in Gundersen and Ziliak (2004), who used CPS data from 1980–1999 and found that the depth and severity of after-tax and (in-kind) transfer poverty among female-headed families was lower after welfare reform. Mills, Alwang, and Hazarika (2001) used semiparametric density estimators to compare the 1993 income distribution of single mothers in the CPS to the 1999 income distribution, finding that single moms were better off across the distribution in 1999 (though this is mostly due to the economy).

When post-2000 data are incorporated, the longer-term effects of welfare reform are less encouraging, especially at the low end of the distribution. This is seen descriptively in the fact that (a) TANF fills a smaller share of the so-called poverty gap—the distance between a family's income and their family-size-adjusted poverty line—as demonstrated in Ziliak (2008) and Moffitt and Scholz (2010); (b) there was an increase of over one-third between 2000 and 2005 in the fraction of single mothers disconnected from work and welfare (Blank and Kovak 2009); (c) there was a 50 percentage point reduction from 1996 to 2011 in the number of households with children lifted out of extreme poverty of $2 per day by TANF (Shaefer and Edin 2013); and (d) the evidence of a tempered response by TANF to changing business-cycle conditions (Bitler and Hoynes 2010, forthcoming). This dire set of facts is cause for concern, and also is cause for renewed research to identify the extent to which these relationships are causal. Such work must also confront the challenge of measurement; namely, that reporting rates of TANF have declined over time, especially in the CPS, and the fact that since 70 percent of TANF is nonassistance, we do not as yet have an understanding of whether survey respondents include an estimate of the cash equivalent of some of this in-kind support.

Consumption, Saving, and Material Well-Being

Compared to the voluminous literature on the effects of welfare reform on participation, work, and earnings, research on the consumption, saving, and material well-being of welfare families is limited. As discussed in the theory section, the presence of a consumption floor and asset tests reduces the incentive to save and thus can lead to overconsumption. Hubbard, Skinner, and Zeldes (1995) suggested that this was important within their calibrated dynamic programming model, but as yet these ideas have not been taken directly to the data in the context of estimating an intertemporal consumption function. There was one notable paper that showed that the AFDC program functioned well as a buffer against consumption losses (Gruber 2000), and a couple of others on the transfer system overall as a partial consumption insurance mechanism (Kniesner and Ziliak 2002; Blundell, Pistaferri, and Preston 2008), but nothing using data from the post-welfare-reform era. There have, however, been a few papers on saving, as well as on consumption levels and material hardships more generally, which are discussed below.

Saving.   Powers (1998) offered the first formal test of how saving responds to asset limits, though in her case she focused on the period when limits were federalized as part of OBRA 1981. Prior to this legislation there was considerable variation across states in asset limits, but by 1983 only a few states deviated from the federal liquid asset limit of $1,000. Powers tested how changes in the net wealth of female heads in the National Longitudinal Survey of Young Women changed between 1978 and 1983, concluding that saving decreased by $0.25 for each $1 decrease in the asset limit in 1981.

After the 1996 welfare reform, lower real guarantees, higher asset limits, and higher earning disregards all suggest that saving and the asset position of the typical mother on welfare should be higher in TANF than under AFDC. Hurst and Ziliak (2006) used data from the wealth supplements to the 1994 and 2001 waves of the PSID to test how liquid assets, as well as certain subcomponents such as ownership of checking and saving accounts and vehicles, changed in response to higher liquid asset limits, vehicle limits, and time limits. They found that the saving of female-headed households with children was unresponsive to the welfare-reform-induced changes as part of PRWORA. The upper-bound saving response from the 95 percent confidence interval to a $1,000 increase in the liquid asset limit was $40, and the average response was between $-$80 and $10. Because nearly 85 percent of single-mother families held liquid wealth below one-half of the pre-welfare-reform limit, it suggests that they are rarely binding for most of these families. However, Ziliak (2003), using PSID wealth data for 1984 and 1989, showed means-tested transfers reduce liquid-asset accumulation and precautionary saving motives of those at risk for welfare. This indicates that the consumption floor aspect of welfare is more important than the asset limits per se. There is one exception—welfare reform had a small positive impact on vehicle ownership. This result was corroborated in Sullivan (2006) and McKernan, Ratcliffe, and Nam (2008), though in the latter only from liberalized food stamp vehicle limits. Because car ownership has been shown to be an important causal channel behind the labor market success of low-income workers (Raphael and Rice 2002), the liberalization of vehicle limits may potentially have a long-run benefit, but this has yet to be established.

Consumption and Material Hardship.   Meyer and Sullivan (2004) used data from the Consumer Expenditure Survey (CE) and the PSID from 1984–2000 to estimate the effects of welfare reform at the mean and selected quantiles of the income and consumption distributions. They specified a difference-in-differences model where the treatment group was single women with children and the comparison group was either single childless women or married mothers, and the periods of study were 1984–1990, 1991–1993, 1994–1995, 1996–2000. They found that the level of inflation-adjusted total consumption increased for single mothers, and with a relative increase near the bottom of the consumption distribution for less skilled single mothers. Some of these gains in consumption occurred after 1995, but these changes were smaller and in many cases not statistically significant. Overall, they concluded that the material well-being of single moms did not decline in the five years after PRWORA. However, as highlighted below in Bitler, Gelbach, and Hoynes (2006b), the living arrangements of welfare families is quite complex, and focusing solely on single-mother families may miss important changes in overall household material well-being.

In a follow-up paper, Meyer and Sullivan (2008) used CE data from 1993 to 2003, along with data from the American Housing Survey, the National Time Use Survey, and the American Time Use Survey, to document trends in total spending and separate components. They found that total consumption increased across the distribution by 7 to 12 percent, with most of the increase at the low end of the distribution coming from increased outlays on housing and transportation, with some modest improvements in the quality among the former category.

Kaushal, Gao, and Waldfogel (2007) also used CE data on consumption among single-mother households to compare prereform (1990–1995) years to postreform (1998–2003). They separated the families by education attainment, which is generally deemed to be a fixed characteristic of adults that serves as a good proxy for permanent income, instead of estimating quantiles of the consumption distribution pre- and postreform as in Meyer and Sullivan (2004) because there may be an endogenous change in sample consumption composition in response to reform. They then compared the difference-in-differences in consumption of low-skilled to high-skilled single mothers to that of married mothers who are assumed to be unaffected by reform. The triple-difference estimates suggested that there was no response of total spending after welfare reform among single mothers at risk of welfare, though they did find significant increases in spending on transportation, food away from home, adult clothing, and footwear. The increased spending on "work supports" is consistent with the 2008 paper by Meyer and Sullivan, as well as the vehicle-saving response in Hurst and Ziliak (2006) and Sullivan (2006).

Beyond actual outlays on goods and services, there is interest in measuring material hardships associated with welfare reform. These hardships are intended to capture not only the quality dimension of material well-being, but also the volatility, such as having utilities shut off, pawning items, or engaging in illegal activities to acquire necessary goods and services, and perceptions of economic anxiety. Kalil, Seefeldt, and Wang (2002) used the first two waves of the WES and found that sanctions were significant correlates of these types of material hardships, along with the mother's mental health. Heflin (2006) extended this work to five waves of the WES and to six forms of hardships: food insufficiency, telephone disconnection, utility disconnection, unmet medical needs, improper winter clothing, and housing problems. She reported high levels of hardships, ranging from 20 percent for improper winter clothing to 56 percent for an unmet medical need, and that experiencing the hardship was common (only 10 percent never experience one of the six over a five-year period) and recipients typically faced multiple hardships at the same time (2.6 on average). Cancian and Meyer (2004) in their leaver study of TANF participants in Wisconsin reported that 44 percent of long-term recipients (defined as receiving welfare for at least eighteen months) faced one or more hardships, though this was not qualitatively different from those shorter-term recipients, 41 percent of whom faced at least one hardship. It is a concern that much of our evidence on hardships comes from a couple of area studies, though in an examination of the link between income and material hardship, Sullivan, Turner, and Danziger (2008) reported that the results from WES are comparable to those found in a national sample from the SIPP. To date, however, there is no direct causal evidence on the role that welfare reform had on material hardships.

Health

The concept of "job lock" is most associated with workers' unwillingness to change jobs for fear of loss of health insurance. The corollary facing low-income single mothers was "welfare lock"—the fear of loss of health insurance via Medicaid upon exiting welfare. Categorical eligibility for Medicaid was bestowed upon recipients of AFDC, and this group comprised the largest share of the Medicaid caseload (though spending was higher for poor elderly residing in nursing homes). However, TANF severed the direct link to Medicaid (though families that met AFDC eligibility standards as they existed in 1996 remained eligible). Welfare leavers under TANF whose earnings place them above Medicaid eligibility thresholds retain access to transitional insurance for twelve months after exit. After transitional assistance, the mother is either covered by private insurance (her own policy or employer's) or not at all, and her children are either covered on her plan or by Medicaid or SCHIP, the latter distinction depending on the state of residence, age of children, and income level. If the mother qualifies for Supplemental Security Income upon exit from TANF, then at state discretion she qualifies for Medicaid, and if she is awarded Social Security Disability Insurance, then coverage comes from Medicare after a two-year wait. In short, the anxiety over health coverage can create incentives for long spells on welfare, but these potential spells then confront time limits and work requirements.

Health Insurance.   Several authors have examined the effect of welfare reform on health insurance coverage. This research is comprehensively surveyed in Bitler and Hoynes (2008), and briefly summarized here. Kaestner and Kaushal (2003) were the first to systematically assess this issue, where they estimated a difference-in-difference model of health insurance coverage of the family as a function of welfare waiver and TANF implementation, state caseloads, and person-level and state-level socioeconomic controls. The primary treatment group was low-skilled single mothers (twelve or fewer years of schooling) and the comparison group was either low-skilled, single, childless women or low-skilled married women. Using data from the March CPS for 1992–1999 they found that Medicaid coverage of single mothers fell 7–9 percent after welfare reform, and private insurance rose 6 percent, which on net left fewer mothers insured. They attributed just a small portion of these changes to welfare reform and more to other factors that caused caseloads to decline.

This basic result of lower insurance coverage is corroborated in Bitler, Gelbach, and Hoynes (2005), who used data from the Behavioral Risk Factor Surveillance System (BRFSS) from 1990 to 2000, and in Cawley, Schroeder, and Simon (2006), who used data from 1992 to 1999 in the SIPP. Bitler et al. applied double- and triple-difference estimators to identify the effect of welfare reform on health insurance coverage, where the former models on single women relied solely on state variation over time in policy changes and the latter also utilized married women as an additional comparison group. They found most of the reduced coverage was from Hispanic mothers. Cawley et al. also compared low-skilled (never-married) mothers to low-skilled married mothers, but because they also followed the same family over time they controlled for individual fixed heterogeneity. They found a larger overall effect of TANF, leading to an 8 percent increase in mothers being uninsured postwelfare reform, though they did not provide estimates separately by race and ethnicity. Borjas (2005), using the 1995–2001 March CPS and a triple-difference estimator, found a sizable reduction in Medicaid coverage among immigrants relative to natives, but that coverage overall was stable or even increased because of a large increase in labor supply (and presumably employer-sponsored insurance) among those immigrants most likely affected by the reforms. Holl, Slack, and Stevens (2005), however, found that Hispanics had significantly higher odds than blacks of being uninsured or having a gap in coverage two years after leaving welfare in a random panel of welfare leavers in Illinois, suggesting greater volatility of coverage in this population.

Ham, Li, and Shore-Sheppard (2009) used data spanning 1989–2003 in various panels of the SIPP to reexamine the effect of welfare reform on health insurance coverage among single-mother families. They conducted a battery of tests and actually rejected the use of all previously adopted comparison groups—single childless women, and married women either with or without children. This has important implications for many nonexperimental papers adopting the differences-in-differences estimation strategy as most use the comparison group approach without actually verifying whether or not the treatment and comparison groups have similar "pretreatment" trends in the outcomes of interest. Ham et al. thus estimated their models separately for each group, but also admitted heterogeneity in the effect of reform on insurance coverage by education level of the mother, and whether the mother was an immigrant or native to the United States. The authors found evidence that welfare reform reduced Medicaid coverage among less skilled single mothers, though this loss was somewhat offset by a rise in private coverage. These effects were heavily concentrated among the Hispanic immigrant population, perhaps reflecting the so-called chilling hypothesis. These estimates overall, and for Hispanics, differ from DeLeire, Levine, and Levy (2006), who also estimated models separately by demographic group, and for a similar time period, but used March CPS in lieu of the SIPP. Ham, Li, and Shore-Sheppard (2009) attempted to replicate the DeLeire et al. results in the SIPP, but were unsuccessful. They conjecture that the difference may lie in the timing of questions between surveys—they used monthly data in SIPP while DeLeire et al. used annual data in CPS—and the reference period may be important. Clearly, reconciling these differences in estimates merits research attention.

Mother's Health.   To date there has been much less research on mother's health after welfare reform (child well-being is discussed below). Bitler, Gelbach, and Hoynes (2005) found evidence in the BRFSS of a substantively and statistically significant reduction in health-care utilization of single black and Hispanic women compared to married women, as measured by wellness check-ups, Pap smears, and breast exams. Kaestner and Tarlov (2006) also used data from the BRFSS, but the same identification strategy as employed by Kaestner and Kaushal (2003) in their study of health insurance coverage. Specifically, they identified the effect of welfare reform on health outcomes via its effect on the welfare caseload. They focused on four health behaviors (smoking, binge drinking, diet, and exercise) and four self-reported measures of health (body mass and obesity, days in poor mental health, days in poor physical health, and general health status). Overall, they found little effect of reform on these health outcomes, with the exception of a reduction in binge drinking. Corman et al. (2013) used a variety of data sets to estimate the effects of welfare reform on illicit drug use among low-skilled single mothers. They found that welfare reform led to a 10–21 percent decline in illicit drug use, and a 7–11 percent decline in hospital emergency department episodes. Whether these declines are the result of increased employment, increased work-related drug testing, TANF (or SNAP) policies, or some other mechanism is unknown.

Bitler and Hoynes (2008) used data from five random-assignment demonstrations projects—MFIP, FTP, Jobs First, Iowa's Family Investment Program, and Vermont's Welfare Restructuring Project—that were conducted during the waiver era. Some of these demonstrations had policies like time limits and work requirements, but none are fully translatable to the current TANF structure. Most of the evaluations of health outcomes were conducted three to five years after random assignment, offering a medium-term glimpse of the policy effects. In three of the five experiments they identified increases in the ability to afford a dentist ranging from 2–16 percent, and in four of the five experiments they saw increases in the ability to afford a doctor ranging from 6–16 percent. None of these effects, however, were statistically different from the control group. They also reported that in four of the five demonstrations there was a reduction in the risk of the mother facing depression, with a statistically significant 20 percent effect relative to the baseline in the MFIP program with work incentives only (and not work requirements).

Overall, our knowledge of health effects of welfare reform on the caregiver is limited, both in experimental and nonexperimental settings. The latter arises in part because of the lack of public survey data on health outcomes that provide geographic identifiers necessary to map welfare policies to outcomes, and in part due to relatively small samples in the major health surveys such as NHANES.

Family Structure

All four goals of TANF touch upon family structure, ranging from providing assistance so "children may be cared in their own home," marriage preparation and maintenance, and out-of-wedlock childbearing. This emphasis by policymakers was not because of strong social science evidence that the AFDC program had significant impacts on family matters. Indeed, in his 1992 review Moffitt concludes "the welfare system does not appear capable of explaining most of the long-term trend, or any of the recent trend of increasing numbers of female-headed families in the United States." (1992, 57) Instead, the focus on the family irrespective of the evidence was an example of what Burtless (1990, 76) called "The Economist's Lament," where he noted "Hard evidence about the behavioral consequences of the program evokes at best a shrug outside the behavioral sciences." Regardless, or perhaps in spite of this lack of policy responsiveness to evidence, the research community embraced the cross-state over time changes in the waivers and TANF to reexamine how welfare reform affected marriage, divorce, cohabitation, and fertility.

Living Arrangements.   Bitler et al. (2004) used flow data at the state level to estimate the effect of waivers and TANF on new marriages and new divorces from vital statistics spanning 1989 to 2000. They measured waivers as the share of the year that a state had a major waiver in place and/or that TANF was implemented. Their models controlled for state economic conditions, demographics, and the generosity of the AFDC/TANF benefit, along with fixed state and time effects, and in some cases state linear trends. They found that during the waiver era flows into marriage were about 5 percent lower, and up to 20 percent lower during TANF. At the same time, they found equal size reductions in divorce rates from waivers, and half again the size of marriage rate reductions during TANF. Their results provide mixed evidence in meeting TANF goals—marriages were less likely to dissolve, but also less likely to form. This is somewhat consistent with Schoeni and Blank (2000), who in their analysis of CPS data found that the stock of married mothers increased during the waiver period, but only among less skilled mothers.

However, Fitzgerald and Ribar (2004), who used longitudinal data from multiple waves of the SIPP spanning 1989–2000 to estimate the effects of waivers and TANF on rates of and transitions into and out of female headship, found limited robust effects of welfare reform on any of the female headship outcomes. Graefe and Lichter (2008) likewise examined transitions into marriage, though their focus was on mothers whose first birth was nonmarital, a group of key policy interest. They are unique in their use of 1995 and 2002 waves of the National Survey of Family Growth, which measures marital and fertility histories of a cohort of women prewelfare reform and post. Their difference-in-difference estimates suggest that marriage rates of women whose first birth was out of wedlock compared to women with no child prior to marriage were no higher after welfare reform than before, and those women in the later cohort were more likely to marry men with weaker labor-market potential. Knab et al. (2009) also tested whether the policy reforms affected the likelihood of marriage following a nonmarital birth, though in their case it was marriage to the biological father five years after the birth and was restricted to the post-PRWORA period only via the Fragile Families longitudinal data set. While they found some evidence that higher welfare generosity and strong child support enforcement was associated with lower rates of marriage, these results were quite sensitive to inclusion of state fixed effects because there was little time variation across the fifteen states in the sample.[18]

In a follow-up paper, Bitler, Gelbach, and Hoynes (2006b) used repeated cross sections from the March CPS to examine the effect of reform on the living arrangements of children; that is, whether the child lived with an unmarried parent, with a married parent, or neither. Although they employed similar methods as in their 2004 paper, this project differed not only in the data source, but importantly in that it took the perspective of the child as opposed to the adult caretaker. They do so because the CPS does not document the whereabouts of a mother's child if the child does not reside with the parent. They found that waivers were associated with reductions in the odds that a child lived with an unmarried parent, increases in the chances they resided with a married parent, and increases in the probability of living with neither parent (and instead with a grandparent or nonrelative caretaker). The latter effect was concentrated among black children, while the increased odds of living with a married parent was found largely among Hispanic children. White children had lower odds of living with a married parent before PRWORA, and higher after, painting a mixed picture for this demographic group.

Cherlin and Fomby (2004) used the first two waves of the Three-City Study, which predominantly consists of black and Hispanic families, to examine this same issue and showed that the increase in child residence in two-adult households was via an increase of blended families (biological mother with nonbiological father) and not biological families, and that these blended unions are more unstable and may perhaps lead to long-term challenges for children. Dunifon, Hynes, and Peters (2009) also examined the living arrangements of children using longitudinal data from the SIPP for 1992–1999 along with disaggregated welfare policy measures such as time limits, sanctions, and earnings disregards. Overall, their estimates suggested few consistent effects of welfare policies on the chances of a child living with married, cohabiting, or single parents. Some policies affected certain children only in the waiver period, other policies affected other children only in the TANF period. Perhaps this heterogeneity of treatment is correct, but until such results are verified in more samples and over longer time periods,

---

18. Teitler et al. (2009) also used Fragile Families to examine transitions into marriage after a nonmarital birth, and find that they are lower if currently on welfare, but past welfare usage has no effect on the odds of marriage.

they mainly serve to keep the waters muddied on the effects of welfare reform on marriage.

Fertility. There were several papers that examined the effects of welfare reform on fertility, which have yielded mixed evidence, not unlike in the AFDC research of the 1970s and 1980s. Joyce, Kaestner, and Korenman (2003) used data from Detailed Natality Files for 1990 to 1999 and a difference-in-difference estimator to compare birth rates among a high-welfare risk group of unmarried women with twelve or fewer years of schooling to a comparison group of married women with twelve or fewer years of school or unmarried women with thirteen to fifteen years of school. Their results suggest little effect of welfare reform on fertility, and if anything, there was a slight increase among white and black women. Garfinkel et al. (2003) also used natality files, but spanning 1980–1996. Their focus was comparing cross-state over time changes in the maximum benefit guarantee to state child-support-enforcement efforts. They found that stricter child support enforcement led to a 6–9 percent reduction in fertility, and welfare benefit declines to a 2–4 percent reduction.

Joyce et al. (2004), Kearney (2004), and Horvath-Rose, Peters, and Sabia (2008) focused on the specific role that family caps played on nonmarital childbearing. Joyce et al. employed a triple-difference estimator to estimate the effect of family caps on birth rates and abortion rates. The triple difference comes from comparing family cap to nonfamily cap states before and after implementation, and within these states, births and abortions among those at risk of the cap (at least in the short run) by virtue of their having a prior birth compared to those low-skilled women with no prior birth. They found that birth rates fell and abortion rates rose among women at risk of the cap, but since this was found also in states with no cap, it was not possible to attribute the change to this specific policy (though they cannot rule out a wider welfare reform effect, or no effect at all). Kearney's (2004) estimates using data from Detailed Natality Files reinforced this finding of no family cap effect on fertility, and like the earlier paper by Joyce, Kaestner, and Korenman (2003), she found a perverse positive effect of family caps on higher-order births among unmarried blacks and high school dropout white women. Horvath-Rose, Peters, and Sabia (2008), however, found that nonmarital childbearing is significantly lower after the implementation of family caps, but perversely, marital births were significantly higher. Given the lack of evidence discussed above on the muted effects of welfare reform on marriage, this calls into question the efficacy of the model identification, perhaps as they argue, due to the endogeneity of the family cap policy.

Most of the papers examining family caps estimated the models separately for teenagers and adults. However, there have been a few papers to isolate fertility among teens. Kaestner, Korenman, and O'Neill (2003) compared cohorts of seventeen-year-olds and nineteen-year-olds in the National

Longitudinal Surveys of 1979 and 1997, where the difference-in-difference results were mixed. They found some evidence of increased nonmarital births among seventeen-year-olds, but no effect among nineteen-year-olds. Hao and Cherlin (2004) also used the NLSY, but only the 1997 survey where they used the fertility history rosters to separate fourteen- to sixteen-year-olds prewelfare reform and fourteen- to sixteen-year-olds postreform. The difference-in-difference estimates suggested no effects of welfare reform on teen pregnancy or births. The exceptions are Offner (2005) and Lopoo and DeLeire (2006). Offner used March CPS data on sixteen- and seventeen-year-old girls from 1989 to 2001 and a difference-in-difference estimator where the treatment group was teenage girls in families below twice the poverty line or below the 30th percentile of the income distribution, and the comparison group was girls from higher-income families. He found a decline in teenage out-of-wedlock childbearing of 1.4 percentage points, or 17 percent of the baseline rate. Lopoo and DeLeire used birth data from Detailed Natality Files, to compare birth rates for fifteen- to seventeen-year-olds to eighteen-year-olds before and after welfare reform. The specific policy they isolate is "minor parent rules," whereby teen parents are required to stay in school as a condition of benefit receipt and to reside in a home maintained by an adult caretaker. During the waiver era fifteen states implemented such rules, and thus they exploited the differential timing across states in order to identify the effect. They found a 22 percent decline in annual fertility rates among fifteen- to seventeen-year-olds following implementation of these minor parent provisions.

It is notable that all the evidence to date on the effect of welfare reform on family structure comes from data within five years of implementation of TANF, and thus future research utilizing changes over the past decade is needed.

Child Well-Being

The origins of TANF via the AFDC program, and ADC and Mothers' Pensions before that, lie in improving the well-being of children. Perhaps it is surprising then to close out the review of TANF with research on child-focused outcomes, rather than leading with the topic. Part of this stems from the fact that in the years surrounding welfare reform, most of the policy and research lenses were focused on caseload reductions and employment gains at the expense of broader issues of child and family well-being. Part of it also stems from the fact that the main national surveys that have been employed to conduct observational studies of welfare reform lack child-focused questions (e.g., CPS) or only ask them intermittently (e.g., SIPP). This led many researchers to study the topic using data from demonstration projects, specialized surveys, or to field new longitudinal surveys such as Fragile Families, the Three-City Study, and WES.

Morris et al. (2009) synthesized results on child outcomes from seven random-assignment experiments covering over 30,000 children in the 1990s as part of MDRC's Next Generation Project. They also used the experimental nature of the data to test how welfare policies designed to discourage welfare and encourage work affected children's achievement and school performance. They found that programs with earnings supplements that boost both maternal employment and income improved preschool children's achievement; however, if the program only raised employment and not income then no discernible effects for pre-K children were found. Moreover, programs that supported center-based childcare also resulted in improved achievement for pre-K children relative to children in home-based or other care. Adolescents age eleven and older, on the other hand, experienced worse academic outcomes relative to children in control groups, while no conclusive pattern of effects were found among children ages six to ten. The worse outcomes for older adolescents seem to be linked with maternal employment and the attendant increase in home responsibilities for the older child.

This positive result for young children was recently corroborated in national data by Dahl and Lochner (2012), who showed that the EITC program boosts child achievement among young children, and in the negative corollary result in Heflin and Acevedo (2011), who found lower cognitive achievement among young children on TANF in Fragile Families. Heflin and Acevedo argued that the pathway for this result was from worse mental health of the mother on welfare, which seems to coincide with Herbst's (2013) finding that mothers' subjective well-being was higher after welfare reform via increased attachment to work, and in Morris and Hendra (2009) who reported lower depression among mothers in Florida's FTP program. These positive results for young children are to be contrasted to the nonresults reported in Jacob, Kapustin, and Ludwig (2015) for a housing-voucher experiment in Chicago, in Chase-Lansdale et al. (2003) from the Three-City Study discussed above, and from the negative results reported in Herbst (2014), who used state-time variation in age of child work exemption policy as an instrumental variable for the effect of maternal employment on child achievement in the first year. His estimates from the Early Childhood Longitudinal Study Birth Cohort found that children of mothers who went to work in the first year of life experienced worse cognitive achievement at nine months of age. Moreover, the negative results on adolescents in Morris et al. contrast to the positive mental-health gains for this age group in Chase-Lansdale et al. when the mother transitioned to work after welfare. The difference in the young children's results across studies may lie in the fact that mothers transitioning into work in the Three-City Study, while likely eligible for an earnings supplement like the EITC, may not have taken up the benefit and thus these outcomes look more like those from mothers with employment but no supplement in the Morris et al. (2009) study. The latter do not report on mental-health outcomes of adolescents, so these results are not easily reconciled, and also conflict with the positive results from observational studies on schooling outcomes among teenagers discussed below.

In related leavers studies, Kalil and Dunifon (2007) reported results from five waves of the WES that mothers' employment had no deleterious effects on children's behavior. Osborne and Knab (2007) used a cross-section of Fragile Families at the three-year follow-up survey after the child's birth, and they reported that child outcomes were better after the mother transitioned to work, but this stemmed from positive self-selection of the types of mothers who chose paid work, and not a result of paid work per se. Slack et al. (2007) reported from the Illinois Families Study that children of mothers who were unemployed and off welfare were in better health than similar children whose mothers were working and off welfare, and the latter were comparable to those on welfare regardless of work status. This result is surprising as this is the group generally defined as "disconnected mothers," and it holds even controlling for confounding factors, including higher rates of marriage among the no work/no welfare group. Since their study is based on a small sample in a single state, it is premature to draw any generalizations.

There are several negative child health outcomes from studies using national surveys and standard difference-in-differences estimators. For example, Haider, Jacknowitz, and Schoeni (2003) found rates of breast feeding to be 5.5 percent lower overall after welfare reform, and as much as 22 percent lower among mothers receiving WIC and residing in states with stringent work requirements on new mothers with children six months of age. Kaestner and Lee (2005) reported reductions in first trimester prenatal care, the number of prenatal care visits, and an increase in the fraction of low birth weight babies. Paxson and Waldfogel (2003) reported that in states with stricter lifetime welfare limits and sanctions for noncompliance there was an increase in substantiated child maltreatment. Kalil and Ziol-Guest (2009) found that the gap between low-income children of noncitizens versus natives in terms of children's health and family access to care widened up to 30 percent over the baseline, suggesting that immigrant families face barriers, whether real or perceived, to health care after PRWORA. The exception here is Dunifon, Hynes, and Peters (2006), who used two waves from the SIPP to examine pre- and post-welfare-reform effects and found no consistent effects on child outcomes. This study, however, only employed a difference estimator and thus did not net out potentially confounding trends that could be controlled with a comparison group.

There is a potential bright spot for adolescents (beyond the couple of studies that found lower teen births) in recent work on education attainment. Offner (2005), in the same paper on teen fertility, examined drop-out rates among teens. He reported that drop-out rates among sixteen- and seventeen-year-old teens declined 3.2 percentage points after welfare reform, or 24 percent of the prereform baseline. Dave, Corman, and Reichman (2012) used the schooling supplement of the CPS fielded in October of each year, but restricted attention to the years 1992–2001. They employed a triple-difference estimator that compared pre- and post-welfare-reform periods (waivers and TANF separately) for a group at high risk of welfare (unmarried females ages fifteen to twenty living with one or no parent who had less than a college education) versus a group at low risk (males of similar SES background). They found that welfare reform reduced the odds of a teen girl dropping out of high school by 15 percent. Miller and Zhang (2012), who used a difference-in-difference estimator applied to both October CPS and to administrative data from the Common Core of Data from 1991 to 2005, found a reduction in high school drop-out rates of males and females combined of 20 percent after welfare reform.

4.5   Summary

Welfare reform spawned a flurry of new research—observational studies, demonstration projects, and surveys—that stemmed both from the broad reach of the new TANF program across multiple domains of family life, and from extensive variation in program features across states and over time that facilitated nonexperimental program evaluation. Nearly two decades after passage of the landmark legislation, are we in a position to draw firm conclusions on the effects of welfare reform? With few exceptions, it is still premature to make definitive claims on TANF.

Work and welfare use were the focal research interests in the early days of welfare reform, and to date remain the most widely studied outcomes. The weight of research evidence seems to indicate that welfare reform reduced participation in the TANF program, increased employment and earnings, and decreased total after-tax and transfer incomes, at least in the lower half of the income distribution of single mothers. To be certain there is wide disagreement in the literature on the magnitude of effects vis-à-vis the business cycle and other policy changes such as the expanded EITC, but there is agreement on the direction. This is perhaps as close to consensus as we get at this stage. Within the bundle of welfare reform policies, time limits and work requirements are the two leading reforms that contributed to the decline in welfare use and rise in employment rates, but what role they had on broader measures of earnings and disposable incomes is as of yet unsettled.

Beyond work and welfare, our confidence begins to wane, either because of scarcity of evidence or wide discrepancy of estimates. There is some limited evidence that welfare reform had no effect on saving (except for increased vehicle wealth) or total consumption, and it reduced health insurance coverage and lowered health outcomes (especially among Hispanics). There are also a few studies that show that flows into marriage, teen births, and teen drop-out rates are all lower after welfare reform, but again we are limited on the number of studies using national data and rigorous identification methods to draw firm conclusions.

The areas in which I believe the evidence to date is too mixed, or even nonexistent, includes consumption and labor supply decisions over time, the interaction of work requirements with human capital development and subsequent earnings, health and fertility outcomes of mothers, living arrangements of children, and welfare use across generations. Regarding the latter, a key argument made by policymakers in favor of the TANF program, especially the introduction of time limits and work requirements, was to break the dependence on welfare not only for the current cohort of recipients, but also for their children. To my knowledge there has been no study on the intergenerational transmission of welfare post TANF. I would add to this list a need to sort out some of the current conflicting evidence on child well-being that arises from demonstrations, leaver studies, and observational studies—young children versus adolescents—in terms of physical and emotional health. The historical underpinning of TANF is on improving child welfare, and yet some of our weakest causal evidence to date on welfare reform is in this domain. Some of this is due to lack of national data on child outcomes, some due to underreporting in surveys, and some due to lack of access to geocoded data necessary to link outcomes to local policy environments. This is an area where more widespread access to secure data sites, such as Census Research Data Centers that also house major health surveys, would foster new research on welfare reform.

Our knowledge base of the effects of welfare reform is also limited by the fact that with very few exceptions all the evidence comes from the first five years after the introduction of TANF. This is a real shortcoming because many of the outcomes of interest are likely to be realized only after many years. It is also disconcerting because as depicted in figure 4.9, the flow of new research on welfare reform has tapered off significantly in recent years, and how low-income families and their children have fared during the Great Recession across these domains is largely unknown. Some of this reduced research flow may be from the misguided perception that TANF is now a "small" program in the safety net and thus less interesting to study. To be certain, programs like SNAP, SSI, and the EITC are larger in terms of annual appropriations, but at $30–$35 billion per year, TANF is still a significant player in the safety net, and touches many more American families than caseload figures indicate because the latter only capture cash assistance whereas two-thirds of spending today is on nonassistance. Moreover, there is ongoing discussion among some members of Congress to block-grant SNAP and Medicaid, using TANF as a model. The limited evidence to date suggests that TANF did not respond to the Great Recession, and this lack of business-cycle response contributed to the growth of deep poverty. There has been scant research in the last decade on the implications of TANF financing for state budgets and family well-being. Thus, an expanded research base is needed to not only assess TANF, but also to offer guidance for evidence-based policy discussions on the wider safety net.

References

Ashenfelter, Orley. 1983. "Determining Participation in Income-Tested Social Programs." *Journal of the American Statistical Association* 78 (383): 517–25.

Barr, Nicholas A., and Robert E. Hall. 1981. "The Probability of Dependence on Public Assistance." *Economica* 48 (190): 109–23.

Bartik, Timothy, and Randall Eberts. 1999. "Examining the Effect of Industry Trends and Structure on Welfare Caseloads." In *Economic Conditions and Welfare Reform*, edited by Sheldon Danziger, 119–57. Kalamazoo, MI: Upjohn Institute.

Becker, Gary, and Nigel Tomes. 1979. "An Equilibrium Theory of the Distribution of Income and Intergenerational Mobility." *Journal of Political Economy* 87 (6): 1153–89.

Ben Porath, Yoram. 1967. "The Production of Human Capital and the Life Cycle of Earnings." *Journal of Political Economy* 75 (4): 352–65.

Berger, Mark, and Dan Black. 1992. "Child Care Subsidies, Quality of Care, and the Labor Supply of Low-Income, Single Mothers." *Review of Economics and Statistics* 74:635–42.

Bernal, Raquel, and Michael P. Keane. 2011. "Child Care Choices and Children's Cognitive Achievement: The Case of Single Mothers." *Journal of Labor Economics* 29 (3): 459–512.

Bitler, Marianne P., and Hilary W. Hoynes. 2008. "Welfare Reform and Indirect Impacts on Health." In *Making Americans Healthier: Social and Economic Policy as Health Policy*, edited by Robert F. Schoeni, James S. House, George A. Kaplan, and Harold Pollack, 231–80. New York: Russell Sage Foundation.

———. 2010. "The State of the Safety Net in the Post-Welfare Reform Era." *Brookings Papers on Economic Activity* (Fall):71–127.

———. 2013. "Immigrants, Welfare Reform, and the US Safety Net." In *Immigration, Poverty, and Socioeconomic Inequality*, edited by David Card and Steven Raphael. New York: Russell Sage Foundation.

———. Forthcoming. "The More Things Change the More They Stay the Same? The Safety Net and Poverty in the Great Recession." *Journal of Labor Economics*.

Bitler, Marianne P., Jonah B. Gelbach, and Hilary W. Hoynes. 2003. "Some Evidence on Race, Welfare Reform, and Household Income." *American Economic Review Papers and Proceedings* 93 (2): 293–98.

———. 2005. "Welfare Reform and Health." *Journal of Human Resources* 40:309–34.

———. 2006a. "What Mean Impacts Miss: Distributional Effects of Welfare Reform Experiments." *American Economic Review* 96 (4): 988–1012.

———. 2006b. "Welfare Reform and Children's Living Arrangements." *Journal of Human Resources* 41:1–27.

Bitler, Marianne P., Jonah B. Gelbach, Hilary W. Hoynes, and Madeline Zavodny. 2004. "The Impact of Welfare Reform on Marriage and Divorce." *Demography* 41 (2): 213–36.

Blank, Rebecca. 1989. "Analyzing the Length of Welfare Spells." *Journal of Public Economics* 39 (3): 245–73.

———. 2001. "What Causes Public Assistance Caseloads to Grow?" *Journal of Human Resources* 36 (1): 85–118.

———. 2002. "Evaluating Welfare Reform in the United States." *Journal of Economic Literature* 40 (4): 1105–66.

———. 2009. "What We Know, What We Don't Know, and What We Need to Know about Welfare Reform." In *Welfare Reform and Its Long-Term Consequences for America's Poor*, edited by James P. Ziliak, 22–58. Cambridge, Cambridge University Press.

Blank, Rebecca M., and Brian Kovak. 2009. "The Growing Problem of Disconnected Single Mothers." In *Making the Work-Based Safety Net Work Better: Forward-Looking Policies to Help Low-Income Families*, edited by Carolyn J. Heinrich and John Karl Scholz. New York: Russell Sage Foundation.

Blau, David, and Janet Currie. 2006. "Preschool, Day Care and After-School Care: Who's Minding the Kids." In *Handbook of Economics of Education*, edited by Eric Hanushek and Finis Welch, 1163–278. New York: North Holland.

Blomquist, N. Soren. 1985. "Labor Supply in a Two-Period Model: The Effect of a Nonlinear Progressive Income Tax." *Review of Economic Studies* 52 (2): 515–24.

Bloom, Dan, Pamela J. Loprest, and Sheila R. Zedlewski. 2011. "TANF Recipients with Barriers to Employment." Temporary Assistance for Needy Families Research Synthesis Brief no. 8, Washington, DC, Urban Institute.

Blundell, Richard, Luigi Pistaferri, and Ian Preston. 2008. "Consumption Inequality and Partial Insurance." *American Economic Review* 98 (5): 1887–921.

Bollinger, Christopher, Luis Gonzalez, and James P. Ziliak. 2009. "Welfare Reform and the Level and Composition of Income." In *Welfare Reform and Its Long-Term Consequences for America's Poor*, edited by James P. Ziliak, 59–103. Cambridge, Cambridge University Press.

Borjas, George J. 1999. "Immigration and Welfare Magnets." *Journal of Labor Economics* 17 (4): 604–37.

———. 2005. "Welfare Reform, Labor Supply, and Health Insurance in the Immigrant Population." *Journal of Health Economics* 22 (6): 933–58.

Brueckner, Jan. 2000. "Welfare Reform and the Race to the Bottom: Theory and Evidence." *Southern Economic Journal* 66 (3): 505–25.

Bucklin, Dorothy. 1939. "Public Aid for the Care of Dependent Children in Their Homes, 1932–38." *Social Security Bulletin* 2 (4): 24–35.

Burke, V. 1996. "New Welfare Law: Comparison of the New Block Grant Program with Aid to Families with Dependent Children." Report no. 96–720EPW, Washington, DC, Congressional Research Service.

Burtless, Gary. 1990. "The Economist's Lament: Public Assistance in America." *Journal of Economic Perspectives* 4 (1): 57–78.

Cadena, Brian, Sheldon Danziger, and Kristin Seefeldt. 2006. "Measuring State Welfare Policy Changes: Why Don't They Explain Caseload and Employment Outcomes?" *Social Science Quarterly* 87 (4): 808–17.

Cancian, Maria, Robert Haveman, Daniel Meyer, and Barbara Wolfe. 2002. "Before and after TANF: The Economic Well-Being of Women Leaving Welfare." *Social Service Review* 76 (4): 603–41.

Cancian, Maria, and Daniel R. Meyer. 2004. "Alternative Measures of Economic Success among TANF Participants: Avoiding Poverty, Hardship and Dependence on Public Assistance." *Journal of Policy Analysis and Management* 23 (3): 531–48.

Capps, Randy, Michael Fix, and Everett Henderson. 2009. "Trends in Immigrants' Use of Public Assistance after Welfare Reform." In *Immigrants and Welfare*, edited by Michael Fix. New York: Russell Sage Foundation.

Cawley, John, Mathias Schroeder, and Kosali Simon. 2006. "How Did Welfare Reform Affect the Health Insurance Coverage of Women and Children?" *Health Services Research* 41 (2): 486–506.

Chan, Marc. 2013. "A Dynamic Model of Welfare Reform." *Econometrica* 81 (3): 941–1001.

Chase-Lansdale, P. Lindsay, Robert A. Moffitt, Brenda J. Lohman, Andrew J. Cherlin, Rebekah Levine Coley, Laura D. Pittman, Jennifer Roff, and Elizabeth Votruba-Drzal. 2003. "Mothers' Transitions from Welfare to Work and the Well-Being of Preschoolers and Adolescents." *Science* 299:1548–52.

Cherlin, Andrew J., and Paula Fomby. 2004. "Welfare, Work and Changes in Mothers' Living Arrangements in Low-Income Families." *Population Research and Policy Review* 23 (5–6): 543–65.

Chernick, Howard. 1998. "Fiscal Effects of Block Grants for the Needy: An Interpretation of the Evidence." *International Tax and Public Finance* 5 (2): 205–33.

Chernick, Howard, and Therese McGuire. 1999. "The States, Welfare Reform, and the Business Cycle." In *Economic Conditions and Welfare Reform*, edited by Sheldon Danziger, 275–303. Kalamazoo, MI: Upjohn Institute.

Chief, Elizabeth. 1979. "Need Determination in AFDC Program." *Social Security Bulletin* 42 (9): 11–21.

Child Trends. 2014. *Births to Unmarried Women: Indicators on Children and Youth.* http://www.childtrends.org/wp-content/uploads/2012/11/75_Births_to_Unmarried _Women.pdf.

Corman, Hope, Dhaval Dave, Dhiman Das, and Nancy Reichman. 2013. "Effects of Welfare Reform on Illicit Drug Use of Adult Women." *Economic Inquiry* 51 (1): 653–74.

Council of Economic Advisers. 1997. "Explaining the Decline in Welfare Receipt, 1993–1996." Technical Report, Washington, DC, Executive Office of the President.

———. 1999. "The Effects of Welfare Policy and the Economic Expansion on Welfare Caseloads: An Update." Technical Report, Washington, DC, Executive Office of the President.

Dahl, Gordon, and Lance Lochner. 2012. "The Impact of Family Income on Child Achievement: Evidence from the Earned Income Tax Credit." *American Economic Review* 102 (5): 1927–56.

Danielson, Caroline, and Jacob Klerman. 2008. "Did Welfare Reform Cause the Caseload Decline?" *Social Service Review* 82 (4): 703–30.

Danziger, Sandra K., Mary Corcoran, Sheldon Danziger, Colleen Heflin, Ariel Kalil, Judith Levine, Daniel Rosen, Kristin Seefeldt, Kristine Siefert, and Richard Tolman. 2000. "Barriers to the Employment of Welfare Recipients." In *Prosperity for All?* edited by Robert Cherry and William Rodgers, 239–72. New York: Russell Sage Foundation.

Danziger, Sheldon, Colleen Heflin, Mary Corcoran, Elizabeth Oltmans, and Hui-Chen Wang. 2002. "Does it Pay to Move from Welfare to Work?" *Journal of Policy Analysis and Management* 21 (4): 671–92.

Danziger, Sheldon, and Hui-Chen Wang. 2005. "Does it Pay to Move from Welfare to Work? Reply to Robert Moffitt and Katie Winder." *Journal of Policy Analysis and Management* 24 (2): 411–17.

Dave, Dhaval, Hope Corman, and Nancy Reichman. 2012. "Effects of Welfare Reform on Education Acquisition of Adult Women." *Journal of Labor Research* 33 (2): 251–82.

De Jong, Gordon F., Deborah Roempke Graete, Shelley K. Irving, and Tonja St. Pierre. 2006. "Measuring State TANF Policy Variations and Change after Reform." *Social Science Quarterly* 87 (4): 755–81.

DeLeire, Thomas, Judith A. Levine, and Helen Levy. 2006. "Is Welfare Reform Responsible for Low-Skilled Women's Declining Health Insurance Coverage in the 1990s?" *Journal of Human Resources* 41 (3): 495–528.

Duncan, Greg J., Hans Bos, Lisa L. Gennetian, and Heather Hill. 2009. "New Hope: A Thoughtful and Effective Approach to 'Make Work Pay.'" *Northwestern Journal of Law and Social Policy* 4 (1): 100–15.

Duncan, Greg J., Aletha C. Huston, and Thomas S. Weisner. 2008. *Higher Ground: New Hope for the Working Poor and their Children.* New York: Russell Sage Foundation.

Dunifon, Rachel, Kathryn Hynes, and H. Elizabeth Peters. 2009. "State Welfare Policies and Children's Living Arrangements." *Social Service Review* 83 (3): 351–88.
Dyke, Andrew, Carolyn J. Heinrich, Peter R. Mueser, Kenneth R. Troske, and Kyung-Seong Jeon. 2006. "The Effects of Welfare-to-Work Program Activities on Labor Market Outcomes." *Journal of Labor Economics* 24 (3): 567–608.
Ellwood, David. 1999. "The Impact of the Earned Income Tax Credit and Social Policy Reforms on Work, Marriage, and Living Arrangements." *National Tax Journal* 53 (4, part 2): 1063–1105.
Falk, Gene. 2012. "The Temporary Assistance for Needy Families (TANF) Block Grant: A Primer on TANF Financing and Federal Requirements." CRS Report for Congress, Congressional Research Service, Washington, DC.
Fang, Hanming, and Michael P. Keane. 2004. "Assessing the Impact of Welfare Reform on Single Mothers." *Brookings Papers on Economic Activity* 2004:1–116.
Fang, Hanming, and Dan Silverman. 2009. "Time-Inconsistency and Welfare Program Participation." *International Economic Review* 50 (4): 1043–77.
Figlio, David N., and James P. Ziliak. 1999. "Welfare Reform, the Business Cycle, and the Decline in AFDC Caseloads." In *Economic Conditions and Welfare Reform*, edited by Sheldon Danziger, 17–48. Kalamazoo, MI: Upjohn Institute For Employment Research.
Fishback, Price, and Melissa Thomasson. 2006. "Social Welfare: 1929 to the Present." In *Historical Statistics of the United States: Colonial Times to the Present*, Millennial Edition On Line, edited by Susan B. Carter, Scott Sigmund Gartner, Michael R. Haines, Alan L. Olmstead, Richard Sutch, and Gavin Wright, 700–19. Cambridge: Cambridge University Press.
Fitzgerald, John. 1991. "Welfare Durations and the Marriage Market: Evidence from the Survey of Income and Program Participation." *Journal of Human Resources* 26(3): 545–61.
Fitzgerald, John M., and David C. Ribar. 2004. "Welfare Reform and Female Headship." *Demography* 41 (2):189–212.
Fix, Michael E., and Jeffrey S. Passel. 1999. "Trends in Noncitizens' and Citizens' Use of Public Benefits Following Welfare Reform: 1994–1997." Research Report, Washington, DC, Urban Institute.
Fording, Richard C., Joe Soss, and Sanford F. Schram. 2007. "Devolution, Discretion, and the Effect of Local Political Values on TANF Sanctioning." *Social Service Review* 81 (2): 285–316.
Fraker, Thomas, Robert Moffitt, and Douglas Wolf. 1985. "Effective Tax Rates and Guarantees in the AFDC Program, 1967–1982." *Journal of Human Resources* 20 (2): 251–63.
Frogner, Bianca, Robert Moffitt, and David Ribar. 2009. "How Families are Doing Nine Years after Welfare Reform: 2005 Evidence from the Three-City Study." In *Welfare Reform and Its Long-Term Consequences for America's Poor*, edited by James P. Ziliak, 140–71. Cambridge: Cambridge University Press.
Garfinkel, Irv, Chien-Chung Huang, Sara S. McLanahan, and Daniel S. Gaylin. 2003. "The Roles of Child Support Enforcement and Welfare in Non-Marital Childbearing." *Journal of Population Economics* 16 (1): 55–70.
Gelbach, Jonah. 2004. "Migration, the Life Cycle, and State Benefits: How Low in the Bottom?" *Journal of Political Economy* 112 (5): 1091–130.
Germanis, Peter. 2015. "TANF is Broken! It's Time to Reform 'Welfare Reform.'" Unpublished Manuscript. http://mlwiseman.com/wp-content/uploads/2013/09/TANF-is-Broken.072515.pdf.
Gordon, Linda, and Felice Batlan. 2011. "The Legal History of the Aid to Dependent Children Program." Report, The Social Welfare History Project. Accessed Feb-

ruary 12, 2015. http://www.socialwelfarehistory.com/programs/aid-to-dependent
-children-the-legal-history/.

Graefe, Deborah R., and Daniel T. Lichter. 2008. "Marriage Patterns among Unwed Mothers: Before and after PRWORA." *Journal of Policy Analysis and Management* 27 (3): 479–97.

Gramlich, Edward, and Deborah Laren. 1984. "Migration and Income Redistribution Responsibilities." *Journal of Human Resources* 19 (4): 489–511.

Green Book. 1998. "Section 7-Aid to Families with Dependent Children and Temporary Assistance for Needy Families (Title-IVA)." Background Material and Data on the Programs within the Jurisdiction of the Committee on Ways and Means, US Congress, Washington, DC.

———. 2008. "Section 7-Temporary Assistance for Needy Families (TANF)." Background Material and Data on the Programs within the Jurisdiction of the Committee on Ways and Means, US Congress, Washington, DC.

Grogger, Jeffrey. 2003. "The Effects of Time Limits, the EITC, and Other Policy Changes on Welfare Use, Work, and Income among Female-Headed Families." *Review of Economics and Statistics* 85 (2): 394–408.

———. 2004. "Time Limits and Welfare Use." *Journal of Human Resources* 39 (2): 405–24.

Grogger, Jeffrey, Steven J. Haider, and Jacob Klerman. 2003. "Why Did the Welfare Rolls Fall during the 1990s?" *American Economic Review Papers and Proceedings* 93 (2): 288–92.

Grogger, Jeffrey, and Lynn A. Karoly. 2005. *Welfare Reform: Effects of a Decade of Change*. Cambridge, MA: Harvard University Press.

Grogger, Jeffrey, and Charles Michalopoulos. 2003. "Welfare Dynamics under Time Limits." *Journal of Political Economy* 111 (3): 530–54.

Grossman, Michael. 1972. "On the Concept of Health Capital and the Demand for Health." *Journal of Political Economy* 80 (2): 223–55.

Gruber, Jonathan. 2000. "Cash Welfare as a Consumption Smoothing Mechanism for Single Mothers." *Journal of Public Economics* 75 (2): 157–82.

———. 2003. "Medicaid." In *Means-Tested Transfer Programs in the United States*, edited by Robert Moffitt. Chicago: University of Chicago Press.

Gundersen, Craig, and James P. Ziliak. 2004. "Poverty and Macroeconomic Performance across Space, Race, and Family Structure." *Demography* 41 (1): 61–86.

Hahn, Heather McCallum, and Rachel Frisk. 2010. "Temporary Assistance for Needy Families: Implications of Recent Legislative and Economic Changes for State Programs and Work Participation." Report no. GAO-10-525, US Government Accountability Office, Washington, DC.

Haider, Steven J., Alison Jacknowitz, and Robert F. Schoeni. 2003. "Welfare Work Requirements and Child Well-Being: Evidence from the Effects on Breast-Feeding." *Demography* 40 (3): 479–97.

Haider, Steven J., and Jacob Klerman. 2005. "Dynamic Properties of the Welfare Caseload." *Labour Economics* 12 (5): 629–48.

Haider, Steven J., Robert F. Schoeni, Yuhua Bao, and Caroline Danielson. 2004. "Immigrants, Welfare Reform, and the Economy." *Journal of Policy Analysis and Management* 23 (4):745–64.

Ham, John C., Xianghong Li, and Lara Shore-Sheppard. 2009. "A Reexamination of the Impact of Welfare Reform on Health Insurance among Less-Skilled Women." In *Welfare Reform and Its Long-Term Consequences for America's Poor*, edited by James P. Ziliak, 217–54. Cambridge: Cambridge University Press.

Hansan, John E. 2011. "English Poor Laws: Historical Precedents of Tax-Supported Relief for the Poor." Report, The Social Welfare History Project. Accessed November 10, 2014. http://www.socialwelfarehistory.com/programs/poor-laws/.

Hao, Lingxin, and Andrew J. Cherlin. 2004. "Welfare Reform and Teenage Pregnancy, Childbirth, and School Dropout." *Journal of Marriage and the Family* 66 (1): 179–94.

Haskins, Ronald. 2007. *Work over Welfare: The Inside Story of the 1996 Welfare Reform Law.* Washington, DC: Brookings Institution Press.

———. 2009. "Limiting Welfare Benefits for Noncitizens: Emergence of Compromises." In *Immigrants and Welfare*, edited by Michael E. Fix. New York: Russell Sage Foundation.

Heckman, James, Lance Lochner, and Ricardo Cossa. 2003. "Learning-By-Doing Versus On-the-Job Training: Using Variation Induced by the EITC to Distinguish between Models of Skill Formation." In *Designing Inclusion: Tools to Raise Low-End Pay and Employment in Private Enterprise*, edited by Edmund Phelps, 74–130. Cambridge: Cambridge University Press.

Heflin, Colleen. 2006. "Dynamics of Material Hardship in the Women's Employment Study." *Social Service Review* 80 (3): 377–97.

Heflin, Colleen, and Sharon Kukla Acevedo. 2011. "Welfare Receipt and Early Childhood Cognitive Scores." *Children and Youth Services Review* 33 (5): 634–43.

Herbst, Chris M. 2013. "Welfare Reform and the Subjective Well Being of Single Mothers." *Journal of Population Economics* 26 (1): 203–38.

———. 2014. "Are Parental Welfare Work Requirements Good for Disadvantaged Children? Evidence from Age-of-Youngest Child Exemptions." IZA Discussion Paper no. 8485, Institute for the Study of Labor. http://ftp.iza.org/dp8485.pdf.

Holl, Jane L., Kristin Shook Slack, and Amy Bush Stevens. 2005. "Welfare Reform and Health Insurance: Consequences for Parents." *American Journal of Public Health* 95 (2): 279–85.

Horvath-Rose, Ann E., H. Elizabeth Peters, and Joseph J. Sabia. 2008. "Capping Kids: The Family Cap and Non-Marital Childbearing," *Population Research and Policy Review* 27 (2): 119–38.

Hotz, V. Joseph, Guido Imbens, and Jacob Klerman. 2006. "Evaluating the Differential Effects of Alternative Welfare-to-Work Training Components: A Re-Evaluation of the California GAIN Program." *Journal of Labor Economics* 24 (3): 521–66.

Hoynes, Hilary. 1996. "Welfare Transfers in Two-Parent Families: Labor Supply and Welfare Participation under AFDC-UP." *Econometrica* 64 (2): 295–332.

———. 2000. "Local Labor Markets and Welfare Spells: Do Demand Conditions Matter?" *Review of Economics and Statistics* 82 (3): 351–68.

Hoynes, Hilary, and Thomas MaCurdy. 1994. "Has the Decline in Benefits Shortened Welfare Spells?" *American Economic Review Papers and Proceedings* 84 (2): 43–48.

Huang, Chien-Chung, Irwin Garfinkel, and Jane Waldfogel. 2004. "Child Support Enforcement and Welfare Caseloads." *Journal of Human Resources* 39 (1): 108–34.

Hubbard, R. Glenn, Jonathan Skinner, and Stephen Zeldes. 1995. "Precautionary Saving and Social Insurance." *Journal of Political Economy* 103 (2): 360–99.

Hurst, Erik, and James P. Ziliak. 2006. "Do Welfare Asset Limits Affect Household Saving? Evidence from Welfare Reform." *Journal of Human Resources* 41 (1): 46–71.

Hutchens, Robert. 1978. "Changes in AFDC Tax Rates: 1967–71." *Journal of Human Resources* 13 (1): 60–74.

Jacob, Brian, Max Kapustin, and Jens Ludwig. 2015. "The Impact of Housing Assistance on Child Outcomes: Evidence from a Randomized Housing Lottery." *Quarterly Journal of Economics* 130 (1): 465–506.

Joyce, Theodore, Robert Kaestner, and Sanders Korenman. 2003. "Welfare Reform and Non-Marital Fertility in the 1990s: Evidence from Birth Records." *Advances in Economic Analysis and Policy* 3(1): Article Number 6.

Joyce, Theodore, Robert Kaestner, Sanders Korenman, and Stanley Henshaw. 2004. "Family Cap Provisions and Changes in Births and Abortions." *Population Research and Policy Review* 23 (5–6): 475–511.

Kaestner, Robert, and Neeraj Kaushal. 2003. "Welfare Reform and Health Insurance Coverage of Low Income Families." *Journal of Health Economics* 22 (6): 959–81.

———. 2005. "Immigrant and Native Responses to Welfare Reform." *Journal of Population Economics* 18 (1): 69–92.

Kaestner, Robert, Sanders Korenman, and June O'Neill. 2003. "Has Welfare Reform Changed Teenage Behaviors?" *Journal of Policy Analysis and Management* 22 (2): 225–48.

Kaestner, Robert, and Won Chan Lee. 2005. "The Effect of Welfare Reform on Prenatal Care and Birth Weight." *Health Economics* 14 (5): 497–511.

Kaestner, Robert, and Elizabeth Tarlov. 2006. "Changes in the Welfare Caseload and the Health of Low-Educated Mothers." *Journal of Policy Analysis and Management* 25 (3): 623–43.

Kaiser Commission on Medicaid and the Uninsured. 2012. "Medicaid Financing: An Overview of the Federal Medicaid Matching Rate (FMAP)." Policy Brief no. 8352, The Henry J. Kaiser Family Foundation. http://kff.org/health-reform/issue-brief/medicaid-financing-an-overview-of-the-federal/.

Kalil, Ariel, and Rachel Dunifon. 2007. "Maternal Work and Welfare Use and Child Well-Being: Evidence from Six Years of Data from the Women's Employment Study." *Children and Youth Services Review* 29:742–61.

Kalil, Ariel, Kristin S. Seefeldt, and Hui-chen Wang. 2002. "Sanctions and Material Hardship under TANF." *Social Service Review* 76 (4): 642–62.

Kalil, Ariel, and Kathleen Ziol-Guest. 2009. "Welfare Reform and Health among the Children of Immigrants." In *Welfare Reform and its Long-Term Consequences for America's Poor*, edited by James P. Ziliak, 308–36. Cambridge: Cambridge University Press.

Kassabian, David, Erika Huber, Elissa Cohen, and Linda Giannarelli. 2013. "Welfare Rules Databook: State TANF Policies as of July 2012." OPRE Report no. 2013–27, US Department of Health and Human Services, Washington, DC.

Katz, Michael B. 1986. *In the Shadow of the Poorhouse*. New York: Basic Books.

Kaushal, Neeraj. 2005. "New Immigrants' Location Choices: Magnets without Welfare." *Journal of Labor Economics* 23 (1): 59–80.

Kaushal, Neeraj, Qin Gao, and Jane Waldfogel. 2007. "Welfare Reform and Family Expenditures on Children." *Social Service Review* 81 (3): 369–96.

Kaushal, Neeraj, and Robert Kaestner. 2001. "From Welfare to Work: Has Welfare Reform Worked?" *Journal of Policy Analysis and Management* 20 (4): 699–719.

Keane, Michael, and Robert Moffitt. 1998. "A Structural Model of Multiple Welfare Program Participation and Labor Supply." *International Economic Review* 39 (3): 553–89.

Keane, Michael, and Kenneth Wolpin. 2002a. "Estimating Welfare Effects Consistent with Forward-Looking Behavior. Part I: Lessons from a Simulation Exercise." *Journal of Human Resources* 37 (3): 570–99.

———. 2002b. "Estimating Welfare Effects Consistent with Forward-Looking Behavior. Part II: Empirical Results." *Journal of Human Resources* 37 (3): 600–22.

———. 2010. "The Role of Labor and Marriage Markets, Preference Heterogeneity, and the Welfare System in the Life Cycle Decisions of Black, Hispanic, and White Women." *International Economic Review* 51 (3): 851–92.

Kearney, Melissa Schettini. 2004. "Is There an Effect of Incremental Welfare Benefits on Fertility Behavior?" *Journal of Human Resources* 39 (2): 295–325.

Kennan, John, and James R. Walker. 2010. "Wages, Welfare Benefits, and Migration." *Journal of Econometrics* 156 (1): 229–38.

Klerman, Jacob, and Steven J. Haider. 2004. "A Stock-Flow Analysis of the Welfare Caseload." *Journal of Human Resources* 39 (4): 865–86.

Knab, Jean, Irv Garfinkel, Sara McLanahan, Emily Moududdin, and Cynthia Osborne. 2009. "The Effects of Welfare and Child Support Policies on the Incidence of Marriage Following a Nonmarital Birth." In *Welfare Reform and Its Long-Term Consequences for America's Poor*, edited by James P. Ziliak, 290–307. Cambridge: Cambridge University Press.

Kniesner, Thomas J., and James P. Ziliak. 2002. "Explicit versus Implicit Income Insurance." *Journal of Risk and Uncertainty* 25 (1): 5–20.

Knox, Virginia, Cynthia Miller, and Lisa Gennetian. 2000. *Reforming Welfare and Rewarding Work: A Summary of the Final Report on the Minnesota Family Investment Program.* New York: MDRC.

Lamarche, Carlos, and Robert Paul Hartley. 2014. "Distributional Effects of Welfare Reform Experiments: A Panel Quantile Regression Examination." UKCPR Discussion Paper no. 2014–11, University of Kentucky Center for Poverty Research. http://uknowledge.uky.edu/ukcpr_papers/5/.

Lofstrom, Magnus, and Frank D. Bean. 2002. "Assessing Immigrant Policy Options: Labor Market Conditions and Post-Reform Declines in Welfare Receipt among Immigrants." *Demography* 39 (4): 617–37.

Lopoo, Leonard M., and Thomas DeLeire. 2006. "Did Welfare Reform Influence the Fertility of Young Teens?" *Journal of Policy Analysis and Management* 25:275–95.

Loprest, Pamela J. 2012. "How Has the TANF Caseload Changed over Time?" Temporary Assistance for Needy Families Research Synthesis Brief no. 8, Washington, DC, Urban Institute.

Lower-Basch, Elizabeth. 2011. "Guide to TANF Funds." TANF Policy Brief, Washington, DC, Center for Law and Social Policy.

Lurie, Irene. 1974. "Estimates of Tax Rates in the AFDC Program." *National Tax Journal* 27 (1): 93–111.

Mazzolari, Francesca. 2007. "Welfare Use When Approaching the Time Limit." *Journal of Human Resources* 42 (3): 596–618.

McGuire, Therese, and David F. Merriman. 2006. "State Spending on Social Assistance Programs over the Business Cycle." In *Working and Poor: How Economic and Policy Changes are Affecting Low-Wage Workers*, edited by Rebecca Blank, Sheldon Danziger, and Robert Schoeni. New York: Russell Sage Foundation.

McKernan, Signe-Mary, Jen Bernstein, and Lynne Fender. 2005. "Taming the Beast: Categorizing State Welfare Policies: A Typology of Welfare Policies Affecting Recipient Job Entry." *Journal of Policy Analysis and Management* 24 (2): 443–60.

McKernan, Signe-Mary, Caroline Ratcliffe, and Yunju Nam. 2008. "Do Welfare and IDA Program Policies Affect Asset Holdings?" Opportunity and Ownership Project Brief no. 10 Washington, DC, Urban Institute.

McKinnish, Terra. 2007. "Cross-Border Welfare Migration: New Evidence from Micro Data." *Journal of Public Economics* 91 (3–4): 437–50.

McKinnish, Terra, Seth Sanders, and Jeffrey Smith. 1999. "Estimates of Effective Guarantees and Tax Rates in the AFDC Program for the Post-OBRA Period." *Journal of Human Resources* 34 (2): 312–45.

Michalopoulos, Charles, Doug Tattrie, Cynthia Miller, Philip K. Robins, Pamela Morris, David Gyarmati, Cindy Redcross, Kelly Foley, and Reuben Ford. 2002. "Making Work Pay: Final Report on the Self-Sufficiency Project for Long-Term

Welfare Recipients." Report, Social Research Demonstration Corporation. http://www.srdc.org/publications/Self-Sufficiency-Project-SSP—Making-Work -Pay-Final-Report-on-the-Self-Sufficiency-Project-for-Long-Term-Welfare -Recipients-details.aspx.

Meyer, Bruce D., and Dan T. Rosenbaum. 2001. "Welfare, the Earned Income Tax Credit, and the Labor Supply of Single Mothers." *Quarterly Journal of Economics* 116 (3): 1063–114.

Meyer, Bruce, and James X. Sullivan. 2004. "The Effects of Welfare and Tax Reform: The Material Well-Being of Single Mothers in the 1980s and 1990s." *Journal of Public Economics* 88:1387–420.

———. 2008. "Changes in the Consumption, Income, and Well Being of Single Mother Families." *American Economic Review* 98 (5): 2221–41.

Miller, Amalia, and Lei Zhang. 2012. "Intergenerational Effects of Welfare Reform on Educational Attainment." *Journal of Law and Economics* 55 (2): 437–76.

Mills, Bradford, Jeffrey Alwang, and Gautum Hazarika. 2001. "Welfare Reform and the Well-Being of Single Female-Headed Families: A Semi-Parametric Analysis." *Review of Income and Wealth* 47 (1): 81–104.

Moffitt, Robert A. 1983. "An Economic Model of Welfare Stigma." *American Economic Review* 73 (5): 1023–35.

———. 1987. "Historical Growth in Participation in Aid to Families with Dependent Children: Was There a Structural Shift?" *Journal of Post Keynesian Economics* 9 (3): 347–63.

———. 1990. "Has State Redistribution Policy Grown More Conservative?" *National Tax Journal* 43 (2): 123–42.

———. 1992. "Incentive Effects of the US Welfare System: A Review." *Journal of Economic Literature* 30 (1): 1–61.

———. 1999. "The Effect of Pre-PRWORA Waivers on AFDC Caseloads and Female Earnings, Income, and Labor Force Behavior." In *Economic Conditions and Welfare Reform*, edited by Sheldon Danziger, 91–118. Kalamazoo, MI: Upjohn Institute.

———. 2003. "Temporary Assistance for Needy Families." In *Means-Tested Transfer Programs in the United States*, edited by Robert Moffitt. Chicago: University of Chicago Press.

———. 2015. "Multiple Program Participation and the SNAP Program." In *SNAP Matters: How Food Stamps Affect Health and Well Being*, edited by Judith Bartfeld, Craig Gundersen, Timothy Smeeding, and James Ziliak, 213–42. Redwood City, CA: Stanford University Press.

Moffitt, Robert, Robert Reville, and Anne Winkler. 1998. "Beyond Single Mothers: Cohabitation and Marriage in the AFDC Program." *Demography* 35 (3): 259–78.

Moffitt, Robert A., and John Karl Scholz. 2010. "Trends in the Level and Distribution of Income Support." In *Tax Policy and the Economy*, vol. 24, edited by Jeffrey Brown, 111–52. Chicago: University of Chicago Press.

Moffitt, Robert A., and David W. Stevens. 2001. "Changing Caseloads: Macro Influences and Micro Composition." *Economic Policy Review* September:37–51.

Moffitt, Robert, and Katie Winder. 2005. "Does it Pay to Move from Welfare to Work?" A Comment on Danziger, Heflin, Corcoran, Oltmans, and Wang." *Journal of Policy Analysis and Management* 24 (2): 399–409.

Morris, Pamela, Lisa Gennetian, Greg Duncan, and Aletha Huston. 2009. "How Welfare Policies Affect Child and Adolescent School Performance: Investigating Pathways of Influence with Experimental Data." In *Welfare Reform and Its Long-Term Consequences for America's Poor*, edited by James P. Ziliak, 255–89. Cambridge: Cambridge University Press.

Morris, Pamela, and Richard Hendra. 2009. "Losing the Safety Net: How Welfare Time Limits Affect Families and Children?" *Developmental Psychology* 45 (2): 383–400.

Mueser, Peter R., David W. Stevens, and Kenneth R. Troske. 2009. "The Impact of Welfare Reform on Leaver Characteristics, Employment, and Recidivism: An Analysis of Maryland and Missouri." In *Welfare Reform and Its Long-Term Consequences for America's Poor*, edited by James P. Ziliak. Cambridge: Cambridge University Press.

Murray, Charles. 1984. *Losing Ground: American Social Policy, 1950–1980*. New York: Basic Books.

Office of Family Assistance (OFA). 2013. "TANF Tenth Report to Congress." Administration for Children & Families, US Department of Health and Human Services, Washington, DC. http://www.acf.hhs.gov/sites/default/files/ofa/10th_tanf_report_congress.pdf.

———. 2014. "TANF Contingency Fund Awards, 2014." Administration for Children & Families, US Department of Health and Human Services, Washington, DC. http://www.acf.hhs.gov/programs/ofa/resource/tanf-contingency-fund-awards-2014.

Offner, Paul. 2005. "Welfare Reform and Teenage Girls." *Social Science Quarterly* 86 (2): 306–22.

Osborne, Cynthia, and Jean Knab. 2007. "Work, Welfare, and Young Children's Health and Behavior in the Fragile Families and Child Wellbeing Study." *Children and Youth Services Review* 29 (6): 762-81.

Parrott, Sharon, Liz Schott, Eileen Sweeney, Allegra Baider, Evelyn Ganzglass, Mark Greenberg, Elizabeth Lower-Basch, et al. 2007. *Implementing the TANF Changes in the Deficit Reduction Act: "Win-Win" Solutions for Families and States*. Washington, DC: Center of Budget and Policy Priorities and Center for Law and Social Policy.

Paxson, Christina, and Jane Waldfogel. 2003. "Welfare Reforms, Family Resources, and Child Maltreatment." *Journal of Policy Analysis and Management* 22 (1): 85–113.

Powers, Elizabeth. 1998. "Does Means-Testing Welfare Discourage Saving? Evidence from a Change in AFDC Policy in the United States." *Journal of Public Economics* 68 (1): 33–53.

———. 2000. "Block Granting Welfare: Fiscal Impact on the States." *Economic Development Quarterly* 14 (4): 323–39.

Primus, Wendell, Lynette Rawlings, Kathy Larin, and Kathryn Porter. 1999. "The Initial Impacts of Welfare Reform on the Incomes of Single-Mother Families." Washington, DC, Center on Budget and Policy Priorities.

Raphael, Steven, and Lorien Rice. 2002. "Car Ownership, Employment, and Earnings." *Journal of Urban Economics* 52 (1): 109–30.

Ribar, David, and Mark Wilhelm. 1999. "The Demand for Welfare Generosity." *Review of Economics and Statistics* 81 (1): 96–108.

Riccio, James, and Daniel Friedlander. 1992. *GAIN: Program Strategies, Participation Patterns, and First-Year Impacts in Six Counties*. New York: Manpower Demonstration Research Corporation.

Riccio, James, Daniel Friedlander, and Stephen Freedman. 1994. *GAIN: Benefits, Costs, and Three-Year Impacts of a Welfare-to-Work Program*. New York: Manpower Demonstration Research Corporation.

Robins, Philip K. 1986. "Child Support, Welfare Dependency, and Poverty." *American Economic Review* 76 (4): 768–88.

Ruggles, Patricia, Steve Bartolomei-Hill, Richard Silva, and Gil Crouse. 1998. *Aid to Families with Dependent Children: The Baseline.* Washington, DC: Office of the Assistant Secretary for Planning and Evaluation, US Department of Health and Human Services. http://aspe.hhs.gov/hsp/AFDC/afdcbase98.htm.

Schmidt, Lucie, and Purvi Sevak. 2004. "AFDC, SSI, and Welfare Reform Aggressiveness: Caseload Reductions vs. Caseload Shifting." *Journal of Human Resources* 39 (3): 792–812.

Schoeni, Robert, and Rebecca Blank. 2000. "What has Welfare Reform Accomplished? Impacts on Welfare Participation, Employment, Income, Poverty, and Family Structure." NBER Working Paper no. 7627, Cambridge, MA.

Schott, Liz, LaDonna Pavetti, and Ife Finch. 2012. "How States Have Spent Federal and State Funds under the TANF Block Grant." Washington, DC, Center on Budget and Policy, Priorities.

Schram, Sanford F., Joe Soss, Richard C. Fording, and Linda Houser. 2009. "Deciding to Discipline: Race, Choice, and Punishment at the Frontlines of Welfare Reform." *American Sociological Review* 74 (2): 398–422.

Shaefer, H. Luke, and Kathryn Edin. 2013. "Rising Extreme Poverty in the United States and the Response of Federal Means-Tested Transfer Programs." *Social Service Review* 87 (2): 250–68.

Shaw, Kathryn. 1989. "Life-Cycle Labor Supply with Human Capital Accumulation." *International Economic Review* 30 (2): 431–56.

Skocpol, Theda. 1992. *Protecting Soldiers and Mothers: The Political Origins of Social Policy in the United States.* Cambridge, MA: Harvard University Press.

Slack, Kristen Shook, Jane Holl, Joan Yoo, Laura Amsden, Emily Collins, and Kerry Bolger. 2007. "Welfare, Work, and Health Care Access Predictors of Low-Income Children's Physical Health Outcomes." *Children and Youth Services Review* 29 (6): 782–801.

Smith, Jeffrey, and Petra Todd. 2005. "Does Matching Overcome LaLonde's Critique of Nonexperimental Estimators?" *Journal of Econometrics* 125:305–53.

Soss, Joe, Sanford F. Schram, Thomas P. Vartanian, and Erin O'Brien. 2001. "Setting the Terms of Relief: Explaining State Policy Choices in the Devolution Revolution." *American Journal of Political Science* 45 (2): 378–95.

Sullivan, James X. 2006. "Welfare Reform, Saving, and Vehicle Ownership: Do Asset Limits and Vehicle Exemptions Matter?" *Journal of Human Resources* 41:72–105.

Sullivan, James, Lesley Turner, and Sheldon Danziger. 2008. "The Relationship between Income and Material Hardship." *Journal of Policy Analysis and Management* 27 (1): 63–81.

Swann, Christopher. 2005. "Welfare Reform When Recipients are Forward-Looking." *Journal of Human Resources* 40 (1): 31–56.

Teitler, Julien, Nancy Reichman, Lenna Nepomnyaschy, and Irwin Garfinkel. 2009. "Effects of Welfare Participation on Marriage." *Journal of Marriage and Family* 71 (4): 878–91.

Tekin, Erdal. 2007. "Child Care Subsidies, Wages, and the Employment of Single Mothers." *Journal of Human Resources* 42:453–87.

Turner, Lesley, Sheldon Danziger, and Kristin Seefeldt. 2006. "Failing the Transition from Welfare to Work: Women Chronically Disconnected from Work and Cash Welfare." *Social Science Quarterly* 87 (2): 227–49.

US Department of Health and Human Services (USHHS). 2014. "Welfare Indicators and Risk Factors: Thirteenth Annual Report to Congress." Office of the Assistant Secretary for Planning and Evaluation, Washington, DC.

US Department of Labor. 1965. *The Negro Family: The Case for National Action.* Washington, DC: Office of Policy Planning and Research.

Waite, Linda. 1995. "Does Marriage Matter?" *Demography* 32 (4): 483–507.

Weiss, Yoram. 1972. "On the Optimal Pattern of Labor Supply." *Economic Journal* 82 (2): 1292–315.

Welfare Rules Databook. 2014. "State TANF Policies as of July 2012." OPRE Report no. 2013–27, Washington, DC, Office of Planning, Research and Evaluation, Administration for Children and Families, US Department of Health and Human Services.

Wu, Chi-Fang, Maria Cancian, Daniel R. Meyer, and Geoffrey L. Wallace. 2006. "How Do Welfare Sanctions Work?" *Social Work Research* 30:33–50.

Ziliak, James P. 2002. "Social Policy and the Macroeconomy: What Drives Welfare Caseloads?" *Focus* 22 (1): 29–34.

———. 2003. "Income Transfers and Assets of the Poor." *Review of Economics and Statistics* 85 (1): 63–76.

———. 2007. "Making Work Pay: Changes in Effective Tax Rates and Guarantees in US Transfer Programs, 1983–2002." *Journal of Human Resources* 42 (3): 619–42.

———. 2008. "Filling the Poverty Gap, Then and Now." In *Frontiers of Family Economics*, vol. 1, edited by Peter Rupert, 39–114. Bingley, UK: Emerald Group Publishing.

———. 2014. "Supporting Low-Income Workers through Refundable Child-Care Credits." In *Policies to Address Poverty in America*, edited by Melissa Kearney and Benjamin Harris, 109–18. Washington, DC: Brookings Institution.

———. 2015. "Income, Program Participation, Poverty, and Financial Vulnerability: Research and Data Needs." *Journal of Economic and Social Measurement* 40 (1–4): 27–68.

Ziliak, James P., David Figlio, Elizabeth Davis, and Laura Connolly. 2000. "Accounting for the Decline in AFDC Caseloads: Welfare Reform or the Economy?" *Journal of Human Resources* 35 (3): 570–86.

Ziliak, James P., and Thomas J. Kniesner. 1999. "Estimating Life-Cycle Labor Supply Tax Effects." *Journal of Political Economy* 107 (2): 326–59.

Ziliak, Stephen T. 2004. "Self-Reliance before the Welfare State: Evidence from the Charity Organization Movement in the United States." *Journal of Economic History* 64 (2): 433–61.

Ziliak, Stephen T., and Joan Underhill Hannon. 2006. "Public Assistance: Colonial Times to the 1920s." In *Historical Statistics of the United States: Colonial Times to the Present*, Millennial Edition On Line, edited by Susan B. Carter, Scott Sigmund Gartner, Michael R. Haines, Alan L. Olmstead, Richard Sutch, and Gavin Wright, 693–700. Cambridge: Cambridge University Press.

Contributors

Thomas Buchmueller
Stephen M. Ross School of Business
University of Michigan
701 Tappan Street
Ann Arbor, MI 48109

John C. Ham
Department of Economics
Faculty of Arts and Social Sciences
National University of Singapore
AS2 #06–02, 1 Arts Link, Singapore
   117570

Hilary Hoynes
Richard & Rhoda Goldman School of
   Public Policy
University of California, Berkeley
2607 Hearst Avenue
Berkeley, CA 94720–7320

Robert A. Moffitt
Department of Economics
Johns Hopkins University
3400 North Charles Street
Baltimore, MD 21218

Austin Nichols
Abt Associates
4550 Montgomery Ave. #800N
Bethesda, MD 20814

Jesse Rothstein
Goldman School of Public Policy and
   Department of Economics
University of California, Berkeley
2607 Hearst Avenue
Berkeley, CA 94720–7320

Diane Whitmore Schanzenbach
School of Education and Social Policy
Northwestern University
Annenberg Hall, Room 205
2120 Campus Drive
Evanston, IL 60208

Lara D. Shore-Sheppard
Department of Economics
Williams College
24 Hopkins Hall Drive
Williamstown, MA 01267

James P. Ziliak
Center for Poverty Research and
   Department of Economics
University of Kentucky
550 South Limestone Street
Lexington, KY 40506–0034

Author Index

Subject Index